Marketing

William M.
Pride
Texas A&M University

O. C.
Ferrell
Texas A&M University

Marketing

Basic Concepts and Decisions

Fourth Edition

Houghton Mifflin Company   Boston

Dallas   Geneva, Illinois   Lawrenceville, New Jersey   Palo Alto

To Nancy, Michael, and Allen Pride

To James Collins Ferrell

Contents

Part Two

8

Wholesaling 234

9

Retailing 258

10

Physical Distribution 290

13

Personal Selling and Sales Promotion   386

Part Six

16

The Marketing Environment 472

Political, Legal, and Regulatory Forces 474

19

Organization, Implementation, and Control 582

Part Eight

20

Selected Applications 610

Industrial Marketing 612

Preface

Marketing is a relevant, challenging, and exciting field to study. Our economy, our lifestyles, and our physical well-being are directly or indirectly influenced by marketing activities. We believe that *Marketing: Basic Concepts and Decisions* is successful because it effectively stimulates student interest with its readable style and extensive use of interesting, real-life examples. The depth of coverage in this text provides students with a full understanding of the marketing discipline.

To provide an understanding of the practice of marketing in a changing environment, this book presents a comprehensive framework that integrates traditional concepts with the realities of today. *Marketing: Basic Concepts and Decisions* presents the concepts and applications that are most relevant to the marketing decision maker. While our view is broad enough to encompass marketing in both business and nonbusiness situations, our focus is on the universal concerns of managers who are responsible for marketing decisions.

The study of the dynamic world of marketing requires continuous review, revision, and updating. After a careful review of our text, we made a number of content changes in this edition that will provide students with a greater depth of knowledge of the marketing field. Many topics are discussed in more detail than in earlier editions. Some examples include the consumer buying decision process, types of consumer decision behavior, the organizational buying decision process, computer-assisted telephone interviewing, mall intercept interviewing, generic branding, product adopter categories, demand and cost relationships, experience curve pricing, the relationship between corporate and marketing strategy, and growth strategies. These more highly detailed topics will enhance students' comprehension of marketing issues and activities.

As in earlier editions, the Fourth Edition contains numerous real-world examples, illustrations, cases, and applications. In this edition we have added a new series of longer applications that are cited and set off in the main portion of the chapter. These new applications illustrate or extend the discussions of topics presented in the chapter. Half of the end-of-chapter cases are new; many of the others have been revised. Most of them focus on real, recognizable products and organizations.

To improve students' grasp of the material and to make the study of marketing more interesting and exciting, this new edition is in full color. Many visual illustrations appear in the text in a form similar to the way one experiences them in everyday life.

In making improvements to this new edition, we have not lost sight of our original primary objective—to provide an introductory marketing textbook that is comprehensive, readable, teachable, full of real-world examples and illustrations, and interesting to students. Our book provides numerous features to facilitate student learning.

- Learning objectives at the beginning of each chapter inform the student about what should be achieved by reading the chapter.
- An opening vignette for each chapter provides a marketing situation that relates to issues discussed in the chapter.
- Many real-world examples about familiar products and organizations aid in illustrating and explaining concepts and issues.
- Two longer applications in each chapter provide examples of concepts and decisions. These applications are current and focus on recognizable firms and products.
- Numerous figures, tables, and photographs are used to facilitate learning.
- A complete summary in each chapter covers the major topics discussed.
- A list of important terms alerts the student to the major concepts and issues discussed in the chapter. These terms are highlighted in the text.
- A set of discussion and review questions are provided not only for review but also for thoughtful exploration of the topics covered in the chapter.
- Two concise and provocative cases appear at the end of each chapter.
- A visual framework for organizing the text is repeated at the beginning of each part to tell students how information in that part is related to other material in the text.
- Full color design makes the book come alive and emphasizes the real world practical theme. Full color provides better contrast between art and prose and facilitates the ease of learning.
- The appendices on financial analysis in marketing and on marketing careers provide additional insights in two important areas.
- The name index and the subject index aid in quickly finding topics of interest.

In addition to numerous instructor support materials, the package for this text includes a number of components to aid in both teaching and learning. A study guide, *Understanding Marketing,* is available for use with the text. A casebook, entitled *Marketing Cases,* is also available. It contains 37 short-to-medium length cases designed to facilitate an understanding of how marketing decisions are made. Also prepared to accompany the text is a book of readings entitled *Marketing: Contemporary Dimensions.* This is a collection of 58 readings from the current literature on marketing topics. *Marketer: A Simulation,* a new ancillary, provides student teams with experience in making marketing decisions and is designed for use with Apple II, IBM PC, or TRS-80 microcomputers. CARE MICROSTUDY, a computerized, self-instructional program also for use on Apple II, IBM PC, or TRS-80, aids students' mastery of key marketing concepts.

The eight parts of *Marketing: Basic Concepts and Decisions* are again organized around a managerial framework to give students both an understanding of marketing concepts and an understanding of how to apply them when making decisions and managing marketing activities. In Part One, we discuss general concepts and present an overview of marketing. We also consider types of markets, target market analysis, buyer behavior, and marketing research. Part Two presents product concepts and the development and management of products. In Part Three we examine marketing channels, institutions, and physical distribution. In Part Four we analyze promotion decisions and methods, such as advertising, personal selling, sales promotion, and publicity. The chapters in Part Five are devoted to pricing decisions. In Part Six the text moves from the marketing mix variables to consideration of the environmental variables. Part Seven focuses on marketing management and includes discussions of strategic market planning and organization, implementation, and control. The chapters in Part Eight explore strategic decisions in the areas of industrial, nonbusiness, and international marketing.

Over the years we have received a number of very helpful suggestions for improving the text from professors and students. We invite your comments, questions, or criticisms. We want to do our best to provide materials that enhance the teaching and learning of basic marketing concepts and decisions. Your suggestions will be sincerely appreciated.

William M. Pride

O. C. Ferrell

Acknowledgments

Like most textbooks, this one reflects the ideas of a multitude of academicians and practitioners who have contributed to the development of the marketing discipline. We appreciate the opportunity to present their ideas in this book.

A number of individuals have made many helpful comments and recommendations in their review of this or earlier editions. We appreciate the generous help of these reviewers.

Barbara Unger
Western Washington University

Harrison L. Grathwol
University of Washington

Robert D. Hisrich
Boston College

Charles L. Hilton
Eastern Kentucky University

Roy Klages
State University of New York at Albany

William G. Browne
Oregon State University

Poondi Varadarajan
Texas A & M University

Lee R. Duffus
University of Tennessee

Glen Riecken
East Tennessee State University

W. R. Berdine
California State Polytechnic Institute

Charles L. Lapp
University of Dallas

Thomas V. Greer
University of Maryland

Patricia Laidler
Massasoit Community College

Stan Madden
Baylor University

Elizabeth C. Hirschman
New York University

Peter Bloch
Louisiana State University

Linda Calderone
*State University of New York
Agricultural and Technical College
at Farmingdale*

Barbara Coe
North Texas State University

Alan R. Wiman
Rider College

Donald L. James
Fort Lewis College

Terrence V. O'Brien
Kansas State University

Joseph Guiltinan
University of Kentucky

Kent B. Monroe
Virginia Polytechnic Institute

William Staples
University of Houston—Clear Lake

Richard J. Semenik
University of Utah

Pat J. Calabro
University of Texas at Arlington

James F. Wenthe
University of Georgia

Richard C. Becherer
Wayne State University

Thomas E. Barry
Southern Methodist University

Mark I. Alpert
University of Texas at Austin

Richard A. Lancioni
Temple University

Steven Shipley
Governor's State University

Paul J. Solomon
University of Texas at Arlington

Michael Peters
Boston College

Terence A. Shimp
University of South Carolina

Kenneth L. Rowe
Arizona State University

Allan Palmer
University of North Carolina at Charlotte

Otto W. Taylor
*State University of New York
Agricultural and Technical College
at Farmingdale*

Stewart W. Bither
Pennsylvania State University

John R. Brooks, Jr.
West Texas State University

Carlos W. Moore
Baylor University

Charles Gross
Illinois Institute of Technology

Hugh E. Law
East Tennessee University

Dillard Tinsley
Stephen F. Austin State University

John R. Huser
Illinois Central College

David J. Fritzsche
University of Nevada—Reno

David M. Landrum
Central State University

Robert Copley
University of Louisville

Robert A. Robicheaux
University of Alabama

Sue Ellen Neeley
University of Houston—Clear Lake

Michael L. Rothschild
University of Wisconsin—Madison

Thomas Falcone
Indiana University of Pennsylvania

William L. Cron
Southern Methodist University

Sumner M. White
Massachusetts Bay Community College

Del I. Hawkins
University of Oregon

Ralph DiPietro
Montclair State College

Norman E. Daniel
Arizona State University

Bruce Stern
Portland State University

Beheruz N. Sethna
Clarkson College

Stephen J. Miller
Oklahoma State University

Dale Varble
Indiana State University

William M. Kincaid, Jr.
Oklahoma State University

John McFall
San Diego State University

James D. Reed
Louisiana State University—Shreveport

Ken Jensen
Bradley University

Arthur Prell
*Southern Illinois University at
Edwardsville*

David H. Lindsay
University of Maryland

Claire Ferguson
Bentley College

Joseph Hair
Louisiana State University

Roger Blackwell
Ohio State University

James C. Carroll
University of Southwestern Louisiana

Guy Banville
Creighton University

Jack M. Starling
North Texas State University

Lloyd M. DeBoer
George Mason University

Dean C. Siewers
Rochester Institute of Technology

Benjamin J. Cutler
Bronx Community College

Gerald L. Manning
Des Moines Area Community College

Hale Tongren
George Mason University

Lee Meadow
University of Lowell

Ronald Schill
Brigham Young University

Don Scotton
Cleveland State University

George Glisan
Illinois State University

Jim L. Grimm
Illinois State University

John I. Coppett
Iowa State University

Roy R. Grundy
College of DuPage

Steven J. Shaw
University of South Carolina

Melvin R. Crask
University of Georgia

J. Paul Peter
University of Wisconsin—Madison

Bert Rosenbloom
Drexel University

Terry M. Chambers
Appalachian State University

Rosann L. Spiro
Indiana University

For contributing cases we are indebted to George Glisan, Illinois State University; Wayne Delozier, University of South Carolina; Jon Hawes, University of Akron; Carlos W. Moore, Baylor University; Taylor Simms, Bradley University; Gene Lavengood, Northwestern University; and William G. Zikmund, Oklahoma State University. We especially thank Jim L. Grimm for drafting the financial analysis in marketing appendix.

We wish to express a great deal of appreciation to Robert A. Robicheaux for playing the major role in developing the readings book, *Marketing: Contemporary Dimensions*. Our special thanks go to Charles W. Lamb, Texas Christian University, for creating the casebook, *Marketing Cases*. For creating *Marketer: A Simulation,* we wish to thank Jerald R. Smith, University of Louisville. We would also like to thank Steven Skinner, University of Kentucky, for creating the original CARE (Computer-Assisted Review and Evaluation) program. A great deal of thanks also go to Edwin C. Hackleman for preparing the computerized test preparation program and for creating the current version of CARE MICROSTUDY for personal computers. For many types of technical assistance we thank Jeanette Baldwin, Patricia Davidson, Elizabeth Ensley, Bill Metcalfe, Linda Nafziger, Dan Rajaratnam, and Jes Simmons.

Marketing

Part 1

The Analysis of Marketing Opportunities

In Part One, we introduce the field of marketing and provide a broad perspective from which one can explore and analyze various components of the marketing discipline. In the first chapter, we define and describe marketing and discuss why an understanding of it is useful in many aspects of everyday life, including one's career. We provide an overview of the variables that marketers analyze when making marketing decisions, and we examine the major dimensions of a marketing strategy. Chapter 2 focuses on one of the major steps required in the development of marketing strategies—selecting and analyzing target markets. To satisfy customers' needs, marketers must be aware of some of the factors that affect the behavior of their customers. In Chapter 3, we discuss consumer and organizational buyer decision processes and a number of factors that influence buying decisions. By understanding some of the elements that affect buying decisions, marketers are better able to analyze customers' needs and to evaluate the extent to which specific marketing strategies can satisfy those needs. Through the discussion in Chapter 4, we analyze the role of a marketing information system, and we describe the basic steps in the marketing research process. The four chapters in this part provide a foundation on which to build an understanding of the basic components of a marketing mix.

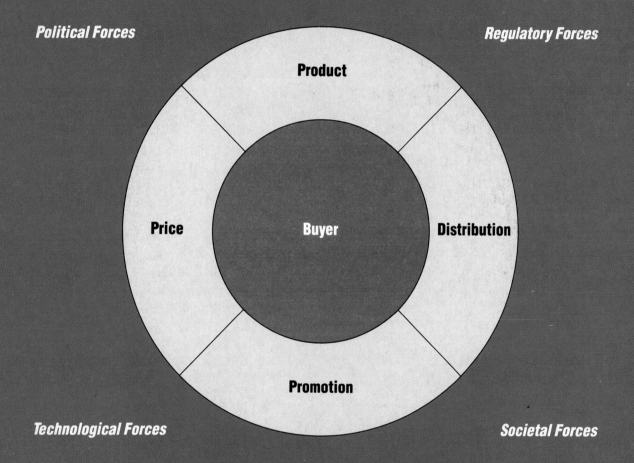

Marketing Environment

Legal Forces

Political Forces

Regulatory Forces

Product

Price

Buyer

Distribution

Promotion

Technological Forces

Societal Forces

Economic Forces

1

Marketing:
An Overview

Objectives

To understand why a person should study marketing.

To learn some representative definitions of marketing, and to understand the definition used in this text.

To gain insight into the basic elements of the marketing concept and its implementation.

To identify the variables that make up the marketing mix.

To recognize and understand the environmental variables that influence marketing decisions and activities.

To understand the definition of a marketing strategy.

General Motors, Ford, Chrysler, Toyota, and Volkswagen have all invested billions of dollars in the belief that consumers and industrial buyers are ready for mini-vans. So far, it appears that their investments are paying off. The mini-van provides more space than a station wagon and more economy and ease of handling than a large van. It measures 14½ feet long and 5½ feet wide, compared with a conventional van's dimensions of 15½ feet by 6½ feet. Figure 1.1 illustrates the Plymouth Voyager.

The front-wheel-drive Plymouth Voyager and Dodge Caravan are based on the Chrysler K car. Ford claims that its Aerovan's rear-wheel drive has more towing power and will appeal to industrial purchasers. General Motors' M van, now the GMC USV and Chevy Astro, also has rear-wheel drive and may appeal to industrial purchasers. On the other hand, Toyota is not trying to appeal to industrial buyers; its van is designed as a family vehicle, with options like a mini-refrigerator, a power sun roof, and separate air conditioning for front and rear passengers. Volkswagenwerk, A.G., was really first in this market and has been selling a small van in the United States since 1952. To compete head-on with the new mini-vans, Volkswagen improved its van's engine to overcome complaints about sluggish performance.[1]

All of these auto manufacturers have taken a slightly different approach to the mini-van. While agreeing that buyers desire a smaller, more efficient van, the automobile manufacturers have developed a selection of distinct engineering designs and marketing efforts to serve several defined markets. The firm that gains the largest market share in the mini-van competition will be the firm that creates quality engineering designs and develops the best marketing strategy.

Figure 1.1   The Plymouth Voyager   *Source: Chrysler/Plymouth news photo.*

1. Charles W. Stevens, "Auto Makers Plan Big Move to Mini-Vans," *Wall Street Journal*, Sept. 27, 1983, p. 1.

In this first chapter, we provide an overview of marketing concepts and decisions that are covered in this text. We look at several reasons why people should study marketing and establish that marketing activities pervade our everyday lives. Marketing is viewed as a diverse group of activities performed by all types of organizations, individuals, and groups to facilitate exchange. We develop a definition of marketing and provide an explanation of each element of the definition. The marketing concept is presented and then we focus briefly on the marketing variables analyzed in this book. Finally, we examine the major components of a marketing strategy.

Why study marketing?

For a society to function, marketing is necessary. It is a fundamental human activity that facilitates and expedites exchange, and exchange benefits individuals, organizations, and society.

Marketing costs consume a sizable part of buyers' dollars

The study of marketing will make you aware that many marketing activities are necessary to provide people with satisfying goods and services. Obviously, these marketing activities cost money. In fact, about one-half of a buyer's dollar goes for marketing costs. A family that has a monthly income of $2,000 and allocates $300 to taxes and savings spends about $1,700 for goods and services. Of this amount, $850 goes for marketing activities. Clearly, if marketing expenses consume that much of your dollar, you should know how this money is used.

Marketing activities are used in many organizations

From 25 to 33 percent of all civilian workers in the United States perform marketing activities. A variety of interesting and challenging career opportunities is available in the marketing field; some of these are personal selling, advertising, packaging, transportation, storage, marketing research, product development, wholesaling, and retailing. In addition, a number of people who work for nonbusiness organizations are involved in marketing activities. For example, as a part of its marketing activities, the American Lung Association used Brooke Shields as a spokesperson to promote non-smoking to teen-age girls. The American Lung Association believed that Shields' reputation as a high-fashion model clearly countered cigarette producers' advertisements associating glamour and sexuality with cigarettes. Marketing skills are also used to promote political, cultural, church, and civic activities. Whether a person earns a living through marketing activities or performs them voluntarily in nonbusiness settings, marketing knowledge and skills are likely to be a valuable asset.

Marketing activities are important to businesses and the economy

A business organization must sell products to survive and to grow. Marketing activities directly or indirectly help to sell the organization's products. By doing so, they also generate financial resources that can be used to develop innovative products. New products allow a firm to better satisfy customers' changing needs, which in turn allows the firm to generate more profits. Procter & Gamble exemplifies this process. It does an excellent job of understanding consumers, creating products to meet their needs, and using innovative marketing. Seven of the top ten packaged-goods products in the United States are Procter & Gamble items.[2] For example, Procter & Gamble's Head & Shoulders is the number-one selling shampoo in the country, with 12 percent of the market.[3]

Our highly complex, industrialized economy depends heavily on marketing activities. They help produce the profits that are essential not only to the survival of individual businesses, but also to the health and ultimate survival of the economy as a whole. Without profits, businesses find it difficult to buy added raw materials, hire more employees, attract more capital, and produce the additional products that in turn make more profits.

Marketing activities should be evaluated

Besides contributing to the well-being of our nation, marketing activities pervade our everyday lives. In fact, they help us to achieve many improvements in the quality of our lives. Still, critics contend that commonplace products are marketed so zealously that they get attention out of all proportion to their merit.[4]

Studying marketing activities allows us to weigh their costs, benefits, and flaws more effectively. We can see where they need to be improved and how to accomplish that goal. For example, if you have had an unsatisfactory experience with a warranty, you may have wished that laws were enforced more strictly to make sellers fulfill their promises. In the same vein, you may have wished that you had more information about a product—or more accurate information—before you made the purchase. Understanding marketing enables us to evaluate the corrective measures (such as laws, regulations, and industry guidelines) that may be required to stop unfair, misleading, or unethical marketing practices.

Marketing defined

If you asked several people what *marketing* is, they would probably respond with a variety of descriptions. Figure 1.2, for example, displays the Celanese Corporation's statement on the purpose of marketing. This statement reflects Celanese's philosophy about the most important elements of marketing in the chemical fiber industry.

Marketing encompasses many more activities than most people think. Remember, though, that any definition is merely an abstract description of a broad concept. No definition perfectly describes the concept to which it refers. Like most developing disciplines, marketing has been, and continues to be, defined in many ways. Here are several definitions:

Marketing consists of the performance of business activities that direct the flow of goods and services from producer to consumer or user.[5]

Marketing is a total system of business activities designed to plan, price,

2. "Well-Run Companies: The Secret of Success," *U.S. News and World Report,* Oct. 10, 1983, p. 74
3. "The Lather Wars Have Shampoo Makers Hunting for Niches," *Business Week,* Jan. 9, 1984, p. 124.
4. "In Today's Marketplace, It's Hype, Hype, Hype," *U.S. News and World Report,* Dec. 5, 1983, p. 51.
5. Committee on Definitions, *Marketing Definitions: A Glossary of Marketing Terms* (Chicago: American Marketing Association, 1960), p. 15.

Figure 1.2
Celanese Corporation's
statement on the pur-
pose of marketing
*Source: Courtesy of
Celanese Corporation.*

*promote, and distribute want-satisfying products and services to present
and potential customers.*[6]

*Marketing is the development and efficient distribution of goods and ser-
vices for chosen consumer segments.*[7]

6. William J. Stanton, *Fundamentals of Marketing,* 7th ed. (New York:
   McGraw-Hill, 1984), p. 7.
7. David L. Kurtz and Louis E. Boone, *Contemporary Marketing,* 4th ed.
   (Hinsdale, Ill.: Dryden Press, 1983), p. 9.

Marketing is the process in a society by which the demand structure for economic goods and services is anticipated or enlarged and satisfied through the conception, promotion, exchange, and physical distribution of such goods and services.[8]

Although these definitions of marketing may be acceptable to some academicians and practitioners, we believe that each is too limited for one or more of the following reasons. First, most of the definitions indicate that marketing consists of business activities; however, marketing also occurs in nonbusiness situations and is practiced by nonbusiness organizations. Second, one definition implies that marketing begins *after* goods and services have been produced; actually, marketing activities begin *before* production activities. Third (as we will see), marketing deals not only with goods and services, but also with ideas, issues, concepts, and even people.

To avoid such limitations, we prefer a broader definition:

Marketing consists of individual and organizational activities aimed at facilitating and expediting exchanges within a set of dynamic environmental factors.

This definition views marketing as a diverse group of activities directed at a varied set of products and performed within a wide range of organizations. In marketing exchanges, any product may be involved and we assume only that individuals and organizations expect to gain a reward in excess of the costs incurred. To fully understand this definition, let us examine its components in more detail.

Marketing consists of activities

A multitude of activities are required to market products effectively. Some activities can be performed by producers; some can be accomplished by intermediaries (who buy from producers or other middlemen in order to resell the products); and some may even be performed by purchasers. Marketing does not include all human and organizational activities. It encompasses only those activities aimed at facilitating and expediting exchanges. Table 1.1 lists several major categories of marketing activities and provides a number of examples for each. This general enumeration should not be considered all-inclusive. Each example could be divided into numerous more specific activities.

Marketing is performed by individuals and organizations

Marketing pervades many relationships between individuals, groups, and organizations. All types of organizations perform marketing activities to facilitate exchanges. Business organizations obviously do so; but so do universities, charitable organizations, political parties, civic clubs, community theaters, hospitals, and religious organizations. The sole owner and operator of a small neighborhood store performs a variety of marketing activities to facilitate exchanges. He or she decides which products will satisfy customers, arranges to have the products delivered to the store, prices them, decides how many to keep in storage and how many to display, advertises, assists customers, and at times even gift wraps and delivers.

8. Marketing Staff of the Ohio State University, "A Statement of Marketing Philosophy," *Journal of Marketing,* Jan. 1965, p. 43.

Table 1.1   Examples of general marketing activities

Category of Marketing Activities	Possible Activities Required
Marketing information	Design and perform marketing experiments; observe and analyze buyer behavior; develop and administer consumer surveys; analyze and interpret routinely collected information such as sales data; perform market tests; evaluate market opportunities; provide managers with information in the form most usable for decision making
Product	Develop and test-market new products; modify existing products; eliminate products that do not satisfy customers' desires; formulate brand names and branding policies; create product warranties and establish procedures for fulfilling warranties; plan packages, including materials, sizes, shapes, colors, and designs
Distribution	Analyze various types of distribution channels; design appropriate distribution channels; design an effective program for dealer relations; establish distribution centers; formulate and implement procedures for efficient product handling; set up inventory controls; analyze transportation methods; minimize total distribution costs; analyze possible locations for plants and wholesale or retail outlets
Promotion	Set promotional objectives; determine major types of promotion to be used; select and schedule advertising media; develop advertising messages; measure the effectiveness of advertisements; recruit and train salespersons; formulate compensation programs for sales personnel; establish sales territories; plan and implement sales promotion efforts such as free samples, coupons, displays, sweepstakes, sales contests, and cooperative advertising programs; prepare and disseminate publicity releases
Price	Analyze competitors' prices; formulate pricing policies; determine method or methods used to set prices; set prices; determine discounts for various types of buyers; establish conditions and terms of sales
Marketing management	Establish marketing objectives; plan marketing activities; coordinate and integrate marketing activities; motivate persons who are implementing marketing efforts; evaluate and control the performance of marketing activities

Universities and their students engage in exchanges. To receive knowledge, entertainment, room, board, and a degree, students give up time, money, effort, perhaps services in the form of labor, and opportunities to do other things. In return, the institution provides instruction, food, medical services, entertainment, recreation, and the use of land and facilities.

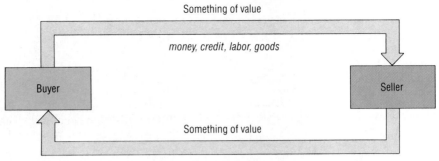

Figure 1.3
Exchange between buyer and seller

Something of value

money, credit, labor, goods

Buyer

Seller

Something of value

goods, services, ideas

Marketing facilitates exchanges

For an *exchange* to take place, four conditions must exist. First, an exchange requires participation by two or more individuals, groups, or organizations. Second, each party must possess something of value that the other party desires. Third, each must be willing to give up its "something of value" to receive the "something of value" held by the other; the objective of a marketing exchange is to receive something that is desired more than what is given up to get it, that is, a reward in excess of costs. Fourth, the parties to the exchange must be able to communicate with each other to make their "somethings of value" available.[9] These four conditions of exchange are illustrated in Figure 1.3. As the arrows indicate, the two parties are communicating to make their "somethings of value" available to each other. Note, though, that an exchange will not necessarily take place just because these four conditions exist. However, even if there is no exchange, marketing activities still have occurred.

The "somethings of value" held by the two parties are most often products and/or financial resources such as money or credit. When an exchange occurs, products are traded for either other products or financial resources. For example, Pan American World Airways traded fifteen of its DC-10s to American Airlines for eight much larger 747 jumbo jets. In this case, both companies benefited by getting planes that they needed on specific routes.[10]

A *product* can be a good, a service, or an idea. A *good* is a physical, concrete something you can touch. A *service* is the application of human and mechanical efforts to people or objects. Services (such as bank services, long-distance telephone services, and air travel) are just as real as goods, but you cannot actually put your hands on them. (The application on page 13 describes some marketing activities of companies competing in the long-distance phone service industry.) Figure 1.4 attempts to visualize such a product—a cash management program tailored to fit the needs of a retailer. This advertisement tries to give the abstract concept of cash management a more tangible image. Products in the form of *ideas* include concepts, philosophies, images, and issues. For instance, Weight Watchers, for a fee, provides its members with ideas to help them lose weight and control their eating habits.

9. Philip Kotler, *Marketing Management: Analysis, Planning, and Control,* 6th ed. (Englewood Cliffs, N.J.: Prentice-Hall, 1984), p. 8.
10. William Curley, "American Air, Pan Am Ready to Swap Planes," *Wall Street Journal,* Oct. 14, 1983, p. 2.

Figure 1.4
Mellon Bank attempts
to visualize the con-
cept of a financial
service
*Source: Brouillard Com-
munications, Division of
J. Walter Thompson
Company.*

Marketing occurs in a dynamic environment

The marketing environment consists of many changing forces: laws, regulations, actions of political officials, societal pressures, changes in economic conditions, and technological advances. Each of these dynamic forces has an impact on how effectively marketing activities can facilitate and expedite exchanges. We will explore such environmental forces later in this chapter and in Chapters 16 and 17.

The marketing concept

During World War II, the U.S. Air Force established a supply base on a South Pacific island. The natives watched the service personnel build the runway, install landing lights, set up a control tower, and erect storage buildings. After the base was completed, the natives enjoyed watching the aircraft land and take off. They especially liked to see supplies being unloaded, because they had developed ways of getting food and other supplies from the storage areas.

After the war was over, the supplies were removed, the facilities were torn down, the landing lights were taken out, and the runway was destroyed. When the last of the U.S. military personnel left the island, the natives—who had become dependent on the supplies—decided that if they could rebuild the base, then the large silver birds would return. So they built crudely thatched storage huts, cleared and smoothed a makeshift runway, and erected a tower-like structure close to it. They lit torches on both

Application

Long-distance Services and Telephone Suppliers Emphasize Marketing

The breakup of AT&T has changed the environment in the long-distance telephone service market. Competition has grown fierce. AT&T has divested itself of its local operating units, and discount competitors such as MCI Communications Corporation and GTE Corporation's Sprint Service have begun to attract some of AT&T's customers. AT&T, in turn, is fighting back.

The $40 billion long-distance market is growing by one-tenth each year and even the one-twentieth of the market gained by smaller companies is significant. AT&T has over one hundred years of experience in this industry of high visibility and public trust. To compete against this image, AT&T's rivals are seeking to establish credibility and recognition. MCI has attempted to do so by promoting its ability to provide new services. It has been enhancing recognition by giving away free three-minute calls at state fairs, at tennis and golf tournaments, and in shopping malls, and by offering thirty minutes of free calls to new subscribers.

Paralleling the competition for long-distance business has been the race to market telephones themselves. However, in this area, there is an added twist—competition from international firms. Until a few years ago, three major U.S. companies manufactured the country's telephones and sold them through a highly limited number of retail outlets. Now, stiff competition from countries such as Korea and Japan is forcing expanded advertising and distribution, as well as analysis of what consumers in this still developing market want in the product.

Source: Based on Virginia Inman, "AT&T Tells Everyone Its Long-Distance Calls Are Better Than MCI's," *Wall Street Journal,* Oct. 27, 1983, pp. 1, 21; and "The Big—and Bruising—Business of Selling Telephones," *Business Week,* March 12, 1984, pp. 103–106.

sides of the runway at night to guide the silver birds to the island. Although the natives waited day after day, the large silver birds never returned.

Some business organizations face a similar problem. They build or acquire facilities, hire personnel, obtain equipment, and make or buy products; yet—like the natives—they fail to attract people with what they have to offer. However, a business that adopts and properly implements the marketing concept should be successful.

The marketing concept is not a second definition of marketing. It is a way of thinking—a management philosophy about an organization's entire activities. This philosophy affects all efforts of the organization, not just the marketing activities.

Basic elements of the marketing concept

According to the *marketing concept* an organization should try to satisfy the needs of customers or clients through a coordinated set of activities that, at the same time, allows the organization to achieve its goals. Customer satisfaction is the major aim of the marketing concept. First, a business organization must find out what will satisfy customers. With this information, the business can create satisfying products. But that is not enough. The business then must get these products into the hands of customers. Nor does the process end there. The business must continue to alter, adapt, and develop products to keep pace with customers' changing desires and preferences. For example, Hewlett-Packard introduces substantially new products at the rate of about eight per week.[11] Essentially, the

11. "Well-Run Companies: The Secret of Success," *U.S. News and World Report,* Oct. 10, 1983, p. 74.

marketing concept stresses the importance of customers and emphasizes that marketing activities begin and end with them.

In attempting to satisfy customers, businesses must consider not only short-run, immediate needs but also broad, long-term desires. Trying to satisfy customers' current needs by sacrificing their long-term desires will only create strong dissatisfaction in the future. For example, people want efficient, low-cost energy to power their homes and automobiles; yet they clearly react adversely to energy producers who pollute the air and water, kill wildlife, or cause disease or birth defects in future generations.

To meet these short- and long-run needs and desires, a firm must coordinate all its activities. Production, finance, accounting, personnel, and marketing departments must work together to ensure customer satisfaction.

Please do not think, however, that the marketing concept is a highly philanthropic philosophy aimed at helping customers at the expense of the business organization. A firm that adopts the marketing concept must not only satisfy its customers' objectives but also achieve its own goals. Otherwise, it would not stay in business for long. The overall goals of a business might be directed toward increasing profits, market shares, sales, or a combination of the three. The marketing concept stresses that a business organization can best achieve its goals by providing customer satisfaction. Implementing the marketing concept should benefit the organization as well as its customers. A firm can only be successful through coordination of all the organization's activities with the aim of meeting business objectives. No matter how effective the marketing strategy, if other areas of the organization fall short, the company can still go bankrupt. Continental Airlines and Braniff Airlines provided excellent consumer service but were forced into bankruptcy because they failed to minimize overhead cost (especially wages and salaries) and concentrate on profitable markets. Their future depends on the ability to coordinate all of the organization's activities and meet their profit objectives.

The Whirlpool advertisement in Figure 1.5 certainly reflects the philosophy of the marketing concept. Whirlpool promises to satisfy customers with "good quality, honest appliances designed to give you your money's worth," and Whirlpool promises to stand behind its products.

Evolution of the marketing concept

The marketing concept may seem like an obviously sensible approach to running a business; but in fact, businesses have not always believed that the best way to make sales, and profits, is to satisfy customers. Despite clear evidence of a shift in consumer preferences, U.S. automobile manufacturers emphasized large cars for far too long. Chrysler almost went bankrupt before government-guaranteed loans and a new market-oriented K car saved the company. Today, Chrysler is a highly profitable consumer-oriented company. Surprisingly, many businesses still have not adopted the marketing concept. This philosophy emerged in the third major era in the history of U.S. business. It was preceded by the production era and the sales era.

The production era

During the second half of the nineteenth century, the Industrial Revolution came into its own in the United States. Electricity, rail transportation, the

We still believe in promises.

use of specialized labor, the assembly line, and mass production made it possible to manufacture products more efficiently. As a result of new technology and new ways of using labor, products streamed out of factories into the marketplace, where consumer demand for manufactured goods was strong. This *production orientation* continued into the early part of this century, encouraged by the scientific management movement, which trained workers to work in a machine-like style to increase their productivity.

The sales era

Beginning in the 1920s, the strong consumer demand for products subsided. Businesses realized that products—which by this time could be made relatively efficiently—would have to be ''sold'' to consumers. From the mid-1920s to the early 1950s, businesses looked on sales as the major means of increasing profits. As a result, this period came to have a *sales orientation*. Business people believed that the most important marketing activities were personal selling and advertising.

The marketing era

By the early 1950s, some business people began to recognize that although they could produce products efficiently and promote them extensively through personal selling and advertising, this did not guarantee that customers would buy them. These businesses, and many others since then, found that they must first determine what customers want and then produce it, rather than simply make products and try to change customers' needs to fit what is produced. As more and more business organizations have realized that the measurement of customers' needs is where everything begins, we have moved into the marketing era, the era of *customer orientation*.

Implementing the marketing concept

A philosophy may look good on paper. It may sound reasonable and noble. But that does not mean it can be put into practice easily. The marketing concept is a case in point. To implement it, an organization must focus on some general conditions. It must also be cognizant of several problems. For this reason, the marketing concept has yet to be fully accepted by business organizations. For example, Atari, Timex, and Texas Instruments overestimated home-computer demand and quickly saturated the low-priced end of the market. Texas Instruments withdrew from this market, while the other companies have tried to better understand home-computer buying motives and are hiring executives from consumer-oriented companies such as Procter & Gamble and Philip Morris to help direct more consumer-oriented marketing.[12]

We will first discuss some conditions that must be met if the marketing concept is to work and then turn our attention to some problems in its implementation.

Making the marketing concept work

Since the marketing concept affects all types of business activities, not only marketing activities, the top management of an organization must adopt it wholeheartedly. Forrest Mars, from the giant candy maker of the same name, was a fanatic about quality and once hurled a batch of poorly wrapped candy into a glass panel in the board room. He spent an immense amount of time checking product quality in the factory and in stores.[13] High-level executives must incorporate the marketing concept into their personal philosophies of business management so completely that they serve as the bases for all the goals and decisions they set for their firms. They must convince other members of the organization to accept the changes in policies and operations that flow from their acceptance of the marketing concept.

As the first step, management must establish an information system that enables it to discover customers' real needs and to use that information internally to create satisfying products. For instance, to develop the right image when selling beer, Stroh's uses extensive consumer research to determine emotional reactions to different representations of its product.[14] Since an information system of this sort is almost always expensive, management must be willing to commit a substantial amount of money and time for development and maintenance.

Without an adequate information system, an organization cannot be customer oriented. Within the last fifteen years, for example, a number of old downtown hotels have failed; yet many new ones have been constructed and are thriving. Why have some of the old ones gone under? One reason, among many, is that their information systems were inadequate. They failed to determine what customers wanted and thus were unable to provide the products desired.

12. "Home Computer Firms Begin to See Marketing as Industry's Salvation," *Wall Street Journal,* Sept. 21, 1983, p. 1.
13. "Well-Run Companies: The Secret of Success," *U.S. News and World Report,* Oct. 10, 1983, p. 74.
14. "Marketing Emphasis Is on Consistent Imagery When Selling Beer: Stroh Exec," *Marketing News,* Mar. 4, 1983, p. 10.

Management's second major task may well be restructuring the organization. We have already pointed out that if a firm is to satisfy customers' objectives as well as its own, it must coordinate all activities. To achieve this coordination, the internal operations and the overall objectives of one or more departments may need restructuring. If the head of the marketing unit is not a member of the organization's top-level management, the situation should be rectified. Some departments may have to be abolished and new ones created. Implementing the marketing concept demands the support not only of top management but also of managers and staff at all levels in the organization. At Walt Disney Productions, all employees, including the president, wear a name tag with only their first name on it. The aim is to increase the intensity of communication.[15]

Problems in implementing the marketing concept

Even when the basic conditions of establishing an information system and reorganizing the firm are satisfied, it is not certain that the firm's new marketing approach will function perfectly. First of all, there is a limit on a firm's ability to satisfy customers' needs for a particular product. Each person has a unique idea of what a specific product should be. In a mass production economy, however, most business organizations cannot tailor products to fit the exact needs of each customer. Second, although a firm may try to learn what customers want, it may be unable to do so; and even when a firm correctly identifies customers' needs, the firm's personnel often have a hard time actually developing a product to satisfy those needs. Many companies spend considerable time and money to research customers' needs yet still create some products that do not sell well.

Third, by satisfying one segment of society, a firm sometimes contributes to the dissatisfaction of other segments. Government and nonbusiness organizations also experience this problem.

Fourth, a firm may have trouble maintaining employee morale during any restructuring that may be required to coordinate the activities of various departments. Change can be highly upsetting to employees and can affect their productivity. Management must clearly enunciate the reasons for the changes and communicate its own enthusiasm for the marketing concept.

Adoption of the marketing concept

You may wonder how many organizations have adopted the marketing concept. Research generally indicates that the marketing concept—especially its customer orientation—has been implemented by a number of business organizations. Larger businesses have seemed more willing to adopt the marketing concept than smaller ones. However, as business people become more aware of their social responsibilities and as an increasing number of individuals and groups pressure businesses to be more responsive to societal needs, we can expect more organizations to adopt the marketing concept.

15. Thomas J. Peters and Robert H. Waterman, Jr., "In Pursuit of Excellence," *Continental*, Mar. 1983, p. 70.

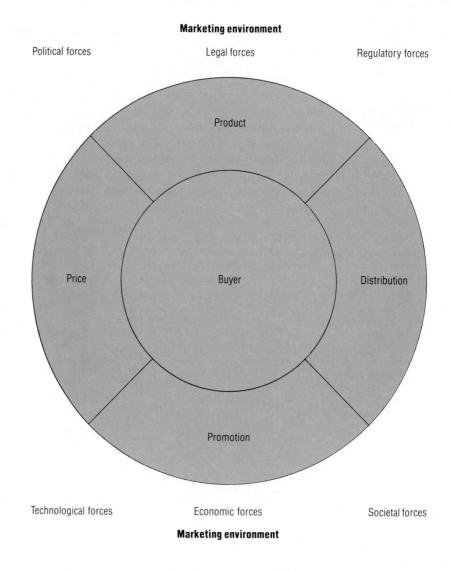

Figure 1.6
Variables of the
marketing mix and the
marketing environment

Marketing environment

Political forces   Legal forces   Regulatory forces

Product

Price   Buyer   Distribution

Promotion

Technological forces   Economic forces   Societal forces

Marketing environment

The marketing variables

Our definition of marketing states that various activities are performed to facilitate and expedite exchanges. Marketing activities are affected by two general kinds of variables: those relating to the marketing mix and those relating to the marketing environment. As shown in Figure 1.6 the marketing mix variables (factors over which an organization has control) are affected in many ways and to varying degrees by the marketing environment variables (aspects of the general business environment over which the firm has little or no control).

Marketing mix variables

The *marketing mix* consists of four major components: product, distribution, promotion, and price. These components are called marketing decision variables because a marketing manager can vary the type and amount of each element. One primary goal is to create and maintain a marketing mix that satisfies consumers' needs for a general product type. Notice in Figure 1.6 that the marketing mix is built around the buyer (as is stressed by the marketing concept). By making decisions and managing activities to relate to each marketing mix variable, a marketing manager can create a satisfying and thus successful mix.

Marketing mix variables often are viewed as "controllable" variables because they can be changed. However, there are limits to how much these variables can be altered. They are not totally controllable. For example, because of economic conditions or government regulations, a manager may not be free to adjust prices from one day to the next. Changes in sizes, colors, shapes, and designs of most tangible goods are expensive; therefore such product features cannot be altered very often. In addition, promotional campaigns and the methods used to distribute products ordinarily cannot be changed overnight.

Now let us look more closely at the decisions and activities related to the marketing mix variables (product, distribution, promotion, and price).

The product variable

As noted earlier, a product can be a good, a service, or an idea. The actual physical production of products is not a marketing activity. However, marketers do research consumers' product wants and design a product to achieve the desired characteristics. They may also create and alter packages and brand names. This aspect of the marketing mix is known as the *product variable*. Figure 1.7 illustrates the creation of a package and brand name to provide a French-import image for a Wisconsin cheese product.

Product variable decisions and related activities are important because they are involved directly with creating want-satisfying products. To maintain a satisfying set of products that will help an organization to achieve its goals, a marketer must be able to develop new products, modify existing ones, and eliminate those that no longer satisfy buyers and yield acceptable profits. For example, the Delco Electronics Division of General Motors and Bose Corporation spent $12 million to develop a new automobile stereo system because they perceived that there was high demand for studio-sound quality in an automobile system. The new system is available for approximately $895 on many General Motors automobiles. In the first year, it exceeded General Motors sales estimates, with 25 percent of Oldsmobile buyers and 84 percent of Corvette buyers ordering the unit.[16]

The distribution variable

To satisfy consumers, products must be available at the right time in a convenient and accessible location. In dealing with the *distribution variable,* a marketing manager attempts to make products available in the quantities desired to as many customers as possible and to hold the total inventory, transportation, and storage costs as low as possible. A marketing manager may become involved in selecting and motivating intermediaries (wholesalers and retailers), establishing and maintaining inventory control procedures, and developing and managing transportation and storage systems.

As an example of the importance of the distribution variable in the marketing mix, management at Adolph Coors Company has dramatically

16. Thomas Pezinge, Jr., "GM Wins Back Music Fans by Developing a High-Quality Stereo for Its Automobiles," *Wall Street Journal,* Aug. 29, 1983, p. 15.

Figure 1.7
The creation of a
unique product
through branding and
packaging
*Source: Besnier USA,
Inc.*

increased sales by expanding distribution of its product to six southeastern states. These states make up the fastest-growing beer market in the United States. Instead of relying on inexperienced wholesalers, Coors tapped into an existing network of Schlitz distributors that needed extra business. This distribution strategy allowed Coors to gain 10 percent of the Florida market in a very short time.[17]

The promotion variable

The **promotion variable** is used to facilitate exchanges by informing one or more groups of people about an organization and its products. Promotion is used for various reasons. For example, it might be used to increase public awareness of an organization or a new product or brand. In addition, promotion is used to educate consumers about product features or to urge

17. John J. Curran, "Beer Stocks with Yeasty Promise," *Fortune*, Oct. 17, 1983, pp. 179–180.

people to adopt a particular position on a political or social issue. It may also be used to renew interest in a product whose popularity is waning. The International Coffee Organization and the National Coffee Association recently spent $20 million in advertising to encourage the 18–34 age group to drink coffee. Lately, people between the ages of twenty and twenty-nine have averaged only 1.3 cups of coffee daily, compared with 3.4 cups twenty years ago. In this promotional campaign, television advertising shows celebrities such as Jane Curtin, quarterback Ken Anderson, and Ann and Nancy Wilson, of the rock group Heart, drinking coffee, working hard, and pursuing goals and achievements. The advertisements indicate that coffee gives both serenity and vitality.[18]

Part 4 looks closely at such promotion activities as advertising, publicity, personal selling, and sales promotion.

The price variable

Consumers are interested in a product's price because they are concerned about the value obtained in an exchange. In the area of the *price variable,* marketing managers usually have a hand in establishing pricing policies and determining product prices. Because price is important to consumers, it is a critical component of the marketing mix. It often is used as a competitive tool; in fact, extremely intense price competition sometimes leads to "price wars." New airlines such as People Express, Muse, and Southwest have touched off air fare price wars that have caused some larger, higher-cost airlines to go bankrupt or lose millions of dollars.

Price also helps to establish a product's image. For instance, if the makers of Chanel No. 5 tried to sell that perfume in a one-gallon jug for $3.95, consumers probably would not buy it. That price would destroy the image of Chanel No. 5.

Marketing environment variables

Marketing decisions and activities do not occur in a vacuum. They are affected by variables in the marketing environment, such as political, legal, regulatory, societal, economic, and technological forces.

As was shown in Figure 1.6, the *marketing environment* surrounds both the buyer and the marketing mix. The variables of the marketing environment affect in three general ways a marketer's ability to facilitate and expedite exchanges. First, the marketing environment influences consumers. It affects lifestyles, standards of living, and preferences and needs for products. Since a marketing manager tries to develop and adjust the marketing mix variables to satisfy consumers, the effects of environmental variables on consumers also have an indirect impact on the marketing mix variables. Second, forces in the marketing environment directly influence whether and how a marketing manager can perform certain marketing activities. Third, marketing environment variables may affect a marketing manager's decisions and actions by influencing consumers' reactions to the firm's marketing mix or mixes.

Although forces in the marketing environment sometimes are called uncontrollables, they are not totally uncontrollable. A marketing manager

18. Kathleen A. Hughes, "Coffee Makers Hope New Ads Will Reverse Declining Sales," *Wall Street Journal,* Sept. 1, 1983, p. 21.

can often influence one or more of them. However, marketing environment variables fluctuate quickly and dramatically, which is one reason why marketing is so interesting and challenging. Since these variables are highly interrelated, a change in one of them may cause others to change.

Even though environmental variables produce uncertainty for marketers and, at times, have severe adverse effects on marketing efforts, they also can create opportunities. For example, technological advances in fabrics have simultaneously put some firms out of business and provided other firms with opportunities to enter a market. Thus marketers must be aware of changes in environmental variables—not only to be able to adjust to and influence them but also to capitalize on the opportunities provided. The remainder of this section briefly describes the dynamic environment in which marketing decisions and activities occur. Chapters 16 and 17 analyze environmental variables in detail.

Political forces
Our political institutions enact laws and create regulatory units that affect business organizations. More broadly, the actions of *political forces* strongly influence the economic and political stability of our country, not only through decisions that affect domestic matters, but also through their authority to negotiate trade agreements and determine foreign policy. If government officials have negative opinions about a firm or an industry, they may pass and enforce laws that place severe constraints on an organization's ability to market products. In addition, the government purchases many products in tremendous quantities and offers several kinds of loans that can aid businesses. Political officials thus may affect the financial position of a firm by awarding or failing to award a government contract or loan. Obviously, it is important to impress political officials favorably. Businesses demonstrate their awareness of this fact by the number and magnitude of their efforts to use political support to influence elected officials.

Legal forces
Legislation and the interpretation of laws give rise to *legal forces*. Marketing decisions and activities are restrained and controlled by a multitude of laws established by political institutions. Many laws were enacted either to preserve a competitive atmosphere or to protect consumers. They tend to influence marketing activities directly, but the real effects of these provisions on the marketing mix variables depend largely on how marketers and the courts interpret such provisions. For example, wide-open competition in the drug market is one result of an unanimous decision of the U.S. Supreme Court in favor of generic medications. This decision permits pharmacists to substitute a less expensive form of a drug for a brand-name medication when filling prescriptions.[19]

Regulatory forces
Regulatory forces arise from regulatory units at the local, state, and federal levels. These units create and enforce numerous regulations that affect

19. Pravat Choudhury, "High Court Clears the Way for Generic Drug Competition," *Marketing News,* Mar. 4, 1983, p. 6.

marketing decisions. For example, since deregulation of airlines and the trucking industry, air fares have gone down and truck rates have decreased. On the other hand, many workers in both industries have taken wage cuts and companies have had to develop better marketing approaches to cope with the new, more competitive market.

At times government regulatory agencies, especially at the federal level, sponsor meetings to encourage firms in a particular industry to develop guidelines to stop questionable practices. Industry leaders usually cooperate in such cases, for they recognize that the next step may be government regulation.

Government is not the only source of regulations affecting marketers, however. Individual firms and trade organizations also exert regulatory pressures on themselves and their members.

Societal forces

A large majority of American consumers have a high standard of living and an enjoyable quality of life. *Societal forces* pressure marketers to provide such living standards and lifestyles through socially responsible decisions and activities.

For many years, Ralph Nader was a key advocate of consumer issues. Today, there are thirty to forty thousand local consumer groups that are well prepared and educated to fight industries on an issue-by-issue basis.[20] This proliferation is just one example of how people in our society form interest groups to let marketers know what they want. In general, such groups desire a high standard of living but do not want to live in a profane or defaced environment. They also insist on honest marketing and attention to product safety. Marketers must attend to such social concerns. Figure 1.8 illustrates that Nutech, a consultant to the nuclear energy, electric utility, and construction industries, recognizes that support of basic American values is important in coping with societal forces. This advertisement emphasizes the promise of good living standards. It implies that Nutech will be socially responsible in achieving these goals.

Economic forces

To a large extent *economic forces* determine the strength of a firm's competitive atmosphere. Some businesses operate under highly competitive conditions. For example, the deregulation of telecommunications, more specifically the AT&T breakup, has completely changed the nature of competition to provide long-distance telephone service.

The intensity of competition is affected by three primary factors: the number of businesses that control the supply of a product; how easily a firm can enter the industry; and how much demand there is for the product relative to supply.

Economic factors affect the impact of marketing activities because they determine the size and strength of demand for products. Two general determinants of demand are buyers' ability to purchase and their willingness to purchase. Changes in the state of the economy have a great bearing

20. John Elkins, "Social Trends Dictate Changes in American Approach to Business," *Marketing News*, June 24, 1983, p. 16.

Figure 1.8
Nutech communicates that it is a socially responsible company in supporting good living standards
*Source: Nutech, Inc.;
Photographer: Jay
Maisel; Ad agency:
Drummond Advertising.*

THE LAND AND THE PROMISE.

"A country puts its dreams and its ideals into symbols—a flag, a plot of ground, a monument. The people grow to love these symbols, fight for them, die for them. A symbol and what it stands for must stay together. They are indivisible."

—Thomas Crawford, sculptor of The Freedom Statue that surmounts the great dome of the Capitol.

You'll see one in front of the post office. The school down the street. The fire station. The cemetery. There may even be one on your neighbor's front porch. And out in center field there will be one gently rippling in the summer breeze. The next time you see the American Flag, spend a few moments with it. And reflect on what it represents. Unity and independence. Our purpose as a nation. Freedom. Democracy. And the land and the promise.

The promise is still alive. But to fulfill it we must meet today's energy needs, as well as those of the future. At NUTECH we are investing in the personnel and the technologies that will help meet those needs. As a full-service consultant to the nuclear power, electric utility, and construction industries, we are successfully applying our unique problem-solving talents to many of the industry's most complex engineering and construction projects.

nutech™

A limited-edition poster of The American Flag, photographed by Jay Maisel, is available by writing: Nutech, 6835-N Via del Oro, San Jose, CA 95119. Please enclose $2.10 for postage and handling.
Copyright 1983 Nutech, Inc.

on these two factors. They can curtail or enhance marketers' effectiveness in facilitating exchanges. During prosperous times buyers usually have more buying power and are more willing to spend. In recessionary periods customers have less ability to buy and frequently are less willing to use that limited buying power.

Technological forces

There are two ways in which *technological forces* influence marketers' decisions and activities. First, they have great impact on people's everyday lives. For instance, home computers are being developed that will allow most appliances to be programmable, will process and store household information, and will permit people to pay bills and purchase groceries and other items while sitting in their kitchens. Technology affects our lifestyles and standards of living which, in turn, influence not only our desires for products but also our reactions to the marketing mixes offered by business organizations. Second, technological developments may have a direct impact on creating and maintaining a marketing mix, because they may affect all its variables: product, distribution, promotion, and price. The technologies of communication, transportation, computers, energy, medicine, fabrics, metals, and packaging have influenced the types of products produced as well as advertising, personal selling, marketing research, pricing, packaging, transportation, storage, and the use and processing of credit.

Many organizations, for example, are taking advantage of the opportunities provided by the new communication technology known as WATS—Wide Area Telecommunications Service. Quaker Oats used an 800 number as part of a contest to promote Cap'n Crunch that generated 15 million responses. The Campbell Soup Company uses WATS to determine viewers' responses to new television commercials. American Express has recently employed WATS to allow individuals to apply for American Express services. Parents can call Beech-Nut baby food's toll-free number for recorded bulletins on infant care.[21] Technology is changing so fast in the telecommunications field that equipment that formerly enjoyed a thirty-year life cycle is becoming obsolete almost as soon as it is installed. The competitive market is forcing companies to automate more functions.[22]

These brief descriptions of marketing environment variables point out some general effects of such forces on marketing decisions and activities. If they hope to create and maintain an effective marketing strategy, marketers must recognize and analyze the effects of the marketing environment on marketing decisions and activities. They must be able to adjust the marketing strategy to major changes in the marketing environment.

Developing a marketing strategy

Strategy, a word derived from the ancient Greek *strategia* (which meant "the art of the general"), is concerned with the key decisions required to reach an objective or set of objectives. A marketing strategy forms the core of a successful marketing plan. It articulates a plan for the best use of the organization's resources and advantages to meet its objectives. Specifically, a **marketing strategy** encompasses selecting and analyzing a target market (the group of people whom the organization wants to reach) and creating and maintaining an appropriate marketing mix (product, distribution, promotion, and price) that will satisfy those people. We will now examine what is involved in formulating a marketing strategy.

Selecting and analyzing target markets

A **target market** is a group of persons for whom a firm creates and maintains a marketing mix that specifically fits the needs and preferences of that group. When choosing a target market, marketing managers try to evaluate possible markets to see how entering them would affect the firm's sales, costs, and profits. Marketers also attempt to determine if the organization has the resources to produce a marketing mix that meets the needs of a particular target market and whether satisfying those needs is consistent with the firm's overall objectives. They also analyze the size and number of competitors who already are selling in the possible target market.

21. Bill Abrams, "Coke Drinkers Talk a Lot . . . 'Lite' Is Hot . . . So Is WATS," *Wall Street Journal,* Oct. 22, 1981, p. 25.
22. "Telecommunications: The Global Battle," *Business Week,* Oct. 24, 1983, p. 126.

Marketing managers may define a target market to include a relatively small number of people, or they may define it to encompass a vast group of people. For example, a women's swimwear manufacturer may select as its target market young women athletes in high school and college and in professional competition, or this firm may try to reach all women who swim for recreation. Although it may focus its marketing efforts on one target market through a single marketing mix, a business often focuses on several target markets by developing and employing multiple marketing mixes. Compare Bic's strategy with Ronson's, for example. Bic produces one type of disposable butane lighter and directs it at one target market. The maker of Ronson lighters, however, aims at several market groups by manufacturing several types of lighters, promoting them in a variety of ways, selling them at different prices, and distributing them through numerous types of outlets.

Creating and maintaining a satisfying marketing mix

Marketing managers must develop a marketing mix that precisely matches the needs of the people in the target market. Before they can do this, they have to collect in-depth, up-to-date information about those needs. The information might include data regarding the age, income, race, sex, and educational level of people in the target market; their preferences for product designs, features, colors, and textures; their attitudes toward competitors' products, services, advertisements, and prices; and the frequency and intensity with which they use the product. With these kinds of data, marketing managers are better able to develop a product, distribution, promotion, and price that satisfy the people in the target market. The Application on page 27 discusses why McDonald's must develop and maintain a marketing strategy that satisfies a broad target market.

The organization of this book

Figure 1.6 is a map of the overall organization of this book. We focus initially on the center of Figure 1.6 by analyzing markets, buyers, and marketing research (in Chapters 2, 3, and 4, respectively). Chapters 5 through 15 explore the marketing mix variables, starting with the product variable and moving around Figure 1.6 in a clockwise direction. Then Chapters 16 and 17 focus on the outer portion of Figure 1.6, which contains the variables in the marketing environment. Starting with political forces (shown in the upper left part of Figure 1.6), we again move in a clockwise direction to analyze each major variable in the marketing environment. Chapters 18 and 19 discuss strategic market planning, organization, implementation, and control. Marketing decisions and activities that are unique to industrial marketing, international marketing, and nonbusiness marketing are considered in Chapters 20, 21, and 22. If, as you are reading, you wonder where the text is leading, look again at the map in Figure 1.6.

Summary

About half of each consumer dollar is spent in marketing activities. You should be aware of what marketing is because its activities permeate our lives. They are performed by business firms and also by nonbusiness organizations such as political, social, church, cultural, and civic groups. Moreover, marketing activities help business organizations to generate profits, the lifeblood of a capitalist economy. Finally, the study of marketing will help you evaluate marketing activities.

Application

McDonald's— Making Marketing Strategy Decisions

Since 1955 McDonald's has been at the top of the fast-food industry, but competition has intensified, and the company needs to respond. McDonald's competitors are diversifying and wooing new market segments. Wendy's is moving into chicken; and Burger King is trying to attract adults. In addition, many small chains have sprung up that offer ethnic menus and promote more healthful food. Pricing, too, is a crucial variable. If burgers are priced low, consumers question their quality. Buyers' tastes and willingness to pay for quality are also changing. This shift has created a niche for chains that offer more stimulating food.

In this environment, McDonald's faces major challenges such as opening new stores, developing new products, setting competitive prices, and developing promotion that will yield a public perception of quality. The company is generally conservative in introducing new products. McDonald's only successful new offering since 1977 has been Chicken McNuggets. McDonald's has traditionally outstripped its competitors in service and efficiency; and its large number of outlets (6,000 in this country, 1,500 overseas) offer convenience of access that competitors such as Burger King (with less than half as many outlets) cannot match. However, McDonald's size means that it is difficult to introduce many new products without sacrificing service and efficiency.

In spite of McDonald's excellent financial position, the company has crucial marketing strategy decisions to make—decisions that involve the marketing mix variables of product, price, promotion, and distribution.

Source: Based on "The Fast-Food War: Big Mac Under Attack," *Business Week*, Jan. 30, 1984, pp. 44–46.

Marketing is defined as individual and organizational activities aimed at facilitating and expediting exchanges within a set of dynamic environmental forces. Four conditions must exist for an exchange to occur: (1) an exchange requires participation by two or more individuals, groups, or organizations; (2) each must have something of value desired by the other; (3) each must be willing to give up what it has to receive the valued item held by the other; and (4) the parties to the exchange must be able to communicate with each other to make their "somethings of value" available. In an exchange, products are traded either for other products or for financial resources, such as cash or credit. Products can be goods, services, or ideas.

The marketing concept is a management philosophy that affects all activities of a business organization. According to this philosophy, a business organization should try to satisfy customers' needs through a coordinated set of activities that, at the same time, allows the organization to achieve its goals. Customer satisfaction is the major objective of the marketing concept. The organization first must determine consumers' needs and then try to satisfy those needs through a coordinated set of activities. An organization achieves its own goals by satisfying customers. To make the marketing concept work, top management must accept it as an overall management philosophy. Implementing the marketing concept requires an efficient information system and, possibly, the restructuring of the organization.

One primary goal of a marketing manager is to create and maintain a marketing mix that satisfies consumers' needs for a particular kind of product. The variables that make up the marketing mix are product, distribution, promotion, and price. Within limits, a marketing manager can alter marketing mix variables as consumers' preferences and needs change.

The marketing environment variables include political forces, legal forces, regulatory forces, societal forces, economic forces, and technological forces. These factors influence the marketing mix variables in several ways. Forces within the marketing environment affect consumers' lifestyles, standard of living, and preferences and needs for products. The impact of the marketing environment variables on consumers often necessitates changes in marketing mixes. Finally, marketers' decisions and their abilities to perform certain marketing activities are affected by variables in the marketing environment.

The development of a marketing strategy encompasses two steps: (1) selecting and analyzing target markets and (2) creating and maintaining a marketing mix that satisfies the needs and preferences of the target market.

Important terms

Marketing
Exchange
Product
Good
Service
Marketing concept
Production orientation
Sales orientation
Customer orientation
Marketing mix
Product variable
Distribution variable

Promotion variable
Price variable
Marketing environment
Political forces
Legal forces
Regulatory forces
Societal forces
Economic forces
Technological forces
Marketing strategy
Target market

Discussion and review questions

1. Why should most people study marketing?
2. In what important ways does the definition of marketing used in this text differ from the other four definitions given? How did you define marketing before you read this chapter?
3. Discuss the basic elements of the marketing concept. Which businesses in your area employ this concept? Why do you believe that these businesses have adopted the marketing concept?
4. Identify several business organizations in your area that obviously have not adopted the marketing concept. What characteristics of these organizations indicate nonacceptance of the marketing concept?
5. Why are the elements of the marketing mix known as variables?
6. What are some marketing activities associated with the product component of the marketing mix? the distribution component? the promotion component? the price component?
7. Why is promotion an important element in the marketing mix? Identify several current advertisements that seem to be aimed at improving the sponsoring firms' images.
8. What are the variables in the marketing environment? How much control does a marketing manager have over environmental variables?
9. Should marketers be concerned with societal forces and their effects? Why or why not? What are businesses doing today that you believe will have negative effects on society in the future? What is society doing to limit these effects?

10. Discuss several ways that economic forces affect marketing. What effect does the current state of our national economy have on what consumers are buying?
11. What are some effects of technological forces on marketing decisions and activities? Which elements of the marketing mix are affected by technological forces?
12. Describe the major components of a marketing strategy. What is the relationship among the components?

Cases

Case 1.1

Levi Strauss & Co. Introduces Women's 501® Jeans[23]

Levi Strauss & Co.'s Womenswear Division markets several lines of casual sportswear, including jeans, slacks, knit and woven tops, blazers, and skirts. Although new products are continuously being introduced by Levi Strauss & Co., the recent introduction of the Women's 501® jeans has been particularly successful.

The marketing strategy for the new product launch was based on studies identifying two consumer clusters as primary targets. The first consumer group consisted of women whose median age was 25, who had sophisticated tastes and were appreciative of the latest styles, and who had progressive lifestyles and a high degree of brand consciousness. The second group consisted of women whose median age was 28, who followed a traditional lifestyle, and who preferred practical clothes. Research showed that the product attributes most important to these two consumer groups were quality, value, comfort, and fit.

The product was a new version of the original Levi's® jeans that set apparel standards for gold-seeking forty-niners more than one hundred years ago. The new garment retains all features of the original, including copper rivets on the front pockets, metal buttons on the fly, and the all-cotton denim fabric that in three washings shrinks to fit individual body contours. With additional washings the 501® jean becomes lighter in color, softer and more comfortable, yet retains its durability.

In contrast with the general practice of advertising after product distribution was completed, "consumer-pull" advertising and intense promotion stimulated distribution. Distribution was also facilitated by good communication with retailers. For example, although quality and value were inherent in the product, fit testing needed to be more rigorous than usual because a garment designed for the male figure was being converted for women. Since the product actually does "shrink when washed," the consumer education program was also more intensive than usual, with much of the information based on advance interviews with major retailers.

Promotional references to the company's origin and the aura surrounding the Old West were strong selling features. The advertising—"designed to create a sensation"—did. Most memorable was a TV commercial which featured an attractive, self-assured young woman in 501® jeans. Photo-

23. Many of the facts in this case are based on the *1982 Levi Strauss & Co. Annual Report.*

graphed against a backdrop of stark Texas countryside, she says only six words: "Travis, you're a year too late!" This cryptic statement generated such intense public interest that it proliferated dramatically through word-of-mouth and frequent editorial mentions. Letters and phone calls inquiring about the identity of Travis deluged the company.

The Levi image was maintained in competitive pricing to provide an image of quality, durability, and good value for the money. The Women's 501® jeans rapidly became a new product success, with first-year shipments more than doubling optimistic projections. The successful promotional efforts for the Women's 501® also generated renewed interest in the entire women's denim line. Individuals closely involved in the product's inception say that the launch was outstanding because of superb teamwork by all involved.

Questions for discussion

1. How did Levi Strauss & Co. make the marketing concept work in launching Women's 501® jeans?
2. Define the target market and marketing mix used in the Levi's® Women's 501® jeans marketing strategy.
3. Why do you think that a jean's product that is physically similar to the 100-year-old original Levi's® jeans was so successful in this 1980s new introduction?

Case 1.2

Pillsbury Restaurants[24]

The Pillsbury Company is a diversified international food company operating in three major segments of the food industry: consumer foods, restaurants, and agriproducts. Included in the area of consumer foods is the entire line of Pillsbury brand products, Green Giant vegetables, and Häagen-Dazs ice cream. Pillsbury's restaurant group includes Steak and Ale, Bennigans Tavern and Restaurant, and Burger King. The agriproducts division is involved with grain merchandising and the production of industrial foods such as flour and bakery products.

Pillsbury's restaurants prospered in the early 1980s. Steak and Ale experienced a 22 percent sales increase last year. Management programs focused on maintaining continued sales growth. New menu items were added to satisfy continuing customer demand for quality and variety; wine sales were strongly promoted, with an emphasis on premium brands; and new creative advertising was developed for television, featuring "lifestyle" themes. Sixty-two restaurants were remodeled to incorporate the latest decor, and 22 units were sold as part of an ongoing asset-management program. High-potential locations, in terms of sales and returns on investment, have been determined for restaurant expansion.

Bennigans restaurants experienced a 65 percent rate of expansion with 43 new restaurant openings last year. This rapid expansion was achieved through high quality site selection and the successful recruiting and training of management personnel. Both television and radio advertising were

24. Facts in this case are from the *Pillsbury 1983 Annual Report*.

used to support sales. A major feature of Bennigans is its broad menu that emphasizes price and value. Menu changes are made continuously to ensure that consumers' evolving needs are satisfied. Another feature that Bennigans promotes heavily is the celebration of certain holidays. Restaurant attendance is increased through the popularity of occasions such as Halloween, St. Patrick's Day, and New Year's.

Burger King, promoted as a high quality fast-food restaurant chain, attained a 19 percent sales increase last year. During that year, the company opened 270 new restaurants, achieving a worldwide total of 3,502. Burger King franchises were responsible for 227 of the 270 new restaurant openings, which demonstrates the company's strong support of the franchise system. New restaurants were made smaller in size to take advantage of current demographic and economic trends. The newer restaurants required fewer operators and less construction time; yet they could produce yearly sales of $1 million per unit and could be expanded as increased sales warranted the change.

Television advertising has proved to be very successful and innovative for Burger King. Advertising slogans, such as "Aren't You Hungry?" and the "Battle of the Burgers" and "Broiling is Better" promotions created increased sales and new awareness of the restaurants. The company distributed coupons that made a free Whopper available when a customer purchased one and said, "The Whopper beat the Big Mac." Many restaurants reported 100 percent increases in sales due to this promotion.

New product introductions have also helped sales. The Bacon Double Cheeseburger, the Whopper, and the 23-item salad bar have been offered as attractive, new menu alternatives. Emphasis has also been placed on operating excellence with Burger King's "Shape-Up" program concentrating on new standards of quality, training, and service.

While Burger King has maintained a highly successful domestic concept, its international operations have produced substantial operating losses. Executive management is concentrating on transferring basic marketing, operations, franchising, and financial strategies that have proved successful in the United States to Canada and other international markets.

Questions for discussion
1. Has Pillsbury been practicing the marketing concept?
2. What societal or economic trends may have caused Pillsbury to sell some restaurants, such as Poppin' Fresh featuring desserts and sandwiches, and expand others, such as Burger King?
3. Identify the differences in the target market for Burger King versus Bennigans?

2

Selecting and Evaluating Target Markets

Objectives

To understand the definition of a market.

To find out what types of markets exist.

To learn how firms identify target markets.

To gain an understanding of market potential.

To understand the definition of a company sales forecast.

To become familiar with sales forecasting methods.

Note that the product in Figure 2.1 is not aimed at everyone; it is not directed at you, unless you are a parent with young children. The advertisement stresses effective decay prevention and other features that parents look for in a toothpaste. The advertisement helps Procter & Gamble to zero in on a particular group of customers. Although there is a wide range of toothpastes in the marketplace, Crest is aimed at parents who want "kids without cavities."

A company identifies or singles out groups of customers for its products and directs some or all of its marketing activities at those groups. It develops and maintains a marketing mix (consisting of a product, a distribution system, promotion—such as the advertisement in Figure 2.1—and price) that effectively meets customers' needs.

In this chapter, we initially discuss the characteristics of a market and the major types of markets. Then, we examine two major approaches to selecting target markets. Next, the major issues associated with market measurement and evaluation are considered. Finally, we describe the primary techniques used in sales forecasting.

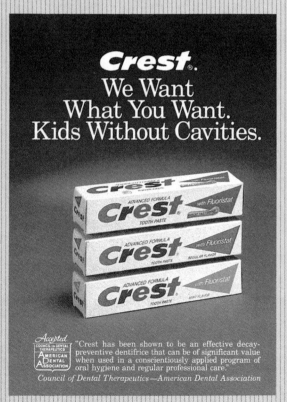

Figure 2.1 Advertisement aimed at a specific customer group
Source: Courtesy of Procter & Gamble Company.

What are markets?

The word *market* has a number of meanings. People sometimes use the word to refer to a specific location where products are bought and sold. A large geographic area may also be called a market. Sometimes "market" refers to the relationship between the demand and supply of a specific product. It has this meaning, for example, in the question, "How is the market for diamonds?" At times "market" is used to mean the act of selling something.

As used in this book, a **market** is an aggregate of people who, as individuals or as organizations, have needs for products in a product class and who have the ability, willingness, and authority to purchase such products. At times, "market" refers to the total population—or mass market—that buys products in general. However, our definition is more specific; it refers to persons seeking products in a specific product category. Obviously, there are many different markets in our complex economy. In this section, we will identify and describe several general groups of markets.

Requirements of a market

For an aggregate of people to be a market, it must meet four requirements.

1. The people must need the product; if the people in the aggregate do not desire the particular product, then that aggregate is not a market.
2. The people in the group must have the ability to purchase the product. Ability to purchase is a function of their buying power, which consists of resources such as money, goods, and services that could be traded in an exchange situation.
3. The people in the aggregate must be willing to use their buying power.
4. Individuals in the group must have the authority to buy the specific products.

At times, individuals have the desire, the buying power, and the willingness to purchase certain products but they are not authorized to do so. Young teen-agers may have the desire, the money, and the willingness to buy liquor. However, a liquor producer does not consider them a market because they are not authorized by law or social custom to buy alcoholic beverages. If, then, an aggregate of people lacks any one of these four requirements, it does not constitute a market.

Types of markets

Markets fall into one of three categories: (1) consumer markets, (2) industrial markets, or (3) reseller markets. These categories are based on the characteristics of the individuals and organizations that make up the specific market. Personal computers, for instance, are aimed at two distinct markets—homes and offices. The machines sold in each market bear little resemblance in price, distribution, or promotion. Whereas the home computer purchase is more faddish or impulsive, office buyers study the purchase and justify it by estimating what the machine will do for their productivity.[1] Since appropriate marketing activities depend on the type of market aimed at, it is important to know the general characteristics of the three categories noted.

1. "Mass-Marketing the Computer," *Fortune,* Oct. 31, 1983, pp. 61–62.

Consumer Markets

A *consumer market* consists of purchasers and/or individuals in their households who intend to consume or benefit from the purchased products and who do not buy products for the main purpose of making a profit. Each of us belongs to numerous consumer markets. The combined force of millions of individuals with the ability, willingness, and authority to buy make up a multitude of consumer markets for such products as housing, food, clothing, vehicles, personal services, appliances, furniture, and recreational equipment. As individual buying power increases and our population rises, we can expect the size and number of consumer markets to expand.

Industrial markets

An *industrial market* consists of individuals, groups, or organizations that purchase a specific kind of product for direct use in producing other products or for use in day-to-day operations. For example, a lamp producer that buys electrical wire to use in the production of lamps is a part of the industrial market for electrical wire. This same firm purchases dust mops to clean its office areas. Although the mops are not used in the direct production of lamps, they are used in the operations of the firm; thus, this manufacturer is part of the industrial market for dust mops.

Compared with other consumers, industrial buyers tend to be more knowledgeable about the products they consider. Normally, industrial buyers purchase large quantities of a relatively limited assortment of products on a periodic basis. They must be well informed about these products in order to buy the most appropriate ones at the best price. Industrial marketers often must provide their customers with a great deal of information.

Since a number of individuals and organizations are involved in producing and processing all the materials and parts that eventually result in consumer products, more exchanges occur in industrial markets than in consumer markets. There are many different types of industrial markets. For purposes of analysis we have divided them into three categories: producer, government, and institutional.

Producer markets. Individuals and business organizations that purchase products for the purpose of making a profit by using them to produce other products or by using them in their operations are classified as *producer markets*. Producer markets include buyers of raw materials as well as purchasers of semifinished and finished items used to produce other products.

Grocery stores are part of the producer markets for numerous support products—paper bags, counters, scanners, floor-care products, and the like. The stores buy and use such products indirectly to make profits. Farmers are part of the producer markets for machinery, fertilizer, seed, and livestock. A broad array of industries—from agriculture, to construction, to communication—make up producer markets.

Manufacturers, which make up a sizable part of producer markets, are geographically concentrated. Large proportions of them are located in California and in the Midwestern and Middle Atlantic states. This geographic concentration of manufacturers sometimes allows an industrial marketer to serve industrial users more efficiently.

Government markets. Federal, state, county, and local governments make up *government markets*. They spend billions of dollars annually for a variety of goods and services to support their internal operations and to provide citizens with such products as highways, education, water, national defense, and energy. For example, in 1981 the federal government spent over $175 billion on defense, about $122 billion on health, and about $27 billion on education.[2]

In addition to the federal government, there are 50 state governments, 3,042 county governments, and 18,856 city governments.[3] The amount spent by federal, state, and local units over the last thirty years has increased so rapidly for several reasons. First, the total number of government units has increased. Second, governments are providing more services. Third, the costs of providing these services have increased. In Table 2.1, notice that the federal government spends over half of the total amount spent by all governments.

The types and quantities of products purchased by government markets reflect societal demands on various government agencies. As citizens' needs for government services change, so does the demand for products by government markets. Because government agencies spend public funds to buy the products needed to provide services, they are accountable to the public. This accountability explains their relatively complex set of buying procedures. Some firms don't even try to sell to government buyers because they do not want to deal with so much red tape. However, a number of marketers learn to deal efficiently with government procedures and do not find them a stumbling block. The U.S. Government Printing Office publishes and distributes several documents explaining buying procedures and describing the types of products purchased by various federal agencies.

Government purchases are made through bids or through negotiated contracts. To make a sale under the bid system, a firm must appear on a list of qualified bidders. When the government unit wants to buy, it sends

Table 2.1   Annual expenditures by government units for selected years (in billions of dollars)

Year	Total Government Expenditures	Federal Government Expenditures	State and Local Expenditures
1960	151	90	61
1970	333	185	148
1975	560	292	268
1980	816	447	369
1981	924	517	407

Source: *Statistical Abstract of the United States: 1984,* p. 274.

2. *Statistical Abstract of the United States* (1984), pp. 103, 139, 274.
3. U.S. Department of Commerce, *1977 Census of Government, Preliminary Report #1* (Washington, D.C.: Government Printing Office, 1978), p. 1.

out a highly specific description of the desired products to qualified bidders. Businesses that wish to sell such products submit bids. The government unit usually is required to accept the lowest acceptable bid.

When buying nonstandard or highly complex products, a government unit often uses a negotiated contract. Under this procedure, the government unit selects only a few firms and then negotiates specifications and terms; it eventually awards the contract to one of the negotiating firms. Most large defense-related purchases are made through negotiated contracts.

Although government markets can be complicated in their requirements, they can also be very lucrative. When the Postal Service, Social Security Administration, and other government agencies modernize obsolete computer systems, successful bidders can gain a billion dollars over the life of a contract, usually five years or more. One computer service company, Electronic Data Systems Corporation, is trying to use federal contracts to make itself the industry leader.[4]

Institutional markets.   Organizations that seek to achieve goals other than normal business goals such as profit, market share, or return on investment constitute *institutional markets*. Members of institutional markets include churches, private schools and hospitals, civic clubs, fraternities and sororities, charitable organizations, and foundations. Institutions purchase millions of dollars' worth of products annually to provide goods, services, and ideas to congregations, students, patients, club members, and others. Because institutions often have different goals and fewer resources than other types of organizations, marketers may employ special marketing activities to serve these markets.

Reseller markets
Reseller markets consist of intermediaries, such as wholesalers and retailers, who buy finished goods and resell them to make a profit. (Wholesalers and retailers are discussed in Chapters 8 and 9.) Except for minor alterations, resellers do not change the physical characteristics of the products they handle. With the exception of items that producers sell directly to consumers, all products sold to consumer markets are also sold to reseller markets. Approximately 382,837 wholesalers and 1,304,000 retailers make up reseller markets.[5]

When making purchase decisions, resellers consider several factors. They evaluate the level of demand to determine in what quantity and at what price the products can be resold. They determine the amount of space required to handle a product relative to its potential profit. Retailers, for example, sometimes evaluate products on the basis of sales per square foot of selling area. Since its own customers often depend on a reseller to have a product when they need it, a reseller typically evaluates a supplier's ability to provide adequate quantities when and where needed. More broadly, when resellers consider the purchase of a product not previously carried, they try to determine whether the product competes with or complements products currently being handled by the firm. These types of concerns

4. "Ross Perot's Raid on Washington," *Fortune,* Oct. 31, 1983, p. 124.
5. *Statistical Abstract of the United States: 1984,* pp. 802, 808.

distinguish reseller markets from other markets. Marketers dealing with reseller markets must recognize these needs and be able to serve them.

Selecting target markets

Regardless of what general types of markets a firm focuses on, marketing management faces two major problems: (1) how to select a specific market or markets and (2) how to approach that market. This section analyzes several possible approaches.

In Chapter 1, we said that a marketing strategy has two components: (1) the selection of the organization's target market, and (2) the creation and maintenance of a marketing mix that satisfies the market's needs for a specific product. We will now examine two general approaches to identifying target markets—the total market approach and the market segmentation approach.

The total market approach

An organization sometimes defines the total market for a particular product as its target market. When a company designs a single marketing mix and directs it at an entire market for a particular product, it is using a *total market* (or *undifferentiated*) *approach*. Notice in Figure 2.2 that the organization is aiming a single marketing mix at the total market for the product. This approach assumes that individual customers in the target market for a specific kind of product have similar needs and, therefore, that the organization can satisfy most customers with a single marketing mix. This single marketing mix consists of one type of product with no (or very little) variation, one price, a promotional program aimed at everyone, and one distribution system to reach all customers in the total market. Products that can be marketed successfully with the total market approach include staple food items such as sugar and salt, certain kinds of farm produce, and some other products that most customers think of as homogeneous (no different from any other product of the same type). Morton's table salt, for instance, is aimed at the total market. One marketing mix can satisfy most consumers of this product.

The total market approach can be effective under two conditions. First, a large proportion of customers in the total market must have similar needs for the product. A marketer who uses a single marketing mix for a total market of customers with a variety of needs will find that the marketing mix satisfies very few people. Anyone could predict that a "universal shoe" that "fits everyone" would satisfy very few customers' needs for shoes because it would not fit most people. Second, the organization must be able to develop and maintain a single marketing mix that satisfies customers' needs. The company must be able to identify a set of product needs that are common to most customers in a total market, and it must have the resources and managerial skills to reach a sizable portion of that market. If customers' needs are dissimilar or if the organization is unable to develop and maintain a satisfying marketing mix, then a total market approach is likely to fail.

Companies that take the total market approach frequently attempt to use promotional efforts to differentiate their own products from competitors' products. They hope to establish in customers' minds that their products are superior and preferable to competing brands. This strategy is

Figure 2.2
Total market approach

Organization   Single marketing mix   Target market

(Single marketing mix labels: Product, Price, Distribution, Promotion)

called *product differentiation* because a marketer tries to differentiate the product, in consumers' minds, from competitive brands.[6] Premium Saltines are promoted as "The All Goodness Family Cracker." The reclosable bags that help keep the crackers fresh are promoted to differentiate the product.

A marketer who uses product differentiation rarely designs a product that is very different physically from other brands. After all, consumers have relatively similar needs for the product. Because the product actually is not much different from competing brands, marketers rely heavily on promotional efforts to emphasize one or several small differences. Unleaded gasoline, for example, has a broad appeal. Millions of consumers use it. Yet most unleaded gasolines are not much different physically from other unleaded gasolines. Therefore, oil companies differentiate their unleaded gasolines from competing brands by promoting greater mileage, additives, or economy. The effectiveness of product differentiation is determined largely by whether the features used to distinguish one brand from another are credible and important to a large number of customers in the total market.

Although customers' needs for some products, such as staple food items, may be similar, there are a multitude of products for which customers' needs are decidedly different. In these cases, a company should not use the total market approach; instead, it should use the market segmentation approach.

The market segmentation approach

Markets made up of individuals with diverse product needs are called *heterogeneous markets*. Not everyone wants the same type of car, house, furniture, or clothes. If you were to ask fifty people what type of home each would like to have, you probably would receive fifty different answers, many of them quite distinct. The automobile market is another example of a heterogeneous market. Some individuals want a car that is economical, some see a car as a status symbol, and still others seek an automobile that is roomy and comfortable for travel. For such heterogeneous markets, the market segmentation approach is appropriate.

As shown in Figure 2.3, *market segmentation* is the process of dividing a total market into market groups consisting of people who have relatively similar product needs. The purpose is to design a marketing mix (or mixes) that more precisely matches the needs of individuals in a selected segment (or segments). Market segments arise from the segmentation process. A

6. Wendell R. Smith, "Product Differentiation and Market Segmentation as Alternative Marketing Strategies," *Journal of Marketing,* July 1956, pp. 3–4.

Figure 2.3
Market segmentation
approach

Organization   **Single marketing mix**   **Market**

market segment is a group of individuals, groups, or organizations who share one or more similar characteristics that cause them to have relatively similar product needs.

The principal rationale for using the segmentation approach is that in a heterogeneous market, an organization is better able to develop a marketing mix that satisfies a relatively homogeneous portion of a total market than it is to design a marketing mix that meets the product needs of all people. For example, people who own sports cars or aspire to own one exemplify one market segment. These individuals are similar in that they like the handling, size, style, and image of a sports car.

A gold and silver plated buckle aimed at native born Texans is shown in Figure 2.4. Instead of trying to develop a buckle that would appeal to all people, H.T.S. & Associates designed a product for a unique and loyal group in one geographic area. In this way, the firm's segmentation approach differs from the total approach because it aims one marketing mix at one segment of a total market, rather than directing a single marketing mix at a total market.

The market segmentation approach is widely used. We should, therefore, analyze several of its most important features, including types of market segmentation strategies, conditions required for effective segmentation, selection of segmentation variables, and types of variables used to segment consumer and industrial markets.

Market segmentation strategies

There are two major market segmentation strategies: the concentration strategy and the multisegment strategy.

Concentration strategy. When an organization directs its marketing efforts toward a single market segment through one marketing mix, it is following a *concentration strategy*. The concentration strategy is used, for example, by Rolls-Royce, which concentrates on only the luxury segment of the automobile market.

The concentration strategy has advantages and disadvantages. One primary advantage is that it allows a firm to specialize. By concentrating all marketing efforts on a single segment, the firm has an opportunity to analyze a distinct group of customers' characteristics and needs. The firm can then direct all its efforts toward satisfying this single group of needs. For example, by identifying an available market segment, ''Daytime,'' a cable television show, has attempted to lure women away from soap operas. The

Figure 2.4
Advertisement for the
native-born
Texan market
*Source: H. T. S.
Associates.*

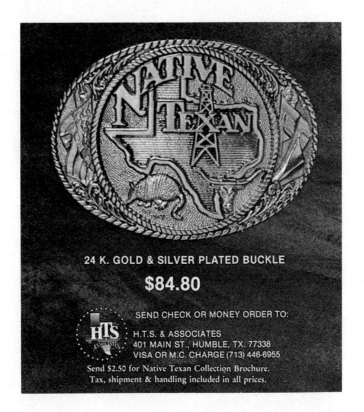

show offers controversial and provocative programming and concentrates on a women's daytime market that is interested in franker treatment of sexual practices, health, and social issues.[7] A firm can generate a large sales volume by reaching such a single segment. In addition, concentrating on a single segment allows a firm with restricted resources to compete with much larger organizations. The application on page 45 describes a concentration strategy used by an AM radio station. Specialization can be a disadvantage too, because the firm puts "all its eggs in one basket." If a company's sales depend on a single segment and that segment's demand for the product declines, then the company's financial strength also declines. Moreover, when a firm penetrates one segment and becomes well entrenched, its popularity may keep it from moving into other segments. For example, Ferrari, which has attempted to maintain the prestigious image shown in Figure 2.5, would have trouble moving into the economy-car segment, whereas Volkswagen would have difficulty entering the luxury-car segment.

Multisegment strategy.   After a firm uses a concentration strategy successfully in one market segment, it sometimes focuses on several segments. A *multisegment strategy* (see Figure 2.6) is one in which an organization directs its marketing efforts at two or more segments by developing a marketing mix for each selected segment. For example, designer

7. Laura Londro, "ABC/Hearst Tries a Provocative Approach to Lure Women to 'Daytime' Cable Show," *Wall Street Journal,* Oct. 22, 1983, p. 25.

fragrances have traditionally been aimed at one segment—women. However, as shown in the ad in Figure 2.7, Halston fragrances for men have a distinct designer image. Halston also produces designer fragrances for women. The marketing mixes used for a multisegment strategy may vary in terms of product differences, distribution methods, promotion methods, and prices.

A business using the multisegment strategy can usually increase its sales in a total market by focusing on more than one segment because the firm's mixes are being aimed at more people. A firm with excess production capacity may find the multisegment approach advantageous because the sale of products to additional segments may absorb excess capacity. However, because the multisegment strategy often requires a greater number of production processes, materials, and skills, production costs may be higher than with the concentration strategy. Keep in mind, also, that a firm ordinarily experiences higher marketing costs because the multisegment approach usually requires several distinct promotion plans and distribution methods. When a business uses the multisegment approach, the costs of planning, organizing, implementing, and controlling marketing activities increase.

Figure 2.6
Multisegment strategy

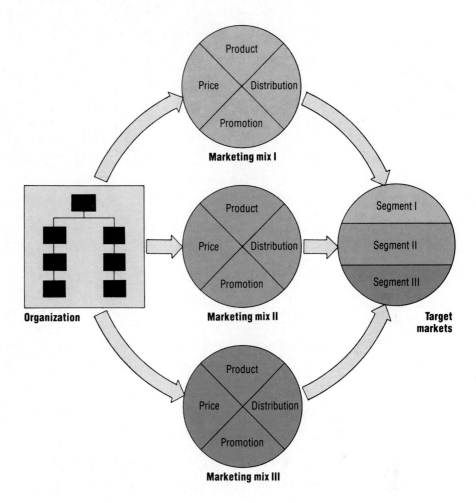

Conditions for effective segmentation

Whether a firm uses the concentration approach or the multisegment approach, several conditions must exist for market segmentation to be effective. First, a company should find out whether consumers' needs for the product are heterogeneous. If they are not, there is little need to segment the market. Second, the segments must be identifiable and divisible. The company must find some basis for effectively separating individuals in a total market into groups that have relatively similar needs for the product. Third, the total market should be divided in such a way that the segments can be compared with respect to estimated sales potential, costs, and profits. Fourth, at least one segment must have enough profit potential to justify developing and maintaining a special marketing mix. Finally, the firm must be able to reach the chosen segment with a particular marketing mix.

Some market segments may be difficult or impossible to reach because of legal, social, or distribution constraints. For instance, marketers of rock albums or jeans are not permitted to sell to a large market in the Soviet Union because of political and trade restrictions. Similarly, the strong demand in the United States for Cuban cigars is not met due to political and trade restrictions.

Choosing segmentation variables

Segmentation variables are the dimensions or characteristics of individuals, groups, or organizations that are used for dividing a total market into segments. For example, location, age, sex, or rate of product usage can be used for segmentation purposes.

Several factors should be considered in selecting a segmentation variable.[8] The segmentation variable should be related to customers' needs for, uses of, or behavior toward the product. That is, people's needs, uses, and actions should vary according to the chosen segmentation characteristic. Automobile producers use income as one means of segmenting the automobile market. Religion is not used as a segmentation variable in the automobile market because one person's automobile needs are not much different from those of persons of other religions. In addition, to classify

8. More than one variable can be used to segment a market. Such multivariable segmentation is discussed later in this chapter.

Application

AM Radio Station Concentrates on Beatles' Fans

KYST, AM, a Houston radio station, plays records featuring only the music of John Lennon, Paul McCartney, George Harrison, and Ringo Starr. It may be the only all-Beatles radio station in the United States.

The music of the Beatles first became popular in the United States over twenty years ago. Since that time, popular music has featured many different music groups and kinds of music. The Beatles disbanded in the late sixties and John Lennon was assassinated in 1980. Nonetheless, KYST's unusual programming increased its listening audience by over 300 percent. KYST directed its marketing efforts toward a single segment—an audience that is emotionally attached to the music of the Beatles. By aiming its marketing mix at this group of listeners, the radio station gained market share in an AM radio market that is declining in the Houston area. In data gathered by the radio station, 92 percent of the people in the target age group, between eighteen and forty-four, said they liked the Beatles, and 80 percent said they would tell a friend about the station's Beatle orientation.

KYST followed a concentration strategy. It defined a new market segment based on similar tastes in music. This market is so unique that no other radio station in Houston is likely to try to compete directly. KYST analyzed its target customers' characteristics and needs and then put all its efforts into satisfying this single group of needs.

Source: Based on Andrew M. Williams, "All Beatle Radio Station Stays Afloat In Houston," *Eagle,* Aug. 28, 1983, p. 3AA; and "Britain Rocks America Again," *Newsweek,* Jan. 23, 1984, pp. 50, 54.

individuals or organizations in a total market accurately, the segmentation variable must be measurable. For example, age, location, and sex are measurable. Such information can be obtained through observation or questioning. However, trying to divide a market on the basis of intelligence is more difficult because this characteristic is harder to measure accurately.

Choosing a segmentation variable is a critical step in segmenting a market. Selecting an inappropriate variable limits the chances of developing a successful strategy. To gain a better understanding of possible segmentation variables, we will consider the major types of variables in more detail.

Variables for segmenting consumer markets

A marketer who uses a segmentation strategy to reach a consumer market can select one or several variables from a broad assortment of possible ones. As shown in Figure 2.8 segmentation variables can be grouped into four categories: (1) socioeconomic variables, (2) geographic variables, (3) psychographic variables, and (4) product-related variables.

Socioeconomic variables.   Socioeconomic characteristics are a broad set of segmentation variables that are commonly used to divide markets. Socioeconomic variables include age, sex, race, ethnicity, income, education, occupation, family size, family life cycle, religion, home ownership, and social class. The application on page 48 illustrates how a socioeconomic variable—age—can be identified and used to segment markets. Socioeconomic characteristics are closely related to customers' product needs and purchasing behavior. Socioeconomic dimensions can also be measured readily through observation or surveys.

Figure 2.8
Segmentation variables
for consumer markets

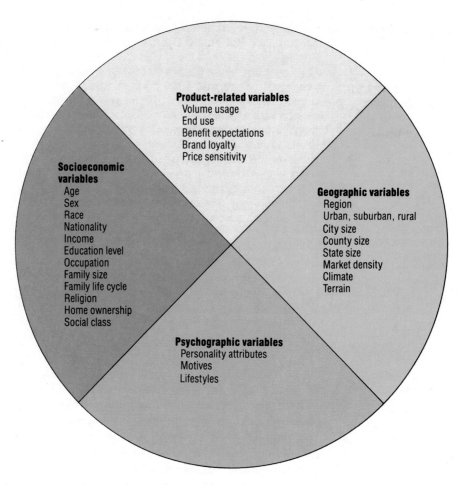

Product-related variables
Volume usage
End use
Benefit expectations
Brand loyalty
Price sensitivity

Socioeconomic variables
Age
Sex
Race
Nationality
Income
Education level
Occupation
Family size
Family life cycle
Religion
Home ownership
Social class

Geographic variables
Region
Urban, suburban, rural
City size
County size
State size
Market density
Climate
Terrain

Psychographic variables
Personality attributes
Motives
Lifestyles

Consider the types of product markets that are segmented according to age. Some examples are clothing, toys, automobiles, and diet foods. Figure 2.9 shows a possible segmentation scheme for the toy market. Notice that with the exception of the twelve-to-adult segment, the segments are relatively narrow. They are narrow because children's needs for toys change rapidly; a toy that entertains children at age two rarely interests them at age five.

A firm's resources and capabilities affect the number and size of segment ranges used. In addition, the type of product and the degree of variation in consumers' needs also dictate the number and size of segment categories for a particular firm's marketing approach. For example, the number and size of the segments in Figure 2.9 may be appropriate for dividing the toy market; clearly, however, the same age ranges would not be satisfactory for segmenting the market for dairy products.

Sex is commonly employed to segment a number of markets, including clothes, soft drinks, nonprescription medications, deodorants, magazines, soaps, and even cigarettes.

Income is often used to divide a market because it strongly influences people's product needs. It affects their ability to buy (discussed in more

Figure 2.9
Segmentation
of the toy market

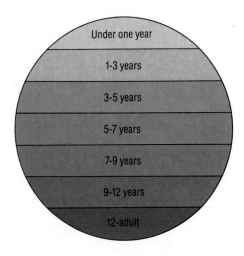

detail in Chapter 17) and their aspirations for a certain style of living. Examples of product markets segmented by income include housing, furniture, clothing, automobiles, food, and certain kinds of sporting goods.

Ethnicity, also, is used to segment markets for products such as food, music, and clothing and for services such as banking and insurance. A striking example of the importance of ethnicity as a segmentation variable is the U.S. Hispanic population. Made up of people with Mexican, Cuban, and Puerto Rican ancestry, and other people of Central and South American heritage, this ethnic group is growing six times faster than the nation as a whole. The Hispanic population is concentrated in nine states, as indicated in Table 2.2. If it continues to grow at its current rate, it will be the largest ethnic group in the country by the year 2020.

The product needs of a household also vary according to marital status and the presence and age of children. These characteristics can be combined into a single variable, sometimes called the family life cycle. The

Table 2.2   Nine states that contain 85 percent of U.S. Hispanics

State	1970	1980	Percent of 1980 Hispanics in USA
California	2,369,292	4,544,331	31.1
Texas	1,840,648	2,985,824	20.4
New York	1,351,982	1,659,300	11.4
Florida	405,036	858,158	5.9
Illinois	393,204	635,602	4.4
New Jersey	288,488	491,883	3.4
New Mexico	308,340	477,222	3.3
Arizona	264,770	440,701	3.0
Colorado	225,506	339,717	2.3

Source: U.S. Census Bureau.

Application

Johnson & Johnson— Affinity for Women Over Forty

In the world of shampoo, Johnson & Johnson is probably best known for Baby Shampoo. Now, however, J&J is promoting its first new shampoo since 1953 with an entirely different image. The company has introduced Affinity Shampoo, aimed at women over forty, into a very competitive market. Revlon, Clairol, Andrew Jergen, and Lever Brothers all have new shampoos. The shampoo market is characterized by a high number of entries, a low market share for each brand, and an exceptionally high failure rate.

Demographers expect that there will be more than 50 million women in the over-forty age group by 1990. Researchers at Johnson & Johnson are convinced that this market has a need for a specialized product that suits older, less flexible hair. The company wants Affinity's image to give older women pride and confidence in their ability to look attractive. In its painstakingly planned promotional efforts for Affinity, J&J has used mature women to stress that women over forty continue to lead exciting lives and deserve to have their product needs met. J&J has identified a target market and it is directing its marketing efforts to meet the needs of that market.

Source: Based on "The Lather Wars Have Shampoo Makers Hunting for Niches," *Business Week*, Jan. 9, 1984, p. 124.

family life cycle has been broken down in several different ways, one of which follows:

1. Young
   a. Single without children
   b. Married without children
   c. Single with children
   d. Married with children
2. Middle-aged
   a. Single without children
   b. Married without children
   c. Single with children
   d. Married with children
   e. Single without dependent children
   f. Married without dependent children
3. Older
   a. Single
   b. Married[9]

Housing, appliances, food, automobiles, and boats are a few of the numerous product markets sometimes segmented by family life cycle stages.

Geographic variables. Geographic variables—climate, terrain, natural resources, population density, and subcultural values—also influence consumer product needs. Markets may be divided into regions because one or more geographic variables cause customers to differ from one region to another. A company that markets products to a national market might divide the United States into the following regions: Pacific, Southwest, Central, Midwest, Southeast, Middle Atlantic, and New England. For instance,

9. Adapted with permission from Patrick E. Murphy and William A. Staples, "A Modernized Family Life Cycle," *Journal of Consumer Research*, June 1979, p. 16.

Pizza Hut changes its pizzas from one region to another because consumer preferences vary by region. Easterners want a lot of cheese, Westerners prefer a greater variety of ingredients, and Midwesterners like both.[10] A firm operating in a one-state or several-state market might also regionalize its market by counties, zip code areas, or other units.

Climate is commonly used as a geographic segmentation variable because it has such a broad impact on people's behavior and product needs. The wide variety of product markets that are affected by climate would include air-conditioning and heating equipment, clothing, yard tools, sports equipment, and building materials.

Market density refers to the number of potential customers within a unit of land area, such as a square mile. Figure 2.10 illustrates projections from the U.S. Census Bureau that the population density of the western United States will increase 45 percent between 1980 and 2000, that the Midwest will remain constant, and that the Northeast will decline. California, Texas, and Florida will be the three most populous states by 2000. Although market density is related generally to population density, the relationship is not necessarily proportional. For example, in two different geographic markets of approximately equal size and population, the market density for denture cleaners might be much higher in one area than another if one area contains a significantly greater proportion of older people. Low-density markets may require different sales, advertising, and distribution activities than high-density markets, which explains why market density is used as a segmentation variable.

Population density itself may influence people's product needs. It is well known that as population density increases, the demand for security devices rises, whereas the demand for lawn and garden supplies declines.

Psychographic variables. Although many psychographic factors could be used to segment markets, the three most common are personality characteristics, motives, and lifestyles. For example, the energy-conscious consumer shows psychographic characteristics of self-confidence, leadership, and reading interests, as well as the belief that increased government control over petroleum products is desirable.[11] A psychographic dimension can be used by itself to segment a market, or it can be combined with other types of segmentation variables.

Examples of personality characteristics used to segment markets are gregariousness, compulsiveness, competitiveness, extroversion, introversion, ambitiousness, and aggressiveness. Personality characteristics are useful when a product is similar to many competing products and consumers' needs are not affected significantly by other segmentation variables.

When attempting to segment a market on the basis of a personality characteristic, marketers face two major problems. First, personality characteristics are difficult, if not impossible, to measure accurately. Existing personality tests were developed for clinical use, not for segmentation

10. Christy Marshall, "Pizza Hut Is Cooking Up Recipe for Future Growth," *Advertising Age,* Feb. 6, 1978, p. 45.
11. Duane L. Davis and Ronald S. Rubin, "Identifying the Energy Conscious Consumer: The Case of the Opinion Leader," *Journal of the Academy of Marketing Science,* Spring 1983, p. 185.

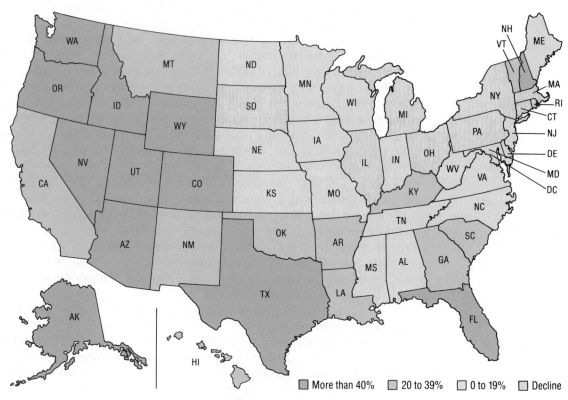

Figure 2.10 U.S. population growth 1980–2000
Source: U.S. Census Bureau.

■ More than 40%   ■ 20 to 39%   □ 0 to 19%   □ Decline

Detailed projections by state

	Population in 2000	Change From 1980		1980 Rank	2000 Rank
Alabama	4,415,300	Up	13.5%	22	24
Alaska	630,700	Up	57.5%	50	49
Arizona	5,582,500	Up	105.4%	29	15
Arkansas	2,835,400	Up	24.1%	33	32
California	30,613,100	Up	29.3%	1	1
Colorado	4,656,600	Up	61.2%	28	21
Connecticut	3,062,400	Down	1.5%	25	29
Delaware	638,200	Up	7.2%	47	48
Dist. of Columbia	376,500	Down	41.0%	—	—
Florida	17,438,000	Up	79.0%	7	3
Georgia	6,708,200	Up	22.8%	13	11
Hawaii	1,277,700	Up	32.4%	39	42
Idaho	1,512,200	Up	60.2%	41	39
Illinois	11,187,500	Down	2.0%	5	6
Indiana	5,679,200	Up	3.4%	12	14
Iowa	2,972,100	Up	2.0%	27	30
Kansas	2,494,400	Up	5.6%	32	34
Kentucky	4,399,900	Up	20.2%	23	25
Louisiana	5,159,800	Up	22.7%	19	19
Maine	1,308,000	Up	16.3%	38	41
Maryland	4,581,900	Up	8.7%	18	22
Massachusetts	5,490,400	Down	4.3%	11	16
Michigan	9,207,600	Down	0.5%	8	8
Minnesota	4,489,400	Up	10.1%	21	23
Mississippi	2,939,200	Up	16.6%	31	31
Missouri	5,080,000	Up	3.3%	15	20
Montana	963,000	Up	22.4%	44	44
Nebraska	1,661,900	Up	5.9%	35	38
Nevada	1,918,800	Up	140.1%	43	36
New Hampshire	1,363,500	Up	48.1%	42	40
New Jersey	7,427,600	Up	0.9%	9	9
New Mexico	1,727,300	Up	32.9%	37	37
New York	14,990,200	Down	14.6%	2	4
North Carolina	6,867,800	Up	16.9%	10	10
North Dakota	682,000	Up	4.5%	46	47
Ohio	10,356,800	Down	4.1%	6	7
Oklahoma	3,944,500	Up	30.4%	26	27
Oregon	4,025,300	Up	52.9%	30	26
Pennsylvania	11,207,600	Down	5.6%	4	5
Rhode Island	925,800	Down	2.3%	40	45
South Carolina	3,907,100	Up	25.3%	24	28
South Dakota	687,600	Down	0.4%	45	46
Tennessee	5,419,600	Up	18.1%	17	17
Texas	20,739,400	Up	45.8%	3	2
Utah	2,777,400	Up	90.1%	36	33
Vermont	625,000	Up	22.2%	48	50
Virginia	6,389,400	Up	19.5%	14	12
Washington	5,832,500	Up	41.2%	20	13
West Virginia	2,067,700	Up	6.1%	34	35
Wisconsin	5,215,500	Up	10.8%	16	18
Wyoming	1,002,200	Up	112.9%	49	43
U.S.	**267,461,600**	**Up**	**18.1%**	**—**	**—**

purposes. Second, even though it seems reasonable that personality characteristics affect buyers' actions, research has yielded little evidence to support this assumption.

When appealing to a personality characteristic, a marketer almost always selects one that is valued positively by many people in our culture. Individuals with this characteristic, as well as those who would like to have it, may be influenced to buy that marketer's brand. For example, a brand may be promoted as "not for everyone" but for those who are "independent," "strong-minded," or "outgoing." Marketers who take this approach do not worry about measuring how many people have the positively valued characteristic, because they assume that a sizable proportion of people in the target market either have or want to have such a characteristic.

A motive is an internal energizing force that moves an individual toward a goal. To some degree, motives influence what people buy and are occasionally used to divide markets. Product durability, economy, convenience, and status are all motives that may affect the types of products purchased and the choice of stores in which they are bought. When a market is segmented according to a motive, it is divided on the basis of consumers' reasons for making a purchase. For example, one motive for the purchase of soft drinks in nonreturnable containers is convenience. It is difficult, at best, to measure motives.

Lifestyle analysis provides a broad view of buyers because it encompasses numerous characteristics related to people's activities, interests, and opinions. Lifestyle segmentation divides individuals into groups on the basis of how they spend their time, the importance of things in their surroundings (their homes or their jobs, for example), their beliefs about themselves and broad issues, and some socioeconomic characteristics such as income and education.[12] Lifestyle analysis focuses on everyday facets of people's lives. Obviously, the manner in which people live affects their product needs. Revlon couples age with lifestyle characteristics to divide the cosmetic market into seven segments. Each segment is served by one of the following Revlon product lines: Classic Revlon, Moon Drops, Natural Wonder, Charlie, Ultima II, Princess Marcella Borghese, and Etherea Fine Fragrances. Charlie is directed at aspiring, self-assured women who are out to shape their own lives and develop their careers. Revlon portrays the Charlie woman as exciting, adventurous, rule-breaking, and earthshaking. The Princess Marcella Borghese line is directed at the fulfilled (rather than aspiring) woman who is very much concerned with fashion, status, and class. This expensive product line is for the "select few." It is promoted by word of mouth and by a limited number of distinctive, subtle advertisements in upscale women's magazines. Compare these two lifestyles in the advertisements in Figure 2.11 for two different product (designer) lines offered by Saks Fifth Avenue. An informal, adventurous lifestyle is provided in the Georges Marciano denim look while a more formal fashion is illustrated by the Bill Blass designer dress.

Psychographic dimensions can effectively divide a market. However, their use has been limited, and probably will continue to be, for several

12. Joseph T. Plummer, "The Concept and Application of Life Style Segmentation," *Journal of Marketing,* Jan. 1974, p. 33.

Red Hot!...the cocktail dress by Bill Blass. Starting from its soft
blouson top, to the slim little spin of its skirt, this is a dress to toast
the evening hours in. And for a final temptation? That fabulous
sash that is just beaded tromp l'oeil—a fantasy for the eyes,
a feast for the senses! In red satin-back silk crepe.
In American Designers Collections.

Figure 2.11   Lifestyles associated with two different Saks Fifth Avenue product lines
Source: Bill Blass—Saks Fifth Avenue; Guess Jeans—Saks Fifth Avenue.

reasons. First, they are more difficult than other types of segmentation variables to measure accurately. Second, the relationships among psychographic variables and consumers' needs are sometimes obscure and unproven. Third, segments that result from psychographic segmentation may not be reachable. For example, a marketer may determine that highly compulsive individuals desire a certain type of clothing. However, no specific stores or specific media vehicles—such as television or radio programs, newspapers, or magazines—appeal precisely to this group and this group alone.

Product-related variables.   Marketers can divide a market on the basis of a characteristic of the consumer's relationship to the product. These characteristics commonly involve some aspect of product use. Thus, a total market may be divided into users and nonusers. Users may then be classified as heavy, moderate, or light. To satisfy a specific group, such as heavy users, a marketer may have to create a distinctive product and initiate special prices, promotion, and distribution activities.

How customers use or apply the product may also be a basis for segmenting the market. To satisfy customers who use a product in a certain way, some feature—say packaging, size, texture, or color—may have to be designed precisely to make the product easier to use, safer, or more convenient. For example, producers of the golf balls illustrated in Figure 2.12 manufacture brightly colored gold balls for golfers who feel they can see them more easily. The company also manufactures white balls for golfers who want a traditionally colored ball. In addition, special distribution, promotion, or pricing activities may have to be created.

Another product-related characteristic is the benefit that consumers expect from the product. *Benefit segmentation* is the division of a market according to the benefits that customers want from the product. Although most segmentation variables show a purported relationship between the variable and customers' needs, benefit segmentation is different in that the benefits sought by customers *are* their product needs. That is, individuals are segmented directly according to their needs. By determining the benefits that consumers want, marketers may be able to divide people into groups that are seeking certain sets of benefits.

The effectiveness of benefit segmentation depends on several conditions. The benefits sought by people must be identifiable. Using these benefits, marketers must be able to group people into recognizable segments. One or more of the resulting segments must be accessible so that the firm's marketing efforts will reach and have impact on the segments.

As this brief discussion shows, consumer markets can be divided on the basis of numerous characteristics. However, some of these variables are not particularly helpful for segmenting industrial and reseller markets.

Variables for segmenting industrial and reseller markets
Industrial and reseller markets, like consumer markets, must sometimes be segmented to satisfy organizations' needs for products. Marketers make this segmentation on the basis of geographic factors, type of organization, customer size, and product use.

Geographic location. We have noted that the demand for some products varies considerably from one geographic area to another as a result of differences in climate, terrain, preferences of ultimate consumers, or similar factors. For example, the producers of certain types of lumber divide their markets geographically because their customers' needs vary regionally. Geographic segmentation may be especially appropriate for reaching industries that are concentrated in certain locations. Furniture producers, for example, are concentrated in the Southeast, while most iron and steel producers are located in the Great Lakes area.

Type of organization. A company sometimes segments a market on the basis of the types of organizations in that market. Different types of organizations often require different product features, distribution systems, and price structures. For example, the trainers for a professional football team may desire a greater range of product features and may place more stringent delivery demands on a manufacturer of athletic tape and equipment than would a neighborhood sporting goods store. Because of these variations, a firm either may concentrate on a single segment with one marketing mix or may focus on several groups with multiple mixes. A carpet pro-

ducer could segment potential customers into several groups, including auto makers, commercial carpet contractors (firms that carpet large commercial buildings), apartment-complex developers, carpet wholesalers, and large retail carpet outlets.

Buying procedures in various kinds of organizations may be sufficiently different that they require special marketing efforts. Marketers who sell to governments, for example, must know how to prepare proposals, bids, and contracts. One or more of a variety of individuals—including chief executives, purchasing agents, and engineers—may have a hand in the buying decisions of a manufacturing organization. Selling to a committee is quite distinct from selling to an individual.

Customer size. The size of customer organizations often differentiates the segments of a total market. Since an organization's size may affect purchasing procedures and the types and quantities of products desired, it can be an effective variable for segmenting an organizational market.

Figure 2.13
Single variable
segmentation

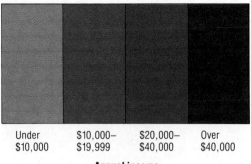

Under | $10,000– | $20,000– | Over
$10,000 | $19,999 | $40,000 | $40,000

Annual income

To reach a particular-sized segment, marketers may have to adjust one or more marketing mix components. For example, customers who buy in extremely large quantities sometimes are charged lower prices. In addition, marketers often have to provide greater personal selling efforts to serve larger organizational buyers properly. Because the needs of larger and smaller buyers tend to be quite distinct, marketers frequently employ different marketing practices to reach various customer groups.

Cook's Industrial Lubricants Company, a marketer of over five hundred metalworking and maintenance lubricants, directs its marketing efforts at light users—firms that use fewer than fifteen drums annually. This segment is almost totally ignored by the larger oil companies such as Shell and Exxon. Yet 85 percent of all potential customers fall into the light user category.[13]

Use of product.   Some products—especially basic raw materials such as steel, petroleum, plastics, and lumber—are used in numerous ways. How a firm uses products affects the types and amounts of the products purchased as well as the method of making the purchase. For example, computers are used for engineering purposes, for performing basic scientific research, and for business operations such as telephone service and airline reservations. A computer producer may segment the computer market by types of use because needs for computer hardware and software depend on the purpose for which the products are purchased.

Selecting the appropriate variable for market segmentation is an important marketing management decision, because the variable is the primary factor in defining the target market. So far, we have discussed segmentation as if only one variable is used, but in fact more than one variable can be used, and marketers must decide on the number of variables to include.

Single-variable or multivariable segmentation
A marketer can divide a market in terms of one variable or several. *Single-variable segmentation* is achieved by using only one variable. The segmentation shown in Figure 2.13 uses only income. (Although the areas shown on the graph are the same size, this does not mean that the segments are

13. "Getting to Know Cook's," *Sales and Marketing Management,* November 1978, p. 28.

Figure 2.14
Multivariable
segmentation

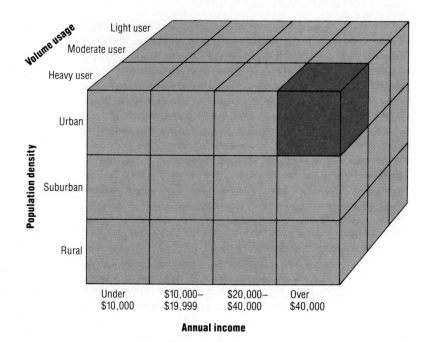

the same size or equal in sales potential.) Single-variable segmentation, the simplest form of segmentation, is the easiest to perform. However, a single characteristic affords marketers only moderate precision in designing a marketing mix to satisfy individuals in a specific segment.

Multivariable segmentation is achieved by using more than one characteristic to divide a total market (see Figure 2.14). Notice in this example that the market is segmented by three variables—income, population density, and volume usage. The people in the shaded segment earn over $40,000, are urban dwellers, and are heavy users. Multivariable segmentation provides more information about the individuals in each segment than does single-variable segmentation. This additional information may allow a marketer to develop a marketing mix that will satisfy customers in a given segment more precisely. More is known about the people in each segment of Figure 2.14 than about those in the segments of Figure 2.13.

The major disadvantage of multivariable segmentation is that the larger the number of variables used, the greater the number of segments. This proliferation reduces the sales potential of many of the segments. Compare, for example, the number and size of the segments in Figure 2.13 with the number and size of those in Figure 2.14.

The use of additional variables can help to create and maintain a more precise and satisfying marketing mix. Playboy Clubs, for example, were started in large U.S. cities in the 1960s and were targeted toward the socioeconomic and lifestyle characteristics of the best-educated, highest-earning, and biggest-spending males in the country. Currently, Playboy is using socioeconomic variables and population density for segmentation purposes. Competition and a changing society is causing Playboy Clubs to move to hotels in small cities. Their settings are smaller and less lavish, with a new focus on appealing to women as well as men who like to visit nightclubs. The clubs are relying on the attraction of the Playboy name, which continues to be perceived as a bit naughty in the heartland of the United States. This multisegmentation approach is helping Playboy develop a more precise and effective marketing mix.[14]

However, when deciding on single- or multivariable segmentation, a marketing manager must consider whether using additional variables will help to create and maintain a more precise and satisfying marketing mix. If using a second or third variable does not provide useful information that allows greater precision, there is little reason to spend more money to gain information about the extra variables.

Evaluating markets and forecasting sales

Whether single-variable segmentation or multivariable segmentation is used, a marketer still must be able to measure the sales potential of the segment or segments. Remember that at least one segment must have substantial sales potential for segmentation to be effective.

Wal-Mart recognized that there was substantial sales potential in these smaller markets.[15] Wal-Mart Stores is a rapidly growing discount chain with more than six hundred stores in eighteen states. Almost all of Wal-Mart's growth is aimed at towns of fewer than 25,000 people, leaving big cities to its competitors. Wal-Mart's revenues are in the billions because it concentrated on a target market that competitors thought was too small to serve.

Developing and maintaining a marketing mix normally consumes a considerable amount of a firm's resources. The target market or markets selected must have enough sales potential to justify the cost of developing and maintaining one or more marketing mixes.

A marketer must evaluate the sales potential in possible target markets as well as in the target markets that the firm currently serves. Moreover, a marketing manager must determine the proportion of this potential that the firm can capture relative to its objectives, resources, and managerial skills. He or she must ponder the question, "To what extent can our company tap this market if the potential is there?"

Demand can be measured along several dimensions, including product level, competitive level, geographic area, and time.[16] With respect to product level, demand can be estimated for specific product items (such as frozen orange juice) or for a product line (such as frozen foods). The competitive level lets us know whether sales are being measured for one firm or for an entire industry. One must decide on the geographic area to be included in an evaluation of demand. For example, demand could be measured for a neighborhood, town, county, state, or nation. In relation to time, demand measurements can be short range (one year or less), medium range (one to five years), or long range (longer than five years).

14. Robert Johnson, "Passe in the Big City, Playboy's Ailing Clubs Search for Profits in America's Hinterlands," *Wall Street Journal,* Sept. 28, 1983, p. 29.
15. Rod Davis, "Wal-Marts Across Texas," *Texas Monthly,* Oct. 1983, p. 168.
16. Philip Kotler, *Marketing Management: Analysis, Planning, and Control,* 5th ed. (Englewood Cliffs, N.J.: Prentice-Hall, 1984), p. 225.

Market and company sales potentials

Market sales potential refers to the amount of a product that would be purchased by specific customer groups within a specified period at a specific level of industrywide marketing activity. Market sales potential can be stated in terms of dollars or units and can refer to a total market or to a market segment. When analyzing market sales potential, it is important to specify a time frame and to indicate the relevant level of industry marketing activities.

Note here that marketers have to assume a certain general level of marketing effort in the industry when they estimate market sales potential. The specific level of marketing effort varies, of course, from one firm to another, but the sum of all firms' marketing activities equals industry marketing efforts. A marketing manager also must consider whether and to what extent industry marketing efforts will change.

Company sales potential is the amount of a product that an organization could sell during a specified period. Several general factors influence a company's sales potential. First, the market sales potential places absolute limits on the size of the company's sales potential. Second, the intensity of industrywide marketing activities has an indirect but definite effect on the company sales potential. Those activities have a direct bearing on the size of the market sales potential. When Texas Instruments advertises calculators, for example, it indirectly promotes calculators in general; it may, in fact, help to sell competitors' calculators. Third, the intensity and effectiveness of a company's marketing activities in proportion to the total industry's marketing efforts affect the size of the company's sales potential. If a company is spending twice as much as any of its competitors on marketing efforts, and if each dollar spent is more effective in generating sales, the firm's sales potential would be quite high compared with its competitors'.

There are two general approaches to measuring company sales potential—the breakdown approach and the buildup approach. In the *breakdown approach,* the marketing manager initially develops a general economic forecast for some future period. The market sales potential is estimated on the basis of this economic forecast. The company sales potential then is derived from the general economic forecast and the estimate of market sales potential. Thus, this approach is called the breakdown approach because the marketer starts with broad, comprehensive estimates of general economic activity and ends up with an estimate of a single firm's sales of a specific product.

In the *buildup approach,* an analyst begins by estimating how much of a product a potential buyer in a specific geographic area, such as a sales territory, will purchase in a given period. Then the analyst multiplies that amount by the total number of potential buyers in that area. He or she does the same thing for each geographic area in which the firm sells products and then adds the totals for each area to calculate the market potential. To determine the company sales potential, the analyst must estimate, on the basis of specific levels of marketing activities, the proportion of the total market potential that the firm can achieve.

For example, the marketing manager of a regional paper company with three competitors might estimate the company sales potential for bulk gift-wrapping paper using the buildup approach. The manager might determine that each of 66 paper buyers in a single sales territory purchases an average of 10 rolls annually. Thus, for that sales territory, the market potential is 660 rolls annually. The analyst follows the same procedure in each of the firm's other nineteen sales territories. He or she then totals the sales potential for each sales territory. Assume that this total market potential is 18,255 rolls of paper (the quantity expected to be sold by all four paper companies). Then the marketing manager would estimate the company sales potential by ascertaining what percentage of the estimated 18,255 rolls the firm could sell, assuming a certain level of marketing effort. The marketing manager might develop several company sales potentials, based on several levels of marketing effort.

Notice that regardless of whether marketers use the breakdown or buildup approach, they depend heavily on sales estimates. To get a clearer idea of how these estimates are arrived at, we need to explore sales forecasting.

Developing company sales forecasts

A *company sales forecast* is the amount of a product that the company actually expects to sell during a specific period at a specified level of marketing activities. When analyzing sales potential, marketers consider what sales levels are possible at various levels of marketing activities, assuming that certain environmental conditions will exist. However, when marketers develop a sales forecast, they concentrate on what the actual sales will be at a certain level of marketing effort.

Many operating units use the company sales forecast for planning, organizing, implementing, and controlling their activities. Managers use sales forecasts when purchasing raw materials, scheduling production, securing financial resources, considering plant or equipment purchases, hiring personnel, and planning inventory levels. The success of numerous activities depends on the accuracy of the company sales forecast.

A sales forecast must be time specific. As indicated earlier, sales estimates can be short range (one year or less), medium range (one to five years), or long range (longer than five years). The length of time chosen for the sales forecast depends on what the forecast will be used for, how stable the market is, and what the firm's objectives and resources are.

To forecast company sales, a marketer can choose from a number of forecasting methods. Some forecasting methods are rather arbitrary; others are more scientific, complex, and time consuming. The method or methods that a firm uses depend on the costs involved, the type of product, the characteristics of the market, the time span of the forecast, the purposes for which the forecast is used, the stability of the historical sales data, the availability of required information, and the expertise and experience of the forecasters.[17] For purposes of analysis, common forecasting techniques can be grouped into five categories: executive judgments, surveys, time series analysis, correlation methods, and market tests. We will explore each of these techniques.

Executive judgment

At times, a company forecasts sales primarily on the basis of *executive judgment*—the intuition of one or more executives. This approach is highly

17. David Hurwood, Elliott S. Grossman, and Earl Bailey, *Sales Forecasting* (New York: Conference Board, 1978), p. 2.

unscientific, but it is expedient and inexpensive. Executive judgment may work reasonably well when product demand is relatively stable and the forecaster has years of market-related experience. However, because intuition is swayed most heavily by recent experience, the forecast may be overoptimistic or overpessimistic. Another drawback to intuition is that the forecaster has only past experience as a guide for deciding where to go in the future.

Surveys

A second way to predict sales is to question customers, sales personnel, or experts regarding their expectations about future purchases.

Customer surveys. Through a *customer forecasting survey,* marketers can ask customers what types and quantities of products they intend to buy during a specific period. This approach may be useful to a business that has relatively few customers, because they can be questioned easily. For example, a transistor producer with fewer than two hundred potential buyers could conduct a customer survey. PepsiCo, Inc., though, has millions of customers and cannot feasibly employ a customer survey to forecast future sales.

Customer surveys have several drawbacks. Customers must be able and willing to make accurate estimates of future product requirements. Although industrial buyers can sometimes estimate their anticipated purchases accurately from historical buying data and their own sales forecasts, many customers cannot make such estimates. For a variety of reasons, customers may not want to participate in a survey. Occasionally, a few respondents give answers that they know are incorrect, making survey results inaccurate. In addition, customer surveys reflect buying intentions, not actual purchases. Customers' intentions may not be well formulated; and even when potential purchasers have definite buying intentions, they do not necessarily follow through on them. Finally, customer surveys consume a great deal of time and money.

Sales-force surveys. In a *sales-force forecasting survey,* members of the firm's sales force are asked to estimate the anticipated sales in their territories for a specified period of time. The forecaster combines these territorial estimates to arrive at a tentative forecast.

Let us trace this process in one manufacturing organization—Ex-Cell-O Corporation, which manufactures machine tools. Machine tools usually are sold through open proposals. These bids are submitted to specific customers for certain types of products. The data in the proposals go into the firm's marketing information system. When the forecast is being prepared, each salesperson receives a summary of his or her proposals, reviews this summary, updates it as needed, and then prepares the forecast for his or her territory for the next five quarters. The sales representatives then send their forecasts to regional managers, who review them and make necessary refinements. The regional managers send the forecasts to the marketing staff at corporate headquarters, where the forecasts are processed; the new forecast is transmitted to Ex-Cell-O's eight manufacturing plants to aid in production and inventory control.[18]

18. Hurwood, Grossman, and Bailey, *Sales Forecasting,* pp. 40–41.

A marketer may survey the sales staff for several reasons. The most important one is that the sales staff is closer to customers on a daily basis than are other company personnel and therefore should know more about customers' future product needs. Moreover, when sales representatives assist in developing the forecast, they are more likely to work toward its achievement. Another benefit of this method is that forecasts can be prepared for single territories, for divisions consisting of several territories, for regions made up of multiple divisions, and then for the total geographic market. This method readily provides sales forecasts from the smallest geographic sales unit to the largest.

Despite these benefits, a sales-force survey has certain limitations. Salespeople can be too optimistic or pessimistic because of recent experiences. Their estimates may be either inflated or low. In addition, salespeople tend to underestimate the sales potential in their territories when they believe that their sales goals are determined usually by their forecasts. Finally, salespeople usually dislike paperwork because it consumes time that could be spent selling. If the preparation of a territorial sales forecast is time consuming, the sales staff may do an inadequate job on it.

Sales-force surveys can be effective, nonetheless, for forecasting sales under certain conditions. If, for instance, the salespeople as a group are accurate—or at least consistent—estimators, the overestimates and underestimates should counterbalance each other. If the aggregate forecast is consistently over or under actual sales, then the marketer who develops the final forecast can make the necessary adjustments. If the survey is well administered, the sales force can really believe that it is making a definite contribution to developing sales goals. Finally, the sales force can be assured that its forecasts are not used to set sales quotas.

Expert surveys.   In an *expert forecasting survey,* a company uses experts to help prepare the sales forecast. These experts are usually economists, management consultants, advertising executives, college professors, or other persons outside the firm who have much experience in a specific market. Drawing on their experience and their analysis of available information about the company and the market, these experts prepare and present their forecasts or attempt to answer questions regarding a forecast.

The use of experts is expedient and relatively inexpensive. However, since they work outside the firm, they may not be as motivated as company personnel to do an effective job.

Time series analysis

Time series analysis is a technique in which the forecaster, using the firm's historical sales data, tries to discover a pattern or patterns in the firm's sales volume over time. If a pattern is uncovered, then it can be used to forecast sales. This forecasting method assumes that the past sales pattern will continue in the future. The accuracy, and thus the usefulness, of time series analysis depends heavily on the validity of this assumption.

To use time series analysis, a forecaster usually performs four types of analysis: trend, cycle, seasonal, and random factor.[19] *Trend analysis* focuses on aggregate sales data, such as a company's annual sales figures,

19. Norbert L. Enrick, *Market and Sales Forecasting: A Quantitative Approach* (San Francisco: Chandler, 1969), pp. 39–40.

over a period of many years to determine whether annual sales are generally rising, falling, or staying about the same. Through *cycle analysis* a forecaster analyzes sales figures (often monthly sales data) over a period of three to five years to ascertain whether sales fluctuate in a consistent, periodic manner. When performing *seasonal analysis,* the analyst studies daily, weekly, or monthly sales figures to evaluate the degree to which seasonal factors such as climate and holiday activities influence the firm's sales. *Random factor analysis* is an attempt to attribute erratic sales variations to random, nonrecurrent events such as a regional power failure, a natural disaster, or the death of a president of the United States. After performing each of these analyses, the forecaster combines the results to develop the sales forecast.

Time series analysis is an effective forecasting method for products that have reasonably stable demand, but it is not very useful for products that have highly erratic demand. Joseph E. Seagram & Sons, importer and producer of liquor and wines, uses several types of time series analyses for forecasting purposes and has found them to be quite accurate. For example, Seagram's forecasts of industry sales volume have proved correct within ±1.5 percent, and the firm's company sales forecasts have been accurate within ±2 percent. However, time series analysis is not always so accurate.[20]

Correlation methods

Like several other techniques, correlation methods are based on historical sales data. When *correlation methods* are used, the forecaster attempts to find a relationship between past sales and one or more variables such as population, per capita income, or gross national product. To determine whether a correlation exists, the analyst uses regression analysis, which analyzes the statistical relationships among changes in past sales and changes in one or more variables. The objective of regression analysis is a formula that accurately describes a mathematical relationship between the firm's sales and one or more variables. A regression formula indicates only an associational relationship, not a cause-and-effect relationship, among sales and one or more factors. Once an accurate formula has been established, the forecaster plugs the necessary information into the formula to derive the sales forecast.

Correlation methods are useful when a precise relationship can be established. However, a forecaster seldom finds a perfect correlation. In addition, this method can be used only when a considerable amount of historical sales data are available. Correlation techniques are ordinarily useless for forecasting the sales of new products.

Market tests

A *market test* consists of making a product available to buyers in one or more test areas and measuring purchases and consumer responses to distribution, promotion, and price. Even though test areas are often cities

20. Hurwood, Grossman, and Bailey, *Sales Forecasting,* p. 61.

with populations of 200,000 to 500,000, test sites can be larger metropolitan areas or towns with populations of 50,000 to 200,000. A market test provides information about consumers' actual purchases rather than about their intended purchases. In addition, purchase volume can be evaluated in relation to the intensity of other marketing activities—advertising, in-store promotions, pricing, packaging, distribution, and the like. On the basis of customer response in test areas, forecasters can estimate product sales for larger geographic units.

When considering the use of a market test, a marketer must weigh the advantages and disadvantages. A market test is an effective tool for forecasting the sales of new products or the sales of existing products in new geographic areas because it has no need for historical sales data. It provides the forecaster with information about customers' real actions rather than intended or estimated behavior. A market test also gives a marketer an opportunity to test various elements of the marketing mix. But a market test is often time consuming and expensive. In addition, a marketer cannot be certain that the consumer response during a market test represents the total market response or that such a response will continue in the future.

Using multiple forecasting methods

Although some businesses depend on a single sales forecasting method, most firms employ several techniques. At Rockwell International, for example, division managers are encouraged to use multiple forecasting methods and are even sent manuals describing numerous sales forecasting methods.[21] A firm is sometimes forced to use several methods when it markets diverse product lines, but even for a single product line, several forecasts may be needed—especially when the product is sold in different market segments. For example, a producer of automobile tires may employ one technique for forecasting new-car tire sales and another to forecast the sales of replacement tires. Variation in the length of the needed forecasts may require the use of several forecast methods; a firm that employs one method for a short-range forecast may find it inappropriate for long-range forecasting. Sometimes a marketer verifies the results of one method by employing one or several other methods and comparing results.

Summary

A market is defined as an aggregate of people who, as individuals or as organizations, have needs for products in a product class and who have the ability, willingness, and authority to purchase such products. There are three types of markets: consumer markets, industrial markets, and reseller markets. A consumer market consists of purchasers and/or individuals in their households who intend to consume or to benefit from the purchased products. An industrial market consists of individuals, groups, or organizations that purchase a specific kind of product for direct use in producing other products or for use in day-to-day operations. Reseller markets

21. Ibid., p. 216.

consist of intermediaries who buy finished products and resell them for the purpose of making a profit.

Industrial markets can be divided in turn into three categories: producer markets, government markets, and institutional markets. Producer markets consist of individuals and business organizations that purchase products for the purpose of making a profit by using them to produce other products or by using them in their operations. Government markets consist of federal, state, and local governments. These government units spend billions of dollars annually for a variety of goods and services to support their internal operations and to provide citizens with such products as highways, education, water, and the like. Institutional markets consist of organizations that seek to achieve goals other than normal business goals such as profit, market share, or return on investment. Institutions purchase millions of dollars' worth of products annually to provide goods, services, and ideas to congregations, students, patients, club members, and others.

Marketers use two general approaches to identify their target markets—the total market approach and the market segmentation approach. When the total market approach is used, the firm designs a single marketing mix and directs it at an entire market for a particular product. The total market approach can be effective under two conditions. First, a large proportion of individuals in the total market must have similar needs for the product. Second, the organization must be able to develop and maintain a single marketing mix that satisfies customers' needs.

Companies that take the total market approach frequently employ a product differentiation strategy. They aim one type of product at the total market and attempt to establish in customers' minds that their product is superior and preferable to competing brands.

The market segmentation approach divides the people in the total market into market groups consisting of people who have relatively similar product needs. The purpose is to design a marketing mix (or mixes) that more precisely matches the needs of individuals in a selected segment (or segments). There are two major types of market segmentation strategies. In the concentration strategy, the organization directs its marketing efforts toward a single market segment through one marketing mix. In the multisegment strategy, the organization directs its marketing efforts at two or more segments by developing a marketing mix for each selected segment.

Certain conditions must exist for market segmentation to be effective. First, consumers' needs for the product should be heterogeneous. Second, the segments of the market should be identifiable and divisible. Third, the total market should be divided in such a way that the segments can be compared with respect to estimated sales potential, costs, and profits. Fourth, at least one segment must have enough profit potential to justify developing and maintaining a special marketing mix for that segment. Fifth, the firm must be able to reach the chosen segment with a particular marketing mix.

A segmentation variable serves as the basis for dividing a total market into segments. The segmentation variable should be related to customers' needs for, uses of, or behavior toward the product. Segmentation variables for consumer markets can be grouped into four categories: socioeconomic variables, geographic variables, psychographic variables, and product-related variables. Segmentation variables for industrial and reseller markets include geographic factors, type of organization, customer size, and product use. Besides selecting the appropriate segmentation variable, a marketer also must decide how many variables to use.

A marketer must be able to evaluate the sales potential in possible target markets as well as in target markets that the firm currently serves. There are two general approaches to measuring company sales potential: the breakdown approach and the buildup approach. Several methods are used to forecast company sales. The executive judgment method—the intuition of one or more company executives—is inexpensive and expedient, yet unscientific. Businesses that use the survey method question customers, experts, or salespeople regarding their expectations about future purchases. Time series analysis is a sales forecasting method based on ascertaining sales patterns over time. Forecasters who use correlation methods develop a mathematical relationship between past sales and one or more variables such as population, per capita income, or gross national product. Finally, a market test can be used to forecast sales. It consists of making a product available to buyers in one or more test areas and measuring purchases and consumer response to distribution, promotion, and price.

Important terms

Market	Multivariable segmentation
Consumer market	Market sales potential
Industrial market	Company sales potential
Producer markets	Breakdown approach
Government markets	Buildup approach
Institutional markets	Company sales forecast
Reseller markets	Executive judgment
Total market approach	Customer forecasting survey
Product differentiation	Sales-force forecasting survey
Heterogeneous markets	Expert forecasting survey
Market segmentation	Time series analysis
Market segment	Trend analysis
Concentration strategy	Cycle analysis
Multisegment strategy	Seasonal analysis
Segmentation variables	Random factor analysis
Market density	Correlation methods
Benefit segmentation	Market test
Single-variable segmentation	

Discussion and review questions

1. What is a market? What are its requirements?
2. In your local area, is there a group of people with unsatisfied product needs who represent a market? Could this market be reached by a business organization? Why or why not?
3. Identify and describe three major types of markets. Give examples of each.

4. What is the total market approach? Under what conditions is it most useful? Describe a present market situation in which a firm is using a total market approach. Is the business successful? Why or why not?
5. Explain the basic characteristics of the product differentiation strategy. What companies are currently using this approach? Is it working for them? Why or why not?
6. What is the market segmentation approach? Describe the basic conditions required for effective segmentation. Identify several firms that employ the segmentation approach.
7. List the differences between the concentration strategy and the multisegment strategy. Describe the advantages and disadvantages of each.
8. When choosing a segmentation variable, what major factors should marketers consider?
9. Identify and describe four major categories of variables that can be used to segment consumer markets. Give examples of product markets that are segmented by variables in each category.
10. What dimensions are used to segment industrial and reseller markets?
11. How do marketers decide whether to use single-variable or multivariable segmentation? Identify examples of product markets that are divided through multivariable segmentation.
12. Why is a marketer concerned about sales potential when trying to find a target market?
13. Describe the relationship between market sales potential and company sales potential.
14. What is a company sales forecast and why is it important?
15. Identify five major types of sales forecasting methods.
16. What are the advantages and disadvantages of using executive judgment as a sales forecasting technique?
17. Explain three types of surveys used for sales forecasting. Compare their benefits and limitations.
18. Compare and contrast correlation forecasting methods with time series analysis.
19. Under what conditions are market tests useful for sales forecasting? Discuss the advantages and disadvantages of market tests.

Cases

Case 2.1

Miller Brewing Company

Miller Beer came to America in 1855 when its founder, Fredrick Miller, came over from Germany. He opened his small brewery in Milwaukee, Wisconsin; the brewery produced about 300 barrels of beer per year. His goal was always to produce a beer of the finest quality.

Miller High Life had only moderate success until 1970, when the company was sold and sales began to increase noticeably. Before 1970, Miller Brewing was production-oriented; its major objective was to produce a high-quality product through highly efficient production methods. In 1970,

Philip Morris purchased the slumping Miller Brewing Company. Miller had a four percent share of the market at that time. Philip Morris had succeeded in the tobacco industry by using market segmentation and emphasizing new product development, packaging, and heavy advertising. When Philip Morris decided to use a similar approach with Miller, the rest of the brewing industry was caught napping. In 1972, there were 192 U.S. breweries, but by 1976 only 49 breweries remained.

When Philip Morris took over in 1970, Miller High Life's target market was the country club set. The brand was labeled the "Champagne of Bottled Beers." Through research, however, Philip Morris discovered that people in this target market did not drink much beer. Further research yielded additional findings. First, 80 percent of all beer is consumed by only 30 percent of the beer drinkers. Second, this group largely consists of men and women aged 18–34. Third, two-thirds of all beer is consumed during the late afternoon and early evening hours. Finally, heavy beer drinkers think of beer as something they can relax with.

These findings indicated that Philip Morris definitely needed to aim Miller High Life at a different target market. Marketers at Miller's decided to aim the brand at working-class people. To avoid customer confusion, the change in target markets was made slowly. The objective of the new advertisements was to not indicate their target market. The advertisements showed outdoor settings and included background music and a narrator. There was no talking by any participants. The theme the narrator stressed was that when the day is done, "It's Miller time."

It was a slow transition, and Miller knew it had to add more group interaction to the commercials. When the time was right, it began showing group interaction, appealing directly to the group it was aiming at, working-class people. The advertisements stressed that no matter what kind of work you do, you do a good day's work and you owe yourself a high-quality beer at the end of the day. Within five years after the Philip Morris takeover, Miller Brewing had more than doubled the market share of Miller High Life.

In 1974, Miller decided to enter another market segment—that for low-calorie beer. In the late sixties there were two entrants in this market, Gablingers and Meister Brau Light. Both of these failed, however, because of their poor taste and because they were targeted at weight-conscious people. Marketers at Miller realized that both of these beers would have been successful had they been able to maintain their first year's sales, but the taste was unacceptable. It took Miller over a year to develop a formula with the desired taste and quality. Miller did this by using a unique fermentation process. It wanted "Lite" to be consumed by heavy beer drinkers, so the advertisements stressed that Lite tasted great and had fewer calories, so one could drink a lot of it without feeling full.

Another segment that Miller wanted to enter was the super-premium segment, which was dominated by Anheuser-Busch's Michelob. In 1975 Miller reached an agreement with Lowenbrau of Munich, Germany, to be the sole distributor of that brand in the United States. The addition of Lowenbrau provided Miller with the potential for competing in the premium-beer segment.

Questions for discussion

1. What segmentation variable or variables did Miller use for segmenting the market for Miller High Life? Evaluate the use of this variable or group of variables.
2. Miller used the multisegment approach. Assess the advantages and disadvantages of using this approach in marketing beer.
3. When Miller introduced Lite and Lowenbrau, was it, in effect, competing with itself?

Case 2.2

Sales Forecasting at Bay State Machine Company

Bay State Machine Company is a medium-sized producer of portable rigs that are used in drilling oil or water wells. Bay State manufactures several standardized models and also custom-designs rigs. Although Bay State began as a small machine shop in 1918, its primary business activities have focused for over forty years on building high-quality portable drilling rigs. Bay State's sales force of thirty-six salespersons is managed by three regional sales managers and one national sales director.

For a number of years, Bay State managers have employed several types of sales forecasting techniques, including sales-force surveys, correlation methods, executive judgments, and expert opinions. The annual sales forecasts arrived at with each method for the last ten years are shown in Table 2.3. The actual sales figures for each year also are presented.

Table 2.3   Bay State's actual and forecasted sales (in millions of dollars)

Year	Actual Annual Sales	Sales Forecasts			
		Sales-force Survey	Correlation Method	Executive Judgment	Expert Opinion
10	42.0	41.1	44.5	37.2	44.1
9	46.2	43.9	48.0	50.4	46.6
8	54.3	52.7	51.0	53.9	58.1
7	57.8	56.6	56.1	54.0	61.3
6	72.4	70.2	77.5	81.9	75.3
5	98.7	93.7	100.1	107.9	99.7
4	114.0	111.9	107.1	113.0	122.0
3	131.8	129.1	127.8	120.7	133.1
2	152.9	148.3	160.5	170.1	159.0
Last year	184.4	180.2	195.4	175.0	189.9

Bay State managers have recently begun to question whether it is really necessary to use four different sales forecasting methods, given that the costs associated with each method have been escalating, especially during the last few years.

Questions for discussion

1. How does Bay State management benefit from using several sales forecasting techniques?
2. Given Bay State's experience over the last ten years, which sales forecasting method should be used if the managers decide to rely on a single method? Explain your answer and be sure to enumerate the major advantages and disadvantages of the method that you recommend.
3. Which combination of sales forecasting methods should Bay State management use if multiple methods are employed? Why?

3

Consumer and Organizational Buying Behavior

Objectives

To understand the types of decision behaviors employed by consumers when making purchases.

To be aware of the stages in the consumer buying decision process and to know the major factors that influence this decision process.

To identify the major characteristics of organizational buyers.

To become familiar with the major components of a buying center.

To understand the major stages of the organizational buying decision process and to be aware of the factors that affect this process.

Changes in our culture and demographic characteristics are resulting in changes in consumption behavior and especially in food consumption behavior. The fastest growing segments in our population are singles, working women, working couples, and older couples. These people want to minimize food preparation time. They eat more meals away from home than their counterparts of twenty years ago. For foods eaten at home, they desire products packaged in single or twin servings. They want high-quality, low-calorie foods that are quick and easy to prepare.

How are marketers responding to these changing food consumption patterns? Stouffer's introduced a line of entrees called "Lean Cuisine" (see Figure 3.1). Swift has launched "International Entrees," a group of frozen, small-portion, gourmet chicken entrees such as Chicken Kiev. Kraft has introduced a single-serving product series called "A La Carte."[1]

Figure 3.1   Advertisement for Stouffer's Lean Cuisine
Source: Copyright 1983 Stouffer Foods Corporation; Lean Cuisine® and Stouffer's® are registered trademarks of the Stouffer Corporation.

1. Theodore J. Gage, "New Tastes Spark Food for Thought," *Advertising Age*, Feb. 22, 1982, M-16.

The demographic and cultural changes cited here represent only a small portion of the total number of dimensions that can influence buying behavior. *Buying behavior* is the decision processes and acts of people involved in buying and using products.[2] Marketers should analyze buying behavior for several reasons. First, buyers' reactions to a firm's marketing strategy have great impact on the firm's success. Second, as indicated in Chapter 1, the marketing concept stresses the idea that a firm should create a marketing mix that satisfies customers. To find out what satisfies buyers, marketers must examine the main influences on what, where, when, and how consumers buy. Third, by gaining a better understanding of the factors that affect buyer behavior, marketers are in a better position to predict how consumers will respond to marketing strategies.

Although marketers attempt to understand and influence buying behavior, they cannot control it. Even though some social critics credit them with the ability to manipulate buyers, marketers have neither special powers nor sufficient knowledge to do so. Their knowledge of behavior comes from what psychologists, social psychologists, and sociologists know about human behavior in general. Even if marketers wanted to manipulate buyers, the lack of laws and principles in the behavioral sciences would prevent them from doing so.

In this chapter we discuss the broad categories of buying behavior—consumer buying behavior and organizational buying behavior. Even though there are differences between the two, some of the factors that influence consumer buying behavior also affect organizational buying behavior.

Consumer buying behavior

Consumer buying behavior refers to the buying behavior of ultimate consumers—those persons who purchase products for personal or household use and not for business purposes. In this part of the chapter, we initially examine the types of decision making that consumers use. Next, we analyze the major stages of the consumer buying decision process. Then we explain some of the factors that are believed to influence the consumer buying decision process.

Types of consumer decision behavior

As we analyze buyer behavior, we will think of buyers as decision makers. Consumers usually have the general objective of creating and maintaining a collection of goods and services that provides current and future satisfaction. To accomplish this objective, buyers make many purchasing decisions. For example, an average adult must make several decisions daily regarding food, clothing, shelter, medical care, education, recreation, or transportation. As they make these decisions, buyers use different decision-making behaviors.

Although the types of consumer decision making vary considerably, they can be classified into one of three broad categories—routine response behavior, limited decision making, and extensive decision making.[3] A consumer uses *routine response behavior* when buying frequently purchased,

2. James F. Engel and Roger D. Blackwell, *Consumer Behavior* (Hinsdale, Ill.: Dryden Press, 1982), p. 9.
3. John A. Howard and Jagdish N. Sheth, *The Theory of Buyer Behavior* (New York: John Wiley & Sons, 1969), pp. 27–28.

low-cost items that require very little search and decision effort. These items are sometimes called low-involvement products. When buying them, a consumer may prefer a particular brand, but he or she is familiar with several brands in the product class and views more than one as being acceptable. Products bought through routine response behavior are purchased quickly with very little mental effort. Most buyers, for example, do not stand at the detergent shelf pondering the detergents for twenty minutes. Instead, they walk by, grab a box, and proceed down the aisle.

Limited decision making is employed for products that are purchased occasionally and when a buyer needs to acquire information about an unfamiliar brand in a familiar product category. This type of decision making requires a moderate amount of time for information gathering and deliberation.

A consumer uses *extensive decision making* when purchasing an unfamiliar expensive product or an infrequently bought item. This process is the most complex type of consumer decision-making behavior. A buyer uses a large number of criteria for evaluating alternative brands and spends a great deal of time seeking information and deciding on the purchase.

The type of decision making that an individual uses when buying a specific product does not necessarily remain constant. In some instances, the first time we buy a certain kind of product we might use extensive decision making. Limited decision making might be used for subsequent purchases of that product. Also, when a routinely purchased, formerly satisfying brand no longer satisfies, we may use limited or extensive decision processes to switch to a new brand.

The consumer buying decision process

As defined earlier, a major part of buying behavior is the decision process used in making purchases. A simplified model of the *consumer buying decision process* and the major factors believed to affect this process appears in Figure 3.2. The five major stages of the consumer buying decision process are problem recognition, information search, evaluation of alternatives, purchase, and postpurchase evaluation. Before examining each stage of the decision process, we should consider several important points. First, note that the actual act of purchasing is only one stage in the process and that the process is initiated several stages prior to the actual purchase. Second, even though, for discussion purposes, we indicate that a purchase occurs, certainly not all decision processes lead to a purchase. The individual may terminate the process during any stage. Finally, not all consumer decisions always include all five stages. Persons engaged in extensive decision making usually employ all stages of this decision process; users of limited decision making and routine response behavior do not include all stages in their decision-making behavior.

Problem recognition
Problem recognition occurs when a buyer becomes aware that there is a difference between a desired state and an actual condition. For example, a consumer may desire an automobile that is reliable. However, when her car will not start in the morning for the third time in a week, she may recognize that a difference exists between the desired state (a reliable car) and the actual condition (a car that refuses to start).

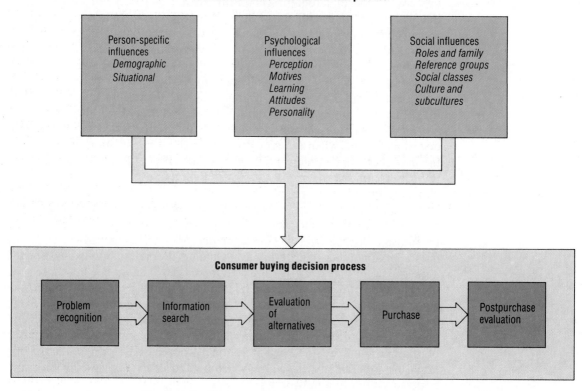

Possible influences on the decision process

| Person-specific influences *Demographic* *Situational* | Psychological influences *Perception* *Motives* *Learning* *Attitudes* *Personality* | Social influences *Roles and family* *Reference groups* *Social classes* *Culture and subcultures* |

Consumer buying decision process

Problem recognition → Information search → Evaluation of alternatives → Purchase → Postpurchase evaluation

Figure 3.2 Consumer buying decision process and possible influences on the process

Sometimes, a problem or need exists for a person, but the individual is not aware of its occurrence. Marketers use sales personnel, advertising, and packaging to aid in triggering the recognition of such needs or problems. The speed of consumer problem recognition can be rather slow or quite rapid.

Information search

After becoming aware of the problem or need, the consumer (if continuing the decision process) searches for information. Information search can focus on numerous dimensions, such as availability of brands, product features, seller characteristics, warranties, operating instructions, and prices. The duration and intensity of search efforts depend on the consumer's experience in purchasing the product and on how important the purchase is to the consumer. If the woman with the unreliable car moves into the information search stage, she is likely to engage in a rather lengthy search. However, if she is buying a blouse, her information search stage will probably be shorter.

When seeking information, a consumer may turn to one or several major sources. One primary source of information is experience. Direct experience with a product can provide selected kinds of information that a consumer may not be able to acquire in other ways. Marketers sometimes attempt to help customers experience products through free samples, demonstrations, and temporary use, such as a test drive of an automobile. Personal sources such as friends, relatives, and associates can also act as sources of information. Since they tend to trust and respect these sources, consumers view them as credible. A third category of information sources is called marketer-dominated sources, which include salespersons, advertising, packaging, and displays. These sources typically do not require that the consumer expend much effort to receive the information. Finally, buyers can use public sources of information, such as government reports, news presentations, and reports from product-testing organizations. Because of its factual and unbiased nature, consumers frequently view information from public sources as being quite credible.

A successful information search yields a group of brands that a buyer views as possible alternatives. This group of products is sometimes called the buyer's evoked set. For example, an evoked set of imported station wagons might include Peugeot, Mercedes-Benz, and Volvo.

Evaluation of alternatives
To evaluate the products in the evoked set that results from information search, a consumer establishes a set of criteria against which to compare the products' characteristics. These criteria are characteristics or features that are desired (or not desired) by the buyer. For example, one car buyer might want a red car, whereas another might have no preference about color except for an intense dislike for the color red. The buyer also assigns a certain level of importance to each criterion; some features and characteristics are more important than others. Using the criteria and considering the importance of each one, a buyer rates and eventually ranks the brands in the evoked set. Evaluation may yield no brand that the buyer is willing to purchase. In this case, further search may be required. If the evaluation yields one or more brands that the consumer is willing to buy, he or she is ready to move on to the next stage of the decision process.

Purchase
The consumer selects the product or brand to be bought during the purchase stage. The choice is based on the outcome of the previous evaluation stage and on other dimensions. Product availability may influence which brand is purchased. For example, if the brand that ranked the highest during evaluation is not available, the buyer may purchase another acceptable brand. During this stage, the consumer determines from which seller he or she will buy the product. The choice of the seller may influence the final product selection, as might the terms of sale, which are negotiated during the purchase decision stage. Issues such as price, delivery, warranties, maintenance agreements, installation, and credit arrangements are discussed and settled. Finally, the actual act of purchase occurs during this stage (unless the consumer terminates the buying decision process prior to purchase).

Postpurchase evaluation
After purchase a buyer will begin to evaluate the purchase. Shortly after the purchase of an expensive product, postpurchase evaluation may result

in cognitive dissonance. *Cognitive dissonance* is dissatisfaction that occurs because the buyer questions whether he or she should have purchased the product at all or would have been better off purchasing another brand that was evaluated very favorably. A consumer who feels cognitive dissonance may attempt to return the product or may seek positive information about it to justify that choice.

As the product is used, the consumer evaluates it to determine if its actual performance meets expected levels. Many of the criteria used in the evaluation-of-alternatives stage are used during postpurchase evaluation. The outcome of this stage is either satisfaction or dissatisfaction, which feeds back to other stages of the decision process and influences subsequent purchases.

Influences on the consumer buying decision process

As shown in Figure 3.2, there are three major categories of factors that are believed to influence the consumer buying decision process: person-specific, psychological, and social. Although we discuss each major factor separately, keep in mind that they are interrelated in their effects on the consumer decision process.

Person-specific influences

A *person-specific factor* is one that is unique to a particular individual. Numerous person-specific characteristics can affect purchasing decisions. In this section, we consider two categories of person-specific factors—demographic and situational.

Demographic factors. *Demographic factors* (also called socioeconomic factors) are individual characteristics such as age, sex, race, nationality, income, family, life-cycle stage, and occupation. (These and other characteristics were discussed in Chapter 2 as possible variables for segmentation purposes.) Demographic factors can influence who is involved in family decision making. For example, findings of a recent study indicated that there is more joint decision making between husbands and wives without children than between those with children.[4] Demographic attributes may influence the speed at which a person moves through the consumer buying decision process. Also, behavior during a specific stage of the decision process is partially determined by demographic factors. For example, during the information stage, a person's age and income may affect the number and types of information sources used and the amount of time devoted to seeking information.

Demographic factors also affect the extent to which a person uses products in a specific product category. For example, the singles demographic group, which is growing rapidly in the United States, accounts for 12.5 percent of consumer spending. Yet singles account for 15 percent of total vacation expenditures, 15.5 percent of expenditures for eating away from home, 15.5 percent of car sales, and 20 percent of alcohol sales.[5] Brand preferences, store choice, and timing of purchases are other areas

4. Pierre Filiatrault and J. R. Brent Ritchie, "Joint Purchase Decisions: A Comparison of Influence Structure in Family and Couple Decision-Making Units," *Journal of Consumer Research,* Sept. 1980, p. 139.
5. Gay Jerrey, "Y & R Study: New Life to Singles," *Advertising Age,* Oct. 4, 1982, p. 14.

Figure 3.3
Is it a bird or a rabbit?
*Source: Gerald H.
Fisher, University of
Newcastle-upon-Tyne,
England.*

influenced by selected demographic factors. Consider, for example, how a consumer's age influences the purchase of clothing. A number of demographic factors are related to a person's needs, product expectations, and behavior toward products.

Situational factors. *Situational factors* are the set of circumstances or conditions that exist when a consumer is making a purchase decision. Sometimes, a consumer engages in buying decision making as a result of an unexpected situation. For example, an individual may be buying an airline ticket hurriedly to spend the last few days with a relative who is mortally ill. A situation may arise that lengthens or causes a person to terminate the buying decision process. A consumer who is considering the purchase of a personal computer, for example, may be laid off during the evaluation-of-alternatives stage. The job loss would certainly slow the buying decision process and might cause the person to reject the purchase entirely. However, if the same person experienced a different circumstance, say a 20-percent salary increase rather than a job loss, then the buying decision process might be completed more quickly than if no pay increase had been received. Situational factors can influence a consumer's actions in any stage of the buying decision process.

Psychological influences
Psychological influences operate within individuals to partially determine their general behavior and thus to influence their behavior as consumers. The primary psychological elements that influence consumer behavior are (1) perception, (2) motives, (3) learning, (4) attitudes, and (5) personality. Even though these behavioral factors operate internally, later in this chapter we will see that they are very much affected by social forces outside the individual.

Perception. Is Figure 3.3 a bird or a rabbit? It could be either one depending on how it is perceived. Different people perceive the same thing at the same time in different ways. Likewise, the same individual at different times may perceive the same item in a number of ways.

Perception is the process of selecting, organizing, and interpreting information inputs in order to produce meaning. A person receives information through the senses: sight, taste, hearing, smell, and touch. *Information inputs* are the sensations that we receive through sense organs. When we hear an advertisement, see a friend, smell polluted air or water, or touch a product, we receive information inputs.

As the definition indicates, perception is a three-step process. Although we receive numerous pieces of information at once, only a few of them reach awareness. We select some inputs and ignore many others because we do not have the ability to be conscious of all inputs at one time. This phenomenon is sometimes called *selective exposure,* because we select inputs that are to be exposed to our awareness. If you are concentrating on this paragraph, you probably are not aware that people or cars are outside making noise, that the light is on, or that you are touching this book. Even though you are receiving these inputs, you ignore them until they are mentioned.

There are several reasons why some types of information reach awareness while others do not. First, an input is more likely to reach awareness if it relates to an anticipated event. Stuckey's uses a series of billboards to encourage travelers to anticipate seeing a Stuckey's store. Even though some motorists may not stop, there is a good chance that they will at least notice the store. Second, a person is likely to allow an input to reach consciousness if the information helps to satisfy current needs. For example, you are more likely to notice food commercials when you are hungry. Conversely, if you have just eaten a large pizza and you hear a Burger King commercial, there is a good chance that the advertisement will not reach your awareness. Third, if the intensity of an input changes significantly, it is more likely to reach awareness. When a store manager reduces a price slightly, we may not notice because the change is not significant. However, if the manager cuts the price in half, we are much more likely to recognize the reduction.

The selective nature of perception leads to two other conditions: selective distortion and selective retention. *Selective distortion* is the changing or twisting of currently received information. This condition can occur when a person receives information that is inconsistent with his or her feelings or beliefs. For example, upon seeing an advertisement promoting a brand that he or she dislikes, a person may distort the information to make it more consistent with prior views. This distortion substantially lessens the effect of the advertisement on the individual. *Selective retention* is a phenomenon in which a person remembers information inputs that support his or her feelings and beliefs and forgets inputs that do not. After hearing a sales presentation and leaving the store, a customer may forget many of the selling points if they contradict prior beliefs.

The information inputs that do reach awareness are not received in an organized form. To produce meaning, an individual must organize them. Ordinarily, this organizing is done rapidly to obtain meaning, and how a person organizes information affects the meaning obtained. For example, depending on how you organize the input in Figure 3.3, you could perceive one of two different forms.

As Figure 3.3 illustrates, an individual can organize inputs in more than one way and obtain more than one meaning. Thus, interpretation—the third step in the perceptual process—is needed to reduce mental confusion. A person bases interpretation on what is familiar. For this reason, a manufacturer that changes a package design faces a major problem. People look for the product in the old, familiar package, and they might not recognize it in the new one.

Several years ago Du Pont test-marketed in several cities a new package design for one of its established automobile polishes. Sales declined significantly because consumers interpreted a different container to mean a different polish. They did not interpret the product as the same polish in a container with a new package design. Unless a package change is accompanied by a promotional program that makes people aware of the change, a firm may lose sales.

Although marketers cannot control people's perceptions, they often try to influence them. Several problems may arise in this attempt. First, a consumer's perceptual process may operate in such a way that a seller's information never reaches that person. For example, a consumer may block out a store clerk's sales pitch. Second, a buyer may receive a seller's information and perceive it differently than was intended. For example, when a toothpaste producer states in an advertisement that "35 percent of the people who use this toothpaste have fewer cavities," a customer could take the statement to mean that 65 percent of the people who use the product have more cavities. Third, a buyer who perceives information inputs that are inconsistent with prior beliefs is likely to forget the information quickly. Thus, if a salesperson tells a prospective car buyer about a highly favorable EPA mileage rating, but the customer does not believe it, the customer probably will not retain the information very long.

It is obvious that how and what consumers perceive strongly affects their behavior toward products, prices, package designs, salespeople, stores, advertisements, and manufacturers. With good reason, then, marketers often concern themselves with how their products are perceived by consumers. As is illustrated in Figure 3.4, organizations sometimes attempt to change customers' perceptions of products.

Motives and motivation research. A *motive* is an internal energizing force that orients a person's activities toward a goal. A buyer's actions at any time are affected by a set of motives rather than just one motive. At a single point in time, some motives in the set are stronger than others, but the strengths of motives vary from one time to another. For example, a person's motives toward having a cup of coffee are much stronger right after waking up than just before going to bed.

Motives can reduce or build tension. When motives drive us toward our goals, they reduce tension. But if some motives impel us toward one goal while other motives pull us toward a different goal, tension may increase because we cannot accomplish either goal.

Many different motives influence buying behavior at once. For example, a person who is purchasing a sofa might be attracted by several characteristics, such as durability, economy, and styling. If a marketer appeals to customers by emphasizing only one attractive characteristic, the effort may fail to generate a satisfactory sales level.

Motives that influence where a person purchases products on a regular basis are called *patronage motives*. A buyer may shop at a specific store, because of such patronage motives as price, service, location, honesty,

Figure 3.4
Advertisement
aimed at changing
customer's perceptions
Source: Ragu Foods, Inc.

product variety, or friendliness of salespeople. To capitalize on patronage motives, a marketer should try to determine why regular customers patronize a store and then emphasize these characteristics in the store's marketing mix.

Motivation research lets marketers analyze the major motives that influence consumers to buy or not buy their products. Motives, which often operate at a subconscious level, are difficult to measure. People ordinarily do not know what motivates them. Therefore, marketers cannot simply ask them about their motives. Most motivation research relies on interviews or projective techniques.

When researchers study motives through interviews, they may use depth interviews, group interviews, or a combination of the two. In a *depth interview* the researcher tries to get the interviewee to talk freely about anything to create an informal atmosphere. The researcher may ask general, nondirected questions and then probe the interviewee's answers by asking for clarification. A depth interview may last for several hours. In a *group interview,* the interviewer—through leadership that is not highly structured—tries to generate discussion on one or several topics among the six to twelve people in the group. Through what is said in the discussion, the interviewer attempts to uncover people's motives relating to some issue, such as the use of a product. The researcher usually cannot probe as deeply in a group interview as in a depth interview. To determine the subconscious motives reflected in the interviews, motivation researchers must be extremely well trained in clinical psychology. Their skill in uncovering subsconscious motives from what is said in an interview determines the effectiveness of their research. Both depth and group interview techniques can yield a variety of information. For example, they might uncover motives about why many customers do not like prunes or why they select high-calorie desserts.

Projective techniques are tests in which subjects are asked to perform specific tasks for particular purposes while, in fact, they are being evaluated for other purposes. Such tests are based on the assumption that subjects unconsciously will ''project'' their motives as they perform the required tasks. Researchers who are trained in projective techniques can analyze the materials produced by a subject and can make predictions about the subject's subconscious motives. Some common types of projective techniques are word-association tests, sentence-completion tests, and balloon tests.

Motivation research techniques can be reasonably effective. They are, however, far from perfect. Marketers who want to research people's motives should obtain the services of professional psychologists who are skilled in the methods of motivation research.

Learning.   *Learning* consists of changes in one's behavior that are caused by information and experience. Variations in behavior that result from psychological conditions such as hunger, fatigue, growth, or deterioration are not considered to be learning. Learning refers to the effects of direct and indirect experiences on future behavior.

The response to an individual's behavior strongly influences the learning process. If actions bring about rewarding or satisfying results, a person may behave in the same way in a subsequent, similar situation. However, when behavior leads to unsatisfying outcomes, a person is likely to behave differently in future situations. For example, when a consumer buys a specific brand of candy bar and likes it, that person is more likely to buy the same brand the next time. In fact, he or she will probably continue to purchase that brand until it no longer provides satisfaction. When the effects of the behavior are no longer satisfying, the person will switch to a different brand.

For a firm to market products successfully, it must help consumers to learn about them. Consumers learn about products directly by experiencing them. As noted earlier, many marketers try to provide consumers with direct experiences before the consumers purchase products.

Consumer learning is also affected by experiencing products indirectly through information from salespersons, advertisements, friends, and relatives. Through sales personnel and advertisements, marketers provide information before (and sometimes after) purchases to influence what consumers learn and to create a more favorable attitude toward the products.

Although marketers may attempt to influence what consumers learn, they seldom fully succeed in significantly affecting buyers' learning processes. Marketers experience problems in attracting and holding consumers' attention, in providing consumers with the kinds of information that are important for making purchase decisions, and in convincing them to try the product.

Attitudes. An *attitude* consists of knowledge and positive or negative feelings about an object. We sometimes say that a person has a "positive attitude," but that statement is incomplete. It has no meaning until we know what the positive attitude relates to. The objects toward which we hold attitudes may be tangible or intangible, living or nonliving. For example, we have attitudes about sex, religion, and politics, just as we do about flowers and beer.

An individual learns attitudes through experience and interaction with other people. Just as attitudes are learned, they can also be changed. However, an individual's attitudes remain generally stable and do not change from moment to moment. Likewise, at any one time, a person's attitudes do not all have equal impact; some are stronger than others.

Consumer attitudes toward a firm and its products greatly influence the success or failure of the firm's marketing strategy. When consumers have strong negative attitudes about one or more aspects of a firm's marketing practices, they may not only stop using the firm's product, but may also implore their relatives and friends to do the same. Since attitudes can play such an important part in determining consumer behavior, marketers should measure consumer attitudes toward such dimensions as prices, package designs, brand names, advertisements, salespeople, repair services, store locations, and features of existing or proposed products.

Not long ago, General Foods realized that consumers' changing attitudes toward desserts affected its dessert line. Consumption of Jello-O pudding and gelatin was declining. Research revealed that consumers wanted quick, low-calorie desserts. To take advantage of this attitude, General Foods created Pudding Pops. They require no preparation time, and a two-ounce Pudding Pop has 100 calories, versus 170 calories in a three-ounce, chocolate-covered vanilla ice-cream bar.[6]

Marketers have several methods available to measure consumer attitudes. One of the simplest ways is to question people directly. An attitude researcher for a watch manufacturer, for example, might ask respondents what they think about the styling and design of the firm's new digital watch. Projective techniques used in motivation research can also be employed to measure attitudes. Marketers sometimes use attitude scales to evaluate attitudes. An *attitude scale* usually consists of a series of adjectives, phrases, or sentences about an object. Subjects are asked to indicate the intensity of their feelings toward the object by reacting to the adjectives, phrases, or sentences in a certain way. For example, if a marketer were measuring people's attitudes toward cable television, respondents might be asked to state the degree to which they agree or disagree with a number of statements such as "Cable television is too expensive." Several computer-assisted analytic approaches (such as multidimensional scaling) are being developed and tested. They hold great promise for future attitude research. However, a discussion of these analytic approaches is beyond the scope of this text.

6. Janet Guyon, "General Foods Gets a Winner with Its Jello-O Pudding Pops," *Wall Street Journal*, Mar. 10, 1983, p. 27.

A marketer can gather many types of information by researching attitudes. One food processor studied dog owners' attitudes toward their dogs and dog foods. Through research, the processor determined that dog owners could be categorized into three attitudinal groups. One group viewed their dogs as performing a utilitarian function such as protecting the family or household, playing with children, or herding farm animals. These consumers wanted a low-priced, nutritious dog food. They weren't interested in a wide variety of flavors. People in the second group were quite fond of their dogs and treated them as companions and as family members. These buyers were willing to pay a relatively high price for dog food and wanted a wide variety of types and flavors so that their dogs would not get bored. Persons in the third group had negative feelings and, in fact, were found to hate their dogs. These customers wanted the cheapest dog food that they could buy and were not concerned with nutrition, flavor, or variety. Because this research determined that other firms were serving these three groups quite effectively, the processor decided not to enter the dog food market after all.

When marketers determine that a significant number of consumers have strong negative attitudes toward an aspect of a marketing mix, they may try to change consumer attitudes to make them more favorable. This task is generally long, expensive, and difficult and may require extensive promotional efforts. When they first entered the U.S. motorcycle market, Honda discovered that many people in this country had negative attitudes toward motorcyclists. People believed that most motorcycle riders were thugs or hoodlums. Honda also determined that people associated motorcyclists with such negative images as crime, black leather jackets, and knives. Knowing this, Honda was able to develop and launch a massive advertising campaign that carried the general theme "You meet the nicest people on a Honda." Although this campaign required considerable effort, time, and money, Honda became a leader in the U.S. motorcycle market. In the same vein, both business and nonbusiness organizations try to change people's attitudes about many things, such as smoking, safety belts, drugs, prices, and product features.

Personality. Some personalities are not as noticeable as others, but everyone does have one. *Personality* is an internal structure in which experience and behavior are related in an orderly way. The manner in which experience and behavior are organized within each individual makes each of us unique. Our uniqueness arises from heredity and our experiences.

Personalities typically are described as having one or more of such characteristics as compulsiveness, ambitiousness, gregariousness, dogmatism, authoritarianism, introversion, extroversion, aggressiveness, and competitiveness. Researchers attempt to find relationships among such characteristics and buying behavior. Even though a few relationships among several personality characteristics and buyer behavior have been determined, the results of many studies have been inconclusive. Despite these inconclusive results, some marketers believe that a person's personality does influence the types and brands of products purchased. For example, the type of clothing, jewelry, or automobile that a person buys may reflect one or more personality characteristics.

At times, marketers aim advertising campaigns at general types of personalities. In doing so, they use positively valued personality characteristics, such as gregariousness, independence, or competitiveness. Products that are promoted in this way include beer, soft drinks, cigarettes, and sometimes clothing.

Social influences

So far we have examined the person-specific and the psychological forces that can influence the consumer buying decision process. Now, let us consider how other people influence buying decisions.

The forces that other people exert on buying behavior are called *social influences*. As we showed in Figure 3.2, they can be grouped into four major areas: (1) roles and family influences, (2) reference groups, (3) social classes, and (4) culture and subcultures.

Roles and family influences.   All of us occupy positions within groups, organizations, and institutions. Associated with each position is a *role*—a set of actions and activities that a person in a particular position is supposed to perform, based on the expectations of both the individual and surrounding persons. For example, even though family roles have changed a good deal, traditionally a married male parent has held two positions in the family: husband and father. The behaviors and activities that make up a man's role as father are determined by the expectations that he, his wife, and his children have regarding the behavior of a father.

Since people occupy numerous positions, they also have many roles. The male in our example not only performs the roles of husband and father but also may perform the roles of plant supervisor, church deacon, Little League coach, and student in an evening college class. In this way several sets of expectations are placed on each person's behavior.

An individual's roles influence not only general behavior but also buying behavior. The demands of a person's many roles may be inconsistent and confusing. To illustrate, assume that the father we have been discussing is thinking about buying a boat. His wife wants him to buy it next year. His fourteen-year-old daughter is hoping for a high-powered skiing boat. His eighteen-year-old son wants a sailboat. His fellow deacons are casually suggesting that he increase his monetary contribution to the church. Several classmates at the college are urging him to buy a specific brand of boat. A coworker indicates that he should buy a different brand, one known for high performance. Thus, an individuals behavior is a function of the input and opinions of significant others (family and friends).

Family roles relate directly to purchase decisions. The male head of household is likely to be involved heavily in the purchase of products like liquor and tobacco. And although female roles also have changed (see related discussion in the Application on p. 85), research shows that women still make buying decisions related to many household items, including health-care products, laundry supplies, paper products, and foods.[7] Husband and wife participate jointly in the purchase of a variety of products,

---

7. *Purchase Influence: Measures of Husband/Wife Influence on Buying Decisions* (New Canaan, Conn.: Haley, Overholser, and Associates, 1975), pp. 13–22.

Application

Advertisers Adjust to Changes in Women's Roles

The roles of women in our society are changing rapidly, and advertisers are trying to reach contemporary women. Images of women in advertisements are slowly becoming more contemporary. Today's woman is more than a person who no longer stays at home; she is a more comfortable, more mature woman with changing attitudes. Women see themselves as being capable individuals, and successful advertisements should portray a more intelligent woman. Advertisements reflecting a positive view toward female imperfections, age, and body size are also more common.

Some advertisers have made errors in attempting to adjust to women's changing roles. One mistake has been to depict a "superwoman," who not only holds a successful career position, but also is able to clean house, do laundry, raise the children, and be prepared to pamper her husband at the end of the day. These advertisements were unsuccessful due to their inability to reach the normal woman.

In adjusting to changes in women's roles, advertisers are trying to avoid traditional stereotypes. They are depicting women in a greater variety of work situations. Also, advertisers are trying to avoid depicting unrealistic total role reversals, in which men are doing all the household jobs that traditionally have been done by women.

Changes in women's roles present a challenge to marketers. Determining where or what a woman is doing today, whether she is in the kitchen or on Wall Street, is not as important as knowing how she performs her roles. Advertisements should support women's perceptions of themselves not as "super-macho," but as capable individuals.

Source: Based on Mary McCabe English, "A Cut Above the Slice of Life Ads," *Advertising Age*, Oct. 3, 1983, pp. M9–M11.

especially durable goods. When two or more family members participate in a purchase, their roles may dictate that each is responsible for performing certain tasks: initiating the idea, gathering information, deciding on whether to buy the product, or selecting the specific brand. The particular jobs performed depend on the types of products being considered. The results of a national survey (see Table 3.1) show the amount of influence that the husband and wife have in certain decisions and tasks related to the purchase of selected durable goods. Children's influence on the purchase of numerous items also must be considered, for it is substantial. In the table, *purchase decision* refers to the decision regarding whether or not to buy a general type of product, such as a typewriter. *Brand decision* deals with the selection of a specific brand.

Marketers need to be aware of how roles affect buying behavior. To develop a marketing mix that precisely meets the needs of the target market, they need to know not only who does the actual buying but what other roles influence the purchase. For example, the data in Table 3.1 indicate that a high proportion of women are the information gatherers for the purchase of carpet. Thus, a carpet producer should design a marketing mix in which much of the advertising is directed toward women. However, because sex roles are changing so rapidly in our country, marketers must be cautious when using data like those in Table 3.1. They must be sure that the information is current and accurate.

Reference-group influence. A group is a *reference group* when an individual identifies with the group so much that he or she takes on many of the

Table 3.1 Relative influence of husband and wife when purchasing selected durable goods and services

| | Purchase Decision Influence[a] | | | |
| | Product Decision | | Brand Decision | |
	Wife	Husband	Wife	Husband
Automotive				
Automobiles	38	62	33	67
Automobile tires	20	80	18	82
Small Appliances				
Electric blender	59	41	53	47
Coffee maker	64	36	64	36
Vacuum cleaner	60	40	60	40
Home Furnishings				
Broadloom carpet	60	40	59	41
Mattress	58	42	59	41
Vinyl flooring	59	41	59	41
Insurance (new policy or increase in coverage)				
Automobile	33	67	31	69
Homeowners'	40	60	39	61
Life	36	64	34	66

[a]Wives' and husbands' influences on purchase decisions = 100 percent (read table across).

values, attitudes, or behaviors of group members. The person who sees a group as a reference group may or may not know the actual size of the group. Most people have several reference groups—families, fraternities, civic organizations, and professional groups like the American Medical Association are examples.

A group can be a negative reference group for an individual. Someone may have been a part of a specific group at one time but later rejected the group's values and members. Also, one can specifically take action to avoid a particular group.[8] However, in this discussion we refer to reference groups as those that are viewed positively by the individual involved.

A reference group may act as a point of comparison and as a source of information for an individual. A customer's behavior may change to be more in line with the actions and beliefs of group members. For example, a person might stop buying one brand of cold medication and switch to another on the advice of members of the reference group. Similarly, an individual may seek information from the reference group about one or more factors affecting a purchase decision, such as where to buy a certain product.

The degree to which a reference group affects a purchase decision depends on an individual's susceptibility to reference-group influence and the strength of involvement with the group. In addition, reference-group influence may affect the purchase decision, the brand decision, or both. For example, the purchase decision for frozen prepared dinners is affected by

8. Henry Assael, *Consumer Behavior and Marketing Action* (Boston: Kent Publishing Company, 1981), p. 318.

Table 3.1   (continued)

	Initiation				Information Gathering			
Product Decision		Brand Decision		Product Decision		Brand Decision		
Wife	Husband	Wife	Husband	Wife	Husband	Wife	Husband
22	78	21	79	18	82	18	82
12	88	11	89	13	87	14	86
67	33	50	50	53	47	52	48
73	27	68	32	64	36	66	34
80	20	69	31	66	34	65	35
82	18	74	26	72	28	69	31
74	26	70	30	67	33	68	32
77	23	66	34	63	37	65	35
21	79	22	78	30	70	28	72
34	66	26	74	37	63	36	64
25	75	23	77	27	73	27	73

Source: *Purchase Influence: Measures of Husband/Wife Influence on Buying Decisions* (New Canaan, Conn.: Haley, Overholser, and Associates, Inc., 1975), pp. 27–29.

reference-group influence, while the brand decision for this product is not. Generally, the more conspicuous a product is, the more likely the brand decision will be influenced by reference groups.

A marketer sometimes tries to use reference-group influence in advertisements by suggesting that people in a specific group buy a product and are highly satisfied with it. In this type of appeal, the advertiser hopes that a large number of people use the suggested group as a reference group and that they will buy (or react more favorably to) the product. The success of this kind of advertising depends on the advertisement's effectiveness in communicating the message, on the type of product, and on the individual's susceptibility to reference-group influence.

Social classes.   Within all societies, people rank others into higher and lower social positions of respect. This ranking results in social classes. A *social class* is an open grouping of individuals who have similar social rank. A class is referred to as "open" because people can move into and out of it. The criteria used to group people into classes vary from one society to another. In our society, we use many factors, including occupation, education, income, wealth, religion, race, ethnic group, and possessions. A person who is ranking someone does not necessarily apply all of a society's criteria. The number and the importance of the factors chosen depends on the characteristics of the individual being ranked and on the values of the person who is doing the ranking.

To some degree, individuals within social classes develop and take on common patterns of behavior. They may have similar attitudes, values,

Table 3.2 Characteristics and buying behavior of persons in various social classes

Class	Percentage of Population	General Characteristics	Patterns of Buying Behavior
Upper	0.2	Socially prominent; possess inherited wealth; may live in large family mansions in mature, exclusive neighborhoods; investors, merchants, and high-level professionals; very active socially; not church goers; college degrees from major institutions	Are not conspicuous consumers; purchase or inherit large homes; buy conservative clothes; patronize exclusive shops and avoid mass merchandisers; travel extensively; purchase expensive, unique products
Upper-middle	10–15	Well educated and career oriented; professionals and middle management; gregarious and socially at ease; have high expectations of their children; tend to join organizations	Buy expensive homes to indicate social position; purchase products such as insurance to achieve financial security; consumption may be conspicuous but cautious to ensure that purchases are socially acceptable; buy high-quality products in pursuit of gracious living
Lower-middle	35	Respectability as major objective; live in suburban tract homes; owners of small businesses; office workers, semiprofessionals, and white-collar workers	Own rather than rent houses to be respectable, houses are well maintained through purchase of do-it-yourself products; furniture bought one piece at a time and likely to be moderately priced, of standard design; highly price sensitive; except for exclusive stores, shopping done in a wide variety of stores; joint shopping by husband and wife more common in this class than in others

Table 3.2 *(continued)*

Class	Percentage of Population	General Characteristics	Patterns of Buying Behavior
Upper-lower	35–40	Blue-collar, semiskilled workers, seek job security; want to improve social position; reside in older, less expensive neighborhoods or suburban tract houses; earn good incomes	Live in small houses or apartments; favor national brands and tend to be brand loyal; spend less on housing and more on household items such as kitchen appliances; spend smaller proportion of income on travel; prefer to shop at nonexclusive department stores and at discount houses; heavy users of credit
Lower-lower	15–20	Poorly educated and poverty stricken; welfare recipients; unskilled workers plagued by high unemployment; live in substandard and slum areas; children expected to be obedient, quiet, and servile; loyal to family and kinfolk; pessimistic about future; apathetic about politics; belong to very few organizations	Purchases are impulsive rather than planned; often pay high prices and interest rates; compared with other classes, spend a larger proportion of income on products to improve personal appearance and less on formal education and cars; prefer to shop in local stores where they know the owner and can get easy credit terms

Sources: Harold M. Hodges, Jr., "Pennisula People: Social Stratification in a Metropolitan Complex," in *Permanence and Change in Social Class: Readings in Stratification,* W. Clayton Lane, ed. (Cambridge, Mass.: Schenkman, 1968), pp. 5–36; James F. Engel and Roger D. Blackwell, *Consumer Behavior* (Hinsdale, Ill.: Dryden Press, 1982), pp. 130–140; and Harold W. Berkman and Christopher C. Gilson, *Consumer Behavior: Concepts and Strategies* (Boston: Kent, 1981), pp. 158–165.

language patterns, and possessions. Social class influences many aspects of our lives. For example, it affects our chances of having children and their chances of surviving infancy. It influences our occupation, religion, childhood training, and educational attainment. Because social class affects so many aspects of a person's life, it also influences buying decisions.

Analysts of social class commonly divide people in our country into five or six classes. The five-class system is outlined in Table 3.2. Note that social class, to some extent, determines the type, quality, and quantity of products that a person buys and uses. Social class also affects an individual's shopping patterns and the types of stores patronized.

Figure 3.5
Luxury aircraft
accommodations
provide
for the upper class
*Source: Courtesy of
Regent Air and
The Lorsch Group.*

Shown above—Regent's lavish cocktail lounge. Private compartments and business conference rooms also available.

DAILY ROUND TRIP FLIGHTS BETWEEN LOS ANGELES AND NEW YORK, EXCEPT SATURDAY.

REGENT AIR

FOR RESERVATIONS CALL THIS NUMBER OR YOUR TRAVEL AGENT.

1-800-538-7587

THIS SERVICE IS PROVIDED BY REGENT AIR AS A CHARTER OPERATOR. THE DIRECT AIR CARRIER FOR THIS SERVICE IS IASCO,
A CAB/FAA LICENSED AIR CARRIER, WHICH HAS OPERATIONAL CONTROL AND SAFETY RESPONSIBILITY FOR YOUR FLIGHT.
THE STANDARD AND QUALITY OF SERVICE HAS BEEN ESTABLISHED BY REGENT AIR.

Marketers sometimes aim marketing mixes at specific social classes. Regent Air, for example, has developed a luxury airline service that provides leather swivel chairs, a barber shop/beauty salon, an art deco lounge, and private compartments (see Figure 3.5). These unrivaled coast-to-coast accommodations are available for a one-way fare of $1,500. The president of Regent Air has stated, "In my youth, the 20th Century Limited was the only way to go by rail to Chicago. Everybody who was anybody rode that train and people used to gather at the station to see who got on the train. That's the kind of service we plan to offer." Regent Air has designed a marketing mix aimed at the upper class.[9]

9. Kevin Higgins, "Airline Will Offer the Ultimate for Bicoastal People,"
   Marketing News, April 1, 1983, p. 1.

Cultural and subcultural influences. *Culture* is everything in our surroundings that is made by human beings. It consists of tangible items (such as foods, furniture, buildings, clothing, and tools) and intangible concepts (such as education, welfare, and laws). Culture also includes the values and a broad range of behaviors that are acceptable within a specific society. The concepts, values, and behavior that make up a culture are learned and are passed on from one generation to the next.

Cultural influences have broad effects on buying behavior because they permeate our daily lives. Our culture determines what we wear and eat, where we reside and travel. It broadly affects how we buy and use products, and it influences our satisfaction from them. For example, in our culture, the problem of time scarcity is increasing because of the increase in the number of females who work and because of the current emphasis we place on physical and mental self-development. Many people do time-saving shopping and buy time-saving products to cope with the scarcity of time.[10]

Since culture, to some degree, determines how products are purchased and used, it in turn affects the development, promotion, distribution, and pricing of products. Food marketers, for example, have had to make a multitude of changes in their marketing efforts. Thirty years ago most families in our culture ate at least two meals a day together, and the mother devoted four to six hours a day to preparing those meals. (See the Application on page 92 for a discussion of related issues.) Today, over 60 percent of the women in the 25–54 age group are employed out of the home, and average family incomes have risen considerably. These two changes have led to changes in the national per capita consumption of certain foods. Consider the following examples:

Per capita consumption of ice milk increased from 1.2 lb. in 1950 to 7.4 lb. in 1976.
Frozen potatoes (used in French fries) went from 6.6 lb. in 1950 to 36.8 lb. in 1976.
Chicken increased from 27.8 lb. to 43.3 lb. per capita between 1950 and 1976.
Pickles went from 4.5 lb. in 1950 to 8.4 lb. in 1976.[11]

When U.S. marketers sell products in other countries, they often see the tremendous impact that culture has on the purchase and use of products. International marketers find that people in other regions of the world have different attitudes, values, and needs, which in turn call for different methods of doing business, as well as different types of marketing mixes. Some international marketers fail because they do not or cannot adjust to cultural differences. The effect of culture on international marketing programs is discussed in greater detail in Chapter 22.

On the basis of geographic regions or human characteristics, such as age or ethnic background, a culture can be divided into parts called *subcultures*. In our country, we have a number of different subcultures: West

10. Leonard L. Berry, "The Time Sharing Consumer," *Journal of Retailing,* Winter 1979, p. 69.
11. Leo J. Shapiro and Dwight Bohmbach, "Eating Habits Force Changes in Marketing," *Advertising Age,* Oct. 30, 1978, pp. 27, 65.

Application

Changes in
Consumers'
Needs
Change
Marketing
Activities

Working mothers, one- or two-person households, an over-fifty-five population segment of more than 15 percent, an increasing number of men living alone—all these characteristics run counter to the traditional perception of the American household. According to the 1980 census, these characteristics as a group predominate in American society today. This fact reflects a dramatic change in the marketing environment and will change the way marketers function.

Mass markets are fragmenting, which means that marketers are having to specialize products to meet the needs of smaller segments. Products and services that appeal to the new demographic segments are proliferating and quite often are very successful. General Electric, for example, redesigned its counter-top microwave oven into a smaller hanging unit that can be suspended under cabinets. In the compressed one- or two-person kitchen, counter space can be at a premium. GE's microwave sales have increased significantly, making the company number two in industry sales.

Other potential buying groups, though, are still being ignored by marketers. Men living by themselves have not been effectively targeted as buyers of household items; nor have teen-age girls who shop for their working mothers. Yet studies have shown that both these groups have market potential.

Because of growing segmentation and complexity in the business environment, marketing is taking on greater importance in corporate strategy. Changing demographics make it harder to pinpoint potential markets, thus increasing the importance of the marketer's role.

Source: Based on "Marketing: The New Priority," *Business Week,* Nov. 20, 1983, pp. 96–106.

Coast, teen-age, and German, for example. Within subcultures there are even greater similarities in people's attitudes, values, and actions than within the broader culture. Relative to other subcultures, individuals in a certain subculture may have stronger preferences for certain types of clothing, furniture, or foods. For example, there is a greater per capita consumption of rice among Southerners than among New Englanders or Midwesterners.

Marketers must recognize that even though their operations are confined to the United States, to one state, or even to one city, subcultural differences may dictate considerable variations in what, how, and when people buy. To deal effectively with these differences, marketers may have to alter their product, promotion, distribution systems or price to satisfy members of particular subcultures.

Organizational buying behavior

Organizational (or *industrial*) *buying behavior* refers to the purchase behavior of producers, government units, institutions, and resellers. Although some of the factors that influence consumer buying behavior definitely influence organizational buying behavior, there are a number of dimensions that are unique to the latter. Specifically, we will examine some general characteristics and concerns of organizational buyers and also look at methods of organizational buying. Then, we will analyze the buying center, the organizational buying decision process, and some of the factors that affect this process.

Characteristics of organizational buyers

We usually think of organizational or industrial buyers as being more rational than ultimate consumers in their purchasing behavior. This view assumes that, compared with ultimate consumers, organizational buyers are more informed about the products they purchase or that they seek more information before purchasing. This assumption is not unfounded. To make purchasing decisions that precisely fulfill an organization's needs, organizational buyers often demand detailed information about the functional features and technical specifications of products.

Marketers may try to appeal to the assumed rationality of organizational buyers. Despite the assumption of rational behavior, however, personal goals still influence organizational buying behavior. Most organizational purchasing agents seek the psychological satisfaction that comes with organizational advancement and financial rewards. Agents who consistently exhibit rational organizational buying behavior are likely to obtain these personal goals, because they are performing their jobs in ways that help their firms achieve organizational objectives. Suppose, though, that an organizational buyer develops a close friendship with a certain supplier. If the buyer values friendship more than organizational promotion or financial rewards, he or she may behave irrationally from the firm's point of view. Dealing exclusively with that supplier regardless of better prices, product qualities, or services offered by competitors may indicate an unhealthy alliance between the buyer and seller.

Primary concerns of organizational buyers

Organizational customers consider a variety of factors when they make purchasing decisions. Many of their primary considerations relate to quality level, service, or price.

Most organizational customers try to achieve and maintain a specific level of quality in the products they offer to their target markets. To accomplish this goal, they often buy their products on the basis of a set of expressed characteristics, commonly called specifications. Thus, an organizational buyer evaluates the quality of the products being considered to determine whether they meet specifications.

Meeting specifications is extremely important to organizational customers. If a product fails to meet specifications and its use results in a product that malfunctions for the ultimate consumer, the organizational customer may become disenchanted with the product and switch to a different supplier. In addition, organizational customers are ordinarily cautious about buying products that exceed specifications, because such products frequently cost more and thus increase an organization's production costs.

Service is important to organizational buyers. The services offered by suppliers directly and indirectly influence industrial customers' costs, sales, and profits. When tangible goods are the same or quite similar—as is the case with most raw materials—the services provided by suppliers may be the primary element that differentiates one product offering from another. The products may be sold at the same price in the same kind of containers and may have the same specifications. Under such conditions the mix of services provided is likely to be the major avenue by which an industrial marketer can gain a competitive advantage.

Even though the importance of specific services varies, those commonly desired include market information, inventory maintenance, on-time delivery, repair services and replacement parts, and credit. Organizational buyers are likely to need technical product information, data regarding demand, information about general economic conditions, or supply and delivery information. Maintaining an inventory is critical because it helps to make products accessible when an organizational buyer needs them and reduces the buyer's inventory requirements and costs. On-time delivery is crucial to organizational buyers because it is usually their responsibility to have the products available and ready for use when needed. By providing reliable, on-time delivery, organizational marketers enable customers to carry less safety stock, thus reducing the customers' costs. Organizational purchasers of machinery are especially concerned about obtaining repair services and replacement parts quickly, because inoperable equipment is costly. For example, Toyota is promoting several maintenance-related services in the fork lift advertisement in Figure 3.6.

Availability of credit can improve an organizational customer's cash flow and reduce the peaks and valleys of capital requirements which, in turn, lowers the firm's cost of capital. Although a single supplier cannot provide every possible service to its organizational customers, a marketing-oriented supplier strives to create the service mix that best satisfies the target market.

Price is obviously important to an organizational customer because it influences operating costs and costs of goods sold, and these costs affect the customer's selling price and profit margin. When purchasing capital equipment, an industrial buyer views the price as the amount of investment necessary to obtain a certain level of return or savings. Thus, an organizational purchaser is likely to compare the price of a machine with the value of the benefits that the machine will yield. Remember, however, that an organizational buyer does not compare alternative products strictly on the basis of price. Other factors, such as product quality and supplier services, are also important elements of the purchase decision. A study of more than one hundred business and medical equipment markets (including copying and data-processing equipment markets) found that the most important factors in user selection of equipment involved customer service, including equipment reliability, quality of performance, field service response time, ease of operation, and cost of service.[12]

Methods of organizational buying

Although no two organizational buyers go about their jobs in the same way, most use one or more of the following purchase methods: description, inspection, sampling, or negotiation.

When the products being purchased are commonly standardized on the basis of certain characteristics (such as size, shape, weight, and color) and are normally graded using such standards, an organizational buyer may be able to purchase simply by describing or specifying quantity, grade, and other attributes. Agricultural commodities often fall into this category. Purchases through description are especially common between a buyer and seller who have established an ongoing relationship built on trust.

12. Dick Berry, "Industrial Marketers Use 'Secret Weapon' Consumer Services for Marketing Success," *Marketing News,* May 1, 1981, p. 8.

Service at new heights

It starts with our high-quality truck. Toyota manufactures more lift trucks than anyone else in the world. Every part* is manufactured by a Toyota Group Company to ensure long-term reliability and economy. This helps maximize uptime. Our documented figures prove how much.

It continues with high-quality support from over 110 dealer locations, nationwide. They determine your lift truck needs, demo on-site and provide Financial Merchandising programs that make your new, used, rental and leasing requirements easier on your budget. We maintain a 95% partsfill rate. Our mechanics serve you fast on-site and at dealer shops. Get in at the top. Call (800) 421-2101**

TOYOTA
No. One makes it Better!

*Batteries and tires are exceptions.
**In California, call (800) 262-1906.

Certain products, such as large industrial equipment, used vehicles, and buildings, have unique characteristics and may vary in terms of their condition. For example, a particular used truck might have a bad transmission. Thus, organizational buyers must base their purchase decisions on inspection of such products.

In buying based on sampling, a sample of the product is taken from the lot and evaluated. It is assumed that the characteristics of this sample represent the entire lot. This method may be appropriate when the product is highly homogeneous—grain, for example—and the examination of the entire lot is not technically or economically feasible.

Some industrial purchasing relies on negotiated contracts. In certain instances an organizational buyer describes exactly what is needed and then asks for sellers to submit bids. When this occurs, the buyer may take the most attractive bids and then negotiate with those suppliers. In other cases, the buyer may not be able to identify specifically what is to be purchased but can only provide a general description. This might be the case for a special piece of custom-made equipment. A buyer and seller might negotiate a contract that specifies a base price and contains provisions for the payment of additional costs and fees. These contracts are most likely to be used for one-time projects such as buildings and capital equipment.

Types of organizational purchases

Most organizational purchases are one of three types: new-task purchase, straight rebuy purchase, or modified rebuy purchase.[13] A *new-task purchase* is one in which an organization is making an initial purchase of an item to be used to perform a new job or to solve a new problem. The industrial buyer usually needs a great deal of information to make such a purchase. A new-task purchase is important to the supplier because, if the industrial buyer is satisfied with the product, the supplier may be able to sell the buyer large quantities of the product over a period of years. A *straight rebuy purchase* occurs when a buyer purchases the same products routinely under approximately the same terms of sale. Buyers require little information for these routine purchase decisions. A *modified rebuy purchase* is one in which a new-task purchase is changed the second or third time it is ordered, or the requirements associated with a straight rebuy purchase are modified. For example, an organizational buyer might seek faster delivery, lower prices, or a different quality level.

The organizational buying decision process

In this section we initially discuss who participates in making organizational purchase decisions. Then we focus on the sequence of stages that are part of this process and the factors that affect it.

The buying center

Relatively few organizational purchase decisions are made by just one person. Instead, they are made through a buying center. Typically, the *buying center* consists of several people in multiple roles, including users, influencers, buyers, deciders, and gatekeepers.[14] One person may perform several of these roles.

Users are those in the organization who actually use the product being acquired. They frequently initiate the purchase process and/or generate the specifications for the purchase. They also evaluate the product's performance relative to the specifications.

Influencers have a definite impact on the purchase decision process. Often, they are technical personnel, such as engineers, who help develop the specifications and evaluate alternative products for possible use.

Buyers are responsible for selecting the suppliers and actually negotiating the terms of the purchases. They may get involved in developing specifications. Buyers are sometimes called purchasing agents or purchasing managers. Their choices of vendors and products are heavily influenced by persons occupying other roles in the buying center.

Deciders actually choose the products and vendors. Although buyers may be the deciders, it is not unusual for these roles to be occupied by

13. Patrick J. Robinson, Charles W. Faris, and Yoram Wind, *Industrial Buying and Creative Marketing* (Boston: Allyn and Bacon, 1967), p. 28.
14. Frederick E. Webster, Jr. and Yoram Wind, *Organizational Buyer Behavior* (Englewood Cliffs, N.J.: Prentice-Hall, 1972), pp. 78–80.

different people. This is especially true when the items being purchased are very expensive. For routinely purchased items, buyers usually are the deciders.

Gatekeepers, such as secretaries and technical personnel, control the flow of information to and among the persons who occupy the other roles in the buying center. Buyers also may be gatekeepers, since they can control the flow of information. The flow of information from supplier sales representatives to users and influencers often is controlled by personnel in the purchasing department.

The number and structure of an organization's buying centers are affected by the organization's size and market position, by the volume and types of products being purchased, and by the firm's overall managerial philosophy regarding exactly who should be involved in the purchase decisions to be made.

Stages of the organizational buying decision process
The stages of the organizational buying decision process are shown on the right side of Figure 3.7. In the first stage, one or more individuals in the organization recognize that a problem or need exists. Problem recognition may arise when a machine malfunctions, when a firm is modifying an existing product or introducing a new one, or under other circumstances. External sources such as trade shows or sales representatives may stimulate problem recognition.

The development of product specifications (the second stage) requires organizational participants to assess the problem or need and determine what will be necessary to satisfy it. By assessing and describing needs, the organization should be able to establish product specifications.

Searching for possible products to solve the problem and locating suppliers of such products is the third stage in the decision process. Search activities may involve looking in company files, contacting suppliers for information, soliciting proposals from known vendors, and examining catalogs and trade publications. The industrial advertisement in Figure 3.8 is an example of information that is available in trade publications. Note that Kodak is suggesting that its chemicals provide solutions to problems.

If all goes well, the search stage will result in a list of several alternative products and suppliers. The fourth stage is that of evaluating the products on the list to determine which ones (if any) meet the product specifications developed in the second stage. Also, during this stage various suppliers are evaluated based on multiple criteria such as price, service, and ability to deliver.

The results of the deliberations and assessments in the fourth stage are used during the fifth stage to select the product to be purchased and the supplier from whom to buy it. In this stage the product is actually ordered.

During the sixth stage the product's performance is evaluated. Actual performance is compared to specifications. Sometimes, it is determined that although the product met the specifications, its performance did not adequately satisfy the problem or need recognized in the first stage. In this case, product specifications must be adjusted. In addition, during the sixth stage, the supplier's performance is evaluated, and if it is found to be unacceptable, the organizational purchaser seeks corrective action from the

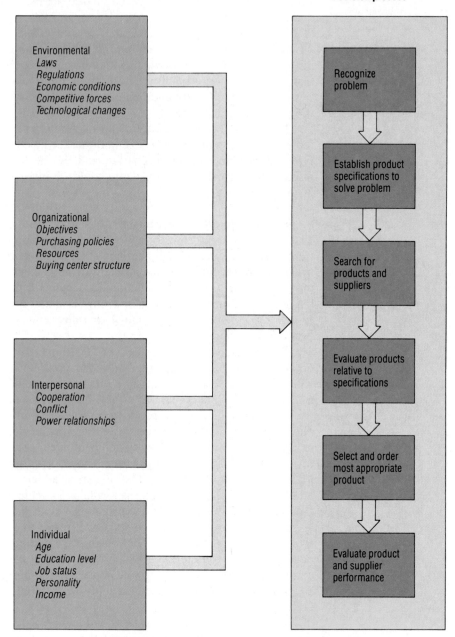

Figure 3.7 Organizational buying decision process and factors that may influence the process *Source: Adapted from Robert Haas,* Industrial Marketing Management *(Boston: Kent Publishing Company, 1982), p. 85; and Frederick E. Webster, Jr., and Yoram Wind,* Organizational Buying Behavior *(Englewood Cliffs, N.J.: Prentice-Hall, 1972), pp. 33–37.*

supplier or searches for a new supplier. The results of the evaluation in this stage become feedback for the other stages and influence future organizational purchase decisions.

This organizational buying decision process is used in its entirety primarily for new-task purchases. Several of the stages are employed for
modified rebuy purchases. The decision process is not used for routine,
straight rebuy purchases.

Influences on organizational buying

As shown in Figure 3.7, there are four major categories of factors that appear to influence organizational buying decisions: environmental, organizational, interpersonal, and individual. Environmental factors are uncontrollable forces such as laws, regulatory actions and guidelines, activities
of interest groups, inflation, competitors' actions, and technological
changes. Organizational factors include the buying organization's objectives, purchasing policies, and resources, as well as the size and composition of its buying center. The interpersonal factors are the relationships

among the people in the buying center. The use of power and the level of conflict among buying center participants, for example, influence organizational buying decisions. These interpersonal dynamics frequently are hidden, making them difficult for marketers to assess. Individual factors are the personal characteristics of individuals in the buying center, such as age, education, personality, position in the organization, and income. How influential these factors are varies depending on the buying situation, the type of product being purchased, and whether the purchase is new-task, modified rebuy, or straight rebuy.

Summary

Since buyers' reactions to a firm's marketing strategy or strategies have great impact on the firm's success, understanding buying behavior is extremely important to marketers and to creating a marketing mix that satisfies customers.

In this chapter we considered both consumer and organizational buying behavior. Although there are many differences between consumers and organizational buyers, some factors that influence consumer buying behavior also affect organizational buying behavior.

Consumer buying behavior refers to the behavior of ultimate consumers—those who purchase products for personal or household use and not for business purposes. The three types of consumer decision making are (1) routine response decision making, used for frequently purchased, low-cost items that require very little search and decision effort; (2) limited decision making, used for products that are purchased occasionally or when a buyer needs to acquire information about an unfamiliar brand in a familiar product category; and (3) extensive decision making, used for purchasing an unfamiliar expensive product or an infrequently bought item.

The five parts of the consumer buying decision process are problem recognition, information search, evaluation of alternatives, purchase, and postpurchase evaluation. Problem recognition occurs when a buyer becomes aware that there is a difference between a desired state and an actual condition. Consumers search for information on such factors as availability of brands, product features, seller characteristics, warranties, and prices. To evaluate alternatives, the consumer establishes a set of criteria found during the information search and uses them to compare product characteristics. When the consumer buys the product, the purchase is completed. After the purchase, the buyer uses postpurchase evaluation to assess the product. The buyer may experience cognitive dissonance— dissatisfaction occurring because the buyer questions whether or not the purchase should have been made at all.

The consumer buying decision process can be affected by three categories of factors: person-specific, psychological, and social. A person-specific factor is one that is unique to a particular individual. Two categories of person-specific factors are demographic factors (also called socioeconomic factors), such as age, sex, race, and nationality; and situational factors, which are the set of circumstances or conditions that exist when a consumer is making a purchase decision.

Psychological influences are perception, motives, learning, attitudes, and personality. Perception is the process by which an individual selects, organizes, and interprets information inputs to create meaning. Motives are internal energizing forces that orient a person's activities toward his or her goals; they sometimes are researched through interviews and projective techniques. Learning consists of changes in one's behavior that are caused by information and experience. An attitude consists of knowledge and positive or negative feelings about an object. Personality is an internal structure in which experience and behavior are related in an orderly way.

The main social influences that affect consumer behavior are roles and family influences, reference groups, social classes, and cultural and subcultural forces. A role is a set of actions and activities that a person in a particular position is supposed to perform. A reference group is a group with which an individual identifies so much that he or she takes on the values, attitudes, and behaviors of group members. A social class is an open aggregate of people with similar social rank. Culture is everything in our surroundings that is made by human beings. A culture consists of several subcultures. Both cultural and subcultural forces influence people's buying behavior.

Organizational buying behavior refers to the purchase behavior of producers, government units, institutions, and resellers. Organizational customers are usually viewed as being more rational than ultimate consumers because organizational buyers are more likely to seek more information about a product's features and technical specifications. When purchasing products, organizational customers are concerned especially about quality, service, and price. Quality is important to an organizational buyer because it directly affects the quality of the products that the buyer's firm produces. Because services can have such a direct influence on a firm's costs, sales, and profits, such things as market information, on-time delivery, availability of parts, and credit can be crucial to an organizational buyer. Although an organizational customer does not depend solely on price to decide which products to buy, price is of prime concern because it directly influences a firm's profitability.

Most organizational buyers use one or more of the following methods: description, inspection, sampling, and negotiation. Most organizational purchases are one of three types: new-task, straight rebuy, or modified rebuy.

Organizational purchase decisions are made through a buying center—a group of several people with multiple roles in the organization, such as users, influencers, buyers, deciders, and gatekeepers. Users are those in the organization who actually use the product. Influencers help develop the specifications and evaluate alternative products for possible use. Buyers are responsible for selecting the suppliers and negotiating the terms of the purchases. Deciders are those who choose the products and vendors. Gatekeepers control the flow of information to and among persons who occupy the other roles in the buying center.

Stages of the organizational buying decision process are problem recognition, establishment of product specifications to solve the problem, search for products and suppliers, evaluation of products relative to specifications, selection and ordering of the most appropriate product, and evaluation of the product's and the supplier's performance. Four categories of factors appear to influence organizational buying decisions: environmental, organizational, interpersonal, and individual.

Important terms

Buying behavior
Consumer buying behavior
Routine response behavior
Limited decision making
Extensive decision making
Consumer buying decision
  process
Cognitive dissonance
Person-specific influences
Demographic factors
Situational factors
Psychological influences
Perception
Information inputs
Selective exposure
Selective distortion
Selective retention
Motive
Patronage motives

Depth interview
Group interview
Projective techniques
Learning
Attitude
Attitude scale
Personality
Social influences
Role
Reference group
Social class
Culture
Subculture
Organizational buying behavior
New-task purchase
Straight rebuy purchase
Modified rebuy purchase
Buying center

Discussion and review questions

1. Why do we think of consumers as decision makers when we analyze buyer behavior?
2. What types of decision making are used by consumers?
3. What are the major stages in the consumer buying decision process? Are all of these stages used in all consumer purchase decisions?
4. How do person-specific influences affect the consumer buying decision process?
5. How does perception determine buyer behavior?
6. How do motives influence a person's buying decisions?
7. What is the role of learning in a consumer's purchasing decision process?
8. How do marketers attempt to shape consumers' learning?
9. Why are marketers concerned about consumer attitudes?
10. How do roles affect a person's buying behavior?
11. Describe reference groups. How do they influence buying behavior?
12. In what ways does social class affect a person's purchase decisions?
13. What is culture? How does it affect a person's buying behavior?
14. Describe your own subculture. Identify buying behavior that is unique to your subculture.
15. Why do some people think that organizational buyers are more rational than ultimate consumers in terms of purchasing behavior?
16. What are the primary concerns of organizational buyers?
17. What are the commonly used methods of organizational buying?
18. What are the major components of a buying center?
19. Identify the stages of the organizational buying decision process. How is this decision process used when making straight rebuys?
20. How do environmental, organizational, interpersonal, and individual factors affect organizational purchases?

Case 3.1

Security Bank & Trust

Security Bank & Trust is located in a medium-sized city. In terms of total deposits, Security is third among the six banks in the trade area. Top-level managers of Security are not happy about being number three. They want to attract new accounts and have placed much of the responsibility for this on Sandra Stinson, vice president of marketing.

To develop a strategy to attract new customer accounts, Stinson, with the help of an independent research company, conducted a telephone survey of residents in the trade area. The group of respondents included both Security customers and customers at other banks. The survey focused on two major dimensions: (1) residents' attitudes regarding general features of the banks in the area and (2) residents' attitudes regarding the relative importance of several characteristics when selecting a bank. Table 3.3 shows

Table 3.3   Percent of responses regarding general bank characteristics

General Features	American State Bank	Citizens Bank	Capital Bank	City National Bank	Security Bank & Trust	Guaranty National Bank	Other	Don't Know	Total
Largest bank	17.0	0.4	1.4	3.2	7.0	59.8	0.4	10.8	100.0
Strongest bank	18.0	1.0	1.6	3.8	5.8	37.4	0.4	32.0	100.0
Bank with most convenient locations	14.2	2.4	7.2	11.2	15.2	33.2	2.2	14.4	100.0
Most progressive bank	19.0	2.6	3.0	2.8	8.2	41.0	0.6	22.8	100.0
Bank catering to the young	24.0	19.8	6.6	3.0	10.6	12.0	0.8	23.2	100.0
Bank for everyone	10.6	2.0	1.4	3.0	6.0	20.0	4.2	52.8	100.0

Table 3.4   Percent of responses regarding the importance of selected bank characteristics

Bank Features	Very Important	Somewhat Important	Not Important	Don't Know	Total
Convenient to home	76.0	14.8	9.2	0.0	100.0
Convenient to work	46.4	21.8	31.6	0.2	100.0
New building	11.0	15.4	72.8	0.8	100.0
Travel department	8.8	17.6	67.2	6.4	100.0
Financial counseling	37.4	28.6	31.4	2.6	100.0
Financial strength	66.2	16.8	12.4	4.6	100.0
Weekend banking services	37.2	24.6	37.2	1.0	100.0
Evening banking hours	48.4	29.6	21.8	0.2	100.0
Drive-in windows	59.0	23.8	16.6	0.6	100.0
Bank credit card	31.6	22.8	43.8	1.8	100.0
Free checking accounts	56.2	19.8	22.8	1.2	100.0
Gives premiums such as stamps or gifts	14.6	15.6	68.8	1.0	100.0
Ease in acquiring loans	44.4	26.4	26.8	2.4	100.0
24-hour cash machines	25.6	19.8	47.8	6.8	100.0

the percentage of respondents who answered with various banks' names when questioned about several general features such as size and strength. The percentage of responses regarding the importance of certain characteristics when selecting a bank are shown in Table 3.4.

Questions for discussion
1. Will the information in Tables 3.3 and 3.4 be useful to Stinson in her efforts to attract new customers? What additional information does she need? Why?
2. Which data in Tables 3.3 and 3.4 are most important for developing a strategy to attract new accounts? Why?
3. On the basis of these findings, what recommendations would you make to Stinson? Why?

Case 3.2

Crown Clothing and Accessories

Crown Clothing, Inc. is the maker of clothing and accessories bearing an unusual crown emblem. Although Crown manufactures a line of men's and women's athletic swimwear, the company focuses primarily on producing and marketing sportswear for the entire family.

Over the last five years, sales of Crown products quadrupled due to the overwhelming popularity of its crown-emblazoned products. However, within the last year, sales of Crown products leveled off and even showed signs of a decline. Some business analysts believe that by the end of the year, sales may be 25% less than last year's sales.

There are several possible explanations for this. During the five years that sales were climbing rapidly, Crown spent most of its resources and efforts emphasizing the crown symbol, and it did not spend as much time monitoring changes in buyer trends or preferences. Also, competitors were quick to produce their own emblemized products, which detracted from the uniqueness of the crown emblem. Competitive emblems ranged from initials to musical instruments. And to make matters worse, some companies Crown had licensed to use the crown emblem did not maintain the high quality level that they had promised, and an image problem was created.

Recently, a research firm conducted a study for Crown to determine the kinds of changes that needed to be made in its sportswear. There were several findings that Crown marketers believed to be important. First, teenagers' and adult females' purchases of sportswear seemed to be heavily influenced by close friends and associates. When asked how they found out about new clothing styles, these respondents reported that they often talked about clothes with friends and that some of these individuals went shopping with them. Second, the findings indicated that clothing buyers had strong feelings about external emblems that clearly identified a brand. Some of the respondents strongly preferred to purchase clothes with an emblem, while others reported that they would not buy a garment bearing an emblem even if they liked all the other features of the garment. Third, the results showed that about 40 percent of the respondents preferred clothes without brand emblems. Four years ago in a similar study, the findings suggested that fewer than 20 percent of sportswear buyers disliked brand emblems.

Currently, Crown is making several changes in its marketing mix. Although it is still producing clothes with the crown emblem, it is also making sportswear without emblems. Looser fitting styles in soft, multi-colored, and striped fabrics are being introduced. To make buyers aware of these new designs, the firm's advertising expenditures have doubled, and Crown's sales force has been increased significantly.

Questions for discussion

1. What kind of buyer decision making do most people use when purchasing sportswear?
2. In what ways do roles influence the purchase of sportswear?
3. How do a person's reference groups influence buying decisions for sportswear?
4. Do you feel that Crown's product adjustments are advisable?

4

Marketing Research and Information Systems

Objectives

To understand the relationship between research and information systems in marketing decision making.

To distinguish between research and intuition in solving marketing problems.

To learn five basic steps for conducting a marketing research project.

To understand the fundamental methods of gathering data for marketing research.

To understand questionnaire construction, sampling, and the design of experiments.

Marketing research played a vital role in the design, development, and marketing of Kodak's disc camera. Kodak's challenge was to market a new camera, even though most consumers were relatively satisfied with the equipment they already owned (94 percent of U.S. families owned at least one camera).

Kodak conducted research to study the fundamentals of photography and the ways in which people take pictures. The company surveyed consumers to determine under what conditions they were using cameras. The findings led to fifteen breakthroughs in Kodak's optics, electronics, and manufacturing technology, and this progress produced a disc-camera concept.

After further research in design and operational details, a market study led to the prototype disc camera, which was shown to people in more than one thousand U.S. homes. Without revealing Kodak's name, researchers asked consumers in these households to comment on the camera's various features. The benefits mentioned by these consumers were integrated, and the result was the disc camera. Amateur photographers could now take pictures in situations where it was previously impossible to do so. Although the disc's long-term success is still to be decided, actual sales of film, cameras, and photofinishing equipment have far exceeded the ambitious sales goals set by Kodak.[1]

Marketing research and systematic information gathering increase the probability of successful marketing. Research findings are essential in planning and developing marketing strategies. Information about target markets provides vital input in planning the marketing mix and in controlling marketing activities. In addition, marketing research helps in determining what product lines deserve the bulk of a company's efforts and resources.[2] In short, the marketing concept—the marketing philosophy of customer orientation—can better be implemented when adequate information about customers is available.

Marketing research and information systems provide the insight for carrying out the marketing concept. With the intense competition in today's marketplace, it is difficult to develop an ingenious invention and then look for a market where it can be profitably sold. The increasing inability of U.S. products to compete successfully with product innovations from other parts of the globe may have its roots in a lack of understanding and application of the marketing concept.[3]

This chapter focuses on the approaches to and processes of gathering information needed for marketing decisions. It distinguishes between

1. "Credit Success of Kodak Disc Camera to Research," *Marketing News*, Jan. 21, 1983, pp. 8–9.
2. David K. Hardin, "Research State-of-Art: Today and Tomorrow," *Marketing Times*, March–April 1983, p. 38.
3. A. Parasuraman, "Hang On to the Marketing Concept," *Business Horizons*, Sept./Oct. 1981, p. 40.

managing information within an organization (a marketing information system) and conducting marketing research projects. We discuss the role of marketing research in decision making and problem solving and compare it with intuition. Next, we examine individual steps in the marketing research process as they relate to analyzing and evaluating research. We look at sampling and experimentation as approaches to reducing error in gathering information. Finally, we describe the major methods of obtaining data (survey, observation, and secondary sources).

Defining marketing research and marketing information systems

Marketing intelligence is a broad term that includes all data gathered as a basis for marketing decisions. **Marketing research,** however, is the part of marketing intelligence that involves specific inquiries into problems. Its purpose is to guide marketing decisions. The thrust of a marketing research effort is to gather information that is not available to decision makers. It is conducted on a special-project basis, and research methods are adapted to the problems studied and to changes in the environment. General Motors, for example, interviews more than 130,000 consumers in surveys to determine consumer behavior, consumer satisfaction, reasons for purchase, loyalty trends, and demographics. The information gathered by marketing research is used in planning the company's marketing activities.[4]

To cite another example, marketers who use music or recording artists as celebrity presenters in their ads must know which music most effectively reaches their target market and why. One marketing research study found that the hard rock segment of the listening public find one type of country music acceptable—outlaw country as performed by Willie Nelson and Waylon Jennings.[5] This specific information could be used to develop a music ad that bridges two music segments.

A *marketing information system (MIS)* establishes a framework for the day-to-day managing and structuring of information gathered regularly from sources both inside and outside an organization. As such, an MIS provides a continuous flow of information about such things as prices, advertising expenditures, sales, competition, and distribution expenses. Figure 4.1 illustrates the chief components of an MIS.

Inputs for an organization's MIS include those information sources (both inside and outside the firm) that are assumed to be useful for future decision making. Processing of information involves classifying, developing categories for meaningful storage, and retrieving information. Marketing decision makers determine which information is useful; that information is used for making decisions and makes up the outputs shown in Figure 4.1. Finally, depending on the information needs of decision makers, feedback enables those who are responsible for gathering internal and external data on a systematic basis to adjust the information intake.

Daily reports of sales by product or market categories, data on inventory levels, and records of the activities of salespersons are all examples

4. "Panelists Provide a Glimpse of Automotive Marketing Research," *Marketing News,* Sept. 30, 1983, p. 3.
5. Thomas E. Turicchi, "Before Using Music, Recording Artists in Ads, Study Music Preferences of Target Audiences," *Marketing News,* May 15, 1981, p. 8.

Figure 4.1
An organization's
marketing information
system

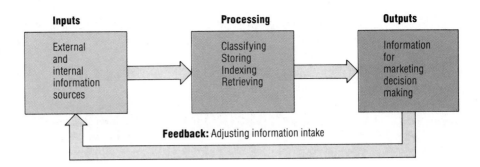

of information flows. In the MIS, the means of gathering data receive less attention than do the procedures for expediting the flow of information. The main focus is on data storage and retrieval, as well as on computer capabilities and the information requirements of management.

J. C. Penney has developed an MIS that provides data for management decisions. Penney has divided the merchandise portion of its business into twenty-eight homogeneous and mutually exclusive profit centers, which include women's sportswear, jewelry, housewares, major appliances, and automotive, among others. Computer-based systems are used to store data by profit center and to ensure the timeliness of reports. Suitable software minimizes the time that reports take and also limits the amount of information produced by summarizing or being selective with what is shown. The MIS provides data for developing models that are close enough to the real world to be a valuable aid to decision making.[6]

Whereas an MIS provides a continuous data input for an organization, marketing research is an information gathering process for specific situations. Nonrecurring decisions that deal with the dynamics of the marketing environment cannot always be structured in the standard MIS. These situations call for a data search that relates to a particular problem and decision. Marketing research is usually characterized by in-depth analyses of major problems or issues. Often, the needed information is available only from sources outside an organization's formal channels of information. For example, an organization may want to know something about its competitors or may want to gain an objective, unbiased understanding of its own customers. Such information needs may require an independent investigation by a marketing research firm. However, data brought into the organization through marketing research do become part of its **marketing data bank,** a file of data collected through both the MIS and marketing research projects.

The information system should aim to store research information so that it will be useful beyond addressing the immediate problem. Organizations are full of research reports forgotten soon after they appear because the information system failed to make the study visible and accessible. Often a research study will generate data that can be analyzed later from an-

6. Allen S. King, "Computer Decision Support Systems Must Be Credible, Consistent, and Provide Timely Data," *Marketing News,* Dec. 12, 1980, p. 11.

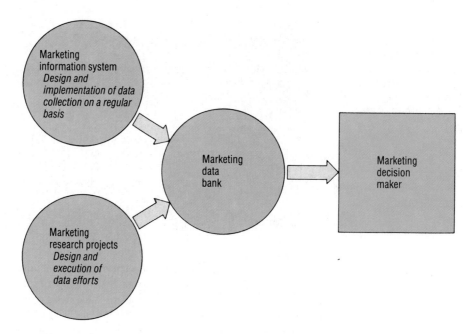

Figure 4.2 Combining marketing research and the marketing information system

other perspective to address a research purpose quite different from that motivating the original study. A large segmentation study for a bank, for example, included a group of benefit questions. Some time after the study was completed, it was necessary to develop a profile of users of traveler's checks, to help select target audiences for a direct mail campaign. A re-analysis of the segmentation data provided an inexpensive and relevant profile.

Orienting market research toward the information system in particular encourages a stream of research over time that tends to be more effective and useful than one-shot projects.[7]

A marketing data bank provides an organization with a large amount of detailed information. In a small organization, the data bank could simply be a large notebook, but in many organizations, a computer storage and retrieval system is needed to handle the volume of data. Figure 4.2 illustrates how marketing decision makers combine research findings with data from an MIS to develop a data bank. Although many organizations do not use the term *data bank,* they still have some system for storing information for later use. While the terms *MIS* and *marketing research* may not be used by smaller organizations, they usually do perform these marketing activities. Decisions can, of course, be made without resorting to these information sources.

After a marketing information system—of whatever size and complexity—has been established, information needs to be related to marketing

7. David A. Aaker and George S. Day, "Increasing the Effectiveness of Marketing Research," *California Management Review,* Winter 1980, p. 62.

Figure 4.3
Nielsen provides
different data sources
to reduce risk in new
product introductions
*Source: Courtesy A.C.
Nielsen Company.*

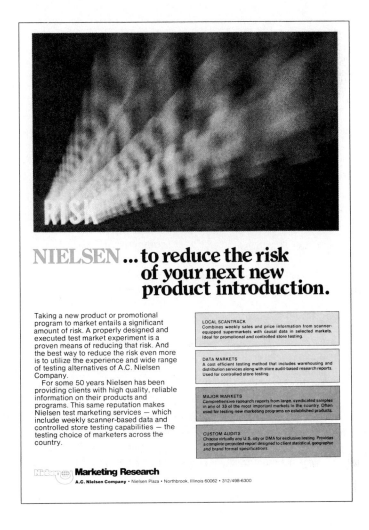

planning. In the next section, we will see how marketers combine marketing information with experience and judgment as they make decisions and how they make some decisions without the aid of research or information systems.

Information needs and decision making

The real value of marketing research and the systematic gathering of information that supports it is measured by improvements in a marketer's ability to make decisions. Figure 4.3 illustrates the role of different data sources in reducing risk in new product introductions. Research and information systems provide customer feedback to the organization. Without feedback, a marketer cannot understand the dynamics of the marketplace. The role of marketing information in decision making is increasing as managers recognize its benefits. The Application on page 114 describes how American Motors used marketing research to develop a successful new-product introduction.

Table 4.1 Information needs during different phases of the marketing planning process[a]

Type of Marketing Intelligence	Assessment of Opportunities	Development of Objectives
Marketing information system (MIS)	Dissatisfactions and needs in relevant market segments Size and trend of demand Industry/market structure and composition, competition, market shares, and profitability Technological and materials innovations Supply conditions and prices	Organizational goals Activities of functional departments such as production, finance, and personnel Resources of the firm
Marketing research	Research project; for example, when a new opportunity or environmental threat suddenly arises	Research projects to assess when and if an objective can be accomplished

[a]This list of information needs is offered only as an example and is not exhaustive.

As we will discuss in Chapter 18, strategic market planning involves assessing opportunities, developing objectives, and formulating strategies. Table 4.1 lists some basic information needs that arise during different phases of the planning process—including implementation and control. This list is not exhaustive, of course. The specific information needs of any organization will depend on its unique situation and environment.

Although no method of decision making can eliminate uncertainty, research provides a more objective and systematic approach. The increase in marketing research activities represents a transition from intuitive to scientific problem solving. In relying on *intuition,* marketing managers do not look for any information other than personal knowledge or experience. However, in *scientific decision making,* managers take an orderly and logical approach to gathering information. They seek facts on a systematic basis; they apply methods other than trial and error or generalization from experience.

Despite the obvious value of formal research, marketing decisions often are made in its absence. It is true that relatively minor problems re-

Table 4.1 *(continued)*

Type of Marketing Intelligence	Formulation of Marketing Strategies	Developing Plans for Implementation and Control
Marketing information system (MIS)	Identifying and tracking current target markets by product category Identifying and tracking market behavior toward present products, promotion, distribution, and prices	The costs and effectiveness of the firm's marketing efforts Firm's sales, by product and market Total industry and product-class sales Compilation and aggregation of operating data to present an accurate picture of performance
Marketing research	In-depth evaluation of existing or potential target markets Testing the appeal of potential product attributes Testing current marketing effectiveness and developing new promotion or price alternatives Evaluating the needs and attitudes of channel members Selecting the most efficient and effective physical distribution alternative	Surveys of consumer awareness, trial, attitudes, preferences, and repurchase rates Research projects when unforeseen events occur or problems develop

Source: Some of this material has been adapted from Harper W. Boyd, Jr., Ralph Westfall, and Stanley F. Stasch, *Marketing Research: Text and Cases,* 5th ed. (Homewood, Ill.: Irwin, 1981), p. 9. © 1981 by Richard D. Irwin, Inc.

quiring immediate attention can and should be handled on the basis of personal judgment and common sense. Research can be worthwhile, though, when immediate decisions are not necessary, and limited research is valuable when it appears that complete data are not needed for good decisions and would be too expensive in relation to the data's usefulness to decision makers. As the number of alternative solutions to a problem increases and the expected economic or social payoffs multiply, the use of research in planning becomes more rewarding and desirable.

We are not suggesting here that intuition has little or no value. Successful decisions blend both research and intuition. Statistics, mathematics, and logic are tools that contribute to problem solving and provide information that decreases the uncertainty of predictions based on limited experience. However, these tools do not necessarily produce all the answers, or even the right ones. Consider one extreme example. A marketing research study conducted for Xerox Corporation in the late 1950s indicated that there was a very limited market for an automatic photo copier. Xerox management judged that the researchers had drawn the wrong conclusions

Application

The Alliance—
American
Motors
Successfully
Uses Marketing
Research

American Motors Corporation's Alliance has been among the top selling automobiles made in this country. AMC's partner is Renault, a French automobile manufacturer, holding 46-percent ownership in the company. The Alliance subcompact was designed with the help of research to appeal to U.S. consumers. AMC used research to successfully market the product.

Prior to deemphasizing the AMC label and naming the automobile Renault Alliance, AMC conducted research that showed that neither the AMC nor the Renault label was popular among potential buyers. Among those questioned, 69 percent rejected the idea of buying a Renault automobile and 55 percent rejected the AMC name. However, the company found that consumers slightly favored the Renault heritage over that of AMC.

AMC carefully researched and planned its advertising—testing consumers to see which product features to emphasize and to determine the best context in which to present the car. However, research had already shown that the company's main concern should be exposure for the product; the product would, in effect, sell itself if advertising could get consumers to look at it because, according to research, its design, construction, and price were extremely well received.

In 1983, *Motor Trend* magazine named the Alliance its car of the year, and AMC quickly released commercials that emphasized this award. The results of the marketing effort for Alliance show that with appropriate exposure, a strong product can overcome negative associations. Of those who have purchased the Alliance, 90 percent have never owned an AMC automobile. Research helped AMC make the right decisions about Alliance's features and how to create public awareness and subsequent acceptance.

Source: Based on Bill Abrams, "Careful Study, Good Product Making AMC's Alliance a Hit," *Wall Street Journal*, April 21, 1983, p. 31.

from the study and decided to launch the product anyway. The first Xerox 914 copier was an instant success. An immediate backlog of orders developed, and the rest is sales history.

The experience and personal judgment of marketing managers are necessary to most marketing decisions. A proper blend of research and intuition is required to make a correct decision. Table 4.2 distinguishes between the roles of research and intuition in decision making.

Table 4.2   Distinction between research and intuition in marketing decision making

	Research	Intuition
Nature	Formal planning and predicting based on scientific approach	Narrow and immediate preference based on personal feelings
Methods	Logic, systematic methods, and statistical inference	Experience and demonstration
Contributions	General hypotheses for making predictions, classifying relevant variables, and carrying out systematic description and classification	Minor problems solved quickly through consideration of experience and practical consequences

The marketing research process

As marketing decisions become more complex, the tasks of identifying, specifying, acquiring, and evaluating information and of making decisions grow more difficult.[8] Marketers should be able to apply effective methods of determining when research is needed and should be able to design projects that will provide useful information to decision makers. They must support practical and understandable procedures to guide the research and to provide a framework for its conduct. Above all, marketers must approach marketing research logically to maintain the control necessary to obtain accurate data. As Figure 4.4 illustrates, the success of marketing research depends on who performs the research. The difference between good research and bad research depends on the input, including effective control over the entire marketing research process.

The five steps shown in Figure 4.5 should be thought of as an overall approach to conducting research rather than as a rigid set of rules to be followed in each project. When they plan research projects, marketers must think about each of the five major steps and how they can best be tailored to fit a particular problem. Therefore, it is important that we look more closely now at the five steps involved in marketing research.

8. Forrest S. Carter, "Decision Structuring to Reduce Management-Research Conflicts," *MSU Business Topics,* Spring 1981, p. 40.

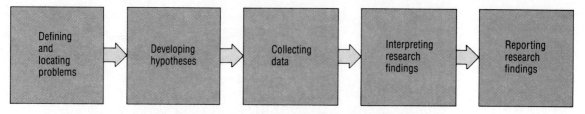

Figure 4.5 The five steps of the marketing research process

Defining and locating problems

Initially, marketers must center their attention on how best to discover the nature and boundaries of a problem. This **problem definition** is the first step toward finding a solution or launching a research study. The first sign that a problem exists is usually a departure from some normal function or appearance, such as conflicts between or failures in attaining objectives. If a corporation's objective is a 12-percent return on investment and the current return is 6 percent, this discrepancy should act as a warning flag. It is a symptom that something inside or outside the organization has blocked the attainment of the desired goal. Decreasing sales, increasing expenses, or decreasing profits are also broad indications of problems. To get at the specific causes of the problem through research, however, marketers must define the scope of the problem and develop problem definitions that go beneath its superficial symptoms.

"The research objective specifies the information required to progress toward the achievement of the research purpose. Managers who do not know fully what they want may have partially or incorrectly defined their problems."[9] Deciding how to refine a broad, indefinite problem into a clearly defined and researchable statement is a prerequisite for the next step in planning the research—developing the type of hypothesis that best fits the problem.

Developing hypotheses

The objective statement of a marketing research project should include hypotheses drawn from previous research and from experience concerning expected research findings.

A **hypothesis** is a guess or assumption about a certain problem or set of circumstances. Essentially, a hypothesis is a reasonable guess or supposition that may be right or wrong. It is based on all the insight and knowledge available about the problem from previous research studies and general information. As information is gathered, a researcher can test the hypothesis. Sometimes, several hypotheses are developed in the course of a study; the hypotheses that are accepted or rejected become the chief conclusions drawn from the study.

Collecting data

Two types of data are available to marketing researchers. **Primary data** are observed and recorded or collected directly from respondents. **Secondary data** are compiled inside or outside the organization for some purpose other than the current investigation. Examples of secondary data would include

9. Aaker and Day, "Increasing the Effectiveness of Marketing Research," pp. 62–63.

Figure 4.6
Approaches
to collecting data

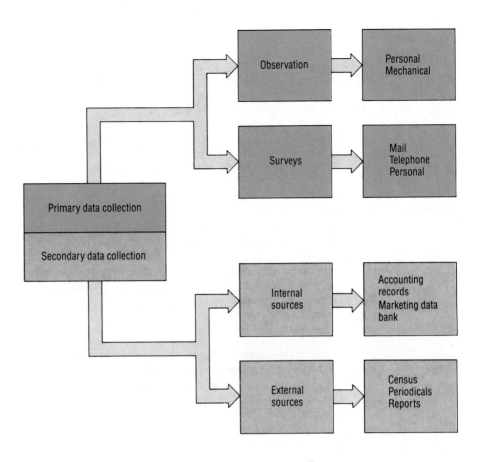

general reports supplied to an enterprise by various data services. Such reports might concern market shares, retail inventory levels, and consumers' purchasing behavior. The Application on page 118 illustrates how ARCO used both secondary and primary research to develop the firm's "cash-only" policy.

Figure 4.6 illustrates how primary and secondary sources differ. Secondary data are usually already available in private or public reports or have been collected and stored by the organization itself. Primary data must be gathered by observing phenomena or surveying respondents.

Both the nature and the type of the hypothesis being tested will determine the choice of a general data gathering approach: exploratory, descriptive, or causal investigations. When more information is needed about the problem and the tentative hypothesis must be made more specific, marketers conduct *exploratory studies*. For instance, a review of information in the organization's data bank or a review of publicly available data may be helpful. By questioning knowledgeable people inside and outside the organization, marketers may get additional insight into the problem. An advantage of the exploratory approach is that it permits marketers to conduct ministudies with a very restricted data base.

Descriptive studies are undertaken when marketers recognize that they must understand the characteristics of certain phenomena to solve a particular problem. Marketers may plan to conduct surveys of consumers'

Application

ARCO Uses Marketing Research to Evaluate Alternatives

Gasoline demand topped off in 1978 and has dropped 15 percent since then. This decline should continue throughout the rest of the century. With the declining market, Atlantic Richfield Company's (ARCO) retail volume fell 25 percent. To study its alternatives, the company decided to conduct marketing research. One study showed that 65 percent of gasoline buyers never used credit cards and only 16 percent were chronic card users. Credit costs were eroding profits.

ARCO rejected the idea of offering a discount for cash payment because, according to research, this dual pricing would confuse the public and would fail to eliminate credit card costs. Research also showed that charging a yearly fee for ARCO card holders would cause 80 percent of them to cancel their cards; so that idea was turned down. Another option was to eliminate credit cards and pass the resulting savings on to customers. Research indicated that two-thirds of ARCO's credit card customers would continue to buy from the company in the absence of credit. ARCO chose this option, thinking it would provide the greatest profitability.

ARCO next used research to carefully design its television commercials, which communicated to the public that ARCO had eliminated credit cards and could thus lower its gas prices. ARCO stations increased sales at a rate two-and-one-half times faster than that of competitors and garnered one billion gallons of new business. ARCO continues to win new customers by using research to examine and meet customers' changing needs.

Source: Based on "How ARCO Used Marketing Research to Go 'Cash-Only' in a Plastic Society," *Marketing News*, Jan. 6, 1984, pp. 1, 26, 27.

education, occupation, or age; they may find out how many consumers purchased Ford Escorts last month; or they may determine how many adults between the ages of eighteen and thirty drink coffee at least three times a week.

Although their purpose is to describe, descriptive studies may require statistical analysis. Some descriptive studies call for predictive tools, too. A researcher trying to find out how many people will vote for a certain political candidate, for example, may have to use sampling, questionnaires, computer tabulations, and estimates of error to predict the correct answer. Descriptive studies generally require much prior knowledge and assume that the problem is clearly defined. The marketers' major task is to find adequate methods for collecting and measuring data.

Hypotheses about causal relationships require a more complex approach than those that can be tested by a descriptive study. In *causal studies,* it is assumed that a particular variable X is the cause of the variable Y. Marketers must plan the research so that the data collected prove or disprove that X causes Y. Moreover, to do so, marketers must try to hold constant all variables except X and Y. For example, to find out whether premiums increase the number of new accounts in a savings and loan association, marketers must try to keep all variables constant except premiums and new accounts.

Interpreting research findings

After collecting data to test their hypotheses, marketers are ready to interpret the research findings.

Interpretation is easier if marketers carefully plan their data analysis methods early in the research process. Marketers should also allow for continual evaluation of the data during the entire collection period. They can then gain valuable insight into areas that ought to be probed during the formal interpretation.

The first step in drawing conclusions from most studies is tabulation of the data. If marketers intend to apply the results to individual categories of the things or people being studied, then cross-tabulation may be quite useful, especially in tabulating joint occurrences.

After the data are tabulated, they must be analyzed. *Statistical interpretation* focuses on what is typical or what deviates from the average. It indicates how widely respondents vary and how they are distributed in relation to the variable being measured. This interpretation is another facet of marketing research that calls for marketers to apply judgment or intuition. Also, when they interpret statistics, marketers rely on estimates of expected error or deviation from the true values of the population.

Reporting research findings

The final step in the marketing research process is preparing a report of the research findings. Before writing the report, the marketer must take a clear objective look at the findings to see how well the gathered facts answer the fundamental research question posed in the beginning. In most cases, it is extremely doubtful that the study will provide everything needed to answer the research question. Thus, a lack of completeness will probably have to be pointed out in the report together with reasons for it.[10]

The analysis of data may lead researchers to accept or reject the hypothesis being studied. Usually, results are communicated in a formal written report. Marketers must allow time for this task when they plan and schedule the project. Since the purpose of the report is to communicate with the decision makers who must use the research findings, researchers also should decide beforehand how much detail and supporting data to include in their report. Often, they will state their summary and recommendation first, especially if decision makers do not have time to get involved in understanding how results were obtained. However, a technical report does allow its users to analyze data and interpret recommendations, since it also describes the research methods and procedures and the most important data gathered.[11]

In a recent survey, top corporate executives indicated that they had a low opinion of marketing research reports. Inefficiency and impracticality of results were chief complaints. Specifically, executives stated that (1) researchers are captivated by techniques and often fit the problem to a favored technique and (2) researchers prefer complex studies, language, and reports to simple ones.[12] Obviously, the researcher must recognize the needs and expectations of the report user and adapt to those expectations.

When marketing decision makers have a firm grasp of research methods and procedures, they are able to integrate reported findings and personal experience. If marketers can spot limitations in research from

10. George E. Breen and Albert B. Blankenship, ''How to Present a Research Report that Gets Action,'' *Marketing Times,* March/April 1983, p. 33.
11. Stewart Henderson Britt, ''The Writing of Readable Research Reports,'' *Journal of Marketing Research,* May 1971, pp. 262–266.
12. Joseph H. Rabin, ''Top Executives Have Low Opinion of Marketing Research, Marketers' Role in Strategic Planning,'' *Marketing News,* Oct. 16, 1981, p. 3.

reading the report, then personal experience assumes more importance in making decisions. The inability of some marketers to understand basic statistical assumptions and data gathering procedures causes them to misuse research findings. Still, report writers should understand the backgrounds and research abilities of those who will use the report to make decisions. Providing adequate explanations in understandable language makes it easier for decision makers to apply the findings and diminishes the likelihood that a report will be misused or ignored entirely. Communicating with potential research users prior to writing a report is most helpful to the researcher in providing information that will, in fact, improve decision making.

Now that we have looked briefly at the factors to consider in planning a research project, let us explore—in general terms—how marketers design research procedures to fit particular problems. The next section discusses how to collect data that will fulfill the design.

Designing the research

That marketers must be able to design research procedures and produce reliable and valid data may seem obvious. However, reliability and validity have precise meanings to researchers that, perhaps, differ from the way many people understand these concepts. First, research techniques must be designed so that they are reliable. A technique has *reliability* if it produces almost identical results in successive repeated trials. Research techniques may be reliable, but that does not necessarily mean that they will be valid. To have *validity,* the method used must measure what it is supposed to measure, not something else. A valid research method provides data that can be used to test the hypothesis being investigated.

Now that we have introduced the basic aims of research design, we are ready to examine some of the main concepts used in designing research.

Sampling

Careful procedures help to increase the reliability of research. The following discussion defines some essential sampling concepts and describes some basic sample designs used in marketing research.

The objective of *sampling* in marketing research is to select representative units from a total population. By systematically choosing a limited number of units to represent the characteristics of a total population, marketers can project the reactions of a total market or market segment from the reactions of the sample. Sampling procedures must be used in studying human behavior as well as in estimating the likelihood of events not connected directly with an activity. For one thing, it would be almost impossible to investigate all members of a population because the time and resources available for research are limited.

A *population,* or "universe," is made up of all elements, units, or individuals that are of interest to researchers for a specific study. For example, if a Gallup poll is to predict the results of a presidential election, the population includes all registered voters in the United States. A representative sample of several thousand registered voters would be selected throughout the country to project the probable voting outcome.

Random sampling

In simple *random sampling,* all the units in a population have an equal chance of appearing in the sample. Random sampling is basic probability sampling. The various events that can occur have an equal or known chance of taking place. For example, a specific card from a deck should have a 1/52 probability of being drawn at any one time. Similarly, if each student at your university or college were given a sequential number, and these numbers were mixed up in a large basket, each student's number would have a known probability of being selected. Sample units are ordinarily chosen by selecting from a table of random numbers statistically generated so that each digit, zero through nine, will have an equal probability of occurring in each position in the sequence. The sequentially numbered elements of a population are sampled randomly by selecting the units whose numbers appear in the table of random numbers.

Stratified sampling

In *stratified sampling,* respondents or sample units are divided into groups according to a common characteristic or attribute. Then a probability sample is conducted within each group. The stratified sample may reduce some of the error that could occur in a simple random sample. By ensuring that each major group or segment of the population receives its proportionate share of sample units, investigators avoid including too many or too few sample units from each of the strata.

Usually, samples are stratified when researchers believe that there may be variations among different types of respondents. For example, many political opinion surveys are stratified by sex, race, and age.

Area sampling

Area sampling involves two stages: (1) selecting a probability sample of geographic areas such as blocks, census tracts, or census enumeration districts; and (2) selecting units or individuals within the selected geographic areas for the sample. This approach is a variation of stratified sampling, with the geographic areas serving as the segments, or primary units, used in sampling. To select the units or individuals within the previously designated geographic areas (blocks or census tracts, for example), researchers may choose every nth house or unit, or random selection procedures may be used to pick out a given number of units or individuals from a total listing within the selected geographic areas. This approach may be used when a complete list of the population is not available.

Quota sampling

Quota sampling is judgmental; that is, the final choice of respondents is left up to the interviewers. A study of consumers who wear eyeglasses, for example, may be conducted by interviewing any person who wears eyeglasses. In quota sampling, there are some controls—usually limited to two or three—over the selection of respondents. The controls attempt to ensure that representative categories of respondents are interviewed.

Quota samples and other judgmental samples are not probability samples; not everyone has an equal opportunity of being selected. Therefore, sampling error cannot be measured statistically. Judgmental samples are used most often in exploratory research, when hypotheses are being developed. Often, a small judgmental sample will not be projected to the total population, although the findings may provide valuable insights into a problem.

Figure 4.7
Relationship between
independent and de-
pendent variables

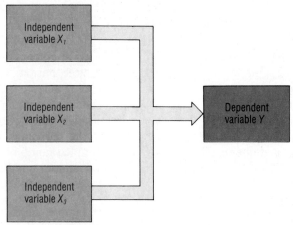

$Y = f(X_1, X_2, X_3)$. (Dependent variable Y is a function of X_1, X_2, and X_3). The independent variables could be X_1 = advertising expenditures, X_2 = number of salespersons, and X_3 = number of dealers. The dependent variable Y could be sales in a specific time period.

Experimentation

Experimentation is a general term for the approach taken in investigating relationships. Finding out which variable or variables caused an event to occur may be difficult unless researchers adopt an experimental approach. *Experimentation* involves maintaining as constants those factors that are related to or may affect the variables under investigation, so that the effects of the experimental variables may be measured. *Marketing experimentation* is a set of rules and procedures under which the task of data gathering is organized to expedite analysis and interpretation.

In the experimental approach, an *independent variable* (a variable free from influence of, or not dependent on, other variables) is usually manipulated and changes are measured in a *dependent variable* (a variable contingent on, or restricted to, one or a set of values assumed by the independent variable). Figure 4.7 shows the relationship between these variables. For example, when a book publisher sets the price of a new dictionary, it may want to estimate the number of dictionaries that could be sold at various prices. The dependent variable would be sales, and the independent variable would be price. Researchers would design the experiment so that other independent variables that might influence sales—such as advertising, distribution, and variation of the product—would be controlled. Experiments may be conducted in the laboratory or in the field. Each setting has advantages and disadvantages.

Laboratory settings

Often, participants or respondents are invited to a central location to react or respond to experimental stimuli. In such an isolated setting, it is possible to control independent variables that might influence the outcome of an experiment. Laboratory settings might include a taste kitchen, video equipment, slide projectors, tape recorders, one-way mirrors, central telephone banks, and interview rooms. In an experiment to determine the influence of price (independent variable) on sales of dictionaries (dependent variable), respondents would be invited to a laboratory—a room arranged with

table, chairs, and sample dictionaries—before the dictionary was available in stores. The dictionary in question would be placed on a table with competitors' dictionaries. Analysts would then query respondents about their reactions to the dictionaries at various prices.

One problem with a laboratory setting is its isolation from the real world. It is simply not possible to duplicate all the conditions that affect choices in the marketplace. On the other hand, by controlling variables that cannot be controlled in the real world, laboratory simulations can focus on variables that marketers think may be significant in ensuring the success of a marketing strategy. Market Facts, Inc., a leading marketing research firm, has reported that test market laboratories are being used more frequently today. Of the largest consumer goods and service companies surveyed, 37% reported using test market laboratories in the preceding year.[13]

Field settings

The experimental approach also can be used in field or survey research. Market Facts has reported that 36 percent of major consumer goods and services companies use controlled store testing.[14] Figure 4.8 illustrates an enterprise—the Marketing Models Group—that specializes in testing products among consumers in real supermarkets. Since field experiments take place in natural surroundings, many factors can influence their results. Some limitations of field experiments follow.

13. Based on a survey conducted by Market Facts, Inc., April 28, 1983.
14. Ibid.

1. Many relevant variables that influence the results are not measurable. For example, the effects of an outside event may inadvertently bias the experiment.
2. Carryover effects on a field experiment tend to be unavoidable. What the respondent has done in prior weeks can exert some influence on what is presently being done.
3. Gaining the interest and attention of the respondent is difficult, and the experiment must be structured to gain respondent cooperation. Usually, the participants in field experiments do not know or understand how they relate to the experiment.
4. Field settings limit the types of manipulation an experimenter can employ. For example, a respondent's exposure to competitors' advertisements cannot be controlled, and this exposure may be difficult to measure.[15]

Experimentation is used in marketing research design to improve hypothesis testing. However, whether experiments are conducted in the laboratory or in the field, many assumptions must be made to limit the number of factors and isolate the causal factors. Marketing decision makers must recognize that these assumptions may diminish the reliability of the research findings.

Simulated test markets for new products can use an experimental approach. For example, one marketing research company, Behavior Scan, has brought a new dimension to experimental research by combining cable television, supermarket scanners, and computers. The company tracks every commercial its panelists watch and every purchase they make in a supermarket or drug store. This procedure permits a projection of the impact of advertising on new product purchases by various consumer groups.[16]

Gathering research data

Marketing research data usually are obtained through surveys, through observation, and from secondary data (data that are stored and already available).

As noted earlier, firsthand information obtained to test the hypothesis under investigation makes up the primary data. Survey results of consumer attitudes toward Coca-Cola's Diet Coke are primary data. Secondary data may be internal accounting records and other information stored in the company's marketing data bank, or they may be collected by such external organizations as the Census Bureau and trade associations.

Most marketing research investigations use a combination of primary and secondary data sources. A massive search of internal records and past studies is particularly useful in determining which additional data should be gathered by primary collection methods such as surveys or observation.

15. Adapted from Gerald Zaltman and Philip C. Burger, *Marketing Research: Fundamentals and Dynamics* (Hinsdale, Ill.: Dryden Press, 1975), pp. 352–353. Used by permission.
16. James S. Figuia, "Simulated Test Markets Are an Oasis in an Era of Marketing Research Which Doesn't Deliver," *Marketing News,* Jan. 20, 1984, p. 3.

Survey methods

Survey methods include interviews by mail or by telephone and personal interviews. The selection of an interviewing method depends on the nature of the problem, the data needed to test the hypothesis, and the resources, such as funding and personnel, that are available to the researcher. Table 4.3 summarizes and compares the advantages of the various methods. Researchers must know exactly what type of information is needed to test the hypothesis and what type of information can be obtained through interviewing. Table 4.4 describes the consumer survey techniques that are used most frequently and thus dominate research spending. The data are based on a survey of large American consumer goods and services companies.

Mail surveys

In a mail survey, questionnaires are sent to respondents who are encouraged to complete and return them. This type of survey is used most often when the individuals chosen for questioning are spread over a wide area and funds for the survey are limited. A mail survey is the least expensive

Table 4.3 Comparison of the three basic survey methods

	Mail Surveys	Telephone Surveys	Personal Interview Surveys
Economy	Potentially the lowest cost per interview if there is an adequate return rate; increased postage rates are raising costs	Avoids interviewers' travel expenses; less expensive than personal in-home interviews; most common survey method	In-home personal interviewing is the most expensive interviewing method; shopping-mall interviewing and focus-group interviewing may lower the costs
Flexibility	Inflexible; questionnaire must be short and easy for respondents to complete; no probing questions; may take more time to implement than other survey methods	More flexible than mail surveys because interviewers can ask probing questions to encourage respondents to answer questions; although more rapport may be gained, observations are impossible	Most flexible method; respondents can react to visual materials and can assist in filling out questionnaire; observation is possible, so that age, race, and other demographic data are more accurate; in-depth probes are possible

continued next page

Table 4.3   (continued)

	Mail Surveys	Telephone Surveys	Personal Interview Surveys
Interviewer bias	Interviewer bias eliminated; questionnaires can be returned anonymously	Lack of a face-to-face contact provides some anonymity; may be harder to develop trust among respondents	Face-to-face contact may foster greater trust among respondents; personal attributes of interviewers may bias respondents
Sampling and respondents' cooperation	Obtaining a complete mailing list is difficult; nonresponse or failure of respondents to return questionnaires is a major disadvantage	Sample must be limited to respondents with telephones and listed numbers; busy signals, no answers, and nonresponse— including refusals—are problems	Refusals may be decreased by rapport-building efforts of interviewers; not-at-homes are more difficult to deal with; some cities have made personal interviewing illegal, but focus-group interviews and shopping-mall interviewing may overcome these problems

method as long as the response rate is high enough to produce reliable results. The main disadvantage of this method is the possibility that the response rate may be low.

One problem with mail surveys is that results may be misleading if respondents are significantly different from the population being sampled. As Table 4.4 indicates, only 4 percent of the surveyed firms spent a major portion of their research funds for direct mail surveys. A high response rate usually results when respondents have some motivation to return the questionnaire. They might be regular customers, organization members, or hard-to-interview respondents who have an interest in the topic. Some techniques that have been useful in achieving a 50- to 70-percent response rate include (a) giving advance notification (post card, letter, mailgram, or phone call) prior to mailing the actual questionnaire package; (b) using a questionnaire package that appears to be personalized; (c) letting respondents know the benefits of filling out the questionnaire, making it easy for them to complete, offering them a monetary incentive, and including a self-addressed stamped envelope; (d) sending a follow-up letter two to three

Table 4.4 Survey methods used most frequently and survey spending patterns of the largest consumer goods and services companies

	Percent Using This Technique in the Last Year (a) %	Percent Spending Major Budget Share On (b) %
WATS interviewing	91	44
Shopping mall intercept	90	43
Focus groups	90	6
Local telephone interviewing	61	5
Consumer mail panels	57	13
Consumer purchase diaries	48	8
In-home interviewing	47	9
Trade surveys	39	1
Direct mail surveys	33	4
Average number used	5.6	

(a) Question: Here is a list of a number of research data *collection* methods and techniques. For which of these have you used outside suppliers within the past year?
(b) Question: On which one or two have you spent the most money in the past year?

Source: "A Description of Consumer Market Research Technique Usage Patterns and Attitudes in 1982," a survey conducted by Market Facts, Inc., April 28, 1983. Reprinted by permission.

weeks after mailing the questionnaire; and (e) making the results of the survey available to the respondents upon request.[17]

Premiums or incentives used to encourage respondents to return questionnaires have been effective in developing panels of respondents who are interviewed repeatedly by mail. Mail panels, which are selected to represent a market or market segment, are especially useful in evaluating new products, in providing general information about consumers, and in providing records of consumers' purchases. As Table 4.4 indicates, 57 percent of the consumer goods and services companies surveyed use consumer mail panels, but these panels represent a major budget share for only 13 percent of the companies surveyed. It is interesting that 48 percent of the sample use consumer purchase diaries. (These surveys are similar to mail panels, but consumers only keep track of purchases.) Consumer mail panels and consumer purchase diaries are much more widely used than direct mail surveys.

Telephone surveys
In a telephone survey, respondents' answers to a questionnaire are recorded by interviewers. A telephone survey has some advantages over a mail survey. The rate of response is higher because it usually is easier for respondents to cooperate; it takes less effort to answer the telephone and talk than to fill out a questionnaire.

17. Milton M. Pressley, "Try These Tips to Get 50% to 70% Response Rate from Mail Surveys of Commercial Populations," *Marketing News,* Jan. 21, 1983, p. 16.

If there are enough interviewers, telephone interviews can be conducted very quickly. Political candidates or organizations seeking an immediate reaction to an event may use telephone surveys because they are fast. In addition, this survey technique permits interviewers to gain rapport with respondents and to ask probing questions.

Telephone interviews have disadvantages, too. They are limited to oral communication; visual aids or observation cannot be included; and interpretation of results must make adjustments for subjects who are not at home or who do not have telephones.

WATS (Wide Area Telecommunications Service) significantly reduces the expense of long-distance telephone interviewing. As Table 4.4 indicates, 91 percent of the consumer goods and services companies surveyed had used WATS interviewing during 1982. Also, as Figure 4.9 indicates, computer-assisted telephone interviewing permits an integration of questionnaire, data collection, and tabulations. Computer-assisted telephone interviewing provides data to aid decision makers in the shortest time possible.

In computer-assisted telephone interviewing, the paper questionnaire is replaced by a video screen, or cathode ray tube (CRT). Responses are entered on a typewriter-like keyboard, or the interviewer can use a pen-shaped flashlight (or light pen) to touch the appropriate response on a light-sensitive screen. On the most advanced devices, the interviewer can use a finger to touch the responses on a touch-sensitive CRT. Open-ended responses can be typed on the terminal keyboard or recorded with paper and pencil.

CRT interviewing saves time and facilitates monitoring the progress of interviews. Entry functions are largely eliminated; the computer will determine which question to display on the CRT so as to skip questions that are not relevant. Because the data file is built as the survey proceeds, interim results can be quickly retrieved from the system, which eliminates cumbersome hand computations. With some systems, a microcomputer may be taken to off-site locations for use in data analysis. Some suppliers claim that CRT interviewing—including the cost of the hardware, software, and operations—is less expensive than conventional paper and pencil methods.[18]

Almost one in five households is excluded from telephone directories by choice or because the residents moved after publication of the directory.[19] National estimates indicate that certain types of persons tend to have unlisted telephones. Demographic patterns emerge, with blacks and persons eighteen to thirty-four years of age having a greater-than-average incidence of unlisted telephones. Also, unlisted households are particularly high in the West and in major metropolitan areas. Income groups of $5,000 to $9,999 yearly show a pattern of unlisted telephones.[20] Thus, if households with unlisted numbers are systematically excluded, the resulting

18. Stephen M. Billig, "Go Slow, Be Wary When Considering Switch to Computer-Assisted Interviewing System," *Marketing News,* Nov. 26, 1982, Sec. 2, p. 2.
19. Gerald J. Glasser and Gale D. Metzger, "National Estimates of Nonlisted Telephone Households and Their Characteristics," *Journal of Marketing Research,* Aug. 1975, p. 361.
20. Ibid.

sample will be somewhat older, more rural, more white, more educated, more retired, and more white-collar than the universe of households with telephone service.[21]

These findings have serious implications for the use of telephone samples in conducting surveys. Some adjustment must be made for groups of respondents that may be undersampled because of a smaller-than-average incidence of telephone listings. Nondirectory telephone samples can overcome such bias. Various methods are available, including random-digit dialing (adding random numbers to the telephone prefix) and plus-one telephone sampling (adding one to the last digit of a number in the directory).[22] These methods make it feasible to dial any working number, whether or not it is listed in a directory.

21. Patricia E. Moberg, "Biases in Unlisted Phone Numbers," *Journal of Advertising Research,* Aug./Sept. 1982, p. 55.
22. E. Laird Landon, Jr., and Sharon K. Banks, "Relative Efficiency and Bias of Plus-One Telephone Sampling," *Journal of Marketing Research,* Aug. 1977, pp. 294–299.

Telephone surveys, like mail and personal interview surveys, are sometimes used to develop panels of respondents who can be interviewed repeatedly to measure changes in attitudes or behavior. Use of these telephone panels is increasing.

Personal interview surveys

Traditionally, marketing researchers have favored the face-to-face interview, primarily because of its flexibility. Various audiovisual aids—pictures, products, diagrams, or prerecorded advertising copy—can be incorporated into a personal interview, and rapport gained through direct interaction usually permits more in-depth interviewing, including probes, follow-up questions, or psychological tests. In addition, because face-to-face interviews can be longer, more information can be gathered through them. Finally, respondents can be selected more carefully, and reasons for nonresponse can be explored.

In the past, most personal interviews, which were based on random sampling or prearranged appointments, were conducted in the respondent's home. Today, the nature of personal interviews has changed. As Table 4.4 indicates, most personal interviews are conducted in shopping malls. The shopping mall intercept interview consists of sampling a percentage of persons passing by certain "intercept" points in the mall. Although there are many variations of this technique, Table 4.4 indicates that shopping mall intercept interviewing is the second most popular survey technique used today, next only to WATS interviewing. Ninety percent of the major consumer goods and services companies use this technique. In fact, 43 percent of these companies report that shopping mall intercept interviewing is their major expenditure on survey research.

As with any face-to-face interviewing method, mall intercept interviewing has many advantages. The interviewer is in a position to recognize and react to nonverbal indications of confusion on the part of the respondent. Respondents can be shown product prototypes, video tapes of commercials, story boards, and the like, and reactions can be sought. The mall environment permits the researcher to deal with complex situations, such as those requiring taste tests, by ensuring that all the respondents are reacting to the same product, which can be prepared and monitored from the mall test kitchen or some other facility. Lower cost, greater control, and the ability to conduct tests requiring bulky equipment are the major reasons for the popularity of this survey method.[23]

A panel interview is more efficient than a mall interview when a study requires responses from older people, low-income people, and minorities, as these people are not adequately represented in malls. Also, when a study requires unhurried, thoughtful responses a panel interview is preferable to the mall interview.[24]

A variation of the personal interview technique is the focus-group interview, in which groups, rather than individuals, are interviewed. The object is to observe group interaction when members are exposed to an idea

23. Roger Gates and Paul J. Soloman, "Research Using the Mall Intercept: State of the Art," *Journal of Advertising Research,* Aug./Sept. 1982, pp. 47–48.
24. Judith Langer, "Consumer Research: Critical Step in New Product Development," *Marketing Times,* March/April 1983, p. 29.

or concept. Often, group interviews are conducted on an informal basis without a structured questionnaire. Consumer attitudes, behavior, life-styles, needs, and desires can be explored in a flexible and creative manner through focus-group interviews. Researchers approach consumers without preconceived notions. Questions are open ended and stimulate consumers to answer in their own words. Researchers who hear something they do not fully understand or something unexpected and interesting can probe for insights into deeper thoughts and feelings that explain consumer behavior.[25] Table 4.4 indicates that 90 percent of the firms surveyed use focus-group interviewing, and 6 percent of the firms spend the major share of their budgets on this technique.

Questionnaire construction

The careful construction of a questionnaire is essential to the success of a survey. First of all, questions must be designed to elicit information that meets the data requirements of the study. Questions must be clear, easy to understand, and directed toward a definable objective. Until that objective has been defined, researchers should not attempt to develop a question-naire, for the composition of the questions depends on the nature of the objective and the detail demanded. One common mistake in questionnaire construction is to ask questions that interest the researchers but do not provide information that helps in deciding whether to accept or reject a hy-pothesis. Finally, the most important rule is to maintain an unbiased, ob-jective approach in composing questions. Several kinds of questions can be included: open ended, dichotomous, and multiple-choice. Examples of each follow:

Open-Ended Question
What is your general opinion of the Ford Escort automobile?

_____

_____

_____

Dichotomous Question
Do you presently own a Ford Escort?
Yes   _____
No   _____

Multiple-Choice Question
What age group are you in?
Under 20   _____
20–29   _____
30–39   _____
40–49   _____
50–59   _____
60 and over   _____

Researchers must be very careful about questions that a person might consider too personal or that might result in a respondent's admitting to

25. NFO Research Inc., Advertisement, *Marketing News,* Jan. 21, 1983, p. 20.

activities that other people are likely to condemn. Questions of this type should be worded in such a way as to make them less offensive. For example, Table 4.5 shows how a series of questions can be designed to overcome the potentially objectionable nature of a question about shoplifting. Even though this approach does not guarantee truthful responses, it should improve their probability of occurring. Note that the series of questions in Table 4.5 asks about the importance of shoplifting as a crime. One question deals with knowledge about shoplifting by others. These questions are designed to measure beliefs or behavior indirectly as well as directly.

Observation methods   Various observation methods other than surveys can be used to collect primary data. In using the *observation method,* researchers record the overt behavior of respondents, taking note of physical conditions and events. Direct contact with respondents is avoided; instead, their actions are examined and noted systematically. For example, researchers might use observation methods to answer the question, "How long does the average McDonald's restaurant customer have to wait in line before being served?"

Observation methods can be used to control such retail store factors as inventory, spoilage, and breakage. Observation may also be combined with interviews. For example, during personal interviews, the condition of a respondent's home or other possessions may be observed and recorded, and demographic information such as race, approximate age, and sex can be confirmed by direct observation.

Data gathered through observation sometimes can be biased if the respondent is aware of the observation process. An observer can be placed in a natural market environment, such as a grocery store, without biasing or influencing the actions of shoppers. However, if the presence of a human observer is likely to bias the outcome or if human sensory abilities are inadequate, mechanical means may be used to record behavior. *Mechanical observation devices* include cameras, recorders, counting machines, and equipment to record physiological changes in individuals. For instance, an audimeter is used to record the station to which a television or radio receiver is tuned. Similarly, a special camera can be used to record eye movements of respondents looking at an advertisement. The sequence of reading and the parts of the advertisement that receive greatest attention can be detected.[26]

Observation methods, like survey methods, are used to test hypotheses, discover problems, or provide a continuous flow of information into a data bank. Observation is straightforward, and there is no need to motivate respondents to state their true feelings—a complex problem with survey methods. However, observation tends to be descriptive. When it is the only method of data collection, it may not provide insights into causal relationships. Another limitation is that analyses based on observation are subject to the biases and limitations of the observer or the mechanical device.

26. Harper W. Boyd, Jr., Ralph Westfall, and Stanley F. Stasch, *Marketing Research Text and Cases,* 4th ed. (Homewood, Ill.: Irwin, 1977), p. 136.

Table 4.5 The use of a series of questions to overcome the objectionable nature of a question

Problem

Have you ever shoplifted anything?
   1 no
   2 yes

Revision

As you know, there is now a great deal of discussion about shoplifting in this community, and questions as to how it should be handled. Some people feel it is a serious problem about which something should be done; others feel it is not a serious problem. How about yourself? Do you consider shoplifting to be a serious, moderate, slight, or no problem at all in our community?
   1 serious
   2 moderate
   3 slight
   4 not at all

During the past few years do you think the frequency of shoplifting has increased, stayed about the same, or decreased in this community?
   1 increased
   2 stayed about the same
   3 decreased

Please try to recall the time when you were a teenager. Do you recall personally knowing anyone who took something from a store without paying for it?
   1 no
   2 yes

How about yourself? Did you ever consider taking anything from a store without paying for it?
   1 no
   2 yes

(If yes) Did you actually take it?
   1 no
   2 yes

Source: Don A. Dillman, *Mail and Telephone Surveys: The Total Design Method* (New York: Wiley, 1978), p. 107. Used by permission.

Secondary data collection

In addition to or instead of collecting primary data, marketers may use available reports and other information to study a marketing problem. An organization's marketing data bank may contain helpful information about past marketing activities, such as sales records and research reports, that can be used to test hypotheses and pinpoint problems.

Secondary data also are found in periodicals, government publications, and unpublished sources. Periodicals such as *Business Week, Sales and Marketing Management,* and *Industrial Marketing* print general information that is helpful in defining problems and developing hypotheses. *Survey of Buying Power,* the annual supplement to *Sales and Marketing Management,* contains sales data for major industries on a county-by-county basis. Demographics from the U.S. census can be prepared for specific research uses by a company specializing in demographic analysis. Such information may be especially valuable in tracking changes in age, education, family size, and population density. Many marketers consult government publications, such as the *Census of Business,* the *Census of Agriculture,* and the *Census of Populations.* They can be obtained from the Superintendent of Documents in Washington, D.C.

External sources of information include **syndicated data services.** American Research Bureau (ARB) furnishes television stations and media purchasers with estimates of the number of viewers at specific times. Sell Area Marketing, Inc. (SAMI), furnishes monthly information that describes market shares for specific types of manufacturers. The A. C. Nielsen Company Retail Index gathers data about products primarily sold through food stores and drugstores. This information includes total sales of the product category, sales of the clients' own brands, and sales of important competing brands.[27] The Market Research Corporation of America (MRCA) collects data through a national panel of consumers to provide information about purchases. Therefore, sales by brands can be classified by age, race, sex, education, occupation, and size of family.

Similar organizations operate at the local level. Market Search, a marketing research company in Indianapolis, for example, offers "Indyindex." This monthly omnibus study for small Indianapolis businesses contains information gleaned from three hundred consumer telephone interviews about product preferences, prices, stores, and other marketing topics. Small businesses use this research information to plan their marketing activities.[28] All syndicated data services collect general information that is sold to many clients. Their information is available only to subscribers.

Internal sources of information can contribute tremendously to research. An organization's accounting records make excellent sources of unpublished data but, strangely enough, are often overlooked. The large volume of data collected by the accounting department does not automatically flow to the marketing area. As a result, detailed information about costs, sales, customer accounts, or profits by product category may not be part of the MIS. This condition is especially true in organizations that do not store marketing information on a systematic basis. As was pointed out early in this chapter, such information—collected systematically and continuously through a carefully constructed marketing information system—is essential to the success of marketing efforts.

Marketing research and information systems in practice

Clearly, marketing research and information systems are vital to marketing decision making. In the past, small and medium-sized organizations have relied primarily on intuition in decision making. Today, managers in all types of organizations are recognizing the need for more and better information. For example, the state of Ohio is using marketing research, including focus groups, personal interviews, and surveys, to determine attitudes and perceptions regarding the state's economic development programs. The goal of the research is to encourage businesses to stay in the state and expand, as well as to convince new companies to locate in Ohio.[29]

27. Boyd, Westfall, and Stasch, *Marketing Research,* p. 598.
28. "Marketing Research Briefs," *Marketing News,* Jan. 21, 1983, p. 5.
29. "Research Keys Bid for Tourism and Industry in Buckeye State," *Marketing News,* Oct. 28, 1983, p. 12.

Managers see the benefit of information in avoiding costly marketing mistakes. If a $10,000 research study can prevent the $100,000 loss associated with developing a product that has no market, then the payoff is obvious. Even so, too many firms do not spend enough to develop new marketing strategies before products are brought to the marketplace. As more organizations use marketing research and develop marketing information systems, more scientific approaches to marketing should develop.

Figure 4.10 shows the service provided by one marketing research agency. Often, a research agency will offer many different services, and a firm may purchase one or several, depending on its own abilities to perform research and on the problem to be solved. Firms often find that by purchasing research services from independent agencies, they can obtain more objective answers at less expense than they could by maintaining their own research staffs. On the other hand, most firms have to develop their own marketing information systems. For the day-to-day management and structuring of regularly gathered information, it is the task of a firm's management to decide which information will be useful in making future decisions and therefore should be stored.

One final area of marketing research practice must not go unmentioned. It is imperative that marketers establish acceptable standards of education and ethics. Attempts to stamp out shoddy practices and to establish generally acceptable procedures for conducting research are enhancing the professional image of marketing researchers.

Summary

Marketing research and information systems are essential to an organization's planning and strategy development. The marketing concept cannot be implemented without information about buyers. As acceptance of the marketing concept in planning efforts has increased, higher levels of management have begun using marketing research.

The marketing information system (MIS) provides a framework for the day-to-day managing and structuring of information regularly gathered from sources both inside and outside an organization. Marketing research is the design and execution of specific inquiries to yield results for making marketing decisions. Marketing research usually is characterized by in-depth analysis of a problem, while the MIS focuses on data storage, retrieval, and classification.

Research and information systems are scientific approaches to decision making in marketing. Intuitive managers make decisions on the basis of past experience and personal bias. Scientific decision making is an orderly, logical, and systematic approach. Minor, nonrecurring problems can be handled successfully by intuition. As the number of alternative solutions increases and the payoffs (as well as risks) multiply, the use of research in planning is more rewarding and desirable.

The five basic steps in planning marketing research are (1) defining and locating problems, (2) developing hypotheses, (3) collecting data, (4) interpreting research findings, and (5) reporting research findings. A problem must be stated clearly for marketers to develop a hypothesis, which is a guess or assumption about that problem or set of circumstances. To test the accuracy of hypotheses and to gather data, researchers may use exploratory, descriptive, or causal studies. To apply research to decision making, marketers must interpret and report their findings properly.

Research design involves establishing procedures for obtaining reliable and valid marketing data. A study is valid if it measures what it is supposed to measure.

Sampling is a method of selecting representative units from a total population. Four basic sampling designs for marketing research are random sampling, stratified sampling, area sampling, and quota sampling. The first three sampling methods are based on statistical probability; that is, sample units have a known or equal chance of being chosen. Quota sampling results in judgmental samples.

Experimentation is a procedure for organizing data to increase the validity and reliability of research findings. Experimentation focuses on controlling some variables and manipulating others to determine cause-and-effect relationships. Laboratory settings provide marketers with maximum control over influential factors. Field settings are preferred when marketers want experimentation to take place in natural surroundings.

There are three fundamental ways to obtain data: through surveys (personal, telephone, and mail); through observation; and from secondary data. Surveys gather data through interviews or by having respondents fill out questionnaires, which are instruments used to obtain information from respondents and to record observations. Questionnaires should be unbiased and objective.

Trends in marketing research point to improved interpretation of research findings. Attempts to stamp out shoddy practices and to establish generally acceptable procedures for conducting research are enhancing the professional image of marketing researchers.

Important terms

Marketing research	Validity
Marketing information system (MIS)	Sampling
	Population
Marketing data bank	Random sampling
Intuition	Stratified sampling
Scientific decision making	Area sampling
Problem definition	Quota sampling
Hypothesis	Experimentation
Primary data	Marketing experimentation
Secondary data	Independent variable
Exploratory studies	Dependent variable
Descriptive studies	Survey methods
Causal studies	Observation method
Statistical interpretation	Mechanical observation devices
Reliability	Syndicated data services

Discussion and review questions

1. How do the benefits of marketing research stack up against those of intuitive decision making? How do marketing decision makers know when it will be profitable to conduct research?
2. In what ways do marketing research and the MIS overlap?
3. Give some specific examples of situations in which intuitive decision making would probably be more appropriate than marketing research.
4. What is the MIS likely to include in a small organization? Do all organizations have a marketing data bank?
5. What is the difference between developing a hypothesis and defining the research problem?
6. "Nonresponse" refers to the inability or refusal of some respondents to cooperate in a survey. What are some ways to decrease nonresponse in personal door-to-door surveys?
7. Give some examples of marketing problems that could be solved through information gained from observation.
8. What are the major limitations of using secondary data to solve marketing problems?

9. If a survey of all homes with listed telephone numbers is conducted, what sampling design should be used?

10. List some problems of conducting a laboratory experiment on respondents' reactions to the taste of different brands of beer. How would these problems differ from those of a field study on beer taste preferences?

11. Make some suggestions for encouraging respondents to cooperate in mail surveys.

Cases

Case 4.1

The Sxlool[30]

The Sxlool was a singles bar in Chicago's "Rush Street" area. The Rush Street area, located on Chicago's Near North Side by the Gold Coast, is approximately seven blocks long and three blocks wide, and is a popular area for evening entertainment.

The Sxlool once was one of the most popular spots on "Rush Street." There had always been wall-to-wall people on Friday afternoons, but lately the crowds had begun to go elsewhere.

A marketing research consultant who patronized The Sxlool because it was two blocks from his home knew the manager, Karen Stein, well. After some discussions with The Sxlool's manager, the consultant sent a letter that proposed that The Sxlool conduct some marketing research.

The Sxlool's Marketing Research Proposal

Dear Karen:

Here is a brief outline of what I believe The Sxlool must consider if it is to regain its popularity on Rush Street. As you know, The Sxlool's management has changed the decor and exterior of The Sxlool, hired exceptional bands, and used various other promotions to improve business. In spite of this, a decline in The Sxlool's popularity has been evidenced. As these efforts have not brought back the crowd The Sxlool once had, I suggest The Sxlool undertake a marketing research investigation of consumer behavior and consumer opinions among Rush Street patrons.

I recommend this project because The Sxlool once had what it takes to be a popular bar on Rush Street and should still have the potential to regain this status. Most likely, the lack of patronage at The Sxlool is caused by one or both of the following factors:

1. A change in the people or type of people who patronize Rush Street bars.

2. The opinion of The Sxlool held by people who patronize Rush Street has changed.

30. This case originally appeared in William G. Zikmund, William J. Lundstrom, and Donald Sciglimpaglia, *Cases in Marketing Research* (Hinsdale, Ill.: Dryden Press, 1982). Used with permission of William G. Zikmund. Names are fictitious to protect confidentiality.

The problem for The Sλool's management is to determine the specifics of the change, either in different people, or in the opinions of the regular patrons of Rush Street and The Sλool.

Determining what type of information is desired by The Sλool's management depends upon some underlying facts about the popularity of the bars on Rush Street. An assumption must be made concerning the questions, "Does the crowd (weekend and Wednesday patrons) go where the regulars go or do the regulars go where the crowd goes?" If you believe that the regulars follow the crowd, a general investigation should be conducted to test why the mass goes to the popular bars. If the assumption is made that a popular bar is popular because there are always people (regulars) there, the best method to increase business is to get a regular following which will attract "the crowd."

Of course, the optimal position is to appeal to both the regulars and the crowd. Thus, there are numerous areas for investigation:

Who visits Rush Street bars? What are the group characteristics?

What motivates these people to go to the various bars and thus make them popular? For example, to what extent does the number of stag girls in the bars bring about more patrons? (Note: Remember that The Sλool, Rush-up, Filling Station and Barnaby's had female waitresses at the start of their popularity. Could this have been a factor in their appeal?) How important is bartender rapport with the patrons?

What do drinkers like and dislike about The Sλool?

What is the awareness among beer drinkers of Watney's quality? Do they like it? How does having Bud on tap affect a bar's popularity?

What image does The Sλool project? Is it favorable or unfavorable? Has it lost the image it once had because it is trying to be the Store Annex, Barnaby's, Rush-up, and The Sλool combined? Is the decor consistent? How can a favorable image be put back into Rush Street drinkers' minds? You might think The Sλool can appeal to all Rush Street people, but you can't be all things to all people. A specialization of image and customers may bring back "the crowd" for The Sλool.

How important is it to be first with a new promotion? For example, did Barnaby's idea of starting a wine and chicken feast make it the place to go to—at least in the short run? If a food promotion would go over, what should The Sλool try?

There are many areas where The Sλool would benefit if it conducted a marketing research survey. Of course, the above suggestions for investigation are not all-inclusive, as I have not had a chance to talk with you to determine which areas are the most important. If you would like to have me submit a formal research proposal to determine how The Sλool can improve its business, I will be happy to talk with you any evening.

Sincerely yours,
Robert Millanes

Questions for discussion
1. Has the problem been adequately defined?
2. Evaluate the research proposal.
3. What should happen in each step of the marketing research process?

Case 4.2

A. C. Nielsen Company[31]

A. C. Nielsen Company and its subsidiaries provide worldwide business services that help clients to make factually based decisions on matters relating to marketing, production, distribution, product and package design, and sales and promotional programs.

The company's major resources include the Marketing Research Group which provides continuous measurement of consumer response at the point of sale. The Neodata Services Group maintains computerized circulation lists for magazine publishers and others. The Media Research Group provides measurement of national and local television audiences. The Clearing House Group processes merchandise coupons for retailers and manufacturers and provides inquiry services for advertisers and magazine publishers. The Petroleum Information Corp. provides statistical data to make oil and gas exploration more efficient. Dataquest, Inc. provides comprehensive information for use in evaluating technology and marketing developments in industrial markets.

Major services provided by the Marketing Research Group include measuring consumer reaction at the actual point of sale. In the U.S. there are more than 7,000 stores equipped with scanners that electronically read the zebra-striped bar codes appearing on most packaged grocery products. Nielsen auditors regularly visit a national sample of retail stores and use these checkout scanners as a source of consumer sales information. The Nielsen auditors also obtain marketplace information such as retail inventories, brand distribution, out-of-stock conditions, prices and displays. Since audits are repeated regularly, all important trends are tracked by the Marketing Research Group.

New products or new ideas can be tested on a limited scale to minimize their risk. Nielsen's E.R.I.M. Consumer Research evaluates the performance of brands using a new technique. Special television advertising messages about new products or select brands are transmitted by cable television to select households in a small geographic area. By collecting data from scanning cash registers in stores where these sample households shop, information about the effect of these commercials on consumer purchase patterns is obtained. This new technique enhances the value of test marketing research.

Nielsen's clients are continually being informed about their products' sales performance and market share either for the entire country or by regions, store type and size, and package sizes. The Nielsen Warehouse Inventory Service, which is also provided by the Marketing Research Group, helps manufacturers of health and beauty aids to gain a more complete knowledge of how their products move through the distribution pipeline from factory to retail stores. The Marketing Research Group also provides a computerized management system to help manufacturers organize the ever-increasing quantities of market data and to utilize these data more effectively.

31. The facts in this case are based on the A. C. Nielsen Company *1983 Annual Report.*

Nielsen's Marketing Research Group has worldwide sales of $363 million. Its worldwide market review service provides clients with access to market-development information on selected product categories in a large number of countries. All the services provided by A. C. Nielsen Company have a common objective—to help clients market their products more profitably.

Questions for discussion
1. In what ways does the comprehensive marketing information provided by the Nielsen Marketing Research Group help its clients?
2. How do Nielsen marketing services impact on the ultimate users of products that are surveyed?
3. Is it best for a company to conduct its own marketing research efforts or purchase marketing research services from a firm such as A.C. Nielsen?

Product Decisions

Having examined markets and marketing opportunities, we now are prepared to analyze the decisions and activities associated with developing and maintaining effective marketing mixes. In Parts Two, Three, Four, and Five we focus on the major components of the marketing mix—product, distribution, promotion, and price. Specifically, in Part Two we explore the product ingredient of the marketing mix. Chapter 5 introduces basic concepts and relationships that must be understood in order to make effective product decisions. Branding, packaging, and labeling are also discussed in this chapter. In Chapter 6, we analyze a variety of dimensions regarding product management, such as the ways that a firm can be organized to manage products, the development and positioning of products, product modification, and the phasing out of products.

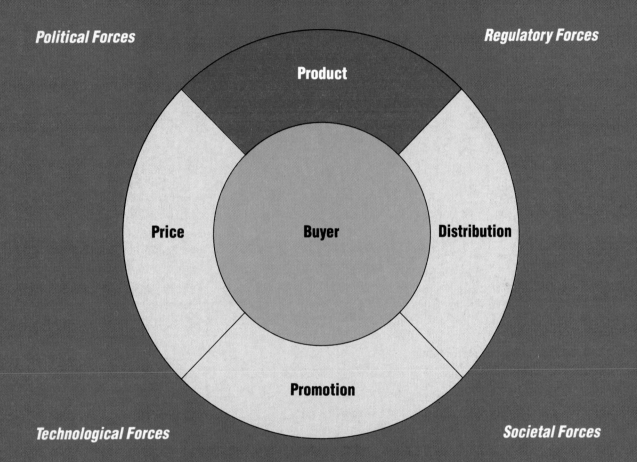

Marketing Environment

Legal Forces

Political Forces

Regulatory Forces

Product

Price

Buyer

Distribution

Promotion

Technological Forces

Societal Forces

Economic Forces

5

Product Concepts

Objectives

To learn how marketers define products.

To understand how to classify products.

To see how product mix and product line policies are developed.

To develop an understanding of the concept of product life cycle.

To grasp the basic product identification concepts as they relate to branding, packaging, and labeling.

Marketing research conducted over a two-and-a-half-year period indicated that customers want pizza for lunch if they can get it quickly. In test markets, the new Personal Pan Pizza dramatically increased lunch sales. Pizza Hut spent $20 million to advertise its new product in the first year, and half of that was spent during the first month (see advertisement in Figure 5.1).

Personal Pan Pizza's guaranteed serving time is five minutes, or the customer's next personal pizza is free. Pizza Hut sells two versions of the six-inch pizza. Each $1.99 supreme pie comes with five toppings—pepperoni, mushroom, onion, green pepper, and pork or beef. A single topping pie, priced at $1.49, also is available. Pizza Hut selects the topping based on preferences determined through research. Personal Pan Pizza is available from 11 A.M. to 4 P.M. Monday through Saturday, although the five-minute guarantee is good only from 11:30 to 1:30.

Figure 5.1   Advertisement for Personal Pan Pizza
Source: Courtesy Pizza Hut

The new menu item was tested in seventeen markets for quality, satisfaction and value. Pizza Hut has invested more than $130 million on developing equipment, redesigning kitchens, and other costs associated with the new product.

Although lunch time business accounts for an estimated 35 percent of all restaurant meals, lunch time trade has only contributed 15 to 18 percent of Pizza Hut's total revenue. The five-minute guarantee strategically positions Pizza Hut as an alternative to other fast food restaurants. Personal Pan Pizza offers a significant opportunity for increasing Pizza Hut's market share.[1]

Products are among a firm's most important and most visible contacts with buyers. If a company's products do not meet the desires and needs of buyers, then—unless adjustments are made—the company will fail. Developing a product that meets the desires and needs of consumers requires knowledge of fundamental marketing and product concepts. The product is an important variable in the marketing mix, and other variables (promotion, distribution, and price) must be coordinated with product decisions.

The fundamental product concepts and definitions that we discuss first in this chapter help clarify what a product is and how buyers view products. Product planners must consider what other products their company offers in the marketplace. Thus, an examination of the concepts of product mix and product line will help us understand product planning. However, a product is not created in a vacuum, nor does it exist in one. Therefore, we must look at product life cycles, the various stages a product moves through from birth to death. Each specific life cycle stage generally requires a specific marketing strategy, assumes a certain competitive environment, and has its own profit pattern. Finally, since branding and packaging are vital components of a product—in fact, they help create the product—we explore these topics, along with labeling, an important informational device.

What is a product?

A *product* is everything (both favorable and unfavorable) that one receives in an exchange; it is a complex of tangible and intangible attributes including functional, social, and psychological utilities or benefits.[2] A product can be an idea, a service, a good, or any combination of these three. This definition includes supporting services that go with goods, such as installation, guarantees, product information, and promises of repair or maintenance. Goods help us to perform mechanical and functional tasks. Ideas provide psychological stimulation that helps us solve problems or adjust to our environment.

When buyers purchase a product, they actually are buying the benefits and satisfaction they think the product will provide. In practice, even the most tangible product cannot be reliably tested or experienced in advance.

1. "Pizza Hut Asserts Presence in Lunch Market," *Marketing News,* April 29, 1983, p. 4.
2. Part of this definition is adapted from S. H. Rewoldt, J. D. Scott, and M. R. Warshaw, *Introduction to Marketing Management,* 4th ed. (Homewood, Ill.: Irwin, 1981), p. 253.

Buyers purchase intangible products—insurance, education, health care, accounting, and air travel, for instance—on the basis of promises of satisfaction. Promises, together with the images and appearances of symbols, help consumers to make judgments about both tangible and intangible products.[3] Since a product meets (or fails to meet) so many consumer needs, it is important for marketers to understand what a product means to consumers and to understand consumers' expectations for that product.

Classifying products

Products fall into one of two general categories, depending on the buyers' intentions. Products purchased to satisfy personal and family needs are *consumer products*. Those bought for use in a firm's operations or to make other products are *industrial products*. Consumers buy products to satisfy their personal wants, while industrial buyers seek to satisfy the goals of their organizations.

The buyer's intent—or the ultimate use of the product—determines the classification of an item as either a consumer or an industrial product. Note that the same thing can be both a consumer product and an industrial product. For example, an electric light bulb is a consumer product if it is used in someone's home. However, the same light bulb is an industrial product if it is purchased either to produce other products or to light an assembly line. After a product is classified as either a consumer or an industrial product, it can be categorized further as a certain type of consumer or industrial product. In this section, we will examine the characteristics of several product classifications and explore the marketing activities associated with some of them.

You may wonder why we need to know about product classifications. The primary reason is that certain classes of products are aimed at particular target markets, and a product's classification affects the kinds of distribution, promotion, and pricing that are appropriate in marketing the product. Industrial products, for example, usually require less advertising than consumer products do. Also, the types of marketing activities and efforts needed differ among the classes of consumer or industrial products. In short, the entire marketing mix can be affected by how a product is classified. The following sections will make this clear.

Classification of consumer products

Although there are several approaches to classifying consumer products, the traditional and most widely accepted approach consists of three categories: convenience products, shopping products, and specialty products. This approach is based primarily on characteristics of buyers' purchasing behavior. One problem associated with the approach is that not all buyers behave in the same way when purchasing a specific type of product. Thus, a single product can fit into all three categories. To minimize this problem, marketers think in terms of how buyers *generally* behave when purchasing a specific item. In addition, they recognize that a product may fall into more than one category and that the "correct" classification can be determined only by considering the target market toward which a particular firm

3. Theodore Levitt, "Marketing Intangible Products and Product Intangibles," *Harvard Business Review*, May–June 1981, pp. 94–102.

is aiming its marketing efforts. With these thoughts in mind, let us examine the three traditional categories of consumer products.

Convenience products

Convenience products are relatively inexpensive, frequently purchased items for which buyers want to exert only minimal effort. Examples include bread, gasoline, newspapers, soft drinks, and chewing gum. The buyer spends little time either in planning the purchase of a convenience item or in comparing available brands or sellers. Even a buyer who prefers a specific brand will readily choose a substitute if the preferred brand is not conveniently available.

Classifying a specific product as a convenience product has several implications for a firm's marketing strategy. A convenience product normally is marketed through many retail outlets. Since sellers experience high inventory turnover of a convenience item, per unit gross margins can be relatively low. Producers of convenience products such as Coca-Cola and Crest toothpaste can expect little promotional effort at the retail level and thus must provide it themselves in the form of advertising. Packaging is an important element of the marketing mix; the package may have to sell the product, since a majority of convenience items are available only on a self-service basis at the retail level.

Shopping products

Shopping products are items for which buyers are willing to expend considerable effort in planning and making the purchase. Buyers allocate considerable time for comparing stores and brands with respect to prices, product features, qualities, services, and perhaps warranties. Appliances, upholstered furniture, men's suits, bicycles, and stereos are examples of shopping products. These products are expected to last for a fairly long time and thus are purchased less frequently than convenience items. Even though shopping products are more expensive than convenience products, few buyers of shopping products are particularly brand loyal.

To market a shopping product effectively, a marketer should consider several key issues. Shopping products require fewer retail outlets than convenience products do. Because shopping products are purchased less frequently, inventory turnover is lower and middlemen expect to receive higher gross margins. Although rather large sums of money may be required to advertise shopping products, a greater percentage of resources are likely to be used for personal selling. Usually, a producer and the middlemen expect some cooperation from one another with respect to providing parts and repair services and performing promotional activities.

Specialty products

Specialty products possess one or more unique characteristics, and a significant group of buyers is willing to expend considerable purchasing effort to obtain them. Buyers actually plan the purchase of a specialty product; they know exactly what they want and will not accept a substitute. In searching for specialty products, purchasers do not compare alternatives. They are concerned primarily with finding an outlet that has a preselected product available.

The fact that an item is a specialty product can affect a firm's marketing efforts in several ways. Specialty products are often distributed through a limited number of retail outlets. Like shopping goods, they are purchased infrequently, causing inventory turnover to be lower and thus requiring gross margins to be relatively high.

Industrial products

As we have noted, industrial products are purchased to produce other products or for use in a firm's operations. Purchases of industrial products are based on an organization's goals and objectives. Usually, the functional aspects of the product are much more important than the psychological rewards that sometimes are associated with consumer products. On the basis of their characteristics and intended uses, industrial products can be classified into several categories: raw materials, major equipment, accessory equipment, component parts, process materials, supplies, and services.[4]

Raw materials

Raw materials, which are basic materials that actually become part of a physical product, are provided from mines, farms, forests, oceans, and recycled solid wastes. Other than the processing required to transport and physically handle the products, raw materials have not been processed when a firm buys them. Raw materials are usually bought and sold according to grades and specifications. Purchasers frequently buy raw materials in relatively large quantities.

Major equipment

Major equipment includes large tools and machines used for production purposes. Examples of major equipment are lathes, cranes, and stamping machines. Usually, major equipment is expensive and is intended to be used in a production process for a considerable length of time. Some major equipment is custom made to perform specific functions for a particular organization, but other items are standardized products that perform one or several tasks for many types of organizations. Because of the high cost of major equipment, purchase decisions often are made by high-level management. Marketers of major equipment frequently must provide a variety of services including installation, training, repair and maintenance assistance, and even aid in financing the purchase.

Accessory equipment

Accessory equipment does not become a part of the final physical product but is used in production or office activities. Examples include hand tools, typewriters, fractional-horsepower motors, and calculators. Compared with major equipment, accessory items are usually much less expensive, are purchased routinely with less negotiation, and are treated as expense items, rather than as capital items, because they are not expected to be used as long. Accessory products are standardized items that generally can be used in several aspects of a firm's operations. More outlets are required for accessory equipment, but sellers do not have to provide the multitude of services expected of major-equipment marketers.

4. Richard M. Hill, Ralph S. Alexander, and James S. Cross, *Industrial Marketing,* 2nd ed. (Homewood, Ill.: Irwin, 1975), p. 37.

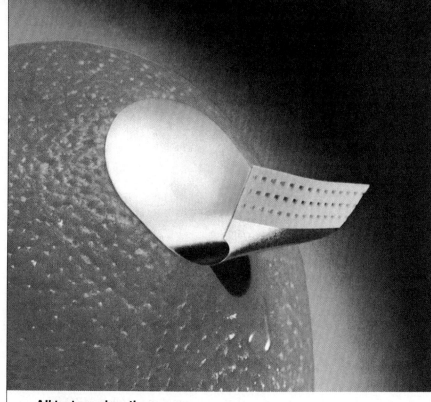

Component parts

Component parts become a part of the physical product and either are fin-ished items ready for assembly or are products that need little processing before assembly. Although they become part of a larger product, compo-nent parts often can be identified and distinguished easily. Spark plugs, tires, clocks, and switches are all component parts of the automobile. Even the familiar 3M "Scotchtab" closure tape shown in Figure 5.2 is a com-ponent part. Buyers purchase such items according to their own predeter-mined specifications or to standards common within an industry. In pur-chasing component parts, buyers expect the parts to consistently be of specified quality and to be delivered on time so that production is not slowed or stopped. Producers that are primarily assemblers, such as most lawn-mower manufacturers, depend heavily on the suppliers of component parts.

Process materials

Process materials are used directly in the production of other products; unlike component parts, however, process materials are not readily identifiable. For example, Reichhold Chemicals, Inc., markets a treated fiber product—a phenolic-resin, sheet-molding compound—that is used in the manufacture of production parts. This material is used by a major aircraft manufacturer in flight deck instrument panels and cabin interiors. Although this material is not identifiable in the finished panels and interiors, it reduces the rate of burning, smoke, and toxic-gas formation if molded components are subjected to fire or high temperatures.[5] Like component parts, process materials are purchased according to industry standards or to the specifications of the individual purchaser.

Supplies

Supplies facilitate production and operations, but they do not become part of the finished product. Paper, pencils, oils, cleaning agents, and paints are examples. Since such supplies are standardized items used in a variety of situations, they are purchased by many different types of organizations. Usually, supplies are sold through numerous outlets and are purchased routinely. To ensure that supplies are available when needed, buyers frequently deal with more than one seller. Because supplies can be divided into three categories—maintenance, repair, and operating (or overhaul) supplies—they are sometimes called *MRO items*. For example, Parker-Hannifin Corporation formed a separate MRO sales organization to sell packings and seals for equipment maintenance, repair, and overhaul.[6] These products were widely available through various industrial distributors.

Industrial services

Industrial services are the intangible products that many organizations use in their operations. Examples include financial products, legal services, marketing research services, and janitorial services. Purchasers must decide whether to provide their own services internally or to hire them from outside the organization. This decision depends greatly on the costs associated with each alternative and on how frequently the services are needed. Most users of the industrial service provided by Ariane, shown in Figure 5.3, would not want to provide their own service.

Product mix and product line

Marketers must understand the relationships among all of an organization's products if they are to coordinate the marketing of the total group of products. The following concepts help to describe the relationships among an organization's products. A *product item* is a specific version of a product that can be designated as a distinct offering among an organization's products. A *product line* includes a group of closely related products that are considered a unit because of marketing, technical, or end-use considerations.

Consider the Gerber line of baby foods. A single item in the product line would be Gerber's strained bananas. Gerber's nonfood product line includes baby clothes, nursery equipment, vaporizers, and hygiene aids.

5. Reichhold Chemicals, Inc., *Annual Report, 1980*, p. 11.
6. Parker-Hannifin Corporation, *Annual Report, 1980*, p. 8.

Figure 5.3
Example of an organi-
zation that provides a
unique industrial
service
*Source: Courtesy
Arianespace.*

This nonfood product line is an interrelated unit because it is usually sold in a single area or department in a retail store. Also, television advertisements and other promotional activities treat the nonfood product line as a distinct group because all the products are used in caring for babies but have different characteristics than the products in the baby food line. A ***product mix*** is the composite of products that an organization makes available to consumers. Gerber sells hundreds of items in its total product mix. These products include adult foods and other items that are not made for babies.

The product mix

No matter how large an organization is, there is a limit to the number and variety of products that it can offer to buyers. Usually the ***depth*** of a product mix is measured by the number of different products offered in each product line. On the other hand, the ***width*** of the product mix measures the number of product lines in the company. Figure 5.4 illustrates these concepts by showing the width of the product mix (number of product lines) and the depth of the product line (number of items in each product line) for selected Procter & Gamble products.

Detergents	Toothpaste	Bar soap	Deodorants	Disposable diapers	Coffee
Ivory Snow 1930	Gleem 1952	Ivory 1879	Secret 1956	Pampers 1961	Folger's 1963
Dreft 1933	Crest 1955	Camay 1927	Sure 1972	Luvs 1976	Instant Folger's 1963
Tide 1946		Lava 1928			High Point Instant 1975
Joy 1949		Kirk's 1930			Folger's Flaked Coffee 1977
Cheer 1950		Zest 1952			
Oxydol 1952		Safeguard 1963			
Dash 1954		Coast 1974			
Cascade 1955					
Duz 1956					
Ivory Liquid 1957					
Gain 1966					
Dawn 1972					
Era 1972					
Bold 3 1976					
Solo 1979					

Product line depth (vertical axis)

Product mix width (horizontal axis)

Figure 5.4   The concepts of product mix width and product line depth applied to selected Procter & Gamble products

Some companies—such as Perrier—have a very narrow and shallow product mix; that is, its width and depth are very limited. On the other hand, if a company like Baskin Robbins sells only ice cream but offers thirty-one flavors, it has a narrow product mix but, in terms of the options available, considerable depth.

The product line

A product line—that is, a related group of products in a product mix—is developed on the basis of marketing or technical considerations. Marketers must understand buyers' organizational resources and goals if they hope to come up with the optimum product line. Specific items in a product line usually reflect the desires of different target markets or the different needs of consumers. Look at Figure 5.4 again. Items in Procter & Gamble's toothpaste product line appeal to different target markets. Gleem is aimed at those concerned mainly with appearance and personal appeal; Crest stresses cavity prevention and good dental hygiene.

Procter & Gamble is known for using differential branding, packaging, and consumer advertising to promote individual items in its detergent product line. Tide, Bold, Gain, Bonus, Dash, Cheer, Oxydol, and Duz—all Procter & Gamble detergents—share the same distribution channels and similar manufacturing facilities. Yet each is promoted as distinctive, and this claimed uniqueness adds depth to the product line.

Product life cycles

Products are like living organisms. They are born, they live, and they die. A new product is introduced into the marketplace; it grows; and when it loses appeal, it is terminated. Remember that our definition of a product focuses on both tangible and intangible attributes. Thus, the total product might be not just a good, but also the ideas and services attached to it. Packaging, branding, and labeling techniques alter or help to create prod-

Figure 5.5
The four stages of the
product life cycle

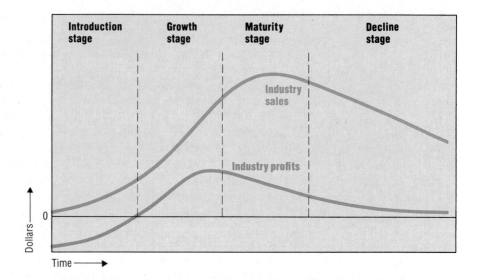

ucts. And just as biological cycles progress through growth and decline, so do the life cycles of products; but product life cycles can be modified by marketers.[7] (The marketing strategies for different life cycle stages are discussed in Chapter 6.)

As shown in Figure 5.5, a ***product life cycle*** has four major stages: (1) introduction, (2) growth, (3) maturity, and (4) decline. As a product moves through its cycle, the strategies relating to competition, promotion, distribution, pricing, and market information must be periodically evaluated and possibly changed. Astute marketing managers use the life cycle concept to make sure that the introduction, alteration, and termination of a product are timed and executed properly. By understanding the typical life cycle pattern, marketers (theoretically) can maintain profitable products and drop unprofitable ones. We will now examine the four stages of a product life cycle.

Introduction

The ***introduction stage*** of the life cycle begins at a product's first appearance in the marketplace, when sales are zero and profits are negative. Profits are below zero because initial revenues are low at the same time that the firm usually must cover large expenses for promotion and distribution. Notice in Figure 5.5 how sales should move upward from zero, while profits should move from below zero. In this stage, it is important to communicate product benefits to buyers. Very few new products represent major inventions. More typically, product introductions involve a new packaged convenience food, a new automobile model, or a new fashion in clothing, to name a few.

During the introduction stage, potential buyers must be made aware of the product's features, uses, and advantages. Two difficulties may arise at this point. There may be only a few sellers with the resources, technological knowledge, and marketing know-how to launch the product successfully; and higher prices may be required initially to recoup expensive mar-

7. Chester R. Wasson, *Dymnamic Competitive Strategy and Product Life Cycles* (St. Charles, Ill.: Challenge Books, 1974), p. 2.

keting research or development costs. Given these difficulties, it is not surprising that many products never get beyond the introduction stage.

For example, recently Procter & Gamble was either introducing or test marketing in one or two cities all of the following: Cinch dishwashing liquid, Rejoice liquid soap, Brigade automatic toilet bowl cleaner, Abound hair conditioner, Certain moistened toilet paper, a butter flavor of Crisco shortening, Pert rinse/conditioner, Solo liquid detergent/fabric softener, Pace dentrifice gel, Roasted High Point decaffeinated coffee, and Crest gel toothpaste, as well as other new products.[8] Not many of these products made it nationally. Crest gel toothpaste did, as did some of the others. The rest of the products, however, never got beyond the introduction stage.

One study indicates that insufficient and poor marketing research is the leading cause of new-product failure. Cited next most often as reasons for failure are technical problems in design or production, and errors in timing the product introduction.[9] To exemplify a technical problem, the Rely tampon, introduced by Procter & Gamble a few years ago, was withdrawn from the market after initial success when the product was associated with toxic shock syndrome.

Growth

During the *growth stage,* sales rise rapidly; profits reach a peak and then start to decline (see Figure 5.5). The growth stage is critical to a product's survival because competitive reactions to the product's success during this period will affect its life expectancy. Profits decline late in the growth stage as more firms enter the market, driving prices down and creating the need for heavy promotional expenses. At this point a typical marketing strategy encourages strong brand loyalty and competes with aggressive emulators of the product. During the growth stage an enterprise tries to strengthen its market share by identifying the product's benefits and by emphasizing these benefits to develop a competitive niche.

Aggressive promotional pricing—including price cuts—is typical during the growth stage. Texas Instruments, for instance, lowered its prices for electronic calculators almost monthly as many competitors entered and attempted to grab a share of the market. By adjusting its prices competitively, Texas instruments was able to maintain its market lead during the growth stage. It thus extended the life expectancy of its product far beyond that of marginal competitors.

Maturity

During the *maturity stage* the sales curve peaks and starts to decline as profits continue to decline (see Figure 5.5). This stage is characterized by severe competition as many brands enter the market. Competitors emphasize improvements and differences in their versions of the product. As a result, during the maturity stage, weaker competitors are squeezed out or lose interest in the product.

For example, as the jogging boom leveled off with about 20 million runners in the United States, a shake-out occurred in the running-shoe industry. However, Nike, the industry leader with 50 percent of the market,

8. "Vibrant Is P & G's Latest," *Advertising Age,* Oct. 5, 1981, p. 2.
9. David Hopkins, "Survey Finds 67% of New Products Succeed," *Marketing News,* Feb. 8, 1980, p. 1.

remained strong as smaller companies went out of business or closed production facilities.[10]

Those who remain in the market make fresh promotional and distribution efforts; advertising and dealer-oriented promotion are typical during this stage of the product life cycle. Nike, for example, added new products such as basketball shoes, racquet-sport shoes, and children's shoes to its product line during this stage of the product life cycle.

Decline

During the *decline stage* sales fall rapidly (see Figure 5.5). New technology or a new social trend may cause the product to take a sharp turn downward in terms of sales. When this happens, the marketer considers pruning items from the product line to eliminate those not returning a profit. At this time, the marketer may cut promotion efforts, eliminate marginal distributors, and, finally, plan to phase out the product.

Using the life cycle concept

The life cycle concept indicates that most products will eventually become unprofitable. For example, Timex sold mainly mechanical watches in the early 1970s. The company was slow to adopt the new digital watches, and competition hurt sales. Mechanical watches had reached the decline stage of the product life cycle. Today, Timex is very successfully selling technologically superior digital and quartz watches to stay competitive. This example demonstrates the need for firms to conduct research continually and to evaluate market opportunities. As opportunities develop, the firm should be prepared to launch new products or extend the life of existing ones.

Since most enterprises have a product mix, a firm's destiny is rarely tied to one product. A composite of life cycle patterns is formed when various products in the mix are at different life cycle stages.[11] As one product is declining, other products are in the introduction, growth, or maturity stages. Since a product's life span is too short from the firm's viewpoint, marketers must deal with the dual problem of prolonging existing products and introducing new products to meet organizational sales goals.[12] For example, General Mills has prolonged the product life cycle of Bisquick prepared biscuit mix by materially improving the product since it was introduced in the mid-1930s. Also, products such as Tuna Helper, Snackin' Cake, and Buc Wheats cereal are more recent General Mills products that satisfy changing consumers' preferences. We will examine approaches to developing new products and managing products in their various life cycle stages in the next chapter.

Branding

Marketers must make many product decisions associated with branding, such as brands, brand names, brand marks, trademarks, and trade names. A *brand* is a name, term, symbol, design, or a combination thereof, that identifies a seller's products and differentiates them from competitors'

10. Victor F. Zonana, "Jogging's Fade Fails to Push Nike Off Track," *Wall Street Journal,* March 5, 1981, p. 27.
11. David J. Luck, *Product Policy and Strategy* (Englewood Cliffs, N.J.: Prentice-Hall, 1972), p. 14.
12. Ibid.

products.[13] A **brand name** is that part of a brand which can be spoken—including letters, words, and numbers—such as 7UP. A brand name is often a product's only distinguishing characteristic. Without the brand name, a firm could not identify its products. To consumers, brand names are as fundamental as the product itself. (Consider the examples in the Application on p. 158.) Brand names simplify shopping, guarantee quality, and allow self-expression.[14] The element of a brand that cannot be spoken, often a symbol or design, is called a **brand mark**. An example is the inscribed anchor on Anchor Hocking glassware. A **trademark** is a legal designation indicating that the owner has exclusive use of a brand or a part of a brand and that others are prohibited by law from using it. In the United States, an organization must, to protect a brand name or brand mark, register it with the U.S. Patent Office. Finally, a **trade name** is the legal name of an organization, such as Ford Motor Company or Safeway, rather than the name of a specific product.

Benefits of branding

Branding can provide benefits to both buyers and sellers. Brands aid buyers by identifying specific products that they like and do not like, which in turn facilitates the purchase of items that satisfy individual needs. Without brands, product selection would be rather random, since buyers could not be assured that what they purchased was the preferred item. A brand also assists buyers in evaluating the quality of products, especially when a person lacks the ability to judge a product's characteristics. A brand symbolizes a certain quality level to a purchaser, and the person in turn allows that perception of quality to represent the quality of the item.

As an example, a car buyer associates certain quality levels with the automobile brands Plymouth, Ford, and Chevrolet. Although the buyer goes through a "ritual" of door slamming, kicking tires, and starting the engine to judge a car's quality, the brand name is among the main indicators of quality to that person; the ritual provides little information to most car buyers.

Another benefit a brand can provide is the psychological reward that comes from owning a brand that symbolizes status. Certain brands of watches, automobiles, and shoes, for example, fall into this category.

Sellers benefit from branding because each firm's brands identify its products, which facilitates repeat purchasing by consumers. To the extent that buyers become loyal to a specific brand, the firm's market share for that product achieves a certain level of stability. A stable market share allows a firm to use its resources more efficiently. When a firm develops some degree of customer loyalty for a brand, it can charge a premium price for the product. The producer of Bayer aspirin enjoys this position. Branding also aids an organization in introducing a new product that carries the name of one or more of its existing products, for buyers are already familiar with the firm's existing brands. Finally, branding facilitates promotional efforts because the promotion of each branded product indirectly promotes all other products that are branded similarly.

13. Adapted from Committee on Definitions, *Marketing Definitions: A Glossary of Marketing Terms* (Chicago: American Marketing Association, 1960), p. 8. Used by permission.
14. James U. McNeal and Linda Zeren, "Brand Name Selection for Consumer Products," *MSU Business Topics,* Spring 1981, p. 35.

Application

Pac-Man and Donkey Kong are entering the cereal market in an attempt to steal the hearts of children from Cap'n Crunch and other magical friends on cereal boxes. New brands of presweetened cereals on the market are identified with video games and popular characters in children's entertainment. Among the most popular new cereals are Pac-Man, Donkey Kong, Smurfs, and Strawberry Short-cake. This branding method is a new step for cereal manufacturers, who for the last fifteen to twenty years have generally tried to achieve unique brand identity for their products. The initial demand for the new cereals has been tremendous.

Since they carry familiar names, these new cereals do not require extensive marketing to create brand identity. The strategy also carries a risk, though, in that the cereals are based on another product's success and may not continue to do well if the characters and games adopted turn out to be short-lived fads. Also, some consumers worry that cereal producers are not concerned enough about nutritional value and that they are trying to exploit children.

Still, consumer response to the new brands has been so positive that manufacturers have not been able to produce enough cereal to keep pace with demand. Assuming that there is not an uprising among consumer activists and that specific game and character names remain popular, this approach to branding children's cereal may continue to be successful.

Source: Based on "Move Over Cap'n Crunch: Pac-Man and His Pals Are Taking Over," *Business Week,* July 18, 1983, p. 174.

Types of brands

There are two categories of brands: manufacturer brands and private distributor brands. *Manufacturer brands* are initiated by producers and make it possible for producers to be identified with their products at the point of purchase. Green Giant, Sylvania, and Exxon are examples. A manufacturer brand usually requires a producer to get involved with distribution, promotion, and, to some extent, pricing decisions. Brand loyalty is created by promotion, quality control, and guarantees; it is a valuable asset to a manufacturer. The producer tries to stimulate demand for the product, which tends to encourage middlemen to make the product available.

Private distributor brands, or *private brands,* are initiated and owned by resellers (marketing organizations that buy products for the purpose of reselling them). The major characteristic of private brands is that manufacturers are not identified on the products. Retailers and wholesalers use private distributor brands to develop more efficient promotion, to generate higher gross margins, and to improve store images. Private distributor brands give retailers or wholesalers freedom to purchase products of a specified quality at the lowest cost without disclosing the identity of the manufacturer.

Wholesaler brands include IGA (Independent Grocers' Alliance) and Topmost (General Grocer). Familiar retailer brand names include Kenmore (Sears, Roebuck), Ann Page (A&P), and Penncraft (J. C. Penney). Many successful private brands are distributed nationally. Sears' Die-Hard battery is at least as well known as most manufacturer brands. The private-brand tires sold by such stores as K mart and J. C. Penney are manufactured by major tire companies—Firestone, Goodrich, Goodyear, Uni-Royal, and others. Sometimes retailers with successful distributor brands start manufacturing their own products in the hope of increasing profits and gaining even more control over their products.

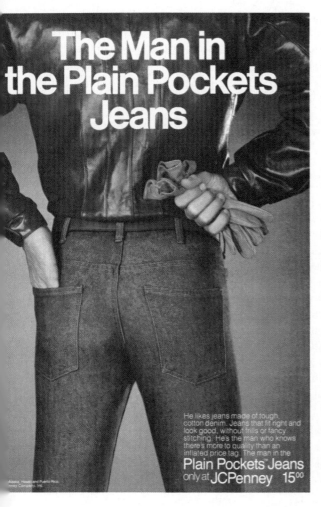

Figure 5.6   A private distributor brand and a manufacturer brand
Source: Ad (left) prepared by McCuffrey & McCull advertising for the J.C. Penney Company; ad (right) ©Levi Strauss & Co., 1982. All rights reserved.

Competition between manufacturer brands and private distributor brands (sometimes called "the battle of the brands") is becoming more intense in several major product categories. For example, Sears' and J. C. Penney's private brands of jeans have half as much market share as does Levi Strauss, the market leader.[15] Figure 5.6 depicts the manufacturer brand (Levi's) and one of the challengers, J. C. Penney's Plain Pockets Jeans, which is a private distributor brand.

Developing multiple manufacturer brands and distribution systems has been an effective means of combating the increased competition from private brands. By developing a new brand name, manufacturers can adjust various elements of the marketing mix to appeal to a different target market. At the same time, they can tailor their product to a target market that tends to purchase private brands.

15. "It's Back to Basics for Levi's," *Business Week,* March 8, 1982, p. 77.

It is difficult for manufacturers to ignore the market opportunities to be gained by producing private distributor brands. Usually, if a manufacturer refuses to produce a private brand, a competing manufacturer will get the business. Also, the production of private distributor brands allows the manufacturer to use excess capacity during periods when its own brands are at nonpeak production. The final decision about whether to produce a private or a manufacturer brand depends on an enterprise's resources, production capabilities, and goals.

Selecting and protecting a brand

The choice of a brand is a critical decision because the name affects customers' images and attitudes toward a product (and sometimes a firm); thus, it ultimately affects purchase decisions. Nissan Motors Corporation, U.S.A., is dropping its well-known Datsun brand name and replacing it with the Nissan corporate name. Datsun has an 85-percent recognition rate compared with 10–15 percent for Nissan, but a company representative stated, "It's essential to unify the name of the company and the brand name in order to pursue our global strategy and to fulfill the kind of social responsibility requested by society and governments."[16] At the time, Nissan was selling products under different corporate identities in 130 countries. This situation apparently complicated expanding overseas operations.

Marketers should consider a variety of issues when they select a brand name. The name should be easy for customers to say, spell, and recall (including foreign buyers, if the firm intends to market its products in other countries). Short, one-syllable names like Cheer often satisfy this requirement. If possible, the brand name should allude to the product's uses and special characteristics in a positive way, and negative or offensive references should be avoided. For example, a deodorant spray to protect against underarm body odor should not be called "B.O." Instead, it should be branded with a name that connotes freshness, dryness, or perhaps long-lasting protection. The name should be descriptive of the product's major benefits. In a recent survey of large, consumer goods producers, almost 60 percent of the respondents reported that this issue is a major criterion in brand name selection.[17]

If a marketer intends to use a brand on several products in a product line, the brand must be designed so that it is compatible with all products in the line. The manufacturer of Hotpoint products (a brand originally used on kitchen ranges) may have had some misgivings about the name when it introduced Hotpoint room air conditioners. Finally, a brand should be designed so that it can be used and recognized in all types of media.

To protect the firm's exclusive rights to a brand, the company should be certain that the selected brand is not likely to be considered an infringement on any existing brand already registered with the U.S. Patent Office. This task may be complex, because infringement is determined by the courts. They base their decisions on whether a brand causes consumers to be confused, mistaken, or deceived about the source of the product.[18] In

16. "A Worldwide Brand for Nissan," *Business Week,* Aug. 24, 1981, p. 104.
17. James U. McNeal and Linda M. Zeren, "Brand Name Selection for Consumer Products," *MSU Business Topics,* Spring 1981, p. 37.
18. George Miaoulis and Nancy D'Amato, "Consumer Confusion and Trademark Infringement," *Journal of Marketing,* April 1978, pp. 48–49.

recent years, the producers of such brands as Ultra Brite, Tylenol, Scrabble, Tic Tac, and Playboy have initiated infringement charges against competing brands. Coca-Cola, with a trademark research department of twenty-five people, files forty to sixty suits annually to protect its brands.[19]

The marketer should also design a brand that can be protected easily through registration. Because of their designs, some brands can be legally infringed upon more easily than others. Although registration protects trademarks domestically for twenty years and can be renewed indefinitely, a firm should develop a system that ensures that its trademarks will be renewed as needed. One hazard that a marketer must guard against is allowing a brand name to become a generic term used to refer to a general product category. Generic terms cannot be protected as exclusive brand names. For example, names such as *cellophane, linoleum,* and *shredded wheat*— all brand names at one time—eventually were declared to be generic words that refer to general product classes; thus, they no longer could be protected. To keep a brand name from becoming a generic term, the firm should spell it with a capital letter and should use it as an adjective to modify the name of the general product class, as in "Lysol Disinfectant."[20] Including the word *brand* just after the brand name is also helpful. Note that in the advertisement in Figure 5.7, the makers of Kitty Litter always use the term *brand* after the brand name. An organization can deal with this problem directly by advertising that its brand is a trademark and should not be used generically. The firm can also indicate that the brand is trademarked by placing the symbol ® near it, as Kitty Litter has done in Figure 5.7.

A U.S. firm that tries to protect a brand in a foreign country frequently encounters problems. In many foreign countries, brand registration is not possible; the first firm to use a brand in such a country has the rights to that brand. In some instances, a U.S. company has actually had to buy its own brand rights from a firm in a foreign country, because the foreign firm was the first user in that country. In Italy (one of the world's biggest producers of counterfeit brands) one can purchase fake Cartier watches, Marlboro cigarettes, and Levi's jeans (the fake Levi's do not fade); none of the products are made by the U.S. firms that own these brands.

Branding policies   In attempting to establish branding policies, the first decision to be made is whether the firm should brand its products at all. When an organization's product is homogeneous and is similar to competitors' products, it may be difficult to brand. Raw materials—such as coal, sand, and farm produce— are hard to brand because of the homogeneity of such products and also because of their physical characteristics.

Some marketers of products that have traditionally been branded have embarked on a policy of not branding, often called generic branding. A *generic brand* indicates only the product category (such as aluminum foil) and does not include the company name or other identifying terms. Many supermarkets are selling generic brands at lower prices than they sell

19. Frank Delano, "Keeping Your Trade Name or Trademark Out of Court," *Harvard Business Review,* March–April 1982, p. 73.
20. "Trademark Stylesheet," U.S. Trademark Association, No. 1A.

branded items in the same product categories. The sales of generic-branded grocery items are rising rapidly. It is estimated that in 1985 generic brands will represent 10 percent of all grocery sales—at the expense of manufacturer brands.[21]

Assuming that a firm chooses to brand its products, marketers may opt for one or more of the following branding policies: individual branding, overall family branding, line family branding, and brand-extension branding.

Individual branding is a policy in which each product is named something different. A major advantage of individual branding is that, when an organization introduces a poor product, the negative images associated with it do not contaminate the company's other products. An individual branding policy facilitates market segmentation when a firm wishes to enter many segments of the same market. Separate, unrelated names can be used, and a specific brand can be aimed at a specific segment. As mentioned earlier, Procter & Gamble relies on an individual branding policy for its line of detergents, which includes Tide, Bold, Gain, Bonus, Dash, Cheer, Oxydol, and Duz.

21. "Metamorphosis: Now They're with Names, Colorful Labels," *Marketing News,* April 30, 1982, p. 1.

In *overall family branding,* all of a firm's products are branded with the same name or at least part of the name. Examples include Sealtest and General Electric. In some cases a company's name is combined with other words to brand items. Sara Lee, for example, has Sara Lee Pound Cake, Sara Lee Banana Cake, Sara Lee Orange Cake, and others. Unlike individual branding, overall family branding means that the promotion of one item with the family brand promotes the firm's other products.

Sometimes an organization uses family branding only for products within a line rather than for all its products. This policy is called *line family branding.* The same brand is used within a line, but the firm does not use the same name for a product in a different line. Colgate Palmolive, for example, produces a line of cleaning products including a cleanser, a powdered detergent, and a liquid cleaner, all of which carry the Ajax name. Colgate also produces several brands of toothpaste, none of which carry the Ajax brand.

Brand-extension branding occurs when a firm uses one of its existing brand names as part of a brand for an improved or new product that is usually in the same product category as the existing brand. The makers of Arrid deodorant eventually extended the Arrid name to Arrid Extra-Dry and Arrid Double-X. There is one major difference between line family branding and brand-extension branding. With the former, all products in the line carry the same name. This is not the case with brand-extension branding; the producer of Arrid deodorant also makes other brands of deodorants.

Marketers are not limited to a single branding policy for the entire organization. Instead, branding policy is influenced by the number of products and product lines produced by the firm, the characteristics of its target markets, the number and types of competing products available, and the size of the firm's resources. Anheuser-Busch, for example, employs both individual and brand-extension branding. Notice in Figure 5.8 that most of the brands are individual brands. However, the Michelob Light brand is an extension of the Michelob brand.

Packaging

Packaging involves the development of a container and a graphic design for a product. A package can be a vital part of a product. It can make the product more versatile, safer, or easier to use. Like a brand name, a package influences customers' attitudes toward a product, which in turn affects their purchase decisions.

James B. Beam Distilling Company has made packaging an important part of its product. When the company had an excess supply of Jim Beam bourbon, it began to offer it in decanters made from fine china and glass. Lavish bottles incorporated designs related to politics, sports, and animals. Every four years Beam produces a variant on the political donkey/elephant theme. The collectible packaging has resulted in increased sales and at least 120 Jim Beam bottle clubs in the United States and several foreign countries.

In one packaging study, respondents perceived potato chips packaged in a polyvinyl bag to be significantly crisper and tastier than those packaged in a wax-coated paper bag (which was much easier to open), even

Figure 5.8
Illustration of individual
brands and a brand
extension
*Source: Courtesy of the
Anheuser-Busch
Companies.*

DECISIONS, DECISIONS, DECISIONS.

ANHEUSER-BUSCH, INC • ST LOUIS ❧ THE WORLD'S LEADING BREWER.

though the chips in both types of bags were the same with respect to taste and crispness.[22]

As the foregoing examples indicate, buyers' impressions of a product, formed at the point of purchase or during use, are significantly influenced by package characteristics. In this section, we will examine the major functions of packaging and consider several major packaging decisions. We will also analyze the role of the package in a market strategy.

Packaging functions   Effective packaging involves more than simply putting products in containers and covering them with wrappers. Packaging materials serve several primary functions. First, they protect the product or maintain its functional form. Product tampering recently has become a problem for

22. Carl McDaniel and R. C. Baker, "Convenience Food Packaging and the Perception of Product Quality," *Journal of Marketing,* October 1977, pp. 57–58.

Figure 5.9
Tamper-resistant pack-
ages used for pain
relievers
*Source: Photo by James
Scherer.*

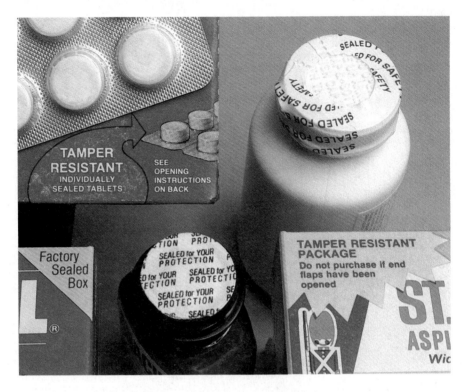

marketers of many types of products, and several packaging techniques are being used to counter such activity (see Figure 5.9). Fluids such as milk, orange juice, and hair spray need packages that preserve and protect them. The protection of the product should be effective in reducing damage that could affect its usefulness and increase costs (economy). Second, consumers often look for convenience. The size or shape of a package may relate to the product's storage, convenience of use, or replacement rate. (See the Application on p. 166 for related issues.) Small, single-serving cans of vegetables may prevent waste and facilitate storage. The third function of packaging is to promote a product by communicating its features, uses, benefits, and image.

***Major packaging
considerations***

Marketers must consider many factors as they develop packages. Obviously, one major consideration is cost. Although a variety of packaging materials, processes, and designs are available, some are rather expensive. In recent years buyers have shown a willingness to pay more for improved packaging, but there are limits. Marketers should try to determine through research just how much customers are willing to pay for packages.

Marketers must also decide whether to package the product singly or in multiple units. Multiple packaging is likely to increase demand because it increases the amount of the product available at the point of consumption (in one's home, for example). However, multiple packaging is not appropriate for infrequently used products, since buyers do not like to tie up their dollars or store these products for a long time. Multiple packaging *can,* however, make products easier to handle and store (just think of six-

Application

New
Package Gives
Ocean Spray a
Competitive
Edge

The paper bottle, an aseptic container in which both product and package are sterilized separately, is one of the newest forms of food packaging in the United States. Retailers across the country are clamoring for Ocean Spray's juices in paper bottles. The paper container was chosen to keep production costs down. Ocean Spray juices are premium-priced, and the company was concerned about pricing its products out of the market with high packaging costs. To gain a competitive advantage, Ocean Spray used a 250-milliliter size, rather than the traditional 200-milliliter size offered by competitors such as Coca-Cola and Borden.

When Ocean Spray came out with paper bottles for juice products, marketers tracked the results with scanners. The scanning service is based on electronic cash registers that read the universal product code on an item, flash the price on a display screen, print it on the customer's receipt, and make a purchase record for the retailer to assist in inventory control. Ocean Spray conducted home-placement tests in Los Angeles, Boston, and Minneapolis; these areas were selected for their geographical and attitudinal diversity.

To make buyers aware of the unique package, television commercials were used to teach consumers about the paper bottle. These commercials compared it to conventional bottles or cans, and pointed out that the juice tasted as good, but was cheaper. The scanner data indicated that these television commercials helped Ocean Spray achieve consumer acceptance of the paper bottle. Sales tripled after television created consumer awareness of the paper bottle. Scanning results showed that cranapple juice was the number-one single-serving item in the fruit juice/drink category and that Ocean Spray grapefruit juice was the number one product in the single-serving category as a whole. Scanners also indicated that sales were better when the product was shelf-positioned in the single-serving category than when it was positioned with Ocean Spray products.

By using a new package, Ocean Spray has remained competitive. One must remember, though, that there are risks associated with introducing totally different forms of packaging. Typically, there are major costs. More important, however, is that buyers may not accept a new form of packaging. Ocean Spray was willing to bear some risks to reap the benefits offered by a new package.

Source: Based on Rayna Skolnik, "Scanners Juice Up Ocean Spray's Test," *Sales and Marketing Management,* March 15, 1982, pp. 80–81.

packs used for soft drinks); and special price offers, such as a two-for-one sale, are facilitated through multiple packaging. In addition, multiple packaging may increase consumer acceptance of a product by encouraging the buyer to try it several times. On the other hand, since they must buy several units when multiple packaging is used, customers may hesitate to try the product in the first place.

When developing packages within an organization, marketers should consider how much continuity among package designs is desirable. No continuity may be the best policy, especially if a firm's products are unrelated or are aimed at vastly different target markets. To promote an overall company image, a firm may decide that all packages are to be similar or are to include one major element of the design. This approach is called *family packaging*. Sometimes, this approach is used only for lines of products, as can be seen with Campbell's soups, Weight Watchers foods, and Planter's nuts.

The promotional role of a package should be considered. It can be used to attract customers' attention and encourage them to examine the product. Through verbal and nonverbal symbols the package can inform potential buyers about the product's content, features, uses, advantages, and hazards. A firm can create desirable images and associations by its choice of color, design, shape, and texture. Many cosmetics manufacturers, for example, design their packages to create impressions of richness, luxury, and exclusiveness. A package may perform a promotional function when it is designed to be safer or more convenient to use, if such characteristics help stimulate demand.

To develop a package that has a definite promotional value, a designer must consider size, shape, texture, color, and graphics. Beyond the obvious limitation that the package must be large enough to hold the product, a package can be designed to appear taller or shorter. Vertical thin lines, for example, make a package appear taller, while horizontal wide stripes make it look shorter. In some cases a marketer may want a package to appear taller because many people perceive something that is taller as being larger.

The shape of the package can help to communicate a particular message. Research and successful promotions have led marketers to stereotype the sexes; they offer men packages with angular shapes and wood or burlap textures; women's packages, on the other hand, have rounded, curved shapes and soft, fuzzy textures.

Colors on packages are often chosen to attract attention. People associate certain feelings and connotations with specific colors. Red, for example, is linked with fire, blood, danger, and anger; yellow suggests sunlight, caution, warmth, and vitality; blue can imply coldness, sky, water, and sadness.[23]

When selecting packaging colors, marketers must first decide whether a particular color will evoke positive or negative feelings when it is used with a specific type of product. Rarely, for example, do processors package meat or bread in green materials, because customers may associate green with mold. A sunburn ointment is more likely to appear in a soothing blue package than in a fiery red one. Marketers must also decide whether a specific target market will respond favorably or unfavorably to a particular color. Cosmetics for women are much more likely to be sold in pastel packaging than are personal care products for men. Packages designed to appeal to young children often use primary colors and bold designs.

Packaging and marketing strategy

Packaging can be a major component of a marketing strategy. A unique cap or closure, a better box or wrapper, or a more convenient container size may give a firm a competitive advantage. Usually, however, there is a direct relationship between a product's package and its cost. The marketer must manage this trade-off to provide the desired benefits.

As package designs improve, it will be harder for any one product to dominate on the basis of packaging. For example, Stouffer's frozen foods were packaged in orange boxes so that they would visually dominate the frozen food section where they compete.[24] The typical large store stocks

23. James U. McNeal, *Consumer Behavior: An Integrative Approach* (Boston: Little, Brown, 1982), pp. 221–222.
24. Bill Abrams and David P. Garino, "Package Design Gains Stature as Visual Competition Grows," *Wall Street Journal*, Aug. 6, 1981, p. 25.

15,000 items. The product that "stands out" is more likely to be purchased. Today skilled artists and package designers, who have experience in marketing research, test packaging to see what sells well, not just what is esthetically appealing.[25]

Resellers (wholesalers and retailers) consider whether a package facilitates transporting, storing, and handling of the product. In some cases, resellers refuse to carry certain products because their packages are too troublesome. Leslie Salt Company, for example, changed from multi-walled paper bag containers to rectangular boxes for its salt products because of pressure from resellers. The firm's resellers complained that their mechanized handling systems could not cope with the multiwalled paper bags.[26]

Packaging of consumer products is extremely important at the point of sale. When Kendall Oil found more of its motor oil sales coming from supermarkets and hardware stores than from service stations, the company redesigned its packages to appeal to do-it-yourselfers.[27] Manufacturers of beer, detergents, and most packaged foods spend a great deal of money to research consumers' reactions to packages.

Labeling

Labeling, too, is an important dimension related to packaging, not only for promotional and informational reasons, but also from a legal perspective. The Food and Drug Administration and the Consumer Product Safety Commission can require products to be labeled or marked with warnings, instructions, certifications, and manufacturer's identifications. Federal laws require disclosure of such data as textile identifications, potential hazards, and nutritional information. Del Monte Corporation introduced nutritional labeling before it was required by federal law. In this case, the eventual legal requirement worked to the advantage of the marketer. Consumers responded favorably to the nutritional information, and Del Monte gained a competitive edge over manufacturers who did not disclose nutritional values. Labels also can be used to promote other products of the manufacturer or to encourage proper use of products and therefore greater satisfaction with them.

Color and eye-catching graphics on labels overcome the jumble of words—known to designers as "mouse print"—that have been added to satisfy government regulations. More direct cues—often a striking photograph of the product itself—about what a product is or does are now found on the front panel.[28]

Since so many similar products are available, an attention-getting device, or "silent salesperson," is needed to attract interest. As one of the most visible parts of a product, the label is an important element in the marketing mix.

25. Ibid.
26. "Retailers Cause Shift from Bag to Box," *Modern Packaging,* February 1977, p. 25.
27. Ibid.
28. "Packaging Design Seen as Cost-Effective Marketing Strategy," *Marketing News,* Feb. 20, 1981, p. 1.

Other product-related characteristics

When developing products, marketers make many decisions. Some of these involve the physical characteristics of the product, while others focus on less tangible supportive services that are very much a part of the total product.

Physical characteristics of the product

A major question that arises during product development is how much quality to build into the product. A major dimension of a product's quality is its durability. Frequently, higher quality calls for better materials and more expensive processing, which increase production costs and, ultimately, the product's price. In determining the specific level of quality, a marketer must know or ascertain approximately what price the target market views as acceptable. In addition, a marketer usually tries to set a level for a specific product that is consistent with the firm's other products that carry a similar brand.

A product's physical features require careful consideration by marketers. The prime basis for decisions about them should be the desires of target market members. If marketers do not know what physical features people in the target market want in a product, then it will be an accident if the product is satisfactory. Even a firm whose existing products have been designed to satisfy target market desires should assess these desires periodically to determine whether they have changed enough to require alterations in such features as textures, colors, or sizes. Product modification will be discussed in more detail in Chapter 6.

Supportive product-related services

All products, whether they are goods or not, possess a certain amount of intangibility. The service component of a product—warranty and repairs, for example—is hard to test in advance. When you buy a new personal computer, you are buying a promise of repair, software, and possibly programming assistance. "When prospective customers can't experience the product in advance, they are asked to buy what are essentially promises—promises of satisfaction. Even tangible, testable, feelable, smellable products are, before they're bought, largely just promises."[29] Here, we will provide a brief discussion of three product-related services: warranties, repairs and replacements, and credit. There are, of course, many other product-related services and product intangibles.

The type of warranty that a firm provides can be a critical issue for buyers, especially when expensive, technically complex products such as appliances are involved (see Figure 5.10). A *warranty* specifies what the producer will do if the product malfunctions. In recent years, government actions have required a warrantor to state more simply and specifically the terms and conditions under which the firm will take action. (Specific legislation is discussed in Chapter 16.) Because warranties must be more precise today, marketers are using them more vigorously as tools to give their brands a competitive advantage.

A marketer must be concerned with establishing a system to provide replacement parts and repair services. This support service is especially important for expensive, complex products that buyers expect to last a

29. Levitt, "Marketing Intangible Products and Product Intangibles," p. 96.

long time. Although the producer may provide these services directly to buyers, it is more common for the producer to provide such services through regional service centers or through middlemen. Regardless of how services are provided, it is important to customers that they be performed quickly and correctly.

Finally, a firm must sometimes provide credit services to customers. Even though doing so places financial burdens on an organization, it can yield several benefits. Providing credit services can help a firm obtain and maintain a stable market share. Many major oil companies, for example, have competed effectively against gasoline discounters by providing credit services. For marketers of relatively expensive items, offering credit services allows a larger number of people to buy the product, thus enlarging the market for the item. Another reason for offering credit services is to earn interest income from customers who do not pay during the ''interest-free'' period. The types of credit services offered depend on the characteristics of target market members, the firm's financial status, the type of products sold, and the types of credit services offered by competitors.

Summary

A product is much more than a physical object or a service rendered. It includes everything that a customer receives in an exchange; it is a complex set of tangible and intangible attributes including functional, social, and psychological utilities or benefits. Functional utilities include ideas, services, and performance, as well as a product's physical properties and attributes. When buyers purchase a product, they actually are buying the benefits and satisfaction they think the product will provide.

Products fall into one of two general categories: consumer products and industrial products. Consumer products satisfy personal and family needs. Industrial products are purchased for use in a firm's operations or to make other products. Consumer products can be subdivided into convenience, shopping, and specialty products. Industrial products can be subdivided into raw materials, major equipment, accessory equipment, component parts, process materials, supplies, and industrial services.

The product mix is the composite or total group of products that an organization makes available. The product line refers to a related group of products within the product mix. The product item within the product line is a unique offering. Product lines are based on marketing, technical, or end-use considerations.

The product life cycle is a concept that explains how product items in an industry move through (1) introduction, (2) growth, (3) maturity, and (4) decline. The life cycle concept is used to evaluate product strategy and adjust the marketing strategy to particular situations. The sales curve is at zero at introduction, rises at an increasing rate during growth, peaks at maturity, and then declines. The life expectancy of a product is based on buyers' wants, the availability of competing products, and other environmental conditions. Products move through various stages of their life cycles according to saturation of market potential. Placing a product at a particular stage in its life cycle is a matter of judgment. Some enterprises have a composite of life cycle patterns for various products. A major marketing task is to manage existing products and to develop new products to keep the overall sales performance at a desired level.

A brand is a name, term, symbol, design, or a combination thereof, that identifies a seller's products and differentiates them from competitors' products. Branding can benefit both marketers and customers. A manufacturer brand is initiated by a producer and makes it possible for producers to be identified with their products at the point of purchase. A private distributor brand is initiated and owned by a reseller. When selecting a brand, a marketer should choose one that is easy to say, spell, and recall, and also one that alludes to the product's uses, benefits, or special characteristics. Branding policies include individual branding, overall family branding, line family branding, and brand-extension branding.

Packaging serves the functions of protection, economy, convenience, and promotion. When developing a package, marketers must consider packaging costs relative to the needs of target market members. Other considerations include both whether or not to employ multiple packaging and family packaging and how to design the package so that it is an effective promotional tool. Labeling is used on packages to provide instructions, contents, certifications, and manufacturer identifications. Labels can perform both informational and promotional functions.

When creating products, marketers must take into account other product-related considerations, such as physical characteristics and less tangible supportive services. Specific physical product characteristics that require attention are the level of quality, product features, textures, colors, and sizes. Supportive services that may be viewed as part of the total product include warranties, repairs and replacements, and credit services.

Important terms

Product
Consumer products
Industrial products
Convenience products
Shopping products
Specialty products
Raw materials
Major equipment
Accessory equipment
Component parts
Process materials
Supplies
MRO items
Industrial services
Product item
Product line
Product mix
Depth (of product mix)
Width (of product mix)
Product life cycle

Introduction stage
Growth stage
Maturity stage
Decline stage
Brand
Brand name
Brand mark
Trademark
Trade name
Manufacturer brands
Private distributor brands
Generic brand
Individual branding
Overall family branding
Line family branding
Brand-extension branding
Family packaging
Labeling
Warranty

Discussion and review questions

1. List the tangible and intangible attributes that a bottle of mouthwash provides. Compare the benefits of mouthwash with those of an intangible product like life insurance.
2. Products have been referred to as a "psychological bundle of satisfaction." Is this a good definition of a product?
3. Is a roll of shag carpeting in a store a consumer product or an industrial product? Defend your answer.
4. How do convenience products and shopping products differ? What are the distinguishing characteristics of each?
5. Would a four-channel receiver that sells for $869 be a convenience, shopping, or specialty product?
6. With respect to industrial products, how do component parts differ from process materials?
7. How does an organization's product mix relate to its development of a product line? When should an enterprise add depth to its product lines rather than width to its product mix?
8. How do industry profits change as a product moves through the four stages of its life cycle?
9. What is the relationship between the concepts of product mix and product life cycle?
10. What is the difference between a brand and a brand name? Compare and contrast the terms *brand mark* and *trademark*.

11. How does branding benefit an organization?
12. What are the distinguishing characteristics of private distributor brands? At what point should a manufacturer make private brands?
13. Given the competition between private distributor brands and manufacturer brands, should manufacturers be overly concerned about the increasing popularity of private distributor brands? How should manufacturers fight back in the brand battle?
14. The brand name Xerox is sometimes used generically. How can Xerox Corporation protect this brand name?
15. Identify and explain four major branding policies and give examples of each. Can a firm use more than one policy at a time? Explain.
16. Describe the functions that a package can perform. Which function is most important? Why?
17. Why is the determination of a product's quality level an important decision? What major factors affect this decision?

Cases

Case 5.1

Softsoap[30]

Americans consume approximately $1.3 billion worth of soap annually. For nearly a century they have traditionally bought their soap in bar, or cake, form. In 1980 Minnetonka, a small Minnesota firm, began offering hand soap in liquid form. The liquid soap was packaged in an attractive plastic container with a pump dispenser and was named Softsoap. The product was such an immediate hit with the consuming public that there are now approximately fifty competing products available.

After grabbing a quick 9 percent of the soap market, the liquid soap market share has begun to stabilize at about 8 percent. Retailers have begun to react by reducing the number of brands they carry. Several liquid soap producers have started offering coupons, trade allowances, and price reductions to increase their individual shares of the market and to induce retailers to handle their brands.

Further clouding the picture for Minnetonka is the fact that consumers use the liquid soap only for cleaning hands. Most of the soap that is bought, approximately 75 percent, is used in the tub or shower. As a result, the market potential for Softsoap seems limited at the present—and this will continue as long as it sits on consumers' sinks.

There is also evidence of consumer dissatisfaction. Independent researchers are finding some consumer resentment at the price of Softsoap. Minnetonka has claimed that although Softsoap is expensive to purchase, it is economical on a per-use basis. Unfortunately, *Consumer Reports* magazine, in a study of soaps, has disputed this claim.

To intensify Minnetonka's concerns, marketing stalwarts Procter & Gamble and Armour-Dial have test marketed their own versions of liquid.

30. Contributed by George Glisan, Illinois State University, and Jon Hawes, University of Akron. Sources: ". . . Is Liquid Soap Field Saturated?" *Wall Street Journal*, June 18, 1981, p. 25; "The World Waits as Orlando Tests Shower Mate Soap," *Orlando* (Fla.) *Sentinel Star*, Dec. 20, 1981, p. 1; and "Liquid Soap's Bubble May Be Bursting," *Business Week*, Mar. 1, 1982, pp. 24–25.

soap. Procter & Gamble has introduced a competing product which carries its Ivory brand. The primary concern is that the large firms possess the potential to overwhelm smaller competitors, including Minnetonka, with their marketing skills, larger resources, and strong channels of distribution.

Reacting to these problems, Minnetonka has taken the offensive. They have launched a new product for the tub and shower segment. The new product, called Shower Mate, is essentially the same as Softsoap except for its package. The new package is designed to hang on a shower curtain rod or any similar horizontal rod/bar configuration. The firm is considering several other possibilities for liquid soap, including the following:

1. *Liquid soap for children.* Enter into licensing agreements to create packages that resemble figures popular among children, such as Walt Disney characters or Smurf figures.
2. *Liquid soap for "dirty hands."* Develop a liquid soap for individuals whose hands get extremely soiled with dirt, oil, grease, and so on. This segment may further be subdivided into a consumer market and an industrial market.
3. *Liquid soap for the health conscious.* Develop a liquid soap with properties that dermatologists might recommend for various groups of users. For example, develop a unique formulation for teenagers concerned about skin blemishes. Create another formulation for older consumers who are especially concerned about excessive drying of their skin.
4. *Liquid soap for the beauty conscious.* Develop a liquid soap containing moisturizers and fragrances.

Questions for discussion
1. What stage of the product life cycle does liquid soap appear to be in? What evidence supports this conclusion?
2. Evaluate the four possibilities for a multisegment strategy. Which possibility seems best?
3. What additional products, if any, would you develop if you were responsible for Procter & Gamble or Armour-Dial product management?

Case 5.2

Rebuilding the Tylenol Brand and Package[31]

McNeilab, Inc., a subsidiary of Johnson & Johnson, introduced adult strength Tylenol in 1961. McNeil launched Tylenol's first major consumer advertising campaign in 1976, after its first non-aspirin competitor, Datril, was introduced by Bristol-Myers Co. Between 1976 and 1982 Tylenol's annual sales rose from $50 million to $400 million. By 1982, the Tylenol name was on twelve different pain-relieving products. It was the number one analgesic, dominating 37 percent of the pain reliever market.

31. The facts in this case are from "Johnson & Johnson Reincarnates a Brand," *Sales and Marketing Management,* January 16, 1984, p. 63; Thomas Moore, "The Fight to Save Tylenol," *Fortune,* November 29, 1982, pp. 44–49; "Johnson & Johnson Will Pay Dearly to Cure Tylenol," *Business Week,* November 29, 1982, p. 37; and "The Rise—and Fall?" *Advertising Age,* October 11, 1982, p. 78.

On September 30, 1982, multiple deaths in the Chicago area were found to have been caused by the ingesting of Tylenol extra-strength capsules laced with cyanide. McNeil spent approximately $100 million to buy back Tylenol products from retailers and consumers and to dispose of these recalled products. Tylenol sales dropped by 80 percent.

Some market analysts and marketing experts would have advised McNeil against attempting to keep the Tylenol brand. However, marketers at Johnson & Johnson and those at McNeilab believed that a product that had once been so successful could be revived.

The first major step taken was to make the package tamper-resistant. As a result of the Tylenol incident, the federal government required that over-the-counter medicines be sold in tamper-resistant packages. The new Tylenol package included glued end flaps, a plastic neck seal, and an inner foil seal; although any one of these precautions would have complied with the government regulation. In addition, every package carried a warning label that read, "Do not use if safety seals are broken." A massive production and distribution effort was launched to make the newly packaged products available nationally in a short time period.

To help in rebuilding consumer confidence in the product, the makers of Tylenol created and implemented an intensive promotional program. Shortly after the package was redesigned, McNeil held an unprecedented national press conference through closed-circuit television to communicate with news personnel about the new package. This press conference reached over a thousand media representatives in thirty cities. Newspaper advertisements offered consumers a $2.50 coupon to replace products they may have discarded. (A survey had shown that over 35 percent of Tylenol users had discarded their Tylenol products.) Consumers also could call a toll-free number to receive a coupon. Advertisements with the theme "Continue to trust Tylenol" were used. In addition, McNeil resumed the use of feature-oriented advertisements similar to those employed prior to the crisis.

Johnson & Johnson closely monitored public sentiments regarding important dimensions associated with the Tylenol incident. At about the point that the new promotional program was being launched, a survey revealed several issues. Ninety-four percent of the adults in the United States knew about the Tylenol incident, and 90 percent believed that it was not the fault of the makers of Tylenol. Of those surveyed, 93 percent felt that the problem could have occurred for any brand of over-the-counter capsule, and 90 percent were aware that only capsules were involved.

In less than 60 days after the Tylenol incident, Johnson & Johnson had re-launched the Tylenol brand. Within six months, Tylenol's market share had rebounded to 27 percent, and within a year Tylenol had a 32 percent market share. Although the costs exceeded $100 million, the makers of Tylenol were able to revive a $400-million-a-year brand.

Questions for discussion
1. What type of branding policy is being used for Tylenol products?
2. To what extent did the strong brand loyalty prior to the poisoning incident aid the makers of Tylenol in helping to revive the brand?
3. How can consumer product companies protect themselves against future incidents of this type?

6

Developing and Managing Products

Objectives

To develop an awareness of organizational alternatives for managing products.

To understand the importance and role of product development in the marketing mix.

To become aware of how existing products can be modified.

To learn that product deletion can be employed to improve product mixes.

To gain insight into how businesses develop a product idea into a commercial product.

To acquire knowledge about product positioning and the management of products during the various stages of their life cycles.

Frito-Lay, which was started only about twenty years ago, is the leader in the salty snack industry with sales of approximately $2 billion. Some of its brands are Ruffles, Cheetos, Lay's Potato Chips, and Doritos. Frito-Lay faces fierce competition from regional snack food producers and from national snack producers such as Nabisco, Procter & Gamble, and Borden.

One major dimension of Frito-Lay's competitive strategy is to overwhelm competitors through the development and introduction of new products. Recently, Frito-Lay increased its salty snack production capacity by 30 percent. This added capacity allowed Frito-Lay to launch Tostitos. Frito-Lay also plans to introduce a line of cookies through a recently purchased subsidiary called GrandMa's Foods. In addition, to respond to new consumer preferences for healthful, lower-calorie foods, Frito-Lay has introduced "light" versions of its corn-based products. Notice also that Frito-Lay is promoting the nutritional value of its chips in the advertisement in Figure 6.1.[1]

Frito-Lay is a good example of an organization that is successfully managing its product mix. To compete effectively and achieve its goals, an organization must be able to adjust its product mix to be consistent with changes in buyers' preferences. These adjustments in the product mix may make it necessary to modify existing products, introduce new products, or eliminate products that were successful, perhaps only a few years ago.

A number of years ago, Shell introduced the Shell Pest Strips, a very successful product. Subsequently, Shell launched a related product called Can Care. This product, which fits inside garbage cans, was designed to kill ants, flies, gnats, and roaches and to mask unpleasant orders. Because the Shell Pest Strip was so successful, Shell performed rather limited test marketing for Can Care. Unfortunately, Can Care did not succeed because it did not satisfy customers needs. Perhaps customers in the target market did not have significant insect and order problems with their exterior covered garbage cans, or they did not see killing insects in garbage cans as a desired benefit.

Effective product management is a major requirement for successful marketing strategies. This chapter examines how enterprises are organized to develop and manage products. We look at several ways to improve a product mix, including product modification, product deletion, and new-product development. We also examine product positioning—how marketers decide where the product should fit into the field of competing products and which unique benefits to emphasize. Finally, we consider some of the decisions that must be made to manage a product through its life cycle.

1. Frito-Lay May Find Itself in a Competitive Crunch," *Business Week*, July 19, 1982, p. 186.

Facts about our chips and calories that you and your scholar should know.

She's a good kid. She may not spend as much time on her school work as you'd like, but the pep rallies, school plays, and after-school sports are all part of being a well-rounded student.

But while "well-rounded" looks good on a report card, it doesn't always look terrific in a mirror. So she's constantly watching her weight. That's why we label the calorie content on every bag of our corn chips and potato chips. So she knows exactly what she's getting in every ounce.

Fewer calories than you think.

What she's getting in every ounce may surprise you. With one ounce of Lay's® or Ruffles® Brand Potato Chips, for example, (about 15-20 good-sized chips), she gets only 150 Calories.

A look at other teen favorites will put those 150 Calories in perspective. You'll find they're 100 Calories less than 1 cup of ice cream. 70 Calories more than an apple. And about the same as 3 chocolate chip cookies.

A lot of people expect potato chips to be much higher than any of those.

So even if she eats more than one ounce, and sometimes kids do, the calories don't add up quite as fast as you thought.

You're concerned about nutrients.

While your daughter counts calories, she may not be so concerned about a balanced diet. As a mother, you are. And while we're not going to tell you that our chips are the answer to total nutrition, we will tell you that they can be part of it.

Our potato chips, like the potatoes they come from, are a good source of Vitamins C and B₆. A one ounce serving contains at least 13 widely recognized nutrients. One ounce of our corn chips contains at least 11.

What about salt?

One ounce of our potato chips contains less sodium than a lot of foods you'd never think of. Like a ½ cup of cottage cheese. Or a 6-ounce glass of tomato juice. And our corn chips have even less salt. Chips *taste* salty because the salt is on the outside.

The facts about cholesterol and preservatives.

The regular flavor Frito-Lay chips shown below contain no cholesterol. None. They're fried only in vegetable oils that are high in polyunsaturates and contain no cholesterol.

The chips flavored with cheese or sour cream seasonings contain the small amount of cholesterol that comes from real cheese and sour cream.

And there are no preservatives in any of these chips, regular or flavored.

We put this information on the backs of the bags. No one said we had to. But when it comes to giving you the facts, we've done our homework.

GOOD THINGS TO KNOW ABOUT GOOD THINGS TO EAT

For more information about nutrition and our chips, write for our brochure. Frito-Lay, P.O. Box 35034, Dept. 1M, Dallas, Texas 75235.   ©Frito-Lay, Inc., 1982

Figure 6.1   Frito-Lay advertisement promoting nutritional dimensions of their chips
Source: Frito-Lay, Inc.

Organizing to manage products

A firm must often manage a complex set of products and/or markets. It frequently finds that the functional form of organization traditionally used by businesses does not fit its needs. A manager—or a group of managers—must find an organizational approach that accomplishes the tasks necessary to develop and manage the products. No single approach is best. Alternatives to the functional form of organization include the product manager approach, the market manager approach, and a combination approach.

A *product manager* holds a staff position in a multiproduct company in which the number of products makes it difficult to use other organizational forms. Product managers are responsible for a product, a product line, or several distinct products that make up an interrelated group. A *brand manager* is a type of product manager who is responsible for a single brand. General Foods, for example, has one brand manager for Maxim coffee and one for Maxwell House coffee. A product or brand manager operates cross-functionally to coordinate the activities, information, and strategies involved in marketing an assigned product. Product managers plan marketing activities to achieve objectives by coordinating a mix of distribution, promotion (especially sales promotion and advertising), and price. The areas they must consider include packaging, branding, and the coordination of research and development, engineering, and production. Marketing research enables product managers to understand consumers and to find target markets.

A *market manager* is an individual who is responsible for managing the marketing activities that are necessary to serve a particular group or class of customers. This organizational approach is especially useful when a firm uses different types of marketing activities to provide products to several diverse customer groups. For example, a firm might have one market manager for industrial markets and another for consumer markets. In addition, these broad categories might be broken down into more detailed subcategories.

A *venture team* is an organizational innovation designed to create entirely new products that may be aimed at unfamiliar markets.[2] Unlike a product manager or a market manager, a venture team is responsible for all aspects of a product's development: research and development; production and engineering; finance and accounting; and marketing. Venture teams work outside established divisions to create inventive approaches to new products and markets. As a result of this flexibility, new products can be developed to take advantage of opportunities in highly segmented markets. Whereas a product manager usually is limited to planning and coordination, a venture team has authority to execute plans for product development.

The members of a venture team come from different functional areas of an organization. When the commercial potential of a new product has been demonstrated, the members may return to their functional areas, or they may join a new or existing division to manage the product. The new product may be turned over to an existing division, a market manager, or a product manager.[3] A venture department is a separate and formalized department or division formed to find, develop, and commercialize promising new-product or new-business areas.[4]

Managing the product mix

To provide products that satisfy people in a firm's target market(s) and achieve the organization's objectives, a marketer must develop, alter, and maintain an effective product mix. Seldom can the same product mix be effective for long.

Several factors in an organization's product mix may need adjustment. Because customers' product preferences and attitudes change, their desire for a product may dwindle. For example, Wheaties cereal, which was introduced in 1934, has lost half of its market share in the last ten years.[5] Changes in consumer preferences are quite apparent when we think about such products as clothing. People's fashion preferences obviously change quite often, but individuals' preferences and attitudes change with respect to almost all products.

In some cases a firm needs to alter its product mix to adjust to competition. A marketer may have to delete a product from the mix because one or more competitors dominate that product's specific market segment.

2. Richard M. Hill and James D. Hlavacek, "The Venture Team: A New Concept in Marketing Organization," *Journal of Marketing,* July 1972, p. 41.
3. Ibid., p. 49.
4. Dan T. Dunn, Jr., "Venture Groups Redefined," *Akron Business and Economic Review,* Fall 1980, pp. 7–11.
5. Lawrence Ingrassia, "General Mills Hoping Humor Can Get Wheaties into Shape," *Wall Street Journal,* Aug. 29, 1981, p. 21.

Similarly, an organization may have to introduce a new product or modify an existing one to compete more effectively. A marketer may expand the firm's product mix to take advantage of excess marketing and production capacity. Regardless of why a product mix is altered, the product mix must be managed.

The management of the product mix is often referred to as the product portfolio approach to marketing strategy formulation. The **product portfolio approach** attempts to create specific marketing strategies to achieve a balanced mix of products that will produce maximum long-run profits. General Electric uses the portfolio approach to manage its products. In any portfolio analysis, the most time-consuming task is the collection of data on the items in the portfolio and on their performance along selected dimensions. This evaluation requires hard data from company records (for instance, on sales and profitability) and from outside sources (for instance, on market share and industry growth). In addition, of course, management's judgment is a key element of the portfolio approach.[6]

The product portfolio concept provides a useful framework for analyses and judgments in managing the marketing mix.[7] We will examine product portfolio models in Chapter 18 in the discussion of strategic market planning. At this point, we will look into three major ways to improve a product mix: the modification of an existing product, the deletion of a product, and the development of a new product.

Modifying existing products

Product modification refers to changing one or more of a product's characteristics. It is most likely to be employed in the maturity stage of the product life cycle to give a brand a competitive advantage.

This approach to altering a product mix entails less risk than developing a new product. Product modification can effectively improve a firm's product mix under certain conditions. First, the product must be modifiable. Second, existing customers must be able to perceive that a modification has been made, assuming that a modified item is still aimed at them. Third, the modification should make the product more consistent with customers' desires so that it provides greater satisfaction. For example, Kraft has been very successful with its Light n' Lively low-calorie cheese products.

Existing products can be changed in three major ways: quality modifications, functional modifications, and style modifications.

Quality modifications

Quality modifications are changes that relate to a product's dependability and durability and usually are executed by alterations in the materials or production process employed. Reducing a product's quality may allow an organization to lower the price and direct the item at a larger target market. For example, the least expensive Polaroid OneStep camera, a modified version of a more expensive camera, provides low-cost, but not the highest-quality, instant photography. On the other hand, the Polaroid 600

6. Yoram Wind and Vijay Mahajan, "Designing Product and Business Portfolios," *Harvard Business Review,* Jan.–Feb. 1981, p. 163.
7. George S. Day, "Diagnosing the Product Portfolio," *Journal of Marketing,* April 1977, p. 38.

instant camera competes with the Eastman Kodak Instamatic 110. Polaroid claims that its outdoor photos are as good as those taken with Japanese-made 35mm cameras.[8]

Increasing the quality of a product may give a firm an advantage over competing brands. In fact, some experts claim that quality improvement is a major means of successfully competing with foreign marketers.[9] It may also allow (or force) a firm to charge a higher price.

Functional modifications

Changes that affect a product's versatility, effectiveness, convenience, or safety are called *functional modifications;* they usually require redesigning the product. Typical product categories in which we have seen considerable functional modifications include kitchen appliances, office and farm equipment, and vacuum cleaners. Functional modifications can make a product useful to more people, which enlarges the market for it. This type of change can place a product in a favorable competitive position by providing benefits not offered by competing items. Functional modifications can also help an organization to achieve and maintain a progressive image.

Style modifications

Style modifications are directed at changing the sensory appeal of a product by altering its taste, texture, sound, smell, or visual characteristics. Since a buyer's purchase decision is affected by how a product looks, smells, tastes, feels, or sounds, a style modification may have a definite impact on purchases. Hallmark, for example, has had to modify its Valentine's Day cards by replacing Cupid with butterflies, puppies, kittens, birds, rainbows, flowers, and contemporary photographs. Hallmark determined that young romantics view Cupid as being too traditional and too trite.[10] Through style modifications, a firm can differentiate its product from competing brands and perhaps gain a sizable market share for such a unique product. The major drawback in using style modifications is that their value is determined subjectively, and although a firm may modify a product to improve the product's style, customers may find the modified product to be less appealing.

Deleting products

Generally, a product cannot indefinitely continue to satisfy target market customers and contribute to achieving an organization's overall goals. To maintain an effective product mix, a firm has to get rid of some products, just as it has to modify existing products or introduce new ones. This is called *product deletion*. A weak product costs the firm financially. In addition, too much of a marketer's time and resources are spent trying to revive it. This effort, in turn, reduces the time and resources available for modifying other products or developing new ones. Shorter production runs, which can increase per unit production costs, may be required for a

8. Mitchell C. Lynch, "Selling New Polaroid 600 Line May Require Teaching Camera Users Why They Need It," *Wall Street Journal*, June 29, 1981, p. 23.
9. Frank S. Leonard and W. Earl Sasser, "The Incline of Quality," *Harvard Business Review*, Sept.–Oct. 1982, p. 171.
10. "Cupid Has Lost the Hearts of the Young," *The Eagle*, Jan. 30, 1983, p. 6D.

marginal product. Finally, when a weak product generates unfavorable images among customers, the negative ideas may rub off onto some of the firm's other products.

Most organizations find it difficult to delete a product. For example, Procter & Gamble, in spite of huge losses, has hesitated to kill Pringle's potato chips. Pringle's lags far behind competing brands.[11] A decision to drop a product may be opposed by management and other employees who feel the product is necessary in the product mix. Salespeople who still have some loyal customers are especially upset when a product is dropped. Sometimes, considerable resources and effort are spent trying to change the product's marketing mix to improve its sales and thus avoid having to abandon the item.

Although some organizations drop weak products only after they have become severe financial burdens, a better approach is some form of systematic review in which each product is evaluated periodically to determine its impact on the overall effectiveness of the firm's product mix. Such a review should analyze a product's contribution to the firm's sales for a given period. It should include estimates of future sales, costs, and profits associated with the product, and a consideration of whether changes should be made in the marketing strategy to improve the product's performance. Through a systematic review an organization is better able to improve the performance of products in its mix and to ascertain when to delete products, thus maximizing the effectiveness of the product mix.

Several alternatives exist for deleting a product, but basically it can be phased out, run out, or dropped immediately (see Figure 6.2). A phase-out approach lets the product decline without changing the marketing strategy. No attempt is made to give the product new life. A runout policy exploits any strengths left in the product. By increasing marketing efforts in core markets or by eliminating some marketing expenditures such as advertising, the product may provide a sudden spurt of profits. This approach is often used for technologically obsolete products, such as calculators, computers, and cassette recorders. Often the price is reduced to get a sales spurt before the product inventory is depleted. An immediate-drop decision results in sudden termination of an unprofitable product. Johnson & Johnson used this approach when it got out of the disposable diaper business.[12] A plant that produced 3.8 million diapers a day was simply shut down. This strategy is appropriate when losses are too great to prolong the life of a product.

***Developing
new products***

Developing and introducing new products is frequently expensive and risky. Thousands of new products are introduced annually. Depending on how one defines it, the failure rate for new products ranges between 33 percent and 90 percent. Although it is often reported that 90 percent of new products end up as failures, a recent study of industrial and consumer-oriented firms indicates that only 33 percent of the new products actually introduced to the marketplace fail. This same study, conducted by the Conference Board, reports that medium and large-sized firms obtain 15

11. Dean Ratbart, "In Spite of Huge Losses, Procter & Gamble Tries Once
 More to Revive Pringle's Chips," *Wall Street Journal*, Oct. 7, 1981, p. 25.
12. Lee Smith, "J and J Comes a Long Way, Baby," *Fortune*, June 1, 1981, p. 58.

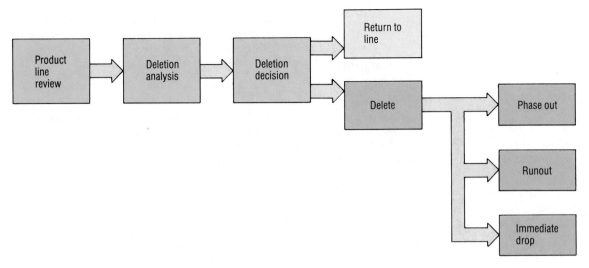

Figure 6.2 Product deletion process
Source: Martin L. Bell, Marketing Concepts and Strategy, *3rd ed., p. 267. Copyright © 1979, Houghton Mifflin Company. Used by permission.*

percent of their sales volume from new products introduced in the last five years. Lack of research is the leading cause of new product failure. Cited most often as reasons for failure are technical problems in design or production and errors in timing the product's introduction.[13]

Although new product development is risky, failure to introduce new products can also be risky. Consider Polaroid. The demand for instant cameras today is less than one-third what it was five years ago. In response to this decline in demand, Polaroid has been doing what retired founder Edwin Land did not want it to do. It has been developing several "not-so-instant" camera products, including a disc camera and a 35mm camera with a separate film processing unit. The risks Polaroid would have taken by not developing new products were too high.[14]

The amount of time required to get a new product to a market can be extensive. Consider some extreme examples. It took sixteen years to research and introduce the first automatic transmission, twenty-two years for instant coffee, and thirty-three years for fluorescent lights.[15]

The term *new product* can have several meanings. The genuinely new product—such as Crest with fluoristat or the RCA videodisc—offers innovative benefits. New products that were different, but distinctly better, include Pampers improved-absorbency diapers and Chiffon soft margarine. Me-too new products are considered less likely to succeed, but Pepsi-Cola was an enormously successful me-too product.[16] For our purposes, a new

13. David Hopkins, "Survey Finds 67% of New Products Succeed," *Marketing News,* Feb. 8, 1980, p. 1.
14. Gay Jervey, "Polaroid: No Longer in an Instant," *Advertising Age,* Jan. 10, 1983, p. 63.
15. Tommy Greer, "Look for These Specialists in Better Mousetrap Building," *Marketing Times,* March–April 1978, p. 11.
16. Peter H. Engel, "How Over-Achievers Kill 6 Sacred Cows of New Item Theory," *Marketing Times,* July–Aug. 1981, p. 2.

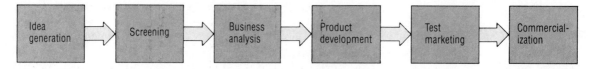

Figure 6.3   Phases of new product development

product is one that a given firm has not marketed previously, although similar products may have been available from other organizations. (Consider Levi's new product mentioned in the Application on p. 185.) Before a new product is introduced, it goes through the six phases shown in Figure 6.3, which depicts the evolutionary nature of *new product development* and outlines the major tasks in each phase. The phases are (1) idea generation, (2) screening, (3) business analysis, (4) product development, (5) test marketing, and (6) commercialization. Many ideas for new products are abandoned before the introductory launching and a product can be dropped at any stage in its development. To gain a clearer understanding of the process, we will follow a well-known and successful product developed by General Foods through the phases shown in Figure 6.3.[17]

To see the various responsibilities involved in product development, in this section we will look at the activities of a General Foods staff group that was formed to come up with ideas for new products. A committee was established to pool ideas and pull together different viewpoints. The committee was involved in developing plans and making recommendations to the chief marketing executive.

Idea generation
Businesses and other organizations seek product ideas that will help them achieve their objectives. This activity is *idea generation*. The difficulty of the task is illustrated by the fact that only a few ideas are good enough to be commercially successful.

New-product ideas can come from several sources. Although some organizations get their ideas almost by random chance, firms that are trying to maximize product mix effectiveness usually develop systematic approaches for generating new product ideas. New ideas may come from internal sources—marketing managers, researchers, engineers, or other organizational personnel. For example, the idea for the highly successful 3M Post-it adhesive-backed yellow notes (see Figure 6.4) came from a 3M employee. As a church choir member, he used slips of paper for marking songs in his hymnal. Because they would fall out, he suggested an adhesive-backed note.[18] New-product ideas may also arise from sources outside the firm—competitors, advertising agencies, management consultants, private research organizations, and customers. For example, customers or users developed 67 percent of the new process machines employed in the semiconductor industry. The Pillsbury Bake-Off, a recipe contest, has gen-

17. The techniques used to develop this product are not intended to represent how General Foods develops new products today.
18. Lawrence Ingrassia, "By Improving Scotch Paper, 3M Gets New Product Winner," *Wall Street Journal,* March 31, 1983, p. 27.

"A new life with Levi's" is the theme of Levi's new fall advertising campaign. Statistics show that the current trend in population growth is expected to continue through the 1980s. Levi's womenswear division, encouraged by these statistics, is penetrating the maternity apparel market for the first time.

Levi's saw an opportunity to diversify its womenswear product line, and did not hesitate to investigate. Marketers at Levi's found that manufacturers of maternity clothing catered to either the upper end or the lower end of the market. Surprisingly, the middle range is virtually ignored. In addition, by questioning pregnant women about their likes and dislikes regarding maternity wear, it was revealed that durability was the quality most sought, yet least found, in clothing for pregnant women.

Levi's has confidence that its expanded line of maternity wear will do well. To reach its target market, Levi's is advertising in women's magazines and using point-of-sale promotional materials. Special premium items that are being offered include denim-bound diaries and pregnancy calendars.

Source: Based on "No Pregnant Pause at Levi's," *Advertising Age*, Sept. 26, 1983, p. 14.

erated several recipes that Pillsbury has commercialized.[19] The Application on page 187 provides another example of new product acquisition.

Brainstorming and incentives or rewards for good ideas are typical intrafirm devices used to encourage the development of ideas. Sometimes, potential buyers of a product are questioned in depth to discover what attributes would appeal to them. In looking at available ideas, the General Foods new-product committee discovered a valuable idea from an unexpected source. The company had been supporting medical researchers at Johns Hopkins University who discovered that when coconut oil is agitated in combination with other ingredients, it whips up very much like fresh cream. The researchers were not trying to make a substitute for whipped cream; they were trying to develop a coconut-oil plasma substitute. To them the fact that coconut oil whipped like cream was only a casual observation. However, General Foods marketers saw that this might lead to a successful new product.

Screening ideas

In the process of *screening ideas,* those that do not match organizational objectives are rejected. Those with the greatest potential are selected for further development. Screening product ideas involves a general assessment of the organization's resources. Through forecasting techniques, an early projection of economic payoffs is made. The firm's overall ability to produce and market the product is analyzed. Other aspects of an idea that should be weighed are the nature and wants of buyers, the competition, and environmental factors. Compared with other phases of the development process, the largest number of product ideas are rejected during screening.

At times, a checklist consisting of requirements for new products is used when making screening decisions. It encourages evaluators to be systematic, thus reducing the possibility that they might overlook some fact.

19. Eric von Hippel, "Get New Products from Customers," *Harvard Business Review,* March–April 1982, p. 118.

The type of formal research that is described in Chapter 4 may be needed if a critical checklist factor remains unclear. Note that the product idea can be dropped at any point in its development.

After screening many ideas, the General Foods new-product committee decided to explore the possibilities of developing a substitute for whipped cream.

Business analysis

Business analysis provides a tentative sketch of a product's compatibility in the marketplace, including its probable profitability. Compatibility factors include the company's manufacturing and marketing capabilities, financial resources, and management's attitude toward the product.[20]

20. Fritz A. Schumacher, "Successful New Product Ideas Require Right Marketing, Financial 'Fit,' Corporate 'Champion,' " *Marketing News,* Oct. 16, 1981, p. 1.

Although American Home Product's earnings rose 8.3 percent during a recent quarter, the increase is not up to par for a company whose quarterly growth is traditionally expressed in two digits. The future for the company looks like an uphill climb, as three of its big-selling products—the drugs Ativan, Serax, and Inderal—are under patents that expired. As a result, American Home is seeking new products and trying to find ways to maintain the market shares held by Ativan, Serax, and Inderal when imitations reach the market. Besides prescription drugs, American Home produces such items as Woolite, Anacin, Dristan, Black Flag insecticides, and Ekco kitchen ware.

One approach for acquiring new products by American Home is to buy smaller firms with proven products. American Home has also spent considerable resources developing unknown products, such as Anacin (which was known by few outside dentistry when the company bought it in 1930), into familiar well-accepted brands. Although American Home in the past has not spent as much as its competitors on research and development, it is now allocating larger amounts of resources to this area. This new thrust is expected to yield numerous new product ideas.

Source: Based on Susan Fraker, "American Home Products Battles the Doubters," *Fortune,* July 25, 1983, pp. 59–64.

During a business analysis, evaluators ask questions such as those listed below:

1. Is market demand strong enough to justify entering the market? Will the demand endure?
2. How will the introduction and marketing of this product affect the firm's sales, costs, and profits?
3. Are the organization's research, development, engineering, and production capabilities adequate?
4. If new facilities must be constructed to manufacture the product, how quickly can they be built? If it is possible to use existing facilities, the product idea usually has a better chance of survival.
5. Does the product fit in with the organization's existing product mix?
6. Is the necessary financing for development and commercialization on hand or obtainable at terms consistent with a favorable return on investment?
7. What types of environmental and competitive changes can be expected, and how will these changes affect the product's future sales, costs, and profits?

During business analysis, General Foods sought information about the market for whipped cream. A poll of consumers, together with secondary data about the purchase of fresh whipping cream and pressurized products, supplied some information for estimating potential sales, costs, and profits. A research-budget meeting explored the financial objectives and related considerations for the whipped coconut-oil product. The new-product committee got budget clearance to proceed with development only after a panel of consumers was enthusiastic about the concept of a whipped coconut-oil topping. The panel described the most meaningful benefits as quality, lower calories, inexpensive cost, convenience of storage, and ease of preparation.

Product development

In the development phase, the company must first find out if it is technically feasible to produce the product and if the product can be produced at costs low enough to result in a reasonable price. If a product idea makes it to the development point, it is then transformed into a working model. To test its acceptability, the idea or concept is converted into a prototype. The prototype should reveal tangible and intangible attributes associated with the product in consumers' minds. The design, mechanical features, and intangible aspects of the product must be linked to wants in the marketplace. The development phase of creating a new product is frequently lengthy and expensive; thus a relatively small number of product ideas are put into development.

However, the development stage is not restricted to mechanical or production aspects of the product. During this stage the various ingredients that will make up the marketing mix must also be tested. Management must review copyrights, preliminary advertising copy, packaging, and labeling to see if there are any legal problems. Management must also plan for personal selling and distribution. The aim is to ensure the effective integration of all elements in the marketing mix.

In our example, General Foods assigned engineering and production to determine whether production was feasible. One problem was readily apparent: how would they convert the paste-like coconut lard into something that tasted like cream. Since the whipped coconut cream tasted soapy, the solution to this problem was difficult. After considerable work, company chemists achieved a tasty formulation. In addition, engineering and production discovered that the product could be converted into a powder that could be whipped with milk or water. The conversion used a spray-drying process in which coconut liquid was sprayed into the top of a gigantic thermos bottle (five stories high); at high temperatures the mixture dehydrated and fell to the tower floor as a finished product.

The General Foods new-product committee chose the name Dream Whip after screening hundreds of possibilities. They chose the name primarily for its descriptive quality, phonetic appeal, and aura of novelty and glamour. After its selection, the corporation's legal department determined that another manufacturer already owned a copyright on the brand name and had a trademark that went along with it. General Foods had to purchase the name from that copyright owner.

An outside consulting firm evaluated proposed package designs, which had been developed by another consulting group. The package that was adopted was the one that had the best results of the three prototypes tested. Initially, marketers at General Foods strongly favored a design that proved to have little appeal when it was presented to consumers in a survey. The package design that consumers favored moved off retail shelves faster than expected, even before advertising began.

Still another outside consulting group helped to determine the proper price. After conducting a test among consumers, this group selected an introductory price. A price below the established level seemed to create an impression of cheapness at the expense of quality, and a price above this level caused a direct comparison with cream. The price selected gave General Foods a good return on its investment.

Test marketing

Test marketing is a limited introduction of a product in areas chosen to represent the intended market. Its aim is to determine probable buyers' reactions. Test marketing is not an extension of the screening and development stages. It is a sample launching of the entire marketing mix. Test marketing should be conducted only after the product has gone through development and after initial plans regarding the other marketing mix variables have been determined. Test marketing is used by companies of all sizes to minimize the risk of product failure. The dangers of introducing an untested product include undercutting already profitable products and (should the new product fail) loss of credibility with distributors.

Test marketing provides several benefits. It allows marketers to expose a product in a natural marketing environment to obtain a measure of its sales performance. While the product is being marketed in a limited area, it is possible to identify weaknesses in the product or in other parts of the marketing mix. Marketers can experiment with variations in advertising, price, and packaging in different test areas and can measure the extent of brand awareness, brand switching, and repeat purchases that result from alterations in the marketing mix.

A product weakness that is discovered after a nationwide introduction can be very expensive to correct, and if initial reactions among consumers are negative, the marketers may not be able to convince consumers to try the product again. Thus, making adjustments after test marketing can be crucial. Examples of variables that could be altered after test marketing include product line extensions; sales potential at different spending and distribution levels; and pricing strategy, product formulation, advertising copy and strategy, package design, and shelf location.[21]

Selection of appropriate test areas is a major influence on the accuracy of test-marketing results. Table 6.1 lists some of the most popular test-market cities. The criteria used for choosing test cities are dependent on the characteristics of the product, the target market's characteristics, and the organization's objectives and resources. Even though the selection criteria will vary from one firm to another, the general issues raised through the questions in Table 6.2 can be useful when assessing a potential test market.

Test marketing is not without risks, however. Not only is it expensive, but a firm's competitors may try to interfere with an experiment. A competitor may try to "jam" the test program by increasing advertising, lowering prices, and offering special incentives, all to combat the recognition and purchase of a new brand. For example, a Reynolds Metals advertisement in test-city newspapers for its new plastic wrap prompted Saran Wrap to offer a special incentive to consumers in the same newspapers.[22] Any such devices can invalidate test results. Sometimes, too, competitors copy the product in the testing stage and rush to introduce a similar product. Schick, for example, introduced a double-bladed razor less than six months after Gillette brought out Trac II. Therefore, it is desirable to move quickly and commercialize as soon as possible after testing.

21. Joel R. Robinson, "Simulated Test Marketing Reduces Risk in New Brand Introductions, Line Extensions," *Marketing News,* Sept. 18, 1981, p. 3.
22. "Reynolds Rolls, Plastic Wrap," *Advertising Age,* Sept. 28, 1981, p. 10.

Table 6.1   Popular test markets for new products

Albany–Schenectady–
  Troy
	Green Bay, WI	Quad Cities: Rock
		  Island & Moline, IL;

Albuquerque	Houston	Davenport &
Amarillo	Indianapolis	Bettendorf, IA
Atlanta	Jacksonville, FL	(Davenport–Rock
Binghamton, NY	Kansas City, MO	Island–Moline SMSA)
Boston	Lexington, KY	Rochester, NY
Buffalo	Lubbock, TX	Sacramento-Stockton
Charleston, WV	Memphis	San Francisco
Charlotte	Miami	St. Louis
Chicago	Milwaukee	San Antonio
Cincinnati	Minneapolis–St. Paul	San Diego
Cleveland	Nashville	Seattle-Tacoma
Columbus, OH	Oklahoma City	South Bend
Dallas–Forth Worth	Omaha	Spokane
Dayton	Orlando–Daytona	Syracuse
Denver	Beach	Tampa–St. Petersburg
Des Moines	Peoria	Tucson
Erie, PA	Phoenix	Tulsa
Fargo, ND	Pittsburgh	Wichita
Fort Wayne	Portland, ME	
Fresno	Portland, OR	
	Providence	

Source: "The Nation's Most Popular Test Markets," copyright 1983 *Sales and Marketing Management*. Used by permission.

If we examine the test marketing of General Foods' Dream Whip, we should see the value of test marketing. Before going into the five cities selected for test marketing (Indianapolis, Huntington, Louisville, Columbus, and Cincinnati), the marketers conducted a survey to learn about the existing market for whipped-cream products. Management was pleased with the tangible evidence from test marketing, and another research program was launched immediately to determine Dream Whip's penetration among customers and the effectiveness of promotional devices.

Dream Whip was introduced in the test markets in October; by June, however, inventory started building up, and management questioned plans for nationwide introduction. Consumer mail about the product's flaws started coming in, including a flood of complaints about whipping failures. Researchers went to the test-market areas and confirmed that hot weather had caused a high failure rate in whipping. Faced with this finding, General Foods delayed nationwide introduction, and to trim inventory, a few additional test markets were opened in Boston, Detroit, and Pittsburgh during the cold-weather months. Finally, one year after the whipping problems were discovered, technical research came up with a solution, and the formula was modified. Dream Whip was successful in the test markets during the next period of warm weather. The product was ready for nationwide introduction.

Commercialization

During *commercialization*, plans for full-scale manufacturing and marketing must be refined and settled, and budgets for the project must be prepared.

Table 6.2 Questions to Consider When Choosing Test Markets

1. Is the area typical of planned distribution outlets?
2. Is the city relatively isolated from other cities?
3. Are local media available and cooperative?
4. Does the city contain a diversified cross section of ages, religions, and cultural/societal preferences?
5. Are the purchasing habits atypical?
6. Is the city's per capita income typical?
7. Does the city have a good record as a test city?
8. Would testing efforts be easily "jammed" by competitors?
9. Does the city have stable year-round sales?
10. Does the area have a dominant TV station; does it have multiple newspapers, magazines, and radio stations?
11. Are retailers that will cooperate available?
12. Are research and audit services available?
13. Is the area free from unusual influences, such as one industry's dominance or heavy tourist traffic?

Source: Adapted from "A Checklist for Selecting Test Markets," copyright 1982 *Sales and Marketing Management*. Used by permission.

In the early part of the commercialization phase, marketing management analyzes the results of test marketing to find out what changes in the marketing mix are needed before the product is introduced. The results of test marketing may tell the marketers, for example, to change one or more of the product's physical attributes, to modify the distribution plans to include more retail outlets, to alter promotional efforts, or to change the product's price.

The organization gears up for large-scale production during the commercialization phase. This activity may require sizable capital expenditures for plant and equipment, and the firm also may need to hire additional personnel.

The product is introduced into the market during commercialization. During product introduction marketers often spend enormous sums of money for such promotional efforts as advertising, personal selling, and sales promotion. These expenses, coupled with capital expenditures, can make the commercialization phase extremely costly; such expenditures may not be recovered for several years.

Commercialization is significantly easier when customers accept the product rapidly. Marketers have a better chance of success if they can make customers aware of a product's benefits. The following stages of the *product adoption process* are generally recognized as those that buyers go through in accepting a product:

1. *Awareness.* The buyer becomes aware of the product.
2. *Interest.* The buyer seeks information and is receptive to learning about the product.
3. *Evaluation.* The buyer considers the product's benefits and determines whether to try it.
4. *Trial.* The buyer examines, tests, or tries the product to determine its usefulness.

5. *Adoption*. The buyer purchases the product and can be expected to use it to solve problems.[23]

This adoption model has several implications for the commercialization phase. First, promotion should be used to create widespread awareness of the product and its benefits. Samples or simulated trials should be arranged to help buyers make initial purchase decisions. At the same time, marketers should emphasize quality control and provide solid guarantees to reinforce buyer opinion during the evaluation stage. Finally, production and physical distribution must be linked to patterns of adoption and repeat purchases. The product adoption process is discussed in Chapter 11 also.

Products are not usually introduced nationwide overnight. Most products are introduced in stages, starting in a set of geographic areas and expanding the introduction into adjacent areas over a period of time. It may take several years to market the product nationally. Sometimes, the test cities are used as initial marketing areas, with the introduction being a natural extension of test marketing. For example, Sacramento, Denver, Dallas, St. Louis, and Atlanta are shown on the map in Figure 6.5. A firm using these test cities could initiate stage 1 of the introduction in them. Stage 2 could include expansion to statewide market coverage in the states in which test cities are located. In stage 3, marketing efforts could be extended into the adjacent states surrounding those in stage 2. All remaining states would then be covered in stage 4. Even though Figure 6.5 shows product introduction on a state-by-state basis, do not assume that gradual introductions always occur state by state; other geographic combinations are used as well.

Gradual product introduction is popular for several reasons. It reduces the risk associated with introducing a new product. If the product fails, the firm will experience smaller losses when the item has been introduced in only a few geographic areas than when it has been marketed nationally. Usually, it is impossible for a company to introduce a product nationwide overnight. The system of wholesalers and retailers necessary to distribute the product cannot be established that quickly. The development of a distribution network may take considerable time. Keep in mind, also, that the number of product units needed to satisfy the national demand for a successful product can be enormous, and a firm usually cannot produce the required quantities in a matter of a few days.

Even though there are good reasons for introducing a product gradually, marketers realize that this approach creates some problems from a competitive standpoint. A gradual introduction allows competitors to observe what a firm is doing and to monitor results, just as the firm's own marketers are doing. If competitors see that the newly introduced product is successful, they may enter the same target market quickly with similar products. Also, as a product is introduced on a region-by-region basis, competitors may expand their marketing efforts to offset the activities promoting the new product.

23. Adapted from *Diffusion of Innovations* by Everett M. Rogers (Copyright © 1962 by The Free Press, a Division of Macmillan Publishing Co., Inc.), pp. 81–86.

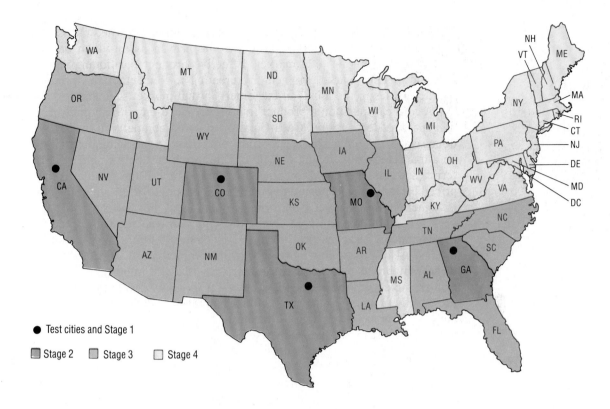

Figure 6.5 Stages of expansion into the national market during commercialization
Source: Adapted from Business: An Involvement Approach, *by Herbert G. Hicks, William M. Pride, and James D. Powell. Copyright © 1975 by McGraw-Hill. Used with permission of McGraw-Hill Book Company.*

Introducing new products is, at best, risky. Many of them fail. To minimize losses and to maximize the effectiveness of its product mix, an organization should establish an approach that includes detailed planning and strict control of new-product development.

The commercialization of Dream Whip relied on national distributors to make the product available. The following product characteristics were stressed to consumers: stays fresh on the shelf; needs no refrigeration; can be whipped hours before serving; will not wilt, separate, or sour; has great taste but is low in calories; and is low priced. Initially successful, Dream Whip sold over half a million cases during the first full year of introduction.

Product positioning

The term ***product positioning*** refers to the decisions and activities that are directed toward trying to create and maintain a firm's intended product concept in customer's minds. When marketers introduce a product, they attempt to position it so that it seems to possess the characteristics most desired by the target market. This projected image is crucial. A product's "position" refers to the customers' concept of the product's attributes relative to their concept of competitive brands. For example, Crest is positioned as a fluoride toothpaste that fights decay, while Ultra Brite is positioned as a whitening toothpaste that increases the user's sex appeal.

Product positioning is a part of a natural progression when market segmentation is used. Segmentation allows the firm to aim a given brand at only a portion of the total market. Effective product positioning helps to serve a specific market segment by creating a concept of the product's characteristics in the minds of customers in that market segment.

A firm can position a product to compete head-on with another brand, as Pepsi has done against Coca-Cola, or to avoid competition, as 7UP has done relative to other soft drink producers. Head-to-head competition may be a marketer's positioning objective if the product's performance characteristics are at least equal to competitive brands and if the product is lower priced. Head-to-head positioning may be appropriate even when the price is higher, if the product's performance characteristics are superior. Conversely, positioning to avoid competition may be best when the product's performance characteristics are not significantly different from competing brands. Also, positioning a brand to avoid competition may be appropriate when that brand has unique characteristics that are important to buyers. For example, 7UP positioned itself away from many competitors (see Figure 6.6) by claiming to have no caffeine, no artificial color, and no artificial flavor. The makers of 7UP are trying to position their product in buyers' minds as being in a category by itself.

Avoiding competition is critical when a firm introduces a brand into a market in which it already has one or more brands. In this situation, marketers usually want to minimize the extent to which the new brand cannibalizes the sales of the firm's existing brands, unless the new brand generates substantially larger profits. When Schlitz introduced light beer, it attempted to position the new brand so as to minimize its adverse effects on the sales of the company's existing brands.

If a product has been planned properly, its attributes and its brand image will give it the distinct appeal needed. Style, shape, construction, quality of work, color—all elements of the product component of the marketing mix—assist in creating the image and the appeal. If the benefits can be identified easily by buyers, then, of course, they are more likely to purchase the product. When some preferred attributes are not being offered, then room exists for a new product or for repositioning of an existing product.

Managing products after commercialization

Most new products start off slowly and seldom generate enough sales to produce profits immediately. As buyers learn about the product, marketers should be alert for product weaknesses and should make corrections quickly. Such actions can prevent the early death of the product or a dissolution of demand.[24] Distribution channels, promotion, and pricing should have been designed to attract the market segment that is most interested and that has the fewest obstacles to overcome.[25] If any of these factors needs to be adjusted, this action, too, must be taken quickly to sustain de-

24. Chester R. Wasson, *Dynamic Competitive Strategy and Product Life Cycles* (St. Charles, Ill.: Challenge Books, 1974), p. 7.
25. Ibid.

Some hard news about soft drinks.

These soft drinks have caffeine.

These soft drinks are artificially colored.

These soft drinks have artificial flavor.

No Caffeine.
No Artificial Color.
No Artificial Flavor.
No wonder 7UP has
a clean, refreshing,
unspoiled taste.

**Don't you feel
good about 7UP?**

For four coupons worth $1.00 off your next purchases of 7UP or Diet 7UP (limit one per household), and for more information about ingredients in all soft drinks, write: Consumer Affairs, Dept. C, The Seven-Up Company, 121 S. Meramec, St. Louis, Mo. 63105

Figure 6.6 Advertisement to position 7UP away from competitors *Source: 7UP.*

mand. As the sales curve moves upward and the breakeven point is reached, the growth stage begins.

Dream Whip sales leveled off a few years after commercialization, but higher advertising expenditures and more national television advertising increased sales again. Advertisements stressed the product's advantages over fresh whipped cream and urged consumers to use it frequently on a variety of desserts. New competition appeared in the form of Lucky Whip, a similar whipped topping mix that aggressively entered the market.

Marketing strategy in the growth stage

As sales increase, management must support the momentum by adjusting the marketing strategy. The goal is to establish the product's position and to fortify it by encouraging brand loyalty. As profits increase, the organization must brace itself for the entrance of aggressive competitors who may make specialized appeals to selected market segments.

Product

During the growth stage, products might be expanded to appeal to more specialized markets. For example, Wendy's—which has over two thousand hamburger restaurants—views the chicken segment of the restaurant business as a good growth area. Wendy's has successfully introduced a chicken sandwich in its hamburger restaurants and is opening The Sisters International, Inc., restaurants with more elegant dining rooms than Church's or Kentucky Fried Chicken.[26] Marketers should analyze the product position in terms of competing products and should correct weak or omitted attributes.

Distribution

Gaps in the marketing channels should be filled during the growth period. It may be easier to obtain new distribution outlets once product acceptance has been established. Sometimes marketers have a tendency to move from an exclusive or selective exposure to a more intensive network of dealers. Marketers must also make sure that the physical distribution system is running efficiently and delivers supplies to distributors before their inventories are exhausted. Since competition increases during the growth period, service adjustments and prompt credit for defective products are important marketing tools.

Promotion

Promotional efforts should stress brand loyalty during the growth stage, but as sales increase, promotion costs should drop as a percentage of total sales. A falling ratio between promotion expenditures and sales should contribute significantly to increased profits. Although the advertising expenditures for Dream Whip increased during the growth stage, the level of advertising as a percentage of sales decreased.

Price

After recovering development costs, a business may be able to lower prices. As sales volume increases, efficiencies in production can result in lower costs. These savings may be passed on to buyers. If price cuts are possible, they can facilitate price competition and discourage new competitors from entering the market. As was mentioned earlier, Texas Instruments made continuous price cuts on its minicalculators as sales increased. If demand remains strong and there are few competitive threats, prices tend to remain stable.

Marketing strategy for mature products

Since many products are in the maturity stage of their life cycles, marketers must deal with these products and must be prepared to improve the marketing mix constantly. During maturity the competitive situation stabilizes, and some of the weaker competitors drop out.

Product

Marketers may need to alter the product's quality or otherwise modify the product. Producers of Underwood Deviled Ham—once a cracker topping for hors d'oeuvres—turned the product into a sandwich spread after research revealed that the heaviest buyers used it that way.[27] A product may

---

26. Michael King, "Wendy's New Management Cooks Up Plans for Growth and Diversification," *Wall Street Journal,* March 27, 1981, p. 12.
27. Theodore Karger, "5 Ways to Find Ideas—Re-evaluate Ideas—Re-evaluate Your Old Products," *Marketing Times,* July/Aug. 1981, p. 18.

be rejuvenated through different packaging, new models, or style changes. Sales and market share may be maintained or strengthened by informing buyers about new uses for the product or by encouraging them to use it more frequently. Noxzema's makers restructured the product from a skin medicament for occasional use to a beauty-care product for routine use.[28]

Distribution
During the maturity stage of the cycle, marketers actively encourage dealers to support the product. Dealers may be offered promotional assistance and help in lowering their inventory costs. In general, marketers go to great effort to serve dealers and provide incentives for selling the manufacturer's brand, in part because private brands are a threat at this time. As we said earlier, private brands present an opportunity as well as a threat to manufacturers, who may be able to sell their product through recognized private brands as well as their own. However, private brands frequently undermine manufacturers' brands. If manufacturers refuse to sell to private-brand dealers, their competitors usually take advantage of this opportunity.

Promotion
Large advertising expenditures are often necessary during the maturity stage to maintain market share. As competition increases, sales promotion and aggressive personal selling may be potent marketing tools. When Dream Whip reached maturity, the promotional aspect of packaging was used to attract and maintain interest in the product.

Price
There is a greater mixture of pricing strategies during the maturity stage. Marketers develop price flexibility to differentiate offerings in product lines. Markdowns and price incentives are more common, but price increases are likely to occur if distribution and production costs increase.

Marketing strategy for declining products

As a product's sales curve turns downward, profits almost always fall. A business can justify maintaining a product as long as it contributes to profits or enhances the overall effectiveness of a product mix. When a product becomes unprofitable, marketers eventually reduce production. At this stage, marketers must determine when to eliminate the product. This can be an extremely important decision.

Product
Usually a declining product has lost its distinctiveness because similar, competing products have been introduced. Competing products engender increased substitution and brand switching as buyers become insensitive to minor differences in products. For these reasons, marketers do little to change style, design, or other attributes of a product during its decline. New technology, product substitutes, or environmental considerations may also indicate that the time has come to delete a product.

28. Ibid.

Distribution

During a product's decline, outlets with core sales (the most loyal buyers) are maintained, and unprofitable outlets are weeded out. An entire marketing channel may be eliminated if it does not make an adequate contribution to profits. Sometimes a new marketing channel, such as a factory outlet, will be used to liquidate remaining inventory of an obsolete product. As sales decline, the product tends to become a specialty item, and loyal buyers may seek out dealers who carry it.

Promotion

Promotion loses its importance during the decline stage. However, advertising may slow the rate of decline, and sales incentives—such as coupons and premiums—may regain buyers' attention. As the product continues to decline, the sales staff shifts its emphasis to more profitable products.

Price

The fact that a product returns a profit may be more important to a firm than maintaining a certain market share through repricing. To squeeze out all possible remaining profits, marketers may maintain the price despite declining sales and competitive pressures. Prices may even be increased as costs rise if a loyal core market still wants the product. In other situations, the price may be cut to reduce existing inventory so that the product can be deleted.

Summary

Developing and managing products is critical to an organization's survival and growth. Although several organizational approaches to product management are possible, they share common activities, functions, and decisions necessary to guide a product through its life cycle. Product managers coordinate efforts and become the strategy center for the product in all markets. Market managers focus on products for specific markets. A venture team is sometimes used to develop new products. Members of the venture team come from different functional areas within the organization and have authority to execute plans. Product planning requires the coordination of such functional areas as research and development, production and engineering, finance and accounting, and marketing. Each of these areas has functional authority over some aspect of the product.

To maximize the effectiveness of a product mix, an organization usually has to alter its mix through such methods as new-product development, modification of existing products, deletion of a product, or the development of a new product.

Product modification refers to changing one or more of a product's characteristics. This approach to altering a product mix can be effective when the product is modifiable, when customers can perceive the change, and when the modification is desired by customers. Products can be changed through quality, functional, or style modifications.

To maintain an effective product mix, a firm has to get rid of weak products. Although a firm's personnel may oppose product deletion, weak products are unprofitable, consume too much time and effort, may require shorter production runs, and can create an unfavorable image of the firm's other products. A systematic review should be employed to determine when to delete products. Products to be deleted can be phased out, run out, or dropped immediately.

New-product development involves generating ideas, screening to determine which ideas to develop, expanding an idea through business analysis, developing a product into a demonstrable concept, test marketing, and commercialization. The decision to enter the commercialization or introduction phase means that the product begins full-scale production and that a complete marketing strategy is developed. The adoption process that buyers go through in accepting a product includes awareness, interest, evaluation, trial, and adoption.

Developing marketing strategies as a product moves through its life cycle may require continual adaptation. In the growth stage, it is important to develop brand loyalty and a market position. In the maturity stage, a product may be modified or new market segments may be developed to rejuvenate its sales. A declining product may be maintained as long as it makes a contribution to profits or enhances the product mix.

Important terms

Product manager
Brand manager
Market manager
Venture team
Product portfolio approach
Product modification
Quality modification
Functional modification
Style modification

Product deletion
New-product development
Idea generation
Screening ideas
Business analysis
Test marketing
Commercialization
Product adoption process
Product positioning

Discussion and review questions

1. What organizational alternatives are available to a firm with two product lines having four product items in each line?
2. When is it more appropriate to use a product manager than a market manager? When is an alternative or combined approach used?
3. What type of organization might use a venture team to develop new products? What are the advantages and disadvantages of such a team?
4. Do small firms that manufacture one or two products need to be concerned about developing and managing products? Why or why not?
5. Why is product development a cross-functional activity within an organization? To put the question in other terms, why must finance, engineering, manufacturing, and other functional areas be involved?
6. Develop some information sources for new product ideas for the automobile industry.
7. Some firms believe that they can omit test marketing. What are some advantages and disadvantages of test marketing?
8. Under what conditions is product modification an appropriate alternative to changing a product mix? How does a quality modification differ from a functional modification? Can an organization make one without making the other?
9. Why might an organization be unable to eliminate an unprofitable product? Give several reasons.

10. What kinds of problems are created by a weak product in a product mix?
11. Why is product positioning important in developing an introductory marketing strategy? Give examples of how some consumer products have been positioned.
12. Why is it desirable to develop strong brand loyalty during the growth stage of a product's life cycle? How is brand loyalty developed?
13. Discuss the appropriate product, promotion, distribution, and price components of a product in the late maturity stage of its life cycle. Give some examples of such a product.
14. Assume that Dream Whip suddenly experiences a rapid sales decline. Which of the marketing strategies discussed in this chapter would you recommend? Why?

Cases

Case 6.1

Coleco's Cabbage Patch Kids[29]

Recently, Coleco Industries, Inc. introduced its first doll product, the Cabbage Patch Kid, and it became an overwhelming success in just a few months. The homely yet appealing Cabbage Patch doll, which sells for about $25 in stores, is a one-of-a-kind doll that comes with a name, birth certificate, adoption papers, and the promise of a birthday card to be sent by Coleco Industries on the doll's first birthday. Even though the doll does not look like a real baby, it has babyish features such as big eyes, rounded cheeks, and pudgy arms and legs. The dolls, originally called Little People, were created by Xavier Roberts, a Georgia-based sculptor who was inspired by local folk artists. Interestingly, Mattel and Fisher-Price had evaluated and rejected the dolls a year prior to Coleco's introduction.

Cabbage Patch Kids are quite appealing for several reasons. Child psychologists indicate that the doll helps fulfill children's needs to hold and cuddle something. The doll arouses the nurturing needs in both children and adults. In addition, the scarcity of the product generated by the 1983 Christmas buying panic, and enhanced by intense news coverage, made the product even more desirable.

Coleco conducted research during the early stages of product development. The findings indicated that parents were looking for a more huggable, non-battery-operated toy for their children. Later, Coleco assembled focus groups so that researchers could observe the reactions of adults and children as they played with prototypes of the Cabbage Patch Kids. The results showed that the dolls appealed to both males and females and to adults as well as children. A limited number of dolls were produced and shown to marketers at major retail chains such as Sears, J. C. Penney, and Toys Я Us. These retailers' initial responses were quite favorable.

29. The facts in this case are from "Oh, You Beautiful Dolls," *Newsweek*, December 12, 1983, pp. 81–84; "Kids Rake In the Cabbage," *Sales and Marketing Management*, Jan. 16, 1984, p. 51; and "The Billion-Dollar Cabbage Patch in Cleveland, Georgia," *Fortune*, Dec. 26, 1983, p. 108.

The dolls were promoted in several different ways. Television commercials put across a very warm and homey appeal. Rather than emphasizing that these dolls were just for little girls, the commercials included boys, girls, and adults to enhance the broad appeal of the Cabbage Patch Kids. (Demand increased so rapidly that the advertising schedule was shortened.) Several publicity releases included statements by two prominent child psychologists who attested to the belief that the dolls had sufficient "play value." Dr. Joyce Brothers endorsed the Cabbage Patch Kids as being healthy toys for young children. A press conference was held at the Boston Children's Museum where children were given free dolls for participating in a mass "adoption" ceremony.

Coleco is hoping that the Cabbage Patch dolls become classics like Barbie, Raggedy Ann, and Teddy, which are children's products that sell year-round. To achieve this objective, Coleco is trying to keep supply slightly less than demand. During the first year of the product's introduction, Coleco sold 2.5 million Cabbage Patch Kids and generated $46 million in revenues. Coleco plans to sell twice as many dolls in its second year. In addition, Coleco plans to introduce related Cabbage Patch products that can be used with the dolls.

Questions for discussion

1. What type of test marketing did Coleco conduct prior to the introduction of the Cabbage Patch Kids? Why did Coleco take this approach?
2. Did Coleco position the product to compete head-on with other products in the doll product category? Discuss.
3. What is Coleco doing to lengthen the product life cycle of the Cabbage Patch Kids?

Case 6.2

Product Positioning of Breyers and Sealtest Ice Cream[30]

Until the 1960s, most ice cream marketers based their marketing strategies and product positionings on either a pricing incentive or a claim of superior quality. By the late 1960s, Kraft, the producer of Breyers and Sealtest ice creams, realized that competition based primarily on price appeal was not an acceptable strategy for long-term growth and profitability. The company also realized that something more was needed than an overall quality umbrella based on the traditional reputation of a product's brand name and its distribution network. To be successful, Kraft knew that somehow it would have to convince retailers that they could maximize the profitability of ice cream by offering consumers a mix of premium brands along with their own, lower-priced, private labels. Of course, this product mix argument rested on one critical assumption: that Kraft could, in fact, develop and

30. Adapted from Samuel R. Gardner, "Successful Market Positioning—One Company's Example," in *Product-Line Strategies,* Report No. 816, ed. Earl L. Bailey (New York: The Conference Board, 1982), pp. 40–41. Used by permission.

successfully market the kind of products that would generate consumer demand for reasons not related primarily to a low price.

In the late 1960s Kraft was marketing Breyers ice cream in the New York, Philadelphia, and Baltimore-Washington areas. It has always been a fine product, made in virtually the same way for more than one hundred years. Like most other well-known local brands, Breyers ice cream was positioned as a premium-quality product. The reputation of its brand name constituted its primary distinction from other brands. But in the 1960s a significant difference in Breyers' formulation became the focus for a new product-positioning strategy. The new formulation and positioning strategy was spelled out in a pledge of purity that appeared on every carton. Breyers ice cream does not contain *any* kind of artificial flavoring, nor does it contain any added coloring. And, more significantly, it does not contain any stabilizers or emulsifiers, which provide a degree of creaminess that is impossible without their aid.

This new Breyers positioning caught on quickly, and in three years the sales in its traditional marketing areas had doubled. Kraft then realized that it could use this strategy effectively to introduce the brand into new markets where the all-natural positioning had not yet been exploited to its fullest. This was a great idea, but how could Kraft justify the introduction of a new premium ice cream, Breyers, when it was already well represented in these markets by Sealtest, another premium quality brand? What would induce the trade to make room for both of Kraft's premium ice creams, especially when stores already had trouble accepting the rationale for allowing even one of them to compete with their own labels?

To appreciate the development of Kraft's Sealtest positioning, it is important to know that many Americans believe that ice cream from an ice cream parlor is somehow superior in quality to products distributed in supermarkets. Right or wrong, this perception persists for many; and, in fact, it has flourished lately with the increasing number of retail establishments that have opened during the past few years. It is also interesting that during this period, total sales of ice cream sold through supermarkets declined, while sales through ice cream parlors increased. And ice cream parlor sales were not all in the form of cones either.

The entrenched, top-quality image of the ice cream parlors' ice cream has been responsible, no doubt, for the surprisingly high tonnage sold to consumers in the form of packaged half gallons, usually at two, and sometimes three, times the price of half gallons distributed through supermarkets—and that includes Sealtest ice cream. Blind product testing confirmed that Sealtest compared favorably on taste with "ice-cream-parlor" ice creams. The results of this research gave Kraft a potentially meaningful price-value advantage over the products sold through ice cream parlors (which were competing directly against Kraft's customers, the supermarkets). An exciting positioning strategy thus presented itself for the Sealtest brand.

Sealtest became "The Supermarket Ice Cream With That Ice Cream Parlor Taste." This positioning gave Kraft a strong sales argument for the trade, as well as a powerful consumer appeal that would be compelling on its own merits without necessarily conflicting with Breyers' natural-ingredient appeal.

To prove its claim (which was crucial to its positioning strategy), Kraft ran dramatic television advertising featuring hidden-camera interviews with real consumers who, after testing both Sealtest and ice cream parlor ice cream, could not tell the difference. This advertising, as well as quality packaging, helped to establish the credibility of this positioning.

Questions for discussion
1. How did the positioning of Breyers and Sealtest ice creams relate to market segmentation?
2. How did Kraft's marketing activities create the image and appeal that resulted in the product position for Sealtest and Breyers?
3. How could Kraft position ice milk and cottage cheese?

Part 3

Distribution Decisions

Providing customers with satisfying products is important but not sufficient for successful marketing strategies. These products also must be available in adequate quantities in accessible locations at the times when customers desire them. The chapters in Part Three deal with the distribution of products and the marketing channels and institutions that provide the structure for making products available. In Chapter 7, we discuss the structure and functions of marketing channels and present an overview of institutions that make up marketing channels. Chapter 8 analyzes the types of wholesalers and the functions that they perform. Then we focus on retailing and retailers in Chapter 9. Specifically, we examine the types of retailers as well as their roles and functions in marketing channels. Finally, in Chapter 10, we analyze the decisions and activities associated with the physical distribution of products, such as inventory planning and control, transportation, warehousing, materials handling, and communications.

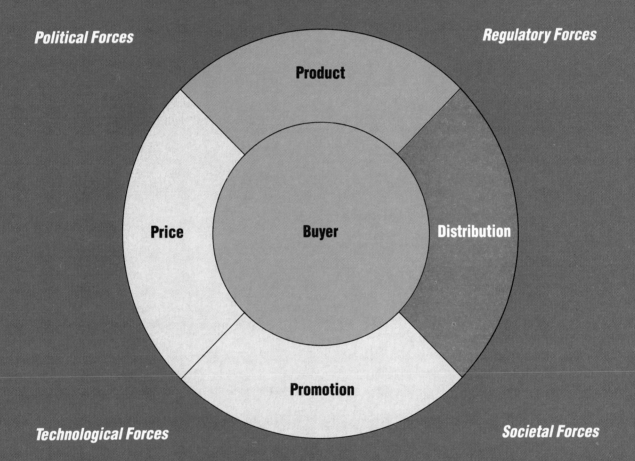

Marketing Environment

Legal Forces

Political Forces

Regulatory Forces

Product

Price

Buyer

Distribution

Promotion

Technological Forces

Societal Forces

Economic Forces

7

Marketing Channels

Objectives

To understand the marketing channel concept and the types of marketing intermediaries in the channel.

To discuss the justification of channel members.

To examine the structure and function of the channel system.

To explore the power dimensions of channels, especially the concepts of cooperation, conflict, and leadership.

International Business Machines entered the personal computer market with a new distribution method that radically departed from the company's previous marketing practices. Rather than using its own sales force, IBM sold its machines through retailers like ComputerLand. IBM did so because it needed to develop a new marketing channel to compete with Apple Computer, Tandy Corporation's Radio Shack, and other marketers of personal computers. IBM used Sears, Roebuck, too, as an outlet for its new line.[1]

Figure 7.1 is an advertisement that shows ComputerLand's emphasis on wide product selection and service to assist computer buyers in over six hundred stores worldwide. ComputerLand serves as a retailer of computers to consumers and as a dealer for office and business customers.

We've helped more kinds of people buy more kinds of computers than any other store in the world.

Make friends with the future.™
Over 600 Stores Worldwide.

Figure 7.1   Retailer that distributes IBM computers
Source: ComputerLand Corporation.

1. Some facts adapted from "IBM's New Line Likely to Shake Up the Market for Personal Computers," *Wall Street Journal*, Aug. 13, 1981, p. 21.

Apple Computer has also shown its ability to adjust its distribution. For example, Apple made a mistake in selecting its target market when it originally planned to sell the Lisa directly to major corporations and to limit retail sales to a few dealers. When the corporate sales failed to develop, Apple cut the price of the Lisa and deleted some of its software. When the Lisa was made available through retail dealers, sales more than doubled.[2]

When Coleco introduced its $600 computer, complete with letter-quality printer, high-speed tape memory, and a built-in word-processing program, as well as video game capacity, the company used mass merchandise retailers, including Toys ℜ Us.[3] This distribution approach was taken to see if ordinary consumers would pay $600 for a home computer. As the computer industry becomes more competitive, even more innovative distribution channels will probably develop.

The selection of marketing channels is one of the most critical decisions in developing a marketing strategy. In this chapter, we first present the concepts used to describe and analyze marketing channels. We illustrate the main types of channels and discuss their structures. Then we justify the existence of intermediaries and explain the sorting activities of channel members. Next, we discuss the functions of intermediaries and facilitating agencies, as well as the intensity of market coverage and considerations affecting channel selection. Finally, we examine the behavioral dimensions of channels—including the concepts of cooperation and conflict.

IBM's decision to sell a personal computer through retail stores indicates a major change in the firm's marketing channels. This development helped IBM reach new target markets. Apple's ability to adjust the distribution of its Lisa computer to double sales indicates effective marketing channel management. Such effectiveness is also shown by Coleco's use of the mass marketing approach, with which it is familiar because of its toy and game products.

The nature of marketing channels

A *marketing channel,* or *channel of distribution,* is a group of interrelated intermediaries who direct products to customers. The marketing intermediary, or middleman, performs the kinds of activities described in Table 7.1. The activities are designed to move products from producers to consumers or industrial buyers. There are two major types of *marketing intermediaries*, merchants and agents. *Merchants* take title to merchandise and resell it, whereas *agents* and *brokers* receive a commission or fee for expediting exchanges.[4]

Both wholesalers and retailers are classified as intermediaries. They can be either merchants or agents. Agents and brokers do not take title to products, but they do negotiate transfer of ownership or possession of

2. Erik Larson and Carle Dolan, "Once All Alone in Field, Apple Computer Girds for Industry Shakeout," *Wall Street Journal,* Oct. 4, 1983, p. 31.
3. Peter D. Petre, "Mass Marketing the Computer," *Fortune,* Oct. 31, 1983, p. 65.
4. Ralph S. Alexander, *Marketing Definitions: A Glossary of Marketing Terms* (Chicago: American Marketing Association, 1960).

Table 7.1 Marketing channel activities performed by intermediaries

Category of Marketing Activities	Possible Activities Required
Marketing information	Analyze and interpret routinely collected information such as sales data; perform or commission marketing research studies
Marketing management	Establish objectives; plan activities; manage and coordinate financing, personnel, and risk-taking functions; evaluate and control channel activities
Facilitating exchange	Match the needs of buyers to production and sorting activities to provide meaningful product assortments
Promotion	Set promotional objectives, coordinate advertising, personal selling, sales promotion, publicity, and packaging
Price	Establish pricing policies; establish conditions and terms of sales
Physical distribution	Physical movement and inventory-holding activities, including transportation, warehousing, materials handling, inventory control, and communication

products. Agents and brokers perform fewer marketing activities than most merchants. In this chapter, all wholesalers should be considered merchants unless specifically designated as agents or brokers.

Channel members share certain significant characteristics. Each member has different responsibilities within the overall structure of the distribution system, but mutual profit and success can be attained only if channel members cooperate in delivering products to the market.

Although channel decisions need not precede other marketing decisions, they do exercise a powerful influence on the rest of the marketing mix. In addition, relationships among channel members (producers, wholesalers, and retailers) usually involve relatively long-term commitments.[5]

A major change in a firm's marketing channel can have a profound impact on sales. Ten years ago, U-Haul International, Inc. abandoned a thirty-year strategy of relying on commissioned dealerships (mainly service stations). It began to focus on a company-owned chain of moving centers that offered truck and trailer rentals as well as other services. U-Haul's commissioned dealership networks dropped from a peak of 14,000 in 1974 to 5,600 in 1981.[6] At the same time, Jartran Inc., founded by James A. Ryder in 1978, began using the service stations U-Haul had abandoned. Its sales increased very rapidly as it captured former U-Haul dealers. Now U-Haul has reversed its decision and is regaining its service stations and other independent dealers. It is, in general, shifting marketing efforts away from its own moving centers and back to commissioned dealers.[7]

5. Philip Kotler, *Marketing Management: Analysis, Planning and Control*, 5th ed. (Englewood Cliffs, N.J.: Prentice-Hall, 1984), p. 539.
6. "U-Haul: A Strategy Reversal Moves It Back to Gas Stations," *Business Week*, May 4, 1981, pp. 162–164.
7. Ibid.

Figure 7.2
Typical marketing
channels for consumer
products

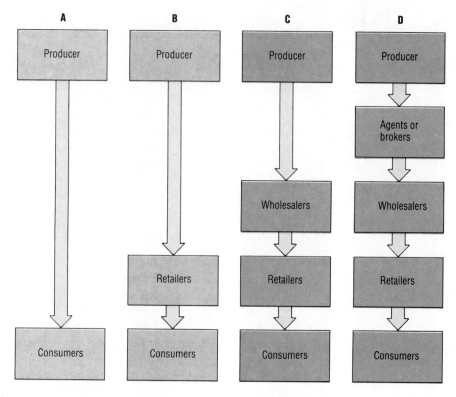

This example illustrates the importance of marketing channel decisions. In the future, U-Haul will continue to operate both moving centers and commissioned dealerships to maintain more than one marketing channel to reach its customers.

Availability benefits the total product. Marketing channel members make products available at the right time, in the right place, and in the right quantity by providing such product-enhancing functions as transportation and storage. Although consumers do not see the distribution of a product, they evaluate the availability that distribution makes possible. The U-Haul experience points out the need to make products available in the right place—that is, where customers go to rent equipment. In another example, Days Inns of America, Inc., made a location decision to build budget motels along interstate highways from the Northeast and the lower Ohio valley to Orlando, Florida, home of Walt Disney World. Today the eighteen Days Inn motels in Orlando are the largest provider of lodging in the area.[8] Now the company has a new distribution strategy designed to push development through the Sun Belt and the remaining parts of the North.

Types of channels

The marketing channel structure defines the arrangement and linkage of its members. Consumers may want—and organizations can design—almost any number of different distribution paths. (See the Application on page 213 for a description of two innovative distribution channels.) In any chan-

8. "Days Inns: Looking for a Berth in a Crowded National Field," *Business Week*, Oct. 31, 1983, p. 70.

Figure 7.3
Typical marketing
channels for industrial
products

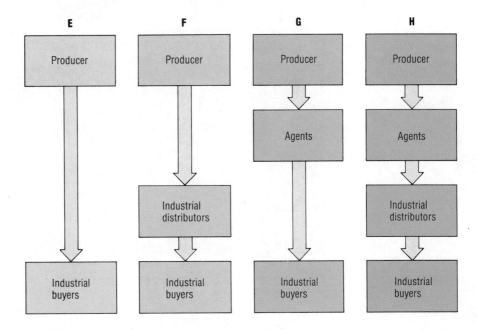

nel, however, the various links are the merchants (including producers) and agents who have managerial responsibility for a product as it moves through the channel.

Channels for consumer products

Several typical channels for consumer products are depicted in Figure 7.2. Channel A illustrates the direct movement of a product to consumers; there are no intermediaries. Farmers who sell small quantities of vegetables directly to consumers typify this channel. Likewise, producers who sell products directly to the factory provide a direct marketing channel to consumers.

Channel B—producer to retailers to consumers—is a common choice for products like automobiles. Using such a channel structure, large retailers like J. C. Penney and K mart sell many products such as stereos and tires, which they buy directly from producers.

Channel C—producer to wholesalers to retailers to consumers—is one of the most traditional channels. Typical products distributed on this basis include manufacturer-brand refrigerators, beer, and tobacco products.

Channel D—producer to agents to wholesalers to retailers to consumers—is typically used for products, like candy, that are distributed on an intensive basis. Candy often is sold to wholesalers by brokers or agents, who facilitate negotiations by bringing buyers and sellers together. Wholesalers then supply the product to retail stores, vending machines, and other outlets that sell to ultimate consumers.

Channels for industrial products

Figure 7.3 illustrates typical channels for industrial products. Products that are sold to large industrial buyers are often sold directly (Channel E). If the number of customers increases, then a direct distribution approach may not be effective. For example, Mitsubishi Aircraft International, Inc.,

MITSUBISHI'S NEW DIAMOND I BUSINESS JET. BECAUSE IN TODAY'S ECONOMY, YOU NEED AN AIRCRAFT THAT'S ALL BUSINESS.

Now, more than ever, the decision to upgrade to a new business jet is significant. The distance it can help put between you and your competition can be highly rewarding.

The business tool perfected for just this application is the new Mitsubishi Diamond I fan-jet. The business jet conceived, designed and built expressly for the way business is transacted today. Swiftly, economically, comfortably. The Diamond I performs very economically at speeds up to 500 mph. On missions of 1000 nautical miles or more, it's most economical. But in the area in which you work most — between 300 and 500 nautical miles, — its efficiency betters nearly every other business jet flying.

And it functions this way due to a host of state-of-the-art efficiencies built in. As in the sophisticated aerodynamics and high-speed swept wing, the low fuel burn engines and modular systems all working in concert to squeeze the most from the least.

Appreciating this, it comes as no surprise that the Diamond I offers its business travellers a most spacious, truly comfort-

able, handsomely appointed, C.E.O.-class cabin. One with ample room for seven to nine passengers to stretch out and get down to business. Room to relax without cramping a thing. And thanks to Mitsubishi's highly advanced airframe design and mechanics, the sound of the engines has been virtually engineered out of this very, very quiet workspace. So whispers can still keep confidential information confidential.

You owe it to yourself to investigate the Diamond I. Certainly one of the most efficient business tools you could hope to own. One that doesn't cost, but earns. One that's always ready to keep the distance between you and your competition considerable.

For further information, call our Product Information Line at *(214) 239-9275* today.

MITSUBISHI
QUALITY TAKES WING

For detailed information, write our Corporate Headquarters:
Mitsubishi Aircraft International, Inc., One Lincoln Centre, 5400 LBJ Freeway, Suite 1500, Dept. IJ13, Dallas, TX 75240. Tel. (214) 387-5600. TLX 73-2575
European Office: Holidaystraat 7, 1920 Diegem, Brussels, Belgium. Tel. 02-720 80 95. TLX 62189 MAI B
Regional Offices: Houston, Windsor Locks, Los Angeles. *District Offices:* Nationwide. *Distributors:* Worldwide

a Dallas-based subsidiary of Mitsubishi Heavy Industries, sells its Diamond I corporate fan jet (illustrated in Figure 7.4) direct to corporate buyers (Channel E). In contrast, when Mitsubishi decided to market industrial and construction products such as fork-lift trucks, it used industrial distributors—merchants who take title to products, as shown in Channel F—to reach this market.

Agents are appropriate in industrial channels when products are standardized and when selling functions and information gathering are important. For example, Channel G might be suitable for selling soybeans to animal food processors.

Channel H is used, for example, by export agents who sell electronic components from Japan to distributors serving small manufacturers or service dealers in the United States.

Since industrial purchasers use products to produce other products, retailers rarely appear in the industrial channel. (Industrial buyers may occasionally purchase products in retail stores, though.) However, if an in-

Application

A Florist and
a Veterinarian
Develop
Innovative
Distribution

Felly's Flowers and Ray and Deborah Craft's Petvacx mobile veterinary service have a basic operating principle in common. Both base their marketing strategy on offering customers convenience of access and availability.

Al Felly, a florist in Madison, Wisconsin, saw that there was an availability and access limitation for customers who want to send flowers via FTD—by far the country's largest long-distance flower delivery service. Felly has introduced a twenty-four-hour toll-free telephone number so that customers can place orders for flowers whenever they want. Before, customers had been restricted by the business hours of local FTD florists, through whom they had to order. The six stores in the Felly's Flowers chain sell $2.5 million worth of flowers per year, and Felly believes he can garner sales of $25 million with his toll-free number 1–800–FLORIST.

The Crafts, of Wheaton, Maryland, both veterinarians, decided to take veterinary care to the patients. Their customized van contains everything needed for routine pet care—they can perform blood tests, vaccinations, minor surgery, and other procedures that do not require general anesthesia. The Crafts make house calls and also set up shop in designated parking lots at preappointed times. Because they do not have to support the overhead of an actual clinic, the mobile vets' fees are only about 50 percent of what stationary vets' are. Customers thus benefit from both convenience and economy.

In their separate ways, Felly and the Crafts illustrate the successful use of marketing channel integration. Felly acts as a more available intermediary by making floral services available nationally twenty-four hours a day. The Crafts have developed an innovative distribution channel that brings their product closer to customers at a reduced cost.

Source: Based on Bill Abrams, "Mr. Felly Hopes People Dial Florist," *Wall Street Journal*, Jan. 20, 1983, p. 25; and Carol Dilks, "Business on the Move," *Nation's Business*, March 1984, pp. 66–68.

dustrial buyer uses the industrial product as a component of a consumer product, then a new marketing channel is created. The final product may pass through wholesalers and retailers on its way to consumers. More information on industrial marketing channels appears in Chapter 20.

Multiple marketing channels

Multiple marketing channels provide different intermediaries to direct products to customers. Consider the Application on page 216 which concerns the marketing channels needed for a simple product like rubber bands. Mitsubishi Corporation, Japan's biggest industrial, trading, and banking conglomerate, relies on multiple marketing channels to distribute its products in the United States. Figure 7.5 indicates a few of the many marketing channels for Mitsubishi products. For example, in a recent year Mitsubishi Motor Sales sold hundreds of thousands of automobiles to Chrysler Corporation for U.S. distribution through Chrysler dealers. These Mitsubishi products are marketed as the Dodge Colt, Plymouth Champ, Plymouth Sapporo, and Dodge Challenger. Recently, Mitsubishi began to develop its own U.S. dealership network to compete directly with Chrysler. Mitsubishi is developing the dual marketing channels for automobiles because Chrysler now has a full line of its own small cars and because the Mitsubishi dealerships will be protected if Chrysler does not focus its efforts on Mitsubishi products. The Mitsubishi Bank of California serves large U.S. industrial customers directly and has developed a twenty-three-

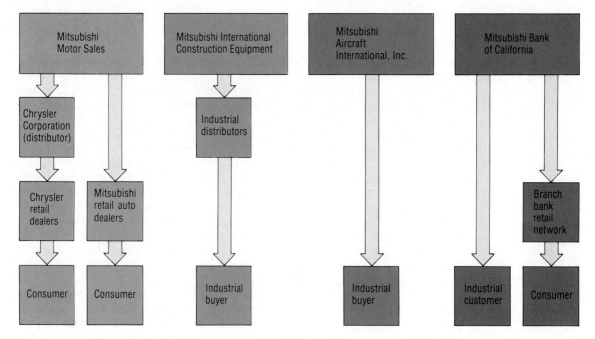

Figure 7.5 Marketing channels for selected Mitsubishi Corporation subsidiaries

branch retail network through acquisitions.[9] Other Mitsubishi products include Nikon cameras, Kirin beer, and the Bonaventure Hotel in Los Angeles. It should be obvious that with such diverse products, the firm must carefully structure its marketing channels to maximize availability of its products. Many firms use multiple marketing channels even if they each sell only a few products.

Justifications for intermediaries

Even if producers and buyers are located in the same city, there are costs associated with exchanges. If five buyers purchased the products of five producers, then twenty-five transactions could be needed for the buyers to obtain their products. If one intermediary serves both producers and buyers, the number of transactions could be reduced to ten, as shown in Figure 7.6.

The press, consumers, public officials, and other marketers freely criticize wholesalers in principle. The critics accuse wholesalers of being inefficient and parasitic. Since suggestions to eliminate them come from both ends of the marketing channel, wholesalers must be careful to perform only those marketing activities that are truly desirable.

Consumers often are obsessed with making the distribution channel as short as possible. They assume that the fewer the intermediaries, the lower the price. To survive, therefore, wholesalers must be more efficient and/or more service oriented than alternative marketing institutions.

Critics who suggest that eliminating wholesalers would result in lower prices for consumers do not recognize that eliminating wholesalers would not do away with the need for the services they provide. Other institutions

9. "Mitsubishi: A Japanese Giant Plans for Growth in the U.S.," *Business Week*, July 20, 1981, p. 128.

Figure 7.6
Efficiency in ex-
changes provided by
an intermediary

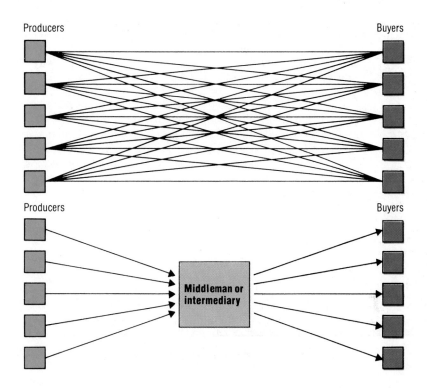

Producers   Buyers

Producers   Buyers

**Middleman or
intermediary**

would have to perform those services, and consumers would still have to
pay for them. In addition, all producers would have to deal directly with
retailers or consumers, meaning that every producer would have to keep
voluminous records and hire enough personnel to deal with every customer. Even in a direct channel, consumers might end up paying a great
deal more for products because prices would reflect the costs of inefficient
producers' operations.

To illustrate the efficient service that wholesalers provide in the market
system, assume that all wholesalers were eliminated. Since there are over
2.8 million retail stores, widely purchased consumer products—say candy—
would require an extraordinary number of sales contacts, possibly over a
million, to maintain the current level of product exposure. For example,
Mars, Inc. would have to deliver its candy, purchase and service thousands of vending machines, establish warehouses all over the country, and
maintain fleets of trucks. Selling and distribution costs for candy would
skyrocket. Instead of a few contacts with food brokers, large retail organizations, and various merchant wholesalers, candy manufacturers would
face thousands of expensive contacts with and shipments to small retailers.
Such an operation would be highly inefficient, and its costs would be
passed on to consumers. Candy bars would cost more, and they would be
harder to find. Wholesalers are more efficient and less expensive not only
for manufacturers, but also for consumers.

**Functions of
intermediaries**

Before we examine the functions of intermediaries, we should define some
key terms.

An *assortment* is a combination of similar or complementary products
put together to provide benefits to a specific market. The lack of consis-

Application

Marketing Channels for Rubber Bands

The distribution of most products reflects the unique nature of the products and their target markets. Consider the different marketing channels necessary for a simple product like rubber bands. Multiple marketing channels are needed because of variations in the size of orders and the end-use requirements. (See Figures 7.2 and 7.3.) The postal service is the largest U.S. purchaser of rubber bands and can be reached through Channel E. The newspaper industry uses the second-highest number of rubber bands, which go through Channel F. The rubber bands that you purchase in an office supply store may go through Channel C. Also, some buyers go through different distributors because of their desire to obtain red rubber bands, crepe rubber bands, pure gum rubber bands, or superior service. One avocado grower in California was in danger of losing a crop if he did not receive 3,000 pounds of rubber bands within one day. In this case, air-freighted rubber bands at a high cost were satisfactory.

Source: Based on Geraldine Brooks, "Here's a Trade War That May Stretch Your Imagination," *Wall Street Journal*, Sept. 9, 1983, pp. 1, 22.

tency or completeness in an assortment calls for sorting activities.[10] **Sorting activities** allow channel members to divide roles and separate tasks, including the roles of sorting out, accumulating, allocating, and assorting products (see Figure 7.7). Consider a supermarket. Meat, frozen vegetables, produce, canned goods, and dairy products come from different producers and require unique handling; therefore, the supermarket usually depends on different wholesalers for different kinds of supplies. If the supermarket itself attempted to perform the wholesaling function for these diverse products, its risks and investment would increase. Instead, the distribution network makes it possible to develop specialized mass production and yet satisfy the differentiated tastes of consumers.[11] To perform this function, as we have noted, intermediaries perform four main tasks: sorting out, accumulation, allocation, and assorting.

Sorting out

Sorting out is the first step in developing an assortment; it involves breaking down conglomerates of heterogeneous supplies into relatively homogeneous groups. The conglomerates of heterogeneous supplies are so diversified that they are unrelated to one another in functional structure or usefulness to ultimate buyers.

Sorting out is the primary step in marketing agricultural and extractive products. Grading eggs exemplifies the sorting process. It makes relatively homogeneous products available for the next step, accumulation.

Accumulation

Through **accumulation**, a bank or inventory is developed of homogeneous products that have similar production or demand requirements. It would be illogical, for example, to develop large inventories of both chain saws and packaged food products, because these products come from different manufacturers and usually are sold by different retailers. On the other

---

10. Wroe Alderson, *Marketing Behavior and Executive Action* (Homewood, Ill.: Irwin, 1957), p. 216.
11. Ibid., p. 217.

Figure 7.7
Sorting activities
conducted by
intermediaries

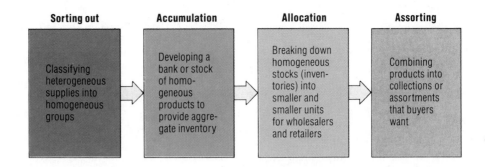

Sorting out	Accumulation	Allocation	Assorting
Classifying heterogeneous supplies into homogeneous groups	Developing a bank or stock of homogeneous products to provide aggregate inventory	Breaking down homogeneous stocks (inventories) into smaller and smaller units for wholesalers and retailers	Combining products into collections or assortments that buyers want

hand, all power tools manufactured by a company could be developed into an inventory so that the tools could be allocated to stores according to their customers' needs.

Allocation

Allocation is the breaking down of large homogeneous inventories into smaller lots. Wholesalers typically break down large lots and then apportion products to other channel members. Often, a wholesaler buys efficiently in truckload or carload lots and then divides products into case lots to sell in smaller quantities. Tobacco wholesalers, for example, provide the bulk-breaking service for competing tobacco companies, affix state tobacco tax stamps, and deliver an entire tobacco assortment to retailers.

Wholesalers serve as a depot and allocate products according to market demand. They supply products that meet consumers' needs. For example, retailers purchase collections of products from wholesalers; these collections contain competing brands so that retailers can develop suitable assortments for consumers.

Assorting

Assorting is combining products into collections or assortments that buyers want available at one place. Assorting thus combines products in ways that satisfy buyers, especially at the retail level. Retailers strive to create assortments that match the demands of consumers who patronize their stores. A convenience grocery, for example, is expected to have an assortment of fresh dairy products such as milk, butter, and cheese.

The number and kind of intermediaries in the marketing channel are influenced by the kinds of assortments desired by buyers and by the efficiency of channel arrangements. The assortment of products desired at one location usually relates to some task that buyers want to perform or some problem that they want solved.

Functions of facilitating agencies

The total marketing channel is more than a continuum from producer to intermediary to buyer. Figure 7.8 illustrates that *facilitating agencies*—transportation companies, insurance companies, advertising agencies, marketing research agencies, and financial institutions—may perform activities that enhance channel functions. Note, however, that any of the functions performed by these facilitating agencies may be taken over by regular marketing intermediaries in the marketing channel (wholesalers and retailers).

Also notice in Figure 7.8 that the basic difference between channel members and facilitating agencies is that members perform the negotiatory

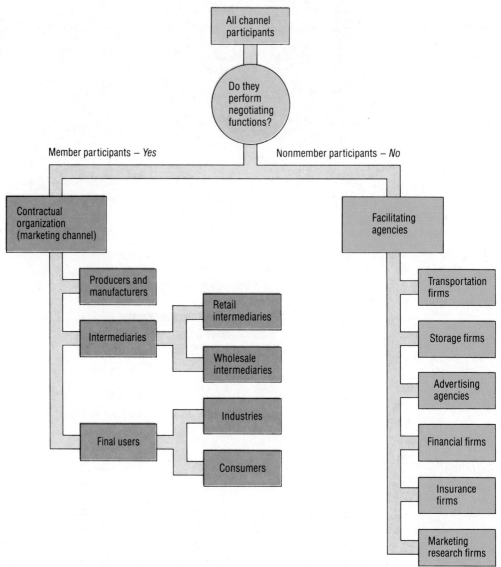

Figure 7.8   Classification of channel participants
Source: Marketing Channels: A Management View *by Bert Rosenbloom. Copyright © 1978 by the Dryden Press. Reprinted by permission of The Dryden Press, CBS College Publishing.*

functions (buying, selling, and transferring title), whereas facilitating agencies do not.[12] In other words, facilitating agencies, participants who do not engage in negotiation, assist in the operation of the channel but do not sell products. The channel manager may view the facilitating agency as a subcontractor to whom various distribution tasks can be "farmed out" on the principle of specialization and division of labor.[13] Channel members (pro-

12. Bert Rosenbloom, *Marketing Channels: A Management View* (Hinsdale, Ill.: Dryden Press, 1978), p. 21.
13. Ibid.

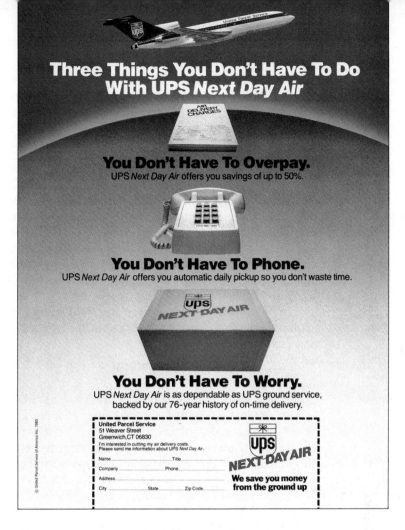

ducers, wholesalers, or retailers) may rely on facilitating agencies because they believe that these independent businesses will perform various activities more efficiently and more effectively than they themselves could.

Marketing research agencies, financial institutions, insurance companies, warehouses, and transportation companies perform essential services that add value and develop benefits that buyers want. Facilitating agencies are functional specialists performing special tasks for channel members without getting involved in directing or controlling channel decisions. They have no control over the path that products take as they move from producers to buyers.

Many people fail to recognize the value added by major channel members and facilitating agencies. Developing assortments of products when and where buyers want them creates important product benefits. Buyers must pay for the labor, energy, and other resources needed to perform this task. Although intermediaries can be eliminated, an enterprise cannot dispense with the activities they perform. Figure 7.9 illustrates the transportation services offered by United Parcel Service, which acts as a facilitating agency providing not only transportation services, but also assistance in communication and inventory control.

Channel functions may be passed on to buyers, or producers may perform the activities themselves instead of passing them on to other channel members. The next section examines how channel members can either combine and control most activities or pass them on to another intermediary. Remember, though, that the channel member cannot eliminate functions. No channel functions disappear when wholesalers, for example are eliminated.

Channel integration

Many marketing channels are determined by consensus. Producers, facilitating agencies, and intermediaries coordinate their efforts for mutual benefit. Some marketing channels, however, are organized and controlled by a single leader, who could be a producer, a wholesaler, or a retailer.[14] The channel leader may establish channel policies and coordinate the development of the marketing mix. Sears, for example, is a channel leader for some of the many products that it sells.

The various links or stages of the channel may be combined under the management of a channel leader either horizontally or vertically. Integration may stabilize supply, reduce costs, and increase coordination of channel members.[15]

Vertical channel integration

Combining two or more stages of the channel under one management is *vertical channel integration*. One member of a marketing channel may purchase the operations of another member, or it may simply take over the functions that member performed. This integration eliminates the need for an intermediary. For example, a large mass merchandiser, such as a discount house, may store and transport products purchased from the producer and eliminate the need for a wholesaler. Total vertical integration would include control of all functions from production to the final buyer. Some oil companies typify this kind of integration in that they own oil wells, transportation facilities, refineries, and terminals that sell direct to retailers.

Integration has proved successful in professionally managed and centrally controlled marketing channels called *vertical marketing systems* (VMS).[16] The corporate VMS combines successive channel stages from production to consumers under one ownership. Figure 7.10 illustrates a shift from the conventional channel to a vertical marketing system.

In an administered VMS, informal coordination brings about a high level of interorganizational management. Decision making takes into account the goals of the system, but authority still remains with individual channel members—as it does in conventional marketing channels (review Figure 7.2 and Figure 7.3). Examples of administered marketing channels

14. George Fisk, *Marketing Systems: An Introductory Analysis* (New York: Harper & Row, 1967), p. 226.
15. Frederick D. Sturdivant, "Determinants of Vertical Integration in Channel Systems," in *Science, Technology, and Marketing,* ed. Raymond M. Haas (Chicago: American Marketing Association, 1966), pp. 472–479.
16. Bert C. McCammon, Jr., "Perspectives for Distribution Programming," in *Vertical Marketing Systems,* ed. Louis P. Bucklin (Glenview, Ill.: Scott, Foresman, 1970), p. 43.

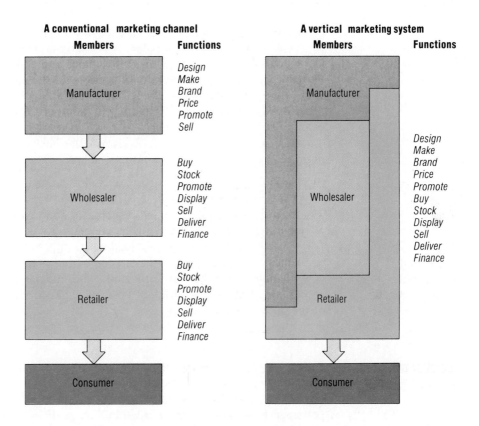

A conventional marketing channel

Members | **Functions**

Manufacturer
Design
Make
Brand
Price
Promote
Sell

Wholesaler
Buy
Stock
Promote
Display
Sell
Deliver
Finance

Retailer
Buy
Stock
Promote
Display
Sell
Deliver
Finance

Consumer

A vertical marketing system

Members | **Functions**

Manufacturer

Wholesaler

Retailer

Design
Make
Brand
Price
Promote
Buy
Stock
Display
Sell
Deliver
Finance

Consumer

Figure 7.10 Comparison of a conventional marketing channel and a vertical marketing system   *Source: Strategic Marketing, by David J. Kollat, Roger D. Blackwell, and James F. Robeson. Copyright © 1972 by Holt, Rinehart and Winston, Inc. Reprinted by permission of Holt, Rinehart and Winston, CBS College Publishing.*

include Sears (retailer), Kellogg (cereal), and Magnavox (television and other electronic products).

Under a contractual VMS, interorganizational relationships are formalized through contracts or other legal agreements. This arrangement is best illustrated by franchise organizations like McDonald's and Kentucky Fried Chicken. Several stages are linked together by legal agreements concerning the rights and obligations of channel members. (Franchisers are discussed in Chapter 9.) Most vertical marketing systems are organized with the objective of improving distribution by combining individual efforts.

Horizontal channel integration

Combining institutions at the same level of operation under one management constitutes ***horizontal channel integration***. Store chains such as Dayton-Hudson Corporation illustrate horizontal integration at the retail level. Dayton-Hudson, one of the nation's largest retailers, has moved horizontally by expanding from a regional department store chain (Hudson's, Dayton's, Diamond's, John A. Brown) into Target discount stores and B. Dalton bookstores. More recently, Dayton-Hudson has been opening off-price (brand-name merchandise at discount prices) fashion outlets. Dayton-Hudson is expanding at the same level in a retailing channel.[17]

Horizontal integration allows efficiencies and economies of scale in advertising, marketing research, purchasing, and the employment of specialists. An organization can effect horizontal integration by merging with other organizations or by expanding the number of units (retail stores, for example) at one channel level.

Horizontal integration is not always the best managerial approach to improving distribution. Its limitations include

1. Difficulties in coordinating an expanded number of units
2. A decrease in flexibility
3. An increase in planning and research to cope with larger-scale operations and more heterogeneous markets

Unless the organization that is combining units can perform the specific channel activities more efficiently than independent stores can, horizontal integration will not reduce costs or enhance the competitive position of the organization.

Intensity of market coverage

Characteristics of the target market and product characteristics determine the kind of coverage a product should get—that is, the number and kinds of outlets in which it is sold. To achieve the desired intensity of market coverage, distribution must correspond to the behavior patterns of buyers. Chapter 5 divided consumer products into three categories—convenience products, shopping products, and specialty products. A specific product is classified according to how consumers make purchases. Consumers view products in terms of replacement rate, product adjustment (services), duration of consumption, searching time to find the product, and similar factors.[18] These variables directly affect the intensity of market coverage.

Three major levels of market coverage are intensive, selective, and exclusive distribution. *Intensive distribution* is a form of market coverage in which all available outlets are used for distributing a product. In *selective distribution,* only some available outlets in an area are chosen to distribute a product. *Exclusive distribution* is a type of market coverage in which only one outlet is used in a relatively large geographic area.

Intensive distribution

Intensive distribution is appropriate for convenience products such as bread, chewing gum, beer, and newspapers. To consumers, availability means a nearby store location as well as a minimum of searching time for the product at the store. Sales may have a direct relationship to availability. The successful sale of bread and milk at service stations or of gasoline at convenience grocery stores has shown that the availability of these

17. John Curley and Lawrence Ingrassia, "Big Retailer Seeks Profits in Discounting," *Wall Street Journal,* Oct. 26, 1982, p. 29.
18. Leo Aspinwall, "The Marketing Characteristics of Goods," in *Four Marketing Theories* (Boulder: University of Colorado Press, 1961), pp. 27–32.

products is more important than the nature of the outlet. Convenience products have a high replacement rate and require almost no service. To meet these demands, intensive distribution is necessary, and multiple channels may be used to sell through all possible outlets.

Intensive distribution is one of the key strengths of Procter & Gamble. It is fairly easy for this company to formulate marketing strategies for many of its products, in all types of food and convenience stores, since consumers desire availability that is provided quickly on an intensive basis. Under such conditions, a new product line can be available to almost every consumer in a very short time. For example, Citrus Hill orange juice, in both frozen concentrate and chilled, ready-to-serve form, was launched nationally after only one year of testing in Indiana. Desired market coverage was possible because Procter & Gamble already had an intensive distribution system in place.[19]

Selective distribution
Selective distribution is appropriate when consumers shop around for products. Durable goods such as typewriters and stereos usually fall in this category. Such products are more expensive than convenience goods. Consumers are willing to spend greater searching time visiting several retail outlets to compare prices, designs, styles, and other features.

Selective distribution is desirable when a special effort—such as customer service from a channel member—is important. Many industrial products are sold on a selective basis to maintain a certain degree of control over the distribution process. For example, herbicides (chemicals that kill weeds) are distributed to farmers on a selective basis because dealers must offer services to buyers, such as instructions about how to apply the herbicides safely.

Exclusive distribution
Exclusive distribution is suitable for products that are purchased rather infrequently, that are consumed over a long period of time, or that require service or information to fit them to buyers' needs. Exclusive distribution is used often as an incentive to sellers when only a limited market is available for products. The Trojan Yacht in Figure 7.11 is an example of a product that is distributed very exclusively. Purchasers of this product may travel thousands of miles for an inspection and trial run.

Behavior of channel members
The marketing channel is a social system with patterned and recurrent behavior. Each channel member has a position with rights, responsibilities, rewards, and sanctions for nonconformity. In addition, each channel member has certain expectations of every other channel member. Retailers expect wholesalers to maintain adequate inventories and to provide on-time deliveries. Wholesalers expect retailers to honor payment agreements and to keep them informed about inventory levels. For the channel to function as a social system, role differentiation must result in a division of labor.

19. "P&G Dives into Orange Juice with a Big Splash," *Business Week,* Oct. 31, 1983, p. 50.

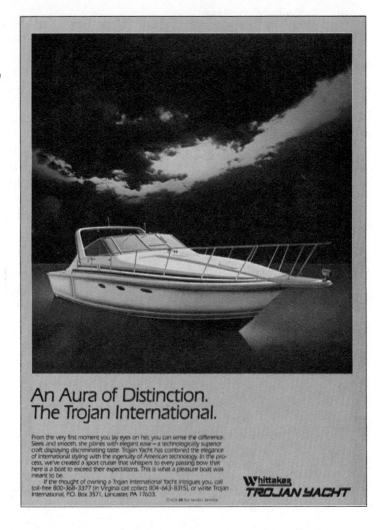

An Aura of Distinction.
The Trojan International.

From the very first moment you lay eyes on her, you can sense the difference. Sleek and smooth, she planes with elegant ease—a technologically superior craft displaying discriminating taste. Trojan Yacht has combined the elegance of International styling with the ingenuity of American technology. In the process, we've created a sport cruiser that whispers to every passing bow that here is a boat to exceed their expectations. This is what a pleasure boat was meant to be.

If the thought of owning a Trojan International Yacht intrigues you, call toll-free 800-368-3377 (in Virginia call collect 804-643-8315), or write Trojan International, P.O. Box 3571, Lancaster, PA 17603.

Whittaker
TROJAN YACHT

Channel cooperation   *Channel cooperation* is required if each channel member expects to gain something from other members.[20] It is necessary for the attainment of overall channel goals and individual member goals. Unless a channel member can be replaced, the failure of one link in the chain could destroy the channel. This vulnerability means that policies must be developed to ensure the welfare and survival of all necessary channel members.

An example of channel cooperation would be licensing a product to open up new markets. Miller Brewing licensed Carling O'Keefe, Ltd., Canada's fastest-growing brewer, to brew and market Miller beer products. It was estimated that Miller accounted for 9 percent of Canadian consumption after just four months on the market. Since Canada restricts the importation of beer, the licensing agreement was the best way to enter this market, and Carling O'Keefe was able to dramatically increase its market share.[21]

20. Wroe Alderson, *Dynamic Marketing Behavior* (Homewood, Ill.: Irwin, 1965), p. 239.
21. John J. Cunon, "Beer Stocks With Yeasty Promise," *Fortune*, Oct. 17, 1983, p. 180.

Channel conflict   Since roles are the means of integration and coordination, role deviance or malfunction is a major source of *channel conflict*. Each role in the channel represents an expected mode of conduct and defines the contribution of that unit in the system.[22] For example, wholesalers expect producers to take care of quality control and production scheduling, and they expect retailers to merchandise products effectively. It is the responsibility of wholesalers, in turn, to conform to the expectations of both retailers and producers by providing coordination, functional services, and communication. If wholesalers or producers failed to deliver products on time, that would constitute channel conflict. A common conflict develops when producers attempt to bypass an intermediary to gain efficiency. Conflicts also develop when dealers decide to place too much emphasis on competing product lines.

Adolph Coors Company has attempted to control both the number of distributors that sell its beer and the territories those distributors can serve. To maintain its proper taste, Coors beer must be refrigerated at all times. Coors believes that unless it exerts tight control over distribution some beer might be shipped without refrigeration. Channel conflict developed when Coors beer was being sold in Missouri before the brewer had selected its own distributors.[23] The Missouri shipments were shipped by a distributor that seemed to be more interested in expanding sales than in cooperating with the brewer to maintain quality control. Coors expressed unhappiness publicly at the unauthorized shipping and encouraged consumers to boycott its product until proper distribution could be assured.[24]

The following statement summarizes one approach to decreasing conflict and increasing cooperation in marketing channels.

Two conditions are necessary to minimize and contain conflict and increase cooperation among channel members. First, the role of each channel member has to be specified. In reality, role specification is a specification of performance expectation from each channel member for the functions he performs. Role specification enhances the ability of channel members to predict one another's behaviors. Therefore, role specification, clarification, and agreement enhance the potential of cooperation in channel relations. Role ambiguity and disagreement enhance the potential of conflict among channel members. Second, certain measures of channel coordination have to be undertaken. Coordination in an interorganizational setting requires leadership and the exercise of control. Control is a two-edge sword. If exercised benevolently, it enhances channel member cooperation. Otherwise, it may fuel conflict among the channel members.[25]

22. Louis W. Stern and Ronald H. Gorman, "Conflict in Distribution Channels: An Exploration," in *Distribution Channels: Behavioral Dimensions,* ed. Louis W. Stern (Boston: Houghton Mifflin, 1969), p. 157.
23. Robert E. Weigand, "Policing the Marketing Channel—It May Get Easier," in *Contemporary Issues in Marketing Channels,* ed. Robert F. Lusch and Paul H. Zinszer (Norman, Okla.: University of Oklahoma Press, 1979), pp. 105–109.
24. Ibid., p. 105.
25. Adel I. El-Ansary, "Perspectives on Channel System Performance," in *Contemporary Issues in Marketing Channels,* ed. Robert F. Lusch and Paul H. Zinszer (Norman, Okla.: University of Oklahoma Press, 1979), p. 50.

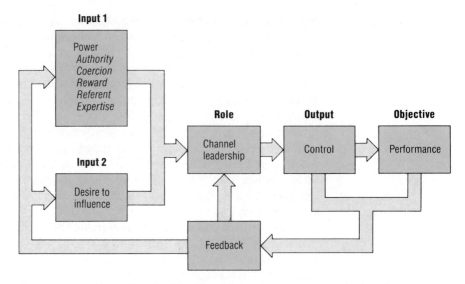

Figure 7.12 Channel leadership: Exercising power to attain desired performance
Source: Adapted from Robert Robicheaux, "Control in a Distribution Channel: A Field Study," Ph.D. Dissertation, Louisiana State University, Baton Rouge, La., 1974.

Channel leadership

One important role usually found in marketing channels is ***channel leadership***. Figure 7.12 illustrates that different power bases may be used to achieve desired objectives.[26] These power bases include authority, coercion, rewards, referents (reference groups or organizations that channel members try to please), and expertise about products, markets, or technology. ***Channel power*** relates to the ability of one channel member to influence the goal achievement of another channel member. Sears, for example, is the central power in the marketing of its private-label power tools, paints, tires, motor oil, batteries, and appliances. In this case, Sears exercises two types of power (see Figure 7.12). First, it provides the profit reward to producers that supply power tools, paint, tires, motor oil, and appliances. Second, it gains power from its marketing expertise. Many of the producers depend on Sears to perform all marketing activities. Note, too, in Figure 7.12 that to assume leadership a channel member must desire to influence and control overall channel performance.

Several conditions are necessary for the emergence of channel leadership. A channel member has to command a comfortable margin of power over other channel members with regard to issues of channel relations, e.g., price, discount structure, and promotional expenditures. Next, this channel member has to have the desire to influence the behavior of other channel members and actually use this power. Finally, other channel members have to tolerate the use of power to achieve control. Channel members' tolerance of control depends to a large extent on their satisfaction with

26. Robert Robicheaux, "Control in a Distribution Channel: A Field Study," Ph.D. dissertation, Louisiana State University, 1974.

their own power position and the payoff or rewards they reap as a result of improved channel performance. In other words, control will be tolerated only if benefits of such control are understood, realized, and shared equitably by the channel members involved.[27]

The following examples illustrate that retailers, producers, or wholesalers can assume the leadership role.

K mart, J. C. Penney, and Sears base their channel leadership on wide public exposure and on consumer confidence in their products. These retailers control many brands and sometimes replace uncooperative producers.

Manufacturers can also exert leadership. Consumer acceptance of Tide, Bold, Cheer, Gain, and other Procter & Gamble detergents allows that manufacturer to structure channel policy and exert considerable control over how retailers make these products available. Many stores allocate the most desirable positions on display shelves to Procter & Gamble products. This producer is in a good position to offer promotional assistance and expert knowledge about markets.

Independent Grocers' Alliance (IGA) is one of the best-known wholesaler-leaders in the United States. Wholesaler-leaders such as IGA provide independent business owners with marketing assistance regarding advertising, pricing, and purchasing. IGA's exercise of power is based on expert knowledge.

Summary

A marketing channel is a group of interrelated intermediaries, including wholesalers and retailers, who direct products to customers. Channel members perform functions necessary to move products from producers to customers, and the channel structure delineates the arrangement of members according to their responsibilities in the distribution process. Most firms have dual or multiple channels that adjust the distribution system to various target markets.

Basic functions of intermediaries include sorting out, accumulating, allocating, and assorting for buyers. The number and characteristics of intermediaries are determined by the assortments required and by the expertise needed to perform distribution activities. Although intermediaries can be eliminated, the functions they perform are essential in developing product assortments. These activities must either be performed by someone in the marketing channel or be passed on to customers.

Integration of marketing channels brings various activities under the management of one channel member. Vertical integration combines two or more stages of the channel under one management. Horizontal integration combines institutions at the same level of operation under a single management. The vertical marketing system is managed centrally and is controlled for the mutual benefit of all channel members.

Channel management concerns product exposure and channel leadership in the division of functional tasks. Intensive distribution strives to

27. El-Ansary, "Perspectives on Channel System Performance," p. 50.

make a product available to all possible dealers. Selective distribution screens dealers to select those most qualified to properly expose a product. Exclusive distribution usually gives one dealer exclusive rights to sell a product in a large geographic area.

A marketing channel is a structured behavioral system with an overall goal that links individuals and organizations. The positions of channel members are associated with rights, responsibilities, and rewards for cooperation. The ability of one channel member to facilitate or hinder attainment of other members' goals indicates its channel power. Power can be based on authority, coercion, rewards, referents, or expertise. Role deviance and competition for rewards can lead to channel conflict.

Channel leaders exert power over other channel members. Retailers gain channel control through consumer confidence, wide product mixes, and intimate knowledge of consumers. Producers are in an excellent position to structure channel policy and to use technical expertise and consumer acceptance to influence other channel members. Wholesalers become channel leaders when they take command and coordinate functions to match supply with demand.

Important terms

Marketing channel
Channel of distribution
Marketing intermediaries
Merchants
Agents and brokers
Assortment
Sorting activities
Sorting out
Accumulation
Allocation
Assorting

Facilitating agencies
Vertical channel integration
Vertical marketing systems
Horizontal channel integration
Intensive distribution
Selective distribution
Exclusive distribution
Channel cooperation
Channel conflict
Channel leadership
Channel power

Discussion and review questions

1. Why do consumers often blame intermediaries for inefficiencies in distribution?
2. When does an organization need multiple channels?
3. "Shorter channels are usually a more direct means of distribution and therefore are more efficient." Comment on this statement.
4. How does the number of intermediaries in the channel relate to the assortments needed by retailers?
5. Can one channel member perform all channel functions?
6. What are the major distinctions between intermediaries and facilitating agencies? Do these units perform different channel functions?
7. Name and describe firms that use (a) vertical integration and (b) horizontal integration in their marketing channels.
8. How does the vertical marketing system (VMS) differ from the traditional marketing channel?
9. Explain the differences among intensive, selective, and exclusive methods of distribution.

10. "Channel cooperation requires that members support the overall channel goals in order to achieve individual goals." Comment on this statement.

11. How do power bases within the channel influence the selection of the channel leader?

Cases

Case 7.1

Developing Marketing Channels for AMF Voit Flying Discs[28]

For over fifty years, AMF Voit, Inc.—the world's largest manufacturer of inflated balls—has made recreational products that have been used by millions of people. W. J. Voit founded the company in 1921 as a small business in a suburb of Los Angeles, California. In 1957, the company became a subsidiary of American Machine & Foundry Company as part of its leisure products group. Product lines include inflated balls; exercise, track and field, court sports, and water sports equipment; institutional products; and sport discs.

AMF Voit entered the flying disc market after research and investigation revealed much potential for growth. Disc throwing has emerged as one of the fastest growing sports in the world. It is estimated that over 20 million people will play with flying discs by the end of 1985.

Wham-O Manufacturing Co., makers of the Frisbee brand discs, have nearly an 80 percent market share. AMF Voit is challenging Wham-O Manufacturing Co., with a new line of technically advanced discs that covers all major product applications. AMF Voit's patented two-piece disc represents the latest in design and is especially adaptable to freestyle maneuvers. The one-piece product line includes a model for every sports event in the competitive arena. AMF Voit hopes to capitalize on its reputation for quality and on the unique design of its discs.

Disc sports have become very competitive throughout the world. Since the 1960s, over twelve competitive sports have been adapted to fit disc capabilities. Some of these sports are Double Disc Court, Ultimate, Guts, Disc Golf and Freestyle, which are played in 14 countries. Disc sports do not directly complete with seasonal sports, and tournaments are held throughout the year. Annually, the Pasadena Rose Bowl is filled to capacity as network television covers World Championship and Freestyle competitions which include the popular dog competitions.

The majority of disc sales occurs during early spring and fall when the college student market is targeted. During summer, the resort- and beachgoer segments have the greatest volume in sales.

Disc users fit into four basic categories. The pro and champion players are the elite of the disc world; they approximate 1,000 players who own an average of over a hundred discs each and travel over 5,000 miles a year for tournaments. These players are looking for better products all the time,

28. Many of the facts in this case are from the 1982 AMF Voit Fact Sheet on Flying Disc Marketing.

and new games, techniques, and trends start with them. The weekend players number over a million, own an average of fifteen to fifty discs each, and play three to five times per week. They attend all local and regional tournaments. The next group consists of the average players, who are typically high school and college students. These players number over 3 million and they own an average of four to ten discs each, play twice a week, and attend local tournaments. This group is aware of top quality discs and the differences in performance. The fourth category consists of the general public, who are recreational, Sunday afternoon, and novice players. They number over 14 million and each own one to three discs. They play one to three times per month.

The primary target customers for the AMF Voit discs are active users within the United States who have technical knowledge about discs. These customers understand the innovations designed into the AMF Voit disc product line, and they have demonstrated a willingness to buy. They own many discs for many different uses and are continually searching for new and better products. By establishing substantial consumer preference in this key group, AMF hopes to gain the endorsement and crucial word-of-mouth promotion that is needed to sell the product to the secondary market—the recreational and novice disc throwers in the 16- to 25-year-old age category.

Wham-O Manufacturing Co. distributes its Frisbee disc nationally through toy stores, mass merchants, and large sporting goods stores. AMF Voit's goal for its Sport Disc line is to establish nationwide distribution through various channels and gain dealer and player acceptance.

Questions for discussion

1. What marketing channels should AMF Voit use to reach each of the four categories of disc users? Specify the type of intermediaries.
2. Should AMF Voit use intensive, selective, or exclusive distribution or a combination of distribution approaches?
3. Why are marketing channels so important for AMF Voit in selling sports discs?

Case 7.2

Distribution of Ralston Purina Company's Diverse Products[29]

Ralston Purina Company, founded in 1894, began as a small animal feed business in St. Louis. Today, it is the world's largest producer of dry dog foods, dry and soft-moist cat foods, and commercial feeds for livestock and poultry. It is a major producer of soybean meal and oil, and it also operates fast-service restaurants. The company's product lines fall into four categories: Grocery Products, Agricultural Products, Restaurants, and Diversified Businesses. Approximately 56,000 employees around the world produce the many products that bear the famous red and white checkerboard

29. Many of the facts in this case are based on the Ralston Purina Company *1983 Annual Report.*

Figure 7.13
Ralston Purina's
diverse products
*Source: 1983 Ralston
Purina Company Annual
Report*

design, the company's principal trademark since 1900. Figure 7.13 shows the diversity of new products that Ralston Purina is responsible for producing.

As Table 7.2 indicates, pet foods account for approximately two-thirds of total grocery sales. They include the Purina Dog Chow®, Chuck Wagon®, Butcher's Blend®, Purina Cat Chow®, Tender Vittles®, and Happy Cat® brands. Grocery products are marketed primarily in the United States through direct sales forces to grocery chains and other customers. The principal competitors are national and regional manufacturers whose products compete with those of the company for shelf space and consumer acceptance. Another product within the grocery category is Chicken of the Sea® tuna. This product is sold primarily in the United States to grocery stores through a network of independent food brokers.

In the Agricultural Products category are primarily Purina Chow® formula feeds manufactured in 126 plants worldwide. Other agricultural products are soybean meal and oil, poultry products, animal health products,

Table 7.2 Sales to unaffiliated customers by major product line[a]

	1983	1982	1981
Grocery Products			
Pet Foods	$1,293.5	$1,279.0	$1,220.4
Sea Foods	270.4	290.3	388.3
Cereals	233.4	222.9	210.6
Other	64.5	74.1	82.5
Agricultural Products			
Animal and Poultry Feeds	$1,678.0	$1,698.3	$1,969.2
Soybean Meal and Oil	279.4	258.7	327.2
Other	147.0	138.3	165.9
Restaurants			
Fast Service	531.7	490.2	455.4
Dinner Houses	137.6	133.9	122.9
Diversified Businesses			
Soy Protein Products	144.3	132.4	113.5
Other	92.6	84.5	90.5
Total	$4,872.4	$4,802.6	$5,146.4

[a]Dollars in millions.

Source: *1983 Ralston Purina Company Annual Report*, p. 22.

grain merchandising, and breeding hogs. Feed products are distributed primarily through a network of approximately 6,000 independent dealers domestically, and more than 3,200 outside the United States. The company competes with other large feed manufacturers, cooperatives, and single-owner establishments and with government feed companies in international markets.

In the Restaurant category, Ralston Purina's subsidiary, Foodmaker, Inc., operates Jack-in-the-Box fast service restaurants, offering hamburgers, chicken sandwiches, shrimp salads, tacos, French fries, steak dinners, and crescent breakfasts. Located primarily in the Western and Southwestern United States, the 774 Jack-in-the-Box units provide drive-through and inside-seating service. The company competes with other national/regional chains and local individually owned and operated restaurants offering low and medium-priced food. (The company recently sold its specialty dinner houses.)

The Diversified Businesses category consists primarily of food protein and industrial polymer products. Also included is Ralston Purina's Keystone Resort and Food Enterprise division which manufactures products for the food service industry.

It should be obvious that Ralston Purina has many marketing channels for its grocery products, agricultural products, restaurants and diversified businesses. Making decisions about the best way to distribute products is extremely important to Ralston Purina.

1. Why does Ralston Purina use a direct sales force to sell grocery products to grocery chains and a network of independent dealers to sell agricultural products?
2. Why do you think that Jack-in-the-Box restaurants operate primarily in the West and Southwest? How does this fact relate to a marketing channel decision?
3. Why are there different marketing channels for Purina's pet foods and its Chicken of the Sea tuna?

8

Wholesaling

Objectives

To understand the nature of wholesaling in the marketing channel.

To learn about the activities of wholesalers.

To understand how wholesalers are classified.

To examine organizations that facilitate wholesaling.

To explore changing patterns in wholesaling.

Certified Grocers of California Limited is the nation's second largest cooperative wholesaler, supplying over 2,000 supermarkets concentrated in southern California but extending north to San Francisco, east to Nevada and Arizona, and west to Hawaii and the South Pacific. (Figure 8.1 shows a Certified Grocers warehouse.) Certified Grocers maintains diversification through their grocery division, frozen foods division, meat division, produce distribution center, creamery, central bakery, specialty foods line, and nonfoods line. The nonfood category includes health and beauty aids, automotive products, beverage glassware, Hispanic cooking ware, stationery, office supplies, toys, brooms and mops, and glass bakeware. Certified has long been recognized as a paragon of wholesaling efficiency; it delivers goods at sharply competitive prices while providing a diversity of products. Certified offers independents everything from retail counseling to store development. Through its store development department, it assists independents in obtaining new locations, acquiring former chain locations, and expanding existing locations. For retailers in the market for new equipment, the financing and leasing department of Certified offers loans of up to $1 million, with only 10 percent down. Certified also offers on a regular basis seminars and specialized educational programs designed to help members with their own retail employee training programs.[1]

Figure 8.1   Photo of a Certified Grocers Warehouse
Source: Certified Grocers of California Ltd.

1. "Certified Grocers of California Turns Up the Power," *Progressive Grocer*, Sept. 1983, pp. 31–64.

These examples illustrate successful wholesaling activities in the grocery industry. In this chapter, wholesaling is viewed as all exchange activities among organizations and individuals except for transactions with ultimate consumers. We will first examine the importance of wholesaling and list activities performed by wholesalers. Next, we will discuss the activities and role of wholesalers in the marketing channel. Then we will classify various types of wholesalers and, finally, explore changing patterns in wholesaling.

This chapter focuses on wholesaling and is not restricted to a description of wholesalers. Although wholesalers can be considered an established part of the marketing channel, their activities can be performed by any channel member. Chapter 7 described the structure and function of the marketing channel. This chapter describes and analyzes wholesaling activities within a marketing channel.

The nature and importance of wholesaling

Wholesaling includes all marketing transactions in which purchases are intended for resale or are used in making other products.[2] It does not include exchanges with ultimate consumers. Wholesaling establishments are engaged primarily in selling products directly to industrial, reseller, and institutional users, including other wholesalers who act as intermediaries in buying products for, or selling products to, other middlemen.

One simple way to determine whether a transaction is retail or wholesale is to see whether it requires a retail sales tax, which is levied on sales to ultimate consumers. (However, certain products in some states are not subject to a retail sales tax.) Usually, the end user of a product has to pay a sales tax. A split-function establishment that sells both wholesale and retail must determine what type of buyer is purchasing a product. Businesses that sell to ultimate consumers have a legal obligation to obtain a retail business license and to collect retail sales taxes. The definition may sometimes be blurred, but legitimate wholesalers who are selling finished products do not charge a retail sales tax, even though they may be subject to other taxes. The reason is that sales taxes are usually charged to the ultimate users of the finished product.

There are over 382,837 wholesaling establishments in the United States.[3] Wholesale sales increased from $144 billion in 1960 to $1,176 billion in 1981, a 716-percent increase. Retail sales, in comparison, rose from $216 billion in 1960 to $1,044 billion in 1981, a 383-percent increase.[4]

While there are over 1.2 million retail establishments, they have significantly lower sales volume than the wholesale establishments because all wholesalers' transactions are measured—including multiple transactions. Multiple transactions include all exchanges of a product as it moves from the producer through all intermediaries, including wholesalers and retailers. In recent years, wholesalers have maintained greater increases in sales and profits than have retail chain stores.[5]

2. Theodore N. Beckman, William R. Davidson, and W. Wayne Talarzyk, *Marketing*, 9th ed. (New York: Ronald Press, 1973), pp. 286–291.
3. *Statistical Abstract of the United States, 1984,* pp. 802, 808.
4. *Statistical Abstract of the United States, 1982–1983,* p. 530.
5. Walter H. Heller, "Business Outlook," *Progressive Grocer,* June 1983, p. 17.

Table 8.1 Major wholesaling activities

Activity	Description
Wholesale management	Planning, organizing, staffing, and controlling the institution's operations
Planning and negotiating supplies	Serving as the purchasing agent for customers by negotiating supplies
Promoting	Providing an outside (field) sales force and inside sales, advertising, sales promotion, and publicity
Warehousing and product handling	Receiving, storing and stockkeeping, order processing, packaging, shipping outgoing orders, and materials handling
Transportation	Arranging local delivery and long-distance shipments
Inventory control and data processing	Controlling physical inventory, bookkeeping, recording transactions, keeping records for financial analysis
Security	Safeguarding and protecting merchandise
Pricing	Developing prices and price quotations on the basis of value added
Financing and budgeting	Extending credit, borrowing, making capital investments, and forecasting cash flow
Management and merchandising assistance to clients	Supplying information about markets and products and providing advisory services to assist customers in their sales efforts

Wholesalers perform marketing activities, such as transportation, storage, and information gathering, that are necessary to expedite exchanges. They provide marketing activities for organizations above and below them in the marketing channel. Most of the marketing functions discussed in Chapter 1 can be performed by wholesalers. Some examples of wholesaling firms are Genuine Parts Company in the automotive industry, Bergen Brunswig Corporation in the drug industry, and Foremost-McKesson, Inc., in the drug, grocery, liquor, and health and beauty aid industries.[6]

The activities of wholesalers

Over 50 percent of all goods are exchanged (or negotiated) through wholesaling institutions. Of course, it is important to remember that wholesaling activities must be performed during distribution for all goods, whether or not a wholesaling institution (independent merchant or agent) is involved.[7] Table 8.1 lists some of the major activities performed by wholesalers. Although it is not exhaustive, nor the activities mutually exclusive, the table

6. Louis W. Stern and Adel I. El-Ansary, *Marketing Channels,* 2nd ed. (Englewood Cliffs, N.J.: Prentice-Hall, 1982), p. 144.
7. C. Glenn Walters, *Marketing Channels* (Santa Monica, Calif.: Goodyear, 1977), p. 131.

lists the major wholesaling activities. As we shall see, however, individual wholesalers need not perform every activity listed in Table 8.1.

Services for producers

Producers have a distinct advantage when they use wholesalers because this distribution link provides accumulation and allocation roles for a number of products. This service saves producers money and permits them to concentrate on producing, assembling, and developing quality products to match consumers' wants.

Producers would like close, direct contact with retailers and consumers, but wholesalers often have more direct contact with retailers.[8] For this reason, many producers have chosen to control promotion and influence the pricing of products while shifting transportation, warehousing, and financing functions to wholesalers. To stay in business, wholesalers must be innovative as they perform marketing activities for other channel members.

The following are examples of products whose producers commonly use wholesalers: plumbing supplies, lumber, office furniture, electrical equipment, and construction machinery. In general, wholesalers serve producers of established products. Wholesalers may be slow to introduce new products because of the risks involved and the special product knowledge or service requirements that may be needed. Thus, when a new technical or mechanical product is launched, few wholesalers may be prepared to serve its producer.

Mitsubishi International Corporation of Japan recognized the need to perform its own wholesaling activities when it decided to market industrial and construction products in the United States.[9]

Services for retailers

In most cases, wholesalers specialize in selling. Matching producers' products to the needs of retailers and adding services to products helps to create an assortment of products for the consumer.

Wholesalers help their retailer-customers select inventory. In industries where obtaining supplies is important, skilled buying is essential. A wholesaler who buys is a specialist in understanding market conditions and an expert at negotiating final purchases. The customer's buyer can thus avoid the responsibility of looking for and coordinating supply sources. Moreover, if the wholesaler makes purchases for several different buyers, expenses can be shared by all customers. Another advantage is that a manufacturer's salespersons can offer retailers only a few products at a time, but independent wholesalers have a wide range of products available.

By buying in large quantities and delivering to customers in smaller lots, a wholesaler can perform physical distribution activities—for example, transportation, materials handling, inventory planning, communication, and warehousing—more efficiently and can provide more service than a producer or retailer could with its own physical distribution system. Fig-

8. Wroe Alderson, *Dynamic Marketing Behavior* (Homewood, Ill.: Irwin, 1965), p. 41.
9. "Dealer Support Is Key in Mitsubishi's U.S. Markets," *Industrial Marketing,* Jan. 1976, pp. 68–69.

ANNOUNCING AN L OF A DEAL

FREE FREIGHT

AND A LITTLE SOMETHING ELSE.

Langenscheidt, world's premiere publisher of bilingual dictionaries since 1858, is now in America.
Our 47 titles in 13 languages are just a telephone call away. And delivery is an even better deal.

As a get-acquainted offer, Langenscheidt is offering free freight during the '83 back-to-school season on any size orders placed between June 1 and July 31, 1983. For full details, visit us at the ABA

Show, Booth 2233. Or contact Langenscheidt Publishers, Inc., 46-35 54th Road, Maspeth, NY 11378. Telephone (212) 784-0055.
Langenscheidt. An "L" of a way to increase profits in language dictionaries.

Langen scheidt
Comes to America

Figure 8.2 Free freight is offered as a service to retailers purchasing a new bilingual dictionary *Source: Langenscheidt Publishers, Inc. © 1983.*

ure 8.2 illustrates this concept for purchasers of a new product line of bilingual dictionaries. In this case, free freight is being offered for any size order during a specified period.

Wholesalers are able to provide quick and frequent delivery even when demand fluctuates. They are experienced in providing the fastest delivery at the lowest cost. They provide time and place utility, which lets the producer and the wholesalers' customers avoid risks associated with holding large product inventories.

Because they carry products for many customers, wholesalers can maintain a wide product line at a relatively low cost. For example, a small Chrysler-Plymouth dealer in the Midwest discovered that it was cheaper to let wholesale suppliers provide automobile parts than to maintain a parts inventory at the dealership. Often wholesalers can perform storage and warehousing activities more efficiently and can permit retailers to concentrate on other marketing activities. When wholesalers provide storage and warehousing, they generally take on the ownership function as well. This arrangement frees retailers' and producers' capital for other purposes. Figure 8.3 illustrates how Maverick distributors perform the inventory function and free retailers' capital for other purposes.

Figure 8.3 Clothing distributor provides warehousing and financial services to retailers *Source: Maverick, Division of Blue Bell, Inc.*

Classifying wholesalers

A wide variety of wholesalers meet the different needs of producers and retailers. In addition, new instititutions and establishments develop in response to producers and retail organizations that want to take over wholesaling functions.

Wholesalers adjust their activities as the contours of the marketing environment change. The classification or description of these wholesalers is meaningful only at a point in time; but one fact remains constant: "Wholesaling organizations by nature must count as their most important resource—their intimate knowledge of the product and service requirements of a particular market segment."[10]

In this section, we will discuss three general categories or types of wholesaling establishments: (1) merchant wholesalers, (2) agents and brokers, and (3) manufacturers' sales branches and offices. This classification of wholesalers is based on activities they perform.

Merchant wholesalers

Merchant wholesalers take title and assume risk and generally are involved in buying and reselling products to industrial or retail customers. The two broad categories of merchant wholesalers are full-service wholesalers and limited-service wholesalers. *Full-service wholesalers* provide most services

10. Richard S. Lopata, "Faster Pace in Wholesaling," *Harvard Business Review*, July–Aug. 1969, pp. 130–143.

Figure 8.4
Types of merchant
wholesalers

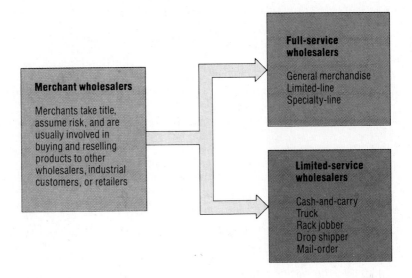

that can be performed by wholesalers. *Limited-service wholesalers* provide only some marketing services and specialize in a few functions. (They pass other functions on to customers, or the other functions are performed by producers.) Figure 8.4 illustrates the different types of merchant wholesalers discussed in this section.

The *Census of Wholesale Trade* indicates that slightly more than half (53.7 percent) of all wholesale sales are conducted by merchant wholesalers.[11] Two-thirds of all wholesale establishments are merchant wholesalers. Figure 8.5 compares the 1969 and 1979 sales of merchant wholesalers by their specific type of business. Sales of merchant wholesalers increased significantly during this period. Taking title to products is the common criterion that distinguishes merchant middlemen from agent middlemen. Some merchant wholesalers are also involved in branding, packaging, and coordinating the marketing strategy of products they carry. IGA merchant wholesalers exemplify this approach.

**Types of
full-service merchant
wholesalers**

Full-service wholesalers provide numerous services to customers. Delivery, warehousing, credit, promotional assistance, and general information about operations may be available to interested customers. There are three categories of merchant wholesalers including general merchandise, limited-line, and specialty-line wholesalers.

General merchandise wholesalers

General merchandise wholesalers are full-service merchant wholesalers who carry a very wide product mix, including such products as drugs, hardware, nonperishable foods, cosmetics, detergents, and tobacco. General merchandise wholesalers typically serve neighborhood grocery stores and small department stores.

11. *Census of Wholesale Trade,* June 1980, pp. 52–55.

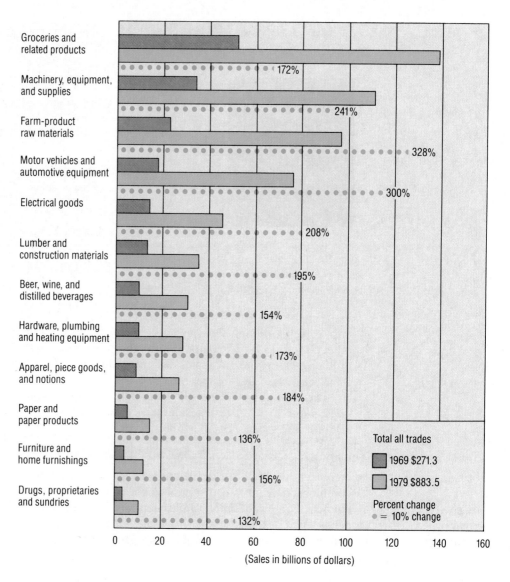

Groceries and related products — 172%
Machinery, equipment, and supplies — 241%
Farm-product raw materials — 328%
Motor vehicles and automotive equipment — 300%
Electrical goods — 208%
Lumber and construction materials — 195%
Beer, wine, and distilled beverages — 154%
Hardware, plumbing and heating equipment — 173%
Apparel, piece goods, and notions — 184%
Paper and paper products — 136%
Furniture and home furnishings — 156%
Drugs, proprietaries and sundries — 132%

Total all trades
■ 1969 $271.3
□ 1979 $883.5
Percent change
● = 10% change

0   20   40   60   80   100   120   140   160
(Sales in billions of dollars)

Figure 8.5   Sales of merchant wholesalers by kind of business
Source: U.S. Bureau of the Census, Monthly Wholesale Trade, December 1979, *BW-79-12 (February 1980), p. 3.*

Limited-line wholesalers

Limited-line wholesalers carry only a few product lines, as opposed to the wide variety carried by general merchandise wholesalers. A limited-line wholesaler might carry only groceries, lighting fixtures, or oil-well drilling equipment. Limited-line wholesalers do, however, offer services similar to those of general merchandise wholesalers. The Application on page 244 illustrates the activities of a limited-line wholesaler of computer equipment and supplies.

Specialty-line wholesalers

Specialty-line wholesalers carry a very limited variety of products. For example, a wholesaler that carries only food delicacies such as shellfish is a

Table 8.2 Various services provided by limited-service merchant wholesalers

	Rack Jobber (service merchandiser)	Mail Order	Truck	Drop Shipper (desk jobber)	Cash and Carry
Physical possession of merchandise	Yes	Yes	Yes	No	Yes
Personal sales calls on customer	Yes	No	Yes	No	No
Information about market conditions	Yes	Yes	Some	Yes	No
Advice to customers	Yes	No	Some	Yes	No
Stocking and maintenance of merchandise in customer's store	Yes	No	No	No	No
Credit to customers	Yes	Some	Some	Yes	No
Delivery of merchandise to customers	Yes	No	Yes	No	No

specialty-line wholesaler. Generally, these merchant wholesalers carry one product line or a few items within a product line to meet their customers' specialized requirements.

Types of limited-service merchant wholesalers

Table 8.2 distinguishes the different services provided by various limited-service merchant wholesalers. Cash-and-carry wholesalers, truck wholesalers, rack jobbers, drop shippers, and mail-order wholesalers are typical limited-service wholesalers.

Cash-and-carry wholesalers

Cash-and-carry wholesalers are limited-service wholesalers that sell to customers who will pay cash and furnish transportation or pay extra to have products delivered. These middlemen usually handle a limited line of products such as groceries, construction materials, electrical supplies, or office supplies.

As an example of a cash-and-carry wholesaler, Makro Self Service Wholesale Corporation has opened a chain of one-stop, cash-and-carry, no-frills wholesale stores for small businesses and professional groups. Self-service reduces personnel requirements for Makro. The cash-only rule eliminates the need for a credit department; and transportation by customers eliminates the need for delivery people and equipment.[12]

12. "Dutch Firm Expands No-Frills Idea to U.S. Self-Service Wholesale Centers," *Marketing News,* Oct. 2, 1981, p. 11.

Application

A Limited-line Wholesaler Gains an Edge in the Computer Disk Market

Leading Edge Products, Inc. (LEP) in Canton, Massachusetts, is a limited-line wholesaler of computer equipment and supplies to retailers. This company has been successful because it foresaw the distribution needs in the computer market.

LEP began its disk marketing by emphasizing price. The company began distributing Memorex disks and opened up nine hundred accounts; it built sales at a rate of 150,000 disks per month and soon became Memorex's largest distributor. LEP next introduced its own label, Elephant Memory Systems, and dropped Memorex. It obtained disks from Dennison KYBE Corporation in Waltham, Massachusetts, and marketed them under the Elephant Memory name. LEP's marketing was geared to the home computer and office computer users who frequent retail stores.

In the first year of its Elephant Memory disks, LEP spent $350,000 on advertising and double that amount in the second year. Elephant Memory's market share grew to about 3 percent of the worldwide disk market.

LEP is a limited-line wholesaler, not a specialty-line wholesaler, because it sells a wide group of products along with computer disks, including printers, modems, and computer screens. As new technologies appear, LEP selects from among many manufacturers the most appropriate items to distribute.

As a wholesaler, LEP has strived to match producers' products to the needs of retailers and consumers. The company demonstrates that a wholesaler needs to understand market conditions, to be knowledgeable and skillful in choosing the right suppliers, and to offer a wide variety of products that are needed in the marketplace.

Source: Based on Bob Davis, "Leader of the Pack," *Inc.*, January 1983, p. 86, 88.

Truck wholesalers

Truck wholesalers provide transportation and deliver products directly to customers for inspection and selection. Usually, a truck wholesaler has a regular route and calls on retail stores and institutions to determine their needs. These middlemen are often small operators who own and drive their own trucks. They play an important part in supplying small grocery stores with such perishable products as fruits and vegetables. Also, meat, potato chips, supplies for service stations, and tobacco products are sometimes supplied by truck wholesalers. Cash purchases and limited services are typical.

Rack jobbers

Rack jobbers (or service merchandisers) are similar to truck wholesalers, but they provide the extra service of placing products on retailers' shelves. Rack jobbers perform purchasing and stocking functions for retailers. They are unique in that they will take back unsold products. Impulse products that have short life cycles, such as toys, may be supplied by rack jobbers to alleviate the producer's and retailer's risk and the inconvenience to retailers of having to deal with unfamiliar products.

Rack jobbers usually specialize in housewares, hardware, drugs, or cosmetics. They physically maintain the goods by refilling shelves, fixing displays, and maintaining inventory records, thus relieving retailers of these chores. Retailers have only to furnish the space. This limited-service wholesaler usually operates on a consignment or cash basis, and other services are limited.

Drop shippers

Drop shippers take title to products and negotiate sales. The distinguishing characteristic of drop shippers is that they do not physically handle products. They are most commonly used to purchase large quantities of items that do not need to be regrouped. The physical inventory may actually remain with the producer or in a public warehouse.

Drop shippers often deal with products that are inefficient to ship or products that could not be sold at competitive prices if the wholesaler had to cover the cost of physically handling them. Drop shippers are concerned mainly with facilitating exchange through selling activities. They assume title to a certain quantity of products that are produced. If the products are not sold, then drop shippers assume the loss.

Mail-order wholesalers

Mail-order wholesalers sell through direct mail by sending catalogs to retail, industrial, and institutional customers—another example of limited-function wholesaling. Wholesale mail-order houses that feature jewelry, cosmetics, specialty foods, or automobile parts usually serve remote geographical areas, where small retailers find mail-order purchasing convenient and efficient. Mail-order wholesalers usually sell small products that can be shipped by United Parcel Service (UPS), the U.S. mail service, or common carriers. Orders are usually paid for in cash or by credit card, and discounts are given for large orders. Figure 8.6 is an advertisement for a computer software company that sells its products by mail order and through telephone orders.

Agents and brokers

Different agents and brokers (see Figure 8.7) negotiate purchases and expedite sales but do not take title to the product; they are *functional middlemen* because they perform a limited number of marketing activities for a commission. Agents, in particular, perform fewer marketing activities than typical merchant wholesalers, retailers, or manufacturers' wholesale operations. These middlemen account for 10.4 percent of the total sales volume of wholesalers.[13]

Brokers perform fewer functions than other intermediaries; their primary one is to bring buyers and sellers together. Brokers are not involved in financing or physical possession, and they assume almost no risks. They exist to seek out buyers or sellers and assist in negotiating exchanges. Brokerage fees are paid by whoever seeks the broker's services.

Agents represent either buyers or sellers on a permanent basis. The services performed by typical agents (manufacturers' agents, selling agents, commission merchants) and brokers (food brokers, real estate brokers, and others) are summarized in Table 8.3 and explained in the following pages.

Manufacturers' agents

Manufacturers' agents represent several sellers and usually offer a complete product line to customers. They enter into agreement with manufacturers regarding territories, selling price, order handling, and terms of sale relating

13. *Census of Wholesale Trade,* June 1980, pp. 52–55.

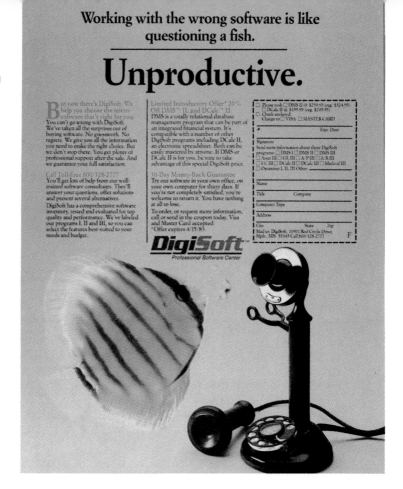
to delivery, service, and warranties. The relationship between an agent and a seller is detailed explicitly in a written agreement.

Most manufacturers' agents are small establishments with only a few employees. They are restricted to a particular territory and perform functions for manufacturers similar to those of a sales office. Professional salespersons who contact potential buyers are highly skilled in selling. A good relationship with customers is the most important benefit manufacturers' agents can offer.

By concentrating on a limited number of products, these middlemen are able to provide an intensified and coordinated sales effort that would be impossible with any other distribution method except producer-owned sales branches and offices. In addition, manufacturers' agents are able to spread operating expenses among noncompeting products and to offer each manufacturer lower prices for services rendered.

The products handled by manufacturers' agents must be noncompeting and complementary. Some agents assist retailers in advertising and in maintaining a service organization. The more services offered, the higher the agent's commission.

Selling agents

Selling agents market either all of a specified product line or a manufacturer's entire output. Selling agents essentially have control over manufac-

Figure 8.7
Types of agents
and brokers

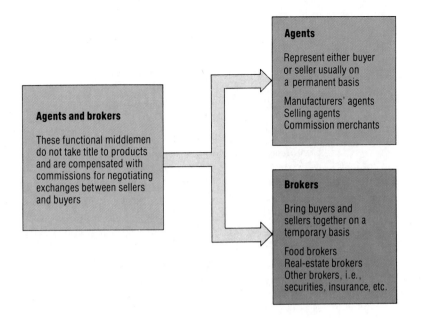

turers' marketing efforts and may be used in place of a marketing department. These agents have full authority with regard to prices, promotion, and distribution. They assume the functions of a sales department for sellers.

Selling agents are used most often by small firms or by manufacturers whose seasonal production or other characteristics make it difficult to maintain a marketing department. These middlemen most often distribute canned foods, household furnishings, clothing, and textiles.

Table 8.3   Various services provided by agents and brokers

	Brokers	Commission Merchants	Selling Agents	Manufacturers' Agents
Physical possession of merchandise	No	Yes	No	Some
Long-term relationship with buyers or sellers	Some	Yes	Yes	Yes
Representation of competing product lines	Yes	Yes	No	No
Limited geographic territory	No	No	No	Yes
Credit to customers	No	Some	Yes	No
Delivery of merchandise to customers	No	Yes	Yes	Some

Selling agents usually assume the sales function for several producers. They avoid conflicts of interest by representing noncompeting product lines. A selling agent is rarely restricted to as narrow a geographical territory as a manufacturer's agent. Selling agents play a key role in advertising, marketing, research, and credit policies, and they may offer advice on product development and packaging.

Commission merchants

Commission merchants are agents who usually exercise physical control over products and negotiate sales. They may have broad powers regarding prices and terms of sale. Arranging delivery and providing transportation are key services offered by commission merchants, who are found most often in agricultural marketing. A commission merchant takes possession of truckload quantities of commodities and transports them to a central market for sale. These agents specialize in obtaining the best price under market conditions; they deduct a commission plus the expense of making the sale and remit the profits to the shipper.

Businesses—including farms—that use commission merchants face one significant problem: They have extremely limited control over pricing. Because large producers must maintain close contact with the market, they have a limited need for commission merchants.

Brokers

Brokers specialize in a particular commodity and give their customers the benefit of established contacts. *Food brokers* sell food and other grocery products to retailer-owned and merchant wholesalers, grocery chains, industrial buyers, and food processors. Buyers and sellers use food brokers to cope with fluctuating market conditions and to obtain assistance in grading, negotiating, and inspecting foods. The Application on page 249 discusses the benefits that a food broker can provide.

Real-estate brokers bring buyers and sellers together to exchange real estate. The broker is a go-between, not a permanent representative of either the buyer or the seller. Real-estate brokers often seek a compromise in negotiations between the buyer and seller. They often obtain an exclusive contract for a stated period, during which they engage in advertising and other promotional activities.

Manufacturers' sales branches and offices

Manufacturers' sales branches resemble merchant wholesalers in their operations. According to the *Census of Wholesale Trade* over one-third (38 percent) of wholesale sales volume is developed through these middlemen.[14] *Sales branches* may offer credit, deliver goods, give promotional assistance, and furnish other services. Customers include other wholesalers, retailers, and industrial buyers. Branch operations are common, for example, in electrical supplies (Westinghouse Electric) and in plumbing (Crane Company and American Standard).[15]

14. *Census of Wholesale Trade,* June 1980, pp. 52–55.
15. Stern and El-Ansary, *Marketing Channels,* 2nd ed., p. 116.

Application

A good broker learns the business of clients and this facilitates a continuing business relationship. For example, in one case, when a shipment of frozen grapes arrived, the buyer who wanted to use the grapes in salads refused to accept them. George R. Lyons Company, of Cleveland, the broker, found a winery that could use the grapes. This knowledge of the market helped both the buyer and the seller.

A broker's experience and diplomacy can prevent hard feelings when difficult situations arise. When one retail buyer refused a line of frozen fish, saying that the packages were too big, Arthur H. Froman & Company involved the buyer in developing smaller packages. In the end, the buyer accepted the frozen fish.

A broker's concern for the welfare of his client sometimes results in lower profits. For example, George R. Lyons Company had a major client to whom they were selling a product in drums. Lyons suggested to the client that it would be less expensive to buy in tank quantities, and the savings of one year would offset the cost of tank installation. The client took the suggestion and it resulted in a drop in the broker's profits from $1,200 to $40. However Lyons regarded the long-term relationship with the client as more important. This decision to focus on long-run customer satisfaction illustrates the spirit of the marketing concept. Later on, this very client came to Lyons for information in selecting a new plant site.

The primary function of brokers is to bring buyers and sellers together. However, the knowledge and experience of brokers can benefit a client in many ways.

Source: Based on Ron Stevens, "Above and Beyond the Call of Duty," *Quick Frozen Foods,* December 1983, pp. 18–19.

Sales offices provide service normally associated with agents. These wholesalers are part of the vertically integrated distribution channel of the producer who owns and controls the sales branch or office. Products that enhance the manufacturer's own product line may be sold by the sales office or sales branch. Hiram Walker, for example, imports wine from Spain to increase the number of products that its sales offices can offer to wholesalers. United States Tobacco Company imports Borkum Riff smoking tobacco from Sweden to add variety to its chewing tobacco and snuff lines.

The sales office or branch usually is reserved for accounts that need its service. Large retail customers may be served directly by the producer, by-passing the organization's wholesaling operation. For example, a major distiller bottles private-label bourbon for California supermarkets. This operation totally by-passes the company's sales office, which serves other retailers.

Organizations that facilitate wholesaling functions

In addition to the three main categories of wholesalers that have been described, there are other highly specialized organizations that perform wholesaling functions. Certain facilitating organizations make it unnecessary for a manufacturer or retailer to utilize a wholesaling establishment. The following sections show ways in which typical wholesaling functions can be performed by such facilitating agencies.

Public warehouses

Public warehouses serve as storage facilities. An organization rents space in a warehouse instead of constructing its own facilities or using a merchant wholesaler's storage services. Public warehouses also provide other whole-saling activities. Many warehouses order, deliver, collect accounts, and maintain display rooms where potential buyers can inspect products. A producer can place products in a bonded warehouse and use them as collateral for a loan.

Field warehouses

Field warehouses are producer-controlled storage spaces that separate part of the inventory into a secure area within the warehouse. A field warehouse manager takes control and becomes responsible for the products. This operation makes it possible for a seller to obtain a warehouse receipt that can be used as collateral for a loan.

Finance companies

Products can be owned by a finance company or a bank while wholesalers or retailers maintain physical possession. Automobile dealers often call this form of financing "floor planning"; it allows them to maintain a large inventory of cars to give customers greater selection and increase sales.

Transportation companies

Rail, truck, air, and other carriers help manufacturers and retailers transport products without the aid of middlemen. For example, freight forwarders combine less-than-full shipments into standard full loads at a savings to customers—perhaps at a carload rate rather than a less-than-carload rate. United Parcel Service is an example of a freight forwarder that provides door-to-door service for small containers and packages.

Trade shows and trade marts

Trade shows and trade marts allow manufacturers or wholesalers to exhibit products to potential buyers and, therefore, assist in the selling and buying functions. *Trade shows* offer both selling and nonselling benefits. On the selling side, they allow vendors to identify prospects; gain access to key decision makers in current or potential customer companies; disseminate facts about their products, services, and personnel; and actually sell products and service current accounts through contacts at the show. The nonselling benefits include opportunities to maintain the company image with competitors, customers, and the industry and to gather information on competitors' products and prices. Other important marketing variables on which trade shows have a positive influence include maintaining or enhancing corporate morale, product testing, and product evaluation.[16]

Trade shows can permit direct buyer-seller interaction and may eliminate the need for agents. For example, more than 35,000 graphic arts company owners and managers convene every fall in Chicago to attend the McCormick Place Graphic Expo.[17] As another example, Honeywell, Inc., collected over four hundred promising sales leads while exhibiting computers at a trade show hospitality suite in Las Vegas.[18]

16. Thomas V. Bonoma, "Get More Out of Your Trade Shows," *Harvard Business Review,* Jan.–Feb. 1983, pp. 75–83.
17. *Official Show Directory,* Graph Expo 81, Sept. 1981, p. 9.
18. Heywood Klein, "Trade Show Hospitality Is Changing," *Wall Street Journal,* Jan. 25, 1983, p. 33.

Magical harmony. Glazed goatskin accessories and desk by Tura.

FRAN MURPHY,

D&D Centre of The Palm Beaches 401 Clematis Street, Florida Phone (305) 659-6200
A Home Furnishings Trade Showroom

Trade marts are relatively permanent facilities that firms can rent to exhibit products year round. In Dallas, the Dallas Market Center, the Dallas Trade Mart, the Homefurnishing Mart, the World Trade Center, the Decorative Center, Market Hall, and the Apparel Mart are housed in six buildings specifically designed for the convenience of professional buyers. Trade marts are located in several major cities, including New York, Chicago, Atlanta, Dallas, and Los Angeles. At these marts, such products as furniture, home decorating supplies, toys, clothing, and gift items are sold to wholesalers and retailers. Figure 8.8 is an advertisement for a home furnishings trade showroom in Palm Beach, Florida.

Changing patterns in wholesaling

The distinction between wholesaling activities that can be performed by any business and the traditional wholesaling establishment is somewhat blurred. Manufacturers, retailers, and facilitating organizations perform wholesaling functions to bridge the gap between manufacturers and consumers. Wholesaling functions can be shifted or shared, but not eliminated.

Wholesaling activities have to be performed by someone or by some institution.

The *Census of Business* statistics on wholesale trade indicate that the growth and sales of wholesaling establishments have been relatively stable since 1929.[19] Wholesale sales are traditionally 140 to 150 percent of retail sales. We will now examine some changes in wholesaling establishments.

Prominence among types of wholesalers

Two kinds of shifts have been taking place in wholesaling activities. First, merchant wholesalers have increased while manufacturers' sales branches have declined. This shift indicates that merchant wholesalers have provided more efficient stocking operations than manufacturers could provide for themselves. (Exceptions to this pattern are seen in industries producing drugs, automobiles, hardware, machinery, and equipment.)[20] Second, the share of trade for manufacturers' sales offices has increased, while agents' and brokers' shares have declined. Manufacturers' sales offices perform essentially the same wholesaling functions as agents and brokers; the shift is from one type of selling operation to another.[21] This movement indicates that manufacturers' sales offices have developed more effective selling methods than independent agents.

In reaction to the integrated wholesaling activities of large corporate chains owned by retailers, voluntary chain wholesalers have evolved and have become strong establishments in the food industry. Voluntary wholesale chains can be formed by independent retailers or independent wholesalers. Associated Grocers (AG) is owned by retailers, Independent Grocers' Alliance (IGA) is owned by wholesalers. Both associations operate as channel leaders for member stores. Through innovative wholesaling methods, small independent food retailers can operate as efficiently and effectively as large chains.

By-passing wholesalers

There is a trend to by-pass traditional wholesaling establishments when alternative channels offer advantages for retailers or manufacturers. New factory outlet malls illustrate the desire of some manufacturers to sell directly to the public. The following environmental conditions favor circumvention of traditional wholesalers:

1. Selling directly to retailers and industrial users becomes more important as unit value, perishability, and the need for service and installation increase.
2. If the manufacturer is strong financially and has a long line of products, direct sales are more feasible.
3. When retailers or users make large-scale purchases or when customers are concentrated, direct sales may be employed.[22]

19. *U.S. Census of Business, 1929, 1939, 1948, 1954, 1963, 1967, 1972.*
20. James C. McKeon, "Conflicting Patterns of Structural Change in Wholesaling," *Economic and Business Bulletin,* Winter 1972, pp. 100–113.
21. Ibid., p. 100.
22. Adapted from James C. McKeon, "Conflicting Patterns of Structural Change in Wholesaling," *Economic and Business Bulletin,* Winter 1972, p. 113. Used by permission.

In general, there is a trend toward simplified marketing channels and fewer distribution points, with a corresponding opportunity for greater centralization and control of distribution.[23] Many producers are opening retail stores to gain a larger share of the market by exposing their product lines to more consumers. Examples include Pepperidge Farm (baked goods), Dannon (yogurt), Texas Instruments (calculators), GAF (duplicating supplies and services), and Sherwin-Williams (paints and home decorating supplies).[24]

New types of wholesalers

The nature of new types of wholesaling establishments that arise will depend on the changing mix of activities that retailers and producers perform and on the innovative efforts of wholesalers to develop efficiency in the marketing channel.[25] The trend toward larger retailers—superstores and the like—will provide opportunities as well as threats to wholesaling establishments. Opportunities will develop from the expanded product lines of these mass merchandisers. A merchant wholesaler of groceries may want to add other low-cost, high-volume products that are sold in superstores. On the other hand, some limited-function merchant wholesalers may not be needed. The volume of sales may eliminate the need for rack jobbers, for example, who usually handle slow-moving products that are purchased in limited quantities. The future of independent wholesalers, agents, and brokers depends on their ability to delineate markets and provide desired services. Wholesalers with low-cost operations are the only ones that will do well.

Summary

Wholesaling includes all marketing transactions in which purchases are intended for resale or are used in making other products. The performance of wholesaling functions can be shifted to or assumed by any channel member, but those functions cannot be eliminated; they must be performed by someone—either by producers, retailers, or consumers, if not by wholesalers.

There are over 385,000 wholesaling establishments in the United States, and their sales volume is significantly higher than that of retail establishments. This high sales volume results from counting multiple transactions as products move through the marketing channel.

Wholesalers' major activities include wholesaling management, planning, and negotiating supplies, promoting, warehousing and product handling, transportation, inventory control and data processing, security, pricing, financing and budgeting, and management and merchandising assistance to clients.

A wide diversity of wholesalers exists to serve the requirements of different market segments. Merchant wholesalers take title and usually are involved in buying, physically handling, and reselling products. Agents and brokers are functional middlemen because they specialize in a limited number of marketing activities, primarily buying and selling. Manufacturers'

23. "Marketing When the Growth Slows," *Business Week,* April 14, 1975, p. 45.
24. Ibid.
25. Bruce Mallen, "Functional Spin-off: A Key to Anticipating Change in Distribution Structure," *Journal of Marketing,* July 1973, p. 22.

sales branches and offices are vertically integrated units owned by manufacturers.

Facilitating organizations that perform wholesaling functions include public warehouses, field warehouses, finance companies, transportation companies, and trade shows and trade marts. In some instances, these organizations eliminate the need for a wholesaling establishment by providing wholesaling functions.

Important terms

Wholesaling	Rack jobbers
Wholesalers	Drop shippers
Merchant wholesalers	Field warehouses
Full-service wholesalers	Trade shows
Limited-service wholesalers	Trade marts
General merchandise wholesalers	Mail-order wholesalers
Real-estate brokers	Functional middlemen
Sales branches	Brokers
Sales offices	Agents
Public warehouses	Manufacturers' agents
Limited-line wholesalers	Selling agents
Specialty-line wholesalers	Commission merchants
Cash-and-carry wholesalers	Food brokers
Truck wholesalers	

Discussion and review questions

1. What is the distinction between wholesalers and wholesaling?
2. Why do wholesaling establishments (excluding wholesaling activities of retailers) have a sales volume greater than retailers?
3. If a friend tells you that a product was purchased from a wholesaler, what questions should you ask to determine if it really was a wholesale transaction?
4. Why shouldn't retailers by-pass wholesalers? What functions are performed by wholesalers?
5. Would it be appropriate for a wholesaler to stock both interior wall paint and office supplies? Under what circumstances would this product mix be logical?
6. Drop shippers take title to products but do not accept physical possession. Commission merchants take physical possession of products but do not accept title. Defend the logic of classifying drop shippers as wholesale merchants and commission merchants as agents.
7. What are the advantages of using agents to replace merchant wholesalers? What are the disadvantages?
8. What, if any, are the differences in marketing functions performed by manufacturers' agents and selling agents?
9. Why are manufacturers' sales offices and branches classified as wholesalers? Which independent wholesalers are replaced by manufacturers' sales branches? Which independent wholesalers are replaced by manufacturers' sales offices?
10. Why do you think merchant wholesalers have increased in number while manufacturers' sales branches have decreased?

11. "Public warehouses are really wholesale establishments." Comment on this statement.
12. Will efficient wholesaling ensure the survival of small independent retailers?
13. How strong is the trend toward by-passing wholesalers? What environmental variables favor direct distribution by manufacturers?

Cases

Case 8.1

Textron Outdoor Products Group[26]

TEXTRON

The Textron, Inc. Outdoor Products Group manufactures E-Z Go, Homelite, and Jacobsen Turf outdoor equipment. Over the past ten years, Textron has been revamping the division's distribution system to increase the exposure and overall availability of its products. Homelite phased out its direct sales method (see Channel E in Figure 7.3) and began selling equipment through wholesalers and industrial distributors who take title to the products. The following distribution methods are used for the Outdoor Products Group:

E-Z Go. Three- and four-wheel gasoline and electric golf cars, utility vehicles, and related parts and accessories are sold through independent distributors and factory distribution centers.

Homelite. Gasoline and electric chain saws, string trimmers, pumps, generators, blowers, and other portable construction equipment are sold to wholesalers and retailers. Homelite also sells lawn and garden equipment and snow throwers under the Jacobsen brand name through wholesalers, other independent distributors, and factory distribution centers.

Jacobsen Turf. Turf maintenance machines, including precision reel mowers, large turf tractors, and rotary mowers and sweepers, are sold through independent distributors to golf courses and other commercial and municipal grounds care customers.

Homelite's widespread distribution network brought about a dramatic increase in sales of Jacobsen lawn and garden equipment. The end result was an increase in Homelite's overall profits.

Homelite has also been reducing overhead by closing some low-income-producing service centers and consolidating a regional distribution center. To enable the Homelite field sales force to devote more of its time to its broadened range of consumer products, such as Jacobsen lawn and garden equipment and snow throwers, Homelite discontinued about thirty marginally profitable products. These products represented nearly 20 percent of the entire Homelite line but accounted for less than 2 percent of sales.

The creative use of Homelite wholesalers and industrial distributors has allowed the Outdoor Products Group to increase profits by getting

26. Facts are from Textron's *1982 Annual Report*, pp. 13–14 and 24.

maximum exposure of its product lines. By discontinuing marginally profitable Homelite products and adding Jacobsen products that can be sold through existing distributors, the company recorded a higher operating profit.

Questions for discussion
1. Why did a shift from direct sales to industrial distributors and wholesalers increase the profits of the Outdoor Products Group?
2. Are there any opportunities for the E-Z Go division to engage in joint distribution with Homelite or Jacobsen?
3. How has the use of wholesalers and industrial distributors affected the marketing strategies of the Outdoor Products Group?

Case 8.2

Dakota Battery Company

Dakota Battery Company of Rapid City, South Dakota, was started over fifty years ago by Paul Moor. Originally the company manufactured automobile batteries, but during the 1950s it got out of that business and began to concentrate on wholesaling batteries on a regional basis. It also opened a few retail stores. Supply contracts were established with General Battery Corporation, the nation's largest battery manufacturer. The Dakota Battery name and brand mark were retained in an effort to maintain brand name recognition and loyalty.

The company concentrated its sales efforts in southwest South Dakota, emphasizing quality products and superior service. A large inventory of all types of batteries enabled the company to provide superior distribution service for its customers. The large inventory provided the customers (usually retailers or commercial users) with the benefit of immediate supply, which was a powerful sales tool.

Over the past thirty years, Dakota Battery Company has prospered and grown. The sales territory now covers most of South Dakota and portions of Wyoming and Montana. The brand is fairly well known by resellers, including service stations and truck service centers, in the three-state area. The company has established itself as an honest organization, and the product has a reputation for quality. The market is segmented into four classes:

1. General automotive resellers (garages, automotive parts dealers): 40 percent
2. Retail consumers: 20 percent
3. Commercial heavy equipment users (farmers, independent truckers, roadgraders): 20 percent
4. Commercial truck fleets: 20 percent

Automotive parts dealers and garages account for the largest single segment of Dakota Company business. Two salespersons cover assigned accounts on a regular basis. Each salesperson attempts to educate the reseller on how best to sell Dakota batteries. The company also monitors inventory levels to assure adequate supplies, makes point-of-purchase displays available, and picks up junk batteries frequently. Dakota even provides joint radio advertising for many customers.

Courses are frequently provided on the best way to make battery sales. Slide and film presentations explain the selling features and benefits of the Dakota batteries. The sales presentation also serves as a basic lesson in sales technique. Resellers are taught what kind of questions to ask prospective buyers in order to close the sale. The emphasis is on how the reseller can "create" new sales.

Dakota sells more than just a battery; it sells a "total battery program." Customers have access to the longest line and largest inventory in the marketing area. The company carries a complete line of automotive, commercial, recreational, and motorcycle batteries. It offers all three types of maintenance-free batteries: the calcium and low-antimony types, and a maintenance-free model designed specifically for commercial use. Since Dakota provides a large, complete source of supply, the customer needs to stock only the fastest-moving batteries. Special orders can be delivered within twenty-four hours in most cases.

Dakota also provides for the customer's own logo if desired. This helps the reseller build repeat sales through product loyalty. The company covers the costs of all battery adjustments. Major oil companies report that it costs them 10 percent to handle adjustments. A reliable source of battery acid is a necessity to resellers. Dakota packages its own acid in both six-quart and five-gallon containers. Battery acid is delivered in any quantity the reseller desires.

In the late 1970s the tide of prosperity turned. Strong promotion efforts by large national retail companies (Sears, Ward's, Penney's) cut deep into Dakota's retail sales. Competition in Dakota's market area was fierce. Out-of-state battery companies were making bids to establish themselves in South Dakota and its regional market. Dakota Battery sales and earnings were declining rapidly.

Questions for discussion
1. In spite of the apparent customer orientation of Dakota Battery Company, sales are declining. Suggest some possible reasons for the decline.
2. Twenty percent of Dakota's sales is derived from its own retail battery stores. Does the Dakota wholesale operation seem to complement or conflict with the retail operation? Should Dakota expand or contract its retail operation?
3. How can Dakota Battery Company improve its marketing strategy and compete more effectively with large national companies?
4. What kind of a promotion program would help Dakota's wholesale *and* retail operations?

9

Retailing

Objectives

To understand the purpose and function of retailers in the marketing channel.

To examine how the environment of a retail store is developed.

To classify retail stores.

To understand nonstore retailing, franchising, and planned shopping centers.

To learn about the wheel of retailing hypothesis, which attempts to explain the evolution and development of retail stores.

To examine retail strategy development.

Sears, Roebuck and Co. is the nation's largest retailer with 845 stores and retail sales of approximately $20 billion.[1] Sears is an all-things-for-all-people retailer, and 65 percent of its sales come from hard-goods like tires, batteries, microwave ovens, washers, dryers, hardware, and paint. Soft-goods lines, especially apparel and linens, have not been as strong as durables, but Sears is trying to improve these product lines so that they will contribute more to sales. In apparel, Sears has added manufacturer brands such as Levi's, Wrangler, Wilson, and McGregor to its private brands, which include Cheryl Tiegs and Arnold Palmer sportswear.

Since two-thirds of all American adults visit a Sears store at least once a year, the basic retailing strategy is to encourage consumers—who are there anyway—to examine products from as many varied product lines as possible. Sears was quick to open telephone departments to sell American Bell products after deregulation of the telephone industry. Sears' service-oriented retail product lines include Allstate Insurance, Dean Witter brokerage firm securities, and Coldwell, Banker & Co. residential real estate. Sears' basic formula for success is to give the consumer quality and value. Rigorous planning, good communications, cost controls, and a contemporary retailing strategy have made Sears the store "Where America Shops."[2]

Sears' success in reaching consumers through both traditional and innovative product lines illustrates that marketing methods that satisfy consumers serve well as the guiding philosophy of retailing. Retailers like Sears form an important link in the marketing channel because they are both marketers and customers. They perform many marketing activities such as buying, selling, grading, risk taking, and developing information about customers' wants. Of all marketers, retailers are the most visible to ultimate consumers. They are, in addition, customers of both producers and wholesalers. Retailers are in a strategic position to gain feedback from consumers and to pass ideas along to producers and to intermediaries in the marketing channel.

Retailing is a very dynamic area of marketing. For example, the American public has gone on a telephone-buying spree since deregulation of the telephone industry. Sales of telephones were expected to reach over $2 billion in 1985. Company phone stores, supermarkets, and department stores, as well as other retail stores, are all fighting for sales once open only to telephone companies. However, the high sales levels are expected to last only a few years. When the sales boom ends, the retailing industry will have to move on to the next major product opportunity to generate sales.[3]

1. *Chain Store Age Executive,* Aug. 1983, p. 25.
2. Ann M. Morrison, "Sears' Overdue Retailing Revival," *Fortune,* April 4, 1983, pp. 133–137.
3. John Morse, "Low-Cost Phones Moving in Supers," *Non-Foods Merchandising,* July 1983, p. 1.

In this chapter, we will examine the nature of retailing, major types of retail stores, nonstore retailers, the wheel of retailing hypothesis, and new developments in retailing.

The nature of retailing

It is fairly common knowledge that retailing is important to the national economy. The *Statistical Abstract of the United States* indicates that approximately 1,304,000 retailers are operating in the United States.[4] While this number has been relatively constant over the past twenty years, sales volume has increased over four times, indicating that the average size of stores has increased. Most personal income is spent in retail stores, and nearly one out of every seven persons employed works in a retail store.

By providing assortments of products that match consumers' wants, retailers create place, time, and possession utilities. They move products from wholesalers or producers to the location of demand (place utility). They make inventories or product stocks available when consumers want them (time utility). And they assume risk through ownership and financing inventories (possession utility).

In the case of service products like hair styling and dry cleaning, retailers develop most of the product utilities. The services of such retailers provide aspects of form utility that are usually associated with the production process. Retailers of service products usually have more direct contact with consumers and more opportunity to alter the product in the marketing mix. Compared with physical goods, the unique aspect of services relates to (1) their intangible nature, which makes consumers' choices more difficult; (2) the fact that the retailer and the product are inseparable, which tends to localize service retailing and to give consumers fewer choices; and (3) the perishability of services, which prevents storage and increases the risk of retailing operations.[5]

Professionals are beginning to offer service products through traditional retail outlets. For example, now there are retail stores that sell legal services. In one store, you can consult with an attorney for $11.95; an additional $13 will purchase a letter or simple phone call; and a variety of packages—wills ($40), name changes ($100), and uncontested divorces ($150)—are the hottest-selling items. This store makes legal services more accessible by using traditional retailing techniques, rather than maintaining the mystique usually associated with a law office.

Retailing focuses on the activities required to facilitate exchanges with ultimate consumers. By definition, retail exchanges are entered into for personal, family, or household purposes.[6] (Although most retailers' sales are to consumers, some non-retail transactions do occur with other businesses.) Retailing activities usually take place in a store or in a service establishment, but in-home selling, vending machines, and mail-order catalogs allow retail exchanges to occur outside of stores.

4. *Statistical Abstract of the United States, 1984,* pp. 802, 808.
5. Richard M. Bessom and Donald W. Jackson, "Service Retailing: A Strategic Marketing Approach," *Journal of Retailing,* Summer 1975, pp. 75–76.
6. William R. Davidson, Alton F. Doody, and Daniel J. Sweeney, *Retailing Management,* 5th ed. (New York: Ronald Press, 1975), p. 4.

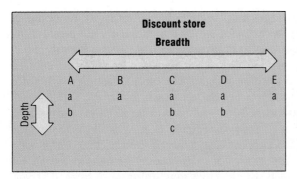

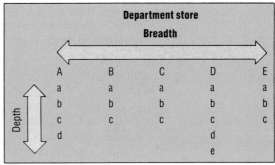

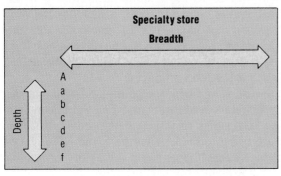

With the capital letters representing number or breadth of product lines, and the small letters depicting the choices in any one product line, it can be seen that discount stores are wide and shallow in merchandise assortment. Specialty stores, at the other extreme, have few product lines, but much more depth in the few they carry. The typical department store falls between these two extremes, having a broad assortment with many merchandise lines and medium depth in each line.

Figure 9.1 Relationship between merchandise breadth and depth for a typical discount store, department store, and specialty store
Source: Robert F. Hartley, Retailing: Challenge and Opportunity, *3rd ed., p. 118. Copyright ©1984 by Houghton Mifflin Company. Used by permission.*

Retailers are positioned in the marketing channel between producers and consumers. As indicated in Chapter 7, retailer leadership in the marketing channel depends on the role and power relationships within the channel. Retailers stand closest to consumers in the channel, but most of the products they sell are developed through the initiative of producers.[7] When producers conduct marketing research and develop products, they are designing products to match consumers' wants. Those producers often coordinate the marketing strategy for products sold at the retail level.

Most retailers develop *product assortments:* that is, they collect a variety of products from several competing producers and wholesalers. This is not always the case, however. A specialty store may provide a narrow selection of products—just women's shoes, for example—and some vertically integrated marketing channels carry only one producer's products. For example, Godiva chocolate stores and Fannie May Candy Shops carry only their own products. Retailers try to provide product assortments that allow consumers to compare, shop, and make purchasing decisions.

As Figure 9.1 illustrates, specialty stores have fewer product lines, but there is much more depth in the lines they do carry. In contrast, discount

7. Wroe Alderson, *Marketing Behavior and Executive Action* (Homewood, Ill.: Irwin, 1957), pp. 333–334.

stores may have a wide product mix (such as housewares, automobile services, apparel, and food). Department stores may have a wide product mix with different product line depths. Nevertheless, it is usually difficult to maintain a wide and deep product mix because of the inventories required. In addition, some producers prefer to distribute through retailers who offer less variety so that their products get more exposure.

A retailer's product assortment is evaluated in terms of (1) purpose, (2) status, and (3) completeness.[8] *Purpose* relates to how well an assortment satisfies consumers and also supports the goals of the retailer. *Status* identifies by rank the relative importance of each product in an assortment. For example, phonograph records would have low status in a store that sells convenience foods. An assortment is *complete* when it includes the products necessary to satisfy a store's customers; it is incomplete when some products are missing. For example, an assortment of convenience foods must include milk to be complete. Most consumers expect to be able to purchase milk when purchasing other food products.

Consumers with different tastes, and with the ability and willingness to purchase, support a variety of retail establishments. The American retail market is splintered, forcing companies to target their products to many new market segments that are being formed.[9] Therefore, the effectiveness and efficiency of the marketing channel depends on the ability of retailers to provide the right product assortment for a specific target market.

Developing the image and atmosphere for a retail store

The ultimate purpose of a retail purchase is sometimes vague to buyers. We discussed the psychological factors and social influences relating to consumer behavior in Chapter 3. It is appropriate to apply some of these concepts as we examine reasons for consumers' patronage. For many consumers, their purchasing is an end in itself; that is, shopping trips are used to escape boredom, to occupy time, or to learn about something new. Because a consumer does not always have a specific reason for going to a retail store, retailers must develop a stimulating and interesting environment for shopping.

Industrial purchases usually are based on economic planning and necessity. Consumer products, on the other hand, are often purchased because of social influences and psychological factors. Consumers usually make a decision to go to one or more of several possible retail stores, most of which have fixed locations, when they search for products. Thus, retailers' marketing efforts are directed toward making desired products available and toward developing a marketing strategy that increases patronage. These goals demand attention to a retail store's image and atmosphere.

The store's image

A retail store must create an image that is acceptable to its target market. Social class and self-concept can be major determinants of patronage. Consumers in lower social classes tend to patronize small, high-margin, high-service food stores—and to prefer small, friendly, high-interest loan com-

8. C. Glenn Walters, *Marketing Channels,* 2nd ed. (Santa Monica, Calif.: Goodyear, 1977), p. 220.
9. "Marketing: The New Priority," *Business Week,* Nov. 21, 1983, p. 96.

Figure 9.2
Saks Fifth Avenue
presents a high-
fashion,
prestige-oriented
image
*Source: Revillon at
Saks Fifth Avenue.*

panies to the more impersonal banks. Saks Fifth Avenue appeals to consumers who are looking for a more distinctive store and a prestige label. Figure 9.2 illustrates the image that Saks Fifth Avenue likes to present to customers. "Different marketing strategies may be required for increasing sales to existing customers and attracting new customers."[10] In other words, customers develop store images based on different characteristics. For example, one study found that the management of Sears should pay attention to "difficulty in finding items" and "friendliness" when trying to get low-frequency shoppers to shop more often. On the other hand, when Sears attempts to gain patronage from K mart customers, honesty and the old-fashioned attributes of K mart seem to affect comparisons between the two. The study found that "high-frequency, low-frequency and non-customers each have different store perceptions."[11] To understand a store's

10. Gerald Albaun, Roger Best, and Del Hawkins, "Retailing Strategy for Customer Growth and New Customer Attraction," *Journal of Business Research,* March 1980, p. 7.
11. Ibid.

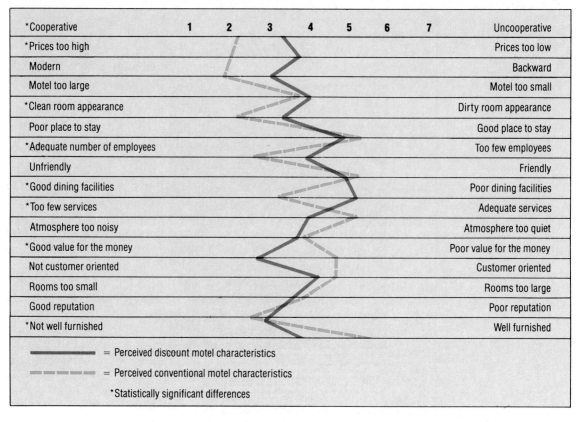

*Cooperative	1	2	3	4	5	6	7	Uncooperative
*Prices too high								Prices too low
Modern								Backward
Motel too large								Motel too small
*Clean room appearance								Dirty room appearance
Poor place to stay								Good place to stay
*Adequate number of employees								Too few employees
Unfriendly								Friendly
*Good dining facilities								Poor dining facilities
*Too few services								Adequate services
Atmosphere too noisy								Atmosphere too quiet
*Good value for the money								Poor value for the money
Not customer oriented								Customer oriented
Rooms too small								Rooms too large
Good reputation								Poor reputation
*Not well furnished								Well furnished

———————— = Perceived discount motel characteristics

– – – – – – – = Perceived conventional motel characteristics

*Statistically significant differences

Figure 9.3 Perceived characteristics (image) of discount versus conventional motels
Source: Ronald F. Bush and Joseph F. Hair, Jr., "Consumer Patronage Determinants, Discount Versus Conventional Motels," Journal of Retailing, *Summer 1976, p. 45.*

image, both shopper characteristics and store characteristics must be understood. Shopper characteristics include demographics, lifestyle, perceptions, and behavior. Store characteristics include clientele, location, promotional emphasis, integrity, convenience, economy, and the clarity and strength of the existing store image.[12]

Figure 9.3 was constructed from 237 personal interviews in four large metropolitan areas. Respondents were a convenience sample of individuals staying at both conventional and discount motels.[13] Discount motels such as Motel 6, Days Inn, Scottish Inns, and Family World have slightly smaller rooms, no elaborate lobbies, and no facilities for conventions and meetings. They also charge up to 50 percent less than conventional motels, such as Holiday Inn and Howard Johnson's. As Figure 9.3 illustrates, perceptions of eight of the characteristics of discount and conventional motels differ significantly, making it possible for a motel to develop an image that appeals to different kinds of customers. A motel with a vague or hazy im-

12. Edgar R. Pessemier, "Store Image and Positioning," *Journal of Retailing,* Spring 1980, pp. 96–97.
13. Ronald F. Bush and Joseph F. Hair, Jr., "Consumer Patronage Determinants of Discount Versus Conventional Motels," *Journal of Retailing,* Summer 1976, p. 45.

age may have difficulty attracting consumers. Similarly, it seems reasonable that store preferences tend to be functions of the degree of "match" between shoppers' perceptions of the store's characteristics and of their own characteristics. Plainly, then, retailers must monitor a store's image in the minds of consumers.

The store's atmosphere

The term *atmospherics* describes the conscious designing of a store's space to create emotional effects that enhance the probability that consumers will buy.[14] The physical aspects of department stores, restaurants, service stations, and shops create an atmosphere that might be perceived as warm, fresh, colorful, or depressing. For example, Figure 9.4 illustrates how the Remington Hotel and restaurant seeks to attract patrons with an atmosphere of old world elegance.

A study indicates that color can physically attract shoppers toward a retail display and provide certain perceptual qualities that affect the image of both the store and the merchandise. In the context of a furniture store, the study showed that subjects may be physically drawn to warm colors such as yellow or red and may sit closer to walls with those colors, which are considered bright and colorful. But they considered these warm colors less attractive and less pleasant than cool colors such as blue and green. Therefore, a good color configuration may be warm colors for a store's exterior or for display cases, with cool colors creating a pleasant environment near product displays.[15] Customers are also affected by a store's interior design and layout.

Filene's of Boston recognized the importance of design and layout when they renovated their cosmetics department. The redesigned department included a fragrance bar, a men's grooming area, and six private consultation areas. Cash registers were hidden behind wooden pillows and the ceilings were lowered to create a warmer, more enclosed, better-lighted environment. The final result was a more personalized, relaxed retail atmosphere where the traditional, brand loyal customer would feel comfortable shopping.[16]

Sound also can be important. A "noisy" environment creates a different atmosphere from one that is characterized by silence or soft music. Even scent may be relevant. Some stores have a distinctive odor of perfume or of prepared food.[17]

Crowding in retail stores is another important part of the environmental psychology. It consists of two components: physical density and perceived crowding.[18] A crowded store may restrict exploratory shopping,

14. Phillip Kotler, "Atmospherics as a Marketing Tool," *Journal of Retailing,* Winter 1973–1974, p. 50.
15. Joseph A. Bellizzi and Ayn E. Crowley, "The Effects of Color in Store Design," *Journal of Retailing,* Spring 1983, pp. 21–25.
16. Phyllis Fine, "Boston Filene's Designed to Draw Cosmetics Customers," *Product Marketing,* Sept. 1983, pp. 1, 6, 8.
17. Edward M. Tauber, "Why Do People Shop?" *Journal of Marketing,* Oct. 1972, p. 47.
18. Gilbert D. Harrell and Michael D. Hutt, "Crowding in Retail Stores," *MSU Business Topics,* Winter 1976, p. 34.

impede mobility, and decrease shopping efficiency. In such a setting, buyers may rely more on familiar brands and may disregard low-priority items.[19]

Retailers should plan a store's atmosphere by first defining the target market and then developing an atmosphere tailored to it. Discount department stores must not seem too exclusive and expensive; high-fashion boutiques might well strive to attain an atmosphere of luxury and novelty. To appeal to multiple market segments, a store may create more than one atmosphere within its departments. The discount basement, the sports department, and the women's shoe department may all have unique atmospheres. Retailers must determine what the target market seeks and then encourage the desired awareness and action in consumers through atmospheric variables.[20]

Major types of retail stores

Retail stores provide assortments to match the shopping preferences of consumers. Figure 9.1 illustrated how the width of product mix and the depth of product line create different types of stores. These factors are important in classifying different types of stores, but there is usually much variation among stores of a particular type. In this section, we will examine the types of retail stores that account for most retail sales.

Department stores

Department stores can be characterized as having a wide product mix; the depth of the product mix may vary, depending on the store. Today, the conventional department stores—Macy's, Hudson's, Bloomingdale's, Marshall Field, Bullock's, or others like them—obtain 75 percent of their sales from apparel and cosmetics.[21] General merchandise, corporate chain department stores—J. C. Penney, Sears, and Montgomery Ward—carry virtually all merchandise lines. These three corporate chain department stores have many more store units and far greater sales volume than certain conventional department store units that usually operate on a regional basis.

Department stores are organized into separate departments—such as cosmetics, housewares, apparel, home furnishings, and appliances—to facilitate marketing efforts and internal management. Recent trends indicate a tendency among general merchandise stores to add departments for automotive, recreational, and sports equipment, as well as services such as insurance, travel advice, and income tax preparation.

Department stores are distinctly service oriented. Their total product includes credit, delivery, personal assistance, merchandise returns, and a pleasant atmosphere. They are, for the most part, shopping stores; that is, consumers compare the price, quality, and service of one store's products with those of competing stores.

General merchandise, corporate chain department stores generate tremendous sales volume, which gives them considerable control over a wide range of the products they sell. For example, Sears has been very success-

---

19. Harrell and Hutt, "Crowding in Retail Stores," p. 34.
20. Kotler, "Atmospherics as a Marketing Tool," p. 62.
21. "The Future of Retailing," *Retailweek,* March 1, 1981, p. 27.

Figure 9.4
Atmosphere that
provides an old world
hospitality image
*Source: Courtesy of
Rosewood Hotel, Inc.*

ful both in integrating marketing activities and in owning or controlling production. Consumers' loyalty and trusted private store brands make Sears extremely powerful in terms of channel leadership and competitive status.

Mass merchandisers Supermarkets and discount stores are mass merchandisers. *Mass merchandisers* tend to offer fewer customer services than department stores and to focus their attention on lower prices, high turnover, and large sales volumes. They generally have a wider—and shallower—product mix than department stores. Mass merchandisers appeal to large heterogeneous target markets. An image of efficiency and economy distinguishes these stores.

Discount stores

Discount stores are self-service, general merchandise stores such as K mart, Wal-Mart, and Target. Table 9.1 lists the top fifteen discount stores. Note that K mart has a commanding lead over second-place Wal-Mart. Many of the discounters, including Wal-Mart, are regional. They carry a wide assortment of products such as appliances, housewares, and

Table 9.1 Top fifteen discount stores (by retail sales)

Rank	Chain (Headquarter State)	Projected Sales for Current Fiscal Year (in millions)
1	K mart (Mich.)	$18,746
2	Wal-Mart (Ark.)	4,325
3	Target (Minn.)	2,774
4	Gemco (Calif.)	2,325
5	T.G.&Y. (Okla.)	1,786
6	Zayre (Mass.)	1,778
7	Hills (Mass.)	1,074
8	Caldor (Conn.)	1,064
9	Bradlees (Mass.)	1,003
10	Meijer (Mich.)	933
11	Payless (Ore.)	830
12	Fred Meyer (Ore.)	792
13	Venture (Mo.)	782
14	Rose's (N.C.)	679
15	Cook United (Ohio)	619

Source: From *Discount Store News,* Sept. 19, 1983. Copyright © Lebhar-Friedman, 425 Park Avenue, New York, N.Y. 10022. Reprinted by permission.

clothing; toys, automotive services, garden supplies, and sports equipment are also found in major discount houses. Often, a food supermarket is operated as a department within a discount store.

In the face of increased competition, discounters have generally improved store services, atmosphere, and location, boosting prices and blurring the distinction between some discount houses and department stores.

In contrast Revco, a leading discount drug chain with 1,630 stores based in Ohio, focuses on price alone, trying to maintain consistently low prices and never running sales. "Everything we do is to try and reinforce the Revco name and reputation as a leading discount drug chain. We established our reputation as a discount outlet from the beginning, and we've attracted numbers by sticking to that image," stated a company spokesman.[22] The Application on page 269 provides an overview of one of Revco's competitors that claims to set prices below even Revco's low prices. In general, however, many better-known discount houses have assumed the characteristics of department stores.

Warehouse showrooms

The *warehouse showroom* is a retail facility incorporating five key characteristics: (1) a large, low-cost building, (2) use of warehouse materials-handling technology, (3) use of vertical merchandise display space, (4) a large on-premises inventory, and (5) minimum services.[23] Most popular

22. "Revco Focuses on Discounts," *Product Marketing,* April 1983, p. 32.
23. Albert D. Bates, "Warehouse Retailing: A Revolutionary Force in Distribution?" *California Management Review,* Winter 1977, p. 75; and Jonathan Goodrich and Jo Ann Huffman, "Warehouse Retailing: The Trend of the Future?" *Business Horizons,* April 1979, pp. 45–50.

Shulman's drugstore in the Eastgate Shopping Center outside Cleveland has an average of thirty thousand customers per week. The store was started in 1975 and current sales are estimated at $20 million a year. According to one study, drug and cosmetic sales were the fourth strongest category of the $74 billion in U.S. discount sales in 1982. Thus, Shulman's ability to become one of the country's most successful discount drugstores, with little advertising, no frills store atmosphere, and seat-of-the-pants, computer-free operation, is impressive. However, Shulman's is no longer the only store of its kind. At least eight other enterprises across the country have started discount drugstores.

Like other discount stores, Shulman's competes on the basis of price. The store buys its merchandise only when drug and cosmetic manufacturers offer a discount, which they are likely to do well over half the time. Shulman's then limits its markup to 20 percent. The result is a business based entirely on high volume. In one week, Shulman's does as much business as a normal discount drugstore like Revco or CVS would do in five months. Impulse buying is important, and at least one of Shulman's imitators has added variety merchandise (the fifth strongest discount sales category) and some foods to increase sales volume.

Shulman's and its imitators are, like superstores, mass merchandisers that offer fewer customer services than more conventional discount drugstores and focus their attention on lower prices, higher turnover, and larger sales volume. Such stores appeal to large heterogeneous target markets and seem to represent a growing segment of the retailing industry.

Source: Based on Bill Abrams, "Discount Drugstores Thriving with Tricky Buying Strategy," *Wall Street Journal*, March 17, 1983, p. 29; and "The True Look of the Discount Industry," *Discount Merchandiser*, May 1983, pp. 40, 106.

warehouse showrooms are large furniture showrooms. Wickes Furniture and Levitz Furniture Corporation have brought sophisticated mass merchandising to the highly fragmented furniture industry. These high-volume, low-overhead operations have reduced personnel and services. Lower costs are effected by shifting some marketing functions to consumers, who must transport, finance, and perhaps store merchandise. Most consumers carry away their purchases in the manufacturer's carton.

Catalog showrooms are another form of warehouse showroom. Consumers select products from a catalog they receive in the mail; they buy at a warehouse where all products are stored out of the buyer's reach. A clerk fills orders from the warehouse, and products are presented in the manufacturer's carton. Operating costs are low because closed inventory rooms reduce shoplifting and display expenses. Catalog showrooms usually sell established brands and models that have little risk of being discontinued. Such showrooms appear to be one of the fastest-growing areas of retailing.

Supermarkets

Supermarkets are large, self-service stores that carry a broad and complete line of food products, and usually some nonfood products as well. They have central checkout facilities. Large grocery supermarkets were the first mass merchandisers. They developed over fifty years ago, but now their total share of the food market is declining. The top ten food chains are listed in Table 9.2.

Table 9.2 The top ten food chains (ranked by sales volume)

Company	1982 Sales
1. Safeway Stores, Inc.	$17,632,821,000
2. The Kroger Company	11,901,892,000
3. Lucky Stores, Inc.	7,972,073,000
4. American Stores Company	7,507,772,000
5. Winn-Dixie Stores, Inc.	7,018,605,000
6. The Southland Corporation	6,782,383,000
7. Jewel Companies, Inc.	5,571,721,000
8. The Great Atlantic & Pacific Tea Company (A & P)	4,607,817,000
9. Albertsons, Inc.	3,940,117,000
10. The Grand Union Company	3,519,341,000

Source: "50 Top Chains," *Supermarket Business,* Oct. 1983, pp. 33–34. Used by permission.

Supermarkets sell a variety of products and feature lower prices than smaller neighborhood grocery stores, which offer convenient locations, personal services, or quality images. One consumer study found that the major reasons for shopping at a particular supermarket were low prices, wide variety, a good selection of quality produce, and convenience of location.[24]

Many supermarkets stock such products as cosmetics and nonprescription drugs and provide such services as check cashing. Supermarkets must be operated efficiently because net profits after taxes are usually less than 1 percent of sales. The future of the supermarket is being challenged by a new competitor, the superstore.

Superstores

Superstores combine features of discount houses and supermarkets. These giant stores carry not only all food and nonfood products ordinarily found in supermarkets, but also most products normally purchased on a routine basis. Such product lines as housewares, hardware, personal care products, garden products, tires, and automotive services complement a complete food line. Compared with supermarkets, superstores have at least double the customer traffic, sales volume per customer, net profit before taxes, and square feet of store space.[25] In addition, superstores have three times the sales and four times as many products as supermarkets.[26] A cluttered atmosphere with pallets of canned goods in boxes is typical. Consumers are most attracted to superstores by lower prices.

Superstores use advanced technology and operating techniques to cut costs and increase sales volume. They often use high-profile shelving and display entire assortments of products to reduce handling costs. Supermarkets' market share is declining because the newly emerging superstores are

24. Jacquelyn Bivens, "Checking Our Consumer Response," *Chain Store Age Executive,* Aug. 1983, p. 19.
25. Walter J. Salmon, Robert D. Buzzell, and Stanton G. Cort, "Today the Shopping Center, Tomorrow the Superstore," *Harvard Business Review,* Jan.–Feb. 1974, pp. 89–98.
26. Ibid.

high-volume, low-margin, low-price stores. Consumers are increasingly concerned with prices, and economic uncertainty makes it difficult for supermarkets to compete. Some superstores, in fact, are little more than warehouses open to the public.[27]

Specialty retailers

Specialty retailers are stores carrying a narrow product mix with deep product lines. The Gap, The Limited, County Seat, Foot Locker, and The Athlete's Foot offer limited product lines but great depth. The Foot Locker, owned by Kinney Shoe Corporation, specializes in running, tennis, and other shoes for sports contests. Florists, bakery shops, and book stores are usually small, independent specialty retailers that appeal to local target markets. Even if this kind of retailer adds a few supporting product lines, the store may still be classified as a specialty store. Usually, such a store is distinguished by its small size and great variety in a few product lines.

Specialty stores usually attempt to provide a unique store image. A strategically positioned retailer may find it easier to compete on the basis of image than to rely on a more flexible variable such as price. The small specialty shop may be unable to compete directly with large retailers in terms of price.[28] Factors relating to fashion, service, personnel, physical characteristics, location, and social class can distinguish small retailers and contribute to favorable consumer attitudes toward them. Figure 9.5 illustrates how a jewelry store maintains a high-fashion, quality image. You would not expect this store to offer discount prices, but to provide the ultimate in service and fine products. Specialty stores give the small business owner an opportunity to provide unique services to match the varied desires of consumers. Specialty stores can, of course, be owned and managed by large corporations. For consumers dissatisfied with the impersonality of larger retailers, the opportunity for close, personal contact in a small specialty store can be a welcome change.

Nonstore retailing

Nonstore retailing takes place without consumers visiting a store. It includes personal sales (such as in-home and telephone retailing) and nonpersonal sales (such as mail-order, vending, and catalog retailing). Nonstore retailing accounts for a small percentage of retail sales—probably less than 20 percent.[29]

Personal sales

In-home retailing
In-home retailing involves personal contacts with consumers. Organizations such as Avon, Electrolux, and Fuller Brush Company go to homes of preselected prospects. However, some in-home selling still is coordinated

27. Albert D. Bates, "The Superstores: Emerging Innovations in Food Retailing," in *Marketing Strategies in Food Distribution,* ed. Jim L. Grimm (Central Illinois Chapter, American Marketing Association, 1976), pp. 12–21.
28. Leonard Berry, "Retail Positioning Strategies for the 1980s," *Business Horizons,* Nov.–Dec., 1982, p. 45.
29. The organization of this section has been adapted from Don L. James, Bruce J. Walker, and Michael J. Etzel, *Retailing Today* (New York: Harcourt Brace Jovanovich, 1975), p. 12.

"I have the simplest of tastes . . .
I am always satisfied with the best"
Oscar Wilde

©1983 G.J.C.

Uniquely . . . GemLok. The classics of tomorrow.

Lee Michaels
FINE JEWELRY
SHREVEPORT, LA. (318) 869-3078
BATON ROUGE, LA. (504) 926-4644

without information about sales prospects. In-home selling of rugs, draperies, and home improvements is helpful to consumers, since these products need to be blended carefully with the existing interior of a house.

Door-to-door selling based on a canvass represents a tiny proportion of total retail sales—probably less than 1 percent. Because it has so often been associated with unscrupulous and fraudulent techniques, door-to-door selling is illegal in some communities. In general, this technique is regarded unfavorably because so many door-to-door salespersons are undertrained and poorly supervised. A big disadvantage of door-to-door selling is the large expenditure, effort, and time involved. Sales commissions are usually 25 to 50 percent, or more, of the retail price; and consumers often pay more than a product is worth as a result. Door-to-door selling is used most often when a product is unsought and consumers will not make a special effort to go to a store to purchase it. Many encyclopedias are sold in this way. Avon and Fuller Brush, two successful and respected companies, have used door-to-door selling very effectively.

One variation of in-home retailing is the home demonstration or party, a method that is gaining popularity. One consumer acts as host and invites a number of friends to view merchandise at his or her home.

Telephone retailing

Telephone retailing can be based on a cold canvass of the telephone directory, or prospective clients can be screened before calling. Another tactic is to use advertising that encourages consumers to initiate a call or to request information about placing an order. Although this type of retailing represents a small part of total retail sales, its use is growing. In some areas, telephone numbers may be listed with an asterisk to indicate those people who consider sales solicitations a nuisance. Figure 9.6 illustrates direct telephone retailing by Lands' End, a direct sales merchandiser.

Nonpersonal sales

Automatic vending

Automatic vending makes use of machines and accounts for less than 2 percent of all retail sales. Six million vending units generated $13.8 billion in retail sales in 1980.[30]

Coin-operated, self-service machines make a wide assortment of products available, including cigarettes, hosiery, golf balls, insurance policies,

30. Data from *Vending Times* reported by *Wall Street Journal*, Sept. 10, 1981, p. 27.

and hot beverages. Many banks now use vending machines to dispense cash when a credit card is inserted.

Automatic vending is one of the most impersonal forms of retailing. Small, standardized, routinely purchased products can be sold in machines. Consumers usually purchase convenience products such as candy, chewing gum, soft drinks, and coffee at the nearest available location. Machines in areas of heavy traffic—offices, service stations, motels, shopping areas, and the like—provide efficient and continuous services to consumers. The elimination of sales personnel and the small amount of space necessary for vending machines give this retailing method some advantages over stores. Some of the advantages are, nevertheless, offset by the expense of the frequent servicing and repair needed.

Mail-order retailing

Mail-order retailing is a form of selling by description; buyers usually do not see the actual product until it arrives in the mail. Mail-order sellers contact buyers through direct mail, catalogs, television, radio, magazines, and newspapers. A wide asssortment of products such as records, books, clothing, and household items are sold to consumers through the mail.

There has been a growing trend for placement of mail orders to be handled by telephone. American Express, Visa, and Mastercard usually enclose mail-order brochures with their statements. The advantages of mail-order selling include efficiency and convenience. Mail-order houses can be located in remote areas and can forego the expenses of store fixtures. Eliminating personal selling efforts and store operations may result in tremendous savings that can be passed along to consumers in the form of lower prices. On the other hand, mail-order retailing is inflexible, provides limited service, and is more appropriate for specialty products than for convenience products.

Catalog retailing is a type of direct marketing conducted by retailers. Orders may be delivered by mail, or customers may pick them up. Although some catalog orders are placed by in-store visits, most are placed by mail or telephone. Figure 9.7 illustrates catalog retailing at Bloomingdale's.

Franchising

Franchising is an arrangement in which a supplier (franchisor) grants a dealer (franchisee) the right to sell products in exchange for some type of consideration. For example, the franchisor may receive some percentage of total sales. The franchisor helps to furnish equipment, buildings, management know-how, and marketing assistance. The franchisee must agree to operate according to the rules of the franchisor.

Franchised health clubs, exterminators, and campgrounds abound. Figure 9.8 illustrates a program for franchised dental care centers. There are also franchised tax preparers and travel agencies. The real estate industry is experiencing rapid growth in franchising. Also expected to join the franchising ranks in large numbers are hair salons, tanning salons, and professionals such as dentists and lawyers.[31]

31. Franchising types and examples are adapted from Robert F. Hartley, *Retailing: Challenge and Opportunity,* Third Edition, Copyright © 1984 Houghton Mifflin Company. Adapted with permission.

The franchising movement has been one of retailing's major growth areas over the past twenty years. During this period, organizations such as McDonald's Corporation, Holiday Inns Inc., Kentucky Fried Chicken, and Howard Johnson Company restaurants and motels have emerged as major competitive forces in their respective industries. Three basic types of franchising arrangements have been developed. The next three paragraphs describe some well-known examples.[32]

A producer may franchise a number of stores to sell a particular brand of product. This franchising arrangement is one of the oldest, and it prevails in the areas of passenger cars and trucks, farm equipment, shoes, paint, earth-moving equipment, and petroleum. Virtually all new cars and trucks are sold through franchised dealers, while an estimated 90 percent

32. "Franchising—Opening the Doors to Expansion," *Retailweek,* Feb. 1, 1981, p. 29.

Figure 9.8
Dental franchise operation located in shopping malls and other convenient locations
Source: Courtesy of Omnidentix Systems Corporation ® Arnold and Company Marketing and Advertising.

"Going to the dentist should be as convenient as going to the store. That's why we put our dental center where you shop."

David B. Slater,
Chairman & Founder, Omnidentix®

We started Omnidentix® because we wanted to make going to the dentist a pleasure. Instead of a pain.

One way to accomplish this is by putting our dental centers in places that are convenient for you. Like easy-to-get-to shopping malls. And busy downtown areas. Besides our convenient locations, you'll also find our affordable prices, long hours and expert staff a pleasure, too.

Now that Omnidentix has made going to the dentist this convenient, what are you waiting for? Call the number below and set up an appointment.

Omni entix®
Business Systems

Theodore Lax,
DDS, PC.
Member

A whole new way to go to the dentist.

Pyramid Mall, Ithaca, New York 14850. Telephone 257-7733.
Hours Mon.–Sat. 8–9, Sun. 12–5. MasterCard & Visa accepted.

of all gasoline is sold through franchised independent retail service stations. Table 9.3 illustrates the largest franchising sectors, ranked by sales.

A producer may franchise wholesalers to sell to retailers. This arrangement is most common in the soft-drink industry. Most national producers of soft-drink syrups—Coca-Cola, Dr. Pepper, Pepsi-Cola, 7UP, Royal Crown—franchise independent bottlers who then serve retail markets.

Sometimes, rather than franchising a complete product, a franchisor provides brand names, techniques, procedures, or other services. While the franchisor may perform some manufacturing and wholesaling functions, its major contribution is a carefully developed, and controlled, marketing strategy. This is the most common type of franchise today. Examples are many, including Holiday Inn, Howard Johnson's, Maaco, McDonald's, Dairy Queen, Avis, Hertz, Kentucky Fried Chicken, and H & R Block.

Franchising continues to grow at a rapid rate. The Department of Commerce indicates that franchise establishments were doing about $116 billion in sales in 1969. By 1980 sales had increased to approximately $338 billion. The number of new franchises or new businesses that entered the franchising arena increased by about 9 percent each year.

The expansion of the franchise system to many industries highlights the advantages of central management control and coordinated marketing efforts for franchise members. The current trends of franchising growth will probably continue at approximately the same rate. The advantages of

Table 9.3 Largest franchising sectors, ranked by sales

	Sales (millions of dollars)	% of Total Franchise Sales
Automobile and truck dealers	132,171	53.4
Gasoline service stations	52,409	21.2
Fast-food restaurants	17,075	6.9
Soft-drink bottlers	11,044	4.5
Retailing (nonfood)	10,883	4.4
Automotive products and services[a]	6,202	2.5
Other	17,791	7.1
Total	274,575	100.0

[a]Includes tires.
Source: *Franchising in the Economy, 1976–1978,* U.S. Department of Commerce (Washington, D.C.: U.S. Government Printing Office, 1978), pp. 1–2. Based on 1977 sales.

going into business under the protective wing of a company with a proven track record are tremendous. Franchisees are entrepreneurs who have invested their own money and must perform at a high level to protect their investment. Still, like all businesses, franchising does pose risks, and many franchisees have gone out of business as a result of poor management, minimal marketing research, poor marketing planning, or overexpansion.

Planned shopping centers

"Today the shopping center is replacing the central business district as a place for shopping, cultural, or recreational opportunities. This is particularly true with enclosed malls that attract large numbers of people for purposes other than shopping."[33] The planned shopping center is constructed by private owners to contain a complementary mix of stores that provide one-stop shopping for family and household needs. Although shopping centers may vary, the concept of a coordinated and complementary mix of stores that generates consumer traffic is a key factor.

Shopping centers are planned, coordinated, and promoted to appeal to heterogeneous groups of consumers. The joint development of shopping-center management ensures an atmosphere that is comfortable and conveniently set up to serve consumers with a variety of needs. Parking facilities, landscaping, and special events create an overall atmosphere that attracts consumers. Shopping centers are self-contained; they provide a variety of different types of stores where consumers can take care of most shopping needs.

Neighborhood shopping centers

Neighborhood shopping centers usually consist of several small convenience and specialty stores such as small grocery stores, drugstores, gas stations, and fast-food restaurants. Neighborhood shopping centers serve consumers who live less than ten minutes' driving time from the center. Many of these retailers consider their target markets to be consumers who live within a two- to three-mile radius of their stores. Since most purchases are

33. Joseph Barry Mason, "First, Fifth and Fourteenth Amendment Rights: The Shopping Center as a Public Forum," *Journal of Retailing,* Summer 1975, p. 21.

based on convenience or personal contact, the coordination of selling efforts within a neighborhood shopping center usually is limited. Product mixes are usually held to essential products, and depth of the product lines tends to be limited.

Community shopping centers

Community shopping centers include one or two department stores and some specialty stores, as well as convenience stores. They serve a larger geographic area and draw consumers who are looking for shopping and specialty products that are not available in neighborhood shopping centers. Consumers drive longer distances to community shopping centers, which are carefully planned and coordinated to attract shoppers. Special events such as art exhibits, automobile shows, and sidewalk sales are used to stimulate traffic. The overall management of a community shopping center looks for tenants that complement the center's total assortment of products. There are wide product mixes and deep product lines.

Regional shopping centers

Regional shopping centers usually have the largest department stores, the widest product mix, and the deepest product lines of all shopping centers. They carry most products found in a downtown shopping district. The success of regional shopping centers has led to defensive measures by downtown retailers, who have modernized their stores and increased parking facilities. Intracity expressways and improved public transportation have helped many downtown shopping districts to remain competitive.

With 150,000 or more consumers in their target market, regional shopping centers must have well-coordinated management and marketing activities. These large centers usually advertise, have special events, furnish transportation to some consumer groups, and carefully select the mix of stores. For example, in Illinois, the stores in Louis Joliet Mall, including Marshall Field, Sears, and The Limited, employed a retail consultant to develop a marketing program for their mall. The result was several fashion shows, entertainment from a regional dance company, and promotions to highlight merchandise and entertain customers. In one case, jewelers set up specially designed booths in the mall and reportedly sold $15,000 worth of merchandise in a single day during a promotional event entitled "All That Jazz."[34]

Because of financial requirements in regional shopping centers, national chain stores have found it easier to gain leases in them than small independents have.

Nontraditional shopping centers

Two new types of discount malls or shopping centers are emerging that differ significantly from traditional shopping centers. The factory outlet mall features discount and factory outlet stores carrying traditional manufacturer brands, such as Van Heusen, Levi Strauss, International Silver, Munsingwear, Health-Tex, and Wrangler. Manufacturers own these stores and must exert particular effort to avoid conflicting with traditional retailers of their products. Most such shopping centers are found outside prime

34. "Mall Promotion: Show & Sell," *Chain Store Age Executive,* May 1983, pp. 100–101.

retail, metropolitan areas. Manufacturers claim that their stores are in non-competitive locations.[35] Not all factory outlets stock closeouts and irregulars, but almost all seek to avoid comparison with discount houses. The factory outlet mall attracts customers because of lower prices for quality and major brand names.[36]

The factory outlet mall operates in much the same way as regional shopping centers and probably draws traffic from a farther shopping radius than the regional shopping center. Promotional activity is at the heart of these new shopping centers. Craft shows, contests, and special events attract a great deal of traffic.

Another nontraditional shopping center is the miniwarehouse mall. These loosely planned centers sell space to retailers, who operate what are essentially retail stores out of warehouse bays. Some of these miniware-houses are located in high-traffic areas and provide ample parking space for customers, as well as display windows that can be seen from the street. Home improvement materials, specialty foods, pet supplies, garden and yard supplies are often sold in these malls. Unlike the traditional shopping centers, a coordinated promotional program and store mix is usually non-existent in the miniwarehouse mall.

The developers of the miniwarehouse mall may sell space to both wholesalers and retailers, or even to light manufacturers who maintain a retail facility in their warehouse bay. These nontraditional shopping centers do not fit the traditional shopping center scheme. They come closest to a neighborhood or community shopping center.

The wheel of retailing

When new types of retail businesses develop, they hope to find a niche in the dynamic environment that surrounds retailing. One hypothesis attempts to account for the evolution of and future opportunities for new types of retail stores. The *wheel of retailing* hypothesis holds that "new types of retailers usually enter the market as low-status, low-margin, low-price operators." Gradually, they acquire more elaborate establishments and facilities, with both increased investments and higher operating costs. Finally, they mature as high-cost, high-price merchants, vulnerable to newer types who, in turn, go through the same pattern."[37] For example, supermarkets have undergone many changes since their introduction in 1921. Initially, they provided limited services in exchange for lower food prices. However, a variety of new services have developed over time, including delicatessens, free coffee, gourmet food sections, and children's areas with cartoon films.

Two new developments in food retailing are superstores and box stores. As discussed earlier superstores are huge mass merchandisers who operate on a low cost, self-service basis and carry most routinely purchased goods as well as groceries. Superstores have increased product choices over the original supermarket offerings and make lower prices available again.

35. Alyson Fendel, "The Newest Malls: Factory Outlets," *Stores,* March 1981, p. 38.
36. Ibid.
37. Stanley C. Hollander, "The Wheel of Retailing," *Journal of Marketing,* July 1960, p. 37.

Figure 9.9

The wheel of retailing explains the entry and evolution of new types of retail stores
Source: Adapted from Robert F. Hartley, Retailing: Challenge and Opportunity, *3rd ed. (Boston: Houghton Mifflin, 1984), p. 42.*

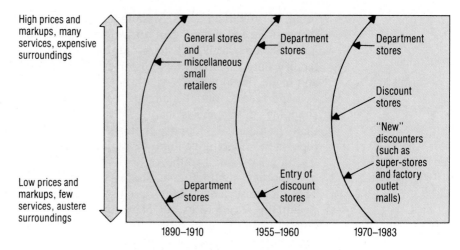

High prices and markups, many services, expensive surroundings

Low prices and markups, few services, austere surroundings

| 1890–1910 | 1955–1960 | 1970–1983 |

If the "wheel" is considered to be turning slowly in the direction of the arrow, then the department stores around 1900 and the discounters later can be viewed as coming on the scene at the low end of the wheel. As it turns slowly, they move with it, becoming higher-price operations, and at the same time leaving room for lower-price types of firms to gain entry at the low end of the wheel.

Box stores, also called no-frills warehouses, leave their merchandise in boxes sitting on shipping pallets. The prices are very low, and the services provided are minimal. Prices are specified above each box, but customers must transfer the price onto each item they buy. Customers must also provide their own bags and bag their merchandise. Box stores can usually undersell conventional supermarkets by as much as 20 percent. Their main innovation is lower price.[38]

Figure 9.9 illustrates the wheel of retailing for department stores and discount houses. Department stores such as Sears developed as high-volume, low-cost merchants to compete with general stores and other small retailers. Discount houses developed in response to the rising expenses of services in department stores. Many discount houses now appear to be following the wheel of retailing by offering more services, better locations, quality inventories, and, therefore, higher prices. In some cases, it is hard to distinguish discount houses from department stores. The wheel of retailing, like most hypotheses, may not apply to all developments in its field. A major weakness is that the hypothesis does not predict what innovations will develop or when. Still, the hypothesis works reasonably well in industrialized, expanding economies.

Retail strategy development

From a managerial point of view, retailing is the attempt to manage exchange at the point of ultimate consumption for the benefit of the organization and society.[39] Table 9.4 summarizes our central managerial philosophy—the marketing concept—as it applies to retailers in the 1980s. A

38. Louis E. Boone and David L. Kurtz, "Box Stores: No-Frills Retailing," *Business,* March 1983, pp. 19–22.
39. Joseph Barry Mason and Morris Lehman Mayer, *Modern Retailing,* rev. ed. (Plano, Tex.: Business Publications, Inc., 1981), p. 18.

Table 9.4   The marketing concept as applied to retailing

The marketing concept in retailing has come to mean an understanding of the consumer's wants, needs, and desires so that the store, through its management and its marketing and merchandising plans, is better equipped to serve and satisfy those wants, needs, and desires.

The marketing concept means that merchandise and services that can be profitably offered are selected on the basis of perceived customer and consumer wants, needs, and desires.

The marketing concept means that these wants, needs, and desires must be ascertained before goods and services are offered for sale.

The marketing concept means that recognition of changing customer and consumer needs is paramount if the firm selling the goods and services is to survive, grow, and prosper.

Source: *Promotion Exchange,* National Retail Merchants Association, in New York, Aug. 1979. Used by permission.

marketing strategy for a retailer is the posture or central scheme assumed by management as it attempts to accomplish its objectives. Defining a target market and developing the retailing mix are critical concerns.

Developing a marketing strategy for a retailer involves five basic steps:

1. *Segmenting the market for the type of product or service offering*
2. *Identifying competitive organizations that handle this class of products and assessing their merchandising strengths and differential advantages*
3. *Assessing the resources of the organization in light of the competitive environment*
4. *Defining the specific market target in terms of focal market segment or segments*
5. *Developing the retailing mix that represents a plan for the allocation of available resources among alternative uses in a coordinated manner to maximize the total impact generated to influence the customers in the defined market target*[40]

Variables to monitor in the retail environment include unit sales growth, gross margin performance, and the ratio of operating expenses to sales. Problems in the business environment could be business cycles, inflation, and changing demographic trends. Once changes are detected, the firm must decide whether to make the necessary investment and changes to adapt to its changing environment. When Woolworth liquidated its Woolco discount division it made a decision that continuing the division would require greater risk and resources than the firm wanted to invest.[41] Consider also the changing environment of the retail jewelry market described in the Application on page 282.

40. Louis W. Stern and Adel I. El-Ansary, *Marketing Channels,* © 1977, p. 60. Reprinted by permission of Prentice-Hall, Inc., Englewood Cliffs, N.J.
41. Joseph V. Rizzi, "Prospering in a Changing Retail Environment," *Retail Control,* March 1983, p. 13.

The lucrative retail jewelry market has some new entrants—among them, J. C. Penney, Sears, Montgomery Ward, Target Stores and other big chains. J. C. Penney, for example, now ranks fourth in size among the country's retail jewelry merchants. These retailers are using mass merchandising techniques to take business away from established jewelry retailers, who traditionally have used high markups to earn large profits on low volumes.

Competition between department stores and jewelers is only partial. The department stores have only been making inroads in the market for items under $800, whereas the specialty stores sell the whole range from $300 to $5,000. The lower-priced items, though, account for most of retail jewelry sales. The department stores concentrate on high turnover, and if jewelry sales fall, items are marked down immediately.

Through price cutting and advertising, department stores hope to get consumers to view jewelry as a more routine purchase. This strategy seems to be effective, as both men and working women are buying more jewelry. Analysts predict that the overall market could grow by as much as 100 percent. As it does so, department store chains will continue to seek a growing market share.

These department store chains illustrate the development of a retail strategy. These stores have segmented the jewelry market and have gone after buyers of low-priced, fast-moving items. The stores have identified their competitors, who are independent jewelers, and are using discount pricing to compete with them. The department stores are focusing their marketing effort to maximize their total impact and influence on the target market.

Source: Based on "Chain Stores Strike Gold in Jewelry Sales," *Business Week,* Feb. 6, 1984, pp. 56, 58.

The retailing mix is similar to the marketing mix concept, but it applies more specifically to the field of retailing. It includes location, hours, facilities, organizational structure and strength, merchandise planning and control, pricing, buying, promotion, service, and expense management. As Figure 9.10 indicates, merchandising is the main element of the mix. *Merchandising* involves selling the right products in the right quantities, at the right place, at the right time, and at the right price. Merchandise management involves planning and control of a merchandise inventory to serve target consumers and achieve the profit goals of the retailer.

In a study of sales, contribution to income, and return on assets in a chain of retail stores, the level of inventory had a strong impact on each store's performance. Management needs to insure that individual store units are stocking an adequate product assortment, that stockouts are minimized, and that any unbalanced inventory situations are handled as quickly as possible. Check-out systems with automatic inventory maintenance are helpful in overcoming these problems.[42]

Failure to create a distinctive retailing mix makes it more difficult for a retailer to compete. As shown in Figure 9.11, Burger King continually updates its product mix to differentiate its offerings from those of McDonald's and other competitors. In today's highly competitive, saturated markets, retailers must differentiate themselves by carefully selecting their

42. Richard Hise, J. Patrick Kelly, Myron Gable, and James B. McDonald, "Factors Affecting the Performance of Individual Chain Store Units: An Empirical Analysis," *Journal of Retailing,* Summer 1983, p. 37.

Figure 9.10
Retailing mix
*Source: Adapted from
Louis W. Stern and Adel
I. El-Ansary,* Marketing
Channels, *1977, p. 61.
Reprinted by permission
of Prentice-Hall, Inc.,
Englewood Cliffs, New
Jersey.*

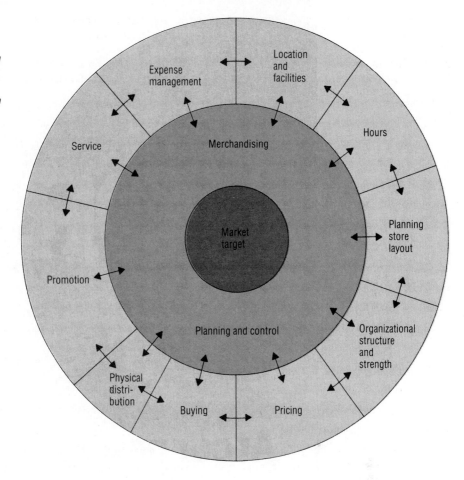

market segments and projecting merchandising images designed to attract specific and well-differentiated markets.[43]

Summary

Retailers form an important link in the marketing channel. They perform many marketing activities and add value to final consumer products. In addition, retailers are customers for wholesalers and producers. Retail institutions provide place, time, possession, and in some cases form utilities.

Manufacturers often develop the marketing strategy for a product, whereas retailers offer an assortment of products from competing manufacturers. The marketing functions that retailers perform depend on the role relationships and the division of labor within the marketing channel.

The environment of a retail store includes the store's image and its atmosphere. In planning these characteristics, retailers must consider the consumers' self-concepts and desires. To create an effective atmosphere, a store's space should be designed to develop an emotional effect that enhances the probability that consumers will buy.

43. Arthur I. Cohen and Ana Loud Jones, "Brand Marketing in the New Retail Environment," *Harvard Business Review,* Sept.–Oct. 1978, p. 142.

Figure 9.11
Merchandising of a
differentiated product
in the highly competi-
tive fast food industry
*Source: Burger King
Corporation.*

This chapter describes major types of retail stores: department stores, mass merchandisers, and specialty stores. It also discusses nonstore retailers, franchisors, and planned shopping centers. Mass merchandisers include discount houses, warehouse showrooms, supermarkets, and superstores. Nonstore retailing pertains to in-home selling, telephone selling, automatic vending, and mail-order selling. Planned shopping centers provide an environment for a complementary mix of retail stores. Such shopping centers include neighborhood, community, and regional and nontraditional shopping centers.

The wheel of retailing hypothesis holds that new retail institutions develop as low-status, low-margin, low-price operators. As they trade up to increase service, they become vulnerable, and newer institutions enter and repeat the cycle. However, like most hypotheses, the wheel of retailing may not apply in every case.

There are five basic steps to developing an overall marketing strategy for a retailer. The last two involve defining the target market and developing a retailing mix. The retailing mix includes location, hours, facilities, organizational structure and strength, merchandise planning and control, pricing, buying, promotion, service, and expense management.

Important terms

Retailing	In-home retailing
Product assortments	Telephone retailing
Atmospherics	Automatic vending
Department stores	Mail-order retailing
Mass merchandisers	Catalog retailing
Discount stores	Franchising
Warehouse showrooms	Neighborhood shopping centers
Catalog showrooms	Community shopping centers
Supermarkets	Regional shopping centers
Superstores	Wheel of retailing
Specialty retailers	Merchandising
Nonstore retailing	

Discussion and review questions

1. Retailers develop product assortments to make final exchanges with ultimate consumers. What marketing activities must be performed to develop product assortments?
2. Retailers develop assortments from several competing manufacturers and serve consumers' interests. What do manufacturers do to ensure that their products are selected at the retail level?
3. Is it possible for a single retail store to have an overall image that appeals to sophisticated shoppers, extravagant ones, and bargain hunters? Why or why not?
4. How does atmosphere add value to products sold in a store? How important is atmospherics for convenience stores?
5. What are the major differences between discount houses and department stores?
6. Furniture warehouse showrooms developed as a new kind of mass merchandiser in the late 1960s and 1970s. List other major shopping products that could be sold using the showroom method.
7. What do specialty retailers have in common? Do they compete with department stores?
8. Why is door-to-door selling a form of retailing? Some consumers feel that direct mail-orders skip the retailer. Is this true?
9. What management assistance does the typical franchisee gain from the franchisor? What are some reasons why many franchisees have gone out of business?
10. What is the hypothesis of the "wheel of retailing"?
11. What impact could the rising cost of gasoline have on the wheel of retailing?
12. Without a distinctive retailing mix it is difficult for a retailer to compete. Do you agree or disagree with this statement? Why?
13. How should one determine the best retail store atmosphere?
14. How does the retail marketing of professional services differ from traditional retail marketing of goods?

Cases

Case 9.1

The Southland Corporation's 7-Eleven Stores[44]

The Southland Corporation operates over 7,400 7-Eleven retail convenience stores in 48 states, the District of Columbia, and five provinces of Canada. 7-Eleven is the country's largest retailer of products such as tobacco products, magazines, beer, and coffee-to-go. In addition, Southland is the largest independent retailer of gasoline in the United States. 7-Eleven self-serve gasoline is available at approximately 3,000 store locations.

Southland opened approximately 3,000 new 7-Eleven stores between 1978 and 1984. However, the corporation is strongly committed to what it considers its "real growth"—that is, increasing sales and earnings in all of its units. It has developed a plan for increasing store productivity by concentrating on several key areas: product mix, personnel, operational efficiency, store location, and advertising and promotion.

The idea that store productivity is closely linked to the number and types of products offered has prompted the constant search for successful new products. Over the past several years, 7-Eleven has introduced Danish pastries, fountain soft-drinks, burritos, juices, and video games, all of which have been very successful. At the same time, it is continuing to promote established products with good sales potential. Its "Slurpee" frozen carbonated drink is an example of a product that found renewed success due to an effective promotional program.

Southland is committed to developing highly motivated personnel to manage and operate its stores. It has found that high quality store managers, franchise owners, and sales personnel have greatly contributed to individual store productivity. For this reason, Southland has launched extensive training programs and offered improved compensation packages.

Southland has also increased productivity by improving store efficiency. This has involved careful attention to product placement and merchandising. Store layout and design has also been improved to achieve a clean and modern look, to control customer traffic, and to make products more accessible and easily visible.

A greater emphasis on store location has led to the acquisition of corner sites for 90 percent of the new stores established within the past five years. These corner sites, though expensive, are a key to greater productivity because they are more accessible and visible. They are also more suitable for selling gasoline, which is responsible for substantial increases in sales and profits.

In addition to this emphasis on location, every store is measured against higher sales and earning standards each year. This means that stores that are in marginal locations or that lack market potential are closed down, leaving a base of competitive, productive stores.

Another area that has contributed to increased productivity for 7-Eleven Stores is advertising and promotion geared toward emphasizing the convenience of shopping there. The advertising theme "America Likes

44. Facts are from the Southland Corporation, *1982 Annual Report* and the November 4, 1983 Marketing Presentation handout from Southland Corporation.

the Freedom of 7-Eleven" has been publicized in television and radio spots and in print advertising.

Southland's plans for the future include a strong commitment to finding products that appeal to the impulse, can be bought with cash, are convenience items, do not require much storage or display space, guarantee an adequate profit per square foot used, can be carried home, require a minimum of employee support, and are preferably, but not necessarily, male-oriented.

Questions for discussion

1. Customers are not aware of the differences between 7-Eleven and other convenience outlets. This is true despite the fact that 7-Elevens carry more products, are cleaner, and have proprietary products. Suggest a solution to this problem.
2. Consumers are unaware of 7-Eleven's competitive pricing on many major product segments: case beer, gallons of milk, carton cigarettes, gasoline. Suggest solutions to this problem.
3. The grocery business is low-profit and highly competitive. What new products and service lines must 7-Eleven look to for future growth?

Case 9.2

W.R. Grace & Co. Specialty Retail Operations[45]

While the largest and most important operation of W.R. Grace & Co. has been specialty chemicals, specialty retailing and restaurants are gaining prominence. A narrow product mix with deep product lines characterizes the specialty retailer. The retailing of items like jewelry, sporting goods, leisure apparel, and home improvement products depends on carefully selected merchandise and a distinctive atmosphere. Table 9.5 shows the spe-

Table 9.5 Specialty Retailing and Restaurant Divisions of W.R. Grace & Co.

Specialty Retailing	Home Centers	Angels, Cashway, Channel, Handy City, Handy Dan, Orchard
	Sporting Goods	Herman's World of Sporting Goods
	Jewelry	J.B. Robinson Jewelers
	Leisure Apparel	Bermans (leather apparel), Sheplers (western wear)
Restaurant	Dinner houses	El Torito, Houlihan's Old Place, Reuben's, Plankhouse, Baxter's, Tequila Willie's, Annie's Santa Fe, Reuben E. Lee, Gorda Liz, Bristol Bar & Grill
	Family Restaurants	Coco's, jojos
	Fast Food	Del Taco

Source: W.R. Grace & Co., *1982 Annual Report,* p. 37.

45. The facts in this case are based on the following sources: Suzanne Wittebarr, "Grace Takes to the Tube," *Institutional Investor,* June 1981, p. 55; W.R. Grace & Co., *1980 Annual Report;* and W.R. Grace & Co., *1982 Annual Report.*

Table 9.6   Sales, numbers of units, and growth rates of W.R. Grace & Co. specialty retailing and
            restaurant groups

	Specialty Retailing				Restaurant			
	Home Centers	Leisure Apparel	Jewelry and Sporting Goods	Total	Family Restaurants	Dinner Houses	Fast Food	Total
Sales ($million)								
1976	$260	$ 76	$139	$ 475	$ 59	$124	—	$183
1978	$407	$ 65	$197	$ 669	$101	$180	$ 1	$282
1980	$685	$104	$274	$1063	$179	$298	$48	$525
1982	$875	$134	$325	$1334	$188	$394	$52	$634
Avg. Annual Growth Rate	21.1%	19.8%	13.3%	18.8%	168%	21.6%	168.5%	225%
Number of Units— Year End								
1976	112	179	84	375	92	115	—	207
1978	175	31	113	319	148	148	21	317
1980	245	58	155	458	219	224	173	616
1982	273	88	169	530	214	256	137	607
Avg. Annual Growth Rate	11.8%	29.8%	10.6%	13.5%	9.7%	14.7%	59.8%	17.6%

Source: W.R. Grace & Co., *1982 Annual Report*, p. 46.

cific stores within W.R. Grace's specialty retailing and restaurant divisions. Table 9.6 shows the sales of the specialty retailing and restaurant groups along with the number of units existing and annual growth rates.

Grace entered the specialty retail area when it purchased Herman's World of Sporting Goods in 1970. Herman's World of Sporting Goods differs sharply from most sports shops. Store design is targeted to appeal to individuals interested in athletic fashion. In avoiding the "locker room-look" of other sporting good shops, Herman's is more appealing due to its warm and pleasant decor and its attractive displays. Today, Herman's is the number one specialty retailer of athletic equipment and sports apparel. Herman's provides a wide assortment of competitively priced sports equipment and clothing. Selective expansion from 3 stores in 1970 with sales of $10 million to 95 stores in 1982 with sales of $275 million has been one of their most successful strategies.

Grace's specialty jewelry retailer is J.B. Robinson. Primarily differentiated by its six-week, money-back guarantee on all merchandise, Robinson's features watches, gold and silver jewelry, diamonds, and other precious gems. Robinson's won the Clio award for advertising excellence in promoting jewelry from the People's Republic of China. The campaign featured sales announcements that were enclosed in fortune cookies and mailed to customers. A unique promotion or special event is not an unusual tactic for J.B. Robinson.

In 1976, Grace acquired Sheplers, a clothing store specializing in western, outdoor, and casual wear. As "the world's largest western store," Sheplers markets a variety of products, including gift items and children's clothing.

In 1979, Grace acquired a chain specializing in leather apparel and leisure wear for men and women. Bermans—The Leather Experts offers practical and unique items. It strives to carry contemporary merchandise at a price that is appropriate for its target market. Bermans operated 78 outlets at the end of 1982, having added 13 stores during the year.

The acquisition of Handy City's 13 stores in 1976 initiated Grace's entry into the home center business. Grace led the do-it-yourself market in 1982 with sales of $875 million, a 10 percent increase over the previous year. Grace's home centers are oriented toward the consumer, offering lumber and building materials, paints, hardware, electrical goods, and numerous other supplies for the do-it-yourselfer. New model stores are being introduced that offer merchandise placed out in front of the stores in "bulk-stacked" displays. These new stores are supported by advertising and promotional programs offering popular items at prices below those of the competition.

Grace operates a 607-unit restaurant group offering many diverse formats and cuisines. Grace develops new restaurant concepts from market research on consumer preferences and trends. For example, Baxter's Restaurant appeals to a segment of the market interested in lighter meals and snacks. With its unique, casual, and entertaining atmosphere, Baxter's has developed a loyal clientele.

One of Grace's most successful restaurants is the Bristol Bar & Grill, a seafood restaurant located in Kansas City and St. Louis. Dinners of fresh oysters, fish fillets, and other seafood items are prepared right in front of customers. The Bristol ships in seafood every day to provide a culinary experience not generally associated with the Midwest. Other features include an open bake shop, luncheon salad bar, and a mahogany lounge with an oyster/appetizer bar.

Grace's fast food division is currently headed by Burger King's former chairperson and chief executive officer. Del Taco Mexican fast-food outlets are located primarily in the Southeast and Texas. Many of these restaurants feature singing waiters and a fiesta-type atmosphere.

Anwar Jolimar, Grace's executive vice president, expects that the company will be specializing in family restaurants and dinner houses.

Questions for discussion

1. Has Grace successfully implemented retail strategy development? Give specific examples.
2. What is the central focus of all Grace food operations?
3. Based on the data presented in Table 9.6 what specialty retailing and/ or restaurant areas should W.R. Grace & Co. expand in the future?
4. What are the advantages and disadvantages associated with franchising Del Taco restaurants?

10

Physical Distribution

Objectives

To understand how physical distribution activities are integrated in marketing channels and in overall marketing strategies.

To become aware of how inventory planning and control are conducted to develop and maintain adequate assortments of products for target markets.

To gain insight into the selection and coordination of transportation modes to bridge the producer-customer gap.

To learn how warehousing facilitates the storage and movement functions in physical distribution.

To illustrate how materials handling is a part of physical distribution activities.

To review the role of communications and data processing in physical distribution.

Payless Cashways, Inc., operates large do-it-yourself, home-improvement stores in a sixteen-state area. The Kansas City–based company is known for saturating a market with 30,000-square-foot stores adjacent to 30,000-square-foot warehouses and 10,000-square-foot covered lumberyards, all usually situated on 6.5 acres. Figure 10.1 shows a Payless Cashways warehouse. Payless services the do-it-yourself market rather than the home-builder market. In other words, Payless focuses on a consumer market, rather than an industrial one. Payless has 83 percent of its inventory—virtually all of which is home-building supplies—shipped directly to the store from the manufacturer. The balance of the inventory is stored in nine regional warehouses. For its smaller stores, Payless has found ways to move inventory quickly over wide geographic areas from its warehouses. Payless is also very price-competitive, owing to its cash-and-carry policy, which shifts delivery expenses to the consumer. The Payless stores are designed as one-stop home-improvement centers, so careful inventory control is necessary to provide a wide assortment of building supplies for the do-it-yourself market.[1]

Figure 10.1 Payless Cashways Inc. warehouse
Source: Payless Cashways.

1. Facts based on "Payless: Zeroing in on Suburbia," *Business Week,* Sept. 7, 1981, p. 104, and *Payless Cashways Annual Report,* 1983.

This example shows that as they develop their marketing strategy, marketers must take careful note of who is to store, transport, and handle goods and process orders. The concept of physical distribution deals with the integration of all these activities, which are necessary to provide a level of service that will satisfy customers. As implied in Chapter 7, the physical movement of products is costly. Physical distribution creates time and place utility, which maximizes the value of products by delivering them when and where they are wanted.

This chapter describes how marketing decisions are related to physical distribution. The major decisions discussed in this chapter include inventory planning and control, transportation, warehousing, materials handling, and communications. When reading this chapter, keep in mind both the importance of customer service considerations in physical distribution and the relationship of physical distribution to marketing channels. Figure 10.2 provides an overview of the major physical distribution activities discussed in this chapter. Closest to the center of the figure are the two major decision areas—physical movement and inventory holding. Arranged around these major decision areas are the specific activities that accomplish them. Before examining these activities in detail, however, we must consider some basic concepts related to physical distribution.

The importance of physical distribution

Physical distribution is an integrated set of activities that deal with managing the movement of products within firms and through marketing channels.[2] Planning an effective physical distribution system can be a significant decision point in developing an overall marketing strategy. A company that places the right goods in the right place, at the right time, in the right quantity, and with the right support services is able to sell more than competitors who fail to accomplish these goals.[3] Physical distribution is an important variable in a marketing strategy, because it can decrease costs and increase customer satisfaction. In fact, speed of delivery, services, and dependability are often as important to buyers as cost.

Physical distribution activities should be integrated with marketing channel decisions. The marketing channel is a group of interrelated organizations that direct products to customers; physical distribution deals with physical movement and inventory holding (storing and tracking inventory until it is needed) both within and among intermediaries. Often, one channel member will arrange the movement of goods for all channel members involved in exchanges. For example, a packing company ships fresh California cherries and strawberries (often by air) to remote markets on a routine basis. Frequently buyers are found while the fruit is in transit.

The physical distribution system is often adjusted to meet the unique needs of a channel member. For example, a dealer of construction equipment who keeps a low inventory of replacement parts will require the fast-

---

2. Adapted from E. Jerome McCarthy and William D. Perreault, *Basic Marketing: A Managerial Approach,* 8th ed. (Homewood, Ill.: Irwin, 1984), p. 439.
3. Thomas Foster, "Bowing Down to the Beancounters," *Distribution,* Sept. 1983, p. 5.

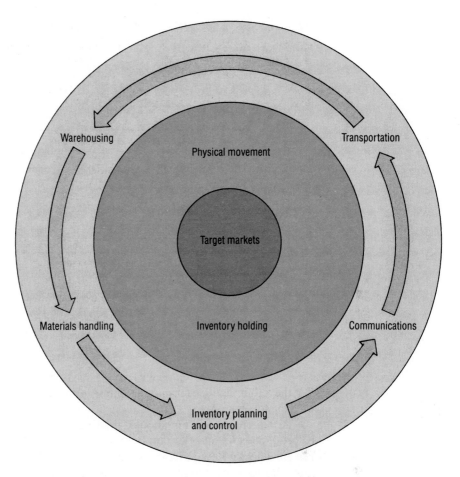

Figure 10.2 Overview of major physical distribution activities

est and most dependable service when the need arises for parts that are not in stock. In such a case, the physical distribution cost may be a minor consideration when compared with service.

For most firms, physical distribution accounts for 19 to 22 percent of the retail price. Of these costs, about two-thirds go for movement of products and one-third is related to inventory holding. Note, though, that physical distribution costs vary by industry. For example, in the food industry, physical distribution costs account for nearly 33 percent of the retail price; such costs average closer to 16 percent of the retail price for wood products and textiles.[4]

Inventory planning and control

Inventory planning and control are physical distribution activities that aid in developing and maintaining adequate assortments of products for the target markets. It is necessary to control the costs of obtaining and maintaining inventory in order to achieve profit goals. For example, it may be an unprofitable use of shelf space to store products that have a slow turnover.

4. Based on statistics obtained from Ronald H. Ballou, *Basic Business Logistics* (Englewood Cliffs, N.J.: Prentice-Hall, 1978), pp. 17–18.

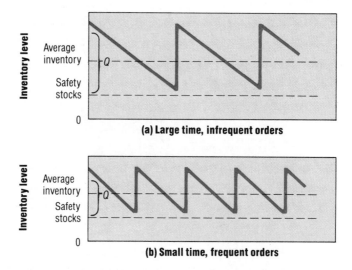

Figure 10.3   Effects of order size on an inventory system   *Source:* Marketing Channels: Systems and Strategies, *by J. Taylor Sims, J. Robert Foster, and Arch G. Woodside: Fig. 14.7 (p. 316). Copyright © 1977 by J. Taylor Sims, J. Robert Foster, and Arch G. Woodside. By permission of Harper & Row, Publishers, Inc.*

On the other hand, *stockouts* (running out of a product) reduce sales and lose customers.

An inventory system should, first of all, be planned so that the number of products sold and the number of products in stock can be determined at certain checkpoints. The control may be as simple as tearing off a code number from each product sold so that the correct sizes, colors, and models can be tabulated and reordered. In many larger stores, cash registers are connected to central computer systems to provide instantaneous updating of inventory and sales records. For continuous, automatic updating of inventory records, Indata Corp. of West Concord, Massachusetts, sells an inventory control system called the Smart Shelf. It uses pressure-sensitive circuits installed under ordinary industrial shelving to weigh what is in the warehouse, convert the weight to units, and display any inventory change on a video screen or computer print-out.[5]

A most significant inventory control decision—in terms of customers and costs—is the average number of units maintained in inventory. If they are to eliminate shortages and avoid having too much capital tied up in inventory, firms must have a systematic method for determining efficient reorder points. The longer a product remains in stock, the greater the probability of obsolescence, pilferage, or damage. Of course, there is a trade-off between inventory-carrying costs and the probability of stockouts. The size of the inventory needed to prevent stockouts is independent of the size that should be reordered for efficient order processing and transportation. The overall *safety stock,* or inventory needed to prevent a stockout, depends on the general level of demand. Individual reorders depend on the

5. *Wall Street Journal,* Sept. 18, 1981, p. 25.

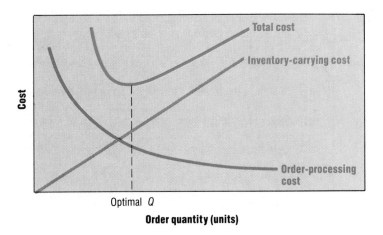

Figure 10.4 Economic order quantity model *Source:* Marketing Channels: Systems and Strategies, *by J. Taylor Sims, J. Robert Foster, and Arch G. Woodside: Fig. 14.8 (p. 318). Copyright © 1977 by J. Taylor Sims, J. Robert Foster, and Arch G. Woodside. By permission of Harper & Row, Publishers, Inc.*

trade-off between the cost of carrying larger average inventory (infrequent orders) and the cost of processing small orders (frequent orders).[6] Figure 10.3 illustrates two order systems involving different order quantities but the same level of safety stocks. Figure 10.3a indicates inventory levels for a given demand of infrequent orders; Figure 10.3b illustrates levels needed to fill frequent orders at the same demand.

There is a trade-off between the cost of carrying the larger average inventory with infrequent orders and the cost of processing many small orders. For this reason, a model for an optimal *economic order quantity (EOQ)* was developed. Figure 10.4 illustrates the EOQ as the order size that minimizes the total cost of ordering and carrying inventory.[7] The EOQ model is accepted widely, and the fundamental relationships that underlie it are the basis of many inventory control systems. Keep in mind, however, that the objective of minimum total inventory cost must be balanced against a customer-service level necessary to maximize profits. Therefore, since increased inventory-carrying costs are usually associated with a higher level of customer service, the order quantity often will lie to the right of the optimal point in Figure 10.4, resulting in a higher total cost of ordering and carrying inventory.

In the 1970s, rising selling prices of inventories tended to offset the cost of financing inventories (financing costs were less than 10 percent).

6. J. Taylor Sims, J. Robert Foster, and Arch G. Woodside, *Marketing Channels: Systems and Strategies* (New York: Harper & Row, 1977), pp. 316–317.
7. The EOQ formula for the optimal order quantity is $EOQ = \sqrt{2DR/I}$, where EOQ = optimum average order size, D = total demand, R = cost of processing an order, and I = cost of maintaining one unit of inventory per year. See Frank S. McLaughlin and Robert C. Pickhardt, *Quantitative Techniques for Management Decisions* (Boston: Houghton Mifflin, 1978), pp. 104–119, for a more complete description of EOQ methods and terminology.

Application

Inventory Planning and Control

One key measure of business health is the level of inventory purchases compared with shipments to customers. Inventories, when excessive, reduce profits because of the interest payments paid to finance them or the cost of capital tied up in inventory.

Inventory management, rather than real demand, is what triggers a build-up of inventory. For example, if the true customer demand for a product increases by 2 percent and a retailer decides to support this higher sales rate by building up inventory, then the demand may be amplified to 4 percent. This amplified demand needs more distributor inventory to support it, and a distributor's supplier receives an 8 percent increase in orders. Thus, all the links in the distribution channel amplify the real demand. Since production capacity is expensive to change, suppliers increase the lead times for delivery. To compensate for increased lead times, distributors place larger orders, and so the process continues.

The Japanese manage their inventories more effectively than comparable U.S. industries, which has allowed them to raise their productivity. Japanese manufacturers communicate the flow rate of products, unamplified by inventory decisions, both up and down the distribution channel. Vendors and customers meet regularly and talk about operating levels. When flow rates are known, additions to capacity in excess of real demand can be minimized.

Inventory planning and control systems should focus on finding the ultimate customer's actual demand. To get accurate information, the inventory expert should visit customers and learn about their requirements and plans. Production capacity can thus be structured to support true demand, and the movement of inventories can be regulated in an effective manner. When inventories are kept to a minimum, the whole business benefits.

Source: Based on Hal F. Mather, "The Case for Skimpy Inventories," *Harvard Business Review,* Jan.–Feb. 1984, pp. 40–42, 46.

Because interest rates have exceeded the rate of inflation in the 1980s, inventories have become the most volatile element in the cost of doing business.[8]

The Federal Trade Commission estimates that a 50 percent reduction in a typical manufacturer's average inventory would increase operating income by about 11 percent. U.S. firms have increased the annual rate of inventory turnover by 20 percent in the past decade.[9]

Many companies have reduced inventories to save money due to inventory-carrying costs, which can run 30 percent or more. In addition to trying to reduce inventory, a company must monitor its inventory's performance. Some warning signals indicate that inventory is not in control: inventory growing at a faster rate than sales; surplus or obsolete inventory; customer deliveries that are consistently late or lead times that are too long; inventory growing as a percentage of assets; and large inventory adjustments or write-offs.[10] The Application on this page discusses the efficient inventory management of many Japanese firms.

It is important to try to properly balance all the conflicting objectives when establishing an inventory system. Inventory management requires a well-tuned communication system and a coordinated effort to make sure

8. Lewis Beman, "A Big Payoff From Inventory Controls," *Fortune,* July 27, 1981, p. 77.
9. Ibid., p. 80.
10. "Watch for These Red Flags," *Traffic Management,* Jan. 1983, p. 8.

Table 10.1 Yearly volume of materials carried by major transportation modes

Mode	Billions of Ton-Miles[a]	Percent of Total
Railways	812	36.3
Pipelines	537	24.0
Motor vehicles	506	22.7
Inland waterways	375	16.8
Airways	5	.2
Total	2,235	100.0

[a]A ton-mile is the movement of 1 ton (2,000 pounds) of freight for the distance of 1 mile.
Source: Association of American Railroads, *Railroad Facts, 1983 Edition,* p. 32.

that the inventory control system supports the overall objectives of marketing and physical distribution. Inventory decisions have a strong impact on physical distribution costs—and on the level of customer service provided.

Transportation

Transportation is an essential and obvious physical distribution activity. As Table 10.1 indicates, there are five major *transportation modes* for moving goods between cities in the United States: railways, pipelines, motor vehicles, inland waterways, and airways. Transportation technology takes advantage of each mode's strength by adopting physical handling procedures that permit the most effective transfers among different types of carriers.

Cost and capability (the ability to handle various products) are not the only considerations in choosing a transportation mode. Reliability and availability are also important. Although a truck can carry a replacement part for a computer system at low cost, air freight may provide more dependable delivery and get the part to the customer in less time. The nature of a product and the needs of its market also determine what type of carrier is selected. Figure 10.5 indicates that the use of railways will be easier in the future. Table 10.2 illustrates some typical transportation modes for various products.

Transportation creates time and place utility for a firm's products. Management must make many transportation decisions during the produc-

Table 10.2 Typical transportation modes for various products

Railways	Motor Vehicles	Waterways	Pipelines	Airways
Coal	Clothing	Petroleum	Oil	Flowers
Grain	Paper goods	Chemicals	Processed coal	Food, highly
Chemicals	Computers	Iron ore	Natural gas	perishable
Lumber	Books	Bauxite		Technical
Automobiles	Fresh fruit			instruments
Iron, steel	Livestock			Emergency
				parts and
				equipment
				Overnight
				mail

tion, storage, and delivery stages of operation. The transportation system links the flow of products among various stages of operation and has a direct impact on the availability of the product. The choice of a transportation mode affects all elements of the physical distribution system. The marketing strategy itself can be based on a unique transportation system.

A firm like Wal-Mart has such a commitment to its transportation system because that level of commitment increases the level of service to its stores and customers while lowering costs. A transportation survey by the U.S. Census indicates that service, especially on-time delivery, is a major factor in a firm's decision to develop its own transportation system. A firm's ability to provide on-time deliveries is part of the total package of benefits that customers want.

Transport selection criteria[11]

Marketers select a transportation mode on the basis of cost, transit time (speed), reliability, capability, accessibility, and security.

Cost

Marketers must determine whether additional services provided by one transportation mode are worth higher costs compared with alternative

11. Some ideas in this section are based on John J. Coyle and Edward Bardi, *The Management of Business Logistics* (St. Paul, Minn.: West, 1976), pp. 150–153.

modes. As long as service is similar, cost differences are an important criterion in selecting a transportation mode. For example, bicycles are often shipped by rail because an unassembled bicycle can be shipped more than a thousand miles that way for as little as $3.60. Therefore, bicycle wholesalers plan their purchases far enough in advance to be able to capitalize on this cost advantage.

Transit time

The total time that a carrier possesses goods is called *transit time;* it includes the time required for pickup and delivery, for handling, and for movement between the points of origin and destination. Transit time obviously affects a marketer's ability to provide service, but there are some less obvious implications as well.

Transit time allows the shipper to process orders for goods enroute. This capability is especially important to agricultural and raw materials shippers. In addition, some railroads allow carloads already in transit to be redirected. A carload of peaches may be shipped to a closer destination if there is danger that the fruit will ripen too quickly.

Reliability

The dependability and consistency of the service provided by a transportation mode make up its total reliability. Transit time and reliability affect a marketer's inventory costs, including sales lost when merchandise is not available. Unreliable transportation makes it necessary to maintain higher inventory levels to avoid stockouts. Marketers must be able to count on their carriers to deliver goods in an acceptable condition and when specified. Figure 10.6 indicates that Flying Tigers, as the world's largest all-cargo airline, provides maximum flights, capacity, and reliability through computer tracking of shipments.

General Motors uses Conrail's overnight service from Kalamazoo, Michigan, to transport auto parts 118 miles to GM's Fisher body and Oldsmobile plant in Lansing, Michigan. Conrail delivers these parts before the commencement of the first shift each morning, thus eliminating the need to stock inventory at the Lansing plant.

Capability

Capability refers to the ability of a transportation mode to provide the appropriate equipment and conditions for moving specific kinds of goods. Many products must be shipped under controlled conditions in terms of temperature or humidity. Others—such as liquids or gases—require special equipment or facilities for shipment. Fifty percent of crude oil production is moved in bulk vessels especially designed for large-volume transport of bulk commodities. These special bulk vessels are the only means of seaborne movement for crude petroleum production.[12]

As an example from a different industry, CSX Corporation uses 45-foot refrigerated trailers and an intermodal concept including both trains and trucks to deliver fresh Florida fruits and vegetables to the East. Figure 10.7 illustrates the service CSX provides and describes the produce delivery system.

12. *Overseas Shipholding Group, Inc. Annual Report, 1980,* pp. 8, 17.

Figure 10.6
Flying Tigers provide
reliability in air cargo
service
*Source: Courtesy of
Flying Tigers.*

Accessibility

The ability of a carrier to move goods over a specific route or network (rail lines, waterways, or regulated truck routes) is the measure of its accessibility. Thus, the inability of a water-borne carrier to serve Great Falls, Montana, would eliminate it from consideration as a possible transportation mode to or from that city. Since Great Falls *is* accessible by rail line, truck routes, and scheduled airline service, those transportation modes are available to marketers there.

Some carriers differentiate themselves by servicing areas not accessed by competitors. For example, GETS—Guaranteed Emergency Transportation Service—is a motor carrier that serves 20,000 points not served by air carriers.[13]

13. Bruce Heydt, "Overnight Over the Road," *Distribution,* Sept. 1983, pp. 101, 102.

Security

Whether or not goods arrive in the same condition in which they were shipped defines the security of a transportation mode. Since the common carrier is held liable for all loss and damage (with limited exceptions), the firm does not incur direct costs when goods are lost or delivered in a damaged condition. Nevertheless, unsafe service and poor security lead to increased costs for the firm as well as foregone profits, since damaged or lost goods are not available for immediate sale or use.

Security problems vary considerably among transportation companies and geographic regions. In the Northeast, for instance, truck hijacking is a

Table 10.3 Ranking of transportation modes by selection criteria, highest to lowest

Cost	Transit Time	Reliability	Capability	Accessibility	Security
Air	Water	Pipeline	Water	Truck	Pipeline
Truck	Rail	Truck	Rail	Rail	Water
Rail	Pipeline	Rail	Truck	Air	Rail
Pipeline	Truck	Air	Air	Water	Air
Water	Air	Water	Pipeline	Pipeline	Truck

Source: Some of this information has been adapted from J. L. Heskett, Robert Ivie, and J. Nicholas Glaskowsky, *Business Logistics* (New York: Ronald Press, 1973). Used by permission.

rapidly growing crime. According to the FBI, approximately 19,000 truck tractors and 47,000 trailers are listed as stolen each year.[14] Hijacking is a security problem that confronts most trucking shippers, but all transportation modes have security problems. Marketers must determine the relative risk associated with each transportation mode in making a final selection. In fact, one of the major benefits of container shipment is increased security.

Table 10.3 illustrates some of the cost and performance considerations that affect decisions concerning transportation modes. Keep in mind that these relationships are a general approximation and that they do vary. There are many trade-offs in the final selection of a transportation mode.

Coordinating transportation services

Since individual transportation companies often specialize in one mode of transportation, marketers must sometimes coordinate and integrate various modes. This task can be handled by the firm or by special transportation agencies. For example, *freight forwarders* consolidate shipments from several organizations into efficient lot sizes. The use of a freight forwarder usually increases transit time and sometimes lowers shipping costs. Figure 10.8 illustrates the services of Transway International Corporation. It is obvious that this company coordinates various transportation and materials handling methods.

Since costs for small shipments (under 500 pounds) are sharply higher than costs for full loads in railroad cars and trucks, consolidated shipments with firms sharing costs and services are increasing.[15] For example, United Parcel Service (UPS) is a specialized transportation agency that efficiently combines shipments of less than 50 pounds, aiding retail deliveries.

The practice of consolidating many items into one container, sealed at the point of origin and opened at the destination, is generally referred to as ***containerization***. Containerization adds great efficiency to shipping, since individual items are not handled in transit. It usually is associated with

14. "Stop Thief," *Traffic Management,* June 1983, p. 84.
15. Walter F. Friedman, "Physical Distribution: The Concept of Shared Services," *Harvard Business Review,* March–April 1975, p. 25.

such words as *piggyback, fishyback,* and *birdyback* services. For example, when loaded containers are placed on railway flatcars or on motor vehicles, it is called a piggyback (see Figure 10.9); if the containers are off-loaded to water carriers, it is called fishyback. Air truck, or birdyback, refers to the exchange of containers between air and truck carriers. (Other aspects of containers are discussed in the section ''Materials Handling'' later in this chapter.) The use of containers and coordinated transportation systems is becoming more popular as transportation costs increase.

Warehousing

Designing and operating facilities to store and move goods are other important physical distribution activities. The following are the essential processing functions performed by a warehouse:

1. *Receives goods.* The warehouse accepts merchandise, delivered from outside transportation or from an attached factory, and assumes responsibility for it.
2. *Identifies goods.* The appropriate stockkeeping units must be recorded, and a record made of the quantity of each item received. It may be necessary to mark the item with a physical code or tag or by other means. The item may be identified by an item code (a code on the carrier or container) or by physical properties.
3. *Sorts goods.* The warehouse may sort merchandise to the appropriate storage areas.
4. *Dispatches goods to storage.* The merchandise must be put away where it can be found later.
5. *Holds goods.* The merchandise is kept in storage under proper protection until needed.
6. *Recalls, selects, or picks goods.* Items ordered by customers, for example, must be efficiently selected from storage and grouped in a manner useful for the next step.
7. *Marshals the shipment.* The items making up a single shipment must be brought together and checked for completeness or for explainable omissions. Order records must be prepared or modified as necessary.

8. *Dispatches the shipment.* The consolidated order must be packaged suitably and directed to the right transport vehicle. Necessary shipping and accounting documents must be prepared.[16]

The expense of maintaining or renting warehouse facilities is a considerable cost of physical distribution. *Private warehouses* are owned and operated by a company for the purpose of distributing its own products. These warehouses may be a distinct and separate operation of the firm or they may be integrated with other activities. The largest user of private warehouses is retail chain stores.[17]

Public warehouses are business organizations whose primary activity is to provide storage and related physical distribution facilities on a rental basis to other firms.[18] Public warehouses may provide such services as reshipping, filling orders, financing, displaying products, and coordinating shipments. In addition, many of them offer services such as providing security for products that are being used as collateral for loans. This service can be provided at a public warehouse or at the site of the owner's inventory. A *field warehouse* is a temporary warehouse established by a public warehouse at the owner's inventory location. The warehouser becomes the custodian of the products and issues a receipt that can be used as collateral for a loan. Also, public warehouses can provide *bonded storage*. In this case, products are not released unless U.S. custom duties, taxes, or other fees are paid by the owners of the products.[19]

Current trends in warehousing seem to indicate a shift from providing space for the storage of goods to offering services for the distribution of goods.[20] Efficiency in materials-handling techniques, better use of space, computer systems, and the holding of large inventories improve warehousing services.

Whether private or public, warehouse facilities represent a cost to the marketer or shipper. With a public warehouse, the cost is variable, since more space has to be rented as the volume of goods increases. On the other hand, private warehouses entail such fixed costs as insurance, taxes, and debt expense. Of course, there also are noncost considerations, such as a firm's resources and the role of the warehouse in the overall marketing strategy.

Private warehouses usually are leased or purchased when a firm believes its warehouse needs are so stable that it can make a long-term commitment to fixed facilities. Retailers like Sears, Radio Shack, and even Burger King often find it economical to integrate the warehousing function

16. Adapted from *Physical Distribution Systems* by John F. Magee. Copyright © 1967 McGraw-Hill, Inc. Used with permission of McGraw-Hill Book Company.
17. James C. Johnson and Donald F. Wood, *Contemporary Physical Distribution & Logistics,* 2nd ed. (Tulsa, Okla.: Penwell Publishing Company, 1982), p. 356.
18. Theodore N. Beckman, William R. Davidson, and W. Wayne Talarzyk, *Marketing,* 9th ed. (New York: Ronald Press, 1973), pp. 488–489.
19. Johnson and Wood, *Contemporary Physical Distribution, p. 355.*
20. Gerry O. Pattino, ''Public Warehousing: Supermarkets for Distribution Services,'' *Handling and Shipping,* March 1977, pp. 59–61.

Figure 10.10
Certified Grocers per-
forms highly auto-
mated warehousing
functions
*Source: Certified Gro-
cers of California, Ltd.*

with purchasing and distribution to retail outlets. When sales volumes are fairly stable, the ownership and control of a private warehouse may provide several gains, including financial ones such as property appreciation and tax shelters realized through depreciation of the facility.

For many firms, the best approach may be a combination of private and public warehousing. For example, a minimum storage area that can always be kept full might be committed to private warehousing, while overflow inventories are placed in public warehousing.[21] In such a case, a firm might lease or buy private facilities on a long-term basis, and then use a nearby public warehouse for seasonal or overflow inventories.

Consider the 635,000-square-foot automated warehouse operated by Certified Grocer's of California, Limited (see Figure 10.10). At any of the 360 stores presently served by this facility, bar codes on shelf tags are electronically scanned, the data are held in an electronic memory, and the order is transmitted to the computers at the Certified headquarters. The dry grocery order is sent to minicomputers at the new mechanized distribution center. Computers analyze and combine orders into batches, with as many as twenty stores being serviced simultaneously. Two computer control stations oversee operations.

21. Albert D. Bates, ''Warehouse Retailing: A Revolutionary Force in Distribution,'' *California Management Review,* Winter 1977, pp. 75–76.

The computer prepares order selection lists for the mechanized portion of the warehouse (the 64 percent of warehouse space containing 5,200 high-volume items that constitute 82 percent of projected volume). It also prepares a list for the conventional portion of the warehouse, which stocks items such as dry dog food that cannot be handled in the mechanized system. Operating simultaneously in fourteen aisles (or "modules"), order selectors then remove cases of products from gravity-fed storage racks.

Cases for a single store's order are then guided by computer and laser beams to a belt that feeds down to one of the warehouse's seventeen main-floor palletizing stations. There the cases are assembled on a standardized (40-by-48-inch) wooden pallet for loading onto a truck. The pallets are critical to improved productivity as they allow bigger "cubes" to be assembled into more secure loads. The platforms on which the workers assemble the pallet loads are designed to rise as work on the pallet proceeds. Thus, an average height of 60 to 74 inches can be achieved. When the order is delivered, the receiving store uses a computer-generated list to check in the merchandise.[22]

<table>
<tr><td>**Materials handling**</td><td>*Materials handling,* or physical handling of products, is important in efficient warehouse operations, as well as in transportation from points of production to points of consumption. The characteristics of the product itself often determine how it will be handled. For example, bulk liquids and gases have unique characteristics that determine how they can be moved and stored. On the other hand, handling processes may alter a product's characteristics or qualities.[23]</td></tr>
</table>

Materials-handling procedures and techniques should increase the usable capacity of a warehouse, reduce the number of times a good is handled, and improve service to customers and increase their satisfaction with the product. Packaging, loading, and movement systems must be coordinated to maximize cost reduction and customer satisfaction.

Chapter 5 noted that the protective functions of packaging are important considerations in product development. Good decisions about packaging materials and methods make possible the most efficient physical handling. Most companies use packaging consultants or specialists to accomplish this important task.

Materials-handling equipment is used in the design of handling systems. *Unit loading* is the grouping of one or more boxes on a pallet or skid and permits movement of efficient loads by mechanical means such as forklifts, trucks, or conveyor systems. Figure 10.11 shows unit loading of palletized freight. The next-sized load in materials handling is the container, discussed earlier. Containers are usually 8 feet wide, 8 feet high, and 10, 20, 25, or 40 feet long. Containerization has revolutionized physical distribution by broadening the capabilities of our transportation system, enabling shippers to transport a wider range of cargoes with speed, reliability, and stable costs. Not only is containerization energy efficient, but it

22. "The Warehouse," *Progressive Grocer,* Jan. 1981, pp. 79–80.
23. Johnson and Wood, *Contemporary Physical Distribution,* p. 322.

PALLETIZED FREIGHT.

ONE OF OUR SPECIALTIES.

Our cargo capacity will lift your spirits as well as your shipments.
Varig's fleet of all-cargo palletized jets can handle just about
anything—from a tiny plant to a power plant—to all of Brazil, and
the world.

And because Brazil is our home, we can carry your cargo to the
most far-flung corners of our country—even places that have no
landing field—through our extensive re-forwarding network covering more than 4,700 Brazilian towns.

So give your cargo to Varig. We'll take it from there.

VARIG *Brazilian Airlines* **CARGO**

Pioneer in palletized cargo in Latin America.

also decreases the need for high-level security measures and cuts down on
losses and damage.

**Communications
and data
processing**

When Bergen Brunswig, a distributor of over-the-counter drugs and medi-
cal/surgical supplies, expanded its computerized customer service programs, sales increased to over $1 billion. The company introduced its phar-
macy and other retail customers to a series of computer based order-entry
programs designed to speed ordering and delivery. These programs helped
broaden the company's drug sales territory.[24]

An information system for physical distribution should link producers,
intermediaries, and customers. Computers, memory systems, display equip-

24. "Bergen Brunswig Writes a Winning Proposition," *Sales and Marketing
    Management,* Jan. 17, 1983, p. 38.

ment, and other communications technology facilitate the flow of information among channel members. The three most frequently computerized functions are order entry, invoicing, and freight bill payment. The least computerized functions include rail costing, site location, private fleet management, and freight budgeting, which are accomplished mostly through planning.[25] The following retail merchandise information systems are in general use.

By definition, an *electronic cash register (ECR)* depends on electronics for its logic and arithmetic functions. A *sophisticated ECR (SECR)* does not accumulate detailed transaction data but may be integrated with any number of peripherals. A *basic ECR (BECR)* is a stand-alone cash register that does not have the capacity for additional totals, features, and so forth. *POS* describes a retailer's *point-of-sale terminal,* which works like an ECR but is connected to a computer or some other device for detailed collection of data for subsequent processing, whether or not it is a stand-alone terminal and regardless of the number of totals it accumulates. An ECR can become a POS terminal when it is so connected.

Universal vendor marking (UVM) is a coding system in which a vendor marks merchandise for individual retailers with a machine-readable code containing such information as department class, size, and color. It is the most common marking code in general merchandise retailing. The *universal product code (UPC)* is the standard source-symbol marking in the food industry. Finally, *electronic funds transfer (EFT)* systems allow electronic transfers of funds between the retailer and financial institutions. They also allow such other functions as credit and check authorization.[26]

The application of advanced computer hardware with appropriate software (computer programs) has greatly increased productivity in communications. These new technologies have manifested themselves in many ways among typical vendors. Automated check-out systems in supermarkets utilize a fixed or hand-held optical scanner, an in-store minicomputer, and an electronic cash register to increase efficiency at the point of sale.[27] When a product is packaged at the factory, it is marked with a symbol that can be read by the optical scanner. When read, the symbol identifies the item down to the level of the individual stockkeeping unit. When it is received at the store, the item is put on a price-marked shelf, but it is not priced individually. The memory bank of the store's minicomputer contains the current price for each unit. As shoppers' purchases are checked out, each item's product code is read by the scanner, the price is looked up by the computer, and details of the item are tabulated and printed by the electronic terminal. At the same time, the computer uses each item's code to update inventory records. There is no need for the clerk to punch individual prices into a cash register.

Other applications of computers in physical distribution include transportation coordination and, to some extent, forecasting of inventory and

25. Tom Foster, "Computerization: Where Are We?" *Distribution,* Sept. 1983, p. 86.
26. J. Barry Mason and Morris L. Mayer, "Retail Merchandise Systems for the 1980s," *Journal of Retailing,* Spring 1980, p. 58.
27. M. S. Moyer and Barry Seitz, "The Marketing Implications of Automated Store Checkouts," *Business Quarterly,* Spring 1975, pp. 68–69.

Jell-O Pudding Pops is one of General Foods' most successful new products ever. The product is frozen pudding on a stick and it is sold in chocolate, vanilla, and banana flavors.

Jell-O Pudding Pops are marketed as a healthy alternative to ice cream novelties. At two ounces, a Pudding Pop has a little less than one-third the calories and only one-tenth the fat of a standard three-ounce stick of chocolate-coated vanilla ice cream.

Jell-O Pudding Pops' success began with a marketing discovery. Jell-O pudding and gelatin were on the decline in sales. General Foods marketing intelligence observed that consumers no longer wanted to spend time making desserts and were also conscious about calories. By freezing low-calorie pudding, General Foods addressed both problems.

In the frozen confection market, much money is spent on transportation, because in general, independent distributors deliver and shelve ice-cream novelties. Frozen foods, however, are shipped through a grocers' warehouse system, which is relatively inexpensive. To save on distribution, therefore, General Foods makes its Pudding Pops with a higher melting point than ice cream; thus, the company can distribute them with its Birds Eye frozen vegetables. Frozen foods are kept at zero Fahrenheit during shipping, whereas ice cream has to travel at 20 below to prevent ice-crystal formation.

Another distribution problem that General Foods faced was grocery store clerks who, because of unfamiliarity with the product, failed to keep Pudding Pops on the shelves. To try to forestall this neglect, General Foods put together a seven-minute film on Pudding Pops that it shows to store personnel.

Jell-O Pudding Pops illustrate how changes in consumer needs and in technology affect physical distribution as a marketing strategy consideration. General Foods made product changes in its pudding and made changes in its physical distribution. These changes contributed to minimization of costs and an increase in sales.

Source: Based on Janet Guyon, "General Foods Gets a Winner With Its Jell-O Pudding Pops," *Wall Street Journal,* March 10, 1983, p. 29.

transportation needs. Low-cost computers and computer systems within firms have increased the use of computers in distribution.

The rapid advance of computer technology is not without problems, however. According to a survey of computer users in distribution, the major problems relate to specific program applications (for example, getting a forecast of warehouse requirements), obtaining timely information, and the reliability of computer hardware.[28] Nonetheless, the trend is toward even more computer applications in the future.

**Marketing
strategy
considerations
in physical
distribution**

Changes in customers or technology may profoundly affect the place of physical distribution in the marketing strategy. Pressures to change service functions or reduce costs can bring about a total restructuring of marketing channel relationships. For example, the tremendous increase in transportation costs in recent years has brought about a careful evaluation of ways to increase efficiency. Consider the Application above, which describes the role of creative physical distribution in developing a marketing strategy for

28. Robert House and George C. Jackson, "Trends in Computer Applications: A Survey," *Handling and Shipping,* June 1977, pp. 52–56.

Speed. Reliability. Economy.
That's what we deliver over 90,000 times every single day.

Excellence. That's what we're committed to at Express Mail Next Day
Service* from the Post Office. We give
you just about everything you could
ask for in overnight delivery. Including
big savings.
 Our 2-Pound Pak, for instance, is
just $9.35. About half what most
others charge.
 That's so little to pay for so much
reliability.
 And for so much convenience, too.
We have over 3,500 Express Mail post
offices across the country. Plus hundreds of collection boxes, for prepaid
items, in most major cities. So when
you need to send something, chances
are, we're just a few steps away.
 To top it all off, we deliver on weekends—at no extra charge. And we
handle packages of up to 70 pounds.
 So next time, send yours with
Express Mail Service from the Post
Office. And we'll deliver it the same
way we deliver over 90,000 others
every day. Quickly. Reliably. And
economically.

EXPRESS MAIL
NEXT DAY SERVICE

The 2-Pound Pak $9.35. We deliver excellence...for less.

© USPS 1983

Jello-O Pudding Pops. In some cases, combining orders and developing
centralized control over the physical movement of products has increased
channel productivity. Independent wholesale distributors, too, can achieve
improved productivity because they usually have a large potential customer base, and standardized product lines; therefore, they can provide
small-quantity unit inventory to customers who require rapid delivery and
service.[29]

 Physical distribution should meet the requirements of an organization's
marketing strategy. Marketers should accept a substantial responsibility
for the design and control of the physical distribution system. While accounting and financial managers may concentrate on minimizing costs,
marketers must relate costs to customer satisfaction. Speed of delivery, reliability, and economy of service are marketing considerations that define
the total product in customers' eyes. Figure 10.12 illustrates how these

29. James D. Hlavacek and Tommy J. McCuiston, "Industrial distributors—
 When, Who and Why?" *Harvard Business Review,* March–April 1983,
 pp. 96–101.

considerations come into play in using Express Mail for overnight delivery of two-pound packages.

Changes in transportation, warehousing, materials handling, and inventory may increase or decrease services such as speed of delivery. Decreasing costs while increasing service should be the main objective in physical distribution. Consumer-oriented marketers analyze the characteristics of the target market and then design a system to provide products at acceptable costs.

Summary

Physical distribution is an integrated set of activities that deal with managing the movement of products within firms and through marketing channels. Physical distribution creates time and place utility by the performance of activities to store, transport, handle, and process orders for products. Our approach to physical distribution focuses on integrating these activities to minimize costs and provide the level of service desired by customers. Physical distribution can be important in an overall marketing strategy; it can be the decision most visible in the marketing mix. But whatever the role of physical distribution in the marketing strategy, distribution decisions must be made for the physical movement of goods. The physical distribution activities discussed in this chapter include inventory planning and control, transportation, warehousing, materials handling, and communications and data processing.

Inventory planning and control require a systematic approach to determine efficient order points that eliminate stockouts and avoid having too much capital tied up in inventory. Although there are trade-offs between the costs of carrying larger average inventories and the costs of frequent orders, this problem can be alleviated by finding an optimal economic order quantity (EOQ).

Various transportation decisions are required during the production, storage, and delivery stages of operation. The major modes of transporting goods between cities in the United States are railways, pipelines, motor vehicles, inland waterways, and airways. The selection of a transportation mode is based on cost, transit time (speed), reliability, capability, accessibility, and security. Because there are many trade-offs in the final selection of a transportation mode, a firm must coordinate its overall transportation process as goods move from production points to customers.

Warehousing involves designing and operating facilities to store and move goods. Private warehouses are owned and operated by a company for the purpose of distributing its own products. Public warehouses are business organizations with the primary activity of providing storage and related physical distribution facilities on a rental basis to other firms. While the variable cost per unit is less for a private warehouse than for a public one, a combination of private and public warehouses can provide a flexible approach to warehousing.

Materials handling, or the physical handling of products, is an important element of physical distribution. Packaging, loading, and movement systems must be coordinated to take into account both cost reduction and customer requirements. The handling systems discussed in this chapter were unit loading on pallets or skids, movement by mechanical devices, and containerization.

Finally, we looked at the role of communications and data processing in physical distribution. Instantaneous inventory updating and stockkeeping, transportation coordination, and forecasting are made possible through computer systems. The increasing use of computers in physical distribution has brought its own problems. Nonetheless, the trend is toward more computer applications because of the availability of low-cost minicomputers and decentralized computer systems within firms.

Important terms

Physical distribution
Inventory planning and control
Stockouts
Safety stock
Economic order quantity (EOQ)
Transportation modes
Transit time
Freight forwarders
Containerization
Private warehouses
Public warehouses

Bonded storage
Field warehouse
Materials handling
Unit loading
Electronic cash register (ECR)
Sophisticated ECR (SECR)
Basic ECR (BECR)
Point-of-sale terminal (POS)
Universal vendor marking (UVM)
Universal product code (UPC)
Electronic funds transfer (EFT)

Discussion and review questions

1. For what two main reasons is physical distribution sometimes a key variable in marketing strategy?
2. Why should physical distribution decisions be integrated with marketing channel decisions?
3. "Like other marketing tasks, physical distribution should be guided by what buyers want." Give some examples to support this statement.
4. What major tasks are involved in inventory planning and control?
5. List several important considerations in a firm's decision to develop its own transportation system.
6. Compare the five major transportation modes in terms of cost, transit time, reliability, capability, accessibility, and security.
7. Under what circumstances should a firm use a private warehouse instead of a public one?
8. In Chapter 9, we discussed miniwarehouses. Think about them in the context of this chapter and suggest some applications that could be discussed.
9. Do you see any conflicts between protective packaging decisions and promotional packaging decisions?
10. What types of products are unsuitable for containerization?
11. What is the likely impact on physical distribution of decentralizing computer systems within firms?
12. Discuss the cost and service trade-offs in developing a physical distribution system.

Cases

SHOP WITHOUT
GOING SHOPPING

Case 10.1

Amway Corporation[30]

Amway Corporation is one of the fastest growing companies in North America. In only a few years it has grown from a small distributor of household products into a complete manufacturing and sales organization with over a billion dollar annual sales volume. This growth includes all areas of operation. The company has completed several phases of a continuing program to increase facilities for research, production, warehousing, and selling. Distributors have rapidly multiplied; and today, over one million independent distributorships are engaged in selling Amway products to homes and industries throughout the United States and 40 other countries and territories.

The corporation was founded by two men with broad experience in direct selling. Jay Van Andel and Richard DeVos each have over 35 years' experience, 10 with Nutrilite Products, Inc., and 25 with Amway, developing direct sales distributorships. Mr. Van Andel is Amway's chairman and Mr. DeVos is its president. But, in fact, these two men serve as co-chief executive officers of the corporation.

Amway's world headquarters and main manufacturing facilities are located on a 300-acre tract of land at Ada, Michigan, about nine miles east of Grand Rapids. Amway's multi-million-dollar complex houses a modern and efficient manufacturing operation, including the most up-to-date equipment for formulating, packaging, bottling, and labeling powder and liquid products. Due to the importance of aerosol packages in the Amway line, the plant includes one of the most completely automatic aerosol filling facilities in existence. A separate $11-million-dollar, state-of-the-art facility makes over 240 personal care items, primarily cosmetics.

Laboratories at the Ada plant are staffed with specialized chemists who carry out extensive testing programs on both raw materials and finished products to assure rigid standards of quality control. In addition, these laboratories carry out research on new and improved products.

Other departments at the Ada plant include: offices where the details and correspondence connected with millions of dollars' worth of annual sales are handled; the creative and printing production department, which turns out hundreds of thousands of magazines, price lists, bulletins, brochures, and other printed pieces each month; and extensive storage facilities for inventories of raw materials and finished goods. Ten regional distribution centers in strategically located cities in the United States and Canada serve distributors. Amway home products include such items as pesticides, auto care products, clothing care products, floor and furniture care products, laundry and kitchen care products, room fresheners, personal care products, nutritional products, and housewares. Amway also manufactures a line of commercial cleaning products.

In the Amway system, products are produced and then sent to a cen-

---

30. From J. Taylor Sims, ''Amway Corporation: Direct Marketing System,'' in M. Wayne Delozier and Arch Woodside, *Marketing Management: Strategies and Cases* (Columbus, Ohio: Merrill, 1978), pp. 376–377. Information updated by Amway in 1984. Reprinted with the permission of Amway Corporation.

tral warehouse on location at the Ada facility. From this warehouse Amway products are shipped to regional distribution centers all over the United States. In other words, the central warehouse handles orders from all of these individual warehouses. The central warehouse performs the transportation function of moving goods from the manufacturer to the regional distribution centers. Transportation of goods from the distribution centers is handled in two ways. The individual salesperson placing an order can arrange to pick it up there. Or, as is more normally the case, the order is trucked from the center to the salesperson's address within seven days after the order is placed. Most distributors have a regular order day and delivery date every week.

Questions for discussion

1. Amway has over one million independent distributorships engaged in distributing Amway products to homes and industries throughout the United States and Canada. Discuss the impact of a direct personal selling system on the physical distribution system.
2. Evaluate the role of efficient warehouse operations in Amway's marketing efforts.
3. Suggest improvements, if needed, for the Amway physical distribution system.

Case 10.2

Wal-Mart Stores, Inc.[31]

WAL-MART

Wal-Mart Stores, Inc. is a chain of 551 discount department stores that operate in 15 states in the Midwest and southern parts of the United States. The first Wal-Mart Discount City store was opened over 20 years ago in Rogers, Arkansas. Since that time, the chain has grown and its annual sales exceed $3.37 billion with a net income of over $124 million. Recently, Dun's *Business Month* ranked the company as one of the five best-managed companies in American industry. *Forbes* magazine, in its *35th Annual Report on American Industry,* ranked Wal-Mart first among all general retailers (including department stores, discount, and variety stores) in terms of profitability and growth.

The stores range in size from 30,000 square feet to 80,000 square feet. They are located primarily in towns having populations of 5,000 to 25,000, although an increasing number of stores are located in and around the metropolitan areas within the chain's regional trade territory. The trading market for most stores covers large rural areas, and Wal-Mart stores are designed to be one-stop shopping centers.

Each Wal-Mart store offers a wide variety of quality merchandise at low everyday retail prices to satisfy most of the clothing, home, recreational, and basic needs of the families in the store's community. Regardless of store size, there are 36 full-line merchandise departments in each store.

31. The facts in this case are from Wal-Mart's *1983 Annual Report.*

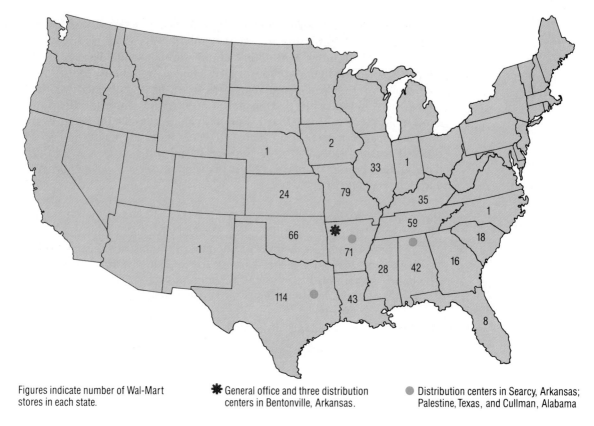

Figures indicate number of Wal-Mart stores in each state.

✳ General office and three distribution centers in Bentonville, Arkansas.

● Distribution centers in Searcy, Arkansas; Palestine, Texas, and Cullman, Alabama

Figure 10.13 Wal-Mart's service area and distribution centers
Source: 1983 Wal-Mart Annual Report

Nationally advertised merchandise accounts for the majority of sales throughout each store, while private label goods are offered only when they provide exceptional value. Wal-Mart offers conveniences for its customers that range from extended shopping hours to free parking, quick checkout lanes, layaway purchase plans, Mastercard and Visa charge services, and customer check-cashing courtesy cards.

To assure a constant flow of products/inventory to its stores, Wal-Mart operates six warehouses that serve as distribution centers. About 82 percent of the merchandise sold in the stores is processed through these distribution centers. Merchandise flows from the manufacturer to the company's distribution centers via a trucking network, including company-owned trucks. Mechanized distribution facilities efficiently sort the large quantities received into outbound shipments to each store. Deliveries are made on Wal-Mart trucks which backhaul inbound merchandise to the distribution centers, eliminating as many miles traveled with empty trailers as possible. Figure 10.13 illustrates the Wal-Mart service area and the location of the six distribution centers. Three distribution centers are in Bentonville, Arkansas.

Approximately 46,000 full- and part-time Wal-Mart employees have the responsibility of meeting the needs of millions of customers. Each employee is made knowledgeable about events throughout the company through training programs, an in-house newspaper, and many programs designed to communicate and recognize individual accomplishments. The company has stuck to its original business philosophy of low everyday prices and guaranteed customer satisfaction in all its marketing efforts.

Questions for discussion
1. Discuss the location and operation of the six Wal-Mart distribution centers. Where should the next distribution center be constructed if growth patterns continue?
2. What impact does Wal-Mart's physical distribution system have on customers and profits?
3. Based on the facts presented in this case, does Wal-Mart integrate physical distribution decisions into its overall marketing strategy? Discuss.

Part 4

Promotion Decisions

Part Four deals with communicating with target market members. A specific marketing mix cannot satisfy people in a particular target market unless they are aware of the product and where to find it. Some promotion decisions and activities are related to a specific marketing mix, while others, broader in scope, focus on the promotion of the whole organization. Chapter 11 presents an overview of promotion. We describe the communication process and the major promotion methods that can be included in promotion mixes. In Chapter 12, we analyze the major steps required to develop an advertising campaign, and we explain what publicity is and how it can be used. Chapter 13 deals with the management of personal selling and the role it can play in a firm's promotion mix. This chapter also explores the general characteristics of sales promotion and sales promotion techniques.

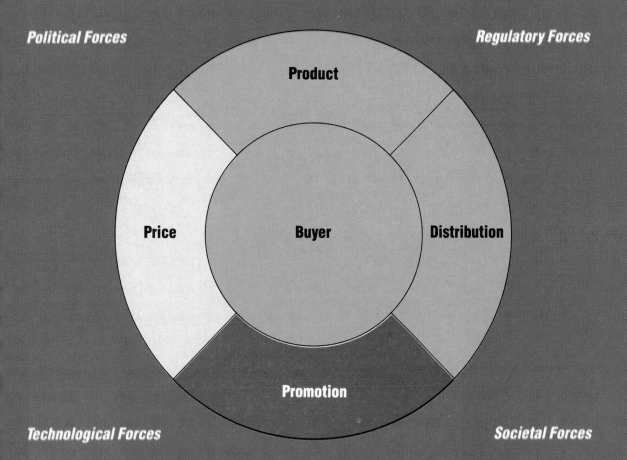

Marketing Environment

Legal Forces

Political Forces

Regulatory Forces

Product

Price

Buyer

Distribution

Promotion

Technological Forces

Societal Forces

Economic Forces

11

Promotion: An Overview

Objectives

To understand the role of promotion in the marketing mix.

To examine the process of communication.

To understand the product adoption process and to learn which promotional efforts to emphasize in its various stages.

To gain an understanding of the promotion mix.

To acquire an overview of the major promotional methods that make up promotion mixes.

To explore factors that affect the choice of promotional methods.

A few years ago, in one of the biggest soft-drink introductions in marketing history, Coca-Cola Company launched Diet Coke. Marketing research at Coca-Cola determined that a product named Diet Coke would appeal to different consumers than the ones who drink the company's leading diet cola, Tab. Consider the following promotional efforts that helped to launch the product effectively.

Outdoor advertising, magazine and newspaper ads, as well as intensive television advertising, were part of the $50-million promotional campaign used for the brand's debut (see the print advertisement in Figure 11.1)

Figure 11.1 Print advertisement for Diet Coke
Source: Illustration courtesy of Coca-Cola USA.

For one of Diet Coke's introductory commercials, Coke planned an advertising extravaganza using the Rockettes of Radio City Music Hall. Diet Coke was the first product promoted on television by the Rockettes in their fifty-five-year history. The thirty-six Rockettes stepped to Diet Coke's "Just for the taste of it" jingle. Coke also invited sales personnel, retailers, distributors, and the news media to the tribute at Radio City Music Hall. In addition to the Rockettes, Coke featured many other celebrities in early commercials, including Bob Hope, Telly Savalas, Susan Anton, Glenn Ford, and Joe Namath.

After the Radio City Music Hall performance, Coke had a party for four thousand people on a pier on New York City's West Side. The crowd ate and drank, and they watched fireworks light the sky with the words **Diet Coke.** *Coke gave the party to generate favorable publicity from the news media, to convince retailers to put the product on their shelves, and to encourage route salespeople to sell it. Coke also used sales promotion efforts including gifts of "commemorative" six packs of Diet Coke, discounts, and special "two bottles for the price of one" coupons.[1]*

Coca-Cola took great pains to develop and implement an effective promotional program to launch Diet Coke. This chapter looks at the general dimensions of promotion. Initially, we consider the role of promotion. Then, to understand how promotion works, we analyze the meaning and process of communication and the product adoption process. The remainder of the chapter discusses the major types of promotional methods and the factors that influence an organization's decision to use specific methods.

The role of promotion

When people think about promotion, they frequently take one of two extreme positions. They may believe that the field of marketing consists entirely of promotional activities such as advertising and personal selling. They believe this primarily because those marketing activities are such a highly visible part of our everyday lives. People who take the other extreme see promotional activities as unnecessary and thus wasteful. They perceive that promotion costs (especially advertising) are high—sometimes excessively so—and believe these costs drive prices higher. Neither opinion is correct.

The role of *promotion* is to communicate with individuals, groups, or organizations to directly or indirectly facilitate exchanges by influencing one or more of the audiences to accept an organization's products. To facilitate exchanges directly, marketers communicate with selected audiences about a firm and/or its goods, services, and ideas. Marketers indirectly facilitate exchanges by focusing communication about company activities and products on interest groups (such as environmental and consumer groups), current and potential investors, regulatory agencies, and society in general. (Consider the promotional role of the jingles and slogans discussed in the Application on page 326.) Viewed from this wider per-

1. Janet Guyon, "Coca-Cola Kicks Off, Diet Coke Campaign with $100,000 Party," *Wall Street Journal*, July 29, 1982, p. 10.

As they soar, so do hearts.

Without voice, their bodies sing songs. Without words, their movements tell stories. Using only motion, ballet dancers can move others. Now, Ballet West, an emerging force in American ballet, is lifting this art form to greater heights. As a major touring company, its members enrich the lives of thousands of Americans. By achieving what most find impossible, they make the heart soar. Phillips Petroleum is glad to help fund them because they help lift the spirits of us all.

For additional information contact Ballet West, 50 West 200 South, Salt Lake City, Utah 84101.

spective, promotion can play a comprehensive communication role. Some promotional activities can be directed toward helping a company to justify its existence and to maintain positive, healthy relationships between itself and various groups in the marketing environment. The advertisement in Figure 11.2, for example, is not aimed directly at selling goods and services. It is designed to improve the relationship between the sponsor and society.

Although a firm can direct a single type of communication—such as an advertisement—toward numerous audiences, marketers often design a communication precisely for a specific audience. A firm frequently communicates several different messages concurrently, each to a different group. For example, a glass producer may direct one communication toward customers for double-paned windows, a second message toward investors about the firm's rapid growth, and a third communication toward society in general regarding what the company is doing to produce strong, safe glass.

To gain the most benefit from promotional efforts, marketers must make every effort to be sure communications are properly planned, implemented, coordinated, and controlled. To develop and implement effective

Figure 11.3
Information flows into
and out of an
organization

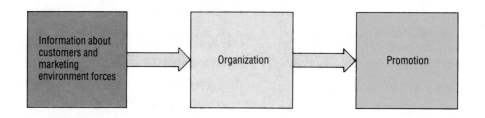

promotional activities, a firm must obtain and use information from the marketing environment (see Figure 11.3). How effectively marketers can use promotion to maintain positive relationships with environmental forces depends largely on the quantity and quality of information taken in by an organization. For example, marketers want to communicate effectively with customers to influence them to buy a particular product. To do so, they must have data about these customers and about the kinds of information these customers use in making purchase decisions for that type of product. Thus, to successfully communicate with selected audiences, marketers must collect and use information about these audiences.

Since the basic role of promotion is to communicate, we should analyze what communication is and how the communication process works.

Promotion and the communication process

Communication can be viewed as the transmission of information. Information is form or pattern. Thus, the sending and receiving of form is communication. According to this description, we are communicating with you when you perceive the following symbols:

在工廠吾人製造化粧品, 在商店吾人銷售希望。[2]

We encounter a problem, however, because this view of communication does not consider the meaningfulness of the pattern that is transmitted.

For promotional purposes, a more useful approach is to define **communication** as a sharing of meaning.[3] Implicit in this definition is the notion of transmission of information, because sharing necessitates transmission. More important, whatever is shared must, to some degree at least, have a common meaning for the individuals involved. Obviously, if we describe communication in these terms, we are not communicating with our readers when we transmit the Chinese symbols shown, because these symbols are not meaningful to most readers. Since this second approach to understanding communication is more comprehensive and realistic, we shall view communication as a sharing of meaning.

As shown in Figure 11.4, communication begins with a source. A **source** is a person, group, or organization that has a meaning which it intends and attempts to share with a receiver or an audience. For example, a source could be a salesperson who wishes to communicate a sales mes-

2. In case you don't read Chinese, this says "In the factory we make cosmetics, and in the drugstore we sell hope." Prepared by Chih Kang Wang.
3. Richard E. Stanley, *Promotion: Advertising, Publicity, Personal Selling, and Sales Promotion* (Englewood Cliffs, N.J.: Prentice-Hall, 1982), p. 136.

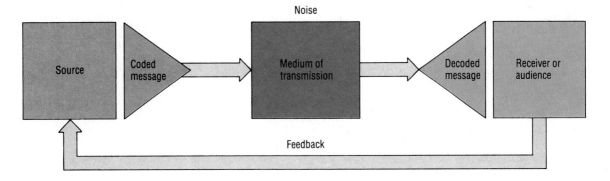

Noise

| Source | Coded message | | Medium of transmission | | Decoded message | Receiver or audience |

Feedback

Figure 11.4   The communication process

sage, or it could be an organization that wants to send a message to thousands of consumers through an advertisement.

To transmit meaning, a source must place the meaning into a series of signs that represent ideas. This is called the **coding process,** or *encoding*. The coding process requires a source to convert the meaning into a series of signs that represent ideas or concepts. For example, in our attempt to communicate with you, we use the words on this page and the symbols in Figure 11.4 as signs that represent meanings we wish to share.

When coding meaning into a message, a source must take into account certain characteristics of the receiver or audience. First, to share meaning most easily, the source should use signs that are familiar to the receiver or audience. Marketers who understand this fact realize how important it is to know their target market and to make sure that an advertisement, for example, is written in language that the target market can understand. If the maker of Visine eye freshener advertises to a general adult audience that the product contains tetrahydrocyline, the company may fail to share meaning. Most of the people in the audience do not use the word *tetrahydrocyline*. They are not likely to know what this substance will do for eyes. In fact, some adults may worry about using a potentially harmful chemical in their eyes. It is important that people understand the language in advertisements.

Second, when coding a meaning, a source should attempt to employ signs that the receiver or audience uses for referring to the concepts intended by the source. Marketers should generally avoid signs that can have several meanings for an audience. A national advertiser of soft drinks, for example, should avoid using the word *soda* as a general term for soft drinks. Although in some parts of the United States *soda* is taken to mean *soft drink,* in other regions it may evoke other concepts in receivers' minds—bicarbonate of soda, an ice-cream treat, or something that one mixes with Scotch whisky, for example.

To share a coded meaning with the receiver or audience, a source must select and use a medium of transmission. A **medium of transmission** carries the coded message from the source to the receiver or audience. Examples of transmission media include ink on paper, vibrations of air waves produced by vocal cords, chalk marks on a chalkboard, and electronically produced vibrations of air waves—in radio and television signals, for example.

Application

Communication Through Jingles and Slogans

Can you identify the products and organizations associated with the following slogans and jingles?

Now you see it, now you don't

Be all that you can be

Welcome to Miller time

Reach out and touch someone

Everything you always wanted in a beer, and less

We bring good things to life

I love New York

Don't leave home without it

Almost one out of every four commercials on the Best TV Commercials list used a slogan or jingle. Successful slogans and jingles are strong selling ideas that imply or state clear benefits in a few catchy words. Powerful jingles have believability, memorability, and often have an emotional appeal as well. Several jingles and slogans have helped products and organizations to be successful. The U.S. Army's "Be all that you can be" is considered to have been highly effective for changing the image of the Army. At the time the jingle came out, entering the army was unpopular. The jingle created an awareness of opportunities for individuals to achieve personal goals, such as further education, while at the same time serving their country. The slogan gave a personal appeal to what would otherwise have been considered a nonpersonal profession.

AT&T's "Reach out and touch someone" is another successful jingle. It has multiple attributes that increase its persuasive strength. The jingle tells the consumer to act and to use the product more often, and it contains an emotional appeal that increases consumer sensitivity to the product. The slogan sells an idea while leaving the consumer with positive, warm feelings.

Source: Based on Merle Kingman, "And Now a Few Words that Sell," *Advertising Age*, Oct. 24, 1983, p. M-28.

When a source chooses an inappropriate medium of transmission, several problems may arise, and marketers should be especially alert to avoid them. A coded message may reach some receivers, but not the right ones. For example, suppose a community theater spends most of its advertising dollars on radio advertisements. If theater goers depend mainly on newspapers for information about local drama, then the theater will not reach its intended target audience. Also, coded messages may reach intended receivers in an incomplete form because the intensity of the transmission is weak. For example, a marketer may choose a printing method that reproduces an advertisement so poorly that people cannot read it. If the advertisement is barely legible, the audience will form an impression of poor quality and associate it with the product or company.

A *receiver,* or audience—another major component of the communication process—is the individual, group, or organization that decodes a coded message. An audience is two or more receivers who decode a message. In the *decoding process,* signs are converted into concepts and ideas.

Seldom does a receiver decode exactly the same meaning that a source coded. When the decoded message is different from what was coded, *noise* exists. Noise has many sources and may affect any or all parts of the communication process. When a source selects a medium of transmission through which an audience does not expect to receive a message, noise is likely to occur. Noise sometimes arises within the medium of transmission itself. Radio static, faulty printing processes, and laryngitis are sources of noise. Interference on viewers' television sets during a commercial is noise and lessens the impact of the advertisement. Suppose the source uses a sign that is unfamiliar to the receiver or one that has a different meaning from the one that the source intended. In that case, noise will occur during decoding. Noise also may originate in the receiver. As discussed in Chapter 3, a receiver's perceptual processes may operate in such a way that a receiver is unaware of the coded message because it is blocked out by perceptual processes.

The receiver's response to the decoded message is *feedback* to the source. Feedback normally occurs and usually is expected by the source, although it may not be immediate. During feedback, the receiver or audience is the source of a message that is directed toward the original source, which then becomes a receiver. It makes sense to think about communication as a circular process.

During face-to-face communication, such as a personal selling situation, both verbal and nonverbal feedback can be immediate. This instant feedback allows communicators to adjust their messages quickly to improve the effectiveness of their communication. For example, when a salesperson realizes through feedback that a customer does not understand a sales presentation, the salesperson adapts the presentation to make it more meaningful to the customer. In interpersonal communication, feedback occurs through talking, touching, smiling, nodding, eye movements, and other body movements.

When mass communication such as advertising is employed, feedback is often slow, which may make it difficult to recognize. For example, if a lawnmower manufacturer were to advertise the benefits of a steam-powered engine, it might be six to eighteen months before the firm could recognize the effects of such advertisements. It could easily take that long for the firm to sense an increase in sales or in customers' interest. Although it is harder to recognize, feedback does exist for mass communication. Advertisers, for example, obtain feedback in the form of changes in sales volume and in consumers' attitudes and product awareness levels.

Each communication channel has a limit regarding the volume of information it can handle effectively. This limit, called *channel capacity,* is determined by the least efficient component of the communication process. Think about communications that depend on vocal speech. An individual source can talk only so fast, and there is a limit to how much a receiver can take in aurally. Beyond that point additional coded messages cannot be decoded; thus meaning cannot be shared. Although a radio announcer can read several hundred words a minute, a one-minute advertising message should not exceed 150 words because most announcers cannot articulate the words into understandable messages at a rate beyond 150 words per minute. This figure is the limit for both source and receiver, and marketers should keep this in mind when developing radio commercials. At times, a firm creates a television advertisement that contains several types of visual materials and several forms of audio messages, all transmitted to viewers at the same time. Such communication may be less than totally effective, because receivers cannot decode all the messages concurrently.

Now that we have explored the basic communication process, let us consider more specifically just how promotion is used to influence individuals, groups, or organizations to accept or adopt a firm's products. Although we introduced the product adoption process in Chapter 6, we explore it more fully in the following section to gain a better understanding of the conditions under which promotion occurs.

Promotion and the product adoption process

Marketers do not promote simply to inform, educate, and entertain. They communicate with individuals, groups, or organizations to facilitate exchanges. One long-run purpose of promotion is to influence and encourage buyers to accept or adopt goods, services, and ideas. At times, an advertisement may be informative or entertaining, yet it may fail to get the audience to purchase the product. For example, some Alka-Seltzer commercials have had this problem. The ultimate effectiveness of promotion is determined by the degree to which it affects product adoption among potential buyers.

To establish realistic expectations about what promotion can do, one should not view product adoption as a one-step process. Rarely can a single promotional activity cause an individual to buy a previously unfamiliar product. The acceptance of a product is a multistep process.

Although there are several ways to look at the *product adoption process,* one common approach is to view it as consisting of five stages: awareness, interest, evaluation, trial, and adoption.[4] In the awareness stage individuals become aware that the product exists, but they have little information about it and are not concerned about getting more. They enter the interest stage when they are motivated to get information about the product's features, uses, advantages, disadvantages, price, or location. During the evaluation stage individuals consider whether the product will satisfy certain criteria that are critical for meeting their specific needs. In the trial stage, they use or experience the product for the first time, possibly by purchasing a small quantity, by taking advantage of a free sample or demonstration, or by borrowing the product from someone. For example, in Figure 11.5, Bigelow Tea addressed the fact that many consumers had not tried Constant Comment tea. To stimulate trial, Bigelow provided a trial offer that included (for $1.00) fifteen tea bags and a 25-cent coupon. During this stage potential adopters determine the usefulness of the product under the specific conditions for which they need it. Individuals move into the adoption stage at the point when they choose that specific product when they need a product of that general type. Do not assume, however, that because a person enters the adoption process, he or she eventually will adopt the new product. Rejection may occur after any stage, including the adoption stage. Both product adoption and product rejection can be temporary or permanent.

4. Many of the ideas in this section are drawn from Everett M. Rogers, *Diffusion of Innovations* (New York: Free Press, 1962), pp. 81–86 and 98–102.

Figure 11.5
Promotion to stimulate
trial of a product
*Source: Courtesy R. C.
Bigelow, Inc.*

For the most part, people respond to different information sources at different stages of the adoption process. Mass communication sources are often effective for moving large numbers of people into the awareness stage. Producers of consumer goods commonly use massive advertising campaigns when introducing new products. They do so to create product awareness as quickly as possible within a large portion of the target market. For example, through advertisements like the one in Figure 11.6, 3M is trying to create awareness of one of its new products called Cold Comfort.

Since people in the interest stage are seeking information, mass communications may also be effective then. During the evaluation stage, individuals often seek information, opinions, and reinforcement from personal sources—relatives, friends, and associates. In the trial stage, individuals depend on salespersons for information about how to use the product properly to get the most out of it. Friends and peers may also be important

Figure 11.6
Advertisement aimed
at generating product
awareness
Source: Courtesy Personal Care Products/3M.

Figure 11.6
Advertisement aimed at generating product awareness
Source: Courtesy Personal Care Products/3M.

sources during the trial stage. By the time the adoption stage has been reached, both personal communication from sales personnel and mass communication through advertisements may be required. Even though the particular stage of the adoption process may influence the types of information sources used, marketers must remember that other factors—such as the product's characteristics, price, uses, and the characteristics of customers—also affect the types of information sources that buyers seek out.

Because people in different stages of the adoption process often will require different types of information, marketers designing a promotional campaign must determine what stage of the adoption process a particular target audience is in before they can develop the message. Potential adopters in the interest stage will need different information than people who have already reached the trial stage.

When an organization introduces a new product, people do not all begin the adoption process at the same time, and they do not move through the process at the same speed. Of those who eventually adopt the product, some enter the adoption process rather quickly. Others start considerably

Figure 11.7
Distribution of product
adopter categories
*Source: Reprinted with
permission of Macmillan,
Inc. From* Diffusion of
Innovations, *Third Edi-
tion, by Everett M. Rog-
ers. Copyright © 1962,
1971, 1983 by The Free
Press, a Division of
Macmillan, Inc.*

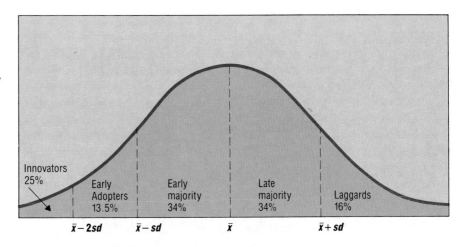

later. (And, of course, for most products, there is a group of nonadopters
who never begin the process.)

The amount of time that people use in adopting a new product can be
employed to classify them into adopter categories. The five major adopter
categories are innovators, early adopters, early majority, late majority, and
laggards.[5] Each adopter category, and the percentage of total adopters that
it represents, are shown in Figure 11.7. *Innovators* are the first to adopt a
new product. They enjoy trying new products and tend to be venturesome,
rash, and daring. *Early adopters* choose new products carefully and are
viewed as being "the people to check with" by persons in the remaining
adopter categories. Individuals in the *early majority* adopt just prior to the
average person; they are deliberate and cautious in trying new products.
Late majority people are quite skeptical of new products; they eventually
adopt new products because of economic necessity or social pressure. *Laggards,* the last to adopt a new product, are oriented toward the past; they
are suspicious of new products, and when they finally have adopted the
innovation, it already may have been replaced by a newer product. When
developing promotional efforts, a marketer should bear in mind that persons in different adopter categories often need different forms of communication and different types of information.

Now, to gain a better understanding of how promotion is used to move
people closer to the acceptance of goods, services, and ideas we will analyze the major promotional methods available to an organization.

The promotion mix

Several types of promotional methods can be used to communicate with
individuals, groups, and organizations. When an organization combines
specific ingredients to promote a particular product, that combination constitutes the promotion mix for that product. In this section, we analyze the
major ingredients that comprise a promotion mix. We also examine the primary factors that influence an organization to include specific ingredients
in the promotion mix for a specific product.

5. Everett M. Rogers, *Diffusion of Innovations* (New York: Free Press, 1983),
   pp. 247–250.

Figure 11.8
Possible ingredients
for an organization's
promotion mix

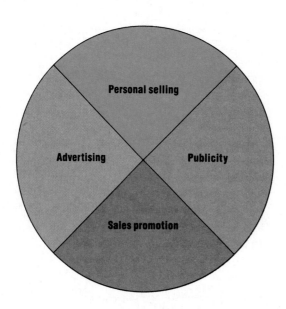

Promotion mix ingredients

The four major ingredients that can be included in an organization's *promotion mix* are advertising, personal selling, publicity, and sales promotion (see Figure 11.8). For some products, firms employ all four ingredients in their promotion mixes. For other products, only two or three are necessary. At this point, we will consider some general characteristics of each promotion mix ingredient. We will analyze the promotion mix ingredients in more detail in Chapters 12 and 13.

Advertising

Advertising is a paid form of nonpersonal communication about an organization and/or its products that is transmitted to a target audience through a mass medium. Individuals and organizations use advertising to promote goods, services, ideas, issues, and people as political candidates. Some mass media commonly selected to transmit advertising are television, radio, newspapers, magazines, direct mail, mass transit vehicles, outdoor displays, handbills, catalogs, and directories. Being a highly flexible promotional method, advertising offers the options of reaching an extremely large target audience or of focusing on a small, precisely defined segment of the population. For example, Figure 11.9 is targeted at a very select, affluent segment of the luxury condominum market. Advertised in *Town and Country,* the condominiums begin at $390,000 for one-bedroom units.

Advertising offers several benefits. It can be an extremely cost-efficient promotional method because it can reach a vast number of people at a low cost per person. For example, the cost of a black-and-white, one-page advertisement in *Time* magazine is $65,275. However, because the magazine reaches 4.6 million subscribers, the cost of reaching 1,000 subscribers is only $14.19. Advertising allows the user to repeat the message a number of times. In addition, advertising a product in a certain way can add to its prestige. The visibility that an organization gains from advertising enhances the firm's public image.

Advertising also has several disadvantages. Even though its cost per person reached may be low, its absolute dollar outlay can be extremely high. The cost can limit, and sometimes preclude, its use in a promotion mix. In addition, advertising rarely provides rapid feedback; measuring its effect on sales is difficult. Moreover, when compared with personal selling, advertising ordinarily has less persuasive impact on customers.

Personal selling

Personal selling is a process of informing customers and persuading them to purchase products through personal communication in an exchange situation. The phrase *purchase products* should be interpreted broadly enough to encompass the acceptance of ideas, issues, and political candidates.

Compared with advertising, personal selling has both advantages and limitations. While advertising is paid, nonpersonal communication aimed at a relatively large target audience, personal selling is aimed at one or several individuals. Reaching one person through personal selling costs considerably more than it does through advertising, but personal selling efforts often have greater impact on customers; and remember that personal selling also provides immediate feedback, which allows marketers to adjust their message to improve communication. It also helps them to determine and respond to customers' needs for information.

When a salesperson and customer communicate face to face, both individuals typically use several types of interpersonal communication. Obviously, the predominating communication form is language—both speech and writing. In addition, a salesperson and customer frequently use *kinesic communication,* or body language. They do this by moving their heads, eyes, arms, hands, legs, or torsos. Winking, head nodding, hand gestures and arm motions are forms of kinesic communication. A good salesperson can often evaluate a prospect's interest in a product or presentation by watching for eye contact and head nodding. *Proxemic communication,* a less obvious form of communication used in personal selling situations, occurs when either party varies the physical distance that separates the two parties. When a customer backs away from a salesperson, for example, that individual may be saying that he or she is not interested in the product or may be expressing dislike for the salesperson. Touching, although it is not as popular in the United States as in many other countries, can also be a form of communication, sometimes called *tactile communication.* Handshaking is a common form of tactile communication in our country.

Publicity

Publicity is nonpersonal communication in news story form, regarding an organization and/or its products, that is transmitted through a mass medium at no charge. Examples of publicity include magazine, newspaper, radio, and television news stories about new retail stores, new products, or personnel changes in the organization. An organization that employs publicity does not pay for the use of the mass medium. One should not, however, view publicity as free communication. There are clear costs associated with preparing news releases and encouraging media personnel to broadcast or print them. A firm that uses publicity regularly must either have employees to perform these activities or must obtain the services of a public relations firm or an advertising agency. Either way, the firm bears the costs of the activities. Although both advertising and publicity are transmitted through mass communication, they differ in that the sponsor does not pay the media costs for publicity and is not identified. The communication is presented as a news story. Publicity must be planned and implemented so that it is compatible with, and supportive of, other elements in the promotion mix.

Sales promotion

Sales promotion is an activity and/or material that acts as a direct inducement, offering added value or incentive for the product, to resellers, salespersons, or consumers.[6] Do not confuse the term *sales promotion* with *pro-*

6. This definition is adapted from John F. Luick and William L. Ziegler, *Sales Promotion and Modern Merchandising* (New York: McGraw-Hill, 1968), p. 4. Copyright © 1968 McGraw-Hill, Inc. Used with permission of McGraw-Hill Book Company.

motion; sales promotion is but a part of the more comprehensive area of promotion. It encompasses efforts other than personal selling, advertising, and publicity. Currently, marketers spend about one and one-half times as much on sales promotion as they do on advertising.

Frequently marketers employ sales promotion to improve the effectiveness of other promotion mix ingredients, especially advertising and personal selling. Although such use is not common, sales promotion can be used as the primary promotion vehicle. Usually, marketers design sales promotion to produce immediate, short-run sales increases. If a company uses advertising or personal selling, it generally employs them on either a continuous or a cyclical basis. However, a marketer's use of sales promotion devices is usually irregular.

Sales promotion methods fall into one of two groups, depending on the intended audience. *Consumer sales promotion methods* are directed toward consumers; coupons, free samples, demonstrations, and contests are typical. Sales promotion methods that focus on wholesalers, retailers, and salespersons are called *trade sales promotion devices*. They are devised to encourage resellers to carry and aggressively market a specific product. Examples include sales contests, free merchandise, and displays.

Having discussed the basic components that can be included in an organization's promotion mix, we must now ask what factors and conditions affect the selection of the promotional methods that a specific organization uses in its promotion mix for a particular product.

Selecting promotion mix ingredients

Marketers vary the composition of promotion mixes for many reasons. Although all four ingredients can be included in a promotion mix, frequently a marketer uses fewer than four. In addition, many firms that market multiple product lines use several promotion mixes simultaneously.

An organization's promotion mix (or mixes) is not an unchanging part of the marketing mix. Marketers can and do change the composition of their promotion mixes. An example is mentioned in the Application on page 336. The specific promotion mix ingredients employed and the intensity at which they are used depend on a variety of factors, including the following: the organization's promotional resources, objectives, and policies; the characteristics of the target market; the characteristics of the product; and the cost and availability of promotional methods.

Promotional resources, objectives, and policies

The quality of an organization's promotional resources affects the number and relative intensity of promotional methods that can be included in a promotion mix. If a company's promotional budget is extremely limited, the firm is likely to rely on personal selling, because it is easier to measure a salesperson's contribution to sales than to measure advertising's contribution. A business must have a sizable promotional budget if it is to employ regional or national advertising and sales promotion activities. Organizations with extensive promotional resources usually can include more ingredients in their promotion mixes. However, that they have more promotional dollars does not imply that they necessarily will use a greater number of promotional methods.

Application

**Amway
Launches
Broader
Promotion Mix**

Traditionally, Amway has used advertising to recruit distributors and promote its corporate image. Now, its advertisements are focusing on products. On the surface, this focus is not unusual, but for Amway it is a major step toward a market orientation for a company that spends less than 1 percent of its total sales volume on advertising. Amway, which uses a direct sales approach, designed a campaign to encourage consumers to approach Amway distributors on their own. In addition, Amway is testing other forms of promotion. The objective is to create a mixture of sales promotion, advertising, and distributor public relations that maximizes consumer-distributor contact.

Instead of encouraging distributors to make the "hard" sell, Amway is promoting products in other ways. For instance, it is researching the benefits of sweepstakes and coupons. Amway will conduct geographic market tests to obtain feedback about its promotional efforts from both distributors and consumers. Marketers at Amway hope that the new mix of promotional efforts will create a favorable climate for Amway distributors.

Source: Based on Ralph Gray, "Amway Discovers the Product Pitch," *Advertising Age,* Oct. 31, 1983, pp. 4, 84.

An organization's promotional objectives also influence the types of promotion employed. If a company's objective is to create mass awareness of a new convenience good, its promotion mix is likely to be heavily oriented toward advertising, sales promotion, and possibly publicity. If a company hopes to educate consumers about the features of durable goods such as home appliances, its promotion mix may consist of a moderate amount of advertising, possibly some sales promotion efforts designed to attract customers to retail stores, and a great deal of personal selling, since this method is an excellent way to inform customers about these types of products. If a firm's objective is to produce immediate sales of consumer nondurables, the promotion mix probably will depend heavily on advertising and sales promotion efforts.

Another element that marketers should consider when they plan a promotion mix is whether to use a push policy or a pull policy. With a *push policy,* the producer promotes the product only to the next institution down the marketing channel. For instance, in a marketing channel with wholesalers and retailers, the producer promotes to the wholesaler, since in this case the wholesaler is the channel member just below the producer (see Figure 11.10). Each channel member, in turn, promotes to the next channel member. A push policy usually relies heavily on personal selling. Sometimes, sales promotion and advertising are used in conjunction with personal selling to push the products down through the channel.

As shown in Figure 11.10, a firm that uses a *pull policy* promotes directly to consumers with the intention of developing a strong consumer demand for the products. If consumer demand is strong enough, consumers will seek the products in retail stores, retailers will recognize the demand and will in turn go to wholesalers or the producer to buy the products. The pull policy is intended to pull the goods down through the channel by creating demand at the consumer level. To stimulate intensive consumer demand, an organization ordinarily must place a heavy emphasis on advertis-

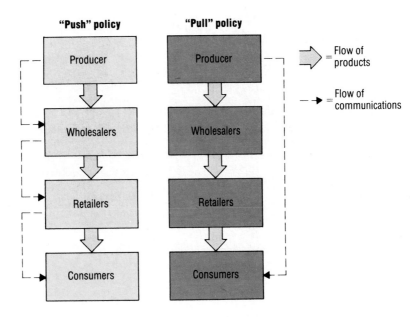

Figure 11.10
Comparison of "push" and "pull" promotional policies

"Push" policy

Producer

Wholesalers

Retailers

Consumers

"Pull" policy

Producer

Wholesalers

Retailers

Consumers

⇒ = Flow of products

- -▶ = Flow of communications

ing, and sometimes on sales promotion. When a major food company recently used a pull policy to introduce a new brand of flaked coffee, it advertised extensively and told consumers to ask for the product at their favorite stores.

Characteristics of the target market

The size, geographic distribution, and socioeconomic characteristics of an organization's target market also help dictate the ingredients included in the promotion mix for a product. The absolute number of persons in a market determines, to some degree, the promotion mix composition. If the size of the market is quite limited, the promotion mix will probably emphasize personal selling, which can be quite effective for reaching small numbers of people. Organizations that sell to small industrial markets and firms that market their products through only a few wholesalers frequently emphasize personal selling as the major component of their promotion mixes. When markets for a product consist of millions of customers, organizations use advertising and sales promotion because these methods can reach masses of people at a low cost per person.

The geographic distribution of a firm's customers can affect the combination of promotional methods used. Personal selling is more feasible if a company's customers are concentrated in a small area than if they are dispersed across a vast geographic region. Advertising may be more practical when the company's customers are numerous and dispersed.

The distribution of a target market's socioeconomic characteristics, such as age, income, or education, may dictate the types of promotional techniques that a marketer selects. For example, personal selling may be much more successful than print advertisements for communicating with less educated people.

Figure 11.11   Advertisement for toys
Source: Copyright 1982 Tyco Industries, Inc.

Characteristics of the product

Generally, promotion mixes for industrial products concentrate heavily on personal selling. For promoting consumer goods, on the other hand, advertising plays a major role. Treat this generalization cautiously, however. Industrial goods producers do use some advertising to promote goods. It is not altogether uncommon to see advertisements for computers, road building equipment, and aircraft; trade-type sales promotion occasionally is used to promote industrial goods. Personal selling is used extensively for consumer durables such as home appliances, automobiles, and houses. Consumer convenience items are promoted mainly through advertising and sales promotion. Publicity appears in promotion mixes both for industrial goods and for consumer goods.

Marketers of highly seasonal products are often forced to emphasize advertising, and possibly sales promotion, because off-season sales will not support an extensive year-round sales force. Although many toy producers have sales forces to sell to resellers, a number of these companies depend to a large extent on advertising to promote their products (see Figure 11.11).

A product's price also influences the composition of the promotion mix. High-priced products call for more personal selling. Since consumers associate greater risk with the purchase of an expensive product, they usually want the advice of a salesperson. Few of us, for example, would be willing to purchase a major appliance such as a freezer from a self-service establishment. For low-priced convenience items, marketers use advertising rather than personal selling at the retail level, because the profit margins on many of these items are too low to justify the use of salespersons, and because most customers do not need advice from sales personnel when buying such products.

The stage of the product life cycle also enters into marketers' decisions regarding an effective promotion mix. In the introduction stage, considerable advertising may be necessary for both industrial and consumer products in order to produce widespread awareness among potential users. For many products, personal selling and sales promotion are also used during this stage. For consumer nondurables, the growth and maturity stages necessitate a heavy emphasis on advertising. Industrial products, on the other hand, often require a concentration of personal selling and some sales promotion efforts during these stages. In the decline stage, marketers usually decrease their promotional activities, especially advertising. Promotional efforts in the decline stage often center on personal selling and sales promotion efforts.

Another factor affecting the composition of the promotion mix is intensity of market coverage. When a product is marketed through intensive distribution, the firm depends strongly on advertising. Sales promotion can also play a major role in the promotion of such products. A number of convenience products such as lotions, cereals, cake mixes, and coffee are promoted through samples, coupons, and cash refunds.

Where marketers have opted for selective distribution, marketing mixes vary considerably in terms of type and amount of promotional methods. Items distributed through exclusive distribution frequently demand more personal selling and less advertising. Expensive watches, furs, and high-quality furniture are examples of products that are promoted heavily through personal selling.

How a product is used affects the combination of promotional methods employed. Manufacturers of highly personal products such as nonprescription contraceptives and hemorrhoid medications depend heavily on advertising for promotion, because many users do not like to talk with salespersons about such products. As Figure 11.12 shows, such advertisements may offer advice from actual professionals such as doctors or pharmacists. An organization attempting to promote such highly personal products through door-to-door selling would probably fail badly.

Cost and availability of promotional methods
The costs of promotional methods are major factors to analyze when developing a promotion mix. National advertising and sales promotion efforts require large expenditures. However, if they are effective in reaching extremely large numbers of people, the cost per individual reached may be quite small, possibly a few pennies per person. Although national advertising campaigns cost a great deal, one should realize that not all forms of advertising are expensive. Many small, local businesses advertise their products through local newspapers, magazines, radio and television stations, and outdoor displays.

Another consideration that marketers must explore when formulating a promotion mix is the availability of promotional techniques. Even though there are a tremendous number of media vehicles in the United States, a firm may find that no available advertising medium effectively reaches a certain market. For example, a feed company may discover that no advertising media precisely reach the turkey growers of Oklahoma. The problem of media availability becomes even more pronounced when marketers try to advertise in foreign countries. Some media, such as television, simply

Figure 11.12
Advertisement for a
highly personal
product
*Source: Warner Lambert
Company.*

may not be available. Other media that are available may not be open to certain types of advertisements. For example, in West Germany, advertisers are prohibited from making brand comparisons in television commercials. Sometimes, too, a firm wishes to increase the size of its sales force but cannot find qualified personnel. In addition, some state laws prohibit the use of certain types of sales promotion activities, such as contests. Those techniques are "unavailable" in those locales.

Summary

The primary role of promotion is to communicate with individuals, groups, or organizations in the environment to directly or indirectly facilitate exchanges.

Communication is a sharing of meaning. The communication process involves several steps. First, the source translates the meaning into code, a process known as coding or encoding. The source must use signs that are familiar to the receiver or audience and should attempt to employ signs that the receiver or audience uses for referring to the concepts or ideas being promoted. The coded message is sent through a medium of transmission to the receiver or audience. The receiver or audience then decodes the message, and usually the receiver supplies feedback to the source. When the decoded message differs from the message that was encoded, a condition called noise exists.

The long-run purpose of promotion is to influence and encourage customers to accept or adopt goods, services, and ideas. The product adoption process consists of five stages. The awareness stage exists when individuals become aware of the product. Next, people move into the interest stage when they seek more information about the product. In the evaluation stage, individuals decide whether the product will meet certain criteria that are critical for satisfying their needs. During the fourth stage, the trial stage, the individual actually tries the product. In the adoption stage, the individual decides to use the product on a regular basis. Rejection of the product may occur at any stage.

The promotion mix for a product may include four major promotional methods: advertising, personal selling, publicity, and sales promotion. Advertising is a paid form of nonpersonal communciation about an organization and/or its products that is transmitted to a target audience through a mass medium. Personal selling is a process of informing customers and persuading them to purchase products through personal communication in an exchange situation. Publicity is nonpersonal communication in news story form, regarding an organization and/or its products, that is transmitted through a mass medium at no charge. Sales promotion is an activity and/or material that acts as a direct inducement, offering added value or incentive for the product, to resellers, salespersons, or consumers.

There are several major determinants of what promotional methods to include in a promotion mix for a product: the organization's promotional resources, objectives, and policies; the characteristics of the target market; the characteristics of the product; and the cost and availability of promotional methods.

Important terms

Promotion
Communication
Source
Coding process
Medium of transmission
Receiver
Decoding process
Noise
Feedback
Channel capacity
Product adoption process
Innovators
Early adopters
Early majority

Late majority
Laggards
Promotion mix
Advertising
Personal selling
Kinesic communication
Proxemic communication
Tactile communication
Publicity
Sales promotion
Consumer sales promotion methods
Trade sales promotion devices
Push policy
Pull policy

1. What is the major task of promotion? Do firms ever use promotion to accomplish this task and fail? If so, give several examples.
2. What is communication? Describe the communication process. Is it possible to communicate without using all the elements in the communication process? If so, which ones can be omitted?
3. Identify several causes of noise. How can a source reduce noise?
4. Describe the product adoption process. Under certain circumstances, is it possible for a person to omit one or more of the stages in adopting a new product? Explain your answer.
5. Describe a product that many persons are in the process of adopting. Have you begun the adoption process for this product? If so, what stage have you reached?
6. Identify and briefly describe the four major promotional methods that can be included in an organization's promotion mix. How does publicity differ from advertising?
7. What forms of interpersonal communication other than language can be used in personal selling?
8. Explain the difference between promotional efforts used with a pull policy and those used with a push policy. Under what conditions should each be used?
9. How do market characteristics determine the promotional methods to include in a promotion mix? Assume that a company is planning to promote a cereal to both adults and children. Along what major dimensions would these two promotional efforts have to be different?
10. How can a product's characteristics influence the composition of its promotion mix?
11. Evaluate the following statement: "Appropriate advertising media are always available if a company can afford them."

Cases

Case 11.1

Michael Jackson, Incorporated[7]

At age 25, Michael Jackson is one of the hottest stars in the pop music world. CBS Records considers him to be its biggest asset. He has won a record-breaking eight Grammy Awards, and his recent *Thriller* LP sold over 27 million copies in the year it was launched. At one point, fans were buying the *Thriller* album at an incredible rate of one million copies every four days.

Why is Michael Jackson so popular? Admittedly, Michael Jackson is a charismatic personality with many talents. However, some credit for his success is due to the promotional efforts that have been aimed at making him a popular entertainer.

Michael Jackson was determined to make *Thriller* a big success. He spent $1.2 million of his own funds to produce the fourteen-minute *Thriller*

7. Some of the information in this case is from Kim Foltz, "Michael Jackson, Inc.," *Newsweek,* Feb. 27, 1984, pp. 66–67; and John Koten, "PepsiCo Gambles Big on an Ad Campaign with Michael Jackson," *Wall Street Journal,* Feb. 28, 1984, p. 1.

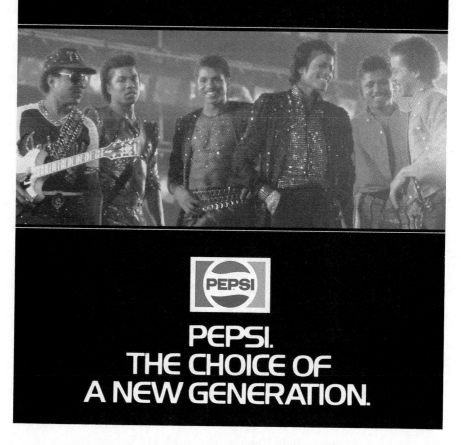

video that was viewed on MTV by audiences across the United States. The video showed him dancing and singing; but there was an added twist—a monster-movie motif. In addition, two separate video presentations were created and performed by Michael Jackson—*Billie Jean* and *Beat It*. Both of these are considered video classics. While MTV is an excellent promotional medium for all music performers, these video excerpts have quadrupled Michael Jackson's worth as a movie musical star.

The *Thriller* LP involved some strategic teamwork. To expand Jackson's listener audience, Eddie Van Halen, the heavy-metal rock musician, performed on the album. Also, in an attempt to create a worldwide appeal, Michael was teamed up with British star Paul McCartney in the duet "The Girl Is Mine."

An extensive array of paraphernalia can be purchased displaying Michael Jackson's sculptured features. One can buy T-shirts, posters, buttons, and trading cards. For $15, a person can purchase a Michael Jackson eleven-inch doll, garbed in the red-and-black outfit he wore for the *Thriller* video. Plans have been made for a new line of leather jackets sporting the

Michael Jackson brand. We soon may even be seeing Michael Jackson's face on a postage stamp issued by a country in the Caribbean.

Anyone attempting to wear a single glove will be considered an imitator because Michael Jackson's symbol is a single, silver-sequined glove. The glove is not new; he has been wearing it for about six years. However, it has only recently become a well-recognized symbol. Invitations sent out for his party in New York's American Museum of Natural History were printed on white gloves.

The *Thriller* success has led to numerous opportunities for the star. Plans have been drawn up for a movie part, a biography, a concert tour with his brothers, and Pepsi commercials. PepsiCo is one of the many companies that have been attracted by Michael Jackson's popularity. Pepsi's "choice of a new generation" ad campaign includes having Michael Jackson and his brothers, the Jacksons, appear in a series of advertisements. Figure 11.13 shows Michael Jackson and his brothers pictured on promotional material for PepsiCo's new ad campaign.

Questions for discussion
1. What forms of promotion are being used in the marketing of Michael Jackson?
2. Which promotion mix ingredient is especially important in the marketing of an entertainer's overall image?
3. Evaluate PepsiCo's decision to spotlight the Jacksons as part of its advertising campaign.

Case 11.2

Harley-Davidson[8]

Harley-Davidson has traditionally been the leader in the heavyweight sector of the U.S. motorcycle market. Harley-Davidson motorcycles (sometimes called hogs) range from 1000 cc to 1340 cc. In 1972, Harley commanded 99.6 percent of the U.S. heavyweight motorcycle market. In 1975, its share dropped to 44.4 percent, and in 1982, although it still led the heavyweight sector, its market share fell to 15 percent. In 1980 Honda closely followed Harley with 26 percent of the heavyweight market. Prices for Harleys range from $3,980 to $9,200, while comparable Honda bikes are about $500 less. Harley differentiates its product by stressing durability, high resale value, and a higher quality product. Harley's sales increased in 1980 to $289 million from $247 million in 1979. However, its profits decreased to $12.3 million in 1980 from $13.3 million in 1979. This decline in profits was attributed to an increase in engineering and development costs and to $2 million in interest rate assistance to dealers. By 1982, sales had dropped to $200 million and the firm suffered a $1 million loss.

Harley has traditionally had two main target markets—the "towers" and the "bikers." The towers are conventional blue-collar workers who tend to take longer trips than buyers of smaller motorcycles. The bikers market is that of the popular conception of the motorcycle gang whose

8. Portions of this case are based on the *1980 AMF Annual Report;* and Steve Kichen, "Thunder Road," *Forbes,* July 18, 1983, pp. 92–93.

members wear leather clothes with insignia. However, the overall Harley marketing emphasis now is on a white-collar image—persons over thirty who like the luxury and durability that Harley provides.

Most of Harley's advertising is done on a local basis; however, some national advertising is done by the corporation. Advertisements displayed in different motorcycle magazines show clean-cut motorcyclists at sporting events. Harley-Davidson also publishes its own news magazine, *Enthusiasts,* which is sent to Harley owners. Local Harley dealers also use ads showing "bikers" and other ads considered appropriate for the local market. Harley's excellent dealer network also permits good personal selling to promote both products and service.

Some Harley owners feel that when you ride a Harley motorcycle, you are more likely to be noticed than if you were on a Honda. Harley believes that everyone wants to be noticed. Both the dealers and the advertisements try to get this idea across to the public. Industry analysts believe Harley-Davidson has been more successful in meeting Japanese competition than automobile and television makers have because it sells more than just a product. Harley sells a special loyalty and recognition.

Questions for discussion

1. Based on this case and your personal knowledge, what are the characteristics of people who make up the target market for Harley-Davidson?
2. What are the major types of promotional methods that Harley-Davidson should use in its promotional mix?
3. Should Harley-Davidson try to broaden its image through promotion to encourage lightweight motorcycle owners to buy a Harley? Why?
4. How can promotion be used to increase market share in the heavyweight motorcycle market?

12

Advertising and Publicity

Objectives

To explore the uses of advertising.

To become aware of the major steps involved in the development of an advertising campaign.

To find out who is responsible for developing advertising campaigns.

To gain an understanding of publicity.

To analyze how publicity can be used.

"A diamond is forever" is the famous advertising slogan used by De Beers Consolidated Mines, Ltd. It has helped De Beers maintain a reputation for being able to stimulate demand for diamonds. The $1.3 billion, South Africa-based company supplies the majority of all diamonds sold in the world. Lately, however, De Beers has suffered some strong buyer resistance. Some observers believe that De Beers may be in serious trouble; diamond sales have been depressed for the past few years.

Realizing the seriousness of the situation, De Beers is revising its advertising campaign. Headlines in print advertisements cleverly emphasize the practical as well as sentimental reasons for buying diamonds (see Figure 12.1). These magazine advertisements also urge buyers to buy the larger, more expensive diamonds. De Beers is devoting 25 percent of its total advertising budget to advertisements that push larger, more profitable stones. This emphasis is another change from past advertising campaigns.

Approximately one-half of the new U.S. campaign will be TV spots. TV commercials are also aimed at convincing customers to trade up. In one

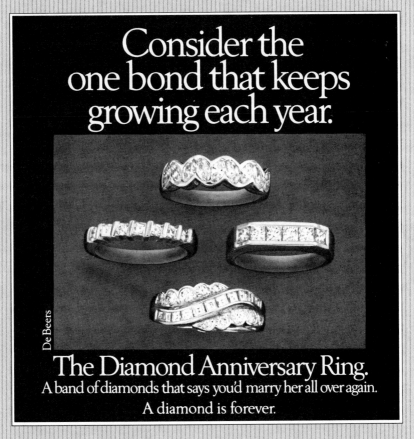

Figure 12.1   De Beers advertisement
Source: Courtesy of DeBeers Consolidated Mines, Ltd., Frank Spinelli, photographer.

advertisement, a husband and wife are thinking back on their earlier years when suddenly he surprises her with a diamond necklace. Just then, an announcer says, "She married you for richer or poorer, let her know how it's going." Other advertisements are geared toward persuading engagement ring buyers to buy larger stones. Advertisements ask, "Isn't two months' salary a small privilege to pay for something that lasts forever?"

De Beers is also exploring new market segments. One new target is the male segment. Twenty percent of the company's U.S. advertising budget goes for advertisements targeted either directly or indirectly, toward men. De Beers is targeting toward the male market with the headline, "Diamonds from a woman to a man."

These advertising campaigns will cost $70 million, the largest advertising expenditure in De Beer's history. It will cover new campaigns for the United States, Taiwan, Thailand, the Philippines, Singapore, Malaysia, and Hong Kong. The U.S. campaign alone will cost $27 million, up 30 percent over last year and 84 percent over the year before last. De Beers has always been a dominant force in the diamond market; this new advertising campaign is aimed at helping De Beers to survive.[1]

Advertising, credited with being the savior of certain companies and the executioner of others, is the subject of numerous "success stories" and a multitude of less visible "failure stories." This chapter explores many dimensions of advertising and publicity. Our discussion initially focuses on how advertising is used; then we consider the major steps involved in developing an advertising campaign. Next, we describe who is responsible for developing advertising campaigns. As we analyze publicity, we compare its characteristics with those of advertising and explore the different forms it may take. Then we consider how publicity is used and what is required for an effective publicity program. Finally, we discuss negative publicity and some of the problems associated with the use of publicity.

The nature of advertising

Advertising permeates our daily lives. At times people view it positively; at other times they curse it. Some of it informs, persuades, or entertains; some of it bores, insults, or deceives.

As indicated in Chapter 11, *advertising* is a paid form of nonpersonal communication that is transmitted to consumers through mass media such as television, radio, newspapers, magazines, direct mail, mass transit vehicles, and outdoor displays. An organization can use advertising to reach a variety of audiences ranging from small, precise groups—such as the paper weight collectors of Wyoming—to extremely large audiences—such as all gumchewers in the United States.

When they think of major advertisers, most people immediately mention business organizations. However, many types of organizations—including government organizations, churches, universities, civic groups,

1. Dennis Chase, "De Beers Changes Ad Tack," *Advertising Age,* July 18, 1983, pp. 42 and 48.

and charitable organizations—take advantage of advertising. In 1982 for example, the federal government was the twenty-ninth largest advertiser in the country, spending over $205 million.[2] So even though we analyze advertising in the context of business organizations, remember that much of what we say applies to all types of organizations.

In deciding when to use it, marketers sometimes give advertising more credit than it deserves. This attitude causes them to use advertising when they should not. There are certain conditions under which advertising can work effectively for an organization. The questions in Table 12.1 raise some general points that a marketer should consider when trying to decide whether advertising could be an effective ingredient in a product's promotion mix. However, this list is certainly not all-inclusive. Numerous factors enter into the decision of whether and how much advertising should be used.

The uses of advertising

Organizations employ advertising in a variety of ways and for many reasons. This section describes some of the ways that individuals and organizations use advertising.

To promote products and organizations

Advertising is used to promote a great many things. For example, it is used to promote goods, services, images, issues, ideas, and people. Depending on what is being promoted, advertising can be classified as either institutional advertising or product advertising. *Institutional advertising* promotes organizational images, ideas, and political issues. *Product advertising* promotes goods and services. It is used by businesses, government organizations, and private nonbusiness organizations to promote the uses, features, images, and benefits of their goods and services.

To stimulate primary and selective demand

Product advertising often serves to stimulate demand directly. When a specific firm is the first to introduce a revolutionary innovation, the marketer uses pioneer advertising to stimulate primary demand. *Pioneer advertising* informs people about a product: what it is, what it does, how it can be used, and where it can be purchased. Since pioneer advertising is used in the introductory stage of the product life cycle, when there are no competitive brands, it neither emphasizes the brand name nor compares brands. The first company to introduce the home videorecorder initially tried to stimulate primary demand by emphasizing the benefits of the product in general rather than the benefits of a specific brand. Product advertising is also sometimes employed to stimulate primary demand for an established product. At times, an industry trade group, rather than a single firm, sponsors advertisements to stimulate primary demand. In Figure 12.2, for example, the Golden Delicious Apple Growers of Washington are trying to stimulate primary demand for their apples.

An advertiser uses competitive advertising to build selective demand, which is demand for a specific brand. *Competitive advertising* points out a brand's uses, features, and advantages that benefit consumers and that

2. "100 Leaders' Advertising as a Per Cent of Sales," *Advertising Age,* Sept. 8, 1983, p. 166.

Table 12.1   Some issues to consider when deciding whether to use advertising

1. **Does the product possess unique, important features?**

   Although homogeneous products such as cigarettes, gasoline, and beer have been advertised successfully, they usually require considerably more effort and expense than other products. On the other hand, products that are differentiated on physical, rather than psychological, dimensions are much easier to advertise. Even so, "being different" is rarely enough. The advertisability of product features is enhanced when buyers believe that those unique features are important and useful.

2. **Are "hidden qualities" important to buyers?**

   If by viewing, feeling, tasting, or smelling the product buyers can learn all there is to know about the product and its benefits, advertising will have less chance of increasing demand. Conversely, if not all product benefits are apparent to consumers on inspection and use of the product, advertising has more of a story to tell, and the probability that it can be profitably employed increases. The "hidden quality" of vitamin C in oranges once helped to explain why Sunkist oranges could be advertised effectively while the advertising of lettuce has been a failure.

3. **Is the general demand trend for the product favorable?**

   If the generic product category is experiencing a long-term decline, it is less likely that advertising can be used successfully for a particular brand within the category.

4. **Is the market potential for the product adequate?**

   Advertising can be effective only when there are sufficient actual or prospective users of the brand in the target market.

5. **Is the competitive environment favorable?**

   The size and marketing strength of competitors and their brand shares and loyalty will greatly affect the possible success of an advertising campaign. For example, a marketing effort to compete successfully against Kodak film, Morton salt, or Campbell's soups would demand much more than simply advertising.

6. **Are general economic conditions favorable for marketing the product?**

   The effects of an advertising program and the sale of all products are influenced by the overall state of the economy and by specific business conditions. For example, it is much easier to advertise and sell luxury, leisure products (stereos, sailboats, recreation vehicles) when disposable income is high.

7. **Is the organization able and willing to spend the money required to launch an advertising campaign?**

   As a general rule, if the organization is unable or unwilling to undertake an advertising expenditure that, as a percentage of the total amount spent in the product category, is at least equal to the market share it desires, advertising is less likely to be effective.

8. **Does the firm possess sufficient marketing expertise to market the product?**

   The successful marketing of any product involves a complex mixture of product and buyer research, product development, packaging, pricing, financial management, promotion, and distribution. If the firm is weak in any areas of marketing, this shortcoming is an obstacle to the successful use of advertising.

Source: Adapted from Charles H. Patti, "Evaluating the Role of Advertising," *Journal of Advertising,* Fall 1977, pp. 32–33. Used by permission.

may not be available in competing brands. Because a number of producers currently sell color televisions, RCA promotes the features and advantages of RCA color television sets to encourage customers to select that specific brand. There is no longer any need to promote the advantages of color television itself.

Figure 12.2
Advertisement to stim-
ulate primary demand
for Golden Delicious
apples
*Source: Washington Ap-
ple Commission.*

WINNING SEASON

PICKED BY THE GOLDEN DELICIOUS APPLE GROWERS OF WASHINGTON. WASHINGTON

One increasingly popular form of competitive advertising is *comparative advertising,* which compares two or more specified brands on the basis of one or more product attributes. Both the sponsored brand and one or more competitive brands are identified in a comparative advertisement. This type of advertising is prevalent among manufacturers of toothpastes, deodorants, tires, automobiles, and a multitude of other products.

To offset competitors' advertising

When marketers advertise to offset or lessen the effects of a competitor's promotional program, they are using *defensive advertising.* Although defensive advertising does not necessarily increase a company's sales or market share, it may prevent a loss in sales or market share. For example, Procter & Gamble, which manufactures Crest toothpaste, tried to limit the impact of Lever Brothers' direct-mail campaign for Aim toothpaste. Lever Brothers sent free samples to households in many parts of the United States, and the Crest television commercials emphasized that there was no need even to try the free sample of the new fluoride toothpaste, since Crest had been so effective. Procter & Gamble used defensive advertising in an attempt to hold on to its sizable share of the toothpaste market. Defensive advertising is employed most often by firms in extremely competitive consumer product markets.

To make salespersons more effective

Business organizations that allot a sizable proportion of promotional effort to personal selling often take advantage of advertising to improve the effectiveness of sales personnel. Advertising that is created specifically to support personal selling activities tries to presell buyers by informing them about a product's uses, features, and benefits and by encouraging them to contact local dealers or sales representatives. This form of advertising helps salespeople to find good sales prospects. Sometimes, advertisements indicate that a person can get more information (or even a free gift) by sending a letter or a completed information blank to a certain address. Salespeople generally view the individuals who send for more information as prospective buyers and contact them. Advertising is often designed to support personal selling efforts for industrial products, insurance, and consumer durables such as automobiles and major household appliances.

To increase the uses of a product

The absolute demand for any product is limited. Persons in a market will consume only so much of a particular product. Because of the absolute limit on demand and because of competitive conditions, marketers can increase sales of a specific product in a defined geographic market only to a certain point. To increase sales beyond this point, they must either enlarge the geographic market and sell to more people or develop and promote a larger number of uses for the product. If a firm's advertising can convince buyers to use its products in more ways, then the sales of its products increase. For years, General Foods has advertised recipes that call for Jell-O brand products. Arm & Hammer has increased demand for its baking soda by promoting additional uses in advertisements like the one in Figure 12.3. When promoting new uses, an advertiser attempts to increase the demand for its own brand without increasing the demand for competing brands.

To remind and reinforce customers

Marketers sometimes use *reminder advertising* to let consumers know that an established brand is still around and that it has certain uses, characteristics, and benefits. *Reinforcement advertising* tries to assure current users that they have made the right choice and tells them how to get the most satisfaction from the product. Both reminder and reinforcement advertising are used to prevent a loss in sales or market share.

To reduce sales fluctuations

The demand for many products varies from one month to another because of such factors as climate, holidays, seasons, and customs. A business cannot be operated at peak efficiency when sales fluctuate markedly. Changes in sales volume translate into changes in the production or inventory, personnel, and financial resources required. To the extent that a marketer can

Figure 12.3
Promotion of Arm &
Hammer Baking Soda
as a dentifrice
*Source: Courtesy of
Church & Dwight Co.,
Inc.*

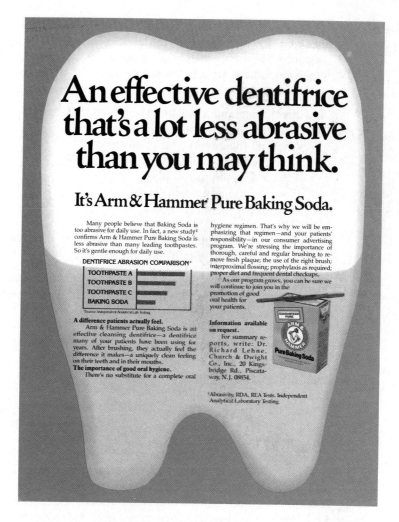

An effective dentifrice that's a lot less abrasive than you may think.

It's Arm & Hammer Pure Baking Soda.

Many people believe that Baking Soda is too abrasive for daily use. In fact, a new study[1] confirms Arm & Hammer Pure Baking Soda is less abrasive than many leading toothpastes. So it's gentle enough for daily use.

DENTIFRICE ABRASION COMPARISON[*]

TOOTHPASTE A	
TOOTHPASTE B	
TOOTHPASTE C	
BAKING SODA	

Source: Independent Analytical Lab Testing

A difference patients actually feel.

Arm & Hammer Pure Baking Soda is an effective cleansing dentifrice—a dentifrice many of your patients have been using for years. After brushing, they actually feel the difference it makes—a uniquely clean feeling on their teeth and in their mouths.

The importance of good oral hygiene.

There's no substitute for a complete oral hygiene regimen. That's why we will be emphasizing that regimen—and your patients' responsibility—in our consumer advertising program. We're stressing the importance of thorough, careful and regular brushing to remove fresh plaque; the use of the right brush; interproximal flossing; prophylaxis as required; proper diet and frequent dental checkups.

As our program grows, you can be sure we will continue to join you in the promotion of good oral health for your patients.

Information available on request.

For summary reports, write: Dr. Richard Lehne, Church & Dwight Co., Inc., 20 Kingsbridge Rd., Piscataway, N.J. 08854.

[*]Abrasivity, RDA, REA Tests. Independent Analytical Laboratory Testing.

generate sales during slow periods, he or she can smooth out the fluctuations. Advertising is often designed to stimulate sales during sales slumps. For example, advertisements promoting price reductions of lawn-care equipment or air conditioners can increase sales during fall and winter months. On occasion, a business organization advertises that customers will get better service by coming in on certain days rather than others. For example, a firm in Texas advertised that customers could get better optical services Tuesdays through Fridays.

During peak sales periods a marketer may refrain from advertising to prevent overstimulation of sales to the point that the firm cannot handle all the demand. When advertising reduces fluctuations a manager can use the firm's resources more efficiently.

A firm's use of advertising depends on the firm's objectives and resources and on environmental forces. The degree to which advertising accomplishes the marketer's goals depends in large part on the advertising campaign. At this point, then, we should analyze the development of an advertising campaign.

Developing an advertising campaign

Several steps are required to develop an advertising campaign. The number of steps and the exact order in which they are carried out may vary according to an organization's resources, the nature of its product, and the types of audiences to be reached, but the major steps in the creation of an advertising campaign include the following:

1. Identifying and analyzing the advertising target
2. Defining the advertising objectives
3. Creating the advertising platform
4. Determining the advertising appropriation
5. Developing the media plan
6. Creating the advertising message
7. Evaluating the effectiveness of the advertising

These general guidelines for developing an advertising campaign are appropriate for all types of organizations.

Identifying and analyzing the advertising target

One basic and important question that marketers must answer as they begin to develop an advertising campaign is: "Whom are we trying to reach with our message?" The *advertising target* is the group of people toward which advertisements are aimed. The advertising target often includes everyone in a firm's target market. Marketers may, however, seize some opportunities to slant a campaign at only a portion of the target market. For example, the maker of a brand of hair care products may define the target market for a shampoo as being females, 12–49 years old. The company may, nonetheless, wish to aim a specific campaign at women in the 35–49 age range. For this campaign, the firm's advertising target would be women 35–49 years old, rather than females in the 12–49 age group.

Advertisers should analyze advertising targets. They need an information base on which to develop a campaign. Information that is commonly needed includes the location and geographic distribution of persons; the distribution of age, income, race, sex, and education; and consumer attitudes regarding the purchase and use both of the advertiser's products and of competing products. The exact kinds of information that an organization will find useful depend on the type of product being advertised, the characteristics of the advertising target, and the type and amount of competition.

Generally, the more that advertisers know about the advertising target, the more able they are to develop an effective advertising campaign. Identifying and analyzing the advertising target is critical because the other steps in developing the campaign are based on this. When the advertising target is not precisely identified and properly analyzed, the campaign has less chance of success.

Defining the advertising objectives

The advertiser's next step is to consider what the firm hopes to accomplish with the campaign. It is imperative that the organization define its advertising objectives.

Advertising objectives should be stated in clear, precise, and measurable terms. Precision and measurability allow advertisers to evaluate advertising success—to judge whether or how well the objectives have been accomplished after the campaign is completed. Imagine that an advertiser sets the following vague objective: "The objective of our campaign is to increase sales." If this advertiser's sales increase by one dollar, has the objective been achieved? Without a reference point, no one knows.

Advertising objectives should contain bench marks giving the current condition or position of the firm. They also should indicate how far and in what direction an advertiser wishes to move from this bench mark. In the above example, the advertiser should state the current sales level (the bench mark) and the amount of sales increase that is sought through advertising. Assuming that average monthly sales are $450,000, this advertiser might set the following objective: "Our primary advertising objective is to increase monthly sales from $450,000 to $540,000."

Although this example may appear to be precise and clear, it is not. An advertising objective also should be specific regarding the time allotted for its achievement. By placing an objective into a time frame, advertisers know exactly how long they have to accomplish their objective. They also know when they should begin to evaluate the effectiveness of the campaign. To make our objective specific as to time, the advertiser could state, "Our primary advertising objective is to increase average monthly sales from $450,000 to $540,000 within twelve months."

Advertising objectives usually are stated in terms of either sales or communication. When an advertiser defines objectives in terms of sales, the objectives focus on raising absolute dollar sales, increasing sales by a certain percentage, or increasing the firm's market share.

Even though the long-run goal of an advertiser is to increase sales, not all campaigns are designed to produce immediate sales. Some campaigns are aimed at increasing product or brand awareness, at making consumers' attitudes more favorable, or at increasing consumers' knowledge of a product's features. These objectives are stated in terms of communication. When Apple, for example, introduced home computers, its initial campaign did not focus on sales, but instead created brand awareness and educated consumers about the features and uses of home computers. A specific communication objective might be to increase product feature awareness from 0 to 40 percent of the target market in the first six months.

Since advertising objectives guide campaign development, advertisers should define the objectives carefully to make certain that the campaign will accomplish what they desire. Advertising campaigns based on poorly defined objectives are seldom successful.

Creating the advertising platform

Before launching a political campaign, party leaders meet and develop a political platform. The platform states the major issues on which the party will base its campaign. Like a political platform, an *advertising platform* consists of the basic issues or selling points that an advertiser wishes to include in the advertising campaign. For example, a motorcycle producer might wish to include economy, speed, ease of handling, and accessories in its advertising platform. A single advertisement in an advertising campaign may contain one or several issues in the platform. Although the platform contains the basic issues, it does not indicate how they should be presented.

A marketer's advertising platform should consist of issues that are important to consumers. One of the best ways to determine what those issues are is to survey consumers to learn what they consider most important in the selection and use of the product involved. The selling features must not only be important to consumers; if possible, they should also be features that competitive products do not have. The safety of their money is important to bank customers. Yet they believe that virtually all banks are equally safe. Thus, the advertising platform for a specific bank should not emphasize safety. In this case, the marketer should look for other selling features that are important to bank customers and that are not available at competing banks.

Research—although it is the most effective method for determining the issues of an advertising platform—is expensive. As a result, the advertising platform is most commonly based on the opinions of personnel within the firm and of individuals in the advertising agency, if an agency is used. This trial-and-error approach generally leads to some successes and some failures.

Because the advertising platform provides a base on which to build the message, marketers should analyze this stage carefully. A campaign can be perfect in terms of the selection and analysis of its advertising target, the statement of its objectives, its media strategy, and the form of its message. The campaign will still fail miserably if the advertisements communicate information that consumers do not consider important when they select and use the product.

Determining the advertising appropriation

The *advertising appropriation* is the total amount of money that a marketer allocates for advertising for a specific time period. It is hard to decide how much to spend on advertising for a month, three months, a year, or several years, because there is no way to measure what the precise effects of spending a certain amount of money on advertising will be.

Many factors affect a firm's decision about how much to appropriate for advertising. The geographic size of the market and the distribution of buyers within the market have great bearing on this decision. As shown in Table 12.2, both the type of product advertised and a firm's sales volume relative to competitors' sales volumes also play a part in determining what proportion of a firm's revenue goes for advertising. Advertising appropriations for industrial products are usually quite small relative to the sales of the products. Consumer convenience items such as soft drinks, tobacco, soaps, drugs, and cosmetics generally have large advertising appropriations.

Of the many techniques used to determine the advertising appropriation, one of the most logical is the *objective and task approach*. Using this approach, marketers initially determine the objectives that a campaign is to achieve and then attempt to list the tasks required to accomplish these objectives. Once the tasks have been identified, their costs are added to arrive at the amount of the total appropriation. There is one main problem with implementing this approach. Marketers usually find it hard to estimate the level of effort needed to achieve certain objectives. A coffee marketer, for example, might find it extremely difficult to determine by how much national television advertising would have to be increased to increase a brand's market share from 8 to 12 percent. Because of this problem, the objective and task approach is not used widely by advertisers.

A common method for establishing the advertising appropriation is the **percent of sales approach**. To use this method, marketers simply multiply a firm's past sales, forecasted sales, or a combination of the two by a standard percentage that is based on both what the firm traditionally spends on advertising and what the industry averages. For example, from the data in Table 12.2 and from experience, a large food processor might determine its total advertising appropriation by multiplying the past year's sales by 4.5 percent (the average for the eighteen food processors shown in Table 12.2). This approach has one major disadvantage. It is based on the incorrect assumption that sales create advertising (rather than that advertising creates sales). A marketer who uses this approach and experiences declining sales will reduce the amount spent on advertising. We must ask how this approach will stimulate lagging sales. It may, in fact, cause a further reduction in sales. Even though this technique is illogical, it has widespread acceptance because it is easy to use and is less disruptive competitively. It stabilizes a firm's market share within an industry.

Marketers usually are concerned about the type and intensity of their competitors' advertising. Another way to arrive at the advertising appropriation is the **competition-matching approach**. Marketers who follow this approach try to match their major competitors' appropriations in terms of absolute dollars or to allocate the same percentage of sales for advertising as competitors do. Although a wise marketer should be cognizant of what competitors spend on advertising, this technique should not be used by itself, because a firm's competitors probably have different advertising objectives and different resources available for advertising.

At times, marketers use the **arbitrary approach**. In using this method, a high-level executive in the firm states how much can be spent on advertising for a certain time period. The arbitrary approach often leads to underspending or overspending. Although it is not a scientific budgeting technique, it is expedient.

Establishing the advertising appropriation is critically important. If it is set too low, then the campaign cannot achieve its full potential in terms of stimulating demand. When too much money is appropriated for advertising, overspending occurs, and financial resources are wasted.

Developing the media plan

As shown in Table 12.3 (on p. 360), advertisers spend tremendous amounts of money on advertising media. These amounts have grown rapidly during the last forty years. To derive the maximum results from media expenditures, a marketer must develop an effective media plan. A **media plan** sets forth the exact media vehicles to be used (specific magazines, television stations, newspapers, and so forth) and the dates and times that the advertisements will appear.

To formulate a media plan, the planner selects the media for a campaign and draws up a time schedule for each medium. The media planner's primary goal is to reach the largest number of persons in the advertising target per dollar spent on media.

Table 12.2 Sales volume and advertising expenditures for the top 100 leading national advertisers

Category	Rank	Company	Advertising	Sales	Ad as Percent of Sales
Food	6	General Foods Corp.	$429.1	$8,256.4	5.2
	9	Nabisco Brands	335.2	5,871.1	5.7
	16	Beatrice Foods Co.	271.0	9,188.2	2.9
	19	McDonald's Corp.	265.5	7,809.0	3.4
	21	General Mills	244.4	5,550.8	4.4
	23	H.J. Heinz Co.	235.7	3,738.5	6.3
	27	Ralston Purina Co.	220.0	4,802.6	4.6
	31	Dart & Kraft	199.2	9,974.0	2.0
	32	Esmark Inc.	197.8	3,389.1	5.8
	33	Norton Simon Inc.	191.2	2,994.3	6.4
	34	Consolidated Foods Corp.	178.0	6,660.0	2.7
	36	Pillsbury Co.	170.4	3,700.0	4.6
	43	Kellogg Co.	154.2	2,370.0	6.5
	52	Campbell Soup Co.	121.0	1,773.0	6.8
	57	Nestle Enterprises	112.5	2,341.0	4.8
	59	Quaker Oats Co.	106.1	2,610.0	4.1
	62	CPC International	96.7	4,091.5	2.4
	97	Wendy's International	44.9	1,632.4	2.8
Automobiles	3	General Motors Corp.	549.0	60,025.6	0.9
	12	Ford Motor Co.	313.5	37,067.2	0.9
	35	Chrysler Corp.	173.0	10,044.9	1.7
	55	Nissan Motor Corp., U.S.A.	117.6	13,346.1	0.9
	58	Toyota Motor Sales	111.3	15,096.3	0.7
	61	Volkswagen of America	98.0	15,200.0	0.6
	64	American Honda Motor Co.	94.9	9,375.7	1.0
	79	American Motors Corp.	72.0	2,878.4	2.5
	82	Mazda Motors of America	70.5	4,248.1	1.7
Pharmaceuticals	10	American Home Products Corp.	325.4	4,580.0	7.1
	15	Warner-Lambert Co.	294.7	3,246.0	9.1
	17	Johnson & Johnson	270.0	3,304.0	8.2
	46	Sterling Drug	140.2	1,796.2	7.8
	50	Richardson-Vicks	129.3	1,115.6	11.6
	51	Schering-Plough Corp.	123.9	1,817.9	6.8
	68	SmithKline Beckman	89.5	2,968.7	3.0
	77	Miles Laboratories	72.3	1,075.6	6.7
	85	Pfizer Inc.	65.7	3,453.6	1.9
Airlines	66	Trans World Corp.	91.6	5,107.9	1.8
	80	Pan American World Airways	72.0	3,716.0	1.9
	81	UAL Inc.	70.6	5,319.7	1.3
	87	AMR Corp.	61.6	4,177.0	1.5
	89	Eastern Air Lines	57.4	3,769.2	1.5
	94	Delta Air Lines	49.3	3,617.7	1.4
Communications and entertainment	25	Warner Communications	232.2	3,990.0	5.8
	41	CBS Inc.	159.0	4,122.8	3.9
	49	Time Inc.	130.1	3,564.0	3.7
	70	MCA Inc.	80.1	1,587.6	5.0

Source: Reprinted with permission from "100 Leaders' Advertising as a Per Cent of Sales," *Advertising Age,* Sept. 8, 1983, p. 166. Copyright 1983 by Crain Communications, Inc.

Table 12.2   (continued)

Category	Rank	Company	Advertising	Sales	Ad as Percent of Sales
	86	20th Century-Fox Film Corp.	$ 65.0	$ 560.7	11.6
	100	American Broadcasting Cos.	42 9	2,664.5	1.6
Tobacco	4	R.J. Reynolds Industries	530.3	13,057.0	4.1
	5	Philip Morris Inc.	501.7	11,716.1	4.3
	24	Batus Inc.	235.0	5,506.7	4.3
	60	Loews Corp.	103.3	4,747.1	2.2
	78	American Brands	72.3	6,505.0	1.1
	91	GrandMet USA	54.0	1,347.3	4.0
Toiletries and cosmetics	30	Bristol-Myers Co.	205.0	3,599.9	5.7
	37	Gillette Co.	163.0	2,239.0	7.3
	48	Chesebrough-Pond's	131.0	1,623.2	8.1
	53	Beecham Group Ltd.	120.7	2,519.6	4.8
	56	Revlon Inc.	113.0	2,351.0	4.8
	93	Noxell Corp.	49.6	261.9	18.9
Wine, beer, and liquor	22	Anheuser-Busch Cos.	243.4	5,185.7	4.7
	44	Seagram Co. Ltd.	153.0	2,826.2	5.4
	76	Brown-Forman Distillers Corp.	74.0	885.0	8.4
	90	Stroh Brewery Co.	55.6	1,318.0	4.2
	98	Hiram Walker Resources Ltd.	44.4	2,759.1	1.6
	99	E&J Gallo Winery	42.9	620.0	6.9
Soaps and cleaners	1	Procter & Gamble Co.	726.1	12,452.0	5.8
	14	Unilever U.S.	304.6	2,954.9	10.3
	18	Colgate-Palmolive Co.	268.0	4,888.0	5.5
	72	Clorox Co.	76.3	867.1	8.8
	75	S.C. Johnson & Son	74.6	2,000.0	3.7
Chemicals and gasoline	11	Mobil Corp.	320.0	64,137.0	0.5
	47	American Cyanamid Co.	133.0	3,453.7	3.9
	65	E.I. du Pont de Nemours & Co.	92.9	33,331.0	0.3
	69	Union Carbide Corp.	83.7	9,061.0	0.9
Appliances, TVs and radios	38	RCA Corp.	160.1	8,237.0	1.9
	40	General Electric Co.	159.0	26,500.0	0.6
	67	North American Phillips Co.	90.6	3,168.1	2.9
Gum and candy	54	Mars Inc.	120.0	1,490.0	8.1
	84	Wm. Wrigley Jr. Co.	67.0	581.5	11.5
	88	Hershey Foods Corp.	60.0	1,565.7	3.8
Photographic equipment	45	Eastman Kodak Co.	142.8	10,815.0	1.3
	95	Polaroid Corp.	47.8	1,293.9	3.7
	96	Canon U.S.A.	47.1	820.2	5.7
Retail chains	2	Sears, Roebuck & Co.	631.1	30,020.0	2.1
	8	K mart Corp.	366.1	16,772.2	2.2
	26	J.C. Penney Co.	230.0	11,414.0	2.0
Soft drinks	13	PepsiCo Inc.	305.0	7,499.0	4.1
	20	Coca-Cola Co.	255.3	6,249.7	4.1
	92	Royal Crown Cos.	50.3	469.0	10.7
Office equipment	71	Xerox Corp.	80.0	8,455.6	1.0
	74	IBM Corp.	75.0	34,364.0	0.2
Telephone equipment	7	AT&T Co.	373.6	65,757.0	0.6
	39	ITT Corp.	159.1	21,921.0	0.7

(continued on next page)

Table 12.2 (continued)

Category	Rank	Company	Advertising	Sales	Ad as Percent of Sales
Miscellaneous	28	Mattel Inc.	$217.9	$1,341.9	16.2
	29	U.S. Government	205.5	NA	NA
	42	Gulf & Western Industries	155.0	6,423.0	2.4
	63	American Express Co.	95.5	8,093.0	1.2
	73	Greyhound Corp.	75.2	5,075.0	1.5
	83	Kimberly-Clark Corp.	69.3	3,000.0	2.3

In making his or her selection, the planner first must decide which general kinds of media to use. The major types of media are radio, television, newspapers, magazines, direct mail, outdoor displays, and mass transit vehicles. After making the general media decision, the planner opts for specific subclasses within each medium. A toothpaste marketer, for example, might decide to use television and magazines. The marketer then must consider whether to use children's, women's daytime, family, and/or late-night adult television programming and whether to use men's, women's, teenagers', children's, and/or general-audience magazines. (See related issues in the Application on page 361.) Finally, the planner must select the specific media vehicles. Having chosen family television programs and women's magazines, the toothpaste marketer must select the exact television programs and stations as well as the specific women's magazines to

Table 12.3 Estimated annual advertising media expenditures for selected years (in millions of dollars)[a]

Medium	1940 $	1940 %	1960 $	1960 %	1980 $	1980 %
Newspapers	815	38.6	3,681	30.8	15,615	28.5
Magazines	186	8.8	909	7.6	3,225	5.9
Farm publications	19	0.9	66	0.6	135	0.2
Television			1,627	13.6	11,330	20.7
Radio	215	10.2	693	5.8	3,690	6.7
Direct mail	334	15.8	1,830	15.3	7,655	14.0
Business papers	76	3.6	609	5.0	1,695	3.2
Outdoor	45	2.2	203	1.7	610	1.1
Miscellaneous	420	19.9	2,342	19.6	10,795	19.7
National total	1,190	56.3	7,305	61.0	30,435	55.6
Local total	920	43.7	4,655	39.0	24,315	44.4
Grand total	2,110		11,960		54,750	

[a]Figures not adjusted for inflation.
Source: Adapted from "Estimated Annual U.S. Ad Expenditures: 1935–1977," *Advertising Age,* Sept. 4, 1978, pp. 32–33, and from Robert J. Coen, "Ad Growth in 1981: Sluggish, Then Bullish," *Advertising Age,* Jan. 5, 1981, pp. 10, 56. Reprinted with permission from the September 1978 and January 1981 issues of *Advertising Age.* Copyright 1978, 1981 by Crain Communications, Inc.

Advertisers are now having difficulty reaching large child audiences. The intrigue of the Saturday morning network programs seems to have vanished. Children are resorting to other forms of entertainment. One is non-network stations. These stations have become more prosperous and are capable of offering fascinating new programs. For advertisers this poses a problem. Advertising on non-network stations is quite expensive and can be difficult.

Cable television channels are another alternative type of amusement that have captured the child audience. Nickelodeon is a children's cable channel and claims that children in subscribing homes spend about 25 percent of their TV viewing time watching its programs. The drawback for advertisers is that Nickelodeon allows no advertisements.

Home video games are also capturing their share of the child audience. Currently, children are intrigued with video games and this interest is expected to increase. It is estimated that video games can be found in 20 percent of American homes and that this figure will reach 40 percent in 1985.

In addition, regulatory changes have added to the advertisers' dilemma. When the Federal Trade Commission dropped its investigation of whether children's advertising is excessive, advertisers increased their budgets. Simultaneously, however, the Federal Communications Commission ended its effort, started under President Carter, to try to get networks to broadcast more children's programs. Accordingly, networks have reduced the number of children's programs being broadcast. This reduction has left advertisers with a short supply of their desired medium and has raised advertising costs.

Source: Based on Geoffrey Colvin, "Children Are Getting Hard to Find," *Fortune*, May 2, 1983, p. 125.

be used. Media planners begin by making rather broad decisions; eventually, however, they must make very specific choices.

Media planners take many factors into account as they devise a media plan. They must analyze the location and demographic characteristics of people in the advertising target, as the various media appeal to particular demographic groups in particular locations. For example, there are radio stations especially for teen-agers, magazines for men in the 18–34 age group, and television programs aimed at adults. Media planners also should consider the sizes and types of audiences reached by specific media. Several data services collect and periodically publish information about the circulations and audiences of various media.

The cost of media is an important but troublesome consideration. Planners should try to obtain the best coverage possible for each dollar spent. Yet there is no way to compare accurately the cost and impact of a television commercial with the cost and impact of a newspaper advertisement.

The content of the message sometimes affects the types of media that are used. Print media can be used more effectively than broadcast media to present many issues or numerous details. If an advertiser wants to promote beautiful colors, patterns, or textures, then media that offer high-quality color reproduction—magazines or television—should be used instead of newspapers. For example, food can look extremely appetizing and delicious in a full-color magazine advertisement, but it might look far less so in black and white. Compare the black and white and color versions of the advertisement in Figure 12.4

When it comes to fancy desserts,
Sara Lee takes the cake.

When it comes to fancy desserts,
Sara Lee takes the cake.

Figure 12.4 Comparison of black-and-white and color advertisements
Source: Sara Lee Cheese Cake and Cake Cart Advertisements.

The information in Table 12.3 indicates that media are used quite differently from one another, and that the pattern of media usage has changed over the years. For example, the proportion of total media dollars spent on magazines has declined slowly but steadily since 1940. This variation in usage arises from the characteristics, advantages, and disadvantages (like the ones shown in Table 12.4) of the major mass media used for advertising. Having to choose from the variety of vehicles within each medium, media planners must deal with a vast number of alternatives; and the multitude of factors that affect media rates obviously add to the complexity of media planning. A ***cost comparison indicator*** allows an advertiser to compare the costs of several vehicles within a specific medium (such as two radio stations or three magazines) in terms of the number of persons reached by each vehicle. For example, the "milline rate" is the cost comparison indicator for newspapers; it shows the cost of exposing a million persons to a space equal to one agate line.[3] A Houston advertiser that can

3. An agate line is one column wide and the height of the smallest type normally used in classified newspaper advertisements. There are fourteen agate lines in 1 column inch.

Application

Use of Sex in Advertising

Sex in advertising can be a very powerful tool, but consumers' reactions can be highly uncertain. For instance, Sanger-Harris department store ran a four-color insert in a major Sunday newspaper that showed women's underwear. The layouts were considered very sexy, and the public reacted negatively. Despite the reactions, sales increased tremendously. Advertisers have been using the sexy sell more often with products (such as coffee and credit cards) that rarely have been associated with sex in advertisements. As a result, the research community has been undertaking studies on the effectiveness of using sex.

Sexy advertisements can get consumers' attention but may not be able to get them to buy products, or even to remember brand names. Comparative studies have supported this conclusion with results showing that sex used simply as an attention-getting device generated the lowest brand recall.

Research efforts have also looked at the differences between male and female responses to sex in advertising. Results have shown that men and women have different responses. Men perceive nudity as being sexy, and women consider romance and fantasy as sexy. Women can also tolerate a high level of sexual arousal and still recall brand names, whereas men cannot remember anything when aroused. This finding explains why there are more advertisements depicting sex and nudity in women's magazines (like *Vogue* and *Cosmopolitan*) than there are in men's magazines like *Playboy*. Even when told to remember a brand name, men could not if it was associated with sexual arousal.

Women's reactions toward sexy advertisements can be further broken down by age and income level. Women from blue collar households react more negatively to fantasy advertisements that do not mesh with their day-to-day realities. Older women are more receptive to sexy commercials than younger women are, because they feel less threatened by sex. A major consideration when using sexy advertisements is to make sure that the sexual themes they convey are consistent with the taste and preferences of persons in the target audience.

Source: Based on B. G. Yovovich, "Sex in Advertising: The Power and the Perils," *Advertising Age*, May 22, 1983, pp. M-4 and M-5.

afford to use only one local newspaper probably will compare the milline rates of the *Houston Post* and the *Houston Chronicle* to determine whether there are cost differences relative to their circulations.

The development of the media plan is crucial to the creation of an advertising campaign. The effectiveness of the plan determines the number of people in the advertising target who are exposed to the message. It also determines, to some degree, the effects of the message on those individuals. Media planning is a complex task that requires thorough analysis of the advertising target.

Creating the advertising message

The basic content and form of an advertising message is a function of several factors. The product's features, uses, and benefits affect the content of the message. Characteristics of the people in the advertising target—their sex, age, education, race, income, occupation, and other attributes—influence the content and form of the message. (The Application above deals with the use of sex in the content and form of messages.) When the American Cancer Society, for example, creates a message that informs fifth- and sixth-graders about smoking hazards, that message differs radically from messages aimed at adults. To communicate effectively, an

Medium	Types	Unit of Sale	Factors Affecting Rates
Newspaper	Morning Evening Sunday Sunday supplement Weekly Special	Agate lines Column inches Counted words Printed lines	Volume and frequency discounts Number of colors Position charges for preferred and guaranteed positions Circulation level
Magazine	Consumer Farm Business	Pages Partial pages Column inches	Circulation level Cost of publishing Type of audience Volume discounts Frequency discounts Size of advertisement Position of advertisement (covers) Number of colors Regional issues
Direct mail	Letters Catalogs Price lists Calendars Brochures Coupons Circulars Newsletters Postcards Booklets Broadsides Samplers	Not applicable	Cost of mailing lists Postage Production costs
Radio	AM FM	Programs: sole sponsor, cosponsor, participative sponsor Spots: 5, 10, 20, 30, 60 seconds	Time of day Audience size Length of spot or program Volume and frequency discounts

Cost Comparison Indicator	Advantages	Disadvantages
Milline rate = cost per agate line × 1,000,000 divided by circulation	Almost everyone reads a daily newspaper; total circulation is increasing; purchased to be read; read by entire family; nationwide geographic flexibility; short lead time; frequent publication; favorable for cooperative advertising; merchandising services	Not selective regarding socioeconomic groups; short life; limited reproduction capabilities; large volume prevents extensive exposure for any one advertisement
Cost per thousand (CPM) = cost per page × 1,000 divided by circulation	Socioeconomic selectivity; good reproduction; long life; prestige; geographic selectivity when regional issues are available; read in leisurely manner	High absolute dollar cost; long lead time
Cost per contact	Little wasted circulation; highly selective; circulation controlled by advertiser; few distractions; personal; stimulates actions; use of novelty; relatively easy to measure performance; hidden from competitors	Expensive; no editorial matter to attract readers; considered junk mail by many; criticized as invasion of privacy
Cost per thousand (CPM) = cost per minute × 1,000 divided by audience size	Highly mobile; low-cost broadcast medium; message can be quickly changed; can reach a large audience; geographic selectivity; socioeconomic selectivity	Provides only audio message; has lost prestige; short life of message; listeners' attention limited because of other activities while listening

(continued next page)

Table 12.4 *(continued)*

Medium	Types	Unit of Sale	Factors Affecting Rates
Television	Network Local CATV	Programs: sole sponsor, cosponsor, participative sponsor Spots: 5, 10, 15, 30, 60 seconds	Time of day Length of program Length of spot Volume and frequency discounts Audience size
Inside transit	Buses Subways	Full, half, and quarter showings are sold on a monthly basis	Number of riders Multiple-month discounts Production costs Position
Outside transit	Buses Taxicabs	Full, half, and quarter showings; space also rented on per-unit basis	Number of advertisements Position Size
Outdoor	Papered posters Painted displays Spectaculars	Papered posters: sold on monthly basis in multiples called "showings" Painted displays and spectaculars: sold on per-unit basis	Length of time purchased Land rental Cost of production Intensity of traffic Frequency and continuity discounts Location

Sources: Some of the information in this table is from S. Watson Dunn and Arnold M. Barban, *Advertising: Its Role in Modern Marketing*, 5th ed. (Hinsdale, Ill.: Dryden Press, 1982), and Robert Barton, *Media in Advertising* (New York: McGraw-Hill, 1964); and Dorothy Cohen, *Advertising* (New York: Wiley, 1972).

advertiser must use words, symbols, and illustrations that are meaningful, familiar, and attractive to those persons who make up the advertising target.

The objectives and platform of an advertising campaign affect the content and form of its messages. If a firm's advertising objectives involve large sales increases, for example, the message demands hard-hitting, high-impact language and symbols. When campaign objectives aim at increasing brand awareness, the message may use much repetition of the brand name and words and illustrations associated with it. The advertising platform consists of the basic issues or selling features to be stressed in the campaign; it is the foundation on which campaign messages are built. A bank, for example, might build an advertising campaign on a platform of such features as convenient locations, "no-charge" checking accounts, twenty-four-hour service, and friendly personnel.

Cost Comparison Indicator	Advantages	Disadvantages
Cost per thousand (CPM) = cost per minute × 1,000 divided by audience size	Reaches extremely large audience; low cost per exposure; utilizes sight and sound; highly visible; high prestige; geographic and socioeconomic selectivity	High-dollar costs; highly perishable message; audience may enjoy commercial but ignore message; size of audience not guaranteed; amount of prime time limited
Cost per thousand riders	Low cost; "captive" audience; geographic selectivity	Does not reach many business and professional persons; does not secure quick or direct results; limited growth
Cost per thousand exposures	Low cost; geographic selectivity; reaches broad, diverse audience	Lacks socioeconomic selectivity; does not have high impact on readers
No standard indicator	Allows for repetition; low cost; message can be placed close to the point of sale; geographic selectivity; operable 24 hours a day	Message must be short and simple; no socioeconomic selectivity; seldom attracts readers' full attention; criticized for being traffic hazard and blight on countryside

The choice of media obviously influences the content and form of the message. Effective outdoor displays and short broadcast spot announcements require concise, simple messages. Magazine and newspaper advertisements can include much detail and long explanations. Because several different kinds of media offer geographic selectivity, a precise message content can be tailored to a particular geographic section of the advertising target. Some magazine publishers produce *regional issues*. For a particular issue, the advertisements and editorial content of copies appearing in one geographic area differ from those appearing in other areas. As shown in Figure 12.5, Playboy publishes six regional issues. A clothing manufacturer that advertises in Playboy might decide to use one message in the Western region and another in the rest of the nation. In addition, a company may choose to advertise in only a few regions. Such geographic selectivity allows a firm to use the same message in different regions at different times.

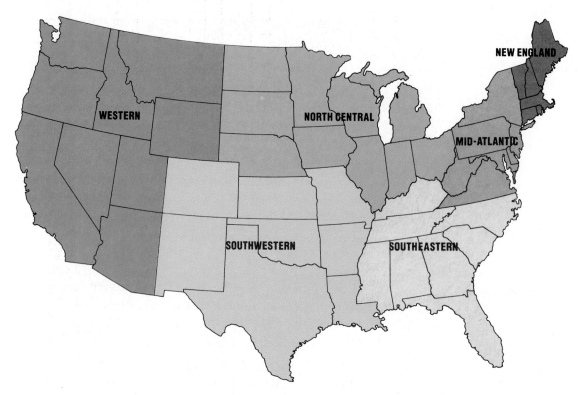

Figure 12.5   Geographic divisions for *Playboy*'s regional issues
Source: Reproduced by special permission of Playboy *magazine; copyright 1983 by* Playboy.

The basic components of a print advertising message are identified in Figure 12.6. The messages for most advertisements depend on the use of copy and artwork. Let us examine these two elements in more detail.

Copy
Copy is the verbal portion of an advertisement. It includes headlines, subheadlines, body copy, and the signature (see Figure 12.6). When preparing advertising copy, marketers should attempt to move readers through a persuasive sequence called AIDA—attention, interest, desire, and action. Not all copy need be this extensive, however.

The headline is a critical component. It is often the only part of the copy that people read. It should attract readers' attention and create enough interest to make them want to read the body copy. The subheadline, if there is one, links the headline to the body copy. It sometimes aids in explaining the headline.

Body copy for most advertisements consists of an introductory statement or paragraph, several explanatory paragraphs, and a closing paragraph. Some copywriters adopt a pattern or set of guidelines to develop body copy systematically: (1) identify a specific desire or problem of consumers, (2) suggest the good or service as the best way to satisfy that desire or solve that problem, (3) state the advantages and benefits of the

Figure 12.6
Basic components of a
print advertisement
*Source: Courtesy Sony
Corporation.*

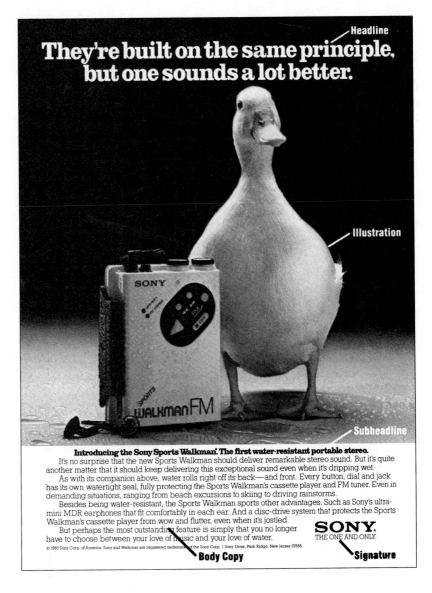

They're built on the same principle, but one sounds a lot better. — Headline

— Illustration

SONY

WALKMAN FM

— Subheadline

Introducing the Sony Sports Walkman. The first water-resistant portable stereo.
It's no surprise that the new Sports Walkman should deliver remarkable stereo sound. But it's quite another matter that it should keep delivering this exceptional sound even when it's dripping wet.
As with its companion above, water rolls right off its back—and front. Every button, dial and jack has its own watertight seal, fully protecting the Sports Walkman's cassette player and FM tuner. Even in demanding situations, ranging from beach excursions to skiing to driving rainstorms.
Besides being water-resistant, the Sports Walkman sports other advantages. Such as Sony's ultra-mini MDR earphones that fit comfortably in each ear. And a disc-drive system that protects the Sports Walkman's cassette player from wow and flutter, even when it's jostled.
But perhaps the most outstanding feature is simply that you no longer have to choose between your love of music and your love of water.
© 1983 Sony Corp. of America. Sony and Walkman are registered trademarks of the Sony Corp. 1 Sony Drive, Park Ridge, New Jersey 07656.

SONY.
THE ONE AND ONLY.

— Body Copy
— Signature

product, (4) indicate why the advertised product is the best for the buyer's particular situation, (5) substantiate the claims and advantages, and (6) ask the buyer for action.[4]

The signature identifies the sponsor of the advertisement. It may contain several elements including the firm's trademark, name, and address. The signature should be designed to be attractive, legible, distinctive, and easy to identify in a variety of sizes.

Since radio listeners often are not fully "tuned in" mentally, radio copy should be informal and conversational to attract listeners' attention, resulting in greater impact. The radio message is highly perishable. Thus,

4. James E. Littlefield and C. A. Kirkpatrick, *Advertising: Mass Communication in Marketing* (Boston: Houghton Mifflin, 1970), p. 178.

Figure 12.7
Parallel format for a tele-
vision script
*Source: Courtesy of
Doyle Dane Bernbach
Inc. Art Director: Roy
Grace; Copywriter: John
Noble; Producer: Susan
Calhoun; Client: Mobil
Oil.*

DOYLE DANE BERNBACH INC. ADVERTISING

437 MADISON AVENUE, NEW YORK, N.Y. 10022 (212) 826-2000

RADIO • TELEVISION

AS RECORDED 6/3/80

program		air date	
client	Mobil Oil Corporation	length	
product	Mobil One	job no.	MBMI-05136
		code #	MBMI-0023
		title	New York to New York

SUPER: Compared to conventional 10W-40 Motor Oils

OPENING SHOT IS CLOSE UP OF TOP OF MOBIL   V.O: This is the oil that saves you gas.
ONE CAN. AN OPENER IS IN THE CAN.
CAMERA TILTS DOWN AND PULLS OUT TO SEE   But it does more.
PRODUCT SHOT OF MOBIL ONE CAN. AS CAN
OPENER IS TAKEN OUT A HAND REACHES FOR
THE CAN.
(ODOMETER BEGINS AND MEASURES MILES THROUGHOUT)
CUT TO A MAN STANDING ON A BUSY NEW YORK   It can take you...
STREET CORNER. HE TAKES THE MOBIL CAN
FROM H.S RIGHT HAND SWITCHES IT TO HIS   NEW YORKER: From New York...
LEFT HAND AND THEN OUT OF THE PICTURE.

CUT TO ENGLISHMAN STANDING IN POURING   ENGLISHMAN: to London...
RAIN UNDER UMBRELLA ON BUSY STREET IN
LONDON...TAKES MOBIL CAN FROM HIS RIGHT
HAND SWITCHES TO HIS LEFT AND OUT OF
PICTURE

CUT TO FRENCH CHEF STANDING IN KITCHEN   FRENCHMAN: to Paris...
TAKING CAN IN HIS RIGHT HAND SWITCHING
TO HIS LEFT AND OUT OF PICTURE. WIPED
CAN OFF WITH TOWEL.

CUT TO SWEDISH GIRL STANDING IN SNOW   SWEDISH GIRL: to Sweden...
STORM TAKING CAN IN HER RIGHT HAND
SWITCHING TO HER LEFT AND OUT OF PICTURE.

CUT TO JAPANESE MAN SURROUNDED BY STEAM JAPANESE MAN: to Tokyo...
TAKING MOBIL CAN IN HIS LEFT HAND
SWITCHING IT TO HIS RIGHT HAND AND OUT
OF PICTURE.

CUT TO HOLLYWOOD MOVIE STAR SITTING IN   MOVIE STAR: to Hollywood....
A CHAIR ON A MOVIE SET. TAKES MOBIL CAN
FROM HER RIGHT HAND TO HER LEFT HAND AND
OUT OF PICTURE.

CUT BACK TO NEW YORK MAN STILL STANDING ON NEW YORKER: ...and back to New York.
SAME STREET CORNER, TAKES CAN FROM HIS
RIGHT HAND AND HOLDS IN HIS LEFT. LITTLE   V.O.: 25,000miles without an oil change.
OLD LADY CROSSING THE STREET PLACES A COIN   Mobil 1.
IN THE CAN.   The oil that saves you gas.
SUPER: 25,000 Miles or one year without   And more.
          an oil change.
          Whichever comes first.
          Add oil as needed. Follow warranty
          for new cars. Follow owner's
          manual for diesels or turbos.

          THE OIL THAT SAVES YOU GAS
               AND MORE

radio copy should consist of short, familiar terms. Its length should not exceed approximately two and one-half words per second.

In television copy, the audio material must not overpower the visual
material and vice versa. However, a television message should make optimal use of its visual portion. As illustrated in Figure 12.7, copy for a television commercial is initially written in parallel script form. The video is
described in the left column, and the audio is set forth in the right column.
When the parallel script is approved, the copywriter and artist combine the
copy with the visual material through use of a *storyboard* (see Figure 12.8),
which depicts a series of miniature television screens to show the sequence
of major scenes in the commercial. Beneath each screen is a description of
the audio portion that is to be used with the video message shown. Technical personnel use the storyboard as a blueprint when they produce the
commercial.

Figure 12.8 Storyboard for a television commercial
Source: Courtesy of Doyle Dane Bernbach Inc. Art Director: Roy Grace; Copywriter: John Noble; Producer: Susan Calhoun; Client: Mobil Oil.

Artwork

Artwork consists of the illustration in an advertisement and the layout of the components of the advertisement (see Figure 12.6). Although *illustrations* often appear in the form of photographs, they also can be presented in forms such as drawings, graphs, charts, and tables. Illustrations are used to attract attention, to encourage the audience to read or listen to the copy, to communicate an idea quickly, or to communicate an idea that is difficult to put into words.[5] Advertisers use a variety of illustration techniques, which are identified and described in Table 12.5.

The *layout* of an advertisement is the physical arrangement of the illustration, headline, subheadline, body copy, and signature. The arrangement

5. S. Watson Dunn and Arnold M. Barban, *Advertising: Its Role in Modern Marketing*, 5th ed. (Hinsdale, Ill.: Dryden Press, 1982), p. 413.

Table 12.5 Illustration techniques for advertisements

Illustration Technique	Description
Product alone	Simplest method; advantageous when appearance is important, when identification is important, when trying to keep a brand name or package in the public eye, or when selling through mail order
Emphasis on special features	Emphasizes special detail or feature; shows special features and advantages; used when product is unique because of special features
Product in setting	Shows what can be done with product; people, surroundings, or environment hint at what product can do; often used in food advertisements
Product in use	Puts action into the advertisement; can remind readers of benefits gained from using product; must be careful not to make visual cliché; should not include anything in illustration that will take away from product; used to direct readers' eyes toward product
Product being tested	Uses test to dramatize product's uses and benefits vis à vis competing products
Result of product's use	Emphasizes satisfaction from using product; can liven up dull product; useful when nothing new can be said

Sources: Dorothy Cohen, *Advertising* (New York: Wiley, 1972), pp. 458–464; and S. Watson Dunn and Arnold M. Barban, *Advertising: Its Role in Modern Marketing,* 5th ed. (Hinsdale, Ill.: Dryden Press, 1982), p. 415.

of these parts in Figure 12.6 is only one possible layout. These same elements could be positioned in many ways. The final layout is the end result of several stages of layout preparation. As the layout moves through the preparation stages, it serves people involved in developing the advertising campaign by helping them to exchange ideas. It also provides instructions to production personnel.

Evaluating the effectiveness of the advertising

There are a variety of reasons for measuring the effectiveness of advertising including the evaluation of advertising objectives achievement; the assessment of effectiveness of copy, illustrations, or layouts; or the evaluation of certain media.

Advertising can be evaluated before, during, and/or after the campaign. Evaluations performed before the campaign begins are called *pretests* and usually attempt to evaluate the effectiveness of one or more elements of the message. To pretest advertisements, marketers sometimes use a *consumer jury,* which consists of a number of persons who are actual or potential buyers of the advertised product. Jurors are asked to judge one

Table 12.5   *(continued)*

Illustration Technique	Description
Dramatizing headline	Appeal in illustration dramatizes headline; can emphasize appeal, but dangerous to use illustrations that do not correlate with headlines
Dramatizing situation	Presents problem situation or shows situation in which problem has been resolved
Comparison	Compares product with "something" established; the "something" must be favorable and familiar to audience
Contrast	Shows difference between two products or two ideas or differences in effects between use and nonuse; before-and-after format is a commonly used contrast technique
Diagrams, charts, and graphs	Used to communicate complex information quickly; may make presentations more interesting
Phantom effects	X-ray or internal view; can see inside product; helpful to explain concealed or internal mechanism
Symbolic	Symbols used to represent abstract ideas that are difficult to illustrate; effective if readers understand symbol; must be positive correlation between symbol and idea
Testimonials	Actually shows the testifier; should use famous person or someone to whom audience can relate

or several dimensions of two or more advertisements. Such tests are based on the belief that consumers are more likely to know what will influence them than advertising experts are.

To measure advertising effectiveness during a campaign, marketers usually take advantage of "inquiries." In the initial stages of a campaign, an advertiser may use several advertisements simultaneously, each containing a coupon or a form requesting information. The advertiser records the number of coupons that are returned from each type of advertisement. If an advertiser receives 78,528 coupons from advertisement A, 37,072 coupons from advertisement B, and 47,932 coupons from advertisement C, advertisement A is judged superior to advertisements B and C.

Evaluation of advertising effectiveness after the campaign is called a *posttest*. Advertising objectives often indicate what kind of posttest will be appropriate. If an advertiser sets objectives in terms of communication—product awareness, brand awareness, or attitude change—then the posttest should measure changes in one or more of these dimensions. Advertisers sometimes use consumer surveys or experiments to evaluate a campaign based on communication objectives. These methods are costly, however.

For campaign objectives stated in terms of sales, advertisers should determine the change in sales or market share that can be attributed to the campaign. Unfortunately, changes in sales or market share that result from advertising cannot be measured precisely; many factors independent of advertisements affect a firm's sales and market share. Competitive actions, government actions, changes in economic conditions, consumer preferences, and weather are only a few factors that might enhance or diminish a company's sales or market share. However, by using data about past and current sales and advertising expenditures, an advertiser can make gross estimates of the effects of a campaign on sales or market share.

Because consumer surveys and experiments are so expensive, and because it is so difficult to determine the direct effects of advertising on sales, many advertisers evaluate print advertisements in terms of the degree to which consumers can remember them. The posttest methods based on memory include recognition and recall tests. Such tests usually are performed by research organizations through consumer surveys. If a *recognition test* is used, individual respondents are shown the actual advertisement and are asked whether they recognize it. If they do, the interviewer asks additional questions to determine how much of the advertisement was read by each respondent. When recall is evaluated, the respondents are not shown the actual advertisement but are asked instead about what they have seen or heard recently. Recall can be measured either through unaided recall or through aided recall methods. In an *unaided recall test,* subjects are asked to identify advertisements that they have seen recently but are not shown any clues to stimulate their memory. A similar procedure is used with an *aided recall test,* except that respondents are shown a list of products, brands, company names, or trademarks to jog their memories. Several research organizations, including Daniel Starch and Gallup & Robinson, provide syndicated research services regarding recognition and recall of advertisements.

The major justification for using recognition and recall methods is that individuals are more likely to buy a product if they can remember an advertisement about it than if they cannot. That individuals remember an advertisement, however, does not mean they will actually buy the product or brand advertised.

Who develops the advertising campaign?

An advertising campaign can be developed by a few individuals, or it can require the efforts of many people. Here, we will consider in more detail exactly who develops a firm's advertising campaign.

An advertising campaign may be handled by (1) an individual or a few persons within the firm, (2) an advertising department within the organization, or (3) an advertising agency.

In very small firms one or two individuals are responsible for performing advertising activities (and many other activities as well). Usually these individuals depend heavily on personnel at local newspapers and broadcast stations for copywriting, artwork, and advice about scheduling media.

In certain types of large businesses—especially in larger retail organizations—advertising departments create and implement advertising campaigns. Depending on the size of the advertising program, an advertising department may consist of a few multiskilled persons or of a sizable number of specialists such as copywriters, artists, media buyers, and technical production coordinators. An advertising department sometimes obtains the services of independent research organizations and also hires free-lance specialists when they are needed for a particular project.

When an organization uses an advertising agency, the firm and the agency usually develop the advertising campaign jointly. How much each participates in the campaign's total development depends on the working relationship between the firm and the agency. The firm ordinarily relies on the agency for copywriting, artwork, technical production, and formulation of the media plan.

An advertising agency can assist a business in several ways. An agency, especially a larger one, supplies the firm with the services of highly skilled specialists such as copywriters, artists, media experts, researchers, legal advisors, and production coordinators. Many persons within an advertising agency have had broad experience in advertising. Also, agency personnel are usually more objective about an organization's products than are the firm's own personnel.

A firm can obtain some agency services at a low or moderate cost because the agency traditionally receives most of its compensation from a 15-percent commission paid by the media. For example, if an agency contracts for $400,000 of television time for a firm, its commission is $60,000. The television station is responsible for paying the commission. Although the traditional compensation method for agencies is changing and now includes other factors, the media commission still offsets some costs of using an agency.

Now that we have explored advertising as a potential promotion mix ingredient, let us consider a related ingredient—publicity.

Publicity

As indicated in Chapter 11, *publicity* is communication in news story form, regarding an organization and/or its products, that is transmitted through a mass medium at no charge. Publicity can be presented through a variety of vehicles, several of which we will examine in this section.

Within an organization, publicity is sometimes viewed as part of public relations—a larger, more comprehensive communication function. *Public relations* is a broad set of communication activities employed to create and maintain favorable relations between the organization and its publics—customers, employees, stockholders, government officials, and society in general.

Publicity and advertising compared

Although publicity and advertising both depend on mass media, they differ in several respects. Whereas advertising messages tend to be informative or persuasive, publicity is mainly just informative. Advertisements sometimes are designed to have an immediate impact on sales; publicity messages are more subdued. Publicity releases do not identify sponsors as their sources. Advertisements do.

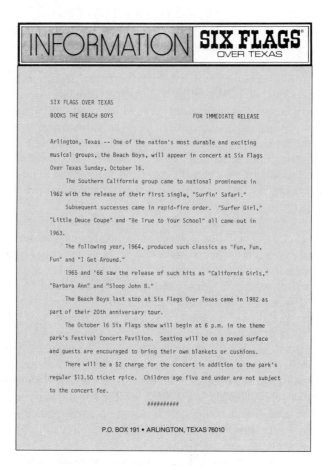

When advertising is used, the sponsor pays for the media time or space. For publicity, an organization does not pay for the use of time or space; communications through publicity usually are included as part of a program or editorial. Advertisements usually are separated from the broadcast programs or editorial portions of print media so that the audience or readers can easily recognize (or ignore) them.

Publicity may have greater credibility than advertising among consumers, since it takes the form of a news story and may appear more objective. Whereas media personnel often provide assistance in preparing advertising messages, they are not as helpful in creating publicity releases. Finally, a firm can use advertising to repeat the same messages or issues as many times as desired; publicity is generally not subject to repetition.

Kinds of publicity

There are several types of publicity mechanisms.[6] The most common is the *news release,* which is usually a single page of typewritten copy containing fewer than three hundred words. Additional information included on a news release is the firm's or agency's name, its address and phone number, and the contact person. Figure 12.9 is an example of a news release. A

6. Richard E. Stanley, *Promotion* (Englewood Cliffs, N.J.: Prentice-Hall, 1982), pp. 245–246.

feature article is a longer manuscript (up to three thousand words) that usually is prepared for a specific publication. A *captioned photograph* is a photograph with a brief description that explains the picture's content. Captioned photographs are especially effective for illustrating a new or improved product with highly visible features.

There are several other kinds of publicity. A *press conference* is a meeting used to announce major news events. Media personnel are invited to a news conference and usually are supplied with written materials and photographs. In addition, letters to the editor and editorials sometimes are prepared and sent to newspapers and magazine publishers. However, newspaper editors frequently allocate space on their editorial pages to local writers and to national columnists. Finally, films and tapes may be distributed to broadcast stations in the hope that they will be aired.

A marketer's choice of specific types of publicity depends on a variety of factors including the type of information being transmitted, the characteristics of the target audience, the receptivity of media personnel, the importance of the item to the public, and the amount of information needing to be presented.

Sometimes, a marketer uses a single type of publicity in a promotion mix. In other cases, a marketer may employ a variety of publicity mechanisms, with publicity being the primary ingredient in the promotion mix.

The uses of publicity

Organizations employ publicity for a variety of reasons. Often it is used to make people aware of a firm's products, brands, or activities. Businesses exploit publicity to maintain a certain level of positive, public visibility. Publicity can enhance a particular image, such as innovativeness or progressiveness. It is also used to overcome negative images.

Some firms use publicity for a single purpose, while others employ it for several purposes. Companies can include a multitude of specific issues in publicity releases; Table 12.6 lists some of them.

Requirements of a publicity program

For maximum benefit, a firm should create and maintain a systematic, continuous publicity program. A single individual or department—within the organization or from its advertising agency or public relations firm—should be responsible for managing the program.

It is important to establish and maintain good working relationships with media personnel. Personal contact with editors, reporters, and other news personnel is often necessary. Without their input, it is difficult to determine exactly how to design an organization's publicity program so as to facilitate the work of media news people.

Media personnel reject a great deal of publicity material because it is not newsworthy or because it is poorly written. If a firm hopes to have an effective publicity program, it must do its best to ensure that these flaws do not afflict its publicity releases. Guidelines and checklists are sometimes helpful in achieving these goals.

Finally, a firm has to evaluate its publicity efforts. Usually, the effectiveness of publicity is measured by the number of releases actually published or broadcasted. To monitor print media and determine which releases are published and how often, an organization can hire a clipping service, a firm that clips and sends published news releases to client

Table 12.6 Possible issues for publicity releases

Marketing developments	Reports on current developments
New products	Reports of experiments
New uses for old products	Reports on industry conditions
Research developments	Company progress reports
Changes of marketing personnel	Employment, production, and sales
Large orders received	statistics
Successful bids	Reports on new discoveries
Awards of contracts	Tax reports
Special events	Speeches by principals
Company policies	Analyses of economic conditions
New guarantees	Employment gains
Changes in credit terms	Financial statements
Changes in distribution policies	Organization appointments
Changes in service policies	Opening of new markets
Changes in prices	**Personalities—names are news**
News of general interest	Visits by famous persons
Annual election of officers	Accomplishments of individuals
Meetings of the board of directors	Winners of company contests
Anniversaries of the organization	Employees' and officers'
Anniversaries of an invention	advancements
Anniversaries of the senior officers	Interviews with company officials
Holidays that can be tied to the	Company employees serving as
organization's activities	judges for contests
Annual banquets, and picnics	Interviews with employees
Special weeks, such as Clean-up	**Slogans, symbols, endorsements**
Week	Company's slogan—its history and
Founders' Day	development
Conferences and special meetings	A tie-in of company activities with
Open house to the community	slogans
Athletic events	Creation of a slogan
Awards of merit to employees	The company's trademark
Laying of cornerstone	The company's name plate
Opening of an exhibition	Product endorsements

Source: Albert Wesley Frey, ed., *Marketing Handbook,* 2nd ed. (New York: Ronald Press), pp. 19–35. Copyright © 1965. Reprinted by permission of John Wiley & Sons, Inc.

companies. No independent monitoring service is available to measure the effectiveness of broadcast news releases. A firm can enclose a card with its publicity releases and request that the station record its name and the dates when the news item is broadcast, but station personnel do not always return these cards.

Dealing with unfavorable publicity

Up to this point, we have discussed publicity as a planned promotion-mix ingredient. However, firms may have to deal with unfavorable publicity regarding an unsafe product, an accident, the actions of a dishonest employee, or some other negative event.

The negative impact of unfavorable publicity can be quick and dramatic. A single negative event that produces unfavorable publicity can wipe out a firm's favorable image and destroy consumer attitudes that took years to build through promotional efforts. To protect an organization's goodwill and favorable images, it is important to avoid unfavorable publicity or, at least, to lessen its effects. First and foremost, the organization can reduce negative incidents and events through safety programs, inspections, and effective quality control procedures. Since firms obviously cannot eliminate all negative occurrences, it is important that they establish policies and procedures for the news coverage of such events. These policies should be designed to lessen negative impact.

In most cases, organizations should expedite news coverage of negative events rather than trying to discourage or block it; the facts are more likely to be reported accurately. If news coverage is discouraged, there is a chance that rumors and misinformation will be passed along. An unfavorable event can easily balloon into a scandal or a tragedy. It could even result in public panic.

Six Flags Over Texas, a theme amusement park, has established a set of policies and procedures to be used when a negative event occurs. The policies are aimed at helping news personnel get into the park quickly and providing them with as much information as possible. Not only does this approach tend to lessen the effects of negative events; it also enables the organization to maintain positive relationships with media personnel. Such relationships are essential if news personnel are to cooperate with a firm and broadcast favorable news stories about an organization.

Limitations in using publicity

That media do not charge for transmitting publicity is a double-edged sword. Although it provides a financial advantage, it brings with it several limitations. Media personnel must believe that messages are newsworthy if they are to be broadcast. That means that messages must be timely, interesting, and accurate. Many communications simply do not qualify. Considerable time and effort may be necessary to convince media personnel of the news value of publicity releases.

Although marketers usually encourage media personnel to air a publicity release at a certain time, they control neither the content nor the timing of the communication. Media personnel alter the length and content of publicity releases to fit publishers' or broadcasters' requirements. They may delete the parts of the message that are most important—at least from the firm's perspective. Media personnel generally use publicity releases in time slots and positions that are most convenient for them; so the messages are frequently presented at times or in locations that do not effectively reach the audiences an organization hopes to reach. Despite its drawbacks, properly managed publicity offers significant benefits to an organization.

Summary

Advertising is a paid form of nonpersonal communication that is transmitted to consumers through mass media such as television, radio, newspapers, magazines, direct mail, mass transit vehicles, and outdoor displays. Both nonbusiness and business organizations employ advertising.

Organizations use advertising in many ways. Institutional advertising is employed to promote organizations' images and ideas as well as political issues and candidates. Product advertising focuses on uses, features, images, and benefits of goods and services. To make people aware of a new or innovative product's existence, uses, and benefits, marketers use pioneer advertising in the introductory stage to stimulate primary demand for a general product category. Marketers switch to competitive advertising to increase selective demand by promoting the uses, features, and advantages of a particular brand.

Advertising sometimes is used to lessen the impact of a competitor's promotional program. It is sometimes designed to make the sales force more effective. To increase market penetration, an advertiser sometimes focuses a campaign on promoting an increased number of uses for the product. Some advertisements for an established product remind consumers that the product is still around and that it has certain characteristics and uses. Marketers may try to assure users of a particular brand that they are using the best brand. Marketers also use advertising to smooth out fluctuations in sales.

Although marketers may vary in how they develop advertising campaigns, they should follow a general pattern. First, they must identify and analyze the advertising target. Second, they should establish what they want the campaign to accomplish by defining the advertising objectives. The next step is to create the advertising platform, which contains the basic issues to be presented in the campaign. Next, the advertiser should establish the budget indicating how much money is to be spent on the campaign. Fifth, the marketer must develop the media plan by selecting and scheduling the media to be used in the campaign. In the sixth stage, the advertiser uses copy and artwork to create the message. Finally, the advertiser must devise one or more methods for evaluating the effectiveness of the advertisements.

Advertising campaigns can be developed by personnel within the firm or in conjunction with advertising agencies. When a campaign is created by the firm's personnel, it may be developed by only a few people, or it may be the product of an advertising department within the firm. The use of an advertising agency may be advantageous to a firm, because an agency can provide highly skilled, objective specialists with broad experience in the advertising field at low to moderate costs to the firm.

Publicity is communication in news story form, regarding an organization and/or its products, that is transmitted through a mass medium at no charge. Usually publicity is part of the larger, more comprehensive communication function of public relations. Publicity is mainly informative and usually is more subdued than advertising. There are many types of publicity, including news releases, feature articles, captioned photographs, press conferences, editorials, films, and tapes. Marketers can use one or more of these to achieve a variety of objectives. To have an effective publicity program, someone—either in the organization or in the firm's agency—must be responsible for creating and maintaining systematic and continuous publicity efforts.

An organization should avoid negative publicity by reducing the number of negative events that result in unfavorable publicity. To diminish the impact of unfavorable publicity, an organization should institute policies and procedures for properly handling news personnel when negative events do occur. Problems that surround the use of publicity include reluctance of media personnel to print and air releases and lack of control over the timing and content of messages.

<table>
<tr><td rowspan="1">Important terms</td><td>Advertising</td><td>Regional issues</td></tr>
<tr><td></td><td>Institutional advertising</td><td>Copy</td></tr>
<tr><td></td><td>Product advertising</td><td>Storyboard</td></tr>
<tr><td></td><td>Pioneer advertising</td><td>Artwork</td></tr>
<tr><td></td><td>Competitive advertising</td><td>Illustration</td></tr>
<tr><td></td><td>Comparative advertising</td><td>Layout</td></tr>
<tr><td></td><td>Defensive advertising</td><td>Pretest</td></tr>
<tr><td></td><td>Reminder advertising</td><td>Consumer jury</td></tr>
<tr><td></td><td>Reinforcement advertising</td><td>Posttest</td></tr>
<tr><td></td><td>Advertising target</td><td>Recognition test</td></tr>
<tr><td></td><td>Advertising platform</td><td>Unaided recall test</td></tr>
<tr><td></td><td>Advertising appropriation</td><td>Aided recall test</td></tr>
<tr><td></td><td>Objective and task approach</td><td>Publicity</td></tr>
<tr><td></td><td>Percent of sales approach</td><td>Public relations</td></tr>
<tr><td></td><td>Competition-matching approach</td><td>News release</td></tr>
<tr><td></td><td>Arbitrary approach</td><td>Feature article</td></tr>
<tr><td></td><td>Media plan</td><td>Captioned photograph</td></tr>
<tr><td></td><td>Cost comparison indicator</td><td>Press conference</td></tr>
</table>

Discussion and review questions

1. What is the difference between institutional advertising and product advertising?
2. When should advertising be used to stimulate primary demand? To stimulate selective demand?
3. How can advertising be used as a competitive tactic?
4. Describe the relationship between advertising and personal selling.
5. How does a marketer use advertising to promote year-round sales stability?
6. What are the major steps in creating an advertising campaign?
7. What is an advertising target? How does a marketer analyze the target audience after it has been identified?
8. Why is it necessary to define advertising objectives?
9. What is an advertising platform and how is it used?
10. What factors affect the size of an advertising budget? What techniques are used to determine this budget?
11. Describe the steps required in developing a media plan.
12. What is the role of copy in an advertising message?
13. How is artwork used in the development of a message?
14. What role does an advertising agency play in developing an advertising campaign?
15. Discuss some ways to posttest the effectiveness of advertising.

16. What is publicity? How does it differ from advertising?
17. Identify and describe the major types of publicity.
18. How is publicity used by organizations? Give several examples of publicity releases that you observed recently in local media.
19. How should an organization handle negative publicity? Identify a recent example of a firm that received negative publicity. Did the firm deal with it effectively?
20. Explain the problems and limitations associated with using publicity. How can some of these limitations be minimized?

Cases

Case 12.1

Zale's Jewelry Advertising

After a three-year analysis of its markets, Zale Corporation has completely changed its approach to the jewelry business. Zale still wants to be the premier jeweler for middle America, but an extensive research project hopefully has shown the company how to solidify this position.

A very important key to Zale's success is advertising. Zale has used information from the marketing research study to change its copy strategy, its newspaper advertising program, its television approach, and its catalog philosophy.

A study of customer attitudes showed that customers bear little loyalty to any jeweler, including Zale. Because of the long time between most people's jewelry purchases, customers have no reason to develop strong ties to a store. When they do decide to purchase, the relative competitive positions of jewelry stores are ill-defined, undifferentiated, and unfocused in consumers' minds. What loyalty customers do feel is based on reliability, selection, and sales personnel. Finally, the study showed that there is a high degree of anxiety associated with purchase decisions.

As a result of this research, Zale began developing advertising that was completely different from previous jewelry advertising. Each new idea was rigorously tested. Advertising copy approaches were checked to determine the relative importance of factors like trust, guarantees, value, and price in the reader's evaluation of the message. From these tests, Zale ended up with 12 to 15 copy approaches. These were again narrowed to five which were tested in six markets. The best of the five was then restructured and four extensions were created for the new campaign.

The new spots concentrated on specific merchandise and placed less emphasis on the company itself. Zale completely reallocated its advertising budget. Network television spending was increased by 80 percent, and spending on newspaper advertisements was also increased.

All advertisements featured a "diamond bond" which included a 90-day refund policy, a generous trade-in policy, and a complimentary service policy requiring twice-a-year service to validate a limited five-year warranty against loss or damage.

In addition, Zale created a year-long bridal program, based on the fact that the incidence of weddings is more constant throughout the year than seasonal. The program included 73 insertions in 16 national magazines. Another program set up funds to be used to purchase co-op advertising in 20 markets. Zale and several well-known watch manufacturers advertised on the same television programs to position Zale as a place to buy watches.

Research also led Zale to develop newspaper graphics with greater impact. Using other research findings, Zale developed different catalogs for the east, the central, and the western regions. To aid in assessing the effectiveness of catalogs, Zale did not use a catalog in the southwestern region.

Questions for discussion

1. How did Zale use research in each stage of the development of its advertising campaign?
2. Given the information in the research study, should Zale's new campaign have been effective in reaching middle America?

Case 12.2

Dr Pepper Changes Its Advertising Campaign[7]

For some time, Dr Pepper used its "Be a Pepper" theme in an attempt to position its product as the soft drink for everyone. Recently, the company dropped its "Be a Pepper" theme. Over the last decade, Dr Pepper had used song-and-dance advertising that was later imitated by many competitors. Now, this advertising technique is being left to the competitors.

Dr Pepper's new advertising campaign focuses on the unique product attributes that made Dr Pepper a successful soft drink—its distinctive and uniquely original taste. The new campaign will cost $35 million this year which is a 25% increase in the budget compared to last year. This increase will help to support Dr Pepper's return to network commercials after a year of primarily locally funded television advertisements. Network spots have been purchased for prime-time, day, special, and syndicated programs, as well as the MTV cable station.

The 12–34 age group has been targeted for the commercials, a group with fewer developed tastes and fewer loyalties as compared with older age groups. Dr Pepper's advertising target will be reached during shows such as "Gimme a Break," "Hart to Hart," "The A-Team," "Facts of Life," and "Three's Company." Network specials, such as the "Solid Gold Special"—a one-hour music program with high audience ratings, will provide optimum exposure for Dr Pepper's new campaign, aiding in the rapid and firm establishment of the advertising messages.

According to the Creative Director who guided message development, the ad campaign's appeal is based on its originality and sparkle. The ads suggest that Dr Pepper's distinctive taste and personality will only appeal to people who are ready to explore the unique aspects of life and who are

7. This case is based on information found in Bill Appelman, "1984 Advertising (Dr Pepper)," *Clock Dial,* September/October 1983, pp. 30–35; and Tom Bayer, "Dr Pepper Shucks Off P&G Philosophy," *Advertising Age,* Oct. 10, 1983, pp. 4, 79.

Figure 12.10
Dr Pepper advertise-
ment highlighting its
new campaign
*Source: © Dr Pepper
Company 1984.*

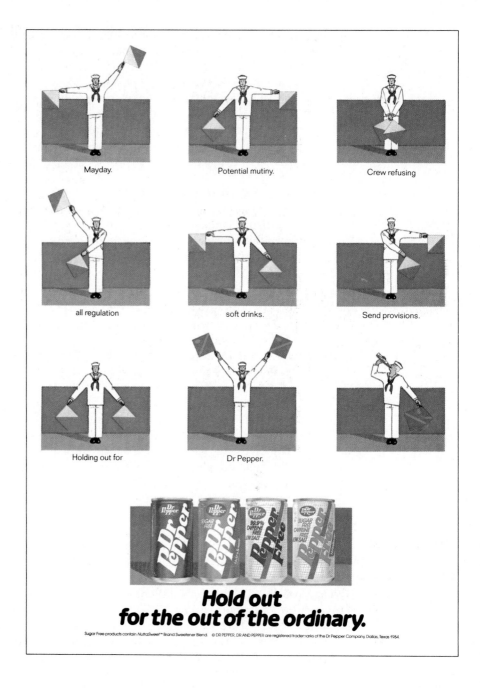

inspired by the unusual. The tag line, ''Hold out for the out of the ordinary,'' is simple and direct and is based on market research on the attributes of Dr Pepper and of the target audience (see Figure 12.10).

The ''Hold out for the out of the ordinary'' campaign is included in
seven television commercials. Three of the commercials support Dr Pepper, two are for Pepper Free, and two are for Sugar Free Dr Pepper. There
are 20-, 30-, and 60-second versions of each. The television commercials
are based on ''twists on history.'' For example, in ''Bell Ringer,'' the for-

lorn hunchbacked bell ringer is surrounded by a crowd that is attempting to decipher his cries. A lovely and sympathetic young woman offers water to the bell ringer, but he rejects this. When she discovers that he is saying "Dr Pepper" and offers him a refreshing bottle of Dr Pepper, the crowd joyously celebrates to the new theme, "Hold out for the out of the ordinary."

In addition to television commercials, Dr Pepper is using radio, print, and outdoor media. The radio commercials include "out-of-the-ordinary" personalities such as Irene Cara and Mickey Gilley. Irene Cara is well known for her title songs to the movies *Fame* and *Flashdance*. Mickey Gilley is famous for his club in Houston.

The commercials were successfully tested through comprehensive interviews with consumers. The tagline, "Hold out for the out of the ordinary" was found to be straightforward and distinct. The approach was considered appropriate for a product as unique as Dr Pepper. In addition, the commercials were highly rated for their originality in not following the current soft drink advertisements that contain burly young men and bikini-clad women frolicking on the beach. The consumer interviews revealed that the Dr Pepper ads were simply enjoyable and would have strong appeal among persons in the targeted group.

Questions for discussion
1. Based on the information in this case and your observations of the advertisements in this campaign, assess whether Dr Pepper's advertising objectives are stated in terms of sales or in terms of communication.
2. What are the primary issues in Dr Pepper's advertising platform?
3. In general, do you believe that this campaign is successful?

13

Personal Selling and Sales Promotion

Objectives

To understand the major purposes of personal selling.

To learn the basic steps in the personal selling process.

To identify the types of salespersons that can be employed in sales forces.

To gain insight into sales management decisions and activities such as setting objectives for the sales force and determining its size; recruiting, selecting, training, compensating, and motivating salespeople; creating sales territories; and routing, scheduling, and controlling sales personnel.

To become aware of what sales promotion activities are and how they can be used.

To become familiar with specific sales promotion methods used.

Standard Register is a major marketer of business forms such as computer-printed statements and communications, pressure sensitive labels, and multiple-copy sales forms (see Figure 13.1). With a 7-percent market share, Standard Register competes directly with Moore Business Forms which has 25 percent of the forms market. Even with the recent sluggish economy, Standard Register has been competing successfully against Moore and other competitors. One reason for its success is its well-managed sales force.

That sales force, consisting of 850 people, is divided among sixty districts and eight regions. Newly hired salespeople are trained in the field and through a two-year correspondence course. Also, within the first three years, a salesperson attends five formal training conferences in Dayton, Ohio. Experienced sales personnel go to such conferences once every two years. These conferences focus on product knowledge and communication skills.

PAPERALYSIS.

Can make an Emergency Room inoperable.

Emergency Room paperwork is often looked upon as a necessary evil. It can slow processing times. Delay treatment. Frustrate patients, relatives and personnel alike. Repetitive paperwork can cause haste and confusion, and under such circumstances, it is a doubtful management tool.

Emergency Room paperwork is vital, but it can also be fast and efficient. And when forms are designed to meet strict standards and specific goals, paperwork can actually help a hospital run more smoothly.

The Orlando Regional Medical Center experienced a welcome turnaround in their ER operations with a redesigned forms system from The Standard Register Company. The busy Florida center previously needed 16 documents to compile and summarize information.

With so many repetitive writings, the process was aggravating and results were slow. But now, a single 7-part ZIPSET® form speeds the entire operation and provides the hospital with more information than ever before. Even more value is realized when the forms reach the hospital Business Office. Each day the data is summarized and the administration receives timely reports enabling them to act immediately when any weak points or unwanted trends appear.

If you think Paperalysis might be making your Emergency Room operations sluggish, today there's an effective antidote. Call on our health care systems specialists at The Standard Register Company. We'll work with you and your staff to solve your paperwork problems. Contact: The Standard Register Co., Dayton, Ohio 45401.

THE STANDARD REGISTER CO.
Health Care Systems Group.
The Standard Register Company is an Equal Employment Opportunity Employer.

Figure 13.1 Advertisement by Standard Register
Source: Courtesy of The Standard Register Company.

For a major account, Standard Register uses a team approach—one senior salesperson and one junior salesperson are assigned. The team approach allows Standard Register to provide its customers with extremely good service.

The company uses salary plus commission to compensate its salespeople. The commission is 5 to 6 percent. Standard Register also employs sales contests and special incentive programs.[1]

Standard Register, like a number of other firms, is using personal selling as one component of a highly effective promotion mix. Much of personal selling today requires highly trained individuals who are called on daily to help customers solve complex problems. Personal selling is becoming more professional and sophisticated as it leans further toward consulting with and advising customers. In a number of business organizations, sales personnel are among the highest-paid individuals. As many salespeople become familiar with their firm's total marketing and company operations, they move up rapidly into managerial positions. Many of today's high-level executives began their careers in sales.

As indicated in Chapter 11, personal selling and sales promotion are two possible ingredients in a promotion mix. Personal selling is the most widely used. Sometimes, it is a company's sole promotional tool. Generally, it works in conjunction with other promotion mix ingredients. Occasionally, personal selling plays a minor role in an organization's total promotional activities.

This chapter focuses on personal selling and sales promotion. Our discussion considers the purposes of personal selling, its basic steps, the types of individuals who make up a sales force and how they are selected, and the major sales management decisions and activities. We first examine several characteristics of sales promotion efforts. Then we look at the reasons for using sales promotion and at the sales promotion methods available for use in a promotion mix.

The nature of personal selling

Business organizations spend more money on personal selling than on any other promotion mix ingredient. Millions of people earn their livings through personal selling.

As defined earlier, ***personal selling*** is a process of informing customers and persuading them to purchase products through personal communication in an exchange situation. Personal selling gives marketers the greatest freedom to adjust a message to satisfy customers' information needs. In comparison with other promotion methods, personal selling is most precise; through it marketers can focus on the most promising sales prospects. Other promotion mix ingredients are aimed at groups of people, some of whom may not be prospective customers. A major disadvantage of personal selling is its cost. In fact, it generally is the most expensive ingredient in the promotion mix. The average industrial sales call, for example,

1. Rayna Skolnik, "Standard Register Sells in Top Form," *Sales and Marketing Management*, Oct. 11, 1982, pp. 49–52.

Application

Computers Assist Salespersons

Computers have been widely used for a variety of business activities from accounting to production. A few companies are even using computers for personal selling to assist their sales forces. For example, during preholiday periods at Enfield Square Mall in Enfield, Connecticut, a computer provides customers with suggestions for gifts and indicates in which mall store they can be purchased. The customer indicates the characteristics of the person he or she plans to buy for and the desired price range. The computer prints out a list of twelve gift suggestions per gift recipient.

A manufacturer of vinyl flooring, Mannington Mills, Inc., has a computer system that assists retail consumers in selecting floor covering styles. The customer answers eight multiple-choice questions regarding room size, furniture style, pattern preference, and traffic volume. The computer then prints out a list of ten styles closely matching the consumer's tastes. The method increases store traffic, speeds up decision making, and helps close sales.

Computers also aid financial planning, real estate, and insurance sales personnel. Balanced Investment Planning, Inc. developed a program to help plan clients' investment strategies. The program cuts forty to fifty hours of work to produce a complete financial analysis to three hours. After a client has completed a questionnaire on his or her needs, the computer is able to construct a fifty-one-page survey of the person's financial situation. In general, consumer response to these types of programs has been quite favorable.

Source: Based on Lawrence Stevens, "When Computers Do the Selling," *Inc*, Nov. 1982, pp. 159–161.

costs about $178, and selling costs are increasing at a faster rate than are advertising costs.[2]

The specific goals of personal selling efforts vary from one firm to another. However, they usually involve finding prospects, convincing prospects to buy, and keeping customers satisfied. Identifying potential buyers who are interested in an organization's products is critical. Later in this chapter, we discuss this issue in more detail.

Although finding prospects is important, it is valueless unless the prospects can be convinced to buy. Since most prospects seek certain types of information before they make a purchase decision, salespersons must ascertain prospects' informational needs and then provide the relevant information. (The Application above focuses on related issues.) To achieve this purpose, sales personnel must be well trained regarding both their products and the selling process in general.

Few businesses survive solely on profits from one-sale customers. For long-run survival most marketers depend, to some degree, on repeat sales. A company has to keep its customers satisfied to obtain repeat purchases. Also, satisfied customers help to attract new ones by telling potential customers about the organization and its products. Figure 13.2 promotes a program whereby new customers can easily communicate with satisfied users.

Even though the whole organization is responsible for providing customer satisfaction, much of the burden falls on salespeople. They are almost always closer to customers than anyone else in the company. The

2. "An Industrial Sales Call Now Costs $178.00," Laboratory of Advertising Performance, McGraw-Hill Research Department, 1982.

Ask Our Users.

about Datsuns. About their astound...
reliability, their toughness, their lack
downtime and their low operating c
That's why we're prepared to give
a full list of national users, or us
from your specific area or indus
They won't mince words. **DATSU**
Write or call today. **FORKLIFTS**
NISSA

Write for users list and for a free do...
Nissan Industrial Equipment Cor
2900 Datsun Drive, P.O. Box 161404, Memphis, TN 3
901-396

Figure 13.2   Advertisement encouraging new customers to talk with satisfied users
Source: Walker and Associates Advertising.

sales force often provides buyers with information and service after the sale. Such activities allow a salesperson to generate additional sales while evaluating the strengths and weaknesses of the company's products and other marketing mix ingredients. These observations are helpful in developing and maintaining a marketing mix that better satisfies both customers and the firm.

A salesperson may be involved with achieving one or several of these general goals. In some organizations, there are individuals whose sole job is to find prospects. This information is relayed to salespeople, who contact the prospects. After the sale, these same salespeople may do the follow-up work, or a third group of employees may have the job of maintaining customer satisfaction. In many smaller organizations, a single person handles all of these functions. Regardless of how many groups are involved, several major sales tasks must be performed to achieve these general goals.

Elements of the personal selling process

The exact activities involved in the selling process vary among salespersons and differ for particular selling situations. No two salespersons use exactly the same selling methods. However, many salespersons—either consciously or unconsciously—move through a general selling process as they sell products. This general selling process consists of seven elements, or steps: prospecting and evaluating, preparing, approaching the customer, making the presentation, overcoming objections, closing, and following up.

Prospecting and evaluating

Developing a list of potential customers is called *prospecting,* and it is the first element in the selling process. A salesperson seeks the names of prospects from several sources, such as the company's sales records, other customers, trade shows, newspaper announcements (of marriages, births, deaths, and the like), public records, telephone directories, trade association directories, and many others. Sales personnel also use responses from advertisements that encourage interested persons to send in an information request form (see Figure 13.3).

After developing the prospect list, a salesperson evaluates each prospect to determine whether the prospect is able, willing, and authorized to buy the product. Based on this evaluation, some prospects may be deleted, while others are deemed acceptable and are ranked relative to their desirability or potential.

Preparing

After developing a list of acceptable prospects, but before contacting them, a salesperson should find and analyze information regarding each prospect's specific product needs, current use of brands, feelings about available brands, and personal characteristics. A salesperson uses this information when he or she selects an approach and puts together a sales presentation. A salesperson with more information about a prospect is better equipped to develop an approach and presentation that precisely communicates with the prospect.

Approaching the customer

The *approach*—the manner in which a salesperson contacts a potential customer—is a critical step in the sales process. The prospect's first impression of the salesperson may be a lasting one, with long-run consequences.

One type of approach is based on referrals; the salesperson approaches the prospect and explains that an acquaintance, an associate, or a relative has suggested the call. The salesperson who uses the cold canvass calls on potential customers without their prior consent. Repeat contact is another common approach; when making the contact, the salesperson mentions a prior meeting. The exact type of approach depends on the salesperson's preferences, the product being sold, the firm's resources, and the characteristics of the prospect.

Making the presentation

During the sales presentation, the salesperson must attract and hold the prospect's attention in order to stimulate interest and stir up a desire for the product. The salesperson should have the prospect touch, hold, or actually use the product. If possible, the salesperson should demonstrate the product and get the prospect more involved with it which, in turn, should stimulate greater interest.

During the presentation, the salesperson must not only talk but also listen. The sales presentation provides the salesperson with the greatest opportunity to determine the prospect's specific needs by listening to

TWO-WAY COMMUNICATIONS IS NOW A THREE-WAY RACE.

FIND OUT WHY JOHNSON IS BEST.
CALL TOLL FREE 800-328-5727 EXT. 122
(IN MINNESOTA 800-742-5685 EXT. 122)

For years, two-way communication was a two-way race. Two companies dominated the industry. Now, a third company is changing the state of the art. That company is Johnson. Not the leader. The challenger.

The leaders in any category are only as good as their competition requires them to be. And Johnson requires a lot in the category of two-way communication.

Johnson was the first in the industry to promise a full one-year warranty on business radio products.

But it didn't stop there. Johnson is pacing the entire industry with its new synthesized dispatch radio line, its Clearchannel LTR™ logic trunked radio, and its pioneering role in the development of the emerging Cellular Mobile Radio Service.

And now, it's about to happen again.

JOHNSON
Radio Products Division
THE CHALLENGER

Please send more information on Johnson. The Challenger.

Name
Title
Company
Address
City
State   Zip
Mail to: E.F. Johnson Company, Radio Products Div., Box 1249, Waseca, MN 56093

---

questions and comments and by observing responses. Even though the salesperson has preplanned the presentation, he or she must be able to adjust the message to meet the prospect's information needs.

Overcoming objections

One of the best ways to overcome a prospect's objections is to anticipate and counter them before the prospect has an opportunity to raise them. However, this approach can be risky. The salesperson may mention some objections that the prospect would not have raised. If possible, the salesperson should handle objections when they arise. They also can be dealt with at the end of the presentation.

An effective salesperson usually seeks out a prospect's objections in order to answer them. If they are not apparent, the salesperson cannot deal with them, and they may keep the prospect from buying.

Closing

Closing is the element in the selling process in which the salesperson asks the prospect to buy the product or products. During the presentation, the salesperson may employ a "trial close" by asking questions that assume the prospect will buy the product. For example, the salesperson might ask the potential customer about financial terms, desired colors or sizes, delivery arrangements, or the quantity to be purchased. The reactions to such questions usually indicate how close the prospect is to buying. A trial close lets propects indirectly respond that they will buy the product without having to state those sometimes difficult words, "I'll take it."

A salesperson should try to close at several points during the presentation, because the prospect may be ready to buy. Often an attempt to close the sale will result in objections. Thus, closing can serve as an important stimulus that uncovers hidden objections.

Following up

After a successful closing, the salesperson must follow up the sale. In the follow-up stage, the salesperson should determine whether the order was delivered on time and installed properly, if installation was required. The salesperson should contact the customer to learn what problems or questions have arisen regarding the product. The follow-up stage also can be used to determine customers' future product needs.

Types of salespersons

To intelligently develop a sales force, a marketing manager must decide which types of salespersons will sell the firm's products most effectively. Most business organizations use several different kinds of sales personnel. Based on the functions they perform, salespersons can be classified into three groups: order getters, order takers, and support personnel. One salesperson can, and often does, perform all three functions.

Order getters

To obtain orders, a salesperson must inform and persuade a prospect to buy the product. The job of *order getters* is to increase the firm's sales by selling to new customers and by increasing sales to present customers. This task sometimes is called creative selling. It requires salespeople to recognize potential buyers' needs and then to provide them with the necessary information. Order-getting activities sometimes are divided into two categories: current customer sales and new-business sales.

Current customer sales

Sales personnel who concentrate on current customers call on people and organizations that have purchased products from the firm at least once. These salespeople seek more sales from existing customers by following up previous sales. Current customers can also be sources of leads for new prospects.

New-business sales

Business organizations depend on sales to new customers, at least to some degree. New-business sales personnel locate prospects and convert them to buyers. Salespersons in many industries help to generate new business, but industries that depend in large part on new-customer sales are real estate, insurance, furniture, appliances, heavy industrial machinery, and automobiles.

Order takers

Taking orders is a repetitive task that salespersons perform to perpetuate long-lasting, satisfying relationships with customers. *Order takers* seek repeat sales. One of their major objectives is to be absolutely certain that customers have sufficient product quantities where and when they are needed. Order takers can be categorized into two groups, inside order takers and field order takers.

Inside order takers

In many businesses, inside order takers, who work in sales offices, receive orders by mail and telephone. Certain producers, wholesalers, and even retailers have sales personnel who sell from within the firm rather than travel into the field. That does not mean that inside order takers never communicate with customers face to face. Salespeople in retail stores are classified as inside order takers.

Mid-Continent Bottlers, a Des Moines soft-drink distributor, has traditionally sold beverages to retailers off its trucks. Sometimes, the brands needed by a retailer were not on the truck. The rising cost of fuel forced Mid-Continent to switch to inside order takers. Today, the bottler telephones 75 percent of its accounts to determine what the retailers need; then the beverages are loaded and delivered. The use of the inside order takers has helped Mid-Continent significantly reduce costs.[3]

Field order takers

Salespersons who travel to customers are referred to as "outside," or "field," order takers. Often a customer and a field order taker develop an interdependent relationship. The buyer depends on the salesperson to take orders periodically (and sometimes to deliver them), and the salesperson counts on the buyer to purchase a certain quantity of products periodically.

However, field or inside order takers should not be thought of as passive functionaries who simply record orders in a machinelike manner. Order takers generate the bulk of many organizations' total sales.

Support personnel

Support personnel facilitate the selling function but usually are not involved only with making sales. They are engaged primarily in marketing industrial products. They are active in locating prospects, educating customers, building goodwill, and providing service after the sale. Although there are many kinds of sales support personnel, the three most common types are missionary, trade, and technical salespersons.

Missionary salespersons

Missionary salespersons, who usually are employed by manufacturers, assist the producer's customers in selling to their own customers. A missionary

---

3. "Mid-Continent Keeps Costs Bottled Up," *Sales and Marketing Management Portfolio,* 1982, p. 7.

salesperson may call on retailers to inform and persuade them to buy the manufacturer's products. If the call is successful, the retailers purchase the products from wholesalers, who are the producer's customers. Manufacturers of medical supplies and pharmaceutical products often use missionary salespersons to promote their products to retail druggists, physicians, and hospitals.

Trade salespersons

Trade salespersons are not strictly support personnel, because they usually perform the order-taking function as well. However, they direct much of their efforts toward helping customers promote the products, especially within retail stores. They are likely to restock shelves, obtain more shelf space, set up displays, provide in-store demonstrations, and distribute samples to store customers. Food producers and processors commonly employ trade salespersons.

Technical salespersons

Technical salespersons direct their efforts toward the organization's current customers by providing technical assistance. They advise customers on applications of the products, on system designs, on product characteristics, and on installation procedures. Since this job is often highly technical, the salesperson needs to have formal training in one of the physical sciences or in engineering. Technical sales personnel often sell technical industrial products such as computers, heavy equipment, steel, and chemicals.

When hiring sales personnel, marketers seldom restrict themselves to a single category; most firms require different types. Several factors dictate how many of each type of salesperson a particular firm should have. A product's uses, characteristics, complexity, and price influence the kind of sales personnel used, as do the number of customers and their characteristics. The kinds of marketing channels and the intensity and type of advertising also have an impact on the selection of sales personnel.

Management of the sales force

In many cases, the effectiveness of sales-force management determines a firm's success, because the sales force is directly responsible for generating an organization's primary input—sales revenue. Without adequate sales revenue, a business cannot survive long.

Our discussion of sales management explores nine general areas, each of which requires numerous decisions and activities. The specific areas analyzed are (1) establishing sales-force objectives, (2) determining sales-force size, (3) recruiting and selecting salespeople, (4) training sales personnel, (5) compensating salespeople, (6) motivating salespeople, (7) creating sales territories, (8) routing and scheduling salespeople, and (9) controlling and evaluating the sales force.

Establishing sales-force objectives

To manage a sales force effectively, a sales manager must develop sales objectives. Sales objectives should be stated in precise, measurable terms and should specify the time period and the geographic areas involved.

Sales objectives usually state goals both for the total sales force and for each salesperson. Objectives for the entire force are normally stated in terms of sales volume, market share, or profit. Volume objectives refer to a quantity of dollar or sales units. For example, the objective for an electric-drill producer's sales force might be to sell $10 million worth of drills annually or to sell 600,000 drills annually. When sales goals are stated in terms of market share, they ordinarily call for an increase in the proportion of the firm's sales relative to the total number of products sold by all businesses in that particular industry. When sales objectives are based on profit, they are usually stated in terms of dollar amounts or return on investment.

Sales objectives for individual salespersons commonly are stated in terms of dollar or unit sales volume. Other bases used for individual sales objectives include average order size, average number of calls per time period, and number of orders relative to number of calls.

Sales objectives tell salespersons what they are expected to accomplish during a specified time period. They give the sales force direction and purpose. They also serve as performance standards for the evaluation and control of sales personnel.

Determining sales-force size

Deciding how many salespersons to use is important because it influences the company's ability to generate sales and profits. In addition, the size of the sales force affects the compensation methods used, salespersons' morale, and overall sales-force management. Sales-force size must be adjusted from time to time. The firm's marketing plans change, as do markets and forces in the marketing environment. There are several methods for determining the optimal size of the sales force. Two analytical techniques are the equalized workload method and the incremental productivity method.

Equalized workload method[4]
The *equalized workload method* allows a marketing manager to base the sales-force size on the condition that every salesperson is assigned a roughly equal set of accounts in terms of the total amount of sales time and effort needed. Marketers must answer several questions if they are considering this method. First, can the manager divide the customers into groups based on size of purchases? Second, is it possible to determine the number of sales calls required to service various account sizes adequately? Third, what is the annual average number of calls per salesperson?

To determine sales-force size through the equalized workload method, a marketing manager must (1) multiply the number of customers in each size group by the number of sales calls required annually to serve those groups effectively, (2) add the products, and (3) divide this sum by the average number of calls made annually by each salesperson.

As a hypothetical case, assume that a company divides its customers into two size groups. It has 300 Class A customers, who each require 20

4. This method, developed by Walter J. Talley, is described in "How to Design Sales Territories," *Journal of Marketing,* Jan. 1961, pp. 7–13.

Table 13.1 Selling costs, sales, and operating margin information for incremental productivity analysis

Number of Salespersons	Total Selling Costs	Sales per Salesperson	Total Sales	Operating Margin
1	$ 25,000	$200,000	$200,000	$175,000
2	50,000	150,000	300,000	250,000
3	75,000	120,000	360,000	285,000
4	100,000	100,000	400,000	300,000
5	125,000	85,000	425,000	300,000
6	150,000	72,000	432,000	282,000

sales calls annually, and 900 Class B customers, who require 12 sales calls annually. The firm's average salesperson makes 600 calls annually. In this case, sales-force size is determined as follows:

$$\frac{300\ (20) + 900\ (12)}{600} = 28$$

Several problems confront the manager who opts for this technique. It is difficult to estimate the number of sales calls required to service an account because, regardless of size, individual customers have different problems and different needs. Moreover, a salesperson's workload depends not only on the number of sales calls, but also on travel time between customers and on the amount of time spent with each account. Although these factors help to determine the average annual number of sales calls per salesperson, there may be marked variations between the average and the actual number of calls that a specific salesperson can make.

Incremental productivity method
As a firm adds salespersons within a geographic market, total sales normally increase. However, total selling costs increase as well. According to the *incremental productivity method,* a marketer should continue to increase the sales force as long as the additional sales increases are greater than the additional selling-cost increases that arise from employing a greater number of salespeople. The optimal sales-force size allows the firm to obtain the greatest operating margin.[5]

The incremental productivity method is illustrated in Table 13.1. Notice that as each of the first four salespersons is added to the sales force, the company experiences increases in its operating margin, the difference between total sales and total selling costs. However, adding the fifth salesperson does not increase the firm's operating margin. Thus, the best sales-force size for this business is four.

The incremental productivity method has several limitations. Its users must be able to estimate accurately how much sales will rise when a sales-

5. Walter J. Semlow developed this method and provides a more detailed analysis of it in "How Many Salesmen Do You Need?" *Harvard Business Review,* May–June 1959, pp. 126–132.

person is added. They must also estimate the incremental selling costs. This method's effectiveness depends on management's ability to develop accurate estimates.

Marketers seldom depend on one technique to determine sales-force size. While they may use one or several analytical methods, marketing managers usually temper their decisions with a good deal of subjective judgment.

Recruiting and selecting salespeople

To create and maintain an effective sales force, a sales manager recruits and selects the right type of salespeople. **Recruiting** is a process by which the sales manager develops a list of applicants for sales positions.

To ensure that the recruiting process produces a usable list, a sales manager should establish a set of qualifications required before beginning to recruit. Although for years marketers have attempted to enumerate a set of traits that generally characterize effective salespeople, there is currently no such set of general characteristics. Therefore, a sales manager must develop a set of characteristics that is especially well suited for the sales tasks in a particular company. Two activities can help establish this set of requirements. The sales manager should prepare a job description that lists the specific tasks to be performed by salespersons. The manager also should analyze the characteristics of the firm's successful salespersons, as well as of those who are ineffective. From the job description and the analysis of traits, the sales manager should be able to develop a set of specific requirements.

A sales manager usually recruits applicants from several sources: departments within the firm, employment agencies, educational institutions, other organizations' personnel, respondents to advertisements, and friends recommended by current employees. The specific sources a sales manager uses depend on the type of salesperson required and the manager's experiences with particular sources.

The process of hiring a sales force varies tremendously from one company to another. In some firms, the selection process consists of a single interview; in others the process may include an initial interview, a written application, a series of secondary interviews, written and oral examinations, an evaluation of recommendations, and a physical examination. Sales management should design a selection procedure that specifically satisfies the company's needs. The process should include enough steps to yield the information that is needed to make accurate selection decisions. However, because each step requires a certain expense, there should be no more steps than necessary. The stages of the selection process should be sequenced so that the more expensive steps, such as a physical examination, are near the end. Fewer people will then move through the higher-cost stages.

Recruitment and selection of salespeople are not one-time decisions. The market and marketing environment change, as do an organization's objectives, resources, and marketing strategies. Maintaining the proper mix of salespeople thus requires continued decision making by the firm's sales management.

Recruitment should not be sporadic. It should be a continuous activity aimed at reaching the best applicants. The selection process should systematically and effectively match applicants' characteristics and needs with the requirements of specific selling tasks. Finally, the selection process should ensure that new sales personnel are available where and when they are needed.

Training salespeople   Both new and experienced salespersons require sales training, even though the types of training may vary considerably. A good number of organizations have systematic training programs. Others depend on on-the-job training. Some systematic training programs are quite extensive; others are rather short and rudimentary. Regardless of whether the training program is to be complex or simple, its developer must consider the questions treated in the following subsections.

Who should be trained and who does the training?

Training programs can be aimed at newly hired salespeople, at experienced salespersons, or at both. Ordinarily, new sales personnel require comprehensive training, whereas experienced personnel need both refresher courses regarding established products and training that provides new-product information. Training programs can be directed at the total sales force or at one segment of it.

Sales managers as well as other salespeople often get involved in giving sales training. Such training may occur daily, on the job, or periodically, in sales meetings. Salespeople sometimes receive training from technical specialists within their own organizations. Also, there are a number of individuals and organizations that sell special sales training programs. Some of these programs consist of actual teaching sessions; others take the form of books and manuals or computerized instructional materials. As shown in Figure 13.4, Xerox Learning Systems offers a sales training program called Professional Selling System III.

Where and when should the training occur?

Sales training may be performed in the field, at educational institutions, in company facilities, or in several of these locations. In some firms, new employees receive the bulk of their training, or at least a substantial amount, before being assigned to a specific sales position. Other business organizations put new recruits into the field immediately. After a brief period, the new salespersons begin their formal training.

Training programs for new personnel can be as short as several days or as long as three years or more. Since sales training for experienced salespeople is commonly a series of recurring training efforts, a firm's sales management must determine the frequency, sequencing, and duration of these activities.

What should be taught?

A sales training program can present the company's general background, plans, policies, and procedures; product information regarding features, uses, advantages, problem areas, parts, service, warranties, packaging,

sales terms, promotion, and distribution; and selling methods. Training
programs often cover all three areas.

Training efforts for experienced company salespersons usually emphasize product information, although salespeople also must be informed
about new selling techniques and any changes in company plans, policies,
and procedures.

How should the information be taught?

Many teaching methods and materials are appropriate for sales training
programs. Lectures, films, texts, manuals, simulation exercises, programmed learning devices, audio and video cassettes, demonstrations,
cases, and on-the-job training can all be effective. The specific methods
and materials employed in a particular sales training program depend on
the type and number of trainees, the program's content and complexity,

the length of the training program, the size of the training budget, the location, the number of teachers, and the teachers' preferences for methods and materials.

Compensating salespeople

To develop and maintain a highly productive sales force, a business must formulate and administer a compensation plan that attracts, motivates, and holds the most effective individuals. A compensation plan should give sales management the desired level of control and provide sales personnel with an acceptable level of freedom, income, and incentive. The sales compensation program should be flexible, equitable, easy to administer, and easy to understand. Good compensation programs facilitate and encourage proper treatment of customers. Even though these requirements appear to be logical and easily satisfied, it is actually quite difficult to incorporate all of them into a simple program; some of them will be satisfied, and others will not. Therefore, in formulating a compensation plan, sales management must strive for a proper balance among these factors.

The developer of a compensation program must determine the general level of compensation required and the most desirable method of calculating it. In analyzing the required compensation level, sales management tries to ascertain a salesperson's value to the company on the basis of the tasks and responsibilities associated with the sales position. The sales manager may consider a number of factors, including salaries of other types of personnel in the firm, competitors' compensation plans, costs of sales-force turnover, and the size of nonsalary selling expenses.

Sales compensation programs usually reimburse salespersons for their selling expenses, provide a certain number of fringe benefits, and deliver the required compensation level. To do that, a firm may use one or more of three basic compensation methods: straight salary, straight commission, or a combination of salary and commission. In a *straight salary compensation plan,* salespeople are paid a specified amount per time period, and this sum remains the same until they receive a pay increase or decrease. In a *straight commission compensation plan,* salespeople's compensation is determined solely by the amount of their sales for a given time period. A commission may be based on a single percentage of sales, or it may be based on a sliding scale involving several sales levels and percentage rates. In a *combination compensation plan,* salespeople are paid a fixed salary and a commission based on sales volume. Some combination programs require a salesperson to exceed a certain sales level before earning a commission; other combination plans are designed so that a commission is paid for any level of sales.

Table 13.2 lists the major characteristics of each sales-force compensation method. Notice that the combination method is most popular. Some methods are especially well suited for certain selling situations. When selecting a compensation method, sales management should weigh the advantages and disadvantages shown in Table 13.2.

Proper administration of the sales-force compensation program is crucial for developing high morale and productivity among sales personnel. To maintain an effective compensation program, sales management should periodically review and evaluate the plan and make necessary adjustments.

Table 13.2 Characteristics of sales-force compensation methods

Compensation Method	Frequency of Use (percent)[a]	Especially Useful	Advantages	Disadvantages
Straight salary	30.3	When compensating new salespersons; when firm moves into new sales territories that require developmental work; when salespersons need to perform many non-selling activities	Provides salesperson with maximum amount of security; gives sales manager large amount of control over salespersons; easy to administer; yields more predictable selling expenses	Provides no incentive; necessitates closer supervision of salespersons' activities; during sales declines, selling expenses remain at same level
Straight commission	20.8	When highly aggressive selling is required; when nonselling tasks are minimized; when company cannot closely control sales-force activities	Provides maximum amount of incentive; by increasing commission rate, sales managers can encourage salespersons to sell certain items; selling expenses relate directly to sales resources	Salespersons have little financial security; sales manager has minimum control over sales force; may cause salespeople to provide inadequate service to smaller accounts; selling costs less predictable
Combination	48.9	When sales territories have relatively similar sales potentials; when firm wishes to provide incentive but still control sales-force activities	Provides certain level of financial security; provides some incentive; selling expenses fluctuate with sales revenue	Selling expenses less predictable; may be difficult to administer

[a]The figures in this column are computed from John P. Steinbrink, "How to Pay Your Sales Force," *Harvard Business Review*, July–Aug. 1978, p. 113. Copyright © 1978 by the President and Fellows of Harvard College; all rights reserved. Reprinted by permission of the *Harvard Business Review*.

Motivating salespeople

A sales manager should develop a systematic approach for motivating salespersons in order to obtain high productivity. Motivation should not be viewed as a sporadic set of activities for use only during periods of sales decline. Effective sales-force motivation is achieved through a continual, organized set of activities performed by the company's sales management.

Although financial compensation is important, a motivational program must also satisfy employees' nonfinancial needs. Sales personnel, like other people, join organizations to satisfy personal needs and to achieve personal goals. A sales manager must become aware of their motives and

Figure 13.5
Advertisement for an
incentive program
*Source: Courtesy of
Princess Cruises and
Grey Advertising.*

goals and then must attempt to create an environment within the organization that allows sales personnel to satisfy their personal needs.

A sales manager can employ a variety of positive motivational incentives other than normal financial compensation. For example, enjoyable working conditions, power and authority, job security, and an opportunity to excel are effective motivators. Sales contests and other devices that provide an opportunity to earn additional rewards can be effective motivators. A firm can develop its own special incentive program, or it can purchase one—like the program advertised in Figure 13.5—from an incentive program supplier. Some organizations also employ negative motivational measures—financial penalties, demotions, even terminations.

Creating sales territories

The effectiveness of a sales force that must travel to its customers is influenced, to some degree, by sales management's decisions regarding sales territories. In deciding on territories, sales managers must consider size, shape, routing, and scheduling.

Size of territory

Sales managers usually try to create territories that have similar sales potentials or that require about the same amount of work. If territories have equal sales potentials, they will almost always be unequal in geographic size. The salespersons who get the larger territories will have to work longer and harder to generate a certain sales volume. When a sales manager attempts to create territories that require equal amounts of work, sales potentials for those territories will often vary. If sales personnel are partially or fully compensated through commissions, they will have unequal income potentials. Rather than relying on a single approach, many sales managers try to balance territorial workloads and earning potentials by employing differential commission rates. Although a sales manager seeks equity when developing and maintaining sales territories, inequities will always prevail to some degree.

Shape of territory

Several factors enter into designing the shape of sales territories. First, sales managers must construct the territories so that sales potentials can be measured. This necessity is why sales territories often consist of several geographic units for which market data are obtainable, such as census tracts, cities, counties, or states. Second, a territory's shape should help the sales force to provide the best possible coverage of customers. Third, the territories should be designed to minimize selling costs. Fourth, the territory shapes should take into account the density and distribution of customers. Fifth, the territory shapes may have to reflect topographical features.

Sales territories seldom form symmetrical patterns. However, sales managers often use geometric shapes as general patterns for sales territories. Circles, rectangles, wedges, and cloverleaves are a few patterns used in designing sales territories.

Routing and scheduling

Someone must route and schedule sales calls in the field. That person must consider the sequence in which customers are called on, the specific roads or transportation schedules to be used, the number of calls to be made in a given period, and what time of day the calls will occur. In some firms, salespeople plan their own routes and schedules with little or no assistance from the sales manager. In other organizations, the sales manager draws up the routes and schedules. No matter who plans the routing and scheduling, the major goals should be to minimize salespersons' nonselling time (the time spent in traveling and waiting) and to maximize their selling time. The planners should try to achieve these goals in a way that also holds a salesperson's travel and lodging costs to a minimum.

Several factors affect the routing and scheduling of sales personnel. The geographic size and shape of a sales territory are most important. Next come the number and distribution of customers within the territory, followed by the frequency and duration of sales calls. Finally, the availability of roads and mass transportation and the location of the salesperson's home base vis-à-vis customers' locations dictate possible routes and schedules.

Controlling and evaluating sales-force performance

To control and evaluate sales-force activities properly, sales management first of all needs information. A sales manager gets information about salespersons from their call reports, customer feedback, and invoices. Since the field sales force cannot be observed by the sales manager on a daily basis, salespersons usually must submit call reports, which identify the customers called on and present detailed information about interaction with those clients. Traveling sales personnel often must file work schedules indicating where they plan to be during specific future time periods.

The dimensions used to measure a salesperson's performance are determined largely by sales objectives. These objectives are normally set by the sales manager. If an individual's sales objective is stated in terms of sales volume, then that person should be evaluated on the basis of sales volume generated. Even though a salesperson may be assigned a major objective, he or she ordinarily is expected to achieve several related objectives as well. Thus, salespeople often are judged along several dimensions. Sales managers evaluate many performance indicators, including average number of calls per day, average sales per customer, actual sales relative to sales potential, number of new-customer orders, average cost per call, and average gross profit per customer.

To evaluate a salesperson, a sales manager may compare one or more of these dimensions with a predetermined performance standard. However, sales management commonly compares one salesperson's performance with the performance of other employees operating under similar selling conditions or compares current performance with past performance. Sometimes, management judges factors that have less direct bearing on sales performance: personal appearance; verbal skills; aggressiveness; cooperativeness; knowledge of the product, company, market, and competitors; etc.

After evaluating salespeople, sales managers must take any needed corrective action, for it is their job to improve the performance of the sales force. They may have to adjust performance standards, provide additional sales training, or try other motivational methods. Corrective action may demand comprehensive changes in the sales force.

Obviously, effective management of sales activities is crucial to an organization's survival. These activities help to generate the revenues that a firm uses to acquire its resources.

The nature of sales promotion

As defined earlier, *sales promotion* is an activity and/or material that acts as a direct inducement, offering added value or incentive for the product, to resellers, salespersons, or consumers.[6] It encompasses all promotional activities and materials other than personal selling, advertising, and publicity. Many sales promotion activities are noncyclical and are designed to produce immediate, short-run effects. For example, cents-off coupons and consumer contests have relatively short deadlines so that consumers must act quickly.

An organization often uses sales promotion activities in concert with other promotional efforts to facilitate personal selling, advertising, or both. For example, people may have to go to a store to enter a consumer contest. This facilitates personal selling by drawing people into the establishment. To improve the effectiveness of advertisements, point-of-purchase displays often are designed to include pictures, symbols, and messages that appear in advertisements.

Sales promotion efforts are not always secondary to other promotion mix ingredients. (See the example in the Application on next page.) Companies sometimes employ advertising and personal selling to support sales promotion activities. For example, marketers frequently use advertising to promote trading stamps, cents-off offers, contests, free samples, and premiums. Manufacturers' sales personnel occasionally administer sales contests for wholesale or retail salespersons. Because the most effective sales promotion efforts and other promotional activities are usually highly interrelated, decisions regarding sales promotion often affect advertising and personal selling decisions, and vice versa.

Sales promotion objectives

Marketers utilize sales promotion for a variety of reasons. A single sales promotion activity may be employed to achieve one or several objectives. On the other hand, several sales promotion activities may be required to accomplish a single goal or set of goals. Marketers draw on sales promotion activities and materials to achieve the following objectives:

1. To identify and attract new customers
2. To introduce a new product
3. To increase the total number of users for an established brand
4. To encourage greater usage among current customers
5. To educate consumers regarding product improvements
6. To bring more customers into retail stores
7. To stabilize a fluctuating sales pattern
8. To increase reseller inventories
9. To combat or offset competitors' marketing efforts
10. To obtain more and better shelf space and displays[7]

Some of these objectives are designed specifically to stimulate resellers' demand and effectiveness; some are directed at increasing consumer de-

6. This definition is adapted from *Sales Promotion and Modern Merchandising* by John F. Luick and William L. Ziegler. Copyright © 1968 McGraw-Hill, Inc. Used with permission of McGraw-Hill Book Company.
7. Richard E. Stanley, *Promotion: Advertising, Publicity, Personal Selling, and Sales Promotion* (Englewood Cliffs, N.J.: Prentice-Hall, 1982), pp. 304–305.

Marketers at Kimberly-Clark have significantly increased their use of sales promotion methods. Kimberly-Clark tries to measure the effectiveness of sales promotion activities, and those activities are included in long-range planning. Management at Kimberly-Clark views sales promotions as having a broad impact on corporate activities in both the production and marketing areas. Shipments, market share, reseller support, and other issues are all affected by sales promotions.

Kimberly-Clark has a professional staff to handle sales promotions. The firm has a director of sales promotions and four assistant sales promotion managers, one for each business unit within the company. The promotion managers perform many functions, including sitting in on sessions regarding branding strategy, market research, distribution, and advertising.

When developing and planning a sales promotion effort, the promotion manager assesses how the effort will affect, during and after the promotion, the shipment of supplies, reseller support, and consumers. The promotion manager tries to estimate how long and to what extent these areas will be affected by the promotion activities. Also during and after the promotion campaign, the increase in sales as a result of the promotion is calculated to determine the costs and benefits of the promotional efforts. Through careful planning and measurement, marketers at Kimberly-Clark are realizing significant benefits from sales promotion activities.

Source: Based on Al Urbanski, "Sales Promotion's New Aura," *Sales and Marketing Management,* Nov. 14, 1983, pp. 48–53.

mand; and others focus on both resellers and consumers. Sales promotion is effective for both offensive and defensive purposes. Whatever its use, the marketer should be certain that the sales promotion objectives are consistent with the organization's overall objectives, marketing objectives, and promotion objectives.

**Sales promotion
methods**

Most sales promotion methods can be grouped into two main categories: consumer sales promotion and trade sales promotion. *Consumer sales promotion techniques* encourage or stimulate consumers to patronize a specific retail store or to try and/or purchase a particular product. Consumer sales promotion techniques can be used to draw people into particular retail stores, to introduce new products, or to promote established products. *Trade sales promotion methods* stimulate wholesalers and retailers to carry a producer's products and to market these products aggressively. Most trade sales promotion techniques provide incentives—money, merchandise, gifts, or promotional assistance—to resellers who purchase products or perform certain activities.

Marketers consider a number of factors before deciding which sales promotion method or methods to use. The objectives of the effort are of primary concern. Marketers must weigh product characteristics—size, weight, costs, durability, uses, features, and hazards—and target market characteristics—age, sex, income, location, density, usage rate, and shopping patterns—before choosing a sales promotion method. How the product is distributed and the number and types of resellers may determine the final outcome. Finally, the competitive environment and legal forces influence the selection of sales promotion methods.

A deeper understanding of sales promotion calls for a thorough examination of several sales promotion techniques. Our analysis divides the major sales promotion methods into four categories: (1) sales promotion methods used by retailers, (2) new-product sales promotion techniques, (3) sales promotion methods for established products, and (4) sales promotion methods aimed at resellers.[8]

Sales promotion methods used by retailers

The variety of sales promotion methods that retailers use fall into four broad categories: retailer coupons, demonstrations, trading stamps, and point-of-purchase displays.

Retailer coupons

Retailer coupons usually take the form of "cents-off" coupons, which are distributed through advertisements or handouts and are redeemable only at specific stores. They are especially useful when price is a primary motivation for consumers' purchasing behavior. For example, a discount supermarket might distribute retailer coupons that allow 30 cents off the price of a specific brand of bread.

Retailer coupons bring customers into a particular store and build sales volume for a specific brand. Competitive counteroffers can significantly reduce the effectiveness of retailer coupons. Taking into account their emphasis on price, there is some question about whether retailer coupons develop loyalty toward retailers.

Demonstrations

Demonstrations are excellent attention getters. They are often used by manufacturers on a temporary basis either to encourage trial use and purchase of the product or to actually show how the product works. Because labor costs can be extremely high, demonstrations are not used widely. They can, however, be highly effective for promoting certain types of products, such as appliances. Recent demonstrations have included those for extrusion pasta machines and microconvection ovens.

Trading stamps

Trading stamps are dispensed in proportion to the amount purchased by a consumer and can be accumulated and redeemed for goods. Retailers use trading stamps to attract consumers to specific stores. In addition, they can increase sales of specific items by giving extra stamps to purchasers of those items. Stamps are attractive to consumers as long as they do not drive up the price of goods. They are effective for many types of retailers.

Point-of-purchase displays

Point-of-purchase materials include such items as outside signs, window displays, counter pieces, display racks, and self-service cartons. These items

---

8. The information in the descriptions of the sales promotion techniques is from *Sales Promotion and Modern Merchandising,* by John F. Luick and William L. Ziegler. Copyright © 1968 by McGraw-Hill, Inc. Used with permission of McGraw-Hill Book Company.

attract attention, inform customers, and encourage retailers to carry particular products. A retailer is likely to use point-of-purchase materials if they are attractive, informative, well-constructed, and in harmony with the store.

New-product sales promotion techniques

Several sales promotion methods can be used to promote new products. Three of the most common techniques are free samples, coupons, and money refunds.

Free samples

Marketers use *free samples* for several reasons: to stimulate trial of a product, to increase sales volume in early stages of the product's life cycle, or to obtain desirable distribution. When Shulton introduced Blue Stratos cologne, for example, 10 million men in the 18–34 target market received samples in the mail just before Father's Day to encourage product trial immediately prior to that heavy gift-giving period.[9]

In designing a free sample, marketers should consider certain factors such as the seasonality of the product, the characteristics of the market, and prior advertising. Free samples are not appropriate for mature products and slow-turnover products. Sampling is the most expensive of all sales promotion methods. Production and distribution through such channels as mail delivery, door-to-door delivery, in-store distribution, and on-package distribution entail very high costs.

Coupons

Coupons are used to stimulate trial of a new or established product, to increase sales volume quickly, to attract repeat purchasers, or to introduce new package sizes or features. Coupons usually reduce the purchase price of an item. For example, a cereal manufacturer might use a 20-cent coupon to promote a new type of cereal. The savings may be deducted from the purchase price or offered as cash. The nature of the product (seasonality, maturity, frequency of purchase, and the like) is the prime consideration in setting up a coupon promotion. Coupons have two disadvantages: fraud or misredemption is possible; and the redemption period can be quite lengthy. For best results, coupons should be easy to recognize and should state the offer clearly.

An increasing number of households are redeeming coupons. A Nielson survey in 1971 indicated that 58 percent of all households were using coupons; a recent similar study revealed that over 76 percent of all households make use of coupons.[10]

Money refunds

With *money refunds,* consumers are mailed a specific amount of money when proof of purchase has been established. Usually, manufacturers demand multiple purchases of the product before a consumer can qualify for

---

9. Steven G. Rothschild, "Hang Gliding Theme Used to Unveil New Fragrance," *Marketing Times,* July/Aug. 1981, p. 32.
10. Mary M. English, "Like 'Em or Not, Coupons Surely Here to Stay," *Advertising Age,* Aug. 22, 1983, p. M-26.

a refund. For example, a money refund may require a consumer to mail in five box tops. This method, used primarily to promote trial use of a product, is relatively low in cost. Nevertheless, because money refunds sometimes generate a low response rate, they have limited impact on sales.

Sales promotion devices for established products

Sales promotion devices for established products are usually aimed at providing additional value for the customer who purchases the item. Four sales promotion methods commonly used to promote established products are premiums, cents-off offers, consumer contests, and consumer sweepstakes.

Premiums

Premiums are items that are offered free or at a minimum cost as a bonus for purchasing. They can attract competitors' customers, introduce different sizes of established products, add variety to other promotional efforts, and stimulate loyalty. For premiums to be effective, they must be easily recognizable and desirable. Premiums usually are distributed through retail outlets or through the mail. They may also be placed on or in packages.

Cents-off offers

When a *cents-off offer* is used, buyers receive a certain amount off the regular price shown on the label or package. This method can provide a strong incentive for trying the product, stimulate the product's sales, yield short-lived sales increases, and promote products in off-seasons. It is an easy method to control and is used frequently. However, it reduces the price to customers who would buy at the regular price, and frequent use of cents-off offers may cheapen a product's image. In addition, the method often requires special handling by retailers.

Consumer contests

In *consumer contests* individuals compete for prizes based on their analytical or creative skill. This method generates traffic at the retail level. Contestants are usually more involved in consumer contests than they are in sweepstakes (discussed next), even though the total participation may be lower. Contests may be used in conjunction with other sales promotion methods such as coupons.

Consumer sweepstakes

The entrants in a *consumer sweepstakes* submit their names for inclusion in a drawing for prizes. Sweepstakes are employed to stimulate sales and, like contests, are sometimes teamed with other sales promotion methods. Sweepstakes are used more often than consumer contests, and they tend to attract a greater number of participants. The cost of a sweepstakes (which is about $3 per 1,000 entrants) is considerably less than the cost of a contest.[11] The advertisement on Figure 13.6 is promoting a consumer sweepstakes.

11. Eileen Norris, "Everyone Will Grab at a Chance to Win," *Advertising Age,* Aug. 22, 1983, p. M-10.

Successful sweepstakes can generate considerable interest and short-term increases in sales or market share. For example, Levi Strauss attracted 1.75 million entries in a two-week sweepstakes; the Benson & Hedges sweepstakes generated 5 million participants; and Cracker Jacks sponsored a $6-million sweepstakes, which helped the firm increase sales by 25 percent in that year.[12] Sweepstakes are, however, prohibited in some states.

Sales promotion methods aimed at resellers

Producers use sales promotion methods to encourage resellers to carry their products and to promote them effectively. Several sales promotion methods are appropriate for these purposes. They include buying allowances, buy-back allowances, counts and recounts, free merchandise, merchandise allowances, cooperative advertising, dealer listings, premium or push money, sales contests, and dealer loaders.

12. Franklynn Peterson and Judi Kesselman-Turkel, "Catching Customers with Sweepstakes," *Fortune,* Feb. 8, 1982, pp. 84–87.

Buying allowances

A *buying allowance* is a temporary price reduction to resellers for purchasing specified quantities of a product. A soap producer, for example, might give retailers $1 for each case of soap purchased. Such offers may provide an incentive to handle a new product, achieve a temporary price reduction, or stimulate the purchase of an item in larger than normal quantities. The buying allowance, which takes the form of money, yields profits to resellers and is simple and straightforward to use. There are no restrictions on resellers regarding their use of the money, and this fact increases the method's effectiveness.

Buy-back allowances

A *buy-back allowance* is a certain sum of money that is given to a purchaser for each unit bought after an initial deal is over. This method is a secondary incentive in which the total amount of money that buyers can receive is proportional to their purchases during the initial trade deal. Buy-back allowances encourage cooperation during an initial sales promotion effort and stimulate repurchase afterwards. The main drawback of this method is its expense.

Count and recount

The *count and recount* promotion method is based on the payment of a specific amount of money for each product unit moved from a reseller's warehouse in a given time period. Units of products in the warehouse are counted at the start of the promotion and again at the end to determine how many units have moved from the warehouse. This method can reduce retail stockouts by moving inventory out of warehouses, clear distribution channels of obsolete products or packages, and reduce warehouse inventories.

The count and recount method can benefit a producer by reducing resellers' inventories, making resellers more likely to place new orders. However, this method is often difficult to administer and may not appeal to resellers who have small warehouses.

Free merchandise

Free merchandise is sometimes offered to resellers who purchase a stated quantity of the same or different products. Occasionally, free merchandise is used as payment for allowances provided through other sales promotion methods. The giving of free merchandise usually is accomplished by reducing the invoice to avoid handling and bookkeeping problems.

Merchandise allowances

A *merchandise allowance* consists of a manufacturer's agreement to pay resellers certain amounts of money for providing special promotional efforts such as advertising or displays. Before paying retailers, manufacturers usually verify their performance. Manufacturers hope that the retailers' additional promotional efforts will yield substantial sales increases.

This method is best suited to high-volume, high-profit, easily handled products. One major problem with using merchandise allowances is that some retailers perform their activities at a minimally acceptable level simply to obtain the allowances.

Cooperative advertising

Cooperative advertising is an arrangement in which a manufacturer agrees to pay a certain amount of a retailer's media costs for advertising the manufacturer's products. The amount allowed usually is based on the quantities purchased. Before payment is made, a retailer must show proof that advertisements did appear. These payments provide additional funds to retailers for advertising. They can, however, put a severe burden on the producer's advertising budget. Some retailers exploit cooperative advertising programs by crowding too many products into one advertisement. Surprisingly, though, not all available cooperative advertising dollars are used. Some retailers cannot afford to advertise. Others can afford it but do not want to advertise. Still others actually do advertising that qualifies but are not willing to do the paperwork necessary to receive reimbursement from producers.[13]

Dealer listings

A *dealer listing* is an advertisement that promotes a product and identifies the names of participating retailers who sell the product. Dealer listings can influence retailers to carry the product, build traffic at the retail level, and encourage consumers to buy the product at participating dealers.

Premium or push money

Premium or *push money* is used in an incentive program designed to push a line of goods by providing additional compensation to salespeople. It is appropriate when personal selling is an important part of the marketing effort; it is not effective for promoting products that are sold through self-service. This method helps a manufacturer to obtain commitment from the sales force. Using push money can be very expensive.

Sales contests

A *sales contest* is designed to motivate distributors, retailers, and sales personnel by recognizing outstanding achievements. To be effective, this method must be equitable for all salespersons involved. One advantage to this method is that it can achieve participation at all levels of distribution. However, results are temporary, and prizes are usually expensive.

Dealer loaders

A *dealer loader* is a gift that is given to a retailer who purchases a specified quantity of merchandise. Often, dealer loaders are used in an attempt to obtain special display efforts from retailers by offering essential display parts as premiums. A manufacturer, for example, might design a display that includes a sterling silver tray as a major component and give the tray to the retailer. Marketers use dealer loaders to obtain new distributors and to push larger quantities of goods.

13. Ed Crimmins, "A Co-op Myth: It Is a Tragedy that Stores Don't Spend All Their Accruals," *Sales and Marketing Management*, Feb. 7, 1983, pp. 72–73.

Summary

Personal selling is the process of informing customers and persuading them to purchase products through personal communication in an exchange situation. The three general purposes of personal selling are finding prospects, convincing prospects to buy, and keeping customers satisfied. The selling process consists of prospecting and evaluating, preparing, approaching, making the presentation, overcoming objections, closing, and following up.

In developing a sales force, marketing managers must consider which types of salespersons will sell the firm's products most effectively. The three classifications of salespersons are order getters, order takers, and support personnel. Order getters inform and persuade prospects to buy. Order getting can be divided into two categories: activities aimed at current customer sales and activities directed toward new-business sales. Order takers seek repeat sales and are divided into two categories: inside order takers and field order takers. Sales support personnel facilitate the selling function but usually are not involved only with making sales. The three types of support personnel are missionary, trade, and technical salespersons.

The effectiveness of sales-force management is an important determinant of a firm's success, because the sales force is directly responsible for generating an organization's primary input—sales revenue. Some major decision areas and activities on which sales managers focus are establishing sales objectives, determining sales-force size, recruiting and selecting salespeople, training sales personnel, compensating salespeople, motivating salespeople, creating sales territories, routing and scheduling salespeople, and controlling and evaluating the sales force.

Sales objectives should be stated in precise, measurable terms and should specify the time period and the geographic areas involved. The size of the sales force must be adjusted from time to time because a firm's marketing plans change, as do markets and forces in the marketing environment. Two techniques that sometimes are used to determine the size of the sales force are the equalized workload method and the incremental productivity method.

Recruiting and selecting salespeople involves attracting and choosing the right type of salesperson to maintain an effective sales force. When developing a training program, one must consider a variety of dimensions, such as who should be trained, where and when the training should occur, what should be taught, and how the information should be presented. Compensation of salespeople involves formulation and administration of a compensation plan that attracts, motivates, and holds the right types of salesperson for the firm. Motivation of salespeople should allow the firm to attain high productivity. Creating sales territories, another aspect of sales-force management, focuses on such factors as size, shape, routing, and scheduling. To control and evaluate sales-force performance, the sales manager must use information obtained through salespersons' call reports, customer feedback, and invoices.

Sales promotion is an activity and/or material that acts as a direct inducement, offering added value or incentive for the product, to resellers, salespersons, or consumers. Marketers use sales promotion to identify and attract new customers, to introduce a new product, and to increase reseller inventories. Sales promotion techniques can be divided into two general categories: consumer and trade. Consumer sales promotion methods encourage consumers to trade at specific stores or to try and/or buy a specific product. Trade sales promotion techniques stimulate resellers to handle a manufacturer's products and to market these products aggressively.

Important terms

Personal selling	Retailer coupons
Prospecting	Demonstrations
Approach	Trading stamps
Closing	Point-of-purchase materials
Order getters	Free samples
Order takers	Coupons
Support personnel	Money refunds
Missionary salespersons	Premiums
Trade salespersons	Cents-off offer
Technical salespersons	Consumer contests
Equalized workload method	Consumer sweepstakes
Incremental productivity method	Buying allowance
Recruiting	Buy-back allowance
Straight salary compensation plan	Count and recount
Straight commission	Free merchandise
compensation play	Merchandise allowance
Combination compensation plan	Cooperative advertising
Sales promotion	Dealer listing
Consumer sales promotion	Premium or push money
techniques	Sales contest
Trade sales promotion methods	Dealer loader

Discussion and review questions

1. What is personal selling? How does personal selling differ from other types of promotional activities?
2. What are the primary purposes of personal selling?
3. Identify the elements of the personal selling process. Must a salesperson include all these elements when selling a product to a customer? Why or why not?
4. How does a salesperson find and evaluate prospects? Do you consider any of these methods to be questionable ethically?
5. Are order getters more aggressive or creative than order takers? Why or why not?
6. What are the similarities and differences between the equalized workload method and the incremental productivity method for determining sales-force size? Can marketers in a new firm use either of these methods to determine the size of the initial sales force? Why or why not?
7. Identify several characteristics of effective sales objectives.
8. How should a sales manager establish criteria for selecting sales personnel? What are the general characteristics of a good salesperson?

9. What major issues or questions should be considered when developing a training program for the sales force?
10. Explain the major advantages and disadvantages of the three basic methods of compensating sales personnel. In general, which method do you most prefer? Why?
11. What major factors should be taken into account in designing the shape of a sales territory?
12. How does a sales manager—who cannot be with each salesperson in the field on a daily basis—control the performance of sales personnel?
13. What is sales promotion? Why is it used?
14. For each of the following, identify and describe three techniques and give some examples: (a) sales promotion methods for retail establishments, (b) new-product sales promotion techniques, (c) sales promotion devices for established products, and (d) sales promotion methods aimed at resellers.
15. What types of sales promotion methods have you observed or experienced recently?

Cases

Case 13.1

Sanders Cutlery Company

Each six months Betty Laven, the sales manager for Sanders Cutlery Company, evaluates the size of the sales force for each of ten geographic areas in which the company's industrial product line is marketed. Currently, Laven is concerned with the number of order getters and support personnel in area C. The size of the order-taker sales force is not of concern now, as this function is mainly handled internally, through telephone contacts. Presently, there are ten order getters and twenty-eight support salespersons in area C.

Sanders manufactures a high-quality line of knives. Its products are not distributed through the usual wholesaler-retailer channels. The company produces a large assortment of knives that provide unique benefits to several different target markets, each of which is serviced directly by the company's sales force. The three principal markets are butcher shops, cafeterias and restaurants, and hospitals.

Laven's staff members have compiled information that they think is needed in order for her to make a decision about the size of the sales force. This information is shown in Tables 13.3 and 13.4.

Questions for discussion
1. Determine the optimum size of the sales force.
2. What additional information do you think the sales force should provide?
3. What methods of salesperson compensation do you think are appropriate for Sanders? Why?

Table 13.3 Estimated total sales and selling costs for the range of 10–18 salespersons

Number of Salespersons	Total Sales	Total Selling Costs
10	$1,500,000	$550,000
11	1,580,000	580,000
12	1,650,000	610,000
13	1,700,000	640,000
14	1,750,000	670,000
15	1,790,000	700,000
16	1,830,000	730,000
17	1,850,000	760,000
18	1,870,000	790,000

Table 13.4 Optimum call frequency and number of customers in each market segment for industrial knife product line

Market Segment	Annual Service Calls Required	Number of Customers
Butcher shops	2	3,000
Restaurants and cafeterias	3	4,800
Hospitals	1	600

Note: Each salesperson should make an average of 1,200 calls a year.

Case 13.2

Avon Products' Sales Organization[14]

With approximately a 15 percent market share, Avon Products Incorporated is the largest producer and distributor of fragrances, cosmetics, and fashion jewelry in the United States. D. H. McConnell, the founder of Avon, took a very bold and radical step when he introduced local women as sales representatives in 1886. These women were the first "Avon ladies." Today, there are 425,000 Avon representatives visiting a total of 21 million homes every two weeks and leaving brochures that describe Avon products. Avon's catalog (see Figure 13.7) reaches more households than does *Reader's Digest* or *TV Guide.*

Avon's sales force can rely on an aggressive product development program. The organization introduces numerous new products annually and drops items that aren't selling. An extensive multi-million dollar advertising campaign helps to support sales representatives' efforts. Recently,

14. This case is based on information from JoAn Paganetti, "An American Best Seller's Story Is Still Direct," *Advertising Age,* March 19, 1984, pp. M4, M5, M44; and Pat Sloan, "Avon Comes Back in Force, Plans Doubled Ad Budget," *Advertising Age,* January 31, 1983, pp. 1, 51.

Figure 13.7
An Avon Catalog
*Source: Courtesy of
Avon Products, Inc.*

AVON CATALOG
SUMMER-FALL, 1984

Avon implemented a system whereby Avon representatives could accept Visa or MasterCard charges as payment.

For almost a hundred years Avon has depended on its direct selling sales organization. Currently, however, Avon is experiencing several problems with its sales force. Due to the growth in the number of women who work out of the home, Avon's traditional approach of calling on housewives is in question because many of these women are no longer at home during the day. Avon's sales force is declining because the firm is finding it difficult to attract and keep effective sales representatives. It is estimated that the average Avon sales representative makes $3 to $6 per hour. Yet, the average Mary Kay (major competitor) salesperson earns $8 to $12 per hour.

To cope with the problem of reaching working women, Avon is testing the use of direct mail. Through direct mail, women would receive the Avon catalog and also be able to order directly from the catalog. Sales representatives would make deliveries, demonstrate products, and take additional orders. Deliveries would be made at night and on weekends. Direct mail also could be employed for sampling Avon products. If Avon decides to use direct mail, these efforts would augment but not replace sales representatives' activities.

Avon also is trying to improve the compensation program for sales representatives. First, Avon is paying a 5 percent bonus (on new representatives' sales) to current representatives who brought the new recruits into the organization. This bonus is built on top of the standard 40 percent commission. Second, each sales group leader receives an additional 3 percent commission on all sales by new recruits. Third, Avon has increased the commission paid to its sales representatives. Under the improved compensation system, an Avon representative should be able to make $5 to $10 per hour.

Questions for discussion
1. What type of compensation method is Avon using?
2. Evaluate Avon's efforts to improve its sales force compensation program.
3. Besides the use of direct mail, what other methods could Avon use to reach women who work out of the home?

Part 5

Pricing Decisions

Obviously, for an organization to provide a satisfying marketing mix, the price must be considered at the least to be acceptable by target market members. Pricing decisions can have numerous effects on other parts of the marketing mix. For example, a product's price can influence how customers perceive it, what types of marketing institutions are used in distributing the product, and how the product is promoted. In Chapter 14, we discuss the importance of price and look at some of the criteria used to establish pricing objectives. Demand schedules, the elasticity of demand, and the relationships among demand, costs, and profits are also considered in this chapter. Chapter 15 focuses on pricing policies and pricing methods. In addition, several unique aspects of pricing industrial products are explained.

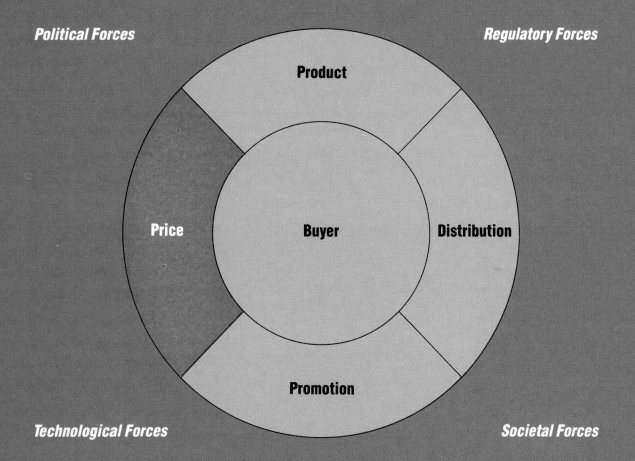

Marketing Environment

Legal Forces

Political Forces

Regulatory Forces

Product

Price

Buyer

Distribution

Promotion

Technological Forces

Societal Forces

Economic Forces

14

Pricing Concepts

Objectives

To understand the nature and importance of price.

To examine the criteria used to establish pricing objectives.

To realize the importance of identifying the target market's evaluation of price.

To gain insight into demand schedules and the elasticity of demand.

To examine the relationships among demand, costs, and profits.

Airline fares exemplify the drastic shift from pricing based on cost to pricing based on competition. In recent years, pricing has become a major factor related to success in the airline business. Before deregulation went into effect, the airlines had to file proposed fare changes with the Civil Aeronautics Board a month in advance. Now they can discount fares radically to fill empty seats and to compete with low-cost carriers. As shown in Figure 14.1, for example, Republic Airlines tries to attract passengers with discounts on first class seating.

Figure 14.1   Republic Airlines attempts to attract first class passengers with discounts   *Source: Campbell-Mithun, Inc. Minneapolis, Minnesota.*

After deregulation, discounts increased from 36 percent to 45 percent off full fares. Deregulation allows the airlines to change fares with only one-day notice. Fares can be raised by 30 percent or decreased by 100 percent from standard levels.

Although the costs of fuel, labor, and other expenses still affect fares, airfare bargains are the order of the day as airlines try to lure passengers away from competitors. This type of price competition costs airlines millions of dollars in revenues. Profits shrink as costs increase and air travel decreases. As long as thousands of airline seats remain empty, however, the discount war will probably continue.[1]

As reflected by pricing practices common to the airline industry, price can be a very important component in a firm's marketing mix. Price, in fact, is probably the most flexible variable in the marketing mix. Marketers can usually adjust their prices more easily and more quickly than they can change any other marketing mix variable. Bear in mind, however, that under certain circumstances, the price variable may be relatively inflexible.

In this chapter, we first survey the nature of the price variable. After that, we concentrate on the first four stages in the process of establishing prices. The remaining stages are discussed in Chapter 15.

The nature of price

To a buyer, *price* is the value placed on what is exchanged. Something of value—usually purchasing power—is exchanged for satisfaction or utility. *Purchasing power* depends on a buyer's income, credit, and wealth. It is a mistake to believe that price is always money paid or some other financial consideration. In fact, trading of products—*barter*—is the oldest form of exchange. Money may or may not be involved.

Buyers' concern for and interest in price is related to their expectations about the satisfaction or utility associated with a product. To illustrate, one study indicates that 25 percent of all meat purchase decisions are based primarily on price.[2] Since buyers have limited resources, they must allocate their purchasing power to obtain the most desired products. Buyers must decide whether the utility gained in an exchange is worth the purchasing power sacrificed.

Almost anything of value—ideas, services, rights, and goods—can be assessed by a price, because in our society the financial price is the measurement of value commonly used in exchanges. Thus, a painting by Picasso may be valued, or priced, at $500,000. Financial price, then, quantifies value. It is the basis of most market exchanges.

1. John Curley, "Decontrol of Airlines Shifts Pricing from a Cost to a Competitive Basis," *Wall Street Journal,* Dec. 4, 1981, p. 25; and Ruth Hamel, "Airlines Specialize to Survive," *USA Today,* Oct. 14, 1983, p. 1.
2. "Yankelovich Says Effort To Up Consumption of Meat Must Focus on Life-Style Changes," *Frozen Food Age,* Nov. 1983, p. 20.

Application

Pricing Bank Services

There has been a trend in the banking industry to court customers who have a lot of money. Favoritism toward large-balance holders can take the form of faster service or special services. This trend has resulted in poorer service to the large segment of customers with small bank accounts; they are paying bigger fees for less service.

The focus on customers with high bank balances has turned away small-account holders from some banks. For example, small-account customers were put off when Citibank experimented with charging them a fee if they chose to see a teller instead of an automatic teller machine. Citibank lost many small customers to a nearby Chemical Bank that advertised personal and friendly customer service. First Community Credit Union in St. Louis, Mo., does not charge checking-account fees, which led to an increase in deposits from $77 million to $175 million within a two-year period.

Many banks whose customers are not affluent are experimenting with reducing expenses through automatic teller machines while trying to maintain the personal touch. Other banks are trying to persuade each customer to consolidate bank accounts into one balance that qualifies for waived fees and special attention.

By lowering prices, banks can attract more customers and increase their volume of accounts just as discount retailers do. By raising prices, banks might lose old customers and customers who are more likely to take loans. The pricing strategy is thus a crucial variable in the marketing mix for services.

Source: Based on Julie Salmon, "Some Banks, Ignoring the Trend, Tout Services for Small Customers," *Wall Street Journal,* April 6, 1983, pp. 33, 41.

Terms used to describe price

Price is expressed in different terms for different exchanges. For instance, auto insurance companies charge a *premium* for protection from the cost of injuries or repairs stemming from an automobile accident. An officer who stops you for speeding writes a ticket and requires you to pay a *fine*. If a lawyer defends you, a *fee* is charged, and if you use a railway or taxi, a *fare* is charged. A *toll* is charged for the use of bridges or turnpikes.

Rent is paid for the use of equipment or for your apartment. A *commission* is remitted to an agent for the sale of real estate. *Dues* are paid to allow membership in a club or group. A *deposit* can be made to hold or lay away merchandise. A *tip* helps pay waitresses or waiters for their services. *Interest* is charged for the loan that you obtain, and *taxes* are paid for government services. Of course, the value of many products is called *price*. In any event, it is important to remember that although price may be expressed in many different ways, the purpose of this concept is to quantify and express the value of the items in a market exchange.

The importance of price to marketers

As pointed out in Chapter 6, it can take a long time to develop a product. It takes time to plan promotion and to communicate the benefits of a product. Distribution usually requires a long-term commitment to dealers who will handle the product. Often, the only thing a marketer can change quickly to respond to changes in demand or to the actions of competitors is price; and price is a key element in the marketing mix because it relates directly to the generation of total revenue. Price, therefore, plays an important part in efficient marketing. The Application above discusses the role of price in the marketing mixes of selected banks.

Figure 14.2
Howard Johnson's pro-
motes good value at a
sensible price
*Source: Howard John-
son Company.*

Because price has a psychological impact on customers, marketers can use it symbolically. By raising a price, they can emphasize the quality of a product and try to increase the status associated with its ownership. By lowering a price, they can emphasize a bargain and attract customers who go out of their way—spending extra time and effort—to save a small amount. Price can have a strong effect on sales. Howard Johnson's recognizes this potential and has developed a price to encourage travelers to compare the value offered by Howard Johnson's with that of so-called expensive hotels (see Figure 14.2).

Figure 14.3
Stages for establishing prices

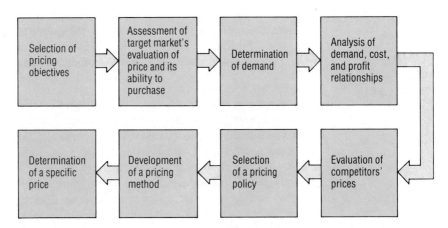

Because price times quantity equals revenue, price is important in determining profits. Efficiency and lower costs can be goals that allow a firm to decrease price and develop a more competitive marketing mix. The economic role of price is to allocate products and match them to market opportunities that develop from increases or decreases in demand.

Stages for establishing prices

Having examined the nature and importance of price, we will move on to the stages in establishing prices. Figure 14.3 identifies these eight stages. You should not consider these stages to be inevitable. They are guidelines that provide a logical way of analyzing the effectiveness of price in the marketing mix and the contributions price makes to an organization's objectives.

The first stage is to develop a pricing objective that dovetails with the organization's overall objectives and its marketing objectives. Other systematic steps should follow. Pricing objectives are based on an organization's philosophy toward its customers. If a firm adopts the marketing concept, then stage 2, assessment of the target market's evaluation of price and its ability to purchase, will be logical and necessary. Next, the nature and elasticity of demand should be examined (stage 3). Stage 4—analysis of demand, cost, and profit relationships—is necessary to estimate the economic feasibility of alternative prices. Evaluation of competitors' prices (stage 5) is helpful in determining the role of price in the marketing strategy. Competitors' prices—and the marketing mix variables that they emphasize—in part determine how important price will be to customers. Stage 6 consists of selecting a pricing policy—the guidelines for using price in the marketing mix. In stage 7, a method for calculating the price charged to customers is selected. Stage 8, determination of the final price, depends on environmental forces and marketers' understanding and use of a systematic approach to establishing prices.

Selection of pricing objectives

In setting prices, marketers should always begin by considering objectives. *Pricing objectives* are overall goals that describe the role of price in an organization's long-range plans. Since pricing objectives will influence decisions in most functional areas—including finance, accounting, and production—the objectives must be consistent with the organization's overall mission and purpose. Because of the many areas involved, a marketer often uses multiple pricing objectives. In this section, we will look at some typical pricing objectives, but do not consider them a complete list.

Survival

A fundamental pricing objective is to survive.[3] Most organizations will tolerate short-run losses, internal upheaval, and almost any other difficulties if they are necessary for survival. Since price is such a flexible and convenient variable to adjust, it sometimes is used to increase sales volume to levels that match the organization's expenses. For example, Continental Airlines, when faced with severe price competition and bankruptcy, was forced to offer discount fares that were significantly below competitors'. This tactic was designed to generate revenue and permit short-term survival. Passenger traffic increased dramatically and the chance of organizational survival improved.

Profit

Although businesses sometimes claim that their objective is to maximize profits for their owners, the objective of profit maximization is rarely operational, since its achievement is difficult to measure. Apple Computer, for instance, is more concerned with long-range survival in the computer industry than with maximizing profits in the short run. The chairman at Apple claims that building good computers is the most important objective at the company.[4] As a result of the difficulty in measurement, profit objectives tend to be set at levels that the owners and top-level decision makers view as "satisfactory." Specific profit objectives may be stated in terms of actual dollar amounts or in terms of percentage change relative to the profits of a previous period.

Return on investment

Pricing to attain a specified return on the company's investment is a profit-related pricing objective. Although General Motors prices for profit objectives, earnings have fluctuated dramatically between 1980 and 1985. Unfortunately, most pricing objectives based on return on investment are achieved by trial and error, because not all cost and revenue data needed to project the return on investment are available when prices are set.

Market share

Market share, which is a firm's sales in relation to total industry sales, is a very meaningful bench mark of success.[5] Many firms establish pricing objectives to maintain or increase market share. For example, a company's pricing objective might be to increase its market share from 22 to 28 percent within the next twelve months.

3. Joel Dean, *Managerial Economics* (Englewood Cliffs, N.J.: Prentice-Hall, 1950), p. 399.
4. Peter Nulty, "Apple's Bid to Stay in the Big Time," *Fortune,* Feb. 7, 1983, p. 36.
5. Martin L. Bell, *Marketing: Concepts and Strategy,* 3rd ed. (Boston: Houghton Mifflin, 1979), p. 398.

Maintaining or increasing market share need not involve industry sales growth or expansion. Remember that an organization can increase its market share even though sales for the total industry are decreasing. For example, in recent years Philip Morris has focused all marketing strategies toward increasing its market share in the cigarette industry. With increased awareness of the negative health consequences of smoking, there is the potential for declining sales in the industry as a whole.[6] On the other hand, an organization's sales volume may, in fact, increase while its market share within the industry decreases.

Cash flow

Some organizations set prices to recover cash as fast as possible. Financial managers are understandably interested in quickly recovering capital spent to develop products. This objective may have the support of the marketing manager who anticipates a short product life cycle.

While it may be acceptable in some situations, the use of cash flow and recovery as an objective oversimplifies the value of price in contributing to profits. A disadvantage of this pricing objective could be high prices, which might allow competitors with lower prices to gain a large share of the market. The introduction of an IBM personal computer, the PCjr, priced at $669, undermined the attempts of competitors to use only cash flow and recovery as their pricing objective.[7]

Status quo

In some instances, an organization may be in a favorable position and therefore—desiring nothing more—may set an objective of status quo. Status quo objectives can focus on several dimensions—maintaining a certain market share, meeting (but not beating) competitors' prices, achieving price stability, or maintaining a favorable public image. A status quo pricing objective can reduce a firm's risks by helping to stabilize demand for its products. The use of status quo pricing objectives sometimes deemphasizes price as a competitive tool, which can lead to a climate of nonprice competition in an industry. For example, makers of high quality bicycles deemphasize price in their marketing mix. Figure 14.4 illustrates a typical Fuji advertisement.

Product quality

A company might have the objective of product quality leadership in the market. This effort normally results in charging a high price to cover the high product quality and the high cost of research and development. For instance, Apple introduced the Lisa computer with a hefty $10,000 price tag. The computer was aimed at the office market and the company hoped that "ease of operation" would set it apart from the competition.[8]

6. "Why Cigarette Makers Are So Nervous," *Business Week,* Dec. 20, 1982, p. 55.
7. Susan Chace, "With Peanut, IBM Plans Attack on Low-Priced Computer Market," *Wall Street Journal,* Jan. 18, 1983, p. 33.
8. Peter Nulty, "Apple's Bid to Stay in the Big Time," *Fortune,* Feb. 7, 1983, p. 36.

Figure 14.4
Fuji deemphasizes
price as a competitive
tool
*Source: Created for Fuji
American by Franges
and Company, Mont-
clair, N.J. Original painting by Hajima Kato,
Paris.*

No. 1 in a limited edition of bicycling
racing art, available from your
authorized Fuji dealer.

Fuji builds twenty-two different
models of bicyles to meet the particular
needs of particular people. See them at
your authorized Fuji bicycle dealer's, or
send for our twenty-six page catalogue.

THE **Fuji.** CLASS

Because "good enough"
just isn't good enough.

©1982 Fuji America,
Div. of Toshoku America, Inc.
118 Bauer Dr., Oakland, NJ 07436

Assessment of the target market's evaluation of price and its ability to purchase

Although we generally assume that price is a significant issue for buyers, the importance of price depends on the type of product and the type of target market. For example, buyers, in general, are probably more sensitive to gasoline prices than to luggage prices. If we look specifically at gasoline as a product category, we find that some gasoline buyers are more price sensitive than others. Gasoline buyers who seek out independent service stations to pay lower prices are probably more price sensitive than those who use oil company credit cards to buy the higher-priced, major brands of gasoline. By assessing the target market's evaluation of price, a marketer is in a better position to know how much emphasis to place on price. The Stroh Brewery Company aims Schlitz and Old Milwaukee brand beers at two different target markets (see Figure 14.5). Consumers expect the price of Schlitz to be higher because of its advertised premium image. Old Milwaukee competes with lower-priced, regional beers and may appeal to consumers who feel their ability to purchase is limited and who are price conscious in selecting a brand of beer. Information about the target market's price evaluation may also aid a marketer in determining how far above the competition a firm can set its prices.

As pointed out in Chapter 2, the people who make up a market must have the ability to buy a product. Buyers must need a product, be willing to use their buying power, and have the authority (by law or social custom) to buy. Their ability to buy, like their evaluation of price, has direct consequences for marketers. The ability to purchase involves such resources

Figure 14.5 The Stroh Brewery Company aims at different markets
Source: © The Stroh Brewery Company, Detroit, MI.

as money, credit, wealth, and other products that could be traded in an exchange. Understanding the purchasing power of customers and knowing how important a product is to them in comparison with other products helps marketers to assess the target market's evaluation of price correctly. The Application on page 432 illustrates off-price retailers' correct assessment that the value-conscious consumers will look for quality at discount prices.

Determination of demand

Determining the demand for a product is the responsibility of marketing research. Techniques for estimating sales potential—the quantity of a product that could be sold during a specific period—are practical approaches to understanding demand. (Chapter 2 described such techniques as surveys, time series analyses, correlation methods, and market tests.) Sales estimates are helpful in establishing the relationship between a product's price and the quantity demanded.

Labels such as Bill Blass, Calvin Klein, and Izod are found on clothes sold in fine department stores. At the same time, many of these brand names are also being sold for 20 to 70 percent less in off-price stores. These off-price stores are providing keen competition for department stores.

Off-price stores buy their goods, exclusively designer labels and brand names, at less than wholesale prices and sell them at less than retail prices. Ordinary discounters, in contrast, buy goods at regular wholesale prices but sell them at lower than the usual markup. The off-price retailers buy irregulars, overruns, cancelled orders, and end-of-season goods, sometimes at a quarter to a fifth of their wholesale prices. Off-price sales currently account for 6 percent of all clothing sold but are expected to reach 20 to 25 percent by the end of the next decade.

Compared with off-price retailers, department stores offer greater assortments in more luxurious atmospheres, which increases their cost structures. Thus, they do not have the pricing flexibility of off-price retailers. The success of off-price retailing has led many traditional retailers to start off-price chains.

Off-price retailers illustrate the successful assessment of a target market's evaluation of price and of its ability to purchase. These retailers are responding to a growing number of consumers who are increasingly value conscious, who rely on brand names for quality, and who are not willing to spend more than is necessary.

Source: Based on Ann M. Morrison, "The Upshot of Off-price," *Fortune,* June 13, 1983, pp. 122–129.

The demand curve

For most products, the quantity demanded goes up as the price goes down; and as price goes up, quantity demanded goes down. There is an inverse relationship between price and quantity demanded. As long as buyers' needs, ability (purchasing power), willingness, and authority to buy remain stable, and as long as environmental situations remain constant, this fundamental inverse relationship will continue.

Figure 14.6 illustrates the effect of one variable—price—on the quantity demanded. As you can see, the classic *demand curve* (D_1) is a line sloping downward to the right, showing that as price falls, quantity demanded will increase. Demand also depends on other factors in the marketing mix, among them product quality, promotion, and distribution. An improvement in any of these factors may cause a shift to, say, demand curve D_2. In such a case, an increased quantity (Q_2) will be sold at the same price (P).

Figure 14.6
Demand curve illustrating the price-quantity relationship and an increase in demand

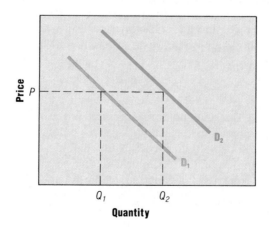

Colorplay
*Jean Schlumberger's winning eighteen karat gold and
enameled bracelets are available exclusively at Tiffany's.*

TIFFANY & CO.

DALLAS, GALLERIA · 13350 DALLAS PARKWAY · 75240 · (214) 458-2800 **HOUSTON**, THE GALLERIA · 5015 WESTHEIMER ROAD · 77056 · (713) 626-0220

There are many types of demand, and not all will assume the classic demand curve shown in Figure 14.6. Prestige products—such as selected perfumes, cosmetics, and jewelry—seem to sell better at high prices than at low ones. For example, the gold and enameled bracelets shown in Figure 14.7 are known to be expensive and prestigious. In fact, these bracelets are desirable partly because their expense makes their owners feel elite. If the price fell drastically and many people owned one, these bracelets would lose some of their appeal. The demand curve in Figure 14.8 shows the relationship between price and quantity for prestige products; demand is greater, not less, at higher prices. For a certain range—from bottom to middle—the quantity demanded (Q_1) goes up to Q_2 when price is increased from P_1 to P_2. After a point, however, raising the price backfires. If the price of a product goes too high, the quantity demanded goes down. In other words, if the price goes even higher, from P_2 to P_3, quantity demanded goes back down from Q_2 to Q_1.

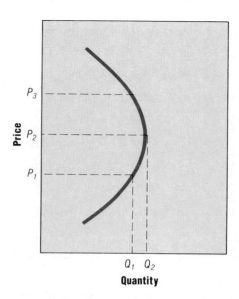

Demand fluctuations

Changes in buyers' attitudes, other components of the marketing mix, and uncontrollable environmental factors can influence demand. Although demand fluctuates unpredictably, some organizations have adjusted to demand fluctuations by correlating demand for a specific product to demand for the total industry or to some other economic variable. If a brand maintains a fairly constant market share, its sales can be estimated as a percentage of industry sales.

Determining elasticity of demand

To this point, we have discussed how marketers identify the target market's evaluation of price and its ability to purchase and examine demand to learn whether price is related to quantity inversely or directly. The next stage in the process is to determine elasticity of demand. *Elasticity of demand* (see Figure 14.9) is the relative responsiveness of changes in quantity demanded to changes in price. The percentage of change in quantity demanded caused by a percentage change in price is much greater for elastic demand than for inelastic demand. For a product such as electricity, demand is relatively inelastic. When its price is increased, say from P_1 to P_2, quantity demanded goes down only a little, from Q_1 to Q_2. For products such as recreational vehicles, demand is relatively elastic. When price rises sharply, from P'_1 to P'_2, quantity demanded goes down a great deal, from Q'_1 to Q'_2.

If marketers can determine *price elasticity,* then setting a price is much easier. By analyzing total revenues as prices change, marketers can determine whether a product is price elastic. Total revenue is price times quantity. For example, ten thousand rolls of wallpaper sold in one year at a price of $10 per roll equals $100,000 of total revenue. If demand is *elastic,* a change in price causes an opposite change in total revenue; an increase in price will decrease total revenue, and a decrease in price will increase total revenue. An *inelastic* demand results in a parallel change in total rev-

Figure 14.9
Elasticity of demand

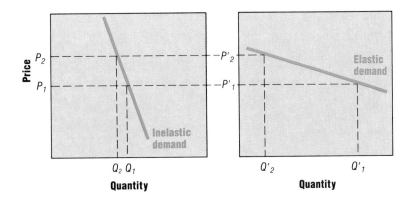

enue; an increase in price will increase total revenue, and a decrease in price will decrease total revenue. The following formula gives the price elasticity of demand:

$$\text{Price elasticity of demand} = \frac{\%\text{ change in quantity demanded}}{\%\text{ change in price}}$$

For example, if demand falls by 8 percent when a seller raises the price by 2 percent, the price elasticity of demand is −4 (the negative sign indicating the inverse relationship between price and demand). If demand falls by 2 percent when price is increased by 4 percent, then elasticity is −½. The less elastic the demand, the more beneficial for the seller to raise the price.

Marketers cannot base prices solely on elasticity considerations. They must also examine the costs associated with different volumes and see what happens to profits. Products without available substitutes and for which there is a strong need perceived by consumers usually have inelastic demand. In the past, for example, there were few substitutes for sugar in the short run, and so the demand for sugar was inelastic. In the long run, however, the demand became more elastic as more people came to use sugar substitutes such as corn syrup, aspartame (NutraSweet), and synthetic sweeteners like saccharin.

Analysis of demand, cost, and profit relationships

Having looked at the role demand plays in setting prices and at various costs and their relationships, we will go on to examine the relationships among demand, cost, and profit. To stay in business, a company has to set prices that cover all its costs. To help set prices, there are two approaches to understanding demand, cost, and profit relationships: marginal analysis and breakeven analysis. Before exploring these two approaches, we will identify several different types of costs.

Types of costs

Costs are associated with the production of any good or service. To determine the costs of production, it is necessary to distinguish fixed costs from variable costs. *Fixed costs* do not vary with changes in the number of units produced or sold. The cost of renting a factory, for example, does not change because production increases from one shift to two shifts a day or because twice as much wallpaper is sold. Rent may go up, but not because

Table 14.1 Costs and their relationships

(1) Quantity	(2) Fixed Cost	(3) Average Fixed Cost (2) ÷ (1)	(4) Average Variable Cost	(5) Average Total Cost (3 + 4)	(6) Total Cost (5) × (1)	(7) Marginal Cost
1	$40	$40.00	$20.00	$60.00	$ 60	
						$10
2	40	20.00	15.00	35.00	70	
						5
3	40	13.33	11.67	25.00	75	
						15
4	40	10.00	12.50	22.50	90	
						20
5	40	8.00	14.00	22.00	110	
						30
6	40	6.67	16.67	23.33	140	
						40
7	40	5.71	20.00	25.71	180	

the factory has doubled production or revenue. *Average fixed cost* is the fixed cost per unit produced. It is calculated by dividing the fixed costs by the number of units produced.

Variable costs do vary directly with changes in the number of units produced or sold. The wages for a second shift and the cost of twice as much paper and dye are extra costs that occur when production is doubled. Variable costs are usually constant per unit; that is, twice as many workers and twice as much material produces twice as many rolls of wallpaper. *Average variable cost* is the variable cost per unit produced. It is calculated by dividing the variable costs by the number of units produced.

Total cost is the sum of fixed costs and variable costs. *Marginal cost (MC)* is the extra cost a firm incurs when it produces one more unit of a product. The *average total cost* is the sum of the average fixed cost and the average variable cost. Table 14.1 illustrates various costs and their relationships. Notice that the average fixed cost declines as the output increases. The average variable cost follows a U-shape, as does the average total cost. Since the average total cost continues to fall after the average variable cost begins to rise, its lowest point is at a higher level of output than that of the average variable cost. The average total cost is lowest at 5 units at a cost of $22, whereas the average variable cost is lowest at 3 units at a cost of $11.67. Marginal cost equals average total cost at the latter's lowest level, between 5 and 6 units of production. Average total cost decreases as long as the marginal cost is less than the average total cost, and it increases when marginal cost rises above average total cost.

Marginal analysis   Marginal analysis involves examining what happens when something is changed by one unit. *Marginal revenue (MR),* therefore, is the change in total revenue that occurs when a firm sells an additional unit of a product.

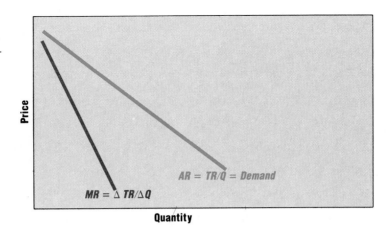

Figure 14.10
Typical marginal revenue and average revenue relationships

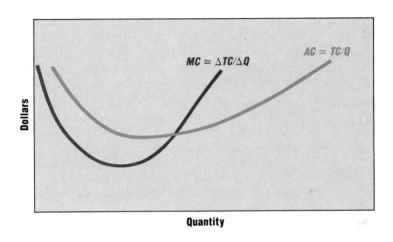

Figure 14.11
Typical marginal cost and average cost relationships

Marginal revenue is depicted in Figure 14.10. The relationship between marginal cost and average cost is shown in Figure 14.11.

The vast majority of firms in the United States face downward sloping demand curves for their products. In other words, they must lower their prices to sell additional units. This situation means that each additional product sold will provide less revenue to the firm than did the previous unit sold. MR would then be less than average revenue, as shown in Figure 14.10. Eventually, MR will reach zero and the sale of additional units would merely hurt the firm.

Before the firm can determine if a unit makes a profit, though, it must know its cost as well as its revenue, since profit equals revenue minus cost. If MR is a unit's addition to revenue and MC is a unit's addition to cost, then MR minus MC tells us whether the unit is profitable or not. Table 14.2 illustrates the relationships between price, quantity sold, total revenue, marginal revenue, marginal cost, and total cost. It indicates where maximum profits are possible at various combinations of price and cost.

Profit is maximized where the MC = MR (see Table 14.2). In this table MC = MR at 4 units. The best price is $37.50 and the profit is $60. Up to

Table 14.2   Marginal analysis: method of obtaining maximum profit-producing price

(1) Price	(2) Quantity Sold	(3) Total Revenue (1) × (2)	(4) Marginal Revenue	(5) Marginal Cost	(6) Total Cost	(7) Profit (3) − (6)
$57.00	1	$ 57	$57	—	$ 60	− $ 3
55.00	2	110	53	$10	70	40
40.00	3	120	10	5	75	45
37.50[a]	4	150	15	15	90	60[b]
32.40	5	162	12	20	110	52
27.80	6	167	5	30	140	37
23.40	7	164	− 3	40	180	24

[a]Best price   [b]Maximum profit

this point, the additional revenue generated from an extra unit of sale exceeds the additional total cost. Beyond this point, the additional cost of another unit sold exceeds the additional revenue generated, and profits decrease. If the price were based on minimum average total cost—$22 (Table 14.1)—it would have resulted in less profit. A profit of only $52 (Table 14.2) for 5 units at a price of $32.40.

Graphically combining Figures 14.10 and 14.11 into Figure 14.12 shows that any unit for which MR exceeds MC is adding to a firm's profits, while any unit for which MC exceeds MR is subtracting from a firm's profits. The firm, therefore, should produce at the point where MR equals MC, because this is the most profitable level of production.

This economic concept gives the impression—which is false—that pricing can be highly precise. If revenue (demand) and cost (supply) remained constant, then prices could be set for maximum profits. In practice, however, cost and revenue are constantly changing.

Between 1982 and 1983, Japanese manufacturers of motorcycles such as Honda and Yamaha overestimated the demand for their products in the United States. As a result, they found themselves with a 12- to 18-month inventory. Price cutting by dealers and manufacturer rebates to both dealers and consumers were used to decrease the supply. Also, imports were reduced dramatically. The massive inventories and discount prices threatened to destroy the one remaining American motorcycle manufacturer—Harley-Davidson. Acting on a recommendation of the U.S. International Trade Commission, the president increased tariffs on imported heavyweight motorcycles (directly competitive with Harley-Davidson). The tariff resulted in a 25-percent increase in the prices of larger motorcycles in an already glutted market. All of these events were clogging the inventory pipeline in a market where supply, demand, and price were not properly coordinated.[9]

The competitive tactics of other firms or government action, as in the case of the motorcycle industry, can quickly undermine expectations of revenue. Thus, the economic concept we have discussed here is only a

9. Bob Woods, "Wheeling and Dealing," *Sales and Marketing Management,* May 16, 1983, pp. 43–50.

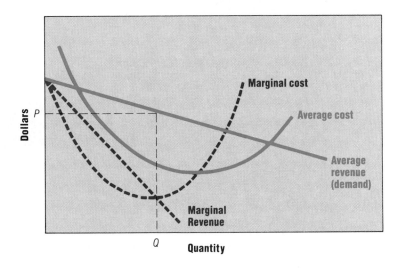

model from which to work. It offers little help in pricing new products before costs and revenues are established. On the other hand, in setting prices of existing products—especially in competitive situations—most marketers can benefit by understanding marginal cost and marginal revenue relationships.

Breakeven analysis

The point at which costs of producing a product equal revenue made from selling the product is the **breakeven point**. If a wallpaper manufacturer has total costs for one year that amount to $100,000 and the same year it sells $100,000 worth of wallpaper, then the company has broken even.

Figure 14.13 illustrates the relationships of costs, revenue, profits, and losses involved in determining the breakeven point. Knowing the number of units necessary to break even is important in setting the price. If a product priced at $100 per unit has an average variable cost of $60 per unit, then the contribution to fixed costs is $40. If total fixed costs are $120,000, here is the way to determine the breakeven point in units:

$$\text{Breakeven point} = \frac{\text{fixed costs}}{\text{per unit contribution to fixed costs}}$$

$$= \frac{\text{fixed costs}}{\text{price} - \text{variable costs}}$$

$$= \frac{\$120,000}{\$40}$$

$$= 3,000 \text{ units}$$

To calculate the breakeven point in terms of dollar sales volume, all one need do is to multiply the breakeven point in units by the price per unit. In the example above, the breakeven point in terms of dollar sales volume would be 3,000 (units) times $100, which would equal $300,000.

Figure 14.13
Determining the break-
even point

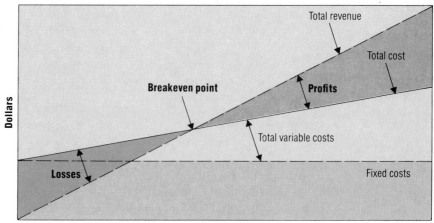

To use breakeven analysis effectively, a marketer should determine the breakeven point for each of several alternative prices. This determination allows the marketer to compare the effects on total revenue, total costs, and the breakeven point for each price under consideration. Although this comparative analysis may not tell the marketer exactly what price to charge, it will identify highly undesirable price alternatives that should definitely be avoided.

Breakeven analysis is simple and straightforward. It does assume, however, that the quantity demanded is basically fixed (inelastic), and the major task in setting prices is to recover costs. This analysis focuses more on how to break even than on how to achieve a pricing objective such as percentage of market share or return on investment. Marketing managers can use this concept to determine more accurately whether a product will achieve at least a breakeven volume. In other words, it is easier to answer the question ''Will we sell at least the minimum volume necessary to break even?'' than to answer the question ''What volume of sales will we expect to sell?''

In the next chapter, we will continue our discussion of price by examining specific policies, methods, and approaches to determining price. Also, we will examine special issues related to the pricing of industrial products.

Summary

Price is the value placed on what is exchanged to gain satisfaction or utility. In most market transactions purchasing power—income, credit, or wealth—is exchanged for some benefit. Barter, the trading of products, involves the exchange of two objects of value. The financial price or money paid for a product is the most widely used value assessment in our society. Financial prices facilitate efficient market exchanges because all products can be assigned a standard, comparable unit of value.

There are eight stages in the process of establishing prices. The first four of these stages—those discussed in this chapter—are (1) the selection of pricing objectives; (2) assessment of the target market's evaluation of price and its ability to purchase; (3) determination of demand; and (4) analysis of demand, cost, and profit relationships.

Pricing objectives are overall goals that describe the role of price in an organization's long-range plans. The broadest and most fundamental pricing objective is survival. Price is easily adjusted to increase sales volume or to combat competition so that the organization can stay alive. Profit objectives, which usually are stated in terms of sales dollar volume or percentage change, are normally set at a satisfactory level rather than at a level designed for profit maximization. A sales growth objective focuses on increasing the profit base by increasing sales volume. Pricing for return on investment has a specified profit as its objective. A pricing objective to maintain or increase market share implies that market position is linked to success. Other pricing objectives include cash flow and recovery, status quo, and product quality.

The second stage in establishing prices is an assessment of the target market's evaluation of price and its ability to purchase. By assessing the target market's evaluation of price, a marketer is in a better position to know how much emphasis to place on price. In addition, this information may aid the marketer in determining how far above the competition the firm can set its prices. Understanding the purchasing power of customers and knowing how important a product is to them in comparison with other products helps marketers to assess the target market's evaluation of price correctly.

In the third stage of setting prices, the organization must determine the demand for its product. The classic demand curve shows an inverse relationship between price and quantity demanded; as the price of the product decreases, the demand increases, and vice versa. In some cases, however, there is a direct positive relationship between price and quantity demanded, as in the case of prestige products, where demand increases as price increases. In setting prices, the organization must learn whether price is related to quantity inversely or directly. Next, elasticity of demand—the relative responsiveness of changes in quantity demanded to changes in price—must be determined. If marketers can determine price elasticity, then setting a price is much easier. The percentage of change in quantity demanded caused by a percentage change in price is much greater for products with elastic demand than for products with inelastic demand. If demand is elastic, a change in price causes an opposite change in total revenue. Inelastic demand results in a parallel change in total revenue when a product's price is changed.

The production of any product results in cost. Average fixed cost is the fixed cost per unit produced. Average variable cost is the variable cost per unit produced. Average total cost is the sum of average fixed cost and average variable cost.

Analysis of demand, cost, and profit relationships, the fourth stage of the process, can be accomplished through marginal analysis or breakeven analysis. Marginal analysis combines the demand curve with a firm's costs to develop an optimum price for maximum profit. This optimum price is the point at which marginal cost—the cost associated with producing one more unit of the product—equals marginal revenue. Marginal revenue is the change in total revenue that occurs when one additional unit of the product is sold. In reality, an organization's cost and revenue relationships are difficult to determine. Therefore, marginal analysis serves only as a model. It offers little help in pricing new products before costs and revenues are established.

The point at which the costs of producing a product equal the revenue made from selling the product is the breakeven point. Knowing the number of units necessary to break even is important in setting the price. To use breakeven analysis effectively, a marketer should determine the breakeven point for each of several alternative prices. This determination makes it possible to compare the effects on total revenue, total costs, and the breakeven point for each price under consideration. Breakeven analysis identifies undesirable price alternatives that should definitely be avoided. This approach assumes, however, that the quantity demanded is basically fixed and that the major task is to set prices to recover costs.

Important terms

Price	Fixed costs
Purchasing power	Average fixed cost
Barter	Variable costs
Pricing objectives	Average variable cost
Market share	Total cost
Demand curve	Marginal cost (MC)
Elasticity of demand	Average total cost
Price elasticity	Marginal revenue (MR)
Total revenue	Breakeven point

Discussion and review questions

1. What is the role of price in the marketing mix?
2. "Price is the exchange of money for something else." Is this statement correct?
3. Describe the price paid for the following services and benefits: (a) fire protection, (b) streets and parks, (c) clean water, (d) Red Cross assistance, and (e) birth control information distributed by a public health clinic.
4. Identify the eight stages that make up the process of establishing prices.
5. How does a pricing objective of sales growth and expansion differ from an objective to increase market share?
6. Why do most demand curves demonstrate an inverse relationship between price and quantity?
7. List the characteristics of products that have inelastic demand. Give several examples of such products.
8. Explain why optimum profits should occur when marginal cost equals marginal revenue.
9. The Chambers Company has just gathered estimates for doing a breakeven analysis for a new product. Variable costs are $7 a unit.

Additional plant will cost $48,000. The new product will be charged $18,000 a year for its share of general overhead. Advertising expenditures will be $80,000, and $55,000 will be spent on distribution. If the product sells for $12, what is the breakeven point in units? What is the breakeven point in dollar sales volume?

Case 14.1

Parsley Patch, Inc.[10]

Parsley Patch, Inc. was founded in Santa Rosa, California by two women who were looking for money to pay for graduate school. Like many food businesses, Parsley Patch, Inc. began in a home kitchen. From spices, herbs, and dried vegetables, one of the founders concocted salt-free seasonings that became an instant success with friends. With this initial success, the founders decided to aim for the retail consumer market. They positioned their products as high-price and high-quality for the affluent gourmet consumer.

About this time, many people were becoming sodium conscious and began to use salt substitutes (see Figure 14.14). Salt or sodium chloride has been medically linked to blood pressure in individuals who are prone to having high blood pressure. Dietary guidelines issued jointly by the U.S. Department of Agriculture and the Department of Health and Human Services advocate that all Americans should moderate their sodium intake.

Figure 14.14
Percentages of shoppers who use lists to avoid salt/sodium
Source: A.C. Nielsen, 1983 Nielsen Review of Retail Grocery Store Trends, *from survey sponsored by the FDA.*

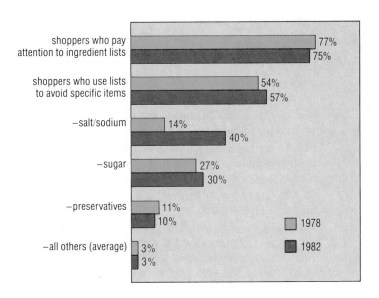

10. The facts in this case are from Sanford L. Jacobs, "A Dash of Cost-Control Savvy Helps Turn Spice Firm Around," *Wall Street Journal,* March 26, 1984, p. 25; "Salt and High Blood Pressure," *Consumer Reports,* Jan. 1984, pp. 17, 21; and "Progressive Grocer's Guide to Usage of Supermarket Products," *Progressive Grocer,* July 1983, p. 39.

Figure 14.15
Low or no sodium new
product introductions
*Source: A.C. Nielsen
Company,* 1983 Nielsen
Review of Retail Grocery
Store Trends.

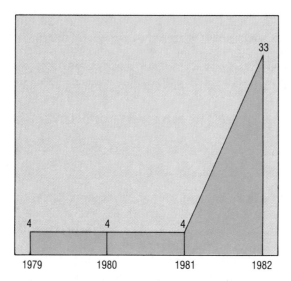

This sodium consciousness led to the introduction of many new brands of salt substitutes in a variety of grocery items (see Figure 14.15).

At the right time, in April 1981, Parsley Patch, Inc. introduced their six spice blends at a gourmet food show in San Francisco. They obtained several thousand dollars' worth of orders. Soon, the founders and their families were working six days, sixty hours a week to manufacture and ship the spices. Five employees were hired and operations expanded to a rented warehouse. The spices gained acceptance in hundreds of gourmet shops and department stores, even in exclusive stores like Neiman Marcus.

The retail price of Parsley Patch, Inc. spices was $4.15 per five-ounce jar, almost double that of rival products. Their wholesale price was $2.75. Pricing had become a crucial marketing mix variable as customers began to mention that the products were good but too expensive. The founders had not paid much attention to costs and pricing. They now took the advice of a consultant and began an inquiry into their products' cost components. They had been buying five-ounce jars at 70 cents a piece and they found that this variable cost could be reduced by using alternative four-ounce jars priced at 17 cents each. They also found that ordering ingredients in larger quantities and less frequently reduced the variable costs even further. The women then set a target gross margin (sales minus cost of goods sold), of 60 percent.

Parsley Patch, Inc. began sales forecasting and breakeven analysis. After considering all the costs and pricing objectives, the final prices were fixed. The wholesale price was fixed at $1.50 per four-ounce jar, and with a markup the retail price became a competitive $2.25. This lower price stimulated sales in health-food stores and facilitated the products' entry into supermarkets. In supermarkets, spices and seasonings are ranked eleventh among food items in terms of frequency of use by consumers. The company's sales began to climb to $700,000 a year and the company posted a profit.

Questions for discussion

1. Will the demand for this product be elastic or inelastic? Explain.
2. If Parsley Patch, Inc. had total variable costs of $1.03 per four-ounce jar and annual fixed costs of $200,000, what would be the breakeven point in units? In dollar sales volume?
3. If variable costs went up to $1.25 per four-ounce jar and annual fixed costs remained at $200,000, what would be the total costs per annum assuming sales of 500,000 units? Should prices be raised?

Case 14.2

How Domestic Compact Cars Are Priced[11]

The U.S. automobile industry has been combating increased competition from foreign automakers. A full 35 percent of the cars sold in the U.S. are imported compacts, and the percentage of imports sold in the U.S. has been as high as 45 percent of the compact market. Japanese cars make up almost 80 percent of all these imports. The 1983 Customer Satisfaction Index indicated that the overall gap between domestic and imported cars did not change for two consecutive years. Imports continued to account for over 85 percent of the above-average index ratings, while domestic cars accounted for nearly 67 percent of the below-average positions.

Pricing competition has been fierce in the automotive industry. The Japanese have a cost advantage of $1,700 or more per small car even after paying $500 for shipping and tariffs. A third of this cost advantage is attributed to cheaper labor and more efficient operations. U.S. automakers have tried to combat this cost advantage by reducing billions of dollars in overhead and by obtaining labor concessions on wages and benefits. Although these measures have cut the cost of building a subcompact by several hundred dollars, they still cannot match the Japanese advantage.

Detroit typically works out the cost of a car in a backward fashion. An automaker researches the market segment for which a new car is positioned about five years in advance. The price of competing models is checked, research is done to find out what features will be desired, and inflationary effects are calculated. All this results in a target price for the still undeveloped car. The company aims at a theoretical profit margin of at least 10 percent. Until the car is introduced, there is a constant shift between desired price and the cost of production. Ultimately, profit is dependent upon sales volume, true production costs, and the need to react to price changes by competition. The cash requirement to put a new small car into production in the U.S. is almost $2 billion. U.S. automakers attempt

11. The facts in this case are from "The All-American Small Car Is Fading," *Business Week,* March 12, 1984, pp. 88–95; Ralph E. Winter, "Rising Tide of Imports Continues To Frustrate U.S. Manufacturers," *Wall Street Journal,* Sept. 23, 1983, p. 35; "Why Detroit Can't Cut Prices," *Business Week,* March 1, 1982, pp. 110–111; and from Amal Nag, "To Build a Small Car GM Tries to Redesign Its Production System," *Wall Street Journal,* May 14, 1984, pp. 1, 12.

Table 14.3 How a small car's price increases from assembly line to showroom

Manufacturing		Overhead		Marketing	
Body	$ 688	Fixed Costs	$ 992	Dealer markup	$1,156
Transmission	112	Profit target	248		
Vehicle assembly	667	R&D special			
Engine	387	tooling	1,537		
Chassis	626				
Total	$2,480	*Total*	$2,777		
		Overall total	**$5,257**	**Overall total**	**$6,413**

Source: Adapted from data of Rath & Strong, Inc.

to break even within four to five years, whereas the Japanese stretch their payback period to eight years. Thus, to compete with the Japanese, domestic automakers will have to cut production costs by as much as $2,200 per car.

Table 14.3 illustrates how the price of a car increases as it moves from the assembly line to the dealer's showroom. The total cost of the car includes both fixed and variable costs incurred through the manufacturing process. The sticker price covers the total cost plus a profit markup by the manufacturer and another profit markup by the dealer.

Cost pressures have left Detroit with few choices short of abandoning the compact car market. General Motors cancelled plans to introduce a front-wheel-drive subcompact because research indicated that a front-wheel-drive replacement from Japan would cost $2,000 less. Foreign produced components are cheaper; and analysts predict that foreign-made auto parts will increase from 6 percent of the U.S. market in 1980 to 15 percent by 1990—a business worth $4 billion a year. General Motors is attempting to redesign its basic production system by introducing modular construction instead of the assembly line and by using intelligent robots to reduce labor costs. The effort has been named "Project Saturn" after the space program that was developed to overcome the Russians early lead in space.

American car manufacturers can benefit by either buying their compact cars from Japanese producers or building them in the U.S. using designs and major components supplied by foreign partnerships. American Motors, for example, through a joint venture with Renault, produced the Alliance. American Motors invested $200 million, which was a tenth of the cost of producing the car on its own. Compact car ventures appeal to foreign manufacturers as they increasingly fear legislative measures that might affect imports into the U.S. Some manufacturers, such as Honda and Nissan of Japan, have set up manufacturing facilities in the U.S. Others have set up joint ventures with U.S. manufacturers, such as Toyota has with General Motors.

Questions for discussion

1. Price alterations are frequently the easiest changes in the marketing mix for competitors to match. Is this a problem for domestic compact cars? Why or why not?
2. Should U.S. automakers increase their pay-back period to eight years to match what Japanese manufacturers have been doing? How would this affect the breakeven point of U.S. automakers?
3. What pricing objectives should domestic compact automakers utilize?

15

Setting Prices

Objectives

To gain some insights into analyzing competitive prices.

To learn about different types of pricing policies.

To examine the major kinds of pricing methods.

To understand that a systematic approach to pricing should determine final price.

To explore selected issues regarding the pricing of industrial products.

Lower prices seem destined to become permanent in the California wine industry. The 1970s was a period of increasing demand as yearly per capita consumption rose to 3.1 gallons. However, after a decade of 10-percent average annual growth, table-wine shipments have flattened out and most California vintners are afflicted by overcapacity. New grape plantings of 153,000 acres in the 1970s, new technologies, and new wineries broke all production records, and prices plummeted. For example, Gallo dropped the price of offers for prime Cabernet Sauvignon grapes from $1,000 to about $650 per ton. Tons of grapes were not picked and premium grape prices will probably continue to fall.

Although per capita wine consumption may increase slightly by 1990, the main problem is relatively flat demand and severe competition in a glutted marketplace. To compound the problem, more imported wines are pouring in from countries as diverse as Yugoslavia, Spain, Algeria, and Argentina, along with the traditional European wines from France and Italy.

American producers have reacted, offering the deepest discounts in memory. A price war is under way among high-volume vintners whose chief products are so-called generic wines—blends sold under such names as Mountain Red and Chablis. Prices of magnum-size jugs have plunged by half; in major food stores, for instance, jug prices have dropped from $5.50 or $6 to less than $3.[1]

Establishing prices and altering them has a definite impact on a firm's marketing mix. It can influence the responses of buyers, resellers, and competitors. In the last chapter we examined the first four stages of establishing prices. Here we examine the last four: analysis of competitors' prices, selection of a pricing policy, development of a pricing method, and determination of a specific price. We also present several issues dealing with such industrial-market pricing practices as discounts, geographic pricing, and price discrimination.

The actual task of pricing falls distinctly in the domain of marketing, because pricing requires creative judgement and a keen awareness of buyers' motivations. Awareness of who the buyers are, why they buy, and how they make their purchase decisions is helpful in determining price. The recognition that buyers differ in these dimensions and are quite diverse is illustrated by Ford Motor Company's Mustang automobile. The Mustang was not designed to be a sports car with all the preconceptions of what a sports car "should be" and then priced to cover costs and provide a target return. Instead, Ford discovered through extensive research that a market segment existed that valued sportiness in a car but was unwilling

1. Gilbert Sewall, "Trouble for California Wine Makers," *Fortune,* April 18, 1983, pp. 55–56.

to pay the price for a sports car. The Mustang was designed to be sufficiently sporty to satisfy this segment, but without those elements of a sports car that would have driven its price out of reach. Ford's pricing strategy was buyer-oriented and very successful.[2]

Evaluation of competitors' prices

The Application on the next page illustrates the important role of price in the competitive environment of the airline industry. In most cases, a marketer is in a better position to establish prices when he or she knows the prices charged for competing brands. Learning competitors' prices may be a regular function of marketing research. Some grocery and department stores, for example, have full-time comparative shoppers who systematically collect data on prices. Companies may also purchase price lists, sometimes weekly, from syndicated marketing research services.

Becoming aware of competitors' prices is not always easy, especially in producer and reseller markets. Competitors' price lists are often closely guarded. Even if a marketer has access to competitive price lists, these lists may not reflect the actual prices at which competitive products are sold. The actual prices may be established through negotiation.

Awareness of the prices charged for competing brands can be very important for a marketer. Marketers in an industry in which nonprice competition prevails need competitive price information to ensure that their organization's prices are the same as competitors' prices. In some instances, an organization's prices are designed to be slightly above competitors' prices to give its products an exclusive image. Another company may employ price as a competitive tool and attempt to price its brand below competing brands. When IBM launched its PCjr, the product had a powerful logo (IBM) representing quality, reliability, and good service, and the base list price was only $669. This price is one-third of the original IBM PC's price. Industry observers estimate 1 million units to be sold in 1985. A key marketing variable that made the PCjr attractive to consumers was its price. Apple II sales may be hurt initially but could increase if PCjrs are stocked insufficiently to meet demand.[3]

Selection of a pricing policy

A *pricing policy* is a guiding philosophy or course of action designed to influence and determine pricing decisions. Pricing policies set guidelines for achieving pricing objectives. They are an important component of an overall marketing strategy. In general, pricing policies should answer this recurring question: How will price be used as a variable in the marketing mix? This question may relate to (1) introduction of new products, (2) competitive situations, (3) government pricing regulations, (4) economic conditions, or (5) implementation of pricing objectives.

Pricing policies relate to price setting in practice. They help marketers to solve the practical problems of establishing prices. Let us examine some of the most common pricing policies.

2. Thomas Nagle, "Pricing as Creative Marketing," *Business Horizons,* July–Aug. 1983, pp. 14–19.
3. Anne B. Fisher, "Winners (and Losers) from IBM's PCjr," *Fortune,* Nov. 28, 1983, pp. 44–48.

Application

Airlines Use Price Differently

Unlike the auto, steel, and electronics companies, which are competing with foreign firms, the airline industry faces keen domestic competition. The new entrants into this industry are small carriers that have lower costs. These carriers have much lower wage rates; their pilots, for example, are younger and have less seniority than the high-salaried pilots of some major airlines like Delta, Eastern, or US AIR. The smaller airlines also purchase used aircraft and crowd their planes with more seats.

People Express is the fastest growing airline in the history of aviation. The company has the lowest expenses per available seat-mile and the highest load factor. The load factor expresses with a percentage the portion of all available seats that are filled with paying customers. For example, People Express' load factor has been 84 percent compared to a 60-percent average for the airline industry. People Express achieves the high load factor through cut-rate fares and no-frills service. Passengers pay for snacks and drinks on board and even to have luggage checked. But fares are as low as $25 between Newark and Boston at off-peak times.

High labor costs associated with a full-service airline service was a major factor that drove Continental Airlines to bankruptcy. The airline negotiated wage and work-rule concessions to keep on flying. Continental, after filing for bankruptcy, offered $49 fares for the first four days on any nonstop flight on its domestic route system. This offer resulted in full (100-percent load factor) flights. Continental then raised the fare to $75 on all its flights for the next three weeks. By engaging in price wars to gain customers, Continental used price to change its marketing strategy. In response, Frontier Airlines, a competitor, promptly offered special $69 tickets for a limited number of seats on all overlapping routes. Later, United Airlines, another competitor, cut its fares in sixty of its Western markets to counter Continental and Frontier.

On the other hand, Braniff Airlines, reorganized by the Hyatt Corporation, launched its air service in 1984 as a full-fare, low-cost airline that offers business passengers excellent service and beautiful cabin interiors. Braniff has no plans for discount fares. Therefore, with a 48-percent load factor it can make a profit.

Airline fares illustrate a radical shift in pricing from pricing based on cost to pricing based on competition. Establishing prices and altering them has a definite impact on the future of a firm's marketing mix. It is obvious that People Express and Braniff use price differently to help formulate their respective marketing strategies. The right price decision can make a difference between survival and extinction in an environment as competitive as the airline industry.

Source: Based on Lucien Rhodes, "That Daring Young Man and His Flying Machines," *Inc.*, Jan. 1984, pp. 42–52; Roy Rowan, "An Airline Boss Attacks Sky-High Wages," *Fortune*, Jan. 9, 1984, pp. 66–73; John Bussey, "United Airlines Is Cutting Fares in West Markets," *Wall Street Journal*, Feb. 15, 1984, p. 6; and "Braniff Is Coming Back to Some Tough Competition," *Business Week*, Feb. 27, 1984, pp. 37, 41.

Pioneer pricing policies

Pioneer pricing—setting the base price for a new product—is a necessary part of formulating a marketing strategy. The base price is easily adjusted (in the absence of government price controls), and its establishment is one of the most fundamental decisions in the marketing mix. The base price can be set high to recover development costs quickly or to provide a reference point for developing discount prices to different market segments.

When they set base prices, marketers also consider how quickly competitors will enter the market, whether they will mount a very strong campaign upon entry, and the effect of their entry on the development of primary demand. If competitors will enter quickly, with considerable marketing force and with limited effect on the primary demand, then a firm may wish to adopt a base price that will discourage their entry.

Price skimming

This pioneer approach provides the most flexible introductory base price. Demand tends to be inelastic in the introductory stage of the product life cycle. *Price skimming* is charging the highest possible price that buyers who most desire the product will pay.

Price skimming can provide several benefits, especially when a product is in the introductory stage of its life cycle. A skimming policy can generate much-needed initial cash flows to help offset sizable developmental costs. The manufacturer of the Kodak disc camera, for example, used a skimming introductory price to help defray large development costs. Price skimming protects the marketer from problems that arise when the price is set too low to cover costs. When a firm introduces a product, its production capacity may be limited. A skimming price can help to keep demand consistent with a firm's production capabilities.

Penetration price

A *penetration price* is a lower price designed to penetrate the market and produce a larger unit sales volume. When introducing a product, a marketer sometimes uses a penetration price to gain a large market share quickly. This approach places the marketer in a less flexible position than price skimming, because it is more difficult to raise a penetration price than it is to lower or discount a skimming price. It is not unusual for a firm to use a penetration price after having skimmed the market with a higher price. Atari used price penetration by extending the memory and lowering price of its home computers, as illustrated in Figure 15.1.

Penetration pricing can be especially beneficial when marketers suspect that competitors could enter the market easily. A penetration price can help in two ways. First, if the penetration price allows one marketer to gain a large market share quickly, competitors might be discouraged from entering the market. Second, entering the market may be less attractive to competitors when a penetration price is used, since the lower per unit price results in lower per unit profit; in turn, this may cause competitors to view the market as not being especially lucrative.

In contrast, environmental conditions can cause a penetration price to become less attractive to consumers. Private-label and generic-brand food products are promoted primarily on the basis of a penetration price advantage. However, their market share has been declining in recent years. An improving economy and an easing of food-price increases are two main reasons given for the decrease in the share of these lower-priced products. This example illustrates that this pricing policy is not always effective in a dynamic environment.[4]

A penetration price is particularly appropriate when demand is highly elastic—meaning that target market members would purchase the product

4. *Frozen Food Age,* November 1983, pp. 1, 32.

if it were priced at the penetration level, but few would buy the item if it were priced above the penetration price. A marketer should consider using a penetration price when a lower price would result in longer production runs, increasing production significantly and reducing the firm's per unit production costs.

Psychological pricing

Psychological pricing is designed to encourage purchases that are based on emotional reactions rather than on rational responses. It is used most often at the retail level. Psychological pricing has limited use in pricing industrial products.

Odd-even pricing

Odd-even pricing assumes that more of a product will be sold at $99.99 than at $100.00. Supposedly, customers will think, or at least tell friends, that the product is a bargain—not $100, mind you, but $99 plus a few insignificant pennies. Also, customers are supposed to think that the store could

Figure 15.2
The five-cent candy
bar of yesteryear
*Source: Courtesy of Her-
shey Foods Corporation.*

have charged $100 but instead cut the price to the last cent, to $99.99 or $99.98 (which is also an odd price, though an even number). Some claim, too, that certain types of customers are more attracted by odd prices than by even ones. Odd prices seem to have little genuine effect on sales, except that they do force the cashier to use the cash register. The daily newspaper is full of examples of odd prices. In fact, even prices are far more unusual today than odd prices.

A second approach to odd-even pricing is based on the attractiveness of the numbers themselves. It is believed that certain numbers are physically more attractive to people. Thus, the symmetrical 8 could be used in the price 88 cents. This is believed by some to be a better price than, say, 77 cents or 44 cents, numbers that have harsh edges and points.

Another pricing theory based on this concept has its roots in the well-known book *The Naked Ape.* Author Desmond Morris declares that human beings are attracted to round figures and letters and that a sign that uses the word *good,* for example, will get more attention than one that uses pinched letters such as *l, f,* or *w.* This is so, Morris writes, since human beings are driven to glance at open figures such as "O" because the primal self is ever alert for eyes that might belong to a predator. Thus, a sign that advertises GOOD FOOD should get more attention than one that reads EAT, and a price of $10.01 should be more visible than one of $9.77.

Customary pricing

In *customary pricing,* certain goods are priced primarily on the basis of tradition. Recent economic uncertainties have made most prices fluctuate fairly widely, but the classic example of the customary or traditional price is the candy bar. For scores of years, the price of a candy bar was 5 cents, as shown in Figure 15.2. A new candy bar would have had to be something

For a full color lithograph, 18″ x 19″, of Ken Davies "Flying Wild Turkey," send $5.00 to Box 929-XX, N.Y., N.Y. 10268.

An Unforgettable Experience

To see a Wild Turkey rising from the forest floor is an awesome sight no man is likely to forget. The bird's wing-beats resound like thunder claps, and its feathers fan out in grand display.

The Wild Turkey is the largest native bird capable of flight and an apt symbol for America's greatest native whiskey—Wild Turkey.

WILD TURKEY / 101 PROOF / 8 YEARS OLD
Austin, Nichols Distilling Co., Lawrenceburg, Kentucky / 1981

very special to sell for more than a nickel. This price was so sacred that manufacturers increased or decreased the size of the candy bar itself rather than change its price as chocolate prices fluctuated. Now, of course, the nickel candy bar has disappeared, probably forever. However, a new customary price has emerged. Most candy bars now sell at this new, and higher, customary price.

Prestige pricing

In *prestige pricing,* prices are set at an artificially high level to provide prestige or a quality image. Pharmacists report that some consumers complain if a prescription does not cost enough. Apparently, some consumers associate a drug's price with its potency. Consumers may also associate quality in beer with high price.

Prestige pricing is used when a higher price is consistent with buyers' attitudes toward the expected cost of a product. Wild Turkey, for instance, is one of the most expensive bourbons on the market. If the producer lowered the price dramatically, it would be inconsistent with the perceived image of the product (see Figure 15.3).

Figure 15.4
Price lining

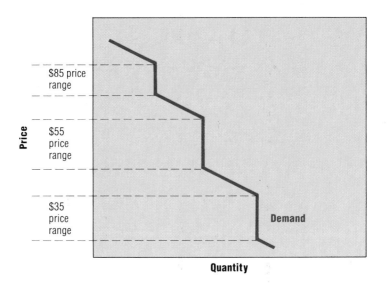

Price

$85 price
range

$55
price
range

$35
price
range

Demand

Quantity

Price lining

When an organization sets a limited number of prices for selected groups or lines of merchandise, it is using a form of psychological pricing called *price lining*. A retailer may have various styles and brands of men's shirts that sell for $15. Another line of shirts may sell for $22. Price lining simplifies consumers' decision making by holding constant one key variable in the final selection of style and brand.

The basic assumption in price lining is that the demand is inelastic for various groups or sets of products. If the prices are attractive, customers will concentrate their purchases without responding to slight changes in price. Thus, if a women's dress shop carries dresses priced at $85, $55, and $35, the store's management is indicating its belief that these are "good" prices and that a drop to, say, $83, $53, and $34 would not attract many more sales. The "space" between the prices of $55 and $35, however, can stir change in consumer response. With price lining, the demand curve looks like a series of steps, as shown in Figure 15.4.

Professional pricing   *Professional pricing* is used by persons who have great skill or experience in a particular field or activity. Professionals who provide such products as medical services feel that their fees (prices) should not relate directly to the time and involvement in specific cases; rather, a standard fee is charged regardless of the problems involved in performing the job (see Figure 15.5). Some doctors' and lawyers' fees are prime examples: $35 for a checkup, $400 for an appendectomy, and $199 for a divorce.

The concept of professional pricing carries with it the idea that professionals have an "ethical" responsibility not to overcharge unknowing customers. In some situations a seller can charge customers a high price and continue to sell many units of the product. Medicine offers several examples. If a diabetic requires one insulin treatment per day to survive, the individual will buy that treatment whether its price is $1 or $10. In fact, the patient surely would purchase the treatment even if the price went higher.

FREE CONSULTATION
COMMON SENSE FEES
ALFORD & BERTRAND
Attorneys at Law
Divorce......................$199
24-hour Divorce $450
Bankruptcy $199
Simple Wills.................$50
Personal Injury Claims

OFFICES IN:
BOSTON
WATERTOWN - QUINCY

926-8800

Open weekdays 'til 8 pm
Saturdays 10 am to 3 pm

In these situations sellers could charge exorbitant fees. Drug companies claim that despite their positions of strength in this regard, they charge "ethical" prices rather than what the traffic will bear.

Promotional pricing

This chapter focuses on price as an ingredient in the marketing mix, and price often is coordinated with promotion. The two variables sometimes are so interrelated that the pricing policy is promotion oriented.

Price leaders

Sometimes a few products are priced below the usual markup or below cost. If some products are sold at less than cost, they are *price leaders;* management hopes that sales of regularly purchased merchandise will rise and increase sales volume and profits. This type of pricing is used most often in supermarkets and department stores to attract consumers by giving them an impression of low prices.

Special-event pricing

To increase sales volume, many organizations coordinate price with advertising for seasonal or special situations. *Special-event pricing* involves advertised sales or price cutting to increase revenue or lower costs. If the pricing objective is survival, then special sales events may be designed to generate the operating capital necessary. Special-event pricing also entails coordination of production, scheduling, storage, and physical distribution. Whenever there is a sales lag, a special sales event may be launched.

Superficial discounting

Superficial discounting, sometimes called "Was-Is pricing" in the trade, is fictitious comparative pricing. "Was $259, Is $199" is an example. The Federal Trade Commission and the Better Business Bureau discourage these deceptive markdowns. Legitimate discounts are not questioned, of course, but when a pricing policy gives only the illusion of a discount, it is unethical and, in some states, illegal.

Superficial discounting is typified by one large retailer that sells 93 percent of its power tools on sale. Discounts range from 10 to 40 percent. Events or sales are planned on a systematic basis so that the tools are sold at sale prices most of the year. To combat such superficial discounting, Canada now requires retailers to post a base price for at least six months before discounting a product.

Experience curve pricing

In *experience curve pricing,* a company fixes a low price that high-cost competitors cannot match, and thus expands its market share. This practice is possible when a firm gains cumulative production experience and is able to reduce its manufacturing costs at a predictable rate through improved methods, materials, skills, and machinery. Texas Instruments used this strategy in marketing both its computers and its calculators. The experience curve depicts the inverse relationship between production costs per unit and cumulative production quantity. To take advantage of the experience curve, a company must gain a dominant market share early in a product's life cycle. An early market share lead, with the greater cumulative production experience that it implies, will place a company farther down the experience curve than its competitors. To avoid antitrust problems, companies must objectively examine the competitive structure of the market before and after implementing experience curve strategy. The strategy should not be anticompetitive and the company must have specific and accurate data that will be unshakable in a court of law. With suitable precaution and sound legal counsel, this method of pricing is perfectly acceptable where it can be successful as a primary policy.[5]

Development of a pricing method

After selecting a pricing policy, a marketer must choose a *pricing method,* a mechanical procedure for setting prices on a regular basis. The pricing method structures the calculation of the actual price. The nature of a product, its sales volume, or the amount of product carried by the organization will determine how prices are calculated. For example, a procedure for pricing the thousands of products in a supermarket must be more direct and simple than that for calculating the price of a new earth-moving machine manufactured by Caterpillar.

Pricing methods provide techniques for actually assigning prices to specific products. Pricing methods must take into account pricing objectives as well as knowledge of buyers, demand, costs, and competition. We will examine three types of market-oriented pricing methods: cost-oriented pricing, demand-oriented pricing, and competition-oriented pricing. Then we will look briefly at intracompany transfer pricing.

Cost-oriented pricing

In using *cost-oriented pricing,* a firm determines price by adding a dollar amount or percentage to the cost of a product. Cost-oriented pricing does not necessarily take into account the economic aspects of supply and de-

---

5. Alan R. Beckenstein and H. Landis Gabel, "Experience Curve Pricing Strategy: The Next Target of Antitrust?" *Business Horizons,* Sept.–Oct. 1982, pp. 71–77.

mand, but cost-oriented pricing methods are simple and easy to implement. They involve calculations of desired margins or profit-margin add-ons to the cost of a product.

A cost-oriented pricing method does not necessarily relate to a specific pricing policy or ensure the attainment of pricing objectives. Two common cost-oriented pricing methods are cost-plus and markup pricing.

Cost-plus pricing

Cost-plus pricing is a pricing method in which the seller's costs are determined (usually during or after a project is completed), and then a specified dollar amount or percentage of the cost is added to the seller's cost to set the price. When production costs are unpredictable or production takes a long time, cost-plus pricing is appropriate. Custom-made equipment and commercial construction projects often are priced by this method. The government frequently uses such cost-oriented pricing in granting defense contracts. One pitfall for the buyer is that the seller may increase costs to establish a larger profit base.

In periods of rapid inflation, cost-plus pricing is popular, especially when the producer must use raw materials that are fluctuating in price. For industries in which cost-plus pricing is common and sellers have similar costs, price competition may not be especially intense.

Markup pricing

A common pricing method among retailers is **markup pricing,** through which a product's price is derived by adding a predetermined percentage of the cost, called *markup,* to the cost of the product. Although the percentage markup in a retail store varies from one category of goods to another (35 percent of cost for hardware and 100 percent of cost for greeting cards, for example), the same percentage often is used to determine the price on items within a single product category, and the same or similar percentage markup may be standardized across an industry at the retail level. Using a rigid percentage markup for a specific product category reduces pricing to a routine task that can be performed quickly.

Markup can be stated as a percentage of the cost or as a percentage of the selling price. To illustrate how percentage markups are determined and to note the differences in the two methods that follow, assume that a retailer purchases a can of tuna at 45 cents, adds 15 cents to the cost, and then prices the tuna at 60 cents. Here are the figures:

$$\text{Markup as a percentage of cost} = \frac{\text{amount added to cost}}{\text{cost}}$$
$$= \frac{15}{45}$$
$$= 33.3\%$$

$$\text{Markup as a percentage of selling price} = \frac{\text{amount added to cost}}{\text{selling price}}$$
$$= \frac{15}{60}$$
$$= 25.0\%$$

Obviously, when discussing a percentage markup, it is important to know whether the markup is based on cost or on selling price.

Markups usually reflect expectations about operating costs, risks, and stock turnovers. Wholesalers and manufacturers often suggest standard retail markups that are considered to be profitable. An average percentage markup on selling price may be as high as 75 percent or more for jewelry or as low as 20 percent for the textbook you are reading. To the extent that retailers use similar markups for the same product category, price competition is reduced. In addition, the use of rigid markups is convenient, which is the major reason that retailers—who face numerous pricing decisions—use it.

Demand-oriented pricing

Rather than basing the price of a product on its cost, marketers sometimes employ a pricing method that is based on the level of demand for the product—*demand-oriented pricing*. This method results in a high price when demand for the product is strong and a low price when demand is weak. To use this method, a marketer must be able to estimate the amounts of a product that consumers will demand at different prices. The marketer then chooses the price that generates the highest total revenue. Obviously, the effectiveness of demand-oriented pricing depends on the marketer's ability to estimate demand accurately. Phone companies have done an excellent job in estimating market response to various long distance rates at different times of the day (see Figure 15.6).

A marketer sometimes uses a demand-oriented pricing method called *price differentiation* when the firm wants to use more than one price in the marketing of a specific product. Price differentiation can be based on several dimensions, such as type of customer, type of distribution channel used, or the time of the purchase.

Here are some examples. A twelve-ounce canned soft drink costs less from a supermarket than from a vending machine. Florida hotel accommodations are more expensive in the winter than in the summer. A homeowner pays more for air-conditioner filters than does an apartment complex owner who purchases the same size filters in greater quantity. Christmas tree ornaments are usually cheaper on December 26 than on December 16.

For price differentiation to work properly, the marketer must be able to segment a market on the basis of different strengths of demand, and then keep the segments separate enough so that segment members who buy at lower prices cannot then sell to buyers in segments that are charged a higher price. This isolation could be accomplished, for example, by selling to multiple, geographically separated segments.

Also, price differentiation can be based on employment in a public service position. For example, USAIR, Inc. as well as most other airlines, permits all U.S. military personnel on active duty, leave furlough, or a pass 50 percent off each regular one-way or roundtrip fare.

Compared with cost-oriented pricing, demand-oriented pricing places a firm in a better position to reach higher profit levels, assuming that buyers value the product at levels sufficiently above the product's cost. To use demand-oriented pricing, however, a marketer must be able to estimate demand at different price levels, which is frequently difficult to do accurately.

If you call long distance after 5PM you'll save 40% and *if you* call after 11PM or on the *weekend* you'll save 60% and your phone bill will get smaller and smaller.

General Telephone GTE

**Competition-oriented
pricing methods**

In using *competition-oriented pricing,* an organization considers costs and revenue secondary to competitors' prices. The importance of this method increases if competing products are almost homogeneous and the organization is serving markets in which price is the key variable of the marketing strategy.

One leading discount retail chain that has stores in the Midwest and South uses a competitive pricing method. Stores price products slightly below other discount outlets in the immediate area. The assistant manager of one Louisiana store goes to competing stores and records the prices of routinely purchased merchandise; this store's prices then are set 1 cent below competitors'. This pricing method is easy to use, and the resulting prices increase store traffic.

Competition-oriented pricing should help attain a pricing objective to increase sales or market share. Competition-oriented pricing methods may be combined with cost approaches to arrive at price levels necessary for a profit.

Transfer pricing

When a unit in a company sells a product to another unit, the pricing that is used is called *transfer pricing*. The price is determined by one of the following methods:

Actual full cost: calculated by dividing all fixed and variable expenses for a period into the number of units produced

Standard full cost: calculated on what it would cost to produce the goods at full plant capacity

Cost plus investment: calculated as full cost plus the cost of a portion of the selling unit's assets used for internal needs

Market-based cost: calculated at the market price less a small discount to reflect the lack of sales effort and other expenses

The choice of a method of transfer pricing depends upon management strategy for the company and the nature of the units' interaction. The company might initially choose to determine price by the actual full cost method and later change to a market-based method or whatever method the management of the company decides is best suited for the company's changed business situation.[6]

Determination of a specific price

Pricing policies and methods should direct and structure the selection of a final price. If they are to do so, it is important for marketers to establish pricing objectives, to know something about the target market, and to determine demand, price elasticity, costs, and competitive factors. In addition to those economic factors, the role of price in the marketing mix will affect the final price.

Although we suggest a systematic approach to pricing, in practice prices often are finalized after only limited planning. Trial and error, rather than planning, may be used to set a price; then marketers determine whether revenue minus costs yields a profit. This approach to pricing is not recommended, because it makes it much harder to discover pricing errors.

In the absence of government price control, pricing remains a flexible and convenient way to adjust the marketing mix. In most situations, prices can be adjusted quickly—in a matter of minutes or over a few days. This flexibility and freedom do not characterize the other components of the marketing mix. Since so many complex issues are involved in establishing the right price, pricing is indeed as much an art as a science.

Pricing for industrial and reseller markets

Industrial markets consist of individuals and organizations that purchase products for the purpose of using them in their own operations or for producing other products. Quoting prices to this category of buyers is sometimes different from setting prices for consumers.

Differences in the size of purchases, geographic factors, and transportation considerations require sellers to make adjustments in prices. Also, the rational purchase motives of industrial customers may limit the use of psychological and some promotional pricing policies.

6. Robert G. Eccles, "Control with Fairness in Transfer Pricing," *Harvard Business Review*, November–December, 1983, pp. 149–161.

Application

Doctors and Hospitals Offer Discount Prices to Groups

The practice of medicine is facing a competitive environment as doctors and hospitals vie for patients. Several factors have contributed to this competition. During the past decade, 40 percent more doctors began practicing in the United States. Hospitals are left with empty beds as increasing numbers of patients are using new outpatient facilities that provide emergency and surgical care. In addition, shifting population and fewer federal funds have caused many hospitals, especially older ones in urban areas, to lose revenue.

Many of the medical bills in the United States are paid by business and government through employee health insurance plans, Medicare, and Medicaid. The federal government, in its efforts to deal with rising medical costs, has placed ceilings on what it will pay hospitals for Medicare patients. Hospitals are therefore expected to counter this loss of revenue by charging more for patients covered by company insurance plans.

Through preferred provider organizations (PPOs) medical providers aim to help companies control their group health insurance bills. In a PPO, doctors and/or hospitals agree to reduce their fees for a contracted company's employees. This contract assures the PPO of a new group of potential patients for whom fees will be paid promptly. Contracting companies offer fuller coverage to employees who see PPO doctors.

The PPO movement illustrates the use of marketing in the practice of medicine. Traditionally, very few doctors have advertised either their prices or their services. By offering reduced prices through company group plans, doctors hope to improve their position in the competition for patients.

Source: Based on Michael Waldholz, "To Attract Patients, Doctors and Hospitals Cut Prices to Groups," *Wall Street Journal,* Nov. 22, 1983, pp. 1, 26.

Price discounting

Discounts off list prices are commonly provided to middlemen by producers. Although there are many types of discounts, they usually fall into one of five categories: trade, quantity, cash, seasonal discounts, and allowances. The Application above illustrates a price discount program that encompasses cash, trade, and quantity discounts.

Trade discounts

A reduction off the list price given to a middleman by a producer for performing certain functions is called a *trade,* or *functional, discount.* A trade discount usually is stated in terms of a percentage or series of percentages off the list price. Middlemen are given trade discounts to compensate them for performing such functions as selling, transporting, storing, final processing, and perhaps providing credit services. Although certain trade discounts become standard practice within an industry, discounts do vary considerably among industries.

Quantity discounts

Deductions from list price that reflect the economies of purchasing in large quantities are called *quantity discounts.* Some of the fixed costs of serving a customer, such as billing and sales contacts, may remain the same—or even go down—as the size of an order increases; and a large purchase reduces per unit selling costs and may shift some of the storage, finance, and risk-taking functions to the buyer. Thus, quantity discounts usually reflect legitimate reductions in costs.

Quantity discounts can be either cumulative or noncumulative. *Cumulative discounts* are quantity discounts that are aggregated over a stated period of time. Purchases of $10,000 in a three-month period might entitle the buyer to a 5-percent, or $500, rebate. Such discounts are supposed to reflect economies in selling and encourage the buyer to purchase from one seller. *Noncumulative discounts* are one-time reductions in prices based on the number of units purchased, the dollar size of the order, or the product mix purchased. Like cumulative discounts, these discounts should reflect some economies in selling or trade functions performed.

Cash discounts

A *cash discount* exists when prompt payment or cash payment results in a price reduction to the buyer. Accounts receivable are an expense and a collection problem for many organizations. A policy to encourage prompt payment is a popular practice and sometimes a major concern in setting prices.

Discounts are based on cash payments or cash paid within a stated period of time. For example, "2/10 net 30" means that a 2 percent discount will be allowed if the account is paid within 10 days and that the balance is due within 30 days without a discount. If the account is not paid within 30 days, interest may be charged.

Seasonal discounts

A price reduction to buyers who buy goods or services out of season is a *seasonal discount*. These discounts allow the seller to maintain steadier production during the year. For example, automobile rental agencies offer seasonal discounts in winter and early spring to encourage firms to use automobiles during the agencies' slow months in their business.

Allowances

Another type of reduction from the list price is an *allowance*—a concession in price to achieve a desired goal. Trade-in allowances, for example, are price reductions given for turning in a used item when purchasing a new one. Allowances help to give the buyer the ability to make the new purchase. This type of discount is popular in the aircraft industry. Another example is promotional allowances, which are price reductions to dealers for participating in advertising and sales support programs that it is hoped will increase sales of a particular item.

For example, because supermarkets, in their own price discount promotions, focus on major brands first, consumers often find that Dr Pepper is priced higher than Coke or Pepsi. This price disadvantage has hurt Dr Pepper's attempts to increase the market share of its noncola in a nation of heavy cola drinkers. To overcome this price disadvantage, Dr Pepper is urging bottlers and retailers to establish new lower prices for its six-packs of ten-ounce bottles. A promotional allowance is offered so that retailers and bottlers can retain their usual profit margins.[7]

7. Al Urbanski, "Dr Pepper Heals Itself," *Sales and Marketing Management,* March 14, 1983, pp. 33–36.

Geographic pricing　　*Geographic pricing* involves reductions for transportation costs or other costs associated with the physical distance between the buyer and the seller. Prices may be quoted as being *F.O.B. (free-on-board) factory,* which is a price that excludes transportation charges and indicates a shipping point. In this case, F.O.B. factory indicates the price of the merchandise at the factory, before it is loaded onto the carrier vehicle. The buyer must pay for shipping. Although this is an easy way to price products, it is sometimes difficult for marketers to administer—especially when a firm has a wide product mix or when customers are dispersed widely. Since customers will want to know about the most economical method of shipping, the seller must keep posted on shipping rates.

To avoid the problems involved with charging different prices to each customer, *uniform geographic pricing,* sometimes called postage-stamp pricing, may be used. This type of pricing results in a fixed average cost of transportation. Gasoline, paper products, and office equipment often are priced on a uniform basis.

Zone prices are regional prices that take advantage of a uniform pricing system; prices are adjusted for major geographic zones as the transportation costs increase. For example, a Florida manufacturer's prices may be higher for buyers on the Pacific Coast and in Canada than for buyers in Georgia.

Base-point pricing is a geographic pricing policy that includes the price at the factory plus freight charges from the base point nearest the buyer. This approach to pricing has been abandoned, as its legal status has been questioned. The policy resulted in all buyers' paying freight charges from one location, say Detroit or Pittsburgh, regardless of where the product was manufactured.

Pricing for a particular customer or geographical area by which the seller absorbs all or part of the actual freight costs is *freight absorption pricing*. The seller might employ this method because of some interest in doing business with a particular customer or to get more business, which would cause the average cost to fall and counterbalance the extra freight cost. A strategy like this is used for market penetration and to retain a hold in an increasingly competitive market.

Price discrimination　　*Price discrimination* is a policy that results in different prices being charged to give a group of buyers a competitive advantage. Price differentiation becomes discriminatory when a seller gives one reseller or industrial buyer an advantage over competitors by providing products at lower prices than other similar customers can obtain. If customers are not in competition with each other, different prices may be charged legally.

Price differentials are legal when they can be justified on the basis of cost savings, when they meet competition in good faith, or when they do not attempt to damage competition. The Robinson-Patman Act prohibits price discrimination that lessens competition among wholesalers and retailers, and it prohibits producers from giving disproportionate services to large buyers. Chapter 16 examines the provisions of the Robinson-Patman Act in greater detail.

For price discrimination to work, the following conditions are neces-

Table 15.1   Principal forms of price discrimination

Main Classes	Bases of Discrimination	Examples
Personal	Incomes of buyers	Doctor's fees
	Earning power of buyers	Royalties paid for use of patented machines and processes
Group	Buyers' socioeconomic characteristics such as age and sex	Children's haircuts, ladies' day at baseball parks, lower admission charges for men in uniform, senior citizen rates
	Location of buyers	Zone prices, in-state vs. out-of-state tuition, lower export prices (dumping)
	Status of buyers	Lower prices to new customers, quantity discounts to big buyers
	Use of product	Railroad rates, public utility rates
Product	Qualities of products	Relatively higher prices for deluxe models
	Labels on products	Lower prices of unbranded products
	Sizes of products	Relatively lower prices for larger sizes (the "giant economy" size)
	Peak and off-peak services	Lower prices for off-peak services; excursion rates in transportation, off-season rates at resorts, holiday and evening telephone rates.

Source: Adapted from Donald S. Watson and Malcolm Getz, *Price Theory and Its Uses,* Second Edition, Copyright © 1968 Houghton Mifflin Company. Used with permission.

sary: The market must be segmentable; the cost of segmenting should not exceed the extra revenue from price discrimination; the practice should not breed customer ill will; competition should not be able to steal the segment that is charged the higher price; and the practice should not be illegal under the law. Table 15.1 shows the principal forms of price discrimination.

Summary

The final four stages of establishing prices include analysis of competitors' prices, selection of a pricing policy, development of a pricing method, and determination of a specific price.

A marketer needs to be aware of the prices charged for competing brands. This allows a firm to keep its prices the same as competitors' prices when nonprice competition is used. If a company employs price as a competitive tool, it can price its brand below competing brands.

A pricing policy is a guiding philosophy or course of action designed to influence and determine pricing decisions. Pricing policies help marketers to solve the practical problems of establishing prices. Two types of pioneer pricing policies are price skimming and penetration pricing. Price skimming means that an organization charges the highest possible price that buyers who most desire the product will pay. This policy provides several benefits, especially when a product is in the introductory stage of its life cycle. It can generate much-needed initial cash flows to help offset sizable development costs. A penetration price is a lower price designed to penetrate the market and produce a larger unit sales volume. Psychological pricing, another pricing policy, encourages purchases that are based on emotional reactions rather than on rational responses. It includes odd-even pricing, customary pricing, prestige pricing, and price lining. A third pricing policy, professional pricing, is used by persons who have great skill or experience in a particular field. Promotional pricing, in which price is coordinated with promotion, is another type of pricing policy. Price leaders, special-event pricing, and superficial discounting are examples of promotional pricing.

A pricing method is a mechanical procedure for setting prices on a regular basis. Pricing methods provide techniques for actually assigning prices to specific products. Three types of pricing methods are cost-oriented pricing, demand-oriented pricing, and competition-oriented pricing. In using cost-oriented pricing, a firm determines price by adding a dollar amount or percentage to the cost of the product. Two common cost-oriented pricing methods are cost-plus and markup pricing. Demand-oriented pricing is based on the level of demand for the product. To use this method, a marketer must be able to estimate the amounts of a product that buyers will demand at different prices. Demand-oriented pricing results in a high price when demand for a product is strong and a low price when demand is weak. When using competition-oriented pricing, costs and revenues are secondary to competitors' prices. Competition-oriented pricing and cost approaches may be combined to arrive at price levels necessary for a profit. Experience curve pricing fixes a low price that high cost competitors cannot match. Experience curve pricing is possible when, through experience, manufacturing costs are reduced at a predictable rate.

Establishing prices for industrial markets differs, in some respects, from setting prices in consumer markets. Sellers must consider differences in the size of purchases, geographic factors, and transportation costs when they set prices for industrial buyers. Price discounting is commonly used by producers in selling to middlemen. When a business unit in a company sells to another business unit in the same company, it is called transfer pricing. There are five main categories of price discounts: trade, quantity, cash, and seasonal discounts, and allowances. Geographic pricing involves reductions for transportation costs or other costs associated with the physical distance between the buyer and seller. Price discrimination occurs when differences in the prices charged give one buyer a competitive advantage over another competing buyer. Price differentials are legal when they can be justified on the basis of cost savings, when they meet competition in good faith, or when they do not attempt to damage competition.

Important terms

Pricing policy
Price skimming
Penetration price
Psychological pricing
Odd-even pricing
Customary pricing

Prestige pricing
Price lining
Professional pricing
Price leaders
Special-event pricing
Superficial discounting

Experience curve pricing	Noncumulative discounts
Pricing method	Cash discount
Cost-oriented pricing	Seasonal discount
Cost-plus pricing	Allowance
Markup pricing	Freight absorption pricing
Demand-oriented pricing	Geographic pricing
Price differentiation	F.O.B. factory
Competition-oriented pricing	Uniform geographic pricing
Transfer pricing	Zone prices
Trade or functional discount	Base-point pricing
Quantity discounts	Price discrimination
Cumulative discounts	

Discussion and review questions

1. Why should a marketer be aware of competitors' prices?
2. For what type of products would a pioneer price-skimming policy be most appropriate? For what type of products would penetration pricing be more effective?
3. Why do consumers associate price with quality? When should prestige pricing be used?
4. Are price leaders a realistic approach to pricing?
5. What are the benefits of cost-oriented pricing?
6. Under what conditions is cost-plus pricing most appropriate?
7. If a retailer purchases a can of soup for 24 cents and sells it for 36 cents, what is the percentage markup on selling price?
8. Compare and contrast a trade discount and a quantity discount.
9. What is the purpose of using the term *F.O.B.*?
10. What is the difference between price discount and price discrimination?

Cases

Case 15.1

AT&T Faces Long-Distance Telephone Service Price Competition[8]

Long distance—the next best thing to being there. But who will dominate in this $44-billion-a-year business? The breakup of American Telephone and Telegraph has spurred fierce competition with MCI, GTE Sprint, All-net, ITT, Western Union, and U.S. Telephone providing alternative services, to name but a few. Table 15.2 shows the breakdown of market share and profits for the major competitors. To increase their market share, competitors are relying heavily on lowering prices and on advertising campaigns. Meanwhile, billions of dollars are also being spent to increase network capacity and improve the quality of communications.

AT&T currently gets about 77 percent of all long-distance calls, with the Bell operating companies handling an additional 17 percent. This leaves only 6 percent of the business to approximately 400 rivals. AT&T's ads stress quality, reliability, and their provision of operator assistance. John Smart, marketing vice president of AT&T states, "We feel that people are

8. The facts in this case are from Manuel Schiffres, "Rivals for Long Distance Snap at AT&T's Heels," *US News and World Report*, Jan. 30, 1984, pp. 53–56; and "Why AT&T Will Lose More Long-Distance Business," *Business Week*, Feb. 13, 1984, p. 106.

Table 15.2 Market Leaders in the Long Distance Industry

	Revenues	Profits	Subscribers
	(millions of dollars)		(thousands)
AT&T	$35,000	$1,430	85,000
MCI	1,520	203	1,550
GTE Sprint	750	66	920
Allnet	180	8	150
ITT	170	8	95
U.S. Telephone	140	−5	80
SBS	70	−145[a]	90

[a]Total corporate losses for data communications as well as long-distance services.
Source: Sanford C. Bernstein & Co. estimates as found in "Why AT&T Will Lose More Long Distance Business," *Business Week*, Feb. 13, 1984, p. 106. Reprinted from *Business Week* by special permission; © 1984 by McGraw-Hill, Inc.

willing to pay a little more for quality and reliability." Competitors, on the other hand, are fighting to give greater discounts and lower prices, even at the risk of cutting profit margins, in order to gain market share. AT&T's competitors will maintain a cost advantage for at least two to three years because they will have to pay only 45 percent of what AT&T pays for each minute they are connected to a local network due to inferior connections to local phone companies.

MCI plans to maintain its price spread with AT&T regardless of varying connection charges. GTE's Sprint has ended monthly subscriptions and instituted discounts on volume for customers making at least $25 a month in calls. AT&T has tested several pricing strategies including a 40 percent discount on night calls for an added $6 per month. Many companies have also experimented with giving away phone time. For example, Allnet in a "Talk Your Head Off" promotion offers an hour of free calling 90 days after becoming a customer.

Joint promotions between long-distance firms are becoming more commonplace. Western Union gives new MetroFone customers 10 free minutes a month for a 6-month duration with the purchase of certain phone models. MCI is promoting its service with American Express and Sears cardholders who are now able to charge their phone bill.

MCI is also fighting AT&T in the pay phone business by placing their own credit card phones inside airports, hotels, and convention centers. AT&T is concurrently testing "Express Phones" that allow a 30-second conversation with anyone in the U.S. for only 50 cents.

What AT&T must contend with is strict regulation and cost disadvantage. AT&T must file formal rate requests before changing prices, whereas competitors do not have to file at all.

Questions for discussion
1. What conclusion should AT&T arrive at after evaluating its competitors' prices?
2. Discuss pricing policies used by AT&T and its competitors.
3. What kind of discounts might be appropriate in pricing long-distance telephone services?

Case 15.2

Bic and Gillette Battle for the Disposable Lighter Market[9]

The Gillette Company is an international consumer products firm that develops, manufactures, and sells a wide range of products for personal care. Major lines include blades and razors, toiletries and grooming aids, Braun electric shavers and small appliances, and lighters. The company is the market leader of blades and razors in North America and in many areas of the world. Holding a major position worldwide through the sale of toiletries, grooming aids, and writing instruments, Gillette's annual sales exceed $2.3 billion. Gillette was the first company to introduce a disposable butane lighter in the U.S. market. In 1972, the Cricket lighter was introduced and became an instant success.

Bic is a diversified company primarily engaged in the manufacture and sale of low-cost disposable plastic consumer products. It is the largest manufacturer and distributor of ball-point pens and butane lighters in America. Its sales have exceeded $218 million. In 1973, when Bic introduced its own lighter, Gillette had already established a strong position in the market.

Although Gillette claimed to have a better product, with an adjustable flame, Bic's flashy "Flick My Bic" ad campaign and overall marketing efforts resulted in an almost equal market share for Bic and Gillette by 1977.

"The time had come in the game for the big play," recalls Bic's vice president, Alexander Alexiades. "We had to decide whether we wanted to just sit back and enjoy substantial short-term profits or go after market share." Bic opted for market share and in mid-1977 slashed the wholesale price of its lighter by 32 percent. Gillette did not reduce prices immediately, largely because its per-unit manufacturing costs were higher than Bic's, and its management was reluctant to give up profits. When Gillette finally did retaliate with a price cut, Bic reduced its price still further—and a price war developed. By the end of 1978 Bic claimed nearly 50 percent of the market. Gillette's market share had slumped to 30 percent. Moreover, in 1978 Bic reported a $9.2-million pretax profit for its lighter division, while Gillette suffered an estimated loss of almost the same amount. See Figure 15.7 for a detailed estimate of Bic sales and market share.

In 1979, despite losses, Gillette tried to improve its position by selling its Cricket lighters at 10 percent below the Bic price. This price change did not substantially hurt Bic's market share. In fact, Bic's market share increased to 53 percent, even though its wholesale price was several cents higher than most of its competitors.

Bic's objective for 1980 was to improve profitability, since the total disposable lighter market was expected to expand. If possible, Bic also wanted to expand market share. During 1980 Bic experienced lighter sales of $85.6 million, market share dropped from 53 to 52 percent, and income before taxes amounted to $15.3 million.

9. The facts in this case are from Linda Snyder Hayes, "Gillette Takes the Wraps Off," *Fortune,* Feb. 25, 1980, p. 149; the *1982 Gillette Company Annual Report;* and the *1982 Bic Corporation Annual Report.*

Figure 15.7
Bic disposable lighter
market
*Source: Bic Pen Corpo-
ration* 1982 Annual Re-
port, *p. 2.*

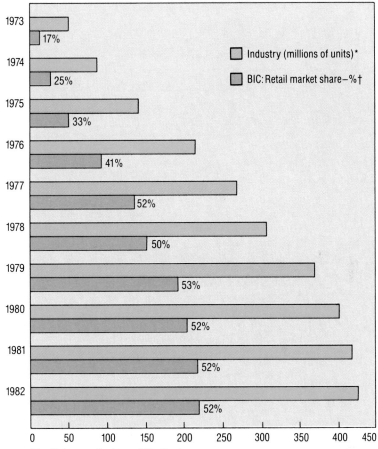

* Total industry unit sales are BIC estimates.
† BIC's market share as reported by independent survey organization.

In 1981, Gillette implemented a program to reduce the cost of production for the Cricket lighter. However, the low price level in the market
place for lighters contributed to losses in 1981 and 1982. Bic's 1981 lighter
sales were $103.3 million and its market share remained at 52 percent. In
1982, the company's lighter sales were $105.2 million and its market share
did not change. This modest increase in sales along with Bic's control of
expenses, produced a 20 percent increase in income before taxes in 1982.

After a phenomenal growth rate over the past ten years, the disposable
lighter market has matured and price competition has increased.

Questions for discussion
1. Have Gillette and Bic successfully implemented the marketing
   concept? Defend your answer.
2. What marketing mix variables did Bic use to develop a successful
   marketing strategy to obtain the largest market share for its lighter?

Part 6

The Marketing Environment

The chapters in Part Six are devoted to a detailed analysis of marketing environment variables. Recall from Chapter 1 that although marketers cannot control environmental variables, they do, at times, attempt to influence them, since these environmental variables affect marketers' decisions and activities. Marketers should understand how environmental forces can affect customers and their responses to marketing strategies. We discuss political, legal, and regulatory forces in Chapter 16 and describe some ways that these forces have an impact on marketing decision making. Chapter 17 describes some of the pressures that societal members place on marketers. We explore several means by which marketers can respond to societal forces and the problems associated with trying to be socially responsive. Also, we describe how economic and technological forces influence marketers' decisions and activities directly and how they indirectly affect marketers by having an impact on consumers.

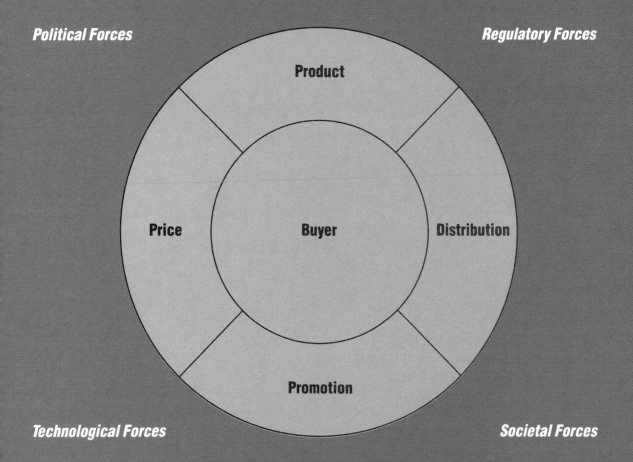

Marketing Environment

Legal Forces

Political Forces

Regulatory Forces

Product

Price

Buyer

Distribution

Promotion

Technological Forces

Societal Forces

Economic Forces

16

Political, Legal, and Regulatory Forces

Objectives

To identify the types of political forces in the marketing environment.

To become aware of the interrelationships among political and legal forces in the marketing environment.

To understand the laws that influence marketing practices.

To explore the problems that arise because of inconsistent judicial interpretations of laws.

To determine how government regulations and self-regulatory agencies affect marketing activities.

To understand some effects of political, legal, and regulatory forces on marketing mix decisions.

To learn how marketers adjust to and influence political, legal, and regulatory forces in the marketing environment.

Traffic-building promotional games may be making a comeback among gasoline retailers. With some recent rule changes, the Federal Trade Commission has made it easier to promote games.[1] In 1969, the FTC initiated disclosure requirements regarding the conduct of such games that made it very expensive to promote them. The rules required a weekly update of radio and television commercials to reflect any changes in prizes and in the odds of winning. Although these requirements still hold for print advertisements, they no longer apply to radio and television commercials.

Under the old rules, when Shell sponsored a thirteen-week run of thirty-second spots for its "Match and Win" game, the cost of changing the advertisements for one market exceeded $13,000. Shell recently tested a new game, but no other companies have followed. Shell believes that although it may be easier to run a game, there will not be much increase in demand for games.

No major oil companies have announced that they plan to start using games, but they are watching the market closely. Game manufacturers and broadcasters remain optimistic because of rumors indicating that several companies are in the developmental stages. If some of the companies start using promotional games, it is likely that others will follow.

This example is only one isolated illustration that raises a very broad, controversial question—What is the role of government in business? The founders of this country generally followed a laissez-faire policy, believing that unrestrained competition would provide the best form of regulation and would benefit everyone, consumers and businesses alike. Noninterference with business worked reasonably well as long as competitors were small and consumers demanded basically simple products. However, improved technology, transportation, and communication complicated our economic system. As those who assumed the risk and management of business sought larger profits and greater shares of the market for themselves, many in the consuming public, and in the business community as well, began to feel that they were being victimized by unscrupulous competitors. The outcry encouraged the government to protect the American "ideal" of free enterprise.

Since the first regulatory legislation was passed, government's role of intervening in our economic system has become increasingly larger and more active. Although there have been some attempts at deregulation, today's political, legal, and regulatory forces still influence many aspects of

1. "New Rule May Fuel Gas Station Games," *Advertising Age,* Jan. 10, 1983, p. 6.

marketing, including product development, branding, packaging, pricing, transporting, storing, wholesaling, retailing, personal selling, advertising, and sales promotion.

In this chapter, we first discuss political forces, which provide the foundation for government actions that influence marketing activities. Then we analyze the effects of laws and regulatory actions on marketing activities. Finally, we examine how marketers deal with political, legal, and regulatory forces.

Politics and the marketing environment

Political and legal forces are closely interrelated aspects of the marketing environment. Legislation is enacted, legal decisions are interpreted by the courts, and regulatory agencies are created and operated, for the most part, by persons who occupy government positions.

When political officials have positive feelings toward particular firms or industries, they are less likely to create or enforce laws and regulations that are unfavorable to those business organizations. If, for example, political officials believe that oil companies are making honest efforts to control pollution, these officials are not likely to create and enforce highly restrictive pollution control laws. There is another reason why business organizations need to be concerned about making a favorable impression on political officials. As we pointed out in Chapter 2, governments are big buyers, and people who hold political office can influence how much a government purchases and from whom. Still another reason to seek political favor is that political officials can play key roles in securing foreign markets.

Many marketers view political forces as beyond their control; therefore, they simply try to adjust to conditions that arise from those forces. However, some firms attempt to influence political events by helping to elect certain individuals to political offices. Much of this help is in the form of campaign contributions. Although laws restrict corporate contributions to campaign funds, corporate money is channeled into campaign funds as personal contributions of corporate executives or stockholders. Not only do such actions violate the spirit of the corporate campaign contribution laws, but they are also unethical. A sizable contribution to a campaign fund may carry with it an implicit understanding that the elected official will perform "political favors" for the contributing firm.

It is not unusual for a corporation to make contributions to the campaign funds of several candidates who seek the same position. Occasionally, it is so important to ensure favorable treatment that certain businesses make direct illegal corporate contributions to campaign funds. Indeed, a former official of American Airlines admitted that the firm illegally contributed $55,000 from corporate funds, not to purchase political favors, but because they feared what might happen if a contribution were not made. Governments can and do take actions aimed at specific industries or companies. However, for many marketers, a primary concern associated with the political environment is its strong influence on the strength and effectiveness of the legal forces with which they must deal.

Table 16.1   Major federal procompetitive laws affecting marketing decisions

Act	Purposes
Sherman Act (1890)	Prohibits contracts, combinations, or conspiracies to restrain trade; establishes as a misdemeanor monopolizing or attempting to monopolize
Clayton Act (1914)	Prohibits specific practices such as price discrimination, exclusive dealer arrangements, and stock acquisitions in which the effect may substantially lessen competition to tend to create a monopoly
Federal Trade Commission Act (1914)	Created the Federal Trade Commission; gives the FTC investigatory powers to be used in preventing unfair methods of competition
Robinson-Patman Act (1936)	Prohibits price discrimination that lessens competition among wholesalers or retailers; prohibits producers from giving disproportionate services or facilities to large buyers
Wheeler-Lea Act (1938)	Prohibits unfair and deceptive acts and practices regardless of whether competition is injured; places advertising of foods and drugs under the jurisdiction of the FTC
Celler-Kefauver Act (1950)	Prohibits any corporation engaged in commerce from acquiring the whole or any part of the stock or other share of the capital or assets of another corporation when the effect substantially lessens competition or tends to create a monopoly
Consumer Goods Pricing Act (1975)	Prohibits the use of price maintenance agreements among manufacturers and resellers in interstate commerce

Laws and their interpretation

Since the passage of the landmark Sherman Act in 1890, a number of laws have been enacted that influence marketing decisions and activities. Various laws affect pricing, advertising, personal selling, distribution, product development, and product warranty and repair policies. For purposes of analysis, laws that directly affect marketing practices can be divided into two categories: (1) procompetitive legislation and (2) consumer protection laws.

Procompetitive legislation

Table 16.1 briefly describes several major procompetitive laws. *Procompetitive legislation* is enacted to preserve competition. At the beginning of the Industrial Revolution in the mid-1800s, many people were fascinated by new production techniques, the introduction of mass production, and the use of new equipment driven by new sources of power. As industrial development continued, an increasing number of people left the farms and became factory workers. By the late 1800s a number of firms had merged or combined with others to form giant business organizations. Business people generally believed that growth was good. Smaller firms combined with others or were driven out of business. Although the Industrial Revolution and the rapid growth in business enterprises may have had some long-run beneficial effects on society, these changes were often devastating to individuals. Masses of workers toiled long, hard hours for little money under bad working conditions. Yet a few industrialists continued to amass tremendous wealth. Eventually, public resentment in the United States became so strong that the Sherman Act was passed.

The Sherman Act

The *Sherman Act* was passed in 1890 to prevent businesses from restraining trade and monopolizing markets. Section 1 of the act condemns "every contract, combination, or conspiracy in restraint of trade." Section 2 prohibits monopolizing or attempting to monopolize. Enforced by the Antitrust Division of the Department of Justice, the Sherman Act applies to firms operating in interstate commerce and to U.S. firms operating in foreign commerce.

The Clayton Act

The Sherman Act was written in general terms, and the courts have not always interpreted it as its creators intended. For this reason, the second major procompetitive act, the *Clayton Act,* was passed in 1914. The Clayton Act prohibits price discrimination (section 2), tying and exclusive agreements (section 3), and the acquisition of stock in another corporation (section 7) "where the effect may be to substantially lessen competition or tend to create a monopoly." In addition, interlocking directorates are deemed unlawful under section 8. Sections 6 and 20 exempt farm cooperatives and labor organizations from antitrust laws.

The Federal Trade Commission Act and the Wheeler-Lea Amendment

The Federal Trade Commission, established by the *Federal Trade Commission Act* (1914), today regulates the greatest number of marketing practices. Like the Clayton Act, the FTC Act was written to strengthen antimonopoly provisions of the Sherman Act. Whereas the Clayton Act prohibits specific practices, the FTC Act more broadly prohibits unfair methods of competition. This act also empowered the FTC to work with the Department of Justice to enforce the provisions of the Clayton Act. Later sections of this chapter discuss the FTC's regulatory activities.

The creators of the FTC Act, like the authors of the Sherman Act, found that the courts did not always interpret it as they had intended. In the Raladam case (1931) the Supreme Court held that a producer's misrepresentation of an obesity cure was not an unfair method of competition because the firm's action did not injure competition.[2] This ruling—among others—spurred Congress in 1938 to enact the *Wheeler-Lea Act,* which amended section 5 of the FTC Act. Essentially, the Wheeler-Lea Act makes unfair and deceptive acts or practices unlawful, regardless of whether or not they injure competition. It specifically prohibits false advertising of foods, drugs, therapeutic devices, and cosmetics and provides penalties for violations and procedures for enforcement. "False advertising" means an advertisement, other than labeling, that is misleading in any material respect.

2. *Federal Trade Commission v. Raladam Company,* 283 U.S. 643, 1931.

The Robinson-Patman Act

During the early 1930s, when the Depression was at its peak, the FTC was alarmed by the buying practices of some chain stores. The commission reported to the Senate that many of the low prices that suppliers offered to chains could not be justified on the basis of cost savings arising from quantity purchases. These markedly lower costs gave chain stores an unfair competitive advantage over independent stores and allowed chain stores to drive many competitors out of business, which led to greater unemployment. Eventually, after several years of economic hardship, pressure from the FTC and popular political support for further legislation led to the enactment of the Robinson-Patman Act in 1936.

The *Robinson-Patman Act* is significant because it directly influences pricing policies. Since many marketers are subject to the act, owners of small businesses as well as marketing executives in large companies risk illegal activity if they are unfamiliar with this law's basic content. The major provisions of the Robinson-Patman Act include the following:

1. Price discrimination among different purchasers of commodities of like grade and quality is prohibited if the effect of such discrimination may lessen competition substantially or tend to create a monopoly.
2. Price differentials are legal if they can be justified as cost savings or as meeting competition in good faith. Price differentials per se are not illegal.
3. Paying, receiving, or accepting anything of value as a commission, brokerage, or other compensation—except for actual services rendered—is prohibited.
4. It is unlawful to knowingly induce or receive discriminatory prices when prohibited by this law.
5. The furnishing of services or facilities to purchasers upon terms not accorded to all purchasers on proportionately equal terms is illegal.[3]

The Robinson-Patman Act deals only with discriminatory price differentials. Price differentials become discriminatory when one reseller, who is competing against other resellers, can acquire similar quantities of commodities of like grade and quality at lower prices than can other purchasers dealing with the same supplier. Such price differentials give that reseller an unfair advantage in the market.

Resale price maintenance laws

Resale price maintenance laws, sometimes called "fair trade laws," were enacted during the Depression. These state laws permitted manufacturers to set the resale prices at which dealers within a state were supposed to sell a firm's products. Lawmakers intended to stop large retailers from selling products at such low prices that smaller, financially weaker retailers could not compete.

3. E. T. Grether, *Marketing and Public Policy* (Englewood Cliffs, N.J.: Prentice-Hall, 1966), pp. 60–61. Used by permission of the author.

The first fair trade laws were enacted in California in 1931. Congress later passed two enabling acts, the Miller-Tydings Act (1937) and the McGuire Act (1952), that legalized and facilitated the use of resale price maintenance agreements in interstate commerce. Eventually, all but four states enacted some form of fair trade laws. However, between the late 1950s and the mid-1970s, a number of states declared their resale price maintenance laws to be unconstitutional.

In 1975, Congress passed the Consumer Goods Pricing Act, which prohibits the use of resale price maintenance laws in interstate commerce. Today, most resale price maintenance agreements among manufacturers and resellers violate the Sherman Act and are illegal.

Unfair trade practices acts

Unfair trade practices acts are state laws enacted in over half the states, that prohibit wholesalers and retailers from selling products below their costs or below their costs plus a certain percentage of markup. Although the exact provisions vary from state to state, retailers must commonly charge at least 6 percent above their costs, and wholesalers must receive at least 2 percent more than their costs. In some states these laws pertain to all products, while in other states such laws apply only to selected products such as liquor, cigarettes, grocery items, or gasoline. Many states with unfair trade practices acts allow firms to sell below their costs for short time periods under certain conditions. Most of these laws were enacted during the Depression to prevent large firms from driving out small ones by selling below cost for extended periods. Most states do not strenuously enforce unfair trade practices acts at the current time.

Consumer protection legislation

The second category of regulatory laws, *consumer protection legislation,* is not a recent development. During the mid-1800s, lawmakers in many states enacted laws to prohibit the adulteration of food and drugs. However, consumer protection laws at the federal level have mushroomed since the mid-1960s. Increased interest in consumer protection has arisen for several reasons. Consumers do not have the time or competence to evaluate all the products that they purchase. Because of cases of inadequate product standards, poor information disclosure, and deceptive marketing techniques, laws to protect consumers have become popular. Recent consumer legislation stems from the efforts of lawmakers, individual consumer advocates, and consumer interest groups. Several federal consumer protection laws are discussed briefly in Table 16.2.

A number of the federal laws are designed to provide consumer safety. For example, the food and drug acts, the flammable fabric law, the child protection acts, and the product safety law were enacted to protect people from actual and potential physical injuries.

To help buyers become better informed, Congress has passed several laws concerning the disclosure of information. Some laws deal with information about specific products such as textiles, furs, cigarettes, and automobiles. Others focus on particular marketing activities—product development and testing, packaging, labeling, advertising, and consumer financing, for example.

Table 16.2   Selected federal consumer protection laws

Act	Purposes
Pure Food and Drug Act (1906)	Prohibits adulteration and misbranding of foods and drugs sold in interstate commerce
Food, Drug, and Cosmetic Act (1938)	Prohibits the adulteration and sale of foods, drugs, cosmetics, or therapeutic devices in a way that may endanger public health; allows the Food and Drug Administration to set minimum standards and to establish guides for food products
Wool Products Labeling Act (1940)	Protects producers, manufacturers, distributors, and consumers from undisclosed substitutes and mixtures in all types of manufactured wool products
Fur Products Labeling Act (1951)	Protects consumers and others against misbranding, false advertising, and false invoicing of furs and fur products
Flammable Fabrics Act (1953)	Prohibits interstate transportation of dangerously flammable wearing apparel and fabrics
Automobile Information Disclosure Act (1958)	Requires automobile manufacturers to post suggested retail prices on all new passenger vehicles
Textile Fiber Products Identification Act (1958)	Guards producers and consumers against misbranding and false advertising of fiber content of textile fiber products
Cigarette Labeling Act (1965)	Requires cigarette manufacturers to label cigarettes as hazardous to health
Fair Packaging and Labeling Act (1966)	Declares unfair or deceptive packaging or labeling of certain consumer commodities illegal
Child Protection Act (1966)	Excludes from sale potentially harmful toys; allows the FDA to remove dangerous products from the market
Truth-in-Lending Act (1968)	Requires full disclosure of all finance charges on consumer credit agreements and in advertisements of credit plans to allow consumers to be better informed regarding their credit purchases
Child Protection and Toy Safety Act (1969)	Protects children from toys and other products that contain thermal, electrical, or mechanical hazards
Fair Credit Reporting Act (1970)	Ensures that a consumer's credit report will contain only accurate, relevant, and recent information and will be confidential unless a proper party requests it for an appropriate reason
Consumer Product Safety Act (1972)	Created an independent agency to protect consumers from unreasonable risk of injury arising from consumer products; agency is empowered to set safety standards
Magnuson-Moss Warranty-Federal Trade Commission Improvement Act (1975)	Provides for minimum disclosure standards for written consumer product warranties; defines minimum content standards for written warranties; allows the FTC to prescribe interpretive rules and policy statements regarding unfair or deceptive practices

Despite the passage of so many consumer protection laws, the question of how effective these laws are in protecting consumers remains unsettled. A number of factors limit their effectiveness. By the time most laws are enacted, their provisions usually have been "watered down" to the point that they do not have the strength or scope that was intended by those who sponsored the legislation. The degree to which business people understand and attempt to comply with these laws and the extent to which consumers avail themselves of the benefits provided largely determine the effectiveness of consumer laws. Their effectiveness also depends on the vigor with which they are enforced. The extent to which consumers can benefit from these laws is affected by court interpretations of them. Finally, when evaluating the effectiveness of consumer protection laws, one must consider the costs to consumers for enforcing these laws compared with the costs of not having such laws.

Interpreting laws

Many laws have the potential to influence marketing activities. Their actual effects are determined by the interpretations of marketers and the courts.

At first glance, laws seem to be quite specific because they contain many complex clauses and subclauses. In reality, however, many laws and regulations are stated in vague terms that force marketers to rely on legal counsel rather than their own understanding and common sense. Because of this vagueness, an organization may operate in a legally questionable way to see how much it can get away with before it is prosecuted under the law. On the other hand, some marketers interpret regulations and statutes very conservatively to avoid violating a vague law.

When firms are charged with violations, the courts must interpret the law. Although the provisions of the laws do not change over the years, court interpretations do (see the Application on the next page). Businesses—and lawyers—have often asked, "What constitutes a monopoly?" The Sherman Act remains the same, but judicial rulings have changed radically over the years.

That a company grows very large or captures a large share of the market may be enough reason to rule that the company is monopolistic. In a case against Aluminum Company of America in 1945, the Supreme Court found the defendant's 90-percent share of the market to be a monopoly.[4] However, the Court has also found much smaller market shares to be monopolistic. For example, the Court decided in 1962 that a merger between Brown Shoe Company and Kinney Shoe Corporation would be unacceptable because the resultant firm would control 5 percent of the market for women's and children's shoes.[5]

Although court rulings have a direct effect on businesses that are being tried for violations, they also have broader, less direct effects on other businesses. When marketers try to interpret laws in relation to specific marketing practices, they often analyze recent court decisions. By being aware of current court interpretations, marketers acquire a better understanding of what the law is intended to do and how the courts are likely to interpret the law in the future.

4. *United States* v. *Aluminum Co. of America,* 148 F.2d 148 (2d Cir. 1945).
5. *Brown Shoe Co.* v. *United States,* 370 U.S. 294 (1962).

Application

Interpretation of Antitrust Legislation May Become More Liberal

Donald Yapp owned a service, Spray-Rite, that sold agricultural herbicides below the manufacturer's suggested retail price. In 1969, Monsanto, one of his major suppliers, cut off his distributorship. Within a few years, Yapp was driven out of business. He filed suit against Monsanto with charges of a conspiracy to fix prices, in reference to an antitrust law that holds manufacturer price fixing as an automatic antitrust violation. Yapp won his case, and it held up in an appeals court. The Supreme Court is reviewing the case.

Several speculations and opinions have arisen out of the controversy over how the Supreme Court will decide the issues. Thinkers at the Chicago Law School say that in some cases it makes sense that price-fixing should be illegal automatically, but some feel that that is true only when the practice's benefits do not offset injury to competition.

Marketing has always been prey to antitrust risks, but today that risk is increasing. Businesses are more willing to sue each other. Scrutiny of marketing practices is growing at both the state and local levels. However, the Monsanto case is an example of the Reagan administration's efforts to liberalize antitrust policy. The government's position in the case contains a philosophy that holds that when a manufacturer sets a price level, retailers are then permitted to provide warranty and other services that add value to the product.

A marketing professor at the University of Pennsylvania argues that the retailers' gain in profitability will not lead to any guarantee that consumers will receive any additional services. Discounters believe that if the Supreme Court holds in favor of Monsanto Company, it will be used as a means of keeping price levels high.

It is uncertain how the Supreme Court will resolve the Monsanto case. The decision to review this and other cases suggests that the justices may be ready to institute changes. If they are not ready, it will put an end to the Reagan administration's current, more liberal, interpretations of antitrust legislation.

Source: Based on "A Powerful Bid to Rewrite the Antitrust Rule Book," *Business Week,* Oct. 10, 1983, pp. 83–90; and "When Lawyers Dictate the Limits of Marketing," *Business Week,* July 14, 1980, p. 76.

Regulatory forces

Interpretation alone does not determine the effectiveness of laws. The level of enforcement by regulatory agencies significantly influences a law's effectiveness.

Some regulatory agencies are created and administered by government units; others are sponsored by nongovernmental sources. Here we first discuss federal, state, and local government regulatory units. Then we focus on regulatory forces that arise from self-regulation.

Federal regulatory agencies

Federal agencies influence many marketing activities, including product development, pricing, packaging, advertising, personal selling, distribution, and storage. For the most part, the people who head federal agencies exert tremendous influence over important economic and social matters. Most federal agencies attempt to be objective, to maintain a consistent pattern of enforcement, and to be flexible enough to attain fair enforcement of laws and guidelines. Of course, there often is a difference between what a business considers fair and what government regulators consider fair.

Regulatory units usually have the power to enforce specific laws, as well as some discretion in establishing operating rules and drawing up regulations to guide certain types of industry practices. Because of this discretion and overlapping areas of responsibility, confusion or conflict as to which agencies have jurisdiction over specific types of marketing activities is not uncommon.

Although these regulatory agencies are often thought of as independent, they really are not. First, the President of the United States appoints the commissioners of these regulatory groups. Since many commissioners traditionally resign when a new president takes office, each president affects the leadership of these agencies markedly, not only through appointments but also by influencing commissioners throughout their terms of office. The philosophy of the current administration, for example, is reflected in the current FTC's approach to questionable practices: The commission's present goal is to seek cooperation rather than prosecution.[6] Second, because these regulatory commissions are created by Congress and submit legislative proposals to Congress for new regulatory powers, Congress defines the scope of their regulatory powers.

In recent years the federal government has attempted to deregulate some industries. Airline routes and fares are one well-known example. The Treasury Department, in accordance with President Reagan's policies, is eager to dismantle its programs to regulate alcoholic beverage advertising and trade practices. However, the alcoholic beverage industry seems to prefer the regulations. Industry executives claim that only full-time specialists, such as those at the Treasury's Bureau of Alcohol, Tobacco, and Firearms, are capable of understanding their problems.[7]

The Federal Trade Commission (FTC)

Of all the federal regulatory units, the Federal Trade Commission has the broadest powers to influence marketing activities. We will now look more closely at this agency.

The *Federal Trade Commission* consists of five commissioners, each appointed for a term of seven years by the President of the United States with the advice and consent of the Senate. Not more than three commissioners may be members of the same political party. Their terms of office are staggered to ensure continuity of experience in the judgment of cases. The FTC has many administrative duties under existing laws, but the policy underlying all of them is the same: "To prevent the free enterprise system from being stifled or fettered by monopoly or anti-competitive practices and to provide the direct protection of consumers from unfair or deceptive trade practices."[8]

A case recently dropped by the FTC illustrates the commission's concern for maintaining a competitive environment. The FTC accused the

6. "The FTC Is Striving to Achieve Cooperation Rather than Confrontation with America's Marketers: Miller," *Marketing News,* Sept. 2, 1983, p. 10.
7. "Liquor Ad Rules: Regulation Hangover," *Advertising Age,* Nov. 23, 1981, p. 18.
8. "Your Federal Trade Commission" (Washington, D.C.: Federal Trade Commission, 1977), pp. 8–9.

Kellogg Company, General Mills, and General Foods, makers of ready-to-eat breakfast cereals, of participating in a "shared monopoly." The term "shared monopoly," which many economists believe to be irresponsible rhetoric on the part of the FTC, gave the impression that the accused companies were employing oligopolistic practices—an impression fostered by the FTC. The FTC charged the three cereal manufacturers with using parallel pricing of highly differentiated products, thereby creating a noncompetitive market structure in the ready-to-eat cereal industry. FTC members believed the companies effected this policy through the use of intense advertising, shelf-space control, and brand proliferation—all in an effort to discourage competition and to create monopoly-level profits. Crucial to the outcome of the case was the absence of any charges of conspiracy. The transcript of testimony (over 75,000 pages) shows that the FTC never accused the companies of conspiring to monopolize the cereal industry. Also important was the lack of evidence showing that the companies earned excessive profits. There was, in addition, no proof that they used parallel pricing of highly differentiated products.[9]

One major function of the FTC is to enforce laws and regulatory guidelines falling under its jurisdiction. When it has reason to believe that a firm is violating a law, the commission issues a complaint stating that the business is in violation. If the company continues the questionable practice, the FTC can issue a cease and desist order, which is simply an order for the business to stop doing whatever caused the complaint in the first place. The firm can appeal to the federal courts to have the FTC order rescinded. The FTC itself has no direct power or authority to imprison or fine. However, provisions added to the Trans-Alaska Pipeline Act of 1973 amended the Federal Trade Commission Act to empower the FTC to seek civil penalties in the courts up to $10,000 a day for each violation if a cease and desist order is violated. Previously, the maximum penalty was $5,000 per day. In addition, the amendment allows the FTC to obtain preliminary injunctions or temporary restraining orders to stop firms from engaging in deceptive or unfair practices. Before passage of the Trans-Alaska Pipeline Act, the FTC had to seek action indirectly through the Justice Department.

The FTC is obligated to provide assistance and information to businesses so that they will know how to comply with laws. Because marketing is continuously changing, many new marketing methods are evaluated every year. As new commissioners are appointed and as other personnel changes occur, FTC decisions as to what is legal and what is not also change. Although the FTC is intended to be a law enforcement agency, its broad powers allow commissioners and lawyers not only to prosecute through the courts but also to explain to businesses what is considered to be unfair, deceptive, or illegal. For example, the FTC recently determined that many home-builder newspaper advertisements did not include adequate information about finance charges, as required by the Truth-In-Lending Act. After writing letters that indicated the requirements to violators, the FTC determined that 80 percent of these home builders' advertise-

9. Ray O. Werner, "Cereal Firm Case Dismissed, As Is 'Shared Monopoly' Idea," *Marketing News*, Oct. 30, 1981, p. 8.

ments were in compliance after a few months.[10] In many areas, moreover, the FTC considers each case on its own merits, rather than strictly applying a single set of guidelines to all firms.

The FTC also investigates industry trade practices. When general sets of guidelines are needed to improve business practices in a particular industry, the FTC sometimes encourages the firms in that industry to establish a set of trade practices voluntarily. The FTC even may sponsor a conference to bring industry leaders and consumers together for the purpose of developing such a set of trade practices.

Although the FTC regulates a variety of business practices, it allocates a large portion of its resources to curbing false advertising, misleading pricing, and deceptive packaging and labeling.

Consumer Product Safety Commission

Few agencies at the federal level exist solely to protect consumers. The *Consumer Product Safety Commission,* however, has been created expressly for this purpose. Since product safety is a basic issue of the consumer movement, the creation of the commission by the Consumer Product Safety Act (1972) was a significant step toward forcing firms to make safer products and to provide more accurate and complete information about them. The Consumer Product Safety Commission sets product standards, tests products, investigates complaints regarding defective products, bans products from the market, and monitors injuries through the National Electronic Surveillance System—a communications system that records injury reports from emergency treatment centers around the nation. If the commission determines that a firm's product is unsafe, it is empowered to order the firm to (1) make the product conform with established safety standards, (2) replace the faulty product with an equivalent product that meets the safety standards, or (3) refund the purchaser's money less a reasonable amount for use.

Other federal regulatory units

While the FTC has broad powers to regulate a variety of business practices, the powers of other regulatory units are limited to specific products, services, or business activities. For example, the Federal Communications Commission (FCC) licenses radio and television stations and develops and enforces regulations regarding their operations. Consider the action taken recently by this agency. The FCC revoked the license of WJIM-TV in Lansing, Michigan, for reasons of misrepresentation and fraud. Gross Telecasting Inc., owner of WJIM, plans to appeal the decision and claims there was no wrongdoing. The judge who ruled in the case refused to renew the license after finding that Gross repeatedly cut out network programming from CBS, of which WJIM is an affiliate, and replaced it with local news and advertising without informing CBS and the FCC. Gross was also charged with using deceptive maps to obtain advertising clients and broad-

10. Stanley E. Cohen, "Education Best Source of Self Regulation," *Advertising Age,* July 11, 1983, p. 30.

Table 16.3 Major federal regulatory agencies

Agency	Major Areas of Responsibility
Federal Trade Commission (FTC)	Enforces laws and guidelines regarding unfair business practices; takes action to stop false and deceptive advertising and labeling
Food and Drug Administration (FDA)	Protects consumers by enforcing laws and regulations to prevent distribution of adulterated or misbranded foods, drugs, medical devices, cosmetics, veterinary products, and particularly hazardous consumer products
Consumer Products Safety Commission	Ensures compliance with the Consumer Product Safety Act; protects the public from unreasonable risk of injury from any consumer product not covered by other regulatory agencies
Interstate Commerce Commission (ICC)	Regulates franchises, rates, and finances of interstate rail, bus, truck, and water carriers
Federal Communications Commission (FCC)	Regulates communication by wire, radio, and television in interstate and foreign commerce
Civil Aeronautics Board (CAB)	Regulates economic aspects of air transport services and encourages development of an air transportation system that fits the needs of commerce, national defense, the postal service, and the general public
Environmental Protection Agency (EPA)	Develops and enforces environmental protection standards and conducts research into the adverse effects of pollution
Federal Power Commission (FPC)	Regulates rates and sales of natural gas producers, thereby affecting the supply and price of gas available to consumers; wholesale rates for electricity and gas; pipeline construction; and imports and exports of natural gas and electricity to and from the United States

casting taped weather reports without notifying the public, as required by the FCC.[11]

As marketing activities become more complex, some responsibilities among various federal units tend to overlap. When authority over a specific product or marketing practice cannot be assigned to a single federal unit, marketers must try to comply with many different regulations.

Table 16.3 outlines the major areas of responsibility of several federal agencies. As you study the table, consider the wide variety of products and business practices that are affected by these agencies.

11. "FCC Judge Rules Against WJIM," *Advertising Age,* Nov. 23, 1981, p. 10.

State and local regulatory agencies

All states—as well as numerous towns and cities—have agencies that enforce laws and rules regarding marketing practices. State and local regulatory agencies try hard not to establish and enforce regulations that conflict with the actions of national regulatory agencies. State and local agencies enforce specific laws dealing with the production and/or sale of particular goods and services. Industries that are commonly regulated by state agencies include banking, savings and loan, insurance, utilities, natural gas, and liquor.

In addition to drafting laws that regulate specific industries and marketing activities, state and local governments are now creating consumer protection units. Almost all states have a consumer protection agency, usually within the attorney general's office, the agriculture department, the commerce department, or the governor's office. State consumer protection offices conduct hearings, draft legislation, receive and process consumers' complaints, and enforce state consumer laws.

Local consumer protection efforts have certain advantages. Local agencies can respond quickly to complaints, and the local level is the most appropriate place to take action to prevent problems before they arise. Consumer education programs and "hot lines," organized at the local level, can be shaped and molded specifically to fit local consumers' needs. It is easiest to inspect weights and measures, control advertising, check personal selling, and regulate retailing right where these activities occur. Putting individuals with problems in direct contact with businesses also promotes faster and better settlement of consumers' complaints. Appeals to business persons to be responsible toward the community can be quite effective at this level.

Nongovernmental regulatory forces

In the absence of governmental regulatory forces and in an attempt to prevent government intervention, some businesses try to regulate themselves. Trade associations in a number of industries have developed self-regulatory programs. Even though these programs are not a direct outgrowth of laws, many are established as an indirect result of legal action or proposed legislation. That is, numerous self-regulatory programs are created to stop or stall the development of laws and governmental regulatory groups that would regulate marketing practices. Sometimes, these programs deal with ethical and social issues. For example, many firms in the cigarette industry agreed, through a code of ethics, not to advertise cigarettes to children and teen-agers.

Self-regulatory programs offer several advantages over governmental laws and guidelines. They are usually less expensive to establish and implement, at least in comparison to government programs, and their guidelines are generally more realistic and operational. In addition, industry self-regulatory programs reduce the need to expand government bureaucracy.

Nongovernmental self-regulatory programs do have some limitations. When a trade association creates a set of industry guidelines, nonmember firms do not have to follow the guidelines. Many self-regulatory programs lack the tools or the authority to enforce guidelines. Finally, guidelines in self-regulatory programs often are less strict than those established by government agencies.

Used in a soap advertisement, *schmuts,* the Yiddish word for dirt is appropriate; used in a men's cologne commercial, the word *stroke* is not; and the phrase "murdering her clothes" cannot be used in a detergent advertisement. These judgments and many more like them are made weekly by the editors (or censors) employed by the three major TV networks—ABC, CBS, and NBC. The task assigned to each individual network group is to ferret out tasteless and deceptive advertising. Whatever fails to meet with their approval will not appear on the networks.

Before an advertisement is screened, a storyboard is presented to an editing group. The group examines the advertisement closely to establish tastefulness and factuality. Advertisers are the first to admit that it has become very difficult to get a commercial on the air. ABC's editing group demands changes in or rejects about 40 percent of commercials. Advertisers go to great lengths to get their commercials approved. Complex demonstrations are often used to prove a product's claims to the editors, and tense discussions are common. However, the process generally remains cordial. Both parties have usually worked together before and will continue to do so. Also, both agencies and editors share the belief that screening is a good thing. Many of the changes editors seek are subtle. One agency was asked to put wedding bands on a couples' hands in a cologne commercial. In another advertisement, bikinis had to be replaced by one-piece swimsuits.

Networks' editors realize that many advertising executives consider their judgments foolish. Editors are tougher on commercials than on programs because commercials are not seen by choice and are repetitious. Despite all the criticism, network rules will remain tough.

Source: Based on Bill Abrams, "The Networks Censor TV Ads for Taste and Deceptiveness," *Wall Street Journal,* Sept. 30, 1982, p. 27.

Collective action may be necessary to prevent violation of industry guidelines, but boycotts are in restraint of trade and are illegal under antitrust statutes—regardless of the motives of the industry group. For this reason, group pressure is hard to apply.[12] In spite of these problems, the threat of increased governmental regulation will result in more self-regulatory actions.

Several programs of self-regulation are successful alternatives to governmental regulation. For example, some degree of self-regulation exists in the manufacturing of automobiles, gas equipment, aluminum windows, appliances, cigarettes, liquor, and home-building supplies. One successful self-regulatory program is sponsored by appliance manufacturers. The American Home Appliance Manufacturers program offers consumers point-of-sale information about installation and maintenance costs. It also provides a complaint system that includes a panel of consumers and consumer advocates who resolve complaints and answer questions about appliance purchases. Consider another example discussed in the Application above.

Better Business Bureaus

The *Better Business Bureau* is perhaps the best-known nongovernmental regulatory group. It is a local regulatory agency that is supported by local

12. William Lazer and Priscilla La Barbara, "Business and Self-Regulation," in *Public Policy Issues in Marketing,* ed. O. C. Ferrell and Raymond LaGarce (Lexington, Mass.: Lexington Books, 1975), p. 121.

Figure 16.1
Advertisement encouraging consumer participation in a self-regulatory program
Source: Courtesy of the National Advertising Review Board

businesses. Today there are over 140 local bureaus that help settle problems among consumers and specific business firms. They also act to preserve good business practices in a locality, although they usually do not have strong enforcement tools to use in dealing with firms that employ questionable practices. When a firm continues to violate what the Better Business Bureau believes to be good business practices, the bureau warns consumers through local newspapers that a particular business is operating unfairly.

National Advertising Review Board

The Council of Better Business Bureaus, a national organization, and three advertising trade organizations have created a self-regulatory unit called the *National Advertising Review Board*. In addition to screening national advertisements to check for honesty, the NARB processes complaints about deceptive advertisements. Figure 16.1 shows how the NARB also encourages consumers to report advertisements that seem misleading or untruthful. The National Advertising Division (NAD) of the Council of Better

Business Bureaus serves as the investigative arm of the NARB. The following describes a typical case handled by NAD/NARB:

A spaghetti sauce, made to be extra thick, was demonstrated alongside a competitor's regular spaghetti sauce by pouring them through kitchen strainers. The NAD found that this was misleading because the competition also made extra thick sauce under the same brand name, a fact not disclosed in the advertising.[13]

The NARB has no official enforcement powers. However, if a firm refuses to comply with its decision, the NARB publicizes the questionable practice and files a complaint with the FTC.

Impact of legal and regulatory forces

Having surveyed a multitude of legal and regulatory forces in the marketing environment, we will now see how these forces affect marketers' decisions and activities. Keep in mind, however, that we have room to discuss only a small portion of their impact on marketing mix decisions.

Product decisions

Legal and regulatory forces have great bearing on decisions and activities that relate to the product variable. When marketers want to add products to their firm's product mix, one alternative is to merge with another business that already produces the desired products. However, the Sherman Act, Clayton Act, and Celler-Kefauver Act (see Table 16.1) prohibit many types of mergers, limiting a firm's ability to expand its product mix through mergers.

When marketing managers choose to expand the product mix by developing products within the firm, they must determine whether the new product violates the patent rights of other firms. They also must ascertain whether the new product can be protected by one or more patents. Although a patent can be in force for 17 years, some product designs are difficult to protect because competitors can imitate the original design while introducing enough variations to avoid violations.

To stay within the limits prescribed by product safety laws and regulations, companies must be concerned about the quality of raw materials, engineering, and work that goes into their products. Laws, regulations, and recent court decisions have caused numerous marketers to be concerned about potential problems associated with product liability. Producers of foods, drugs, cosmetics, and therapeutic devices are restrained by laws and regulations. The Food and Drug Administration occasionally bans the use of certain substances, thus forcing a number of businesses to reformulate their products. For example, soft-drink bottlers had to switch sweeteners when the FDA prohibited the use of cyclamates, and cosmetic companies were forced to alter the composition of many products when the FDA restricted the use of hexachlorophene.

Because marketers make packaging and labeling decisions, they must be aware that the Fair Packaging and Labeling Act requires the following information: (1) type of product; (2) name and location of the producer or processor; (3) net quantity; printed on the major display panel in easily readable type; and (4) number and size of servings, if applicable. In

13. "Report of NARB Panel #34," p. 4.

addition, the labeling of a variety of products such as foods, drugs, cosmetics, textiles, furs, and toys is subject to many laws (see Table 16.2) and regulatory guidelines.

When designing a package, marketers must consider several conflicting forces. The package should be large enough to attract attention and to present all information required by law. Yet if the package is too large relative to the size of the product, the FTC may rule the package to be deceptive as its size may suggest that it contains more than it actually does.

Pricing decisions

Most procompetitive laws influence pricing decisions and activities. Ironically, lawmakers drafted such laws to preserve competition by limiting one tool of competition—pricing. The Sherman Act prohibits conspiracies to control prices. Court interpretations of the Sherman Act have ruled that price fixing among firms in an industry is illegal per se. Marketers not only must refrain from fixing prices but also must develop independent pricing policies and set prices in ways that do not even suggest collusion.

Both the Federal Trade Commission Act and the Wheeler-Lea Act prohibit deceptive pricing. In establishing prices, marketers must not deceive customers.

The Robinson-Patman Act has had great impact on pricing decisions. For various reasons, marketers may wish to sell the same type of product at different prices. Provisions in the Robinson-Patman Act, as well as those in the Clayton Act, limit the use of such price differentials. If price differentials tend to lessen or injure competition, they are ruled discriminatory and are prohibited. Not all price differentials, however, are discriminatory. Marketers can employ price differentials for a product under one of the following conditions:

1. When the price differentials do not injure or lessen competition
2. When the price differentials result from differences in the costs of selling to various customers
3. When the customers are not competitors
4. When the price differentials arise because the firm has had to cut its price to a particular buyer to meet competitors' prices

Until 1975, manufacturers of consumer goods could set and enforce minimum retail prices for their products in some states. Now the *Consumer Goods Pricing Act* of 1975 proscribes the use of price maintenance agreements among the producers and resellers involved in interstate commerce.

Retailers and wholesalers in states that have effective unfair trade practices acts are limited in their use of pricing as a competitive tool. Since such acts place a "floor" under prices that retailers or wholesalers can charge regularly, marketers who compete on the basis of price must be cognizant of legal constraints on their competitors' pricing policies.

Governmental action, at times, strongly influences marketers' pricing decisions. In an attempt to curb inflation, the federal government may invoke price controls. They may "freeze" prices at certain levels or determine the rates at which prices can be increased. In some states, regulatory agencies set the prices of such products as insurance, liquor, dairy products, and electricity.

Distribution decisions

When developing marketing channels, marketers must recognize that any channel structure that tends to restrain trade may violate the Sherman Act. For example, the Justice Department probably would not allow a large food processor to merge with a major retail grocery chain. Marketers most assuredly are not free to create or participate in a distribution channel just because it can be developed.

Legal forces not only affect the overall structure of marketing channels, but also have an impact on the relationships among channel members. For instance, a manufacturer might try to limit the number of competing brands sold by retailers that sell its products. Through *exclusive dealing contracts,* resellers agree to buy only from one supplier, thus relinquishing their right to purchase from the supplier's competitors. The Clayton Act prohibits such arrangements when they tend to lessen competition or to create monopolies. Since the anticompetitive effects of an exclusive dealing agreement are rather obvious, their use is limited.

To increase total sales, some suppliers have tried to encourage dealers to purchase the suppliers' total product lines by using *tying contracts.* Under such an agreement, a supplier agrees to sell certain products to a dealer on condition that the dealer consents to purchase other products sold by the supplier. The Clayton Act prohibits tying contracts when they tend to lessen competition or to create monopolies. Like exclusive dealing contracts, tying arrangements by nature tend to lessen competition, which makes many of them illegal. However, tying contracts are common in franchise agreements. One study indicates that approximately 70 percent of all franchise agreements contain some form of tying arrangements.[14]

There are, on the other hand, a few types of products that may be distributed only through certain outlets. For example, the Food and Drug Administration specifies that prescription drugs can be sold only through registered pharmacies by licensed personnel; and in twenty-one states, liquor is sold at the retail level only through state-owned liquor stores.

Both state and federal laws and regulations may affect the transportation methods employed by a firm. These laws and regulations influence the cost and speed of moving products. The maximum size and weight of shipments are also affected by state and federal laws.

Promotion decisions

Legal and regulatory forces have had (and will continue to have) tremendous impact on decisions regarding advertising, personal selling, and sales promotion. The Wheeler-Lea Act, passed in 1938, strengthened the Federal Trade Commission Act's ability to prohibit unfair or deceptive acts or practices. Together, these two acts have empowered the FTC to develop and enforce regulations that prevent or stop false advertising. The FTC annually issues complaints against a variety of firms regarding misrepresentations in advertisements.

In recent years, the FTC has developed and administered an advertising substantiation program. Under this program, the FTC evaluates advertisements of national advertisers to determine whether their claims are

14. Shelby Hunt and John Nevin, "Tying Agreements in Franchising," *Journal of Marketing,* July 1975, p. 24.

truthful. The FTC believes that it is unfair to advertise a claim that cannot be supported by reasonable proof. Depending on the product and the claim, reasonable proof can range from authoritative opinions to fully documented, rigidly administered, independent scientific tests. If the FTC believes a firm's claims to be questionable, it asks the firm to substantiate them, and the FTC has ordered some firms to run corrective advertisements in which false claims are exposed and consumers are given accurate information.

When advertising prices, marketers must be careful to avoid any form of misrepresentation. FTC rules prohibit several types of price misrepresentation, including "special prices" that are not really lower than regular prices; price comparisons involving an inflated "list price"; and bait pricing, in which a product is advertised at a low price but is unavailable when consumers attempt to buy it. When they use such words as "free," "two for one," "half price," and "wholesale price," marketers must be sure that their claims are absolutely true.

Although the FTC is the major federal advertising watchdog, a number of federal agencies enforce advertising regulations related to specific products, such as securities, stamps, money, alcohol, seeds, insecticides, and packaged meat products. Such agencies include the Securities and Exchange Commission, the Treasury Department, the Agriculture Department, and the Department of Health and Human Services.

Marketers' advertising decisions must also take into account state laws and regulatory agencies. Many states have laws regarding truth in advertising. The basic provisions of most such laws make it a misdemeanor to use untrue, misleading, or deceptive advertising.

Legal and regulatory forces affect personal selling less than they affect advertising. The FTC is forcing larger firms that sell regularly on a door-to-door basis to make their salespersons identify themselves accurately, rather than using false pretenses to gain entrance into a house. In some communities local "green river ordinances" require door-to-door sales personnel to buy licenses, and in other localities door-to-door selling of certain products may be prohibited. Some communities have banned door-to-door selling altogether. "Blue laws" prohibit the sale of nonnecessity products on Sundays in some states. Although provisions vary among states, blue laws usually allow certain products, including food, drugs, and gasoline, to be sold on Sundays.

Regulatory agencies also focus on companies that sell by phone. Not long ago, the FTC filed charges against Allied Publishers Services that resulted in a $140,000 fine. The FTC claimed that Allied sales personnel misrepresented the purpose of sales solicitation phone calls, failed to disclose buyers' rights to cancel, used illegal collection methods, and offered "free" subscriptions that really were not free.[15]

Marketers must be particularly aware of legal and regulatory forces if they are considering the use of promotional allowances to resellers or of consumer sweepstakes. The Robinson-Patman Act states that if a supplier offers promotional allowances to one dealer, the supplier must offer the

15. "Subscription Service Pays FTC Penalty," *Advertising Age,* Sept. 5, 1983, p. 26.

same allowances on a proportional basis to all other dealers. A firm that uses consumer sweepstakes must give away all prizes as advertised and may not misrepresent the chances of winning. Several states have outlawed consumer contests and/or sweepstakes.

Coping with political, legal, and regulatory forces

Legislation, judicial rulings, and regulatory agencies place a wide variety of pressures on marketers. At this point, you may have the impression that marketers are at the mercy of political, legal, and regulatory forces in the environment. Although marketers cannot control these forces, they are not entirely "defenseless" either. Attempts to influence political, legal, and regulatory forces may, in fact, be quite effective.

Generally, marketers try to cope with political and legal pressures either by complying with laws and regulations or by trying to influence them. There are, however, a few marketers who violate laws and flout regulations. Sometimes the profit rewards for violating laws exceed the fines and other sanctions that exist to enforce compliance.

Complying with the law

The vast majority of marketers attempt to comply with the law—something that sounds easy but, in reality, can be quite difficult. As we have pointed out, legal compliance is complicated by the vagueness of many laws and regulatory guidelines. It is difficult to comply with all laws and regulatory guidelines simply because there are so many of them. Furthermore, since the courts' interpretations of laws change over the years, marketers may not know how to comply.

Businesses often rely on professional legal guidance. Larger firms obtain counsel from their own legal staffs and from outside attorneys, and many firms are increasing their legal staffs. Small firms can rarely afford to maintain legal staffs within the organization. Instead, they retain the services of one or more independent lawyers.

Influencing political, legal, and regulatory forces

Even though most marketers strive to comply with legal provisions and guidelines, some of them also attempt to influence political, legal, and regulatory forces. To do this, firms sometimes contribute resources to help elect candidates for office or to affect the outcome of public referendums. In addition, business organizations and industry groups sometimes advertise their positions on specific social and economic issues.

Businesses can also affect legal and regulatory forces by sending company representatives to legislative bodies to speak for or against proposed laws or regulations. In recent years, many companies have sent chief executives to lobby, rather than vice presidents, as was once more common. Firms also hire professional lobbyists who represent their clients' interests by trying to persuade lawmakers to vote a certain way on proposed legislation. Professional lobbyists can be effective because they usually know who the more powerful legislators are.

Sunkist, an agricultural cooperative that controls 75 percent of lemon and orange production in the western United States, successfully lobbied Congress to enact legislation that removed agricultural cooperatives from the jurisdiction of the FTC. The FTC had claimed that several Sunkist practices, such as withholding products from the market to keep prices artificially high, were anticompetitive.[16]

Marketers' willingness to cooperate with government agencies in establishing sets of trade practices indirectly affects the types of legal provisions that lawmakers create. To the extent that firms and industries cooperate with government agencies voluntarily to develop trade practices, agency personnel and lawmakers may not push as hard for strong laws that are highly unfavorable to the firms or industries involved.

Although some firms and trade associations spend much time and money trying to influence the shape of legal forces, they are not always successful. Each year, many laws and guidelines are adopted that are disadvantageous to some firms. Remember that although the automobile industry opposed federal pollution and safety requirements for automobiles, they nevertheless were implemented. Such cases are quite common.

Violating laws and guidelines

Although most marketers consistently abide by the law, a few violate laws and regulatory guidelines either intentionally or unintentionally. They do so for a number of reasons. First, marketers sometimes unintentionally violate laws and guidelines because the provisions are vague. Second, marketers break certain laws or regulatory guidelines simply because they are not aware of them. Third, some marketing executives violate laws that directly affect their businesses because they believe enforcement to be so inadequate that the chances of being caught are slight. Fourth, violations occur when legal restrictions are so harmful that a business cannot survive if it operates within the law. Fifth, marketers at times break laws to garner large profits in the short run, despite the risk of being fined. Even if fines are imposed, the excess profits that result from violating the laws or guidelines often exceed the fines. Marketers should try to operate within the law at all times. Intentional violations are both unethical and socially irresponsible.

Summary

The marketing environment contains political, legal, and regulatory forces that marketers must understand in order to operate successfully. Some marketers view governmental intervention in the marketplace as detrimental; others see it as both good and necessary. Regardless of how one views governmental intervention, its role in our economic system has become increasingly larger and more active.

Political and legal forces are closely interrelated aspects of the marketing environment. The atmosphere in which legal and regulatory forces are developed and implemented is strongly shaped by political forces. The current political feelings of lawmakers are reflected in legislation or the lack of it. Many marketers feel that political forces are uncontrollable, but some marketers attempt to influence political forces by making campaign contributions.

Federal legislation covers all major areas of marketing activities and can be divided into two categories: procompetitive legislation and con-

16. Michael McMenamin and Diane Connelly, "How Sunkist Put the Squeeze on the FTC," *Reason,* November 1981, p. 45.

sumer protection laws. Beginning with very broad procompetitive legislation such as the Sherman Act, these laws have gradually focused more directly on specific marketing practices. The apparent vagueness of the Sherman Act allowed courts to apply its regulations to a variety of situations that had the common characteristic of being harmful to competition. Subsequent legislation such as the Clayton Act, the Federal Trade Commission Act, and the Wheeler-Lea Act were directed more toward specific practices.

Price regulation often arises out of political pressure to curtail certain anticompetitive practices. Legislators at one time considered the differential pricing policies of large chain stores detrimental to competition. They therefore passed the Robinson-Patman Act to correct the situation.

For over forty years, resale price maintenance laws allowed manufacturers of branded consumer goods to set and enforce minimum resale prices, but now the Consumer Goods Pricing Act of 1975 prohibits such practices. Unfair trade practices acts at the state level prohibit wholesalers and retailers from selling below cost or below cost plus a certain percentage of markup.

Since the 1960s there has been a rapid surge in consumer protection legislation. Such laws are based on the belief that consumers have certain basic rights, among them the rights to information and protection from unsafe products.

Laws alone are not enough; court interpretations must be considered. Enforcement is another component of the legal environment. Regulatory agencies also exert considerable force on marketing practices. Often these agencies generate regulatory guidelines that carry considerable weight in the marketplace. For example, the FTC has been active in several areas, including the monitoring and regulation of advertising practices. Although the FTC has no direct power to fine or imprison, it can seek such actions in the courts.

Marketers must not overlook state and local laws and regulatory agencies when considering the legal forces in the marketing environment. State and local laws sometimes place additional restrictions on marketers, and regulatory agencies enforce specific laws dealing with the production and/or sale of particular goods and services.

Industry self-regulation provides another source of concern for marketers. However, this type of regulation is generally more welcome because marketers have a more direct opportunity to participate in the creation of the guidelines. The Better Business Bureau is probably the best-known nongovernmental regulatory group. Self-regulatory groups have several advantages over governmental laws and guidelines. They provide a more operational and often a less expensive regulatory structure. However, compliance with regulations is more difficult to enforce through these groups than through governmental agencies.

Legal and regulatory forces have great bearing on marketing mix decisions. Product decisions are regulated by numerous laws and regulations. The option of adding products to a firm's product mix by merging with another business may be prohibited by provisions of the Sherman Act, the Clayton Act, and the Celler-Kefauver Act. Development of products within a firm is influenced by patent laws, product safety laws, and regulations of the FDA. Packaging and labeling decisions are affected by the Fair Packaging and Labeling Act. Pricing decisions are influenced by many of the procompetitive laws. The Sherman Act prohibits price fixing; the Federal Trade Commission Act and the Wheeler-Lea Act prohibit deceptive pricing; and the Robinson-Patman Act and the Clayton Act limit the use of price differentials. Distribution decisions are regulated by the Sherman Act. Exclusive dealing contracts and tying contracts are restricted by the Clayton Act. Promotion decisions are constrained by the Federal Trade Commission Act, by the Wheeler-Lea Act, and by various governmental agencies.

Marketers are not entirely at the mercy of political and legal forces. They try to adapt to and influence these forces in several ways. The vast majority attempt to comply with the law, but compliance is difficult because of variations in court interpretations, the general vagueness of the laws, and the sheer number of pertinent laws and regulations.

Important terms

Procompetitive legislation
Sherman Act
Clayton Act
Federal Trade Commission Act
Wheeler-Lea Act
Robinson-Patman Act
Resale price maintenance laws
Unfair trade practices acts
Consumer protection legislation

Federal Trade Commission (FTC)
Consumer Product Safety
  Commission
Better Business Bureau
National Advertising Review
  Board (NARB)
Consumer Goods Pricing Act
Exclusive dealing contracts
Tying contracts

Discussion and review questions

1. How are political forces related to legal and governmental regulatory forces?
2. Describe marketers' attempts to influence political forces.
3. What types of procompetitive legislation directly affect marketing practices?
4. What was the major objective of most procompetitive laws? Do these laws generally accomplish this objective? Why or why not?
5. What are the major provisions of the Robinson-Patman Act? Which marketing mix decisions are influenced directly by this act?
6. Do you feel that unfair trade practices acts are fair to retailers? Why or why not?
7. What are the major goals of consumer legislation? What has caused the upsurge in this type of legislation? Do you feel that consumers really benefit from consumer laws? Why or why not?
8. What types of problems do marketers experience as they try to interpret legislation?
9. To what extent are federal regulatory agencies independent? Do the agencies regulate business organizations, or do businesses regulate the agencies?
10. What are the goals of the Federal Trade Commission? List the ways in which the FTC affects marketing activities. Should a single regulatory agency have such broad jurisdiction over so many marketing practices? Why or why not?

11. What does the Consumer Product Safety Commission do? What powers, if any, does it have?
12. Discuss the types of state and local government regulatory agencies that affect marketing practices and consumers.
13. Name several nongovernmental regulatory forces. Do you feel that self-regulation is more or less effective than governmental regulatory agencies? Why?
14. Describe several specific ways that legal and regulatory forces affect each decision variable in the marketing mix. Which decision variable is most affected by these forces? Why?

Cases

Case 16.1

Eli Lilly's Oraflex[17]

Millions of Americans suffer from the annoying pain of arthritis. For these persons, a simple task like opening a jar becomes a difficult process. Eli Lilly & Company, a large manufacturer of pharmaceuticals, developed a drug called Oraflex to help persons who suffer from arthritic pain. On April 19, 1982, the FDA gave Lilly approval to market Oraflex; but less than three months later, Lilly pulled the medication off the market. It had been under pressure from consumer protection groups and regulatory forces who claimed the drug had adverse side effects. This recall cost Lilly $11.4 million dollars. Currently, the Justice Department is conducting an investigation, and a product liability suit against Lilly is pending.

The chemical name for Oraflex is benoxaprofen. Oraflex is an oral prescription medication that is taken once daily. The 400 milligram tablets cost about 94 cents a piece. This is significantly cheaper than another antiarthritic drug, Feldome, that sells at $1.11 for a 20 milligram tablet.

The only side effects that had been known to Lilly were increased sensitivity of skin and nails to the sun. Lilly had submitted an application to the FDA for new drug approval on January 17, 1980. Twenty-eight months later, the FDA, after a routine review process, gave its approval for the marketing of Oraflex. Lilly had estimated that sales of Oraflex would be about $100 million annually.

Although it now takes less time than it did in the past, FDA approval is still a lengthy process. In 1981, a relaxed approval program was put into effect, reducing the previous review time by 20%. Now, any applicant seeking approval of a drug that has already been approved must no longer conduct primary research; a report of 50–200 pages summarizing technical data can be submitted. This has reduced the manufacturer's cost considerably, allowing some generic producers to enter the market. (We have only recently seen generic drugs on the market because, previously, generic producers could not afford to reproduce the studies of the innovator.)

17. The facts in this case are from Lou LaMarca, "FDA Sets Faster Pace for New Drug Review," *Advertising Age,* Sept. 27, 1982, pp. M24, M27; "An Arthritis Drug's Quick Exit," *Newsweek,* Aug. 16, 1982, p. 59; "Oraflex: Behind the Headlines," *Consumers' Research Magazine,* Dec. 1982, pp. 11–14; and Howard Banks, "The Oraflex Fiasco," *Forbes,* Oct. 25, 1982, pp. 41–42.

The new program also allows the FDA to approve competitive brands at the same time. For example, Oraflex was approved along with two similar oral anti-arthritic drugs. In the past, the FDA had released only one of a group of similar drugs, watched its effects, and then a year later approved competitive drugs. The FDA also may begin accepting the results of foreign tests that follow U.S. regulations. This new, relaxed process has only been in effect for a short time. If the Department of Justice uncovers evidence that Oraflex caused fatal effects, the new FDA approval process will be changed back to the old process. Lilly's new drug application will certainly undergo extensive analysis by the FDA.

U.S. officials are considering suing Lilly on the grounds that the FDA was ill-informed about the adverse side effects associated with Oraflex. Shortly after FDA approval, benoxaprofen (sold under the name of Opien in Britain) was associated with sixty-one deaths in Britain. The drug supposedly causes liver and kidney damage that can prove fatal for some persons. In the United States, eleven deaths are under investigation. Although this adverse publicity has hurt Oraflex, nothing definite about the deaths has been proven. Lilly still maintains that if proper dosage is followed, Oraflex is safe and effective.

Questions for discussion
1. What kinds of environmental forces does Eli Lilly have to deal with that may not be as strong for many firms in other types of industries?
2. What types of risks does Eli Lilly (and other pharmaceutical firms) bear when developing and introducing a new drug such as Oraflex?
3. How could a pharmaceutical product like Oraflex pass through all the testing conducted by Eli Lilly, pass all of the FDA tests and requirements, and still have to be recalled after less than three months?

Case 16.2

Nissan Automotive Products

Nissan Motor Co., Ltd. is Japan's second largest automobile producer (Toyota is the largest). Nissan is a worldwide exporter of a full line of automotive products and parts. In the United States and some other foreign markets, Nissan's products are sold under the Datsun, as well as Nissan, name. That name has become respected in many parts of this country due to Nissan's keen awareness of its customers' desires and the ability of its strong engineering staff to make these desires a reality. The legendary Datsun 240Z, the Datsun 200SX, and the Nissan Stanza are examples of this ability. Recently, company officials have decided to sell all products under the Nissan name, and the gradual changing of the name is currently underway.

Nissan has been in the export business since 1934 and has exported over 10,000,000 units. The company has 25 assembly and manufacturing plants located in 20 countries worldwide. At present, Nissan has 174 dis-

tributors and 5,540 dealers in 150 countries. North America is its largest market (45 percent of total exports), followed by Europe (23 percent), and the Middle East (10 percent).

Nissan has three major objectives. First, it wants to continue developing a line of cars that blends safety, economy, and emission control. These three elements are seen as a car's most important aspects. Nissan's second objective is to become a unified multi-national corporation. This is the reason for selling all its products under the Nissan name. By selling all its products under one name, Nissan hopes to increase awareness of its international image. The third objective is to remain aware of what the public is looking for in a car. Styling was previously determined to be lacking in its product line, and emphasis has been given to upgrade this area.

Although Nissan has made major inroads into the U.S. automobile market, this firm may be facing several major problems. High energy costs will sustain demand for energy-efficient cars in the United States but will continue to hurt sales in Japan. Content legislation and import quotas in the United States could also seriously affect Nissan. Content legislation, currently being proposed by the United Auto Workers, would require 75 percent of all parts and labor to be North American for companies selling 200,000 vehicles per year in the United States. This percentage would increase to 90 percent if sales were over 500,000 vehicles per year. This legislation, if passed, would take full effect in 1985. As for quotas, the proposed Danforth-Bentsen bill would limit total Japanese imports for three years to 1,600,000 vehicles.

Questions for discussion
1. Should Congress enact legislation with import quotas or product content requirements in order to protect the jobs of American auto workers? Is this type of legislation in the interests of consumers? Explain.
2. How can Nissan attempt to block passage of legislation that contains import quotas and content requirements?
3. If such legislation were enacted, how could Nissan cope with its effects?

17

Societal, Economic, and Technological Forces

Objectives

To gain a better understanding of what society does and does not want from marketers.

To identify social and ethical issues that marketers must deal with as they make decisions.

To identify the tools by which firms compete.

To understand how economic factors affect buying power.

To explore several economic forces that influence consumers' willingness to spend.

To learn how marketers analyze consumers' spending patterns to better understand spending behavior.

To gain an awareness of the effects of technological knowledge on society.

To understand how technology can influence marketing activities.

To examine factors that determine whether and to what extent businesses use existing technological information.

Intelmatique is beginning to market the "smart card," a European phenomenon, in the United States. Intelmatique is a French government-owned firm set up to promote the French telecommunications industry. A smart card, which looks like a credit card (see Figure 17.1), is a portable computer that relies on an external power source supplied by a card reader or data terminal. The card has a microcircuit chip embedded in it that contains both a coded memory and microprocessor "intelligence." Both are programmed to the requirements of the issuer and user.

The smart card functions as an "electronic checkbook." It stores confidential data and can record up to two hundred transactions, either at home or at the point of sale. The card's memory is updated after each use and cannot be erased. If one loses the card, the memory can be reprogrammed by the issuer. When the user makes purchases, transaction data are recorded both in the card's memory and in the retailer's terminal, usually on a cassette. This data is then transferred from the cassette to a magnetic disc at the bank. Manufacturers believe that the smart card can replace most of the documents and cards Americans carry with them. It could serve as a cash management card, credit card, identification card for automatic teller machines (ATMs), insurance information card, passport, credit application qualification card, home terminal purchase authorization card, student identification card, library card, driver's license, or employee identification card.

Figure 17.1   Smart cards
Source: Reprinted from Marketing News, *November 26, 1982.*

The smart card can provide both the user and issuer with many advantages. The user is assured of security and privacy. The intelligence feature ensures security. The device protects the user memory, guards against fraudulent use, stores the user's private identification number, and provides privacy for user transactions. If the card is lost, it is worthless if found by another party. The card can only be used in conjunction with a personal identification number. The card is said to be tamper-proof. If a thief should attempt to use the card without the proper identification number, the electronics in the card would self-destruct. The card, although it permits immediate electronic funds transfers, also offers float time (the time it takes to debit an account) that can be set by the issuer. For the issuer, the smart card can reduce paperwork, eliminate handling costs and mistakes, and decrease the number of computer thefts using false identification.[1]

The smart card is only one example of how technology affects consumers and marketers. Later in this chapter, we explore the technological forces in the marketing environment and look more closely at the impact of technology on buyers and on marketing decisions and activities.

This chapter first discusses general societal forces in the marketing environment and describes some of the social and ethical issues facing marketers. Then we discuss several types of economic forces that affect the intensity of competition and others that influence consumers' willingness and ability to buy. We also consider the effects of general economic conditions—prosperity, recession, depression, inflation, and shortages. Finally, as mentioned above, we analyze the major dimensions of the technological forces in the environment.

Societal forces

Societal forces comprise the structure and dynamics of individuals and groups and the issues with which they are concerned. The public raises questions about the activities of marketers when the consequences of those activities are felt to be inconsistent with the goals of individuals or of society in general. Even when marketers do a good job of satisfying society, letters of praise or positive evaluation rarely follow. Society expects marketers to provide a high standard of living and to protect the general quality of life that we enjoy. In this section, we examine some of society's expectations, the vehicles used to express those expectations, and the problems and opportunities that marketers experience as they try to deal effectively with society's often contradictory wishes.

Living standards and quality of life

In our society, we want more than just the bare necessities required to sustain life—shelter, food, and clothing. Our homes, schools, factories, stores, and other buildings must provide not only protection from the elements but also comfort and aesthetic satisfaction. Our food must give us the nutrients

1. Bernie Whalen, "The Smart Card: No Longer a Solution in Search of a Problem," *Marketing News,* Nov. 26, 1982, pp. 4–5.

necessary for life and good health, but almost all of us also want it to be readily available in large quantities, in wide varieties, and in easily prepared forms. We use our clothing to cover, protect, and warm our bodies, but most of us also think it necessary to provide ourselves with a variety of clothing for adornment and to project an "image" to others.

We have many other wants, too, beyond the necessities of life. We want vehicles that provide rapid, convenient, and efficient transportation when and where we want to go. We want communication systems that allow us to talk to anyone in the world and that quickly provide us with information from around the globe. We want sophisticated medical services that prolong our life span, make our lives more tolerable, and improve our physical appearance. And we expect our education to equip us to both acquire and enjoy a higher standard of living.

Our society's high material standard of living is not enough; we also want a high degree of quality in our lives. We do not want to spend all our waking hours working. We seek leisure time for recreation, entertainment, amusement, and relaxation. Nor do we wish to spend our lives in a dirty environment. We cannot enjoy the benefits of a high living standard when the water is polluted with raw sewage and industrial wastes or when the air is full of smoke, foul odors, and loud noises. The *quality of life* is enhanced by leisure time, clean air and water, an unlittered earth, conservation of wildlife and natural resources, and security from radiation and poisonous substances.

Our society seeks a multitude of goods and services in addition to healthy environmental conditions. It expects business to provide many elements necessary to both a high standard of living and a satisfying quality of life. Since marketing activities are a vital part of the total business structure, marketers have a responsibility to help provide what societal members want and to minimize what they do not want.

Various interest groups exert pressure on business, government, and public opinion. For example, Action for Children's Television, is a national organization of parents and professionals working to upgrade television for children and to eliminate its commercial aspects. Then there is the Council on Children, Media, and Merchandising, created by Robert Choate to monitor the advertising of food and nutrition to children. These and many other organizations focus on specific issues in an attempt to involve members of society in safeguarding our quality of life.

Consumer movement forces

The *consumer movement* is a diverse group of independent individuals, groups, and organizations that attempts to protect the rights of consumers. The major issues of the consumer movement fall into three categories: environmental protection, product performance and safety, and information disclosure. A recent study, for example, reported that consumers are seeking simpler, gentler, and safer health and beauty aids such as analgesics and shampoos.[2] The major forces of the consumer movement are individual consumer advocates, consumer organizations, consumer education, and consumer laws. Consumer advocates, such as Ralph Nader, take it

2. Bill Abrams, "Hair Care Fears . . . License Plates Locate Customers . . . Sex and Sales," *Wall Street Journal*, Feb. 5, 1981, p. 29.

upon themselves to protect the rights of consumers. They inform and organize other consumers, help businesses to develop consumer-oriented programs, and pressure lawmakers to enact consumer laws. More often, however, consumer advocates band together into consumer organizations, either voluntarily or under government sponsorship. Some organizations operate nationally, while others are active at state and local levels. The results of a recent study indicate that the consumer movement will rely more heavily on local organizations during the 1980s because national organizations do not have public support.[3]

Consumer organizations aid the consumer movement by encouraging consumers to get involved, advising and pressuring legislators to pass stronger consumer laws, encouraging enforcement of existing consumer laws, and establishing consumer education programs. Educating consumers to make wiser purchasing decisions will perhaps be one of the most far-reaching aspects of the consumer movement. Consumer education is increasingly becoming a part of high school and college curricula and adult education programs.

Businesses have responded to the consumer movement in various ways. They have resisted, been indifferent to, or actively accepted the movement's goals. Firms that resist the consumer movement view it as a threat to free enterprise and profits. Some feel that if they ignore the consumer movement, it will—perhaps—fade away. Many firms have created consumer affairs units, and many industries and trade associations have established guidelines and programs to further consumers' interests.

Ethical issues and social responsibility

The advertisement in Figure 17.2 reflects an organization's desire to behave in a socially responsible manner. Seagram's is encouraging Fourth of July celebrators to drink in moderation.

The changing values of society have placed more pressure on marketers to act responsibly and ethically. Such issues as racial injustice, malnutrition, human rights, poverty, and unethical marketing behavior have increased public concern about the role of marketing in society. Payoffs, bribes, and coverups of defective products have eroded public confidence in marketers. For example, one automobile manufacturer was indicted on criminal charges of "recklessly causing the death" of three teenagers in connection with the crash of a subcompact automobile. The jury in this case said the manufacturer was aware that the automobile's fuel tank was unsafe but did nothing about it. Although this decision is highly controversial—since the manufacturer did not actually cause the accident—it does illustrate that some members of society want businesses to take an active role in providing safe products to consumers.

Some firms are recognizing that ethical issues and social responsibility find their expression in the daily decisions of marketers rather than in abstract ideals. According to this view, to preserve their ethical and socially responsible behavior while they accomplish their goals, organizations must monitor changes and trends in society's values. Also, marketers must develop control procedures to ensure that a few unethical employees do not

3. Bill Abrams, "Quieter Consumer Movement Expected," *Wall Street Journal,* Oct. 8, 1981, p. 27.

Figure 17.2
Advertisement that
demonstrates a firm's
social responsiveness
*Source: The House of
Seagram*

This Fourth of July, proceed with caution.

The Fourth of July is a time to celebrate. Unfortunately, sometimes we tend to overindulge. Drinking more than our limit is never wise but it can be especially dangerous over a long holiday weekend. This Fourth of July, if you choose to drink, use common sense. And if you're on the road, watch out for the other guy. The more cautious we are about July Fourth, the more likely we'll be here to remember it on July Fifth.

The House of Seagram

damage the company's relations with the public. An organization's top management must assume some responsibilty for the ethical conduct of employees by establishing and enforcing policies.

Marketing decisions and societal forces

Marketers have a responsibility to act in socially responsible ways as they provide people with satisfying marketing mixes. Unfortunately, some marketers have, at times, succumbed to business pressures and failed to act in socially responsible ways regarding products, pricing, distribution, and promotion.

Society does not want products that are faulty or unsafe. It does not want product warranties that are misleading or that are not backed up by sellers. It does not want durable goods for which replacement parts and repair services cannot be obtained easily. Deceptive packages that are misleading in terms of quantity, size, color, shape, or uses of products are also undesirable, as are labels that inaccurately describe or fail to describe the contents of products. Nor does society want deceptive advertisements that cause consumers to spend money unwisely and to lose confidence in advertising generally; equally objectionable are deceptive selling practices, including dishonest personal selling techniques, unfair consumer contests, and deceptive premium offers. And because prices to some degree determine how far people can stretch their dollars, consumers do not want to be abused by inflated or exploitive prices that yield excessive profits to sellers and by price quotations that include numerous, hidden, additional charges. In addition to all of these constraints on the mix variables, products or packages that increase problems of pollution, litter, or solid waste disposal are undesirable.

Society expresses what it does not want in several different ways. Through its lawmakers, society creates laws and regulatory groups to prohibit or control undesired marketing practices. As we saw in Chapter 16, a wide variety of laws and guidelines relate to product safety, warranties, packaging, labeling, advertising, personal selling, consumer contests, and pricing. In addition, consumer and other special-interest groups pressure marketers to take or change certain actions.

To be socially responsible, marketers not only must determine what product features consumers want, but must also consider product safety and dependability. They must write clear, straightforward warranty statements; establish an efficient distribution system that provides buyers with products, parts, and repair services when and where needed; develop promotion mixes that satisfy consumers' informational needs; and provide these mixes at prices that customers can afford and that yield reasonable profits.

Being socially responsible may be a noble endeavor, but it is not a simple one. To be socially responsible, marketers must confront certain major problems. They must determine what society wants and then predict the long-run effects of their decisions, often by turning to scientists. However, scientists make new discoveries and sometimes do not agree with each other. Forty years ago, marketers promoted cigarettes as being good for one's health. Scientists had not yet discovered that cigarette smoking is linked to cancer. Since society is made up of many diverse groups, finding out what "society" as a whole wants is difficult, if not impossible. In trying to satisfy the desires of one group, marketers may dissatisfy others. Many of the demands of society have costs associated with them. Marketers must evaluate the extent to which members of the society are willing to pay for what they want. For example, consumers may desire more information regarding a product yet be unwilling to pay the costs that the firm sustains in providing it. Thus, marketers who want to make socially responsible decisions may find the task difficult.

Economic forces

The economic forces in the marketing environment influence customers' reactions to a firm's marketing decisions and activities. We have already discussed the basic forces of supply and demand (in Chapter 14). Here we will explore broader economic forces. Specifically, we will examine the effects of competitive forces, buying power, willingness to spend, spending patterns, and general economic conditions.

Table 17.1 Selected characteristics of competitive structures

Type of Structure	Number of Competitors	Ease of Entry	Product	Knowledge of Market	Example
Monopoly	One	Many barriers	Almost no substitutes	Perfect	Dayton (Ohio) Power and Light (electrical service)
Oligopoly	Few	Some barriers	Homogeneous or differentiated (real or perceived differences) products	Imperfect	Philip Morris (cigarettes)
Monopolistic competition	Many	Few barriers	Product differentiation with many substitutes	More knowledge than oligopoly; less than monopoly	Timex, and foreign competitors (digital watches)
Perfect competition	Unlimited	No barriers	Homogeneous products	Perfect	Vegetable farm (sweet corn)

The intensity of competition

Few firms, if any, operate free of competition. Broadly speaking, all firms compete with each other for the buying power of consumers. From a more practical viewpoint, however, a business generally views as *competition* those firms that market products similar to, or substitutable for, its products in the same geographic area. For example, a local supermarket manager views all grocery stores in town as competitors but almost never thinks of all other local or out-of-town stores as competitors. Several factors affect the strength—and thus the importance—of a firm's competitive environment. Let us explore a few of them.

Types of competitive structures

The number of firms that control the supply of a product may affect the strength of competition. When only one or a few firms control the product, competitive factors will exert a different sort of influence on marketing activities than when there are many competitors. Table 17.1 presents four general categories or models of competitive relationships. This *competitive structure* is a continuum; and many types of structures could exist.

A *monopoly* exists when a firm produces a product that has no close substitutes. In this case, a single seller can erect barriers to potential competitors. For example, Dayton (Ohio) Power and Light has a monopoly on sales of natural gas and electricity in its service area. The state Public Utilities Commission sets rates that greatly influence shareholders' return on investment. Therefore, the company focuses on rate hearings and efficient operations rather than on the strength of competition.

An *oligopoly* exists when a few sellers control the supply of a large proportion of a product. In this case, each seller must consider the reactions of other sellers to changes in marketing activities. Products facing oligopolistic competition may be homogeneous, such as aluminum, or differentiated, such as cigarettes and automobiles. There usually are some barriers that make it difficult to enter the market and compete with oligopolies. Few companies or individuals could enter the oil refining or steel industries, for example, because of the tremendous financial resources that are necessary. Moreover, some industries require special technical or marketing skills that block the entry of many potential competitors.

Monopolistic competition exists when a firm with many potential competitors attempts to develop a differential marketing strategy to establish its own market share. This is the course Timex has taken in the digital watch industry. Although a competitor offers the lowest possible prices and a dependable but often stark product, Timex provides many designs and styles to obtain its share of the digital watch market. The firm's marketing strategy is based on dependability, service, design, price, and distribution; it seeks a differential advantage to obtain a partial monopoly in its market. Similarly, Levi's has established a differential advantage for its jeans through a well-known trademark, design, advertising, and a quality image. Although many competing jeans and digital wrist watches are available, these two firms have carved out their market shares through use of differential marketing strategies.

Perfect competition, if it existed at all, would entail a large number of sellers, no one of which could significantly influence price or supply. Products would be homogeneous, and there would be full knowledge of the market and easy entry into it. Something like perfect competition exists in the case of agricultural products, such as sweet corn or tomatoes, that are sold directly to consumers by small vegetable farmers.

Few, if any, marketers operate in a structure of perfect competition. Rather, perfect competition is an ideal at one end of the continuum, with monopoly at the other end. Most marketers function in a competitive environment that falls somewhere between these two extremes.

The tools of competition

Another set of factors that influence the level of competition is the number and types of competitive tools used by competitors. To survive, a firm uses one or several available competitive tools to deal with competitive economic forces. Once a firm has analyzed its particular competitive environment and decided which factors in that environment it can or must adjust to or influence, it can choose among the variables it can control to strengthen its competitive position.

Probably the first competitive tool that occurs to most of us is price. Recognizing this phenomenon, Bic produces disposable products that are similar to competing products but less expensive. There is, however, one major problem with using price as a competitive tool. Frequently competitors will either match or beat your price. This threat is one of the primary reasons for employing nonprice competitive tools that are based on the differentiation of market segments, product offering, promotion, distribution, or enterprise.[4] For example, Caterpillar charges at least 10 percent more than the competition for its earth-moving equipment, but its customers want a reliable product and the best parts and service system in the industry.

By focusing on a specific market segment, a marketer sometimes gains a competitive advantage. Timex is an example. One primary reason it gained a competitive advantage is that it concentrated its initial marketing efforts on a single market segment. Many marketers compete by differentiating their product offerings. Producers often attempt to gain a competitive edge by incorporating into their respective brands product features that make their brands, to some extent, distinctive. Stores sometimes use services as competitive tools. To compete with a large discount store like K mart, a locally owned independent hardware dealer may offer free delivery, gift wrapping, and credit services. Firms employ distinguishing promotional methods to compete, such as advertising and personal selling. A number of marketers use gifts, stamps, and discounts as competitive tools. Competing producers sometimes use different distribution channels to gain competitive advantage over each other. Merchants may compete by placing their outlets in locations that are convenient for a large number of shoppers and by creating unique and appealing atmospheres that make their stores distinctive.

The kind of competitive structure and the types of competitive tools selected by marketers make up one set of forces in a firm's economic environment. We will now examine another significant group of economic forces that influence consumers' spending behavior.

Consumer demand and spending behavior

Marketers must understand what factors determine whether, what, where, and when people buy. In Chapter 3, we looked at behavioral factors that underlie these choices. Here, we focus on economic aspects of buying behavior. Specifically, we analyze buying power and consumers' willingness to purchase, as well as their spending patterns.

Buying power

Think back to the requirements for a market outlined in Chapter 2. One is that people have buying power. The strength of a person's *buying power* depends both on the size of the resources that give that individual the ability to purchase and on the state of the economy. The resources that make up buying power are goods, services, and financial holdings. The state of the economy affects buying power because it influences price levels. During inflationary periods, when prices are rising, buying power is reduced because more dollars are required to buy products. For example, products today cost over two-and-one-half times as much money as they did in 1967. As Figure 17.3 indicates, the consumer price index has nearly tripled during these years. Conversely, in periods of declining prices, the buying power of a given set of resources increases. The following analysis concentrates on the financial sources of buying power: income, credit, and wealth.

4. Wroe Alderson, *Dynamic Marketing Behavior* (Homewood, Ill.: Irwin, 1965), pp. 195–197.

Figure 17.3
The consumer price index (cost of living)

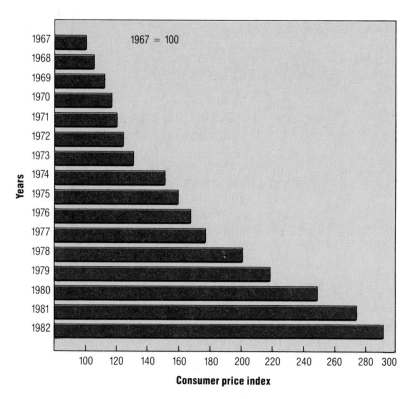

Income and its distribution. From an individual's viewpoint, *income* is the amount of money received through wages, rents, investments, pensions, and subsidy payments for a given period, such as a month or a year. Normally, this money is used for three purposes—paying taxes, spending, and saving. The average annual family income in the United States is approximately $20,000. However, because of the differences in people's educational levels, abilities, occupations, and wealth, income is not equally distributed in this country (or in other countries).

Figure 17.4 shows the estimated percentages of families in various income groups for 1980, 1985, and 1990. Notice that in 1990 a smaller proportion of families will fall into the lower income ranges and a greater proportion will be in the higher income ranges. The fact that an increasing proportion of families is obtaining higher incomes means that a higher standard of living is possible for a greater number of people, assuming that the rate of inflation is less than increases in income. This prediction is very important to marketers, because as a larger proportion of families moves into higher income ranges, consumers' total buying power—and thus the total potential for sales—increases.

Disposable income. Marketers are most interested in the amount of money that is left over after taxes are paid. After-tax income is called *disposable income* and is used for spending or saving. Because disposable income is a ready source of buying power, the total amount available in our country is important to marketers. Several factors affect the size of total

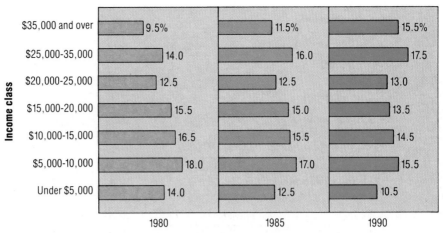

Income class	1980	1985	1990
$35,000 and over	9.5%	11.5%	15.5%
$25,000-35,000	14.0	16.0	17.5
$20,000-25,000	12.5	12.5	13.0
$15,000-20,000	15.5	15.0	13.5
$10,000-15,000	16.5	15.5	14.5
$5,000-10,000	18.0	17.0	15.5
Under $5,000	14.0	12.5	10.5

This chart projects percent distribution of households based on 1978 dollars.

Figure 17.4 Changing income pyramids
Source: Fabian Linden, "The Great Reshuffle of Spending Power," Across the Board, *November 1978. Data from the U.S. Department of Commerce and The Conference Board.*

disposable income; one, of course, is the total amount of income. Total national income is affected by wage levels, rate of unemployment, interest rates, and dividend rates, and these factors, in turn, affect the size of disposable income. Since disposable income is income that is left after taxes are paid, the number of taxes and their amount reduces income, and directly affects the size of total disposable income. When taxes rise, disposable income declines; when taxes fall, disposable income increases.

Discretionary income.   Disposable income that is available for spending and saving after an individual has purchased the basic necessities of food, clothing, and shelter is called *discretionary income*. People use discretionary income to purchase entertainment, vacations, automobiles, education, lawn supplies, pets and pet supplies, furniture, appliances, and so on. Changes in total discretionary income affect the sales of these products, especially of automobiles, furniture, large appliances, and other durable goods. Table 17.2 estimates discretionary income by age of head of household for 1980, 1985, and 1990.

Consumer credit.   Credit transactions allow people to spend future income now or in the near future. Credit increases current buying power at the expense of future buying power. Several factors determine whether consumers use or forgo credit. First, of course, credit must be available to consumers. Interest rates, too, affect consumers' decisions to use credit, especially for expensive purchases such as homes, appliances, and automobiles. When credit charges are high, consumers are more reluctant to purchase expensive items and are more likely to delay such purchases. Because of recent high interest rates on home loans, for example, many people decided not to purchase homes. These decisions hurt the sales of related industries—building materials, appliances, furniture, carpet, and real

Table 17.2 Discretionary income by age of head of household: 1980, 1985, and 1990

			Age of Head of Household					
		Total	Under 25	25–34	35–44	45–54	55–64	65 and Over
1980								
Income:	Percent total	100.0%	5.8%	23.1%	21.4%	21.0%	16.8%	11.8%
	Percent discretionary	100.0	1.0	13.0	27.5	31.0	20.5	7.0
1985								
Income:	Percent total	100.0%	5.4%	24.0%	23.8%	19.0%	15.7%	12.1%
	Percent discretionary	100.0	0.5	16.0	29.0	27.5	19.0	8.0
1990								
Income:	Percent total	100.0%	4.6%	23.1%	25.7%	20.1%	14.2%	12.3%
	Percent discretionary	100.0	1.0	15.5	29.5	28.5	17.5	8.0

Source: Adapted from Fabian Linden, "The Great Reshuffle of Spending Power: The Ages of Affluence," *Across the Board,* December 1978, p. 64. Data from the U.S. Department of Commerce and The Conference Board. Used by permission.

estate. Credit usage also is affected by credit terms such as the size of the down payment and the amount and number of monthly payments. If all these factors are satisfactory, consumers still must consider their ability to use more credit, that is, the amount of future income that already is committed to past credit agreements. Although the use of consumer credit fluctuates, the trend has been toward general growth in credit usage.

Wealth. A person can have a high income and very little wealth. It is also feasible, but not likely, for a person to have great wealth but not much income. *Wealth* is the accumulation of past income, natural resources, and financial resources; it may exist in many forms, including cash, securities, savings accounts, jewelry, art, antiques, real estate, minerals, machinery, and even animals. Like income, wealth is unevenly distributed among people in this country. The significance of wealth to marketers is that as people become more wealthy, they gain buying power in three ways. They can use their wealth not only for current purchases but also to generate income and to acquire large amounts of credit.

Analyzing buying power. Marketers need to analyze buying power because it has a tremendous impact on consumers' reactions to firms' marketing strategies. Marketing managers can use buying power analysis for many purposes: evaluating opportunities in various markets, forecasting sales, establishing sales quotas, and budgeting marketing expenditures, to name only a few. Buying power information is available from government sources, trade associations, and research agencies.

One of the most current and comprehensive sources of buying power data is the *Sales and Marketing Management Survey of Buying Power,* published annually by *Sales and Marketing Management* magazine. As shown in Table 17.3, the *Survey of Buying Power* presents data regarding effective buying income (EBI) and buying power for specific geographic areas including states, counties, and most cities with populations in excess

	Total EBI ($000)	Median Hsld. EBI	Percent of Hslds. by EBI Group				Buying Power Index
			A[a]	B[b]	C[c]	D[d]	
San Francisco Metro Area	19,318,206	26,273	21.4	29.4	19.0	14.5	.8280
Marin County	3,452,136	31,902	17.3	27.5	22.1	22.6	.1376
Novato	564,655	31,836	18.3	29.7	26.0	17.7	.0228
San Rafael	658,597	28,225	20.4	27.3	21.0	17.7	.0342
San Francisco County	7,954,483	21,649	24.7	28.7	14.8	10.3	.3524
•San Francisco	7,954,483	21,649	24.7	28.7	14.8	10.3	.3524
San Mateo County	7,911,587	30,018	18.9	31.1	23.0	16.6	.3380
Daly City	870,700	27,888	21.0	35.1	22.9	10.2	.0450
Redwood City	680,309	25,386	23.9	30.4	20.6	10.9	.0326
San Mateo	1,077,885	28,897	19.6	32.9	22.5	14.3	.0495
South San Francisco	552,200	29,110	17.9	35.8	23.8	11.0	.0237
Suburban Total	11,363,723	30,502	18.5	30.1	22.8	18.3	.4756
San Francisco—Oakland— San Jose Consolidated Area	66,238,123	27,100	20.4	30.4	20.7	13.5	2.8363

[a](A) $10,000–$19,999 [b](B) $20,000–$34,999 [c](C) $35,000–$49,999 [d](D) $50,000 & over
Source: Survey of Buying Power. Copyright 1983 *Sales & Marketing Management*. Reprinted by permission.

of forty thousand. The *Survey of Buying Power* also contains population and retail sales data for the same geographic areas.

The most direct indicators of buying power in the *Survey of Buying Power* are "effective buying income" (EBI) and "buying power index" (BPI). **Effective buying income** is similar to what we call disposable income; it includes salaries, wages, dividends, interest, profits, and rents, less federal, state, and local taxes.[5] The **buying power index** is a weighted index consisting of population, effective buying income, and retail sales data.[6] The higher the index number, the greater the buying power. Like other indexes, the buying power index is most useful for comparative purposes. Marketers can use buying power indexes for a particular year to compare the buying power of one area with the buying power of another area; or they can analyze buying power trends for a particular area by comparing the area's buying power indexes for several years.

Income, wealth, and credit equip consumers to purchase goods and services. Marketing managers should be aware of current levels and expected changes in buying power in their own markets, because buying power directly affects the types and quantities of goods and services that consumers purchase, as we shall see later, in our discussion of spending patterns. Just because consumers have buying power, however, does not mean that they will buy. They must also be willing to use their buying power.

5. *Sales Management 1983 Survey of Buying Power*, p. A-48.
6. Ibid.

Consumers' willingness to spend

A person's *willingness to spend* is, to some degree, related to his or her ability to buy. That is, a person is sometimes more willing to buy if he or she has the buying power. However, a number of other elements also influence willingness to spend. Some affect specific products; others influence spending in general. A product's absolute price and its price relative to the price of substitute products influence almost all of us. At times, the total dollar outlay for an item may seem too great, or a consumer may know of a similar, substitutable item with a much lower price. The amount of satisfaction currently received or expected in the future from a product already owned may also influence a consumer's desire to buy other products. Satisfaction depends not only on the quality of the functional performance of the currently owned product but also on numerous psychological and social forces, as discussed in Chapter 2.

Factors that affect a person's general willingness to spend are expectations about future employment, income levels, prices, family size, and general economic conditions. If a person is unsure whether or how much he or she will be employed, willingness to buy ordinarily declines. During the most recent recession, when unemployment was high and many working people were less than positive that they would have their jobs in the future, the sales of durable goods decreased. Conversely, willingness to buy may increase if a person expects, and is reasonably certain of, a higher income in the future. Expectations of rising prices in the near future may also increase the willingness to spend. Another factor that affects willingness to spend in general is family size. For a given level of buying power, the larger the family, the greater the willingness to buy. One reason for this relationship is that as family size increases, a greater number of dollars must be spent to provide the basic necessities of life to sustain the family members. Lastly, perceptions of future economic conditions in general influence willingness to buy. When economic forecasts predict prosperity, people generally are more willing to make purchases. If a recession or depression is predicted, people often want to hang on to their dollars and thus are less willing to buy. The effects of general economic conditions are discussed in more detail later in this section.

Consumer spending patterns

Marketers must be aware of the factors that influence consumers' ability and willingness to buy, but they should also analyze how consumers actually spend their disposable incomes. Marketers obtain this information by studying consumer spending patterns.

Consumer spending patterns indicate the relative proportions of annual family expenditures or the actual amount of money that is spent on certain kinds of goods and services. Families are usually categorized on the basis of one of several characteristics, including income, age of the household head, geographic area, and family life cycle. There are two types of spending patterns: comprehensive spending patterns and product-specific spending patterns.

Comprehensive spending patterns.   The percentages of family income allotted to the annual expenditures for general classes of goods and services constitute *comprehensive spending patterns*. Comprehensive spending pat-

Table 17.4   Spending patterns based on family size (figures show percent of income)

Product Category	Average Percent	Family Size					
		Single Consumer	2 Persons	3 Persons	4 Persons	5 Persons	6 or More
Food	24.4	24.0	22.9	23.5	23.9	26.0	28.2
Tobacco	1.8	1.4	1.9	1.9	1.8	1.6	1.8
Alcoholic beverages	1.5	2.0	1.8	1.4	1.4	1.3	1.3
Housing	28.9	36.1	30.7	28.0	27.9	27.3	26.3
Clothing	10.4	8.3	8.5	10.4	11.2	11.9	12.2
Personal care	2.9	2.8	2.9	3.0	2.9	2.9	2.9
Medical care	6.8	6.9	8.1	6.9	6.4	6.2	5.6
Recreation	4.0	3.3	3.5	4.1	4.4	4.5	4.0
Reading	0.9	1.1	1.0	0.9	0.8	0.8	0.7
Education	1.1	0.3	0.4	1.2	1.4	1.4	1.7
Transportation	15.1	11.7	16.0	16.5	15.7	13.9	13.4
Other	2.2	2.1	2.4	2.2	2.3	2.1	1.8

Source: *Survey of Consumer Expenditures, 1960–1961*, Department of Labor, Bureau of Labor Statistics, p. 17.

Table 17.5   Spending patterns based on age of family head (figures show percent of income)

Product Category	Average Percent	Age of Family Head						
		Under 25	25–34	35–44	45–54	55–64	65–74	75 and Over
Food	24.4	21.7	23.6	25.2	24.0	24.5	24.9	27.3
Tobacco	1.8	2.1	1.9	1.8	1.9	1.7	1.4	1.1
Alcoholic beverages	1.5	1.2	1.5	1.6	1.5	1.5	1.4	0.8
Housing	28.9	30.4	30.8	27.9	26.7	28.4	32.5	34.6
Clothing	10.4	9.6	9.9	11.5	11.5	9.7	7.4	6.0
Personal care	2.9	2.9	2.8	3.0	3.0	2.9	2.7	2.6
Medical care	6.8	5.8	6.0	5.9	6.2	7.9	9.8	12.9
Recreation	4.0	4.5	4.5	4.4	3.9	3.6	2.7	1.6
Reading	0.9	0.6	0.8	0.9	0.9	0.9	1.0	1.1
Education	1.1	0.9	0.7	1.2	1.9	0.8	0.3	0.1
Transportation	15.1	19.4	16.0	14.6	15.6	15.2	13.3	9.4
Other	2.2	0.9	1.4	1.9	2.8	2.8	2.5	2.6

Source: *Survey of Consumer Expenditures, 1960–1961.* Department of Labor, Bureau of Labor Statistics, p. 18.

terns or the data to develop them are available in government publications and in reports by the Conference Board. Examples of comprehensive consumer spending patterns based on family size and age of the household head are shown in Tables 17.4 and 17.5, respectively.

In Table 17.4, comprehensive spending patterns are classified by family size. As family size increases, consumers spend a larger proportion of their incomes on food, clothing, recreation, and education. The proportion spent on alcoholic beverages and housing declines as family size increases.

Table 17.6 Annual expenditures for toys and play equipment by families in various stages of the family life cycle

Product Category	Total	Families with child under 6		6 or Over only		No Children	
		Some under 6	All under 6	All 6 to 11	Any 12 or over	Husband-Wife	Other
Distribution of all families	100%	14.5%	12.7%	4.6%	25.7%	24.1%	18.4%
Toys and play equipment total	$17.37	$51.94	$36.52	$34.45	$12.52	$1.29	$.76
Dolls and accessories	1.97	5.94	3.57	5.38	1.39	.19	.09
Stuffed toys and infants' toys	.90	1.90	3.26	.70	.57	.10	.05
Tricycles	.61	1.79	2.05	.51	.23	.03	.03
Wagons, skates, sleds	.88	2.34	1.28	2.03	1.05	.06	.03
Games, puzzles, mechanical toys	2.93	7.89	4.32	8.06	3.01	.27	.18
Other toys and equipment	2.72	7.19	6.57	5.78	2.07	.18	.06
Lump-sum expenditures	7.36	24.90	15.46	12.00	4.22	.47	.31

Source: Fabian Linden, *Expenditure Patterns of the American Family* (New York: The Conference Board, 1965), pp. 132–133. Used by permission.

Comprehensive spending patterns by age of the family head are shown in Table 17.5. Families with younger household heads spend a greater proportion of their incomes on tobacco and recreation than do families with older household heads. The proportion of incomes spent on reading material and medical services is higher in families with older household heads than in those with younger household heads. The percentage of income spent on housing appears to be the lowest for households with middle-aged household heads.

Product-specific spending patterns.   While comprehensive spending patterns focus on the proportion of family income that is spent for broad categories of goods and services, *product-specific spending patterns* indicate the annual dollar amounts spent by families for specific products within a general product class. Information sources used to construct product-specific spending patterns include government publications, the Conference Board, trade publications, and consumer surveys. Table 17.6 illustrates a product-specific spending pattern. Notice the differences between this type of spending pattern and the comprehensive ones. The products listed fall into one general product category, and the figures are stated in terms of dollars.

A marketer uses spending patterns to analyze general trends in the ways that families spend their incomes for various kinds of products. For example, an individual who is considering opening a toy store might use the data in Table 17.6 to estimate the demand for various categories of toys and play equipment by families in each stage of the family cycle. By multiplying the number of families in the area that fall into each life cycle stage by the expenditures per family for toys and play equipment, the marketer could determine the annual demand for these products in the area. Such information also could be helpful in determining store location and designing promotional campaigns.

Analyses of spending patterns yield information that a marketer can use to gain perspective and background for decision making. However, spending patterns reflect only general trends and thus cannot be used as the only basis for making specific decisions.

General economic conditions

The overall state of the economy fluctuates in our country and others. These changes in general economic conditions affect (and are affected by) the forces of supply and demand, buying power, willingness to buy, consumer expenditure levels, and the intensity of competitive behavior. Therefore, present-day economic conditions and changes in the economy have a broad impact on the success of organizations' marketing strategies.

Fluctuations in our economy follow a general pattern that is often referred to as the "business cycle." In the traditional view, the business cycle consists of four stages: prosperity, recession, depression, and recovery. Although general economic conditions are largely a function of the business cycle, its effects may be complicated by other factors, such as inflation and shortages of resources. To gain a fuller understanding of the effects of the general economic climate and how marketers can respond to them, let us explore certain characteristics of different stages of the business cycle and the effects of inflation and resource shortages.

Prosperity

During *prosperity*, unemployment is low and aggregate income is relatively high, which causes buying power to be high (assuming a low inflation rate). To the extent that the economic outlook remains prosperous, consumers generally are willing to buy. In the prosperity stage, marketers often expand their product mixes to take advantage of the increased buying power. They sometimes capture a larger market share by intensifying distribution and promotion efforts.

Unfortunately, marketers sometimes become so optimistic about favorable economic conditions that they overspend on marketing activities. Overspending may result in a number of problems. For example, it may result in so much product proliferation that a number of products are unprofitable, or so many resellers that a producer cannot properly service them, or so many advertisements that demand outstrips the firm's supply capabilities.

Recession

Since unemployment rises during a *recession*, total buying power declines. Table 17.7 shows a number of characteristics of eleven recessions in the United States since 1920. Note how gross national product, industrial production, and employment levels are affected by recessions. The pessimism that accompanies a recession often stifles spending by both consumers and

Table 17.7   Selected characteristics of recessions and depressions

	Duration (mos.)	Real GNP (%)	Industrial Production (%)	Nonfarm Employment (%)	Unemployment Rate		Industries with Employment Decline (%)
					High (%)	Increase (%)	
1. The Great Depression (1933)	43	−33	−53	−32	25	+22	100
2. Two major depressions (1921, 1938)	16	−13	−32	−11	16	+10	97
3. Five sharp recessions (1924, 1949, 1954, 1958, 1975)	12	−3	−13	−4	7	+4	90
4. Five mild recessions (1927, 1945, 1961, 1970, 1980)	10	−2	−8	−2	6	+3	78
5. Most recent recession (see note)	16	−3	−12	−3	11	+4	79

Explanation of table:

The first column is the period from the peak of the business cycle to the trough, as determined by the National Bureau of Economic Research. The next three columns show the percentage declines in output or employment from the high month or quarter to the low. For unemployment (columns 5 and 6) the highest monthly figure reached is shown as well as the increase from the low to the high. The last column is the percentage of industries that experienced a decline in employment over a six-month interval. The figure shown is the highest percentage reached during the depression or recession.

All the entries on lines 2, 3, and 4 are averages covering the respective depressions or recessions. Entries on line 5 are for the recession from July, 1981 to November, 1982.
Source: Geoffrey H. Moore, Center for International Business Cycle Research, Columbia University, New York, New York.

business persons. Because of decreased buying power many consumers become more price and value conscious—they look for products that are basic and functional. People ordinarily reduce their consumption of the more expensive convenience foods and exert greater effort to save money by growing and preparing more of their own food. Individuals buy fewer durable goods and more repair and do-it-yourself products.

During a recession some firms make the mistake of drastically reducing their marketing efforts. Such firms may cut out marketing research, stop new-product development, reduce sales forces, or severely decrease advertising expenditures. Any one or several of these actions may significantly damage the firm's ability to survive a recession.

Obviously, though, marketers should consider revising their marketing activities during a recessionary period. Because consumers are more concerned about the functional value of products, a firm must focus its marketing research on determining precisely what product functions are important to buyers and then make certain that these functions are included in the firm's products. Promotional efforts should emphasize value and utility. Through promotion, marketers should encourage consumers to spend rather than to save. Because consumers usually are more price sensitive during recessions, marketers should evaluate the efficiency of their marketing operations to be sure that marketing costs are minimized to keep prices at acceptable levels.

Depression

A *depression* is a period in which there is extremely high unemployment, wages are very low, total disposable income is at a minimum, and consumers lack confidence in the economy. Selected characteristics of three depressions are shown in Table 17.7. Some experts have indicated that depression should not be included in the business cycle.

The federal government has used both monetary and fiscal policies in an attempt to offset the effects of recession, depression, and inflation. Monetary policies are employed to control the money supply, which in turn influences spending, saving, and investment by both individuals and businesses. Through fiscal policies, the government can influence the amounts of savings and expenditures by altering the tax structure and by changing the levels of government expenditures. Some experts believe that effective use of monetary and fiscal policies can eliminate depressions from the business cycle. One fact that supports this position is that we have not had one since the 1930s, even though we have experienced prosperity, recession, and recovery several times since then. This is not to say that we could not have another depression; it still is a possibility.

The government's use of monetary and fiscal policies influences marketers in several ways. An increase in the money supply gives consumers greater buying power; a decline in the supply of money reduces buying power. A tax reduction increases buying power, while increased taxes limit consumers' ability to purchase. Increases in government spending enlarge the sales potential in government markets; a general reduction in government spending leads to a sales decline in government markets. Marketers must be cognizant of the effects of various monetary and fiscal policies and should keep themselves informed regarding the government's current and planned use of monetary and fiscal measures.

Recovery

Recovery is the business cycle stage in which the economy moves from recession to prosperity. During this period, the high unemployment rate begins to decline, total disposable income increases, and the economic gloom that lessened consumers' willingness to buy subsides (Note the discussion of related issues in the Application on p. 523.) Both the ability and the willingness to buy rise.

Marketers face some problems during recovery. One is the difficulty of ascertaining how quickly prosperity will return. It can also be difficult to forecast the level of prosperity that will be attained. In the recovery stage, marketers should maintain as much flexibility in their marketing strategies as possible to be able to make the needed adjustments as the economy moves from recession to prosperity.

Inflation

Inflation is a condition in which price levels increase more rapidly than incomes, causing a decline in buying power. Inflation may accompany any of the business cycle stages; it especially intensifies the adverse effects of a recession, because the higher prices increase the hardships of high unemployment, decrease disposable income, and increase the high level of economic pessimism that is an intrinsic part of a recession.

Inflation affects marketers in several ways. Obviously, when inflation dampens consumers' ability and willingness to purchase, many firms experience declining sales. Inflation also affects production costs, which usually require price adjustments. Marketing costs increase, often forcing a marketing manager to control expenditures more carefully. Generally, prolonged inflationary periods force marketers to reformulate their marketing strategies.

Shortages

In all economic systems and for all organizations in these economic systems, resources are limited. However, because of the tremendous consumption in our country and others, as well as the types and quantities of resources held by other nations, our economy sometimes experiences severe shortages of such basic resources as petroleum, natural gas, electricity, and some metals. Shortages in basic resources lead to shortages of a wide variety of products.

Shortages create a number of problems for businesses. They often magnify inflationary pressures, leading to inflated costs and higher prices. When consumers respond to shortages by rapidly altering their preferences, firms may need to alter one or all marketing mix components. For example, prior to the energy crisis, some U.S. automakers' plants were designed to produce big, expensive, gas-guzzling cars in large quantities. When the energy crisis hit, they were rapidly forced to convert their facilities and their product mixes. Consumers wanted smaller, more efficient automobiles, and they did not want to wait.[7] Changes in consumers' desires also necessitated alterations in the pricing and promotion of automobiles.

Shortages do not affect marketing departments alone; accounting, production, finance, personnel, and purchasing also feel their impact.[8] Not only do shortages cause turmoil within business organizations, but they also create friction among producers, resellers, and consumers regarding nonavailability of products, high prices, slow deliveries, lack of parts, and poor service.

Shortages that have a significant impact on the economy usually force marketers to adjust their marketing activities. In periods that are relatively free of shortages, marketing activities usually focus on finding and satisfying markets, which ultimately increases demand and consumption. During periods of shortages, marketers may have to redirect demand away from products that require scarce resources toward products that are made from

7. Philip Kotler, "Marketing During Periods of Shortage," *Journal of Marketing,* July 1974, p. 21.
8. Ibid.

Application

A Snapshot of Economic Trends During Recovery

Consumers, whether they are financially strapped or materially satisfied, are playing it safe by saving. Despite obvious improvement in the economy and rising consumer confidence, retail prices have been depressed. Consumers have developed a new mind-set from concern over the recession and changes in attitudes toward buying.

Business Week surveyed a wide range of individuals, asking them what they would do if they received a $1,000 windfall. More than half said they would put it in savings, invest it, or use it to pay off bills. A number of consumers believe that they have satisfied all their material needs and that their lives are comfortable.

Consumers also perceive that prices are too high. Car prices seem to be bothering consumers the most. One consumer polled, blamed this on big-car prices that are so high consumers resort to shopping for small cars. Because small cars are not able to meet the needs of their families, they decide to delay car purchases.

Unemployment is a major threat to consumers. A Gallup Poll indicated that one out of ten consumers is out of work, and an additional 10 percent fear losing their jobs. While prices are moderating, consumers are reluctant to spend.

With current economic conditions improving, consumers are financially able to borrow more. However, consumer installment payments are a smaller portion of monthly income than at any time since 1965. In short, consumers are feeling conservative. If their attitude changes, a boost in retail sales will further aid in the economy's recovery.

Source: Based on "Consumers Are Still Playing It Safe," *Business Week*, April 25, 1983, pp. 22–23.

more plentiful materials. They may have to use marketing activities to reduce consumption. This approach is sometimes called "demarketing."[9] During sustained shortages, marketers may be forced to ration or reduce demand, rather than stimulate it. Since periods of shortages call for changes in marketing mixes, marketers must know how to adjust their mixes. A marketer must bear in mind that consumers feel the pinch of shortages in many ways. Therefore, a new marketing mix for a shortage period should strive to minimize consumers' dissatisfaction and alienation.

In recent years the U.S. economy has been stagnating while at the same time experiencing inflation—an economic condition sometimes called "stagflation." Four types of stagflation are: (1) inflation-shortage, (2) inflation-recession, (3) recession-shortage, and (4) inflation-recession shortage.[10] Table 17.8 lists some adaptive strategies and tactics that marketers can implement in periods of shortage, inflation, and recession.

Competitive factors, consumers' ability and willingness to buy, and general economic conditions are among the major economic forces that determine consumers' reactions to a firm's marketing efforts. Since consumers' responses determine a business's long-term survival, a marketing manager should analyze the potential effects of these economic forces on consumers to optimally adjust the firm's marketing strategies.

9. This concept, developed by Philip Kotler and Sidney J. Levy, is discussed in their article "Demarketing: Yes, Demarketing," *Harvard Business Review,* November-December 1971, pp. 74–80.
10. Avraham Shama, "Management of Consumers in an Era of Stagflation," *Journal of Marketing,* July 1978, pp. 43–52.

Table 17.8 Adaptive strategies and tactics in periods of shortages, inflation, and recession

	Shortages Demand Reduction in the Short Run, and Demand Adjustment in the Long Run	Inflation Demand Reduction	Recession Demand Increase
Product	1. Narrow product line. 2. Offer cheaper, more functional products. 3. Purchase shortage materials more carefully and strategically. 4. Make shortage material go further. 5. Invest in researching substitute materials. 6. Introduce substitute products. 7. Avoid quantity discounts.	1. Narrow product line. 2. Offer cheaper, more functional products. 3. Purchase raw material more carefully and strategically. 4. Use less expensive (or lower-grade) material in production. 5. Invest in researching substitute materials. 6. Avoid quantity discounts.	1. Narrow product line. 2. Offer cheaper, more functional products. 3. Cut top of product line. 4. Use less raw materials in production. 5. Offer quantity discounts.
Price	8. Raise prices. 9. Adjust prices periodically (upward). 10. Change price differential among products in the line to decrease demand for shortage goods. 11. Stop price discounting practices. 12. Tighten credit. 13. Centralize price decisions.	7. Raise prices. 8. Adjust prices frequently (upward). 9. Change price differential among products in the line to decrease total demand. 10. Stop price discounting practices. 11. Tighten credit. 12. Centralize price decisions.	6. Lower prices whenever possible. 7. Change price differential to increase total demand. 8. Offer price discounts. 9. Loosen credit. 10. Centralize price decisions.
Promotion	14. Demarketing through promotion.	13. Demarketing through promotion.	11. Remarketing through promotion.

Table 17.8 *(continued)*

	Shortages Demand Reduction in the Short Run, and Demand Adjustment in the Long Run	Inflation Demand Reduction	Recession Demand Increase
	15. Decrease promotion of shortage goods. 16. Increase promotion of more readily available products.	14. Decrease promotion via advertising and personal selling. 15. Push the more profitable products.	12. Increase promotion to stimulate demand. 13. Cultivate every potential account and territory. 14. Motivate sales force to sell more.
Distribution	17. Limit quantity per customer. 18. Limit distribution to make products less available.	16. Limit quantity per customer. 17. Limit distribution to make product less available. 18. Utilize a higher price to achieve product differentiation.	15. Increase distribution outlets. 16. Motivate middlemen to buy more of your product and push it. 17. Offer products directly to consumers.
Consumer Focus	19. Study how consumers and potential consumers are affected. 20. Drop marginal accounts whenever possible. 21. Selective treatment of consumers to maximize loyalty.	19. Study how consumers and potential consumers are affected. 20. Drop marginal accounts whenever possible. 21. Selective treatment of consumers to maximize loyalty.	18. Study how consumers and potential consumers are affected. 19. Cultivate even marginally profitable accounts. 20. Selective treatment of consumers to maximize sales.
Other	22. Innovate. 23. Increase productivity. 24. Diversify.	22. Innovate. 23. Increase productivity. 24. Diversify.	21. Innovate. 22. Increase productivity. 23. Diversify.

Source: Adapted from Avraham Shama, "Management of Consumers in an Era of Stagflation," *Journal of Marketing*, July 1978, p. 47. Reprinted with permission of the publisher, the American Marketing Association.

Technological forces

Even though economic forces influence business survival, the impact of technology on society and businesses is a major factor in the success—or failure—of a business enterprise. Economic forces are related to technology because the pursuit and existence of technological information may affect income, taxation, prices, and consumers' willingness to spend. The effects of technology are broad in scope. Technology today exerts a tremendous influence on our lives. There is every reason to believe that it will continue to do so. In this section, we describe technology, discuss its sources, analyze its effects on society and on marketing activities, and explore the means marketers have for dealing with it.

The rapid technological growth of the last several decades is expected to continue through the 1980s. Areas that hold out the greatest technological promise include solid-state electronics, artificial intelligence, materials research, biotechnology, and geology.

Solid-state electronics will reach new levels of sophistication. As new technologies speed up the computerization of society, semiconductor chips will become increasingly important to our lives. Current research is investigating new forms of chips, computers that are a hundred times faster than current models, and optical computers that use video images rather than digital codes. By 1990, a single chip may be able to hold one million bits of data as compared to the current level of 65,000 bits. Researchers are now working on methods to speed up the switching time of the active elements on chips, making it possible for computers to work faster. It is known, for example, that electrons can travel faster in gallium arsenide, one substance now being tested, than in silicon, the most common semiconductor material in use at present.

In the future, artificial intelligences may be used to explore significant scientific questions at a level greatly exceeding human ability. Some scientists believe that there is no limit to the intelligence that computers can attain. Special-intelligence systems are presently being used in industry and medicine. These systems mimic human experts with astonishing precision. By the 1990s, they may be widely available to professionals in many fields.

Materials research is another booming field. New "microscience" equipment allows scientists to explore the innermost structure of matter and to modify the ninety-two basic elements of the periodic table. Changes are occurring in the materials we use and in the way these materials are made. Research has been done, for example, with ceramics that can conduct electricity and with plastics that are derived from nonpetroleum sources. Supercooling of metals is another area attracting much attention. Molten metal is cooled so rapidly that it does not have time to form a normal crystalline structure but solidifies instead as a glasslike metal. Microscience is also finding new ways to manipulate the surfaces of existing materials at the molecular level to make them more resistant to corrosion and abrasion.

Research in biotechnology has yielded exciting results. New drugs and chemicals are being created by altering the hereditary characteristics of bacteria. Amazing developments in the modification of plant, animal, and human genetics may profoundly affect food production, human health, and medical science. Cloning and gene splicing may be used in the near future to develop varieties of plants that can grow in harsh environments and produce their own fertilizer. Agriculture may be revolutionized by modified plants and livestock. Scientists hope eventually to produce new species of animals, combining the best traits of three or more "parents." In medicine, recombinant DNA technology has already produced a number of important hormones and drugs, including insulin and interferon. Human proteins, on which much research is now focusing, may play a vital role in helping the body fight diseases.

In geology, computers (and computers with artificial intelligence) are employed to locate new sources of minerals and energy more efficiently. Computers can create three-dimensional images of the earth's interior to identify new resources. Seismology, the use of sound waves to map rock layers in the earth's interior, depends on computers more and more often. Satellites are employed to locate new mineral deposits by measuring gravity, the amount of sunlight reflected from the earth's surface, and the strength of the earth's magnetic field. Scientists hope that these new developments in computer technology will enable them to locate billions of dollars' worth of minerals and hydrocarbon fuels located beneath the earth's surface.[11]

These and other technological developments will have a definite impact on buyers and on marketers' decisions. Let us, therefore, take the time to define technology and to consider some of technology's effects on society and on marketers. After that, we will discuss several factors that influence the adoption and use of technology.

Technology defined

The word *technology* brings to mind creations of progress such as spaceships, computers, synthetic fibers, laser beams, and heart transplants. Even though such items are outgrowths of technology, none of them *is* technology. *Technology* is the knowledge of how to accomplish tasks and goals.[12] Often this knowledge comes from scientific research.

Technology is credited with providing the machines, buildings, materials, and processes that allow us to achieve a high standard of living. Yet it is also blamed for pollution, unemployment, crime, and a number of other social and environmental problems. Technology itself is neither good nor bad. Its effects are determined largely by how it is applied. Technology has been used to improve health care so that people can live longer. It has also been used to kill masses of people. It enabled the Nazis, for example, to hideously exterminate millions of people during World War II. In addition, although the potential effects of technology may be significant, the actual effects of certain types of technology are nonexistent unless the technology is used. For example, some technological knowledge that came out of our space explorations has not yet been put to use.

11. "Technologies for the '90s," *Business Week,* July 6, 1981, pp. 48–56.
12. Herbert Simon, "Technology and Environment," *Management Science,* June 1973, p. 1110.

Technology grows out of research performed by businesses, universities, and nonprofit organizations. Much of this research—in fact, over half of it—is paid for by the federal government, which supports investigations in a variety of areas including health, arms, agriculture, energy, and pollution. Because much federally funded research requires the use of specialized machinery, personnel, and facilities, a sizable proportion of this research is done by large business organizations that already possess the necessary specialized equipment and personnel. Also, of course, businesses and foundations conduct technological research in their own facilities, in universities, or in independent research laboratories.

The impact of technology

Marketers must be aware of new developments in technology and their possible effects, because technology can and does affect marketing activities in so many different ways. (Related issues are discussed in the Application on p. 531.) Consumers' technological knowledge influences their desires for goods and services. To provide marketing mixes that satisfy consumers, marketers must be aware of these influences. Technological developments can put some people out of business as they are opening up new business opportunities to others. The introduction and general acceptance of synthetic fabrics drove some sheep raisers, cotton growers, and dry cleaners out of business. Yet this technology provided new market opportunities for synthetic fabric producers, clothing manufacturers, retail clothiers, and self-service laundries. Technology definitely affects the types of products that are offered to consumers. The items that follow are only a few of the thousands of existing products that were not available to consumers fifteen years ago.

Solar-powered pocket calculators
Convection ovens
Supersonic airliners
Videotape recorders for home use
Tuning-fork and quartz-crystal
   wrist watches
Calorie-reduced beer, wine, and
   pasta
Felt-tipped and nylon-tipped
   pens
Low-cost personal computers

The various ways in which technology affects marketing activities fall into two broad categories. It affects consumers and society in general, and it influences what, how, when, and where products are marketed.

The effects of technology on society
When you stop to think about it, technology influences whether you are born, how you live, and how and when you die. In fact, it is difficult to think of any aspect of human life that is untouched by technological developments; we are engulfed by them. One measure of the increasing magnitude of technological applications is the general increase in the number of patents issued (see Figure 17.5). Except during the 1930s and 1940s, the number of patents issued has increased substantially from decade to decade.

Technology determines how we satisfy our physiological needs. In various ways and to varying degrees, eating and drinking habits, sleeping pat-

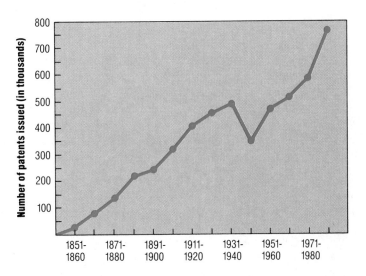

Figure 17.5
Growth in the number of patents issued
Source: Adapted from Statistical Abstract of the United States, *1949, 1964, 1972, 1977.*

terns, sexual activities, and health care are all influenced both by existing technology and by changes in technology. For example, freeze-dried foods, birth control pills, and computerized health information systems have had a definite impact how people satisfy physiological requirements.

Technological developments definitely have improved our standard of living. Through technology, workers are more productive, do less physical labor, and earn larger incomes with which to purchase the extremely large number of technologically improved goods and services available where and when they want them. Technological knowledge also allows producers and manufacturers to create products that help people perform ordinary tasks more easily, thus giving us more leisure time. Education, information, and entertainment have been improved through technology. Home computers, like the Atari in Figure 17.6, are beginning to aid users along these dimensions.

Although improved technologies have these and numerous other favorable effects on society, they often carry with them undesirable side effects—polluted air and water and other health hazards, unemployment, and mental retardation. These unfavorable aspects of technology arise from the physical production of goods and services and from the ways in which society uses products. Technology may provide a high standard of living, but it can detract from the quality of life in our society. Some people believe that further applications of technology can soften or eliminate these undesirable side effects. Others argue that the best way to improve the quality of our lives is to reduce the use of technology.

The impact of technology on marketing activities
Technology affects the types of products that marketers can offer. Technological improvements in production processes and materials sometimes result in more durable, less expensive products. When color television sets, for example, were introduced, they did not work very well and were

Figure 17.6   Atari home computer advertisement
Source: Atari, Inc.

quite expensive. Over the years, technological advances (and competitive pressures) have led to higher-quality, lower-priced sets.

Technology has altered the ways in which marketers inform consumers about goods and services. Because of technological changes in communications, marketers now can reach large masses of people through a variety of media including newspapers, magazines, direct mail, radio, television, transit, and billboards. Also, technology is helping marketers to be more efficient. GTE offers worldwide telemail service (Figure 17.7). This service allows people in the same organization but in different locations to communicate. It can be used for entering orders, managing salespeople, and for other activities.

Technological advances in transportation allow consumers to travel farther and more often in order to shop at a larger number of stores. The greater mobility of consumers has, in turn, affected the sizes and locations of stores. Thirty years ago the owner of a large furniture store would have been reluctant to build a store at the edge of a city. Today, this practice is common. Technological changes in transportation also have affected the producers' ability to get products to retailers and wholesalers. The ability of present-day manufacturers of relatively lightweight products to reach any of their dealers within twenty-four hours (through air freight) would have astounded their counterparts fifty years ago.

Application

Technology Is Changing What Marketers Do

Influenced by technology, marketers are changing their marketing practices, interactions with consumers, and relationships with their organizations. An example of the change in work styles is the way personal computers are becoming standard items in marketing offices. Marketers are also taking portable computers with them when they travel. New technological devices have changed the telephone into a computer communications device. The result is new marketing opportunities for out-of-office sales representatives.

As consumers watch more cable television, marketers need to find new media to present their messages. The new media that are often used arise from technological advances. Videotex is affecting many of the world's large corporations and is one technology that has generated numerous marketing opportunities.

Technology is also influencing retail and office environments. At the retail level, technology has introduced touch-sensitive devices that provide information, electronic catalogs, and new methods of payment. In the office, materials are sent out on transceivers, graphics can be sent through phone lines, and video printers produce slides, transparencies, and prints of computer and video images. These technological advances are all affecting the way marketers operate.

An important issue raised by rapid technological advancements is their effects on both society and the individual. Although technology has helped improve society, it has also created alienation, "intellectual elitism," and a loss of privacy for the individual.

Technology is a driving force behind what marketers are able to do. The companies on the leading edge in technology are demonstrating what many marketers will be doing five years from today. To maintain a competitive posture, marketers need to be aware of what technology is doing and how they can use it.

Source: Based on Bernie Whalen, "Technology: It's Quickly Changing What Marketers Do," *Marketing News,* Nov. 26, 1982, p. 1.

Adoption and use of technology

As we said earlier, businesses will not necessarily use all available technologies. There are a number of reasons why. First, a firm must be capable of using technological information, and consumers must be able and willing to buy the resulting products. A particular firm may not have the resources—capital, land, labor, technical skills, or managerial know-how—to apply new technology. Even if it does have the resources, the resulting products may not—for any one of the reasons we discussed earlier in this chapter—attract consumers' limited dollars. Consumers, for example, have rejected a variety of new products: cereals with freeze-dried fruits; certain types of automobile safety equipment; and more effective, more convenient, safer mousetraps—among others.

A second factor involved in a decision to use technology is its potential effects. Marketing managers try as a matter of course to evaluate the effects of new technology on the firm's costs, sales, profits, and market position. Of course, they are still concerned about such internal effects, but in some firms marketing managers also try to evaluate the broader effects of technology. Through a procedure known as *technology assessment,* managers try to foresee the effects of new products and processes on the firm's operation, on other business organizations, and on society in general. With the information gained through a technology assessment, management tries to estimate whether or not the benefits of using a specific kind of technology outweigh the costs to the firm and to society generally.

The degree to which a business is technologically based also will influence how its management responds to technology. Firms whose products and product changes are outgrowths of recent technology are very much concerned with gathering and using technological information. Many firms—especially in the automotive, electronics, and energy industries—have whole departments responsible for performing technological research and for monitoring the research efforts of other organizations.

A company may also react to whether other firms in an industry use technology as a competitive tool. Technological information may exist that could radically improve a firm's products or other parts of the marketing mix, but the firm may not apply the technology as long as its competitors do not attempt to use it.

Finally, the extent to which a firm can protect inventions that arise from technological information influences the use of technology. Patent laws protect an invention from use by persons or firms other than the inventor while the patent is in force. A patent is enforceable for seventeen years. However, as pointed out in Chapter 16, the amount of protection a patent provides depends on how easily the product can be copied without violating its patent. (In fact, there are some very successful firms that legally copy the ideas of other, more innovative businesses.) If new products and processes cannot be protected through patents, a firm that has spent the time and money to develop them is less likely to make the benefits of its research available to competitors by marketing them.

How a firm uses (or does not use) technology is important for its long-run survival. A firm that makes the wrong decisions may well lose out to its competitors. Poor decisions may also affect a firm's profits by requiring expensive corrective actions. Poor decisions about technological forces may even drive a firm out of business.

Summary

This chapter discusses three major parts of the marketing environment: societal, economic, and technological forces. These forces have a broad impact on consumers and on marketing managers.

Marketers are subjected to a variety of societal forces that express what society wants and what it does not want. Members of our society want a high standard of living and a high quality of life. People expect business organizations to help them obtain what they want. As they attempt to provide what society wants, marketers must also avoid providing what society does not desire. Society does not want faulty and unsafe products, misleading and unsupported warranties, deceptive packages and labels, misleading advertisements, fraudulent selling practices, or unfair and exploitive prices. In trying to be socially responsible, marketers experience two general problems. It is difficult, if not impossible, to determine what society wants because its various groups have diverse wants. Marketers also have a tough job in attempting to estimate the long-run effects of their decisions on society.

The economic factors that can strongly influence marketing decisions and activities are competitive forces, buying power, willingness to spend,

Figure 17.7 Promotion of technologically advanced telemail service
Source: Courtesy of Tandem Computers.

spending patterns, and general economic conditions. Although all business organizations compete for consumers' dollars, a business usually views its competitors as the businesses in its geographic area that market products similar to, or substitutable for, its own products. Several factors influence the intensity of competition in a firm's environment, including the type of competitive structure in which a firm operates and the kinds of competitive tools employed by the organizations in that particular industry.

Consumer demand is affected by consumers' buying power and by their willingness to purchase. Consumers' goods, services, and financial holdings make up their buying power, that is, their ability to purchase. The financial sources of buying power are income, credit, and wealth. Just because consumers have buying power, however, does not mean that they will use it; they also must be willing to spend. Factors that affect the willingness to spend are the product's price; the level of satisfaction that is obtained from currently used products; family size; and expectations about future employment, income, prices, and general economic conditions.

In weighing the effects of consumers' buying power and their willingness to spend, marketers must be aware of consumer spending patterns, which reveal the relative proportion of annual family expenditures or the actual dollar amounts that are spent for certain types of goods and services. Spending patterns depend on certain factors. Accordingly, families usually are grouped into categories based on income, age of the household head, geographic area, or family life cycle.

The general economic conditions in our country affect the forces of supply and demand, buying power, the willingness to buy, consumer expenditure levels, and the intensity of competitive behavior. The overall state of the economy fluctuates in a general pattern known as a business cycle. The various stages of the business cycle are prosperity, recession, depression, and recovery.

Technology is the knowledge of how to accomplish tasks and goals. Technological knowledge grows out of research—much of it paid for by the federal government—performed by businesses, universities, and nonprofit organizations. Technology today exerts a tremendous influence on our lives, on society, and on marketing decisions and activities. The degree to which the effects of technology are good or bad depends on how it is used.

Most aspects of our lives are influenced by technology, including our work, recreation, eating and drinking, sleep, and sexual behavior. Technology has helped us to achieve a high standard of living, but it also carried with it undesirable side effects, such as polluted air and water and other health hazards, unemployment, and mental retardation.

Like all other aspects of our society, marketing decisions and activities are affected by technology. Product development, packaging, promotion, prices, and distribution systems are all influenced directly by technology. Not all businesses, however, are affected in the same way or to the same degree. Several factors determine how much and in what way a particular business will make use of technology, including the firm's ability to use it, consumers' ability and willingness to buy technologically improved products, the firm's perception of the long-run effects of applying technology, the extent to which it is technologically based, the degree to which technology is used as a competitive tool, and the extent to which the business can protect resulting technological applications through patents.

Important terms

Societal forces
Quality of life
Consumer movement
Competition
Competitive structure
Monopoly
Oligopoly
Monopolistic competition
Perfect competition
Buying power
Income
Disposable income
Discretionary income
Wealth

Effective buying income
Buying power index
Willingness to spend
Consumer spending patterns
Comprehensive spending patterns
Product-specific spending patterns
Prosperity
Recession
Depression
Recovery
Inflation
Technology
Technology assessment

Discussion and review questions

1. What living standard does the American public expect? Why does this expectation affect marketers?
2. How does society expect marketers to handle social responsibility and ethical matters?
3. Do you agree or disagree that consumers are manipulated by marketers? Defend your position.
4. Describe the consumer movement. Analyze some active consumer forces in your area.
5. What are the primary factors that affect the strength of competition in a firm's environment?
6. Define income, disposable income, and discretionary income. How does each affect consumers' buying power?
7. How is consumers' buying power affected by wealth and consumer credit?
8. How is buying power measured? Why should it be evaluated?
9. What factors influence a consumer's willingness to buy?
10. What types of information can be gained from the analysis of consumer spending patterns?
11. In what ways can each of the business cycle stages affect consumers' reactions to marketing strategies?
12. What business cycle stage are we experiencing currently? How is this stage affecting business firms in your area?
13. How can marketers adjust their marketing mixes during periods of scarcity?
14. What does the term *technology* mean to you?
15. List and describe some sources of technology.
16. How does technology affect you as a member of society? Do technology's benefits outweigh its costs and dangers?
17. Discuss the impact of technology on marketing activities.
18. What factors determine whether a business organization adopts and uses technology?

Cases

Case 17.1

Kodak Competes Through Technologically Advanced Products[13]

Formerly the fourteenth largest employer and the twelfth largest in net income, Kodak was once considered an American institution. It made its mark on the film industry, manufacturing two principal products—photographic paper and color film. It controlled 85 percent of the U.S. film mar-

13. The information in this case is from Thomas Moore, "Embattled Kodak Enters the Electronic Age," *Fortune,* August 22, 1983, pp. 120–128; "New Video Cameras?" *Business Month,* Feb. 1984, p. 25; "Kodak Takes a Risky Leap into Consumer Video," *Business Week,* Jan. 16, 1984, pp. 92–93; Philip Maher, "Kodak Uses Private Label for Business Product," *Industrial Marketing,* April 1983, pp. 14, 16; and Gay Jervey, "Kodak Nurses Slipped Disc," *Advertising Age,* Oct. 3, 1983, p. 16.

ket and 50 percent of the worldwide film market. Kodak was the dominant supplier in the film industry and managed to maintain its position by being a technological leader and a low-cost producer. However, in the 1980s profit margins slowly began to shrink. In 1982, Kodak's profit margin was 10.7 percent of sales compared to 15.7 percent only ten years earlier; and its stock is now selling at about half of what it was a decade ago. The reasons for Kodak's slump are competition and technology.

Competition in the film industry has become intense. Currently used technology is continually being challenged, and several Japanese manufacturers are entering the film market with prices as low as Kodak's. Kodak has a new strategy to bring the firm out of this slump. Kodak plans to maintain its present market share in the film industry by combining electronic technology with its own expertise. One of Kodak's problems had been poor marketing decisions. For a long time, Kodak did not consider entering other markets unless the rates of return on those markets were above that of the film market. Kodak passed up several inventions such as xerography due to this conservative strategy. While being too conservative in a fast-paced technological field, Kodak also took too long between product conception and product introduction. Kodak realizes the potential financial disaster that could occur if they stick to the old strategy.

In the early 1980s Kodak decided to make the transition from the film business to the electronics business. Kodak entered the instant photography market, but its timing may have been off. The Kodamatic instant camera and the disc camera were both introduced at a time when consumers seemed more interested in high quality 35 mm cameras. Sales have lagged for both instamatic cameras; however, Kodak feels that part of this lag was due to the recession. Kodak has decided to alter its promotional approach for the disc camera by stressing convenience and long use instead of photo quality.

One of Kodak's successes is Trimprint film, a type of instant photography film that is the first of its type. It allows a picture's back to be peeled away so that the instant photo is not so bulky.

Kodak has also entered the video camera market by launching the 8 mm Kodavision camcorder, a lightweight video camera and recorder. To use the camcorder as a VCR, one must purchase a few options. This innovation has been designed especially for recording family gatherings and celebrations rather than for recording TV broadcasts, and it will be advertised accordingly. The camera weighs only 5 pounds, records on 8 mm special magnetic tape, and is priced at $1,600 or at $1,900 if automatic focusing is desired. Expected sales this year are 100,000 units in the U.S. alone, and they are expected to triple next year with the introduction of the camcorder in forty foreign countries.

In line with its new strategy, Kodak has entered the computer industry with several product introductions. One of the more popular products is the KAR-4000 System. This computerized system stores and retrieves microfilmed documents. The micrographics technology used in this system touches on both microfiche and total electronic data storage. This product carries the Kodak brand although the software was created by Acetex and the mini computer that powers the system was manufactured by Applied

Digital Data Systems. The likely customers for the system are banks, insurance companies, and large industrial corporations.

Kodak's Ektaprint copier, developed in the early 1980s, has been doing well. Kodak anticipates a 20 percent growth in its sales this year. Also, Spin Physics, one of Kodak's electronics programming subsidiaries, has produced an ultra-high-capacity "floppy" disk memory to be used with personal computers.

Questions for discussion

1. What are the major forces that have caused Kodak to introduce new products into markets that it previously had not entered?
2. If Kodak were not faced with these major forces, would its new strategy still be useful? Explain.
3. Why do organizations resist or reject technology, as Kodak did with xerography?
4. Do you believe that buyers will accept Kodak's new technologically advanced products? Explain.

Case 17.2

Xerox Corporation Faces Competition[14]

Since 1959, Xerox has dominated the world's copying equipment and supplies markets. Ninety-five percent of Xerox's annual sales result from its copying operations. Recently it has been faced with increased foreign and domestic competition.

Xerox's phenomenal growth started with its introduction of the 914 copier. The 914 was one of the most successful products in the history of American business. By 1969 Xerox had achieved annual sales that were nearly eight times greater than in 1964. For the past five years, Xerox's sales growth has averaged 16 percent annually.

For the first three-fourths of its life, Xerox Corporation had a virtual monopoly in the plain paper copier business. Its basic corporate strategy through the first half of the 1970s was to focus on high-profit, high- and medium-output copiers. At that time the growing market of offices that needed less expensive, low-output copiers was not served adequately.

In the mid-1970s a trio of firms realized that the needs of this significant market segment were not being met. Many offices required only low-output machines and were interested in a less expensive copier. In a joint venture, Savin designed a lower-cost yet efficient plain paper copier, Ricoh manufactured the Savin-designed copiers, and Savin and Nashua marketed them. Working together, they captured the low-priced end of the copier industry.

14. Some of the facts in this case are from "Competition Heats Up in Copiers," *Business Week*, Nov. 5, 1979, p. 115; and from "Xerox Zooms Toward the Office of the Future," *Fortune*, May 18, 1981, p. 45.

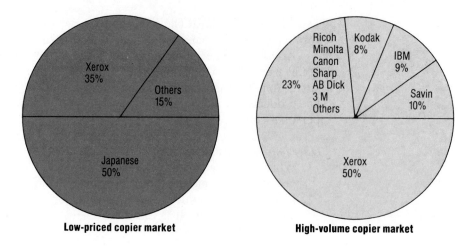

Low-priced copier market

Xerox
35%

Others
15%

Japanese
50%

High-volume copier market

Ricoh
Minolta
Canon
Sharp
AB Dick
3 M
Others
23%

Kodak
8%

IBM
9%

Savin
10%

Xerox
50%

Figure 17.8   Estimated market share for copiers

Reducing Xerox's market share still further, IBM introduced a medium-volume copier in the late 1970s. At the beginning of the 1980s, the copier industry looked like Figure 17.8.

Today Xerox wants to win back market share from Ricoh and other firms in the low-volume market segment. It also hopes to continue to dominate the high-volume copier market.

Several factors make it likely that Xerox will attain its goals. In 1981 an FTC ruling was lifted that had previously required Xerox to maintain uncompetitively high prices to prevent it from acting as a monopoly. Xerox's products are now more competitively priced.

Another important factor is that Ricoh, Nashua, and Savin have ended their partnership. Each of them now plans to go after its own share of the market. Individually they are significantly less threatening than they were when acting as a unit.

In 1981 Xerox moved toward developing retail outlets. Featuring copiers, typewriters, and office supplies, these stores broaden Xerox's coverage of the low-volume market.

Finally, Xerox is enlarging its product mix to include text and data processing machines. The Star, a management-oriented information processing computer, is now the leader in automated office work stations. Xerox's Ethernet, another information systems product, allows integration of terminals, printers, plotters, and processors into one network. It is being closely watched by customers interested in data processing and office automation.

By a combination of environmental factors (the lifted FTC ruling and the Savin, Ricoh, and Nashua breakup) and new strategies (retail outlets and product innovation), Xerox hopes to maintain its dominance of the high-volume segment and increase its low-volume market share.

Questions for discussion

1. Trace the competitive structure that Xerox has developed since 1959. Has Xerox's position on the competitive structure continuum changed? Explain.
2. What features has Xerox incorporated into its marketing strategy that make it, to some extent, distinctive?

Part 7

Marketing Management

We have divided marketing into several sets of variables and have discussed the decisions and activities associated with each variable. By now, you should understand (1) how to analyze marketing opportunities, (2) the components of the marketing mix, and (3) the environmental forces and their impact on marketing decisions and activities. Now it is time to put all these components together in our discussion of marketing management issues. In Chapter 18 we discuss strategic market planning. Specifically, we focus on the planning process, the setting of marketing objectives, the assessment of opportunities and resources, and specific product/market matching approaches to strategic market planning. Chapter 19 deals with other marketing management issues including organization, implementation, and control. Approaches to organizing a marketing unit, issues regarding strategy implementation, and techniques for controlling marketing strategies are explored in this chapter.

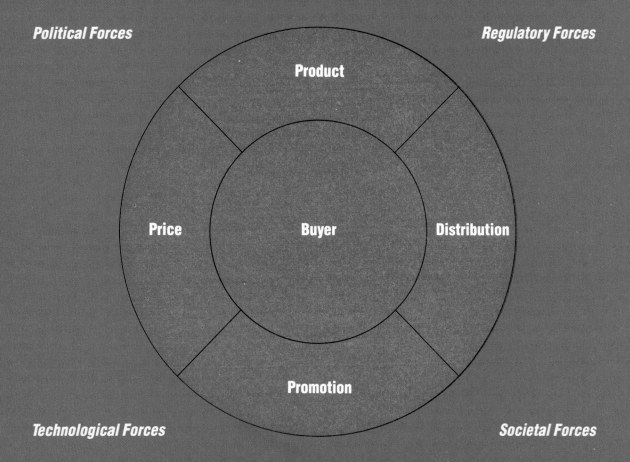

Marketing Environment

Legal Forces

Political Forces

Regulatory Forces

Product

Price

Buyer

Distribution

Promotion

Technological Forces

Societal Forces

Economic Forces

18

Strategic Market Planning

Objectives

To provide an overview of the strategic market planning process.

To define marketing planning and differentiate it from strategic market planning.

To describe three major approaches to strategic market planning including product-portfolio analysis, the market attractiveness/business position model, and PIMS (Profit Impact on Marketing Strategy).

To evaluate strategic market planning and relate it to the development of functional marketing strategies and activities.

AMF Incorporated is a diversified company that includes the following five strategic business units. (Also included are some representative products in each of these major areas of business.)

Automated process equipment
    Microprocessor-controlled
    tobacco processing equipment
    Tire equipment
    Hamburger pattie dispensers
    French fry machines for use in fast
    food restaurants
Electronic controls and systems
    Timers
    Computer-based control systems
Specialty materials
    Purification filters

Energy services and products
    Oil-field inspection and coating
    services
    Digital plotters
    Graphic data processing
Leisure products
    Ben Hogan golf clubs
    Head racquets and skis
    Bowling products
    Sunfish sailboats
    Hatteras yachts

The following statement summarizes AMF's corporate strategy:

AMF's strategy for the balance of the decade is to win maximum results during uncertain economic times by linking our planning and development to identifiable key growth industries. We have aimed our products at vital segments of these businesses. Our marketing efforts are focused on capturing larger shares of our present markets, entering new markets with innovative applications for AMF products and services, and expanding into new geographic areas.

We are shaping long-term programs for improved productivity and cost-effectiveness, adding advanced manufacturing technology, and developing the skills of our people. We believe all these actions strengthen our position for future growth.

Note that the above statement explains the basic thrust of the corporation's effort to deploy resources in order to mold AMF into a flexible corporation, responsive to the demands of industrial customers and consumers. AMF intends to build the company's future by shifting assets from several mature, low-margin, operations into five promising higher-profit core businesses.

Specifically, the proceeds from the divestitures of divisions such as Lawn & Garden, Wheel Goods, and Harley-Davidson were reinvested both in newly acquired businesses in areas such as energy and electronics and in the ongoing development of other profitable AMF operations through product line acquisitions and internal development. Thus, although AMF is a smaller company than a few years ago, restructuring it has multiplied its chances for future profitability and growth.

While the corporate strategy guides the company's mission and areas of business, functional strategies are coordinated to reach corporate goals. For example, AMF's marketing strategy for sports equipment *focuses on quality products at premium prices. These products are promoted in media aimed to appeal to upscale lifestyles and are distributed through dealers that stress performance and value. More specifically, in the golf equipment area a new product line, AMF Ben Hogan Radial Irons, set new sales records for the company. The golf club product line features a four-way cambered sole to help golfers get the ball up quickly, with a solid feel, and to achieve greater distance. This product line was successful because AMF implemented a sound marketing strategy.[1]*

Strategic planning requires a general management orientation, rather than a narrow functional orientation. Nevertheless, market analysis is becoming more and more important, and the lead responsibility for formulating corporate strategy is increasingly being entrusted to the marketing department in many companies. The *corporate strategy* determines the means for utilizing resources in the areas of production, finance, research and development, personnel, and marketing to reach the organization's goals.

Figure 18.1 illustrates how Komatsu attempts to coordinate all functional areas of its business in a way that responds to a dynamic environment in order to reach a corporate goal. Komatsu (Caterpillar's number-one competitor worldwide) intergrates all of its many activities into a strategy that keeps the customer satisfied. This strategy seems to be working, because Komatsu is making progress in gaining a larger market share in the United States.

Corporate strategic planning focuses on the decision-making process that governs the overall direction of the corporation, including many marketing considerations. As we stated in Chapter 1, a *marketing strategy* encompasses selecting and analyzing a target market and creating and maintaining an appropriate marketing mix. Unfortunately, the marketing concept and concerns such as segmentation, product positioning, and marketing research have sometimes been ignored by corporate strategic planners.[2] For example, for many years Bonanza, a budget steakhouse chain, ignored its products, customers, and marketing strategies. Then there was a drop in the consumption of red meat, a primary product for Bonanza, and the firm's shrinking market became primarily older, blue collar, and middle class, and its direct competition became coffee shops. To recover, Bonanza realigned its strategy to place a strong emphasis on strategic market planning. Bonanza added a new product line—"Freshtastiks," a food and salad bar, and fish and poultry were added to the restaurant's offerings. More contemporary design in new restaurants, renovation in old restaurants, a more diversified product line, and in general, a much broader customer base resulted in a more successful Bonanza.[3]

This chapter looks closely at one portion of marketing management—planning. More specifically, we will provide a general overview of planning

1. All facts used in this discussion are taken from the *AMF Annual Report,* 1982. Published in 1983.
2. Yoram Wind, "Marketing and Corporate Strategy," *The Wharton Magazine,* Summer 1982, p. 38.
3. Debra Farst, "Bonanza Begins Comeback Bid," *Adweek,* Oct. 18, 1982, pp. 1, 6.

Figure 18.1
Komatsu integrates all
functional areas to
keep customers
satisfied
*Source: Komatsu Amer-
ica Corporation.*

activities and approaches to strategic market planning. Strategic market planning should guide marketing strategy and marketing planning. Planning of marketing activities strongly affects the overall success of marketing efforts. Other parts of the marketing management process—organizing, implementing, and controlling—will be covered in Chapter 19.

Strategic market planning defined

A *strategic market plan* takes into account not only marketing but all other functional areas of a business unit that must be coordinated, such as production, finance, and personnel, as well as concern about the environment. The concept of the strategic business unit is used to define areas for consideration in a specific strategic market plan. Each *strategic business unit (SBU)* is a division, product line, or other profit center within its parent

Figure 18.2
Exxon Office Systems is a strategic business unit
Source: Exxon Office Systems Company.

company. Each sells a distinct set of products and/or services to an identifiable group of customers, and each is in competition with a well-defined set of competitors. In the context of the parent company, meaningful separation can be made of a SBU's revenues, operating costs, investments, and strategic plans. Exxon office systems, illustrated in Figure 18.2, is a good example of a strategic business unit of the Exxon Corporation. In this case, the office systems SBU contains product lines and is an operating division.

A strategic market plan is *not* the same, therefore, as a marketing plan; it is a plan of *all* aspects of an organization's strategy in the marketplace. A marketing plan, in contrast, deals primarily with implementing the market strategy as it relates to target markets and the marketing mix.[4]

4. Derek F. Abell and John S. Hammond, *Strategic Market Planning* (Englewood Cliffs, N.J.: Prentice-Hall, 1979), p. 10.

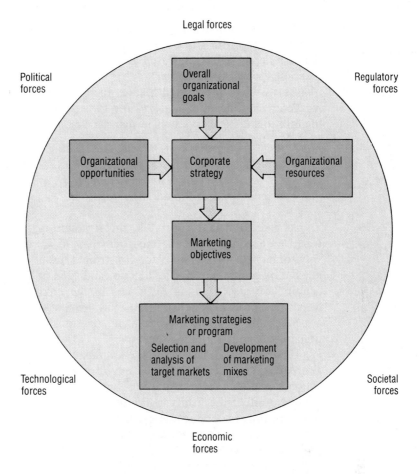

Legal forces

Political forces

Regulatory forces

Overall organizational goals

Organizational opportunities

Corporate strategy

Organizational resources

Marketing objectives

Marketing strategies or program

Selection and analysis of target markets

Development of marketing mixes

Technological forces

Societal forces

Economic forces

Figure 18.3   Components of strategic market planning

A marketing strategy is developed through, and is the result of, *strategic market planning*. Through this process an organization can develop marketing strategies that, when properly implemented and controlled, will contribute to achieving the organization's overall goals. Note that we focus on strategic market planning in this chapter. Development of the marketing strategy is generally based on strategic market planning. To develop a marketing strategy, all aspects of an organization that interface with the marketplace must be considered.

The components of strategic market planning are shown in Figure 18.3. The process is based on the establishment of an organization's overall goals, and it must be within the bounds of the organization's opportunities and resources. When the firm has determined its overall goals and identified its resources, then it can assess its opportunities and develop corporate strategy. Thereafter, marketing objectives must be designed so that their achievement will contribute to the corporate strategy and so that they can be accomplished through efficient use of the organization's resources.

To reach its marketing objectives, an organization must develop a marketing strategy, or a set of marketing strategies, as shown in Figure 18.3.

Usually, several marketing strategies are used simultaneously in an effort to achieve the firm's marketing objectives; the set of marketing strategies that are implemented and used at the same time is referred to as the organization's **marketing program**.

As we have mentioned before, to formulate a marketing strategy the marketer identifies and analyzes the target market and develops a marketing mix to satisfy individuals in that market.

Marketing strategy is best formulated when it reflects overall direction. Then it can become a strategy partner with other organizational functions, such as finance, human resources, and R&D, so that they reinforce each other for best organizational advantage.[5]

As indicated in Figure 18.3, the strategic market planning process is based on an analysis of the environment and is very much affected by it. Environmental forces can place constraints on an organization that can influence its overall goals. The amount and type of resources that a firm can acquire are also affected by forces in the environment. However, such forces do not always constrain or work against the firm; they can also create favorable opportunities that can be translated into overall organizational goals and marketing objectives.

Environmental variables have an impact on the creation of a marketing strategy in several ways. When environmental variables affect an organization's overall goals, resources, opportunities, or marketing objectives, they also affect the firm's marketing strategies, which are based on these goals, resources, opportunities, and marketing objectives. More directly, environmental forces influence the development of a marketing strategy through their impact on consumers' needs and desires. In addition, marketing mix decisions are influenced by a variety of forces in the environment. Figure 18.4 illustrates that White Consolidated Machine Tool Group recognizes the importance of coping with different environmental situations.

In the next several sections, we will discuss the major components of strategic market planning.

Establishing organizational goals

A firm's organizational goals should direct its planning efforts. (Table 18.1 illustrates some typical goals.) A company's overall goals may focus on one or several business activities. Goals specify ends or results that are sought. For example, a firm that is in serious financial trouble may be concerned solely with short-run results needed to stay in business. In recent years, Eastern Airlines and International Harvester both faced this problem. In 1984, Eastern gave its employees 25 percent of its stock in lieu of salary to reduce operating expenses. In this way they were able to obtain financing to continue business and, they hope, solve long-run financial problems. A successful company, however, may want to sacrifice this year's profits for the long run; and it may have other goals at the same time, such as finding new customers. For example, Coca-Cola purchased Columbia Pictures Industries, Inc., believing that the parent company's

5. John G. Keane, "Better Marketing Programs Result by Understanding the Nature of Strategy," *Marketing News,* June 24, 1983, p. 1.

Figure 18.4
White Consolidated Tool Group considers environmental variables in its planning efforts
Source: Courtesy of White Consolidated Industries.

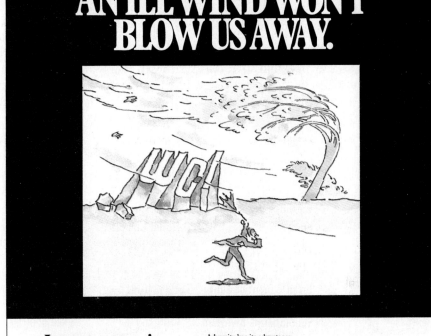

AN ILL WIND WON'T BLOW US AWAY.

In any economic climate, our Group's got the strength to stand its ground.

Adversity has its advantages:

In hard times like these, the strong get a real chance to show off their strength.

So we couldn't imagine a showier time to introduce you to the WCI Machine Tool Group.

Four companies — American Tool/White-BSA, Bullard, White-Sundstrand and the Manufacturing Systems Division — grouped together. Backed by a $2 billion corporation that's unwaveringly committed to the future of the machine tool industry.

Translated into benefits, that means stability for us, security for you. Also, it means we have the resources to develop the highly productive, technologically sophisticated machine tools your future depends on.

Experts tell us the future belongs to a few, large, heavily-capitalized machine tool builders. As one of the ten largest builders in America, and the only builder with WCI behind them, those words don't worry us. Or our customers.

So why worry? Call your nearest Group representative. He'll be there, now and always.

Or write for a brochure to the WCI Machine Tool Group, White Consolidated Industries, Cleveland, Ohio 44111.

 **White Consolidated** *Machine Tool Group*

soft drink profits could not be pushed to grow any faster than 10 percent per year. Coca-Cola hopes to make profits at Columbia grow 20 percent per year.[6]

Organizational opportunities and resources

There are three major considerations in assessing opportunities and resources: market opportunity must be evaluated; environmental forces, discussed in Chapters 16 and 17, must be monitored; and the firm's capabilities should be understood. For example, Eastman Kodak Co. earns 60 percent of its pretax profits and 21 percent of its sales volume from the sale of conventional color film and processing paper.[7] In the large amateur photography market, Kodak has been able to compete successfully against the

6. Myron Magnet, "Coke Tries Selling Movies like Pop," *Fortune,* Dec. 26, 1983, p. 119.
7. "Kodak Fights Back," *Business Week,* Feb. 1, 1982, p. 48.

Table 18.1   Some typical business goals

Possible Attributes	Possible Indices	Targets and Time Frame		
		Year One	Year Two	Year Three
Growth	$ sales	$100 million	$120 million	$140 million
	Unit sales	x units	$1.10x$ units	$1.20x$ units
Efficiency	$ profits	$10 million	$12 million	$15 million
	Profits/sales	.10	.10	.11
Utilization	ROI	.15	.15	.16
of resources	ROE	.25	.26	.27
Contribution to	Dividends	$1.00/share	$1.10/share	$1.30/share
owners	Earnings per share	$2.00/share	$2.40/share	$2.80/share
Contribution to	Price	Equal or better	Equal or better	Equal or better
customers	Quality	than competition	than competition	than competition
	Reliability			
Contributions to	Wage rate	$3.50/hour	$3.75/hour	$4.00/hour
employees	Employment stability	<5% turnover	<4% turnover	<4% turnover
Contributions to	Taxes paid	$10 mil	$12 mil	$16 mil
society	Scholarships awarded	$100,000	$120,000	$120,000

Source: Adapted from C. W. Hofer, ''A Conceptual Scheme for Formulating a Total Business Strategy,'' Case 9-378-726 (Boston: HBS Case Services 9-378-726, 1976), p. 2. Used by permission of the author.

Japanese and nurture its powerful consumer franchise, although its share of this market has decreased in recent years.

Market opportunities for Kodak are changing rapidly, however. Most threatening to Kodak is the possibility that the Japanese will dominate the market for the magnetic tapes and discs that may replace traditional film. If this new technology is successful and if Kodak does not organize its resources to compete with it, then Kodak's market could shrink drastically. The company is marshalling its immense resources in cash, research and development, marketing, and strong employee relations to defend itself in this harsh, new competitive environment. For example, Kodak launched the largest marketing effort in its history to promote its disc film camera, introduced in 1982. This miniature camera uses a fifteen-exposure disc of film instead of film cartridges. Although the company shipped eight million disc cameras the first year, the life cycle for this product is yet to be determined. On the other hand, Ektaprint copiers have become the company's fastest growing product line.[8]

Kodak's capabilities are almost unparalleled in financial strength and technological expertise. Therefore, Kodak's assessment of opportunities and resources is important in developing objectives and in developing or revising marketing strategies. All these activities are a part of strategic market planning.

8. Thomas Moore, ''Embattled Kodak Enters the Electronic Age,'' *Fortune*, Aug. 22, 1983, pp. 122–123.

Figure 18.5
C-E must access market opportunity for waste products
Source: Combustion Engineering, Inc. Advertising Agency: HBM/ Creamer, Inc.

Last year C-E helped turn a potential waste problem into $3 billion worth of energy.

The residue from municipalities and many industrial processes used to be viewed as having little, if any, value. Substances such as wood chips, rice hulls, sugar cane residue and garbage not only were considered waste, but also created large disposal problems.

For many years Combustion Engineering has been designing and selling steam generators that burn these substances as fuel. Today, with C-E's special designs and new equipment, the units also make a significant contribu-

tion in helping to meet local air quality standards.

Last year alone Combustion Engineering systems converted "waste" materials, including the ones shown, into energy that saved the equivalent of 86 million barrels of oil. This works out to a saving of approximately $3 billion...a good start in turning what many consider a liability into a valuable asset.

Combustion Engineering supplies products and services for oil and gas, power generation,

petrochemical, process industries, and other industrial markets worldwide. For more information about our diverse lines of business and a listing of our offices around the world, write: Combustion Engineering, Inc., Dept. 7004-236, 900 Long Ridge Rd., P.O. Box 9308, Stamford, CT, USA 06904.

C-E COMBUSTION ENGINEERING

Energy Technology. Worldwide.

Market opportunity

A *market opportunity* arises when the right combination of circumstances occurs at the right time to allow an organization to take action toward a target market. An opportunity provides a favorable chance or opening for the firm to generate sales from identifiable markets. Figure 18.5 illustrates that Combustion Engineering must assess market opportunity (sales potential) for converting waste products into industrial products to serve power generation, process industries, and other industrial markets. The term *strategic window* has been used to describe what are often only limited periods of optimum fit between the key requirements of a market and the particular capabilities of a firm competing in that market.[9]

For example, Levi Strauss & Co. is facing a fast-changing retail market. Traditionally higher-priced department stores are now toying with discount marketing, and mass merchandisers such as K mart Corp. have set up boutiques to flaunt prestigious labels.

Due to the influence of competitors, Levi Strauss & Co. is assessing its opportunities for future growth. A major competitor, Wrangler, holds an estimated 21 percent market share, compared with Levi's 43 percent, and has been gaining market share. In response to this challenge, Levi Strauss & Co. changed its strategic market planning by creating its David Hunter line of casual men's wear. This line provides a medium-priced alternative to high-fashion labels such as Ralph Lauren's Polo line. Levi's youthwear division is introducing a similar line for boys called Davy Hunter. Other new products include Roegiers' Tourage collection of men's casual wear and Railback's corduroy and denim maternity wear. Neither Tourage nor David Hunter carry the Levi's logo.[10]

This example illustrates that understanding the environment as well as the firm's ability to respond to a market opportunity are important considerations in strategic market planning.

Determinants of the attractiveness of market opportunity include market factors such as size and growth rate and other factors such as competition, financial and economic factors, technological factors, and social, legal, and political factors.[11] Since each industry and product is somewhat different, the factors that determine attractiveness tend to vary. For example, when Motorola decided to enter the market for distributed data processing, it was assumed that the company did not have the needed technology, although the market had great potential. However, after purchasing Four-Phase Systems, Inc., Motorola rounded out its semiconductor operations with the terminals and computers acquired, thus significantly altering its product mix to serve new and growing markets. Motorola now serves the office automation and data processing markets as well as markets for mobile radios and other electronic products.[12]

Market requirements relate to the customers' needs or desired benefits. The market requirement is satisfied by components of the marketing mix that provide benefits to buyers. Of course, buyers' perceptions of what requirements fill their needs and provide the desired benefits determine the success of any marketing effort.

As we mentioned in Chapter 17, market requirements often change as competition offers new benefits to consumers. For example, to encourage more families with children to eat at Burger King, that chain is following McDonald's lead in building more playgrounds at its stores.[13] To meet the

9. Derek F. Abell, "Strategic Windows," *Journal of Marketing,* July 1978, p. 21.
10. "Levi Strauss: A Touch of Fashion—and a Dash of Humility," *Business Week,* Oct. 24, 1983, pp. 85, 86.
11. Abell and Hammond, *Strategic Market Planning,* p. 213.
12. "Motorola's New Strategy," *Business Week,* March 29, 1982, p. 128.
13. Christy Marshall, "BK Hungers for Sales, Starts New Drive," *Advertising Age,* Nov. 30, 1981, p. 6.

intense competition of other fast food companies, Burger King also recently offered, or is considering offering, a breakfast menu, veal sandwich, seafood basket, Mexican dinner basket, and pizza.

Environmental monitoring

Environmental monitoring is the process that seeks information about events and relationships in a company's outside environment, knowledge of which assists marketers in identifying opportunities and planning.[14]

Some corporations have derived substantial benefits from establishing an "environmental scanning (or monitoring) unit" within the strategic planning group or from including line management in teams or committees to conduct environmental analysis.[15] Management is thus integrally involved in the process of environmental forecasting, and the likelihood of successfully integrating forecasting efforts into strategic market planning is considerably enhanced.[16]

Monitoring change in the environment is extremely important if a firm is to avoid crisis management. The Nestlé Company tried ignoring protestors and took activists that questioned the firm's promotion of Nestlé infant formulas to court. The controversy involved the marketing of a product that promoted bottle-feeding over breast-feeding. Allegations developed that babies in less developed countries suffered from diarrhea and malnutrition when fed this product. To deal with this problem Nestlé has formed an audit commission to review complaints and has taken its defense directly to the news media.[17]

An environmental change can suddenly alter a firm's opportunities or resources, and reformulated, more effective strategies may be needed to guide marketing efforts. The impact of an environmental force such as technology can have far-reaching impact on diverse businesses. When video games became popular in the early 1980s, few record companies saw them as a threat. Environmental monitoring should have indicated to record companies that youths were spending money for video games that would otherwise have gone to records.[18] Record companies have now diversified into the video game market (Warner, for example, owns Atari), and many record retailers have transformed their stores into home entertainment centers.[19] Record and tape rental services now are replacing the purchase of records in some cases. Record companies might have predicted these changes if they had monitored the impact of new technology on entertainment. But then in 1983–1984, Michael Jackson almost single-handedly turned record industry sales upward; and youths lost interest in video games—plunging this industry into a recession. Also, popular pay television such as MTV has hurt video game sales. Environmental moni-

14. See Francis Joseph Aguilar, *Scanning the Business Environment* (New York: Macmillan, 1976).
15. Liam Fahey, William K. King, Vodake K. Naraganan, "Environmental Scanning and Forecasting in Strategic Planning—The State of the Art," *Long Range Planning,* Feb. 1981, p. 38.
16. Ibid.
17. Kevin Higgins, "Instant Formula Protest Teaches Nestlé a Tactical Lesson," *Marketing News,* June 10, 1983, p. 1.
18. *Business Week,* Nov. 30, 1981, p. 124.
19. Ibid.

Application
Coleco Industries' Strategic Market Plan

Coleco Industries, Inc. is a major manufacturer of entertainment and recreation products. It is the producer of Colecovision, an expandable video game/home computer system; it manufactures video games hardware and software for systems other than Colecovision; and it is the world's largest maker of portable electronic games. Coleco also manufactures a broad variety of ride-on vehicles for children and is the world's largest manufacturer of above ground swimming and wading pools.

Coleco's successful introduction of new electronic products was due to the effective application of its merchandising strategy. Coleco's merchandising strategy is comprised of four basic elements: understanding what consumers want and responding appropriately to their desires, selectively acquiring and creatively applying popular licenses, making extensive use of advertising to communicate messages in a unique and memorable way, and employing mass-market distribution techniques to make products readily available at a reasonable price. Market research determined the features that were most important to the consumer in the video game market—high resolution graphics, responsive controllers, licensed arcade game software, and expandability to accommodate a home computer module and new technological developments.

Recognizing the positive identification consumers have with well-known arcade games, Coleco negotiated licensing agreements for popular games such as Donkey Kong, Zaxxon, and Turbo. This marketing strategy was applied to a broad range of Coleco products. Perhaps the most easily recognizable example of this is Coleco's use of the Smurf license. Some of the products using the Smurf cartoon character include a video cartridge, snow coaster, stroller, slide, pedal car (smurfmobile), pools, playhouses, and picnic tables. The licensed character is applied to quality goods in a manner that integrates the character and the product in a logical and appealing fashion. Massive advertising and promotion enhances consumer demand.

Coleco's business opportunity will involve developing increasingly sophisticated, interactive and appealing entertainment software delivered by a state-of-the-art hardware system. The use of audio disks, video disks, and the latest in techniques will further enhance the appeal of computerized entertainment software. Coleco will also continue to utilize licensed characters such as Smurfs, the Berenstain Bears, and Dr. Seuss. Although toys play an important role in Coleco's success, its most significant source of growth has been in the electronic business.

Source: Based on Coleco Industries, Inc. *1982 Annual Report.*

toring should identify new developments and determine the nature and rate of change. Consider the Application above which discusses Coleco Industries' creation of product lines to fit a changing environment.

Capabilities and resources of the firm

A firm's capabilities relate to distinctive competencies that it has developed to do something well and efficiently. Figure 18.6 indicates, for example, that Timken wants to be known as a knowledge company with a wealth of ideas and skills that can be put to work. A company is likely to enjoy a differential advantage in an area where its competencies outmatch those of its potential competition.[20]

20. Philip Kotler, "Strategic Planning and the Marketing Process," *Business,* May–June 1980, pp. 6–7.

HOW THINGS COME OUT COULD DEPEND ON WHERE WE COME IN.

THE DECISIONS you make at the drawing board are going to affect your product for the rest of its life. That's why it's so important to use all of the design tools at your company's command.

Think of The Timken Company as one of those tools.

We've put everything we know about helping

you pick just the right bearings into what we call bearing systems analysis.

A blend of computer programming and the very latest bearing technology that helps us predict more accurately than ever before just how long any Timken® tapered roller bearing will last in your product.

And how well it'll do its job in the field.

The real beauty of our bearing systems analysis is that your Timken bearing sales engineer can sit down with your people and, using a uniquely programmed calculator, make those precise predictions on the spot.

Pick our brains right from the start. We think you'll find that it'll pay off in the end.

The Timken Company, Canton, Ohio 44706.

IT'S NOT JUST WHAT WE MAKE. IT'S WHAT WE KNOW.

TIMKEN®

Figure 18.6 Timken promotes its image as an organization possessing technological capabilities and resources *Source: The Timken Company.*

Volvo, Inc., a Swedish motor vehicle manufacturer, has developed a distinctive competency in the area of auto safety. Volvo engineers were committed to researching and improving automobile safety long before it was required by law in the United States. Today Volvo claims to be the model to emulate in auto safety features. Volvo claims that its body creates a kind of cage that surrounds Volvo passengers on all sides with front and rear ''crumple zones'' to absorb impact and to reduce the possibility of injury to passengers. Volvo has emphasized these features to provide a differential advantage in terms of safety benefits.

Besides differentiation of a product feature, firms may develop capabilities in the area of low costs in production and marketing, or they may use a combination of features. For example, in the heavy-duty truck industry Ford and Paccar lead in growth and financial performance. Ford serves the large fleet market, while Paccar sells its Kenworth and Peterbilt trucks to quality-conscious independent truckers. These two heavy-truck manufacturers have succeeded by going after different target markets and by developing different capabilities and resources.

Today marketing planners are especially concerned with resource constraints. Due to shortages in energy and other scarce economic resources, strategic planning options are often limited.

Table 18.2 A framework for viewing resource constraints and opportunities in different planning periods

Present (few or no resource constraints)	**Short/Intermediate-Range Horizon** (increasingly severe resource and social-governmental constraints)
Current products (*benefits*) produced and supplied at currently feasible[a] technology/resource combinations (*costs*)	Somewhat modified products (*benefits*) that will be demanded at *costs* based on feasible[a] extensions of current technology/resource combinations
Intermediate/Long-Range Horizon (extremely severe resource and social-governmental constraints)	**Long-Range Horizon** (resource constraints disappearing, continuing severe social-governmental constraints)
Extensively modified products (*benefits*) that will be demanded at *costs* based on feasible[a] major modifications of current resource/technology combinations	Products (*benefits*) that will be demanded at *costs* based on feasible[a] new resources/new technology combinations

[a]Most advantageous to the corporation in terms of its long-run organizational goals.
Source: Reprinted by permission from *Business* magazine. "Strategic Planning Under Resource Constraints," by Jacob Naor, September–October 1981, p. 18. Copyright © 1981 by the College of Business Administration, Georgia State University, Atlanta.

Table 18.2 provides a framework for viewing opportunities and resources in different planning periods. This framework suggests that individual firms face four distinct planning horizons, each constrained to a different degree in regard to resources, social concerns, and government regulations.[21] These constraints increase from the present to the intermediate long-range period, with resource constraints possibly declining thereafter as radically new technologies and resource applications become commercially available. Crucial to the usefulness of this framework is the ability to predict future technological developments or the likely direction of future breakthroughs. For example, the projected direction of technological innovation could, in effect, suggest the strategic horizons facing firms and industries. In that case, technological forecasting could be a crucial element in the strategic-planning process.

Costs (resulting from various technology/resource combinations) and benefits must go through a series of modifications or extensions as constraints become more severe. As we have already pointed out, scarce resources are not always constraints; they may provide the impetus a firm needs to provide benefits at the most desirable cost. For example, Transamerica Corporation attempts to be a low-cost marketer by reducing costs because its products are closely related and because of operating efficiencies between complementary businesses the firm owns. Transamerica seeks to maximize the benefits of diversification and maintain a compatible mix of companies. This strategy permits the company to provide products (benefits) at resource/technology combinations (costs) to achieve industry leadership in service, reputation, innovation, and overall efficiency.

21. This section is adapted by permission from *Business* magazine. "Strategic Planning Under Resource Constraints," by Jacob Naor, September–October 1981, p. 17. Copyright © 1981 by the College of Business Administration, Georgia State University, Atlanta.

Corporate strategy

Corporate strategy defines the means and direction of reaching organizational goals. The resources of the corporation are matched with the opportunities and risks in the environment. Corporate strategy attempts to define the scope and role of the strategic business units of the firm that are coordinated to reach the ends that are desired. For example, Xerox focuses on reprographics (photocopying, electronic printers), office systems, and work stations. The acquisition of Grum and Forster, a leading property and liability insurance company, represents a major change in the direction of Xerox and provides new opportunities and risks. Xerox does not engage in businesses to produce robots, automobiles, or earth-moving equipment, because they do not fit into the corporate strategy. A corporate strategy determines not only the scope of the business, but also its resource deployment, competitive advantages, overall coordination of production, finance, marketing, and other functional areas. The application on page 558 illustrates how ASEA has developed a most successful corporate strategy.

Tenneco illustrates the payoff of strategic market planning. The company's management assessed its opportunities and resources, saw the threats in the environment, and formulated a corporate strategy that enabled the company to survive and be profitable when falling oil prices and an oversupply of natural gas hurt many corporations in its industry.[22]

Marketing objective

A *marketing objective* is a statement of what is to be accomplished through marketing activities. It specifies the results expected from marketing efforts. It should be expressed in clear, simple terms so that all marketing personnel understand exactly what they are to try to achieve. It should be written in such a way that its accomplishment can be measured accurately. If a company has an objective of increasing its market share by 12 percent, the firm should be able to measure changes in its market share accurately. A marketing objective should also indicate the time frame for accomplishing the objective. For example, a firm that sets an objective of introducing three new products should state the time period in which this is to be done.

A marketing manager who fails to set marketing objectives that are consistent with the firm's general goals not only will be less likely to accomplish the marketing objectives but also may work against the achievement of the firm's overall goals. Suppose a marketing manager sets an objective that requires greater use of consumer credit, but an overall goal of the firm is to reduce bad-debt loss. The two objectives probably will conflict.

Consider the corporate strategy for Transamerica Corporation: Transamerica should focus on key market segments related to primary businesses including insurance and financial services, travel services, and the manufacturing of precision engineered products used in industry. "A key dimension of Transamerica is the value added to our operating companies from being part of a larger corporation."[23] It is obvious that this is a corporate strategy, because it indicates the overall thrust of the corporation.

22. Tenneco 1982 Annual Report. Published in 1983.
23. Transamerica *1982 Annual Report*. Published in 1983, p. 5.

Application

Sweden's ASEA
Challenges
Robotics in
Japan and
U.S.A.

ASEA (Allmana Svenska Electriska or Swedish General Electric Company) is a large industrial conglomerate in Sweden. This 101-year-old company began as a lackluster multinational producer of electrical equipment and home appliances. Today, this highly successful company is an international leader in energy transmission, process and pollution controls, locomotives, and robotics. Annual sales exceed $3.5 billion and profits are over $162 million.

Changes in ASEA's corporate strategy transformed the company from a stagnant, top-heavy conglomerate into forty separate strategic business units. Some of ASEA's traditional domestic businesses were eliminated and factories were closed or sold in Brazil, Denmark, and Greece. Then, the company pumped money into electronics seeking high-profit expansion in world markets. A new robotics plant was opened in Belgium in 1982 and new plants were opened in Japan and in North America.

ASEA has made breakthroughs in the emerging high-technology field of long-distance transmission of high-voltage direct current (HVDC). Since most power lines in the world transmit alternating current, ASEA's conversion device—called a *thyristor*—has opened up 53 percent of the developing world market for its HVDC technology. The company has entered into a contract to connect Brazil's Itaipu Dam, presently the largest hydroelectric project in the world, to São Paulo through a HVDC system. ASEA also sold a $200 million system to the Intermountain Power Agency of Salt Lake City, which will make it possible for a coal-fired power plant in Utah to be connected to Los Angeles.

ASEA is also pursuing other markets, including the industrial controls market. It sold a $1 million control system to Chaparral Steel Company of Midlothian, Texas. ASEA also has 50 percent of the rapidly expanding world market for industrial energy controls, such as controls for recycling waste heat. It claims 12 percent of the market for computer controls used by electrical utilities; and its mass-transit technology has been sold to Amtrak and British Columbia Railways. ASEA also perceives large market potential in pollution controls, especially in Scandinavia and in North America.

This change in ASEA's strategic market planning has contributed to dramatic results. Sales tripled and profits quadrupled in three years. In line with the company's global plans, export revenue accounted for an increasing proportion of the company's business, reaching 68 percent.

ASEA illustrates the use of strategic market planning for competing successfully in the marketplace. The company successfully monitored its environment. It assessed its market opportunities in electronics and other high growth markets. It utilized its resources and experiences in its existing global markets to develop marketing strategies. By dividing its businesses into strategic business units (SBU's) that had clear goals and objectives, ASEA increased its opportunities for profitability. Strategic market planning led to divestment of unprofitable operations and entry into highly profitable diversifications.

Source: Based on "Sweden's ASEA: Its Robots Reach for the U.S. as a High-tech Drive Begins To Pay Off," *Business Week*, Jan. 16, 1984, pp. 104, 105.

Now take a look at a marketing objective of the same corporation:

Achieve a significant market share in each segment of our businesses.[24]

It is evident that achieving a significant market share is a statement of what is to be accomplished through marketing activities. This marketing objective is clear and can be measured accurately once it is quantified. For example, to achieve a 25 percent market share in each segment of their

24. Transamerica *1982 Annual Report*, p. 5.

businesses in the next three years would explain exactly what is to be accomplished and when it is to be done. Also note that the corporate strategy and the marketing objective are consistent. Transamerica Corporation maintains a staff group to focus on strategic planning. Besides setting corporate goals, corporate strategy and marketing objectives, the planning actions of Transamerica encompass all of the strategic market planning activities described in this chapter.

Planning marketing activities

Marketing management is a process of planning, organizing, implementing, and controlling marketing activities in order to facilitate and expedite exchanges effectively and efficiently. "Effectiveness," an important dimension of our definition, refers to the degree to which an exchange furthers an organization's objectives. The quality of exchanges relative to an organization's objectives may range from highly desirable to highly undesirable. One major purpose of the marketing management process is to facilitate highly desirable exchanges. "Efficiency" refers to the minimization of the resources that an organization must expend to achieve a specific level of desirable exchanges. Thus, the purpose of the marketing management process is to facilitate highly desirable exchanges and to minimize as much as possible the costs of doing so.

As we noted at the start, this chapter deals with the planning part of the marketing management definition. So far, we have discussed strategic marketing planning. In this section we describe how the strategic plan is implemented. *Marketing planning* is a systematic process that involves the assessment of marketing opportunities and resources, the determination of marketing objectives, the development of a marketing strategy, and the development of a plan for implementation and control. A *marketing plan* includes the framework and entire set of activities to be performed; it is the written document or blueprint for implementing and controlling an organization's marketing activities. A firm should have a plan for each marketing strategy it develops. Since a firm's plans must be changed as forces in the firm and the environment change, marketing planning is a continuous process.

Because most organizations have existing plans and are engaged in ongoing activities, marketing managers must start with an organization's current situation and performance and then assess future marketing opportunities and constraints. The planning process calls for information about the difference, if any, between objectives and current performance. Probable performance in the future should be assessed; then the current marketing strategy can be altered or objectives changed if forecasted performance does not meet desired objectives in the next planning period. Figure 18.7 illustrates the *marketing planning cycle*. Note that marketing planning is a circular process. Also as the dotted feedback lines in Figure 18.7 indicate, planning is not unidirectional. Feedback is used to coordinate and synchronize all stages of the planning cycle.

When formulating a marketing plan, a new enterprise or a firm with a new product does not have current performance to evaluate or an existing plan to revise. Therefore, its marketing planning would center on analyzing available resources and options to assess opportunities. Managers could then develop marketing objectives and a strategy. In addition, many firms

Figure 18.7
The marketing plan-
ning cycle

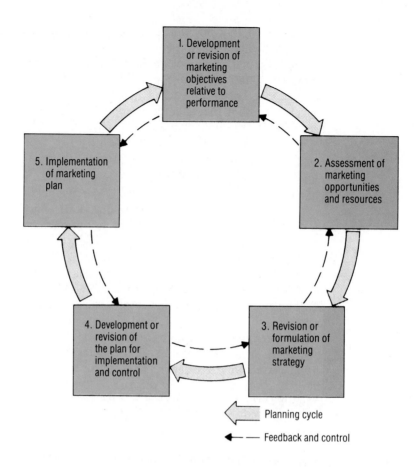

1. Development or revision of marketing objectives relative to performance

2. Assessment of marketing opportunities and resources

3. Revision or formulation of marketing strategy

4. Development or revision of the plan for implementation and control

5. Implementation of marketing plan

⇨ Planning cycle

◄ — — Feedback and control

recognize the need to include information systems in their plans so that they can have continuous feedback and keep their marketing activities oriented toward objectives. Information systems were discussed in Chapter 4.

To illustrate the marketing planning process, consider the decisions that went into the planning of the introduction of a national newspaper—*USA Today*. Table 18.3 lists some of the more important marketing decisions that had to be made in planning the introduction of *USA Today*. Of course, to reach the objective, a detailed course of action was communicated throughout the organization. In short, specific marketing plans should do the following:

1. Specify expected results so that the organization can anticipate what its situation will be at the end of the current planning period.
2. Identify the resources needed to carry out the planned activities, so that a budget can be developed.
3. Describe the activities that are to take place in sufficient detail that responsibilities for implementation can be assigned.
4. Provide for the monitoring of activities and results, so that control can be exerted.[25]

25. David J. Luck and O. C. Ferrell, *Marketing Strategy and Plans,* 2nd ed. © 1985, in press. Adapted by permission of Prentice-Hall, Inc., Englewood Cliffs, N.J.

Table 18.3 Planning for the introduction of a national newspaper: *USA Today*

Objective: Achieve 1 million in circulation by reaching an upscale market, primarily male, holding professional and managerial positions, who made at least one trip of 200 miles or more within the last year.

Opportunity: Paper tends to be a second newspaper purchase for readers. *USA Today* is not in competition directly with local papers and it is not positioned against other national newspapers/magazines.

Market: Circulation within a 200-mile radius of 15 major markets, representing 54% of the U.S. population, including such cities as Chicago, Houston, New York, Los Angeles, and Denver.

Product: Superior graphic quality, appeal to the TV generation with short stories, color weather map and other contemporary features.

Price: Competitive price.

Promotion: Pedestal-like vending machines with attention-grabbing design and positioned higher than competitors to differentiate the paper and bring it closer to eye level. Outdoor advertising and some print advertising promotes the paper.

Distribution: Newsstand and vending machines in high traffic locations.

Implementing and Control: Personnel with experience in the newspaper business who could assist in developing a systematic approach for implementing the marketing strategy and design and information system to monitor and control the results.

Source: Kevin Higgins, "*USA Today* Nears Million Reader Mark," *Marketing News*, April 15, 1983, pp. 1, 5. Reprinted by permission of the American Marketing Association.

The duration of marketing plans vary. Plans that cover a period of one year or less are called *short-range plans*. *Medium-range plans* usually encompass two to five years. Marketing plans that extend for more than five years are generally viewed as *long-range plans*, they sometimes cover a period as long as twenty years. Marketing managers often have short-, medium-, and long-range plans all at the same time.

The extent to which marketing managers develop and use plans also varies. Although planning provides numerous benefits, some managers do not use formal marketing plans because they spend almost all their time dealing with daily problems—many of which would be eliminated by adequate planning. However, planning is becoming more important to marketing managers. They realize that planning is necessary to develop, coordinate, and control marketing activities effectively and efficiently.

Approaches to strategic market planning

In recent years, marketing managers have developed target market/marketing mixes, sometimes called product/market matching approaches to strategic market planning. Because these approaches to planning are widely used today, let us focus briefly on three approaches that can be useful in structuring the overall strategic market plan. The Boston Consulting Group (BCG) product-portfolio analysis and the market attractiveness/business position model are popular approaches to strategic planning. The PIMS (Profit Impact on Market Strategies) project provides data to help direct strategic market planning efforts.

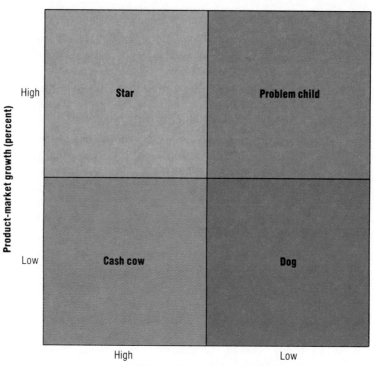

Figure 18.8
Illustrative growth-share matrix developed by the Boston Consulting Group
Source: Adapted from "The Product Portfolio," Perspectives No. 66, The Boston Consulting Group, Inc., 1970. See also George Day, "Diagnosing the Product Portfolio," Journal of Marketing, April 1977, pp. 29–38.

Product-market growth (percent)

High   Star   Problem child

Low   Cash cow   Dog

        High   Low

Market share (actual or relative)

The Boston Consulting Group (BCG) product-portfolio analysis

Product-portfolio analysis, the BCG approach, is based on a philosophy that a product's market growth rate and its relative market share are important considerations in determining its marketing strategy. All the firm's products should be integrated into a single, overall matrix and evaluated to determine appropriate strategies for individual SBUs and the overall portfolio strategies. Just as financial investors have different investments with varying risks and rates of return, firms have a range of products characterized by different market growth rates and relative market shares. However, a balanced product portfolio matrix is the end result of a number of actions, not the result of the analysis alone. Portfolio models can be created based on present and projected market growth rate and proposed market share strategies (build share, maintain share, harvest share, or divest business). Managers can use these models to determine and classify each product's expected future cash contributions and future cash requirements.

In general, managers who use a portfolio model must examine the competitive position of a product (or product line) and the opportunities for improving that product's contribution to profitability and cash flow.[26] The BCG analytical approach is more of a diagnostic tool than a guide for making strategy prescriptions.

Figure 18.8, which is based on work by the Boston Consulting Group, enables the marketing manager to classify a firm's products into four basic

26. Joseph P. Guiltinan and Gordon W. Paul, *Marketing Management: Strategies and Programs* (New York: McGraw-Hill, 1982), p. 31.

Figure 18.9
Illustrative growth-
share matrix for a ciga-
rette company

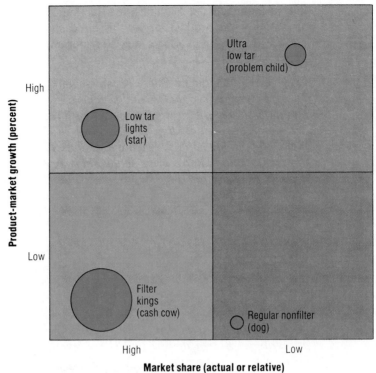

The area of each circle represents dollar sales of the product on the matrix.

types: stars, cash cows, dogs, and problem children.[27] Stars are products with a dominant share of the market and good prospects for growth; they generally generate a lot of cash, but it is used to finance growth, add capacity, and increase market shares. Cash cows have a dominant share of the market but low prospects for growth; typically they generate more cash than is required to maintain market share. Dogs have a subordinate share of the market and low prospects for growth; these products are often found in mature markets. Problem children have a subordinate share of a growing market, and generally require a large amount of cash to build share.

The growth-share matrix in Figure 18.8 can be expanded as in Figure 18.9 to show a firm's whole portfolio by providing for each product: (1) its dollar sales volume, illustrated by the size of a circle on the matrix; (2) its market share relative to competition, represented by the horizontal position of the product on the matrix, and (3) the growth rate of the market, indicated by the position of the product in the vertical direction. Figure 18.9 illustrates the growth-share matrix for a cigarette company. Although total unit sales of cigarettes have been almost constant in recent years, firms that have introduced low-tar and, more recently, ultra-low-tar brands have obtained a larger share of the total cigarette market. In other words, some market segments have been growth areas while others have declined in growth. Brown & Williamson, for example, has extended its product

27. George S. Day, "Diagnosing the Product Portfolio," *Journal of Marketing,* April 1977, pp. 30–31.

line to include Kool Lights, a low-tar menthol cigarette, and Kool Ultra, an ultra-low-tar product, as well as the cash cow Kool Filter Kings brand.

The following passage suggests marketing strategies appropriate for each of the four basic types of products:

Low Growth/Dominant Share (Cash Cows)

These profitable products usually generate more cash than is required to maintain share. All strategies should be directed toward maintaining market dominance—including investments in [process improvements and] technological leadership. Pricing decisions should be made cautiously with an eye to maintaining price leadership. Pressure to over-invest through product proliferation and market expansion should be resisted unless prospects for expanding primary demand are unusually attractive. Instead, excess cash should be used to support research activities and growth areas elsewhere in the company.

High Growth/Dominant Share (Stars)

Products that are market leaders, but also growing fast, will have substantial reported profits but need a lot of cash to finance the rate of growth. [The cash may be needed to add capacity, make process and product improvements, develop products through research and development, and in general to increase market share.] The appropriate strategies are designed primarily to protect the existing share level by reinvesting earnings in the form of price reductions, product improvement, better market coverage, production efficiency increases, etc. Particular attention must be given to obtaining a large share of the new users or new applications that are the source of growth in the market.

Low Growth/Subordinate Share (Dogs)

Since there usually can be only one market leader and because most markets are mature, the greatest number of products fall in this category. Such products are usually at a cost disadvantage and have few opportunities for growth at a reasonable cost. Their markets are not growing, so there is little new business to compete for, and market share gains will be resisted strenuously by the dominant competition.

The slower the growth (present or prospective) and the smaller the relative share, the greater the need for positive action. The possibilities include:

1. *Focusing on a specialized segment of the market that can be dominated, and protected from competitive inroads*
2. *Harvesting, which is a conscious cutback of all support costs to some minimum level which will maximize the cash flow over a foreseeable lifetime—which is usually short*
3. *Divestment, usually involving sale of a going concern*
4. *Abandonment or deletion from the product line*

High Growth/Subordinate Share (Problem Children)

The combination of rapid growth and poor profit margins creates an enormous demand for cash. If the cash is not forthcoming, the product will become a "Dog" as growth inevitably slows. The basic strategy options are fairly clear-cut; either invest heavily to get a disproportionate share of the

Figure 18.10
Coca-Cola and Bacardi are cash cows
Source: Bacardi Imports, Inc.

Love at first sip.

Delicious Bacardi rum and icy cold Coke. They've been winning smiles
since the turn of the century. And today this refreshing pair is America's favorite.
Ahhh Bacardi and Coke, a taste you'll love sip, after sip, after sip.

BACARDI rum. The mixable one. Made in Puerto Rico.

*new sales or buy existing shares by acquiring competitors and thus move
the product toward the "Star" category or get out of the business using
some of the methods just described.*

*Consideration also should be given to a market segmentation strategy,
but only if a defensible niche can be identified and resources are available
to gain dominance. This strategy is even more attractive if the segment
can provide an entree and experience base from which to push for dominance of the whole market.*[28]

The long-run health of the corporation depends on having some products that generate cash (and provide acceptable reported profits) and others that use cash to support growth. Figure 18.10 illustrates two well-
known cash cows that continue to generate the greatest amount of sales in

28. George S. Day, "Diagnosing the Product Portfolio," *Journal of Marketing,*
April 1977, pp. 30–31. Reprinted with the permission of the publisher, the
American Marketing Association.

their respective firms' product lines. This cash permits the Coca-Cola and Bacardi companies to develop new products. Among the indicators of overall health are the size and vulnerability of the cash cows (and the prospects for the stars, if any), and the number of problem children and dogs. Particular attention must be paid to those products with large cash appetites. Unless the company has abundant cash flow, it cannot afford to sponsor many such products at one time. If resources (including debt capacity) are spread too thin, the company simply will wind up with too many marginal products and suffer a reduced capacity to finance promising new product entries or acquisitions in the future. For many years, Zenith was known as a one-product company (television sets). Zenith's acquisition of Heath Company has led to parlaying a hobby computer into an excellent personal computer. Zenith has achieved a leadership position with machines powerful enough to handle software written for IBM personal computers. Today Zenith Data System represents over 12 percent of Zenith's total sales, and this SBU is one of the fastest-growth areas in the company. In addition, Zenith has become the leading seller of video monitors for the computer industry.[29]

Market attractiveness/ business position model

The *market attractiveness/business position model,* illustrated in Figure 18.11, is a two-dimensional matrix. The vertical dimension is labeled *market attractiveness,* which includes all the sources of strength and resources that relate to the market, such as seasonality, economies of scale, competitive intensity, industry sales, and the overall cost and feasibility of entering the market. The horizontal axis is labeled *business position;* it is a composite of factors such as sales, relative market share, research and development, price competitiveness, product quality, and market knowledge as they relate to the product in building market share. A slight variation of this matrix is called General Electric's Strategic Business Planning Grid, because General Electric is credited for extending the product portfolio planning tool to examine market attractiveness and business strength. The best situation is for a firm to have a strong business position in an attractive market.

The upper left area in Figure 18.11 represents the opportunity for an invest/grow strategy, but there is no indication from Figure 18.11 telling how to implement this strategy. The purpose of the model is to serve as a diagnostic tool to highlight SBUs that have an opportunity to grow or that should be divested or approached selectively. SBUs that occupy the invest/grow position can lose their position through faulty marketing strategies.

Decisions on resource allocation in regard to SBUs characterized by medium overall attractiveness should be arrived at on a relative basis. The lower right area is a low-growth harvest/divest area. Harvesting is a gradual withdrawal of marketing resources on the assumption that sales will decline at a slow rate but profits will still be significant at a lower sales

29. "Zenith: The Surprise in Personal Computers," *Business Week,* Dec. 12, 1983, p. 102.

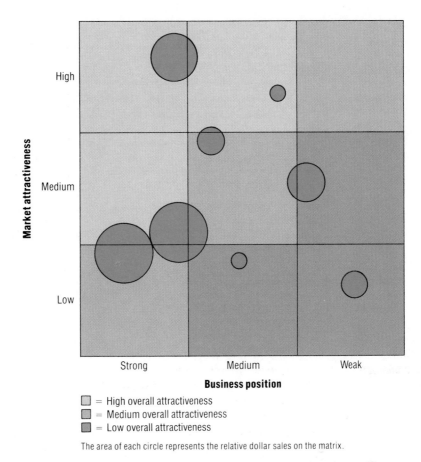

High

Medium

Low

Market attractiveness

Strong   Medium   Weak

Business position

☐ = High overall attractiveness
▨ = Medium overall attractiveness
■ = Low overall attractiveness

The area of each circle represents the relative dollar sales on the matrix.

Figure 18.11   Market attractiveness/business position matrix
Source: Adapted from Derek F. Abell and John S. Hammond, Strategic Market Planning: Problems and Analytical Approaches, © *1979, p. 213. Reprinted by permission of Prentice-Hall, Inc., Englewood Cliffs, N.J.*

volume. Harvesting and divesting may be appropriate strategies for SBUs characterized by low overall attractiveness. For example, Westinghouse has decided to place less emphasis (harvest) on medium- and low-attractiveness sectors in utility businesses in favor of sectors of high overall attractiveness such as services, cable television, robotics, and defense electronics.[30]

PIMS (Profit Impact on Marketing Strategy)

The Strategic Planning Institute (SPI) has developed a data bank of information on over 1,700 products that members provide for the ***PIMS (Profit Impact on Marketing Strategy)*** research program. Over two hundred members of the institute provide confidential information on successes, failures, and marginal products. Figure 18.12 shows a PIMS data form sent to member firms. The data are analyzed to provide reports for member firms on strategy.

30. "Operation Turnaround," *Business Week,* Dec. 5, 1983, p. 124.

Figure 18.12
Sample page from PIMS data forms
Source: PIMS Data Form 1 reproduced by permission of the Strategic Planning Institute (PIMS Program), Cambridge, Massachusetts, 1979.

103: "LIFE CYCLE" STAGE OF PRODUCT CATEGORY

How would you describe the stage of development of the types of products or services sold by this business during the last three years? *(Check one)*

. . . Introductory Stage: Primary demand for product just starting to grow; products or services still unfamiliar to many potential users ☐ 1

. . . Growth Stage: Demand growing at 10% or more annually in real terms; technology or competitive structure still changing ☐ 2

. . . Maturity Stage: Products or services familiar to vast majority of prospective users; technology and competitive structure reasonably stable ☐ 3

. . . Decline Stage: Products viewed as commodities; weaker competitors beginning to exit ☐ 4

104: What was this business's first year of commercial sales? *(Check one)*

Prior to 1930	1930-1949	1950-1954	1955-1959	1960-1964	1965-1969	1970-1974	1975-
☐ 0	☐ 1	☐ 2	☐ 3	☐ 4	☐ 5	☐ 6	☐ 7

105: At the time this business first entered the market, was it . . . *(Check one)*

. . . One of the pioneers in first developing such products or services? ☐ 1

. . . An early follower of the pioneer(s) in a still growing, dynamic market? ☐ 2

. . . A later entrant into a more established market situation? ☐ 3

106-107: PATENTS AND TRADE SECRETS

Does this business benefit *to a significant degree* from patents, trade secrets, or other proprietary methods of production or operation . . .

106: Pertaining to products or services? NO ☐ 0 YES ☐ 1

107: Pertaining to processes? NO ☐ 0 YES ☐ 1

108: STANDARDIZATION OF PRODUCTS OR SERVICES

Are the products or services of this business . . . *(Check one)*

. . . More or less standardized for all customers? ☐ 0

. . . Designed or produced to order for individual customers? ☐ 1

109: FREQUENCY OF PRODUCT CHANGES

Is it typical practice for the business and its major competitors to change all or part of the line of products or services offered . . . *(Check one)*

. . . Annually (for example, annual model changes)? ☐ 1

. . . Seasonally? ☐ 2

. . . Periodically, but at intervals longer than one year? ☐ 3

. . . No regular, periodic pattern of change? ☐ 4

110: TECHNOLOGICAL CHANGE

Have there been *major* technological changes in the products offered by the business or its major competitors, or in methods of production, during the last 8 years? *(If in doubt about whether a change was "major," answer NO.)* NO ☐ 0 YES ☐ 1

Table 18.4 is illustrative information on each business in the PIMS data base. The results of PIMS include both diagnostic and prescriptive information to assist in analyzing marketing performance and formulating marketing strategies. The analysis focuses on options, problems, resources, and opportunities. The unit of observation in PIMS is a SBU.

The data on member firms' experiences have proved useful for evaluating current marketing strategies and examining alternatives. Nine major strategic influences on profitability and net cash flow have been identified. They are the following:

1. Investment intensity. *Technology and the chosen way of doing business govern how much fixed capital and working capital are required to produce a dollar of sales or a dollar of value added in the business. Investment intensity generally produces a negative impact on percentage measures of profitability or net cash flow; i.e., businesses that are mechanized or automated or inventory-intensive generally show lower returns on investment and sales than businesses that are not.*
2. Productivity. *Businesses producing high value added per employee are more profitable than those with low value added per employee. (Definition: "value added" is the amount by which the firm increases the market value of raw materials and components it buys.)*

Table 18.4 Illustrative information on each business in the PIMS data base

Characteristics of the business environment	Structure of the production process
Long-run growth rate of the market	Capital intensity (degree of automation, etc.)
Short-run growth rate of the market	Degree of vertical integration
Rate of inflation of selling price levels	Capacity utilization
Number and size of customers	Productivity of capital equipment
Purchase frequency and magnitude	Productivity of people
	Inventory levels
Competitive position of the business	**Discretionary budget allocations**
Share of the served market	R&D budgets
Share relative to largest competitors	Advertising and promotion budgets
Product quality relative to competitors	Sales force expenditures
Prices relative to competitors	**Strategic moves**
Pay scales relative to competitors	Patterns of change in the controllable elements
Marketing efforts relative to competitors	above
Pattern of market segmentation	**Operating results**
Rate of new product introductions	Profitability results
	Cash flow results
	Growth results

Source: Reproduced by permission of the Strategic Planning Institute (PIMS Program), Cambridge, Mass.

3. Market position. *A business's share of its served market (both absolute and relative to its three largest competitors) has a positive impact on its profit and net cash flow. (The "served market" is the specific segment of the total potential market—defined in terms of products, customers or areas—in which the business actually competes.)*

4. Growth of the served market. *Growth is generally favorable to dollar measures of profit, indifferent to percent measures of profit, and negative to all measures of net cash flow.*

5. Quality of the products and/or services offered. *Quality, defined as the customers' evaluation of the business's product/service package as compared to that of competitors, has a generally favorable impact on all measures of financial performance.*

6. Innovation/differentiation. *Extensive actions taken by a business in the areas of new product introduction, R&D, marketing effort, and so on, generally produce a positive effect on its performance if that business has strong market position to begin with. Otherwise usually not.*

7. Vertical integration. *For businesses located in mature and stable markets, vertical integration (i.e., make rather than buy) generally impacts favorably on performance. In markets that are rapidly growing, declining, or otherwise changing, the opposite is true.*

8. Cost push. *The rates of increase of wages, salaries, and raw material prices, and the presence of a labor union, have complex impacts on profit and cash flow, depending on how the business is positioned to pass along the increase to its customers and/or to absorb the higher costs internally.*

9. Current strategic effort. *The current direction of change of any of the above factors has effects on profit and cash flow that are frequently opposite to that of the factor itself. For example, having strong market share tends to increase net cash flow, but getting share drains cash while the business is making that effort.*

Additionally, there is such a thing as being a good or a poor "operator." A good operator can improve the profitability of a strong strategic position or minimize the damage of a weak one; a poor operator does the opposite. The presence of a management team that functions as a good operator is therefore a favorable element of a business and produces a financial result greater than one would expect from the strategic position of the business alone.[31]

Significance of strategic market planning approaches

The Boston Consulting Group's portfolio analysis, the market attractiveness/business position model, and the profit impact of marketing strategy (PIMS) studies of the Strategic Planning Institute are planning tools only. They should not be viewed as strategic solutions but as diagnostic aids, which is all they are intended to be. The emphasis should be on making sound decisions using these analytical tools.[32]

The key to understanding the approaches to strategic market planning described in this chapter is recognition that strategic market planning takes into account all aspects of an organization's strategy in the marketplace. Whereas most of this book is about functional decisions and strategies of marketing as a part of business, this chapter focuses on the recognition that all functional strategies including marketing, production, and finance must be coordinated to reach organizational goals. Results of a survey, sponsored by the *Harvard Business Review,* of top industrial firms indicate that portfolio planning and other depersonalized planning techniques help managers strengthen their planning process and solve the problems of managing diversified industrial companies. However, the results also indicate that analytical techniques alone will not result in success. Management must blend this analysis with managerial judgment to deal with the reality of the existing situation. Although subjective managerial judgment will remain important, consider the findings concerning portfolio analysis:

Portfolio planning recognizes that diversified companies are a collection of strategic business units each of which makes a distinct contribution to the overall corporate performance and which should be managed accordingly. Putting the portfolio planning philosophy into place takes three steps as the typical company:

1. Redefines businesses for strategic planning purposes as strategic business units (SBUs), which may or may not differ from operating units.

31. *The PIMS Letter on Business Strategy No. 1* (Cambridge, Mass.: The Strategic Planning Institute, 1977), pp. 3–5. Reproduced by permission of the Strategic Planning Institute (PIMS Program), Cambridge, Massachusetts.
32. David W. Cravens, "Strategic Marketing's New Challenge," *Business Horizons,* March–April 1983, p. 19.

2. *Classifies these SBUs on a portfolio grid according to the competitive position and attractiveness of the particular product market.*
3. *Uses this framework to assign each a "strategic mission" with respect to its growth and financial objectives and allocates resources accordingly.*[33]

Besides the approaches to strategic market planning discussed here, there are other approaches. For example, marketing planners have used the product life cycle that is discussed in Chapters 5 and 6 for many years. Many firms have their own approaches to planning that incorporate, to varying degrees, some of the approaches that we have discussed. All strategic planning approaches have some similarity in that some components of strategic market planning outlined in Figure 18.3 (especially market/product relationships) are related to a plan of action for reaching objectives. The PIMS project makes a major contribution by providing data gathered from a broad range of companies to draw conclusions about strategic market planning. The approaches in this chapter are meant to be supplements to, not substitutes for, marketing managers' own judgment. The issues of product/market-share definition, strategic-information procurement, and organizational change will inevitably grow in importance as a result of increased use of strategic market planning concepts.[34]

The approaches presented here should provide you with an overview of the most popular analytical methods used in strategic market planning. The real test of each approach, or any integrated approach, is how well it assists management in diagnosing the firm's strengths and weaknesses and prescribing strategic actions for maintaining or improving performance. The management of many companies has moved strategic market planning to the top of its list of corporate priorities for the 1980s.[35] It should be obvious that an appropriate marketing strategy should evolve from the strategic market planning effort.

Growth strategies for marketing

After evaluating business operations and business performance, the next step in strategic planning is the determination of future business directions and the development of marketing strategies. Growth strategies are an alternative that may be chosen for a business. Figure 18.13 shows growth-strategy alternatives on a product-market matrix. This matrix can be helpful in determining growth strategies that can be implemented through marketing strategies.

Intense growth

Intense growth can take place when current products and current markets have the potential for increasing sales. There are three main strategies for intense growth: market penetration, market development, and product development.

33. Adapted from Philippe Haspeslogh, "A Survey of U.S. Companies Shows How Effective Portfolio Planning Could Be But Often Isn't," *Harvard Business Review*, January-February 1982, p. 61.
34. Ben M. Enis, "GE, PIMS, BCG and the PLC," *Business*, May–June 1980, pp. 17–18.
35. David W. Cravens, *Strategic Marketing* (Homewood, Ill.: Irwin, 1982), p. 91.

Figure 18.13
Growth Strategies
Adapted from Corporate
Strategy *by H. I. Ansoff,*
p. 109. Copyright ©
1965 by McGraw-Hill.
Used with permission of
McGraw-Hill Book
Company.

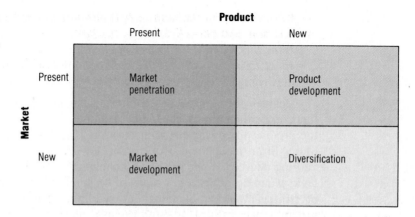

Market penetration is a strategy of increasing sales in current markets with current products. A fast-food chain, for instance, would probably attempt to increase its market share by increasing its advertising budget and the size of its marketing staff.

Market development is a strategy of increasing sales with current products in new markets. For example, a European aircraft manufacturer was able to enter the U.S. market by offering financing to Eastern Airlines that Boeing could not match.

Product development is a strategy of increasing sales by improving present products or developing new products for current markets. A manufacturer of personal care products might pursue product development by introducing a longer lasting deodorant or a new cologne.

Diversified growth

Diversified growth occurs in three ways, depending on the technology of the new products and the nature of the new markets the firm enters. The three forms of diversification are horizontal, concentric, and conglomerate.

When new products that are not technologically related to current products are introduced to current markets, horizontal diversification occurs. An airline might diversify horizontally by starting a chain of hotels at the destinations it serves.

In concentric diversification, the marketing and technology of new products are related to current products, but the new ones are introduced into new markets. For example, a manufacturer of minicomputers for business might decide to introduce a personal computer for home use.

Conglomerate diversification occurs when new products are unrelated to current technology, products, or markets and are introduced to markets new to the firm. If an electronics company were to start a car-rental business, the move would represent conglomerate diversification.

Integrated growth

Integrated growth can occur in the same industry that the firm is in and in three possible directions: forward, backward, and horizontal.

A firm growing through forward integration takes ownership or increased control of its distribution system. For example, a shoe manufacturer might start selling its products through wholly owned retail outlets.

In backward integration, a firm takes ownership or increased control of its supply systems. A newspaper company that buys a paper mill is integrating backward.

Horizontal integration occurs when a firm takes ownership or control of some of its competitors. A hotel chain integrating horizontally might purchase a competing motel chain.

Summary

Strategic planning requires a general management orientation, rather than a narrow functional orientation. Corporate strategy determines the means for utilizing resources in the areas of production, finance, research and development, personnel, and marketing to reach the organization's goals. The concept of a strategic business unit (SBU) is used to define areas for consideration in a specific strategic market plan. Each SBU is a division, product line, or other profit center within its parent company. Each sells a distinct set of products and/or services to an identifiable group of customers, and each is in competition with a well-defined set of competitors. In the context of the parent company, meaningful separation can be made of an SBU's revenues, operating costs, investments, and strategic plans. This chapter deals with strategic market planning and planning processes in marketing management.

When a marketing strategy—which is developed through strategic market planning—is implemented properly, it achieves the organization's marketing objectives; these, in turn, contribute to accomplishing the organization's overall goals. As indicated in Figure 18.3, environmental forces are an important consideration in the strategic market planning process and very much affect it. These environmental forces imply opportunities and threats that influence the overall goals of an organization. The amount and type of resources that a firm can acquire are also affected by forces in the environment. However, such forces need not constrain or work against the firm; they may also create favorable opportunities that can be translated into overall organizational goals.

There are three major considerations in assessing opportunities and resources: market opportunity must be evaluated; environmental forces must be monitored; and the firm's capabilities should be understood. A market opportunity arises when the right combination of circumstances occurs at the right time to allow an organization to take action toward a target market. An opportunity provides a favorable chance or opening for the firm to generate sales from markets. Determinants of market opportunity include market size, market requirements, and the actions of other firms.

Environmental monitoring is the process that seeks information about events and relationships in a company's outside environment, the knowledge of which assists marketers in planning. A firm's capabilities relate to distinctive competencies that it has developed to do something well and efficiently. A company is likely to enjoy a differential advantage in an area where its competencies outmatch those of its potential competition.

Corporate strategy defines the means and direction of reaching organizational goals. Marketing objectives are statements of what is to be accomplished through marketing activities. They should be expressed in clear, understandable, and measurable terms and they must be consistent with an organization's overall goals. Marketing management is the process of planning, organizing, implementing, and controlling marketing activities in order to facilitate and expedite exchanges effectively and efficiently.

Marketing planning is a systematic process that involves the assessment of opportunities and resources, the determination of marketing objectives, the development of a marketing strategy, and the development of plans for implementation and control. A well-written plan clearly specifies when, how, and who is to perform marketing activities. Plans that cover one year or less are called short-range plans. Medium-range plans usually encompass two to five years, and plans that last for more than five years are long-range plans. There are several benefits of marketing planning. Planning forces marketing managers to think ahead, to establish objectives, and to consider future marketing activities. Effective planning also reduces or eliminates daily crises.

In recent years, marketing managers have developed target market/ marketing mixes, sometimes referred to as product/market matching approaches to strategic market planning. These approaches to planning are widely used today to structure the overall strategic market planning process. The Boston Consulting Group (BCG) product-portfolio analysis, the market attractiveness/business position model, and PIMS (Profit Impact on Marketing Strategy) are popular approaches to strategic planning.

The BCG approach is based on a philosophy that a product's market growth rate and its market share are key factors influencing marketing strategy. All of the firm's products should be integrated into a balanced product portfolio. Just as financial investors hold investments with varying risks and rates of return, firms have a variety of products. Managers can use portfolio models to classify products to determine each product's expected future cash contributions and future cash requirements. In general, managers who use a portfolio model must examine the competitive position of a product (or product line) and the opportunities for improving that product's contribution to profitability and cash flow.

The market attractiveness/business position model is a two-dimensional matrix. The vertical dimension—labeled *market attractiveness*—includes all the sources of strength and resources that relate to the market; competition, industry sales, and the cost of competing are among them. The horizontal axis is labeled *business position*. It measures sales, relative market share, research and development, and other factors that relate to the product in building a market share.

The Strategic Planning Institute (SPI) has developed a data bank of information on over 1,700 products that members report on for the PIMS (Profit Impact on Marketing Strategy) research program. Over two hundred members of the institute provide confidential information on successes, failures, and marginal products. The data are analyzed to provide reports for member firms on strategy. The results of PIMS include diagnostic and prescriptive information to assist in analyzing marketing performance and formulating marketing strategies. The analysis focuses on options, problems, resources, and opportunities. The unit of observation in PIMS is a SBU.

The real test of strategic planning is how well it helps in diagnosing a firm's strengths and weaknesses and improving performance. The approaches to strategic market planning covered in this chapter are meant to be supplements to, not substitutes for, the marketing manager's own judgment.

Growth strategies that can be implemented through marketing strategies include intense growth, diversified growth, and integrated growth. Intense growth includes market penetration, market development, or product development. Diversified growth includes horizontal, concentric, and conglomerate diversification. Integrated growth includes forward, backward, and horizontal integration.

Important terms

Corporate strategy	Marketing planning cycle
Marketing strategy	Short-range plans
Strategic market plan	Medium-range plans
Strategic business unit (SBU)	Long-range plans
Strategic market planning	Product portfolio analysis
Marketing program	Market attractiveness/business
Market opportunity	position model
Market requirements	PIMS (Profit Impact
Environmental monitoring	on Marketing Strategy)
Marketing objective	Intense growth
Marketing management	Diversified growth
Marketing planning	Integrated growth
Marketing plan	

Discussion and review questions

1. Why should an organization develop a marketing strategy? What is the difference between strategic market planning and the strategy itself?
2. Identify the major components of strategic market planning, and explain how they are interrelated.
3. In what ways do environmental forces affect strategic market planning? Give specific examples.
4. Why is price flexibility important in implementing the marketing strategy?
5. What are some of the issues that must be considered in analyzing opportunities and resources? How do these elements affect marketing objectives and market strategy?
6. Why is market opportunity analysis necessary? What are the market opportunity determinants?
7. In relation to resource constraints, how can environmental monitoring affect a firm's long-term strategic market planning? Consider product costs and benefits affected by the environment.
8. What is marketing management, and why is it important to the survival of business organizations?
9. What benefits do marketing managers gain from planning? Is planning necessary for long-run survival? Why or why not?
10. How should an organization establish marketing objectives?

11. What are the major considerations in developing the product portfolio grid? Discuss the four basic types of products suggested by the Boston Consulting Group.
12. When should marketers consider using PIMS for strategic market planning?

Cases

Case 18.1

Strategic Market Planning of Sigma Press, Inc.[36]

In 1984 Sigma Press, Inc., a small commercial printer located in Ottawa, Illinois, was reviewing its past performance and charting a new strategy. Twelve years earlier, Sigma Press had moved to new facilities at the intersection of Illinois Route 23 and Interstate 80 on the edge of Ottawa. The prestigious location with its high visibility created a then-unwarranted image of success. Don Sapit, the president of Sigma, was a graduate mechanical engineer with an MBA from the University of Chicago. It seemed apparent to him that Sigma should try to capitalize on its high visibility to change the emphasis of the business and, he hoped, improve its record of growth and profit. Over the next few years, the marketing strategy of the company was oriented toward building a reputation for producing the most creative and highest quality printing in its service area, which had a thirty-five- to forty-mile radius. The firm took a calculated risk. Sapit anticipated that this new direction would give his firm a solid reputation as an expensive quality printer—but one that justified the prices it charged. The strategy paid off, and sales volume increased by 220 percent by 1976.

One of the factors that had prompted the 1972 move was a perceived market for a specialized advertising desk-pad calendar. The calendar, sold to businesses for distribution as a free promotional item, kept an advertising message on their customers' desks at all times (see Figure 18.14). Sales of the calendar had increased slowly but steadily. Management wanted growth, but it wanted it in an orderly and manageable manner, and it wanted it to be more profitable than the industry average of approximately 5 percent on sales. It was becoming obvious that to be successful in the printing business, one had to specialize. After long and deliberate discussion and investigation in 1976, the company management wrote a three-year corporate plan.

The corporate plan emphasized marketing, which was unique for a small commercial printer. The marketing plan focused a major share of the sales and marketing effort on building a market for the Salesbuilder desk calendar. The target market consisted primarily of larger corporate accounts. The marketing mix emphasized product and promotion. Space advertising in sales and marketing-oriented publications created large numbers of inquiries, but sales levels did not follow. Direct mail, primarily to manufacturers, produced a much higher return on investment. Sigma had created a unique product that was very flexible in terms of unusual designs, advertising messages, photographic techniques, and other special requirements.

36. Contributed by Donald Sapit, President, and Tracy Walkup, Vice President of Marketing, Sigma Press, Inc., Ottawa, Illinois.

Figure 18.14
Sigma's desk-top
calendar
*Source: Courtesy Sigma
Press, Inc.*

Within the next few calendar seasons, prime accounts such as General Electric, Serta Mattress, Archway Cookies Inc., Borden Inc., and other blue-chip companies were added to the list of satisfied customers. Reorder rates were very high, usually in the 88 to 90 percent range. Quantities ordered by individual companies tended to increase annually for three or four years and then level off. Total calendar sales had increased at a rate of approximately 40 percent per year during the 1976–1980 period, during which commercial printing sales increased at a much lower rate.

Because of the success of the marketing plan, production capacity was being taxed. In 1979–1980 major capital commitments were made to add a new high-speed two-color press and to purchase, redesign, and rebuild a specialized collating machine to further automate calendar assembly. This opened the way to mass marketing of the Salesbuilder calendar line. Direct mail techniques were improved to allow selection of prospects by S.I.C. number and sales volume. A toll-free phone line encouraged direct response by interested parties. Whenever possible, the company responded to inquiries by sending a sample calendar which contained advertising ideas that related to the respondent's line of business. This sample would be followed up with personal phone calls within two to three weeks. Calendar sales continued to improve until, by 1983, they represented 40 percent of total sales and approximately 75 percent of net profit.

In spite of the success of the calendar marketing programs, Sapit was disturbed by trends in the printing industry that pointed toward a diminishing market and increased competition for the commercial segment. At the same time, Sigma's management was starting to feel comfortable with its experience in product marketing and was experiencing a good reception from small, diverse businesses and the most successful corporations in the United States.

Since specialization had proven so successful, it seemed logical to explore other types of calendars and how they might be planned to best utilize the excess capacity in the first half of the year. A market study considered possible markets and their utility in Sigma's long-range plan. In 1982, Sigma launched a marketing campaign directed at the college market. Based on an August through July monthly format, these collegiate calendars were customized for individual campuses with sports and class schedules printed in school colors. The advantage was the ability to sell and produce these earlier in the year than the standard January through December format.

Progress of the calendar sales and industry trends toward a diminishing and more competitive commercial market led to discussions of switching exclusively to specialization in calendars. A complete switch to specialty printing of desk-top calendars could not be made without a degree of risk. While the commercial part of the business did not appear to have the desired growth and profit potential Sigma wanted, it did comprise approximately 60 percent of total sales and made a substantial contribution to fixed operating costs.

In July 1983, Sigma Press spun off a separate corporation and reallocated assets to support an intense effort to market the Sigma calendar line. Seven distinct calendar products were developed to add more depth to the product line.

Once again, management began to develop strategic market plans for the new Sigma Press. Sapit requested Tracy Walkup, vice president of Marketing, to develop three- and five-year plans for each of the alternatives open to the company.

Questions for discussion

1. Compare and contrast the need for long-range versus short-range marketing planning at Sigma Press.
2. Examine the different marketing strategies at Sigma in 1972–1976, in 1976–1982, and in 1983 and beyond. How was strategic market planning used to coordinate the development of a "new Sigma"?
3. If you were Sigma's marketing consultant, what recommendation would you make for future strategic market planning?

Case 18.2

Transamerica Corporation's Strategic Business Units[37]

 Transamerica is a diversified company concentrating in three areas: insurance on financial services, travel services, and manufacturing. Within each category there are several subsidiaries:

1. *Insurance and financial services*
   Occidental Life
   Transamerica Insurance Co., Inc. (property/casualty insurance)
   Transamerica Title Insurance Co.
   Transamerica Financial Services (consumer lending)
   Fred S. James and Company (insurance brokerage)
   Transamerica Interway, Inc.

37. Many of the facts in this case are based on the Transamerica Corporation *1982 Annual Report.*

2. *Travel services*
   Transamerica Airlines, Inc.
   Budget Rent-A-Car Corp.
3. *Manufacturing*
   Transamerica Delaval Inc. (manufacturing of precision-engineered products)

Transamerica's strategy is to focus on key market segments related to primary businesses, including insurance and financial services, travel services, and the manufacturing of precision products for industrial applications. Transamerica's objectives are to become diversified in businesses benefiting from economic, social, and demographic transitions; to maintain low costs through innovative marketing; to provide first-rate services at a fair price; and to be a responsible employer. The two major objectives of its subsidiaries are (1) to achieve a significant market share in each business segment and (2) to achieve industry leadership in terms of service, reputation, innovation, and efficiency. Subsidiaries of Transamerica benefit from being part of a larger corporation. Funds may be borrowed at a low cost; capital may be allocated between subsidiaries; and a corporate staff provides centralized strategic planning, investment, real estate, cash management, and data processing activities.

Responding to consumer needs, Occidental Life introduced several new products. Two new annuities for funding an individual retirement account and a policy combining the features of term and whole-life insurance were introduced. New product introduction is critical to the success of Occidental Life. Nearly two-thirds of the individual life insurance policies written had been on the market less than three years. The insurance is most actively sold in the growing western and southwestern states. Occidental specializes in low-cost insurance with term-like rates—this type of insurance represents 84 percent of its direct ordinary volume. Occidental insurance is sold through 750 sales offices in the United States and Canada, of which roughly one-half are full-time agents and the other half are independent insurance brokers.

Transamerica acquired Fred S. James & Co., Inc., one of the world's largest insurance brokerage firms. James provides a broad range of services designed to analyze risk and determine proper protection through insurance, self-insurance, captive insurance companies and other risk-financing alternatives. Growth for this division appears to be in the area of innovative domestic property/casualty products, employee benefits, and in the claim administration area.

Transamerica Insurance Company provides property and casualty insurance throughout most of North America. The target market is individuals and small-to-medium-sized businesses in suburban and rural areas. Marketed through local independent agents, Transamerica Insurance emphasizes prompt, efficient service.

Transamerica Financial Corporation operates consumer loan offices in twenty-one states concentrating in the West. Operations tend to be concentrated in regions with favorable market and regulatory conditions. New consumer loan customers are solicited through sophisticated mass-mail marketing techniques followed by direct contact from a branch office employee. Transamerica Financial will continue to concentrate on improving operating efficiency and providing fast individual service to customers. It also will combine its successful strategy of increasing the portion of its loans secured by residential real estate, increasing average loan size and branch receivables, and maintaining a superior credit rating through a conservative balance sheet position.

Transamerica Interway operates a transport equipment leasing business, including cargo containers, piggyback trailers, and over-the-road trailers. Transamerica Interway has two primary divisions: one leases standard dry cargo containers, and the other leases a fleet of piggyback trailers. Transamerica Interway restructured its organization to lease directly to shipper's agents and regional truckers. The company repairs and maintains its own equipment in the United States through company-owned repair shops and mobile-service units. The company enjoys operating cost advantages resulting from economies of scale.

Title Insurance and Escrow Services are provided by Transamerica Title Insurance Company. This division has concentrated its resources in geographic areas where major market shares are attainable. It has increased its skills in the less cyclical industrial and commercial real estate markets, upgraded management development programs, and invested in productivity improvements—such as computerized title plants and shared title plants.

Transamerica Airlines flies to more locations around the world than any other airline. Transamerica's planes fly to nearly five hundred airports in more than one hundred countries, serving both the passenger and cargo markets. To compete in the more competitive market, Transamerica has refurbished many aircrafts. This has resulted in superior passenger accommodations and improved fuel conservation and noise reduction. Diversified services also include military passengers and cargo, scheduled services, and leasing of aircrafts. Transamerica's low-cost approach makes it a major national airline.

Operating as a franchiser, Budget Rent-A-Car provides the same rental services as any other competitor, but at a lower rate. Budget has expanded to provide service at airports. To support dealers, Budget developed a nationwide, toll-free, computerized reservation network. Sears, Roebuck has an exclusive agreement to provide and operate concessions for Budget's automobile rental distribution. To increase profits, the number of company-owned outlets are being increased. This move also makes Budget more responsive to consumer needs. High-volume commercial customers are guaranteed lower rates and the nationwide toll-free network makes reservations more convenient.

Transamerica Delaval manufactures precision-engineered products that run the gamut from small connectors, fasteners, and couplings to large turbines, compressors, diesel engines, condensers, filters, instruments, and control devices. Due to a slowdown in the utility construction industry, orders have dropped. Although this area has not performed up to expectation, the general industrial, marine, and petrochemical markets have steadily increased. Fuel conservation, conversion, and environmental control should benefit several of Transamerica's Delaval product lines—helping to offset the slowdown in the utility market. In a continuing acquisition program, Transamerica Delaval acquired a manufacturer of pumps and submersible electric motors. As the co-owner of Biphase Energy Systems, Transamerica Delaval will continue to develop and market energy-related products and services.

Transamerica is aware that the marketing environment is an important consideration in adapting a product to market needs. Transamerica's marketing strategies are now being examined to determine which areas to expand, develop, or phase out. Transamerica's marketing objective for each subsidiary is to achieve a significant market share in each business unit and to become the industry leader in terms of service, reputation, innovation, and operating efficiencies. Consistent with this strategy, Transamerica is diversifying to achieve low-cost marketing in all areas. But its first priority is its existing business units. Transamerica is currently evaluating how best to proceed with its marketing strategy. Obviously, strategic market planning is important to the corporation.

Questions for discussion
1. Identify the strategic business units that make up Transamerica's total business.
2. Attempt to place various products in each Transamerica strategic business unit in a growth-share matrix to provide portfolio analysis.
3. What does top management at Transamerica do best? In other words, describe the corporate strategy that has worked for the company. How could this strategy be improved?
4. Identify marketing strategies for each Transamerica strategic business unit.

19

Organization, Implementation, and Control

Objectives

To become aware of how the marketing unit fits in a firm's organizational structure.

To become familiar with the ways of organizing a marketing unit.

To examine several issues relating to the implementation of marketing strategies.

To understand the control processes used in managing marketing strategies.

To be aware of how cost and sales analyses can be employed to evaluate the performance of marketing strategies.

WD-40 is a unique, successful product that has been a gold-mine for WD-40 Company's major stockholder, John Barry. He feels the product's strengths are based on the fact that he operates a marketing company and not a manufacturing company. Several major corporations, such as 3M, Borden, and Du Pont, have attempted to penetrate the market with their own products but have failed. (Figure 19.1 is an advertisement for WD-40.)

WD-40 was developed by an in-house chemist to protect the stainless steel skin of Atlas missiles. Employees began taking the product home to use on guns, wet engines, and for other household purposes. During the Vietnam War, WD-40 was put in gift packs and used by thousands of American soldiers to clean their rifles. Those who returned home continued to use it and were sold on the product.

Can WD-40 solve all your problems?

Dissolves tar, won't harm paint.

Cleans and lubricates tracks.

Cleans bike gears.

Loosens hard water deposits.

Loosens sticky locks.

Dissolves crayon marks.

Just about. Because WD-40 helps clean and do repairs in the yard, the garage and all through the house.

Got a problem with window cranks? WD-40 loosens corrosion and rust. Try it on chairs to keep them working quietly. Even unfreeze ski bindings with no problem.

And now your favorite use can win you an exciting prize like a Buick Riviera or a Caribbean cruise in the <u>WD-40 Take Off Sweepstakes</u>. Look for displays at participating stores.

WD-40 Company, San Diego, CA 92110

Figure 19.1 Advertisement for WD-40
Source: Courtesy of WD-40 Company.

Sales and earnings have been increasing dramatically for over twenty years. The company is able to return half of its profits to shareholders. Production of the product is kept at a very simple level. There are a mere thirty-six employees who manufacture the product. It is then shipped to packaging contractors and from there distributed through wholesalers. Of every sales dollar, WD-40 spends 44 cents on raw materials and packaging and 23 cents on overhead and advertising, resulting in 33 cents remaining for taxes and earnings. In the near future, WD-40 Company has no plans for expanding its product line. However, there are plans to aim WD-40 at the female market segment.[1]

WD-40's success has resulted from effective implementation and control of its marketing strategies. This chapter initially focuses on methods of organizing the marketing unit. Then we examine several issues regarding the implementation of marketing strategies. Next, we consider the basic components of the process of control. We discuss the use of cost and sales analyses to evaluate the effectiveness of marketing strategies. Finally, we describe a marketing audit.

Organizing marketing activities

The structure and relationships of marketing personnel, including lines of authority and responsibility that connect and coordinate individuals, strongly affect marketing activities. This section first looks at the place of marketing within an organization and examines the major alternatives available for organizing a marketing unit. Next it shows how marketing activities can be structured to fit into an organization so as to contribute to the accomplishment of overall objectives.

Marketing's place in an organization

Marketing's place within a company is determined largely by whether the firm is production, sales, or marketing oriented. A *production-oriented organization* concentrates either on improving production efficiency or on producing high-quality, technically improved products; it has little regard for customers' desires. In a *sales-oriented organization*, there is a general belief that personal selling and advertising are the primary tools used to generate profits and that most products—regardless of consumers' needs—can be sold if the right quantity and quality of personal selling and advertising are employed. Thus, the sales and advertising managers are at the same level in the company's hierarchy as are the production, financial, and personnel managers, and all participate in top-level management. Upper-echelon sales and advertising executives, along with other executives at the same level, are involved with setting the company's overall objectives and policies. In a *marketing-oriented organization,* as Figure 19.2 shows, the marketing manager is in a position equal to that of the financial, production, and personnel managers. This structure allows the marketing manager to participate in top-level decision making. Note, too, that the marketing manager is responsible for a variety of activities, several of which are under the jurisdiction of other functional managers in production- or sales-oriented firms.

1. Ellen Paris, "The One-Mystique Company," *Forbes,* April 26, 1982, p. 103.

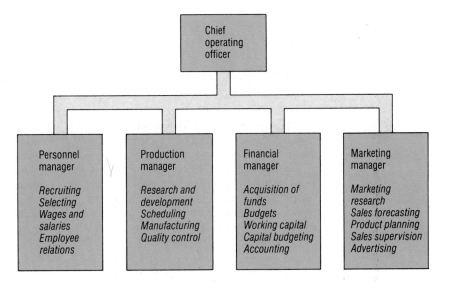

Figure 19.2
Organizational chart of a marketing-oriented firm

Chief operating officer

Personnel manager	Production manager	Financial manager	Marketing manager
Recruiting Selecting Wages and salaries Employee relations	Research and development Scheduling Manufacturing Quality control	Acquisition of funds Budgets Working capital Capital budgeting Accounting	Marketing research Sales forecasting Product planning Sales supervision Advertising

Both the relationships between marketing and other functional areas (such as production, finance, and personnel) and marketing's importance to management depend heavily on the firm's basic orientation. Marketing encompasses the greatest number of business functions and occupies an important position when a firm is marketing oriented; its role in an organization is minimal when the firm is production oriented. (Note that related issues are discussed in the Application on p. 586.) However, that a firm's organization is marketing oriented does not automatically mean that the firm will be. The marketing orientation is not achieved simply by redrawing the organizational chart; management must also adopt and use the marketing orientation as a management philosophy.

Major alternatives in organizing the marketing unit

How effectively a firm's marketing management can plan and implement marketing strategies depends on how the marketing unit is organized. The organizational structure of a marketing department establishes the authority relationships among marketing personnel and specifies who is responsible for making certain decisions and performing particular activities.

In organizing a marketing unit, managers divide the work into specific activities and delegate responsibility and authority for those activities to persons in various positions within the marketing unit. They include, for example, the sales manager, the research manager, and the advertising manager. This internal structure provides the vehicle for directing marketing activities.

No single approach to organizing a marketing unit works equally well in all businesses. A marketing unit can be organized according to (1) functions, (2) products, (3) regions, or (4) types of customers. The specific approach (or approaches) that is (are) best depends on the number and diversity of the firm's products, the characteristics and needs of the people in the target market, and other factors. Let us consider each organizational approach in detail.

Consumers are the focus of Castle and Cooke Food's new marketing orientation. In the past, the company emphasized production and supply, but after experiencing a steady decline of profits and an operating loss, the company shifted its focus to a consumer orientation.

This new emphasis necessitated some reorganizing at Castle and Cooke. Reorganization began with the decentralization of decision making through the establishment of product divisions, each with separate headquarters. The company then reduced its nonprofitable shellfish and salmon operations. The company also added a soft-drink division by purchasing A&W rootbeer. This reorganization was meant to enable the company to better serve consumer needs.

In focusing more closely on the consumer, Castle and Cooke has been forced to change its marketing practices. Branding produce, offering coupons, and developing new products are all a part of the company's marketing orientation. The decentralization of decision making further enhances the company's responsiveness to its markets. The return of profits since the reorganization has been underway is a clear signal of the success of the firm's marketing orientation.

Source: Based on Jennifer Pendleton, "Castle and Cooke Puts Consumer in Driver's Seat," *Advertising Age,* Nov. 7, 1983, p. 4.

Organizing by functions

Some marketing departments are organized by general marketing functions such as marketing research, product development, distribution, sales, advertising, and customer relations. As shown in Figure 19.3, the personnel who direct these functions report directly to the top-level marketing executive. This structure is fairly common because it works well for small businesses with centralized marketing operations. In large firms, with decentralized marketing operations, functional organization can raise severe coordination problems. The functional approach may, however, be useful in a larger centralized company in which the products and types of customers are neither numerous nor diverse.

Organizing by products

For an organization that produces and markets diverse products, the functional approach may be inadequate. The decisions and problems related to a single marketing function for one product may be quite different from those related to the same marketing function for another product. For this

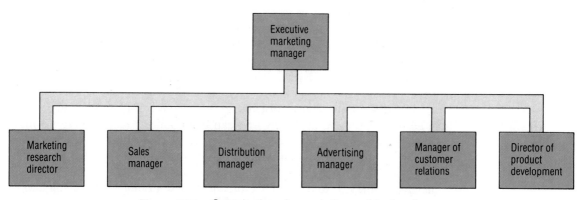

Figure 19.3   Organization of a marketing unit by functions

reason, businesses that produce diverse products sometimes organize their marketing units according to product groups. In this type of organization, a product manager takes full responsibility for the marketing of a product or product group. As Figure 19.4 shows, the product manager for product group C has authority over the functional managers who are lower in the organizational hierarchy. The product manager may also draw upon the resources of specialized staff in the company.

Organizing by product groups gives a firm the flexibility to develop special marketing mixes for different products. The firm can hire specialists to market specific types of products. One disadvantage of organizing by products is that some marketing activities may be duplicated by the different product groups. For example, salespersons from three product groups may call on the same customer in a single day. This form of internal organization was discussed in more detail in Chapter 6.

Organizing by regions

A large company that markets products nationally (and possibly in foreign countries) may organize its marketing activities by geographic regions (see Figure 19.5). All the regional marketing managers report directly to the executive marketing manager. Managers of marketing functions for each region report to their regional marketing manager, as shown for region 2.

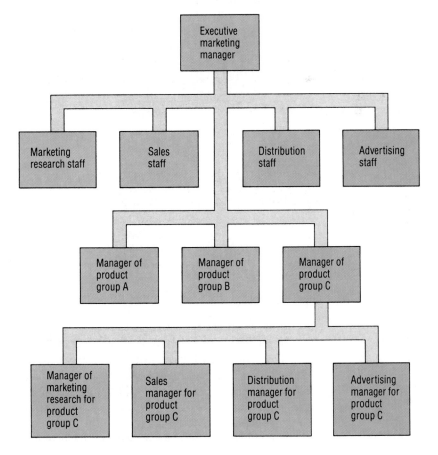

Figure 19.4
Organization of a marketing unit by product group

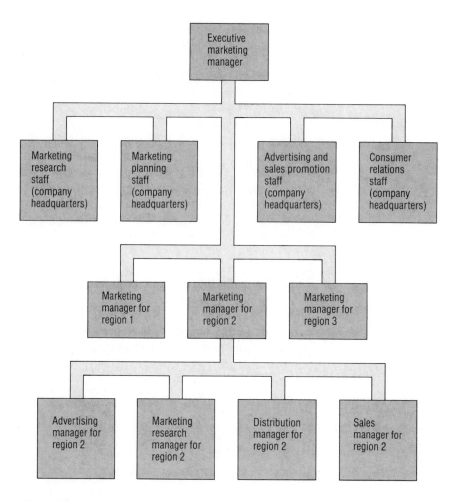

Figure 19.5 Organization of a marketing unit by regions

This form of organization is especially effective for a firm whose customers' characteristics and needs vary greatly from one region to another.

The company depicted in Figure 19.4 has a complete marketing staff at its headquarters to provide assistance and guidance to regional marketing managers. However, not all firms that organize their marketing unit by regions have a complete top-level unit. Companies that try to penetrate the national market intensively sometimes divide regions into subregions.

Organizing by types of customers

Sometimes the marketing unit is organized according to types of customers, as shown in Figure 19.6. This form of internal organization works well for a firm that has several groups of customers whose needs and problems are different. For example, an appliance manufacturer may sell appliances to large retail stores, wholesalers, and institutions. Because the marketing decisions and activities required for these three groups of customers differ considerably, the company may find it more efficient to organize its

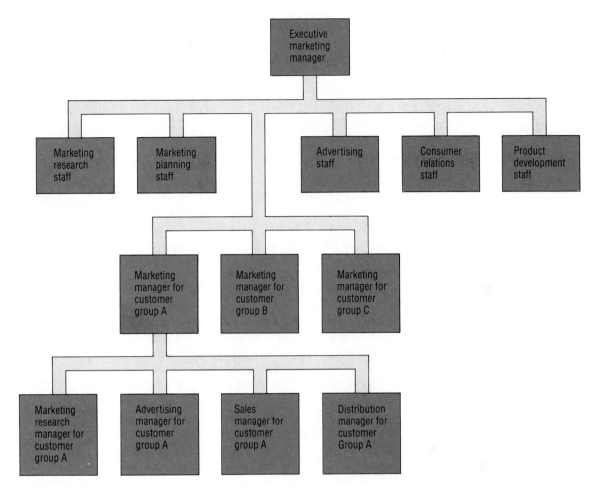

Figure 19.6　Organization of a marketing unit by types of customers

marketing unit by types of customers. Retailers may want more rapid delivery of small shipments and more personal selling by the producer than do either wholesalers or institutional buyers.

As Figure 19.5 shows, the marketing manager for each customer group reports to the top-level marketing executive and directs most marketing activities for that group. Usually, the managers of various marketing functions handle the activities needed to market products to a specific customer group. This structure is illustrated for the manager of customer group A in Figure 19.5.

Using several bases for organizing

You may have noticed that Figures 19.3, 19.4, and 19.5 each show more than one type of organization. The marketing unit in Figure 19.3 is organized by products, but each product manager has authority over functional managers within the product groups. A similar condition exists for the marketing units organized by regions and types of customers.

It is common for a firm to use some combination of organization by functions, products, regions, or customer types. Product features may dictate that the marketing unit be structured by products, while customers' characteristics require that it be organized by geographic region or by types of customers. By using more than one type of organization, a flexible marketing unit can develop and implement marketing plans to match customers' needs precisely.

Implementing marketing activities

The planning and organizing functions provide purpose, direction, and structure for marketing activities. However, until marketing managers implement the marketing plan, exchanges cannot occur. Proper implementation of a marketing plan depends on the coordination of marketing activities, the motivation of personnel who perform those activities, and the effectiveness of communication within the marketing unit. (See the Application on p. 591.) We will examine these three aspects of implementing the marketing plan.

Coordinating marketing activities

Because of job specialization and differences in approaches, interests, and timing related to marketing activities, marketing managers must synchronize individuals' actions to achieve marketing objectives. They must work closely with managers in research and development, production, finance, accounting, and personnel to see that marketing activities mesh with other functions of the firm. Marketing managers must not only coordinate the activities of marketing staff within the firm but also integrate those activities with the marketing efforts of external organizations—advertising agencies, resellers (wholesalers and retailers), researchers, and shippers, among others. Marketing managers can improve coordination by making each employee aware of how one job relates to others and of how each person's actions contribute to the achievement of marketing plans.

Motivating marketing personnel

One important element in implementing the marketing plan is motivating marketing personnel to perform effectively. People work to satisfy physical, psychological, and social needs. Since individuals try to achieve personal goals through the work environment, marketing managers must show each individual how personal goals can be attained within the organization. To motivate marketing personnel, managers must discover their employees' needs and then base their motivation methods on those needs. The degree to which a marketing manager can motivate personnel has a major impact on the success of all marketing efforts.

To put this another way, managers must base their motivational efforts on the value systems of individuals within a specific organization. Various studies have shown that income, power, and the prestige that accompanies a high position in the organization are often motivators.[2] Marketing managers can motivate marketing personnel to perform at a high level if they

2. E. Frank Harrison, *Management and Organizations* (Boston: Houghton Mifflin, 1978), p. 28.

When IBM introduced the PC, Apple Computer, Inc., and Radio Shack were vying for the lead in the fast-growing personal computer market. In just two years, IBM has taken over first place, and industry watchers predict that its market share will continue to grow at a rapid pace.

Because the personal computer market is taking on characteristics of a mature market, marketing skills are becoming more important than the latest technology. The personal computer market, which is now dominated by a few large firms, is quite dynamic and has put some smaller companies into deep trouble. Even Apple Computer is planning new strategies to better compete with IBM. Manufacturers of minicomputers, mainframes, and office equipment makers such as Burroughs and Digital Equipment are coming out with their own products to compete with PC.

Even IBM is surprised at the success of its personal computer. But the success is no accident. IBM did it by effectively implementing a bold, creative, and fortuitous marketing strategy.

Some of the key elements contributing to the success of the IBM PC included advanced design, multichannel distribution using computer retailers as well as IBM's own huge sales force, low-cost manufacturing (IBM's automated factories can make a PC every 45 seconds), and aggressive pricing.

IBM's smaller competitors are having an extremely difficult time just staying afloat in the rugged PC market. IBM is carrying out its marketing strategies so voraciously that its smaller competitors will not be able to increase sales enough to afford the facilities and product development efforts they will need to compete.

Source: Based on "Personal Computers: And the Winner Is IBM," *Business Week,* Oct. 3, 1983, pp. 76–86.

identify employees' goals and provide rewards and some means of goal attainment. It is most important that the plan to motivate personnel be fair, that it provide incentives, and that it be understood by employees. Also keep in mind that what is a minor reward or accomplishment for one employee may be the ultimate fulfillment for someone else.

Communicating within the marketing unit

Without good communication, marketing managers can neither motivate personnel nor coordinate their efforts. Marketing managers must be able to communicate with the firm's high-level management to ensure that marketing activities are consistent with the overall goals of the company. Communication with top-level executives keeps marketing managers aware of the company's overall plans and achievements. It also guides what the marketing unit is to do and how its activities are to be integrated with those of other departments—such as finance, production, or personnel—with whose management the marketing manager must also communicate to coordinate marketing efforts. Marketing personnel must work with the production staff, for example, to help design products that customer groups want. To direct marketing activities, marketing managers must communicate with marketing personnel at the operations level, such as sales and advertising personnel, researchers, wholesalers, retailers, and package designers.

To facilitate communication within a marketing unit, marketing managers should establish an information system within the marketing unit. The information system should allow for easy communication among marketing managers, sales managers, and sales personnel. The information system should aid marketers in preparing internal and external reports. Marketers need an information system to support a variety of activities such as planning, budgeting, sales analyses, and performance evaluations. A useful information system should be designed to expedite communications with other departments in the organization and to minimize destructive competition among departments for organizational resources.[3]

Controlling marketing activities

To achieve marketing objectives, as well as general organizational objectives, it is imperative for marketing managers to effectively control marketing efforts. The *marketing control process* consists of establishing performance standards, evaluating actual performance by comparing it with established standards, and reducing the differences between desired and actual performance. We will discuss these steps in the control process and look at the major problems they involve. Figure 19.7 illustrates the process.

Establishing performance standards

Planning and controlling are closely interrelated because plans include statements about what is to be accomplished. For purposes of control, these statements function as performance standards. A *performance standard* is an expected level of performance against which actual performance can be compared. Examples of performance standards might be the reduction of customers' complaints by 20 percent, a monthly sales quota of $150,000, or a 10 percent increase per month in new customer accounts. Performance standards also appear in the form of budget accounts; that is, marketers are expected to achieve a certain objective without spending more than a given amount of resources.

Evaluating actual performance

To compare actual performance with performance standards, marketing managers must both know what marketers within the company are doing and have information about the activities of external organizations that provide the firm with marketing assistance. (We will talk about specific methods for assessing actual performance later in this chapter.) Information is required about the activities of marketing personnel at the operations level and at various marketing management levels. Most businesses obtain marketing assistance from one or more external individuals or organizations, such as advertising agencies, middlemen, marketing research firms, and consultants. To acquire the most benefit from external sources, a marketing control process must monitor their activities. Although it may be difficult to obtain the necessary information, it is impossible to measure actual performance without it.

Records of actual performance are compared with performance standards to determine whether and how much of a discrepancy exists. For ex-

3. Robert E. Sweeney and Dan A. Boswell, "Obey 10 Commandments When Designing Marketing Info System," *Marketing News,* April 16, 1982, p. 16.

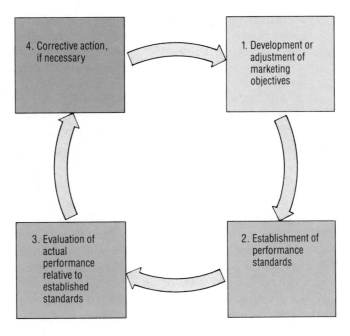

Figure 19.7 The marketing control process

ample, a salesperson's actual sales are compared with his or her sales quota (performance standard) to determine how much difference exists. If a significant negative discrepancy exists, the marketing manager takes corrective action.

In some organizations, electronic data processing equipment enhances a marketing manager's ability to evaluate actual performance. For example, L'eggs hosiery is sold mainly through self-service displays in supermarkets and drugstores. The displays are replenished and cleaned by traveling representatives who drive vans containing inventories of L'eggs products. Drivers pick up the inventories from a local branch warehouse. A local branch manager supervises the warehouse operations and the sales activities of the L'eggs representatives. When servicing a display, the representative records on a special sales form the amounts of various products that have been sold and the types of products that are sold out. This information goes to a centralized data processing center in Atlanta, where it is assembled weekly by display, by account, by route, and by branch warehouse. The company uses these weekly reports not only for billing purposes but also for analyzing the performance of marketing activities from the mill right down to individual display units.[4]

Taking corrective action

To reduce the discrepancy between established performance standards and actual performance, marketing managers can take steps to improve actual performance, can reduce or totally change the performance standard, or do

4. David T. Harrold, ''L'eggs Revisited,'' Point of Purchase Advertising Institute Workshop, Atlanta, Ga., March 24, 1971.

both. Changes in actual performance may require the marketing manager to use better methods of motivating marketing personnel or to employ more effective techniques for coordinating marketing efforts.

Sometimes, performance standards are unrealistic when they are written. In other cases, changes in the marketing environment make them unrealistic. For example, a firm's annual sales goal may become unrealistic if several aggressive competitors enter the firm's market. In fact, changes in the marketing environment may force managers to change their marketing objectives completely.

Requirements for an effective control process

Effective control depends heavily on the quantity and quality of information and the speed at which it is received.[5] The control process should be designed so that the flow of information is rapid enough to allow the marketing manager to detect quickly differences between actual and planned levels of performance. Since a single control procedure is not suitable for all types of marketing activities, a variety of procedures must accurately monitor different kinds of activities. Because internal and environmental changes affect an organization's activities, control procedures should be flexible enough to adjust to these changes. For the control process to be usable, its costs must be low relative to the costs that would arise if there were no controls. Finally, the control process should be designed so that both managers and subordinates can understand it.

Problems in controlling marketing activities

When marketing managers attempt to control marketing activities, they frequently run into several problems. Often, the information required to control marketing activities is unavailable or is available but costly. Even though marketing controls should be flexible enough to allow for environmental changes, the frequency, intensity, and unpredictability of such changes hamper effective control. In addition, the time lag between marketing activities and their effects limits a marketing manager's ability to measure the effectiveness of marketing activities.

Consider the problem of an electric utility company that wanted to build a nuclear power plant. In the face of public concern about nuclear safety in general and increasingly well-organized antinuclear activists, the company mounted a rather expensive advertising campaign to swing public opinion to the side of nuclear energy. The utility company emphasized nuclear safety and fuel independence. Three years after the campaign was launched, public attitudes were, indeed, slightly more favorable toward nuclear energy and toward the utility. How much of this change can the company attribute to its own marketing efforts and how much to extraneous factors—magazine articles on energy resources, high unemployment in the area, and the high costs and technical difficulties of some solar installations? How could the utility measure the impact of each factor?

Since marketing activities often overlap with other business activities, marketing managers cannot determine their precise cost of marketing activities. Without an accurate measure of marketing costs, it is difficult to

---

5. See Theo Haimann, William G. Scott, and Patrick E. Connor, *Management,* 4th ed. (Boston: Houghton Mifflin, 1982), pp. 468–480.

know if the effects of marketing activities are worth their costs. Finally, marketing control may be difficult because it is very hard to develop exact performance standards for marketing personnel.

Methods of evaluating performance

Specific methods exist for assessing and improving the effectiveness of a marketing strategy. A marketer should state, through plans and objectives, what a marketing strategy is to accomplish. These statements should set forth performance standards, which usually are stated in terms of profits, sales, or costs. The actual performance of a marketing strategy must be measured in a similar manner so that comparisons are possible. This section describes sales analysis and cost analysis—two general ways of evaluating the actual performance of marketing strategies.

Sales analysis

With *sales analysis,* sales figures are used to evaluate a firm's current performance. Sales analysis is probably the most common method of evaluation, because sales data both partially reflect the target market's reactions to a marketing mix and often are readily available, at least in aggregate form.

Marketers use current sales data to monitor the impact of current marketing efforts. However, that information alone is not enough. To provide useful analyses, current sales data must be compared with forecasted sales, with industry sales, with specific competitors' sales, or with the costs incurred to achieve the sales volume. For example, knowing that a variety store achieved a $600,000 sales volume this year does not tell management whether or not the marketing strategy is successful. However, if managers know that expected sales were $550,000, then they are in a better position to determine the effectiveness of the firm's marketing efforts. In addition, if they know that the marketing costs needed to achieve the $600,000 volume were 12 percent less than budgeted, they are in an even better position to analyze their marketing strategy precisely.

Types of sales measurements

Although sales may be measured in several ways, the fundamental unit of measurement is the sales transaction. A sales transaction results in a customer order for a specified quantity of an organization's product sold under specified terms by a particular salesperson or sales group on a certain date. Many organizations record these bits of information about their transactions. With such a record, a company can analyze sales in terms of dollar volume or market share.

Firms frequently use dollar volume sales analysis because the dollar is a common denominator for describing sales, costs, and profits. However, price increases and decreases affect total sales figures. For example, if a firm increased its prices by 10 percent this year and its sales volume is 10 percent greater than last year, it has not experienced a real sales increase in terms of the number of units sold. A marketing manager who uses dollar volume analysis should factor out the effects of price changes.

A firm's market share is the firm's sales of a product stated as a percentage of industry sales of that product. For example, Coca-Cola at one time annually sold 38 percent of all the cola sold in this country; thus Coke's market share was 38 percent. Because a firm's market share is a function of its own sales in relation to competitors' sales, market share analysis allows a firm to examine its marketing strategy vis-à-vis the strategies of competitors.

The primary reason for using market share analysis is to estimate whether sales changes resulted from the firm's marketing strategy or from uncontrollable environmental forces. When a company's sales volume declines and yet its share of the market stays the same, the marketer can assume that industry sales declined (because of some uncontrollable factors) and that this decline was reflected in the firm's sales. However, if the firm experiences a sales decline and a decline in market share, the company should consider the possibility that its marketing strategy is not effective.

Even though market share analysis can be helpful in evaluating the performance of a marketing strategy, the user must interpret results cautiously. When attributing a sales decline to uncontrollable factors, a marketer must keep in mind that such factors do not affect all firms in the industry equally. Not all firms in an industry have the same objectives, and some firms change objectives from one year to the next. Changes in the objectives of one firm can affect the market shares of one or all firms in that industry. For example, if a competitor significantly increases promotional efforts or drastically reduces prices to increase market share, then a company could lose market share despite a well-designed marketing strategy. Within an industry, the entrance of new firms and the demise of established ones also affect a specific firm's market share. Market share analysts should attempt to account for the effects of firms entering and leaving an industry.

Bases for sales analysis

Whether evaluation is based on sales volume or market share, sales analysis can be performed on aggregate sales figures or on disaggregated data. Aggregate sales analysis provides an overview of current sales; it gives a broad perspective. Although helpful, aggregate sales analysis is often insufficient, because it doesn't bring to light sales variations within the aggregate. It is not uncommon for a marketer to find that a large proportion of aggregate sales comes from a small number of products, geographic areas, or customers. (This is sometimes called the "iceberg principle," because only a small part of an iceberg is visible above the water.) To find such disparities, total sales figures usually are broken down by geographic unit, salesperson, product, customer type, or a combination of these categories.

In sales analysis by geographic unit, sales data can be classified by city, county, district, state, country, or any other geographic designation for which a marketer collects sales information. When geographic sales analysis is used, actual sales in a geographic unit usually are compared with sales in a similar geographic unit, with last year's sales, or with an estimated market potential for the area. For example, if a firm finds that 18 percent of its sales are coming from an area that represents only 8 percent of the potential sales for the product, then it can be assumed that the marketing strategy is successful in that geographic unit.

Because of the cost associated with hiring and maintaining a sales force, businesses commonly analyze sales by salesperson to determine the contribution each makes. Performance standards for each salesperson often are set in terms of sales quotas for a given time period. To evaluate actual performance, a salesperson's current sales are compared to a pre-established quota or some other standard, such as last period's sales. If actual sales meet or exceed the standard and the sales representative has not incurred costs above those budgeted, that person's efforts are acceptable.

Sales analysis by product group or specific product item is common. Marketers frequently break down their aggregate sales figures by product to determine the proportion that each contributed to total sales. A firm usually sets a sales volume objective—and sometimes a market share objective—for each product item or product group. Sales analysis by product is the only way to measure such objectives. A marketer can compare the breakdown of current sales by product with similar analyses of previous years. In addition, within industries for which sales data by product are available, a firm's sales by product type can be compared with industry averages. To gain an accurate picture of where sales of specific products are occurring, marketers sometimes combine sales analysis by product with sales analysis by geographic area or salesperson.

When sales are analyzed on the basis of customers, they are usually broken down by types of customers. Customers can be classified by the way they use a firm's products, by their distribution level (producer, wholesaler, retailer), by their size, by the size of orders, or by other characteristics. Sales analysis by customer type allows a firm to ascertain whether its marketing resources are allocated in a way that achieves the greatest productivity. For example, sales analysis by type of customer may indicate that a large group of customers served by 60 percent of the sales force actually accounts for only 15 percent of total sales.

A considerable amount of information is needed for sales analyses, especially if disaggregated analyses are desired. The marketer must develop an operational system for collecting sales information; obviously, the effectiveness of the system for collecting sales information largely determines a firm's ability to develop useful sales analyses.

Marketing cost analysis

Although sales analysis is critical for evaluating the effectiveness of a marketing strategy, it gives only part of the picture. A marketing strategy that successfully generates sales may also be extremely costly. To get a complete picture, a firm must know the marketing costs associated with using a given strategy to achieve a certain sales level.

With *marketing cost analysis,* various costs are broken down and classified to determine which costs are associated with specific marketing activities. By comparing costs of previous marketing activities with results generated, a marketer can allocate the firm's marketing resources more effectively in the future. Marketing cost analysis allows a firm to evaluate the effectiveness of an ongoing or recent marketing strategy by comparing sales achieved and costs incurred. By pinpointing exactly where a firm is experiencing high costs, a marketing cost analysis can help to isolate profitable or unprofitable customer segments, products, or geographic areas. In some organizations, personnel in other functional areas—such as production or accounting—think that marketers are primarily concerned with generating sales regardless of the costs incurred. By conducting cost analyses, marketers can undercut this criticism and put themselves in a better position to demonstrate how marketing activities contribute to generating profits.

Determining marketing costs

Frequently, the task of determining marketing costs turns out to be complex and difficult. Simply ascertaining the costs associated with marketing a product is rarely adequate. Marketers must usually determine the marketing costs of serving specific geographic areas, market segments, or even specific customers.

A first step in determining marketing costs is to examine accounting records. Most accounting systems classify costs into accounts such as rent, salaries, office supplies, utilities, and so on—based on how the money was actually spent. Unfortunately, many of these accounts—called *natural accounts*—do not help to explain what functions were performed through the expenditure of those funds. It does little good, for example, to know that $80,000 is spent for rent each year. The analyst has no way of knowing whether the money is spent for the rental of production, storage, or sales facilities. Therefore, marketing cost analysis usually requires that some of the costs in natural accounts be reclassified into *marketing function accounts*. The more common marketing function accounts are transportation, storage, order processing, selling, advertising, sales promotion, marketing research, and customer credit.

In some instances a specific marketing cost is incurred to perform several functions. A packaging cost, for example, could be associated with a production function, a distribution function, a promotional function, or all three. The marketing cost analyst must reclassify such costs across multiple functions.

When attempting to determine marketing costs, three broad cost categories are used: direct costs, traceable common costs, and nontraceable common costs. *Direct costs* are directly attributable to the performance of marketing functions. For example, sales force salaries might be allocated to the cost of selling a specific product item, to the cost of selling in a specific geographic area, or to the cost of selling to a particular customer. *Traceable common costs* can be allocated indirectly, using one or several criteria, to the functions that they support. For example, if the firm spends $80,000 annually to rent space for production, storage, and selling, the rental costs associated with storage could be determined on the basis of cost per square foot used for storage. *Nontraceable common costs* cannot be assigned according to any logical criteria and thus are assignable only on an arbitrary basis. Interest, taxes, and the salaries of top management are often viewed as nontraceable common costs.

The manner of dealing with these three categories of costs depends on whether the analyst uses a full-cost or a direct-cost approach. When a *full-cost approach* is used, cost analysis includes direct costs, traceable common costs, and nontraceable common costs. Proponents of this approach claim that if an accurate profit picture is desired, all costs must be included in the analysis. However, opponents point out that full costing does not yield actual costs because nontraceable common costs have been determined by arbitrary criteria. With different criteria, the full-costing approach yields different results. A cost-conscious operating unit can be discouraged if numerous costs are assigned to it arbitrarily. To eliminate such problems, the *direct-cost approach* is used. This approach includes direct costs and traceable common costs, but it does not include nontraceable common costs. Opponents say that this approach fails to provide an accurate picture of costs because it omits one cost category.

Methods of marketing cost analysis

Marketers can use several methods to analyze costs. The methods vary in their precision. This section examines three cost analysis methods, beginning with the least precise.

Analysis of Natural Accounts.   Marketers sometimes can perform a cost analysis by studying a firm's accounting records or natural accounts. The precision of this method depends heavily on how detailed the firm's accounts are. For example, if accounting records contain separate accounts for production wages, sales-force wages, and executive salaries, the analysis can be more precise than if all wages and salaries are lumped into a single account. An analysis of natural accounts is more meaningful, and thus more useful, when current cost data can be compared with those of previous periods or with average cost figures for the entire industry. Cost analysis of natural accounts frequently treats costs as percentages of sales. The periodic use of cost-to-sales ratios allows a marketer to ascertain cost fluctuations quickly.

Analysis of Functional Accounts.   As indicated earlier, the analysis of natural accounts may not shed much light on the cost of marketing activities. In such cases, natural accounts must be reclassified into marketing function accounts. As shown in the simplified example in Table 19.1, the natural accounts are divided into functional accounts. Note that a few natural accounts, such as advertising, can be reclassified easily into functional accounts because they do not have to be split across several accounts. For most of the natural accounts, however, marketers must develop criteria for assigning them to the various functional accounts. For example, the number of square feet of floor space used was the criterion for dividing the rental costs in Table 19.1 into functional accounts. Whether or not certain natural accounts are reclassified into functional accounts, and the criteria used to reclassify them, depend to some degree on whether the analyst is using direct costing or full costing. After natural accounts have been reclassified into functional accounts, the cost of each function is determined

Table 19.1   Reclassification of natural accounts into functional accounts

Profit and Loss Statement

Sales	$250,000							
Cost of			**Functional Accounts**					
Goods Sold	45,000							
Gross	205,000		Personal			Marketing	Non-	
Expenses		Advertising	Selling	Transportation	Storage	Research	marketing	
(natural accounts)								
Rent	$ 14,000		$ 7,000		$6,000		$ 1,000	
Salaries	72,000	$12,000	32,000	$7,000		$1,000	20,000	
Supplies	4,000	1,500	1,000			1,000	500	
Advertising	16,000	16,000						
Freight	4,000			2,000			2,000	
Taxes	2,000				200		1,800	
Insurance	1,000				600		400	
Interest	3,000						3,000	
Bad debts	6,000						6,000	
Total	$122,000	$29,500	$40,000	$9,000	$6,800	$2,000	$34,700	
Net Profit	$ 83,000							

by summing the costs in each functional account. For example, the cost analysis in Table 19.1 shows that the firm's cost of personal selling was $40,000.

Once the costs of these marketing functions have been determined, the analyst is ready to compare resulting cost figures with budgeted costs, with sales analysis data, with cost data from earlier operating periods, or perhaps with average industry cost figures, if available.

Cost Analysis by Product, Geographic Area, or Customer.   Although marketers ordinarily get a more detailed picture of marketing costs by analyzing functional accounts than by analyzing natural accounts, some firms need an even more precise cost analysis—especially if they sell several types of products, sell in multiple geographic areas, or sell to a wide variety of customers. Activities vary in marketing different products in specific geographic locations to certain customer groups. Therefore, the costs of these activities also vary. By allocating the functional costs to specific product groups, geographic areas, or customer groups, a marketer can find out which of these marketing entities are the most cost effective to serve. In Table 19.2, the functional accounts (derived in Table 19.1) are divided by allocating the functional costs to specific product categories. A similar type of analysis could be performed for geographic areas or for specific customer groups. The criteria employed to allocate the functional accounts must be developed so as to yield results that are as accurate as possible. Use of faulty criteria is likely to yield inaccurate cost estimates which, in turn, lead to less effective control of marketing strategies. Marketers determine the marketing costs for various product categories, geographic

Table 19.2 Functional accounts divided into product group costs

Functional Accounts		Product Groups		
		A	B	C
Advertising	$29,500	$14,000	$ 8,000	$ 7,500
Personal selling	40,000	18,000	10,000	12,000
Transportation	9,000	5,000	2,000	2,000
Storage	6,800	1,800	2,000	3,000
Marketing research	2,000		1,000	1,000
Total	$87,300	$38,800	$23,000	$25,500

areas, or customer groups and then compare them to sales. This analysis allows them to evaluate the effectiveness of the firm's marketing strategy or strategies.

The marketing audit

A *marketing audit* is a systematic examination of the objectives, strategies, organization, and performance of a firm's marketing unit. It is the intelligence system used to gather the information needed to determine whether the marketing strategy is working. A marketing audit identifies what the marketing unit is doing and how it is performing these activities, evaluates the effectiveness of these activities in terms of the organization's objectives and resources, and recommends future marketing activities.[6]

A marketing audit may be specific and focus on one or a few marketing activities, or it may be comprehensive and encompass all of a company's marketing activities. Table 19.3 illustrates numerous dimensions that can be included in a marketing audit. An audit might deal with only a few of these areas, or it might include all of them. The scope of an audit depends on the costs involved, the target markets served, the structure of the marketing mix, and environmental conditions. The results of the audit can be used to reallocate marketing effort and to reexamine marketing opportunities.

The marketing audit should aid evaluation by doing the following:

1. Describing current activities and results related to sales, costs, prices, profits, and other performance feedback
2. Gathering information about customers, competition, and environmental developments that may affect the marketing strategy
3. Exploring opportunities and alternatives for improving the marketing strategy
4. Providing an overall data base to be used in evaluating the attainment of organizational goals and marketing objectives

Like an accounting or financial audit, a marketing audit should be conducted regularly. The marketing audit is not a control process to be used

6. Abe Schuchman, "The Marketing Audit: Its Nature, Purposes, and Problems," in *Analyzing and Improving Marketing Performance*, Report No. 32 (New York: American Management Association, 1959), pp. 16–17.

Table 19.3   Examples of dimensions to include in a marketing audit

Part I. The Marketing Environment Audit

Macroenvironment

A. Economic-Demographic

1. What does the company expect in the way of inflation, material shortages, unemployment, and credit availability in the short run, intermediate run, and long run?
2. What effect will forecasted trends in the size, age distribution, and regional distribution of population have on the business?

B. Technology

1. What major changes are occurring in product technology? In process technology?
2. What are the major generic substitutes that might replace this product?

C. Political-Legal

1. What laws are being proposed that may affect marketing strategy and tactics?
2. What federal, state, and local agency actions should be watched? What is happening in the areas of pollution control, equal employment opportunity, product safety, advertising, price control, etc., that is relevant to marketing planning?

D. Social-Cultural

1. What attitude is the public taking toward business and toward products such as those produced by the company?
2. What changes are occurring in consumer life styles and values that have a bearing on the company's target markets and marketing methods?

Task Environment

A. Markets

1. What is happening to market size, growth, geographical distribution, and profits?
2. What are the major market segments? What are their expected rates of growth? Which are high opportunity and low opportunity segments?

B. Customers

1. How do current customers and prospects rate the company and its competitors, particularly with respect to reputation, product quality, service, sales force, and price?
2. How do different classes of customers make their buying decisions?
3. What are the evolving needs and satisfactions being sought by the buyers in this market?

C. Competitors

1. Who are the major competitors? What are the objectives and strategy of each major competitor? What are their strengths and weaknesses? What are the sizes and trends in market shares?
2. What trends can be foreseen in future competition and substitutes for this product?

D. Distribution and Dealers

1. What are the main trade channels bringing products to customers?
2. What are the efficiency levels and growth potentials of the different trade channels?

E. Suppliers

1. What is the outlook for the availability of different key resources used in production?
2. What trends are occurring among suppliers in their pattern of selling?

F. Facilitators

1. What is the outlook for the cost and availability of transportation services?
2. What is the outlook for the cost and availability of warehousing facilities?
3. What is the outlook for the cost and availability of financial resources?
4. How effectively is the advertising agency performing? What trends are occurring in advertising agency services?

Part II. Marketing Strategy Audit

A. Marketing Objectives

1. Are the corporate objectives clearly stated, and do they lead logically to the marketing objectives?
2. Are the marketing objectives stated in a clear form to guide marketing planning and subsequent performance measurement?
3. Are the marketing objectives appropriate, given the company's competitive position, resources, and opportunities? Is the appropriate strategic objective to build, hold, harvest, or terminate this business?

B. Strategy

1. What is the core marketing strategy for achieving the objectives? Is it a sound marketing strategy?
2. Are enough resources (or too much resources) budgeted to accomplish the marketing objectives?

Table 19.3   (continued)

3. Are the marketing resources allocated optimally to prime market segments, territories, and products of the organization?

4. Are the marketing resources allocated optimally to the major elements of the marketing mix, i.e., product quality, service, sales force, advertising, promotion, and distribution?

Part III. Marketing Organization Audit

A. Formal Structure

1. Is there a high level marketing officer with adequate authority and responsibility over those company activities that affect the customer's satisfaction?

2. Are the marketing responsibilities optimally structured along functional, product, end user, and territorial lines?

B. Functional Efficiency

1. Are there good communication and working relations between marketing and sales?

2. Is the product-management system working effectively? Are the product managers able to plan profits or only sales volume?

3. Are there any groups in marketing that need more training, motivation, supervision, or evaluation?

C. Interface Efficiency

1. Are there any problems between marketing and manufacturing that need attention?

2. What about marketing and R&D?

3. What about marketing and financial management?

4. What about marketing and purchasing?

Part IV. Marketing Systems Audit

A. Marketing Information System

1. Is the marketing intelligence system producing accurate, sufficient, and timely information about developments in the marketplace?

2. Is marketing research being adequately used by company decision makers?

B. Marketing-Planning System

1. Is the marketing-planning system well conceived and effective?

2. Is sales forecasting and market-potential measurement soundly carried out?

3. Are sales quotas set on a proper basis?

C. Marketing Control System

1. Are the control procedures (monthly, quarterly, etc.) adequate to insure that the annual-plan objectives are being achieved?

2. Is provision made to analyze periodically the profitability of different products, markets, territories, and channels of distribution?

3. Is provision made to examine and validate periodically various marketing costs?

D. New-Product Development System

1. Is the company well organized to gather, generate, and screen new product ideas?

2. Does the company do adequate concept research and business analysis before investing heavily in a new idea?

3. Does the company carry out adequate product and market testing before launching a new product?

Part V. Marketing Productivity Audit

A. Profitability Analysis

1. What is the profitability of the company's different products, served markets, territories, and channels of distribution?

2. Should the company enter, expand, contract, or withdraw from any business segments, and what would be the short- and long-run profit consequences?

B. Cost-Effectiveness Analysis

1. Do any marketing activities seem to have excessive costs? Are these costs valid? Can cost-reducing steps be taken?

Part VI. Marketing Function Audits

A. Products

1. What are the product line objectives? Are these objectives sound? Is the current product line meeting these objectives?

2. Are there particular products that should be phased out?

3. Are there new products that are worth adding?

4. Are any products able to benefit from quality, feature, or style improvements?

B. Price

1. What are the pricing objectives, policies, strategies, and procedures? To what extent are prices set on sound cost, demand, and competitive criteria?

Table 19.3 *(continued)*

2. Do the customers see the company's prices as being in line or out of line with the perceived value of its offer?
3. Does the company use price promotions effectively?

C. Distribution
1. What are the distribution objectives and strategies?
2. Is there adequate market coverage and service?
3. Should the company consider changing its degree of reliance on distributors, sales reps, and direct selling?

D. Sales Force
1. What are the organization's sales force objectives?
2. Is the sales force large enough to accomplish the company's objectives?
3. Is the sales force organized along the proper principle(s) of specialization (territory, market, product)?
4. Does the sales force show high morale, ability, and effort? Are they sufficiently trained and are there sufficient incentives?
5. Are the procedures adequate for setting quotas and evaluating performances?
6. How is the company's sales force perceived in relation to competitors' sales forces?

E. Advertising, Sales Promotion, and Publicity
1. What are the organization's advertising objectives? Are they sound?
2. Is the right amount being spent on advertising? How is the budget determined?
3. Are the ad themes and copy effective? What do customers and the public think about the advertising?
4. Are the advertising media well chosen?
5. Is sales promotion used effectively?
6. Is there a well-conceived publicity program?

Source: Philip Kotler, *Marketing Management: Analysis, Planning, and Control,* 5th ed. © 1984, pp. 767–770. Reprinted by permission of Prentice-Hall, Inc., Englewood Cliffs, N.J.

only during a crisis, although a business in trouble may use it to isolate problems and generate solutions.

Marketing audits can be performed by people within a company or outside it. The auditor inside a company may be a top-level marketing executive, a company-wide auditing committee, or a manager from another office or of another function. Although it is more expensive, an audit by outside consultants is usually more effective because external auditors have more objectivity, more time for the audit, and greater experience.

Although there is no single set of procedures for all marketing audits, firms should adhere to several general guidelines. Audits are often based on a series of questionnaires that are administered to the firm's personnel. These questionnaires should be developed carefully to ensure that the audit focuses on the right issues. Auditors should develop and follow a step-by-step plan to guarantee that the audit is systematic. When interviewing company personnel, the auditors should strive to talk with a diverse group of people from many parts of the company. To achieve adequate support, the auditors normally focus on the firm's top management initially, and then they move down through the organizational hierarchy. The results of the audit should be set forth in a comprehensive written document.[7]

The marketing audit allows an organization to change tactics or alter day-to-day activities as problems arise. For example, a regular audit of a

7. Martin L. Bell, *Marketing: Concepts and Strategies,* 3rd ed. (Boston: Houghton Mifflin, 1979), p. 472.

U.S. women's apparel firm operating in South Africa uncovered a counter-productive failure in a sales incentive program. The firm's salesclerks were supposed to receive one free brassiere for every ten sold, but the local warehouse failed to send salesclerks the incentive products they had earned. Although the mistake was an oversight by those in charge of physical distribution, it created negative feelings toward the company. By promptly sending the salesclerks the brassieres they had earned, the company made its sales incentive program function properly again.

The concept of auditing implies an official examination of marketing activities. Many organizations audit their marketing activities informally. Any attempt to verify operating results and to compare them with standards can be considered an auditing activity. Many smaller firms probably would not use the word *audit,* but they do perform auditing activities.

Several problems may arise in an audit of marketing activities. Marketing audits can be expensive in time and money. Selecting the auditors may be difficult because objective, qualified personnel may not be available. Marketing audits can be extremely disruptive, because employees sometimes fear comprehensive evaluations, especially by outsiders.

Summary

The organization of marketing activities involves the development of an internal structure for the marketing unit. The internal structure is the key to directing marketing activities. The marketing unit can be organized in different ways, by (1) functions, (2) products, (3) regions, or (4) types of customers. An organization may use only one approach or a combination.

Implementation is an important part of the marketing management process. Proper implementation of marketing plans depends on the coordination of marketing activities, the motivation of marketing personnel, and effective communication within the unit. Marketing managers must coordinate the activities of marketing personnel and integrate these activities both with those in other areas of the firm and with the marketing efforts of personnel in external organizations. Marketing managers also must motivate marketing personnel. The communication system of an organization must allow the marketing manager to communicate with high-level management, with managers of other functional areas in the firm, and with personnel involved in marketing activities both inside and outside the organization.

The marketing control process consists of establishing performance standards, evaluating actual performance by comparing it with established standards, and reducing the difference between desired and actual performance. A performance standard is an expected level of performance against which actual performance can be compared. Performance standards are established in the planning process. In evaluating actual performance, marketing managers must know what marketers within the firm are doing and have information about the activities of external organizations that provide the firm with marketing assistance. Then actual performance is compared with performance standards. Marketers must decide whether a discrepancy exists and, if so, whether it requires corrective action such as changing the performance standards or improving actual performance.

An effective control process has several requirements. First, it should be designed so that the flow of information is rapid enough to allow the marketing manager to quickly detect differences between actual and planned levels of performance. Second, a variety of control procedures must accurately monitor different kinds of activities. Third, control procedures should be flexible enough to accommodate changes. Fourth, the control process must be economical so that its costs are low relative to the costs that would arise if there were no controls. Fifth, the control process should be designed so that both managers and subordinates are able to understand it.

To maintain effective marketing control, an organization needs to develop a comprehensive control process that evaluates its marketing operations at a given time. The control of marketing activities is not a simple task. Problems encountered include environmental changes that hamper effective control, time lags between marketing activities and their effects, and problems in determining the costs of marketing activities. In addition, it may be difficult to develop performance standards.

Control of marketing strategy can be achieved through sales and cost analyses. For purposes of analysis, sales usually are measured in terms of either dollar volume or market share. For a sales analysis to be effective, it must compare current sales performance with forecasted company sales, with industry sales, with specific competitor's sales, or with the costs incurred to generate the current sales volume. A sales analysis can be performed on the firm's total sales, or the firm's total sales can be disaggregated and analyzed by product, geographic area, or customer group.

Marketing cost analysis involves an examination of accounting records and frequently a reclassification of natural accounts into marketing function accounts. Such an analysis is often difficult because there may be no logical, clear-cut way to allocate natural accounts into functional accounts. The analyst may choose either direct costing or full costing. The cost analysis methods used can focus on an aggregate cost analysis of natural accounts or functional accounts, or on an analysis of functional accounts for specific products, geographic areas, or customer groups.

To control marketing strategies, it is sometimes necessary to audit marketing activities. Auditing is a systematic appraisal and review of activities in relation to objectives. A marketing audit attempts to identify what a marketing unit is doing, to evaluate the effectiveness of these activities, and to recommend future marketing activities.

Important terms

Production-oriented organization
Sales-oriented organization
Marketing-oriented organization
Marketing control process
Performance standard
Sales analysis
Marketing cost analysis
Natural accounts

Marketing function accounts
Direct costs
Traceable common costs
Nontraceable common costs
Full-cost approach
Direct-cost approach
Marketing audit

1. What determines marketing's place within an organization? Which type of organization is best suited to the marketing concept? Why?
2. What factors can be used to organize the internal aspects of a marketing unit? Discuss the benefits of each type of organization.
3. Why might an organization use multiple bases for organizing its marketing unit?
4. How does communication help in implementing marketing plans?
5. Why is motivation of marketing personnel important in implementing marketing plans?
6. What are the major steps of the marketing control process?
7. List and discuss the five requirements for an effective control process.
8. Discuss the major problems in controlling marketing activities.
9. What is a sales analysis? What makes it an effective control tool?
10. Identify and describe three cost analysis methods. Compare and contrast direct costing and full costing.
11. How is the marketing audit used to control marketing program performance?

Cases

Case 19.1

The Place of Marketing at AT&T[8]

On January 1, 1984, AT&T completed its court-ordered breakup—the largest divestiture in U.S. history. Prior to this, the company enjoyed an 80 percent market share, and its main task was that of production. AT&T was simply an order taker, seldom faced with the hustle and bustle of today's competitive environment. Certainly, there were hardly any competitors to force the company to cater to market needs.

Currently, there is an internal war raging at AT&T, a war that started in 1971. It has recently climaxed due to the breakup. The two groups involved in the battle are the manufacturers, or engineers, from Western Electric and the marketers from Information Systems.

Marketers at AT&T argue that the company is still operating under the notion that it is the sole producer in the industry and that customers have no choice but to do business with AT&T. Marketers claim that the company has forgotten that its sole reason for being is its customers. The marketers realize that AT&T is up against some stiff competition in the long-distance service market—from MCI Communications, ITT Longer Distance, Satellite Business Systems' Skyline, and GTE Sprint. AT&T is experiencing difficulty adapting to the idea of competition. The marketers believe that if they are not given free reign, AT&T will not be able to compete.

On the other hand, the manufacturers believe that AT&T has done quite well with a conservative and bureaucratic organization, and it will

8. Most of the facts in this case are from "Changing Phone Habits," *Business Week*, Sept. 5, 1983, pp. 69–75; and Monica Langley, "AT&T Marketing Men Find Their Star Fails to Ascend as Expected," *Wall Street Journal*, Feb. 13, 1984, pp. 1, 12.

continue to do so. Key decisions concerning product distribution and pricing have always been the responsibility of the manufacturers, not the marketers. Manufacturing is shifting its attention to overhauling operations. Part of their new strategy is to speed up product development and cut costs through automation. The manufacturers at AT&T boast that the advanced Telstar call-control system was developed in less than one year. They claim to never have produced anything so rapidly before. Some believe that to get ahead at AT&T, one must have a manufacturing mentality.

Although AT&T announced after the breakup that more aggressive marketing was included in its strategy, actions prove otherwise. Most recently, in the battle over who would control the entrance in the computer business, the marketers lost to the manufacturers. This is AT&T's most exciting and innovative area; yet the manufacturers control both distribution and pricing decisions. Although many employees of the marketing staff have since resigned from AT&T, there still remain a few marketers to wage battle. However, manufacturing is still making marketing decisions.

Questions for discussion
1. Why is AT&T product oriented instead of being marketing oriented?
2. What can AT&T do to become more marketing oriented?
3. What major factors will force AT&T to become more marketing oriented?

Case 19.2

Sea Fresh Seafood Corporation

The Sea Fresh Seafood Corporation is a small seafood processor that currently produces three products. Marketers at Sea Fresh are concerned about whether their marketing strategies for their three products are effective.

The Sea Fresh marketers have decided to analyze the sales and costs of marketing the three products to provide information for assessing their marketing strategies. The income statement for the company for last year is shown in Table 19.4

Questions for discussion
1. What type of sales measurement and bases for sales analysis are used in this case?
2. What types of costs appear on the income statement?
3. What are the implications of the data on the income statement for products A, B, and C?

Table 19.4 Income Statement for Sea Fresh Seafood Corporation

	Total	Product A	Product B	Product C
Sales	$520,000	$120,000	$150,000	$250,000
Costs of goods sold	250,000	55,000	70,000	125,000
Gross profit on sales	270,000			
Marketing costs				
Salespeople's salaries	24,500	8,000	7,000	9,500
Salespeople's commissions	27,500	11,000	6,000	10,500
Advertising	65,000	13,000	13,000	39,000
Transportation and delivery	8,400	2,310	2,520	3,750
Warehouse	4,500	1,500	1,500	1,500
Sales office expenses	14,800	4,900	4,900	5,000
Non-marketing costs	19,110			
General and administrative costs	41,250			
Total costs	$205,060			
Net profit	$ 64,940			

Part 8

Selected Applications

The remaining chapters in this book deal with strategic applications in industrial, nonbusiness, and international marketing. Emphasis is placed on the features and issues that are unique to each of these selected areas of marketing when formulating and implementing marketing strategies. Chapter 20 analyzes industrial marketing strategy development and discusses the decisions and activities that characterize industrial marketing. Chapter 21 explores selected aspects of nonbusiness marketing strategies. In Chapter 22, we focus on the development and implementation of marketing strategies for foreign markets.

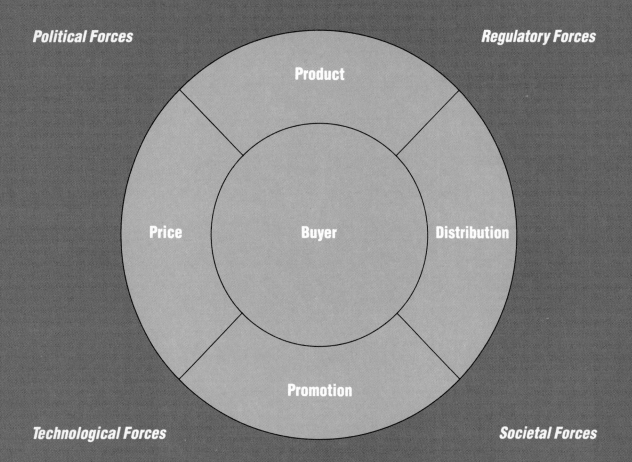

Marketing Environment

Legal Forces

Political Forces   Regulatory Forces

Product

Price   Buyer   Distribution

Promotion

Technological Forces   Societal Forces

Economic Forces

20

Industrial Marketing

Objectives

To understand some unique characteristics of industrial transactions

To see how the demand for industrial products differs from the demand for consumer products.

To learn how to select and analyze industrial target markets.

To find out how industrial marketing mix components differ from the components in consumer product marketing mixes.

Executives at Du Pont view the company's Kevlar as the most important fiber since nylon (see Figure 20.1, next page). Because Kevlar is so light and yet so strong, it was used to support the wings of the Gossamer Albatross, the human-powered airplane that flew across the English Channel. Kevlar cable is strong enough to anchor an oil rig in a heavy sea. Clothing made of Kevlar is as heat resistant as asbestos. Woven into a vest only three-eighths of an inch thick, Kevlar can stop a .38 caliber bullet fired at close range.

In eight years on the market Kevlar, despite its amazing properties, is far from being a marketing success. There are several problems. The solvent used in its manufacture came under suspicion as a carcinogen, which not only delayed Kevlar's introduction for several years but also drove up costs enormously. The production system had to be automated and isolated to protect workers from the possible effects of the solvent. Even worse, the market for which Kevlar was developed—high-priced automobile tires in which Kevlar substitutes for steel—not only is one of the principal victims of the recent recession, but also will probably continue to contract even now that the recession is over.

Du Pont, however, is still counting on Kevlar. The company is tripling its Kevlar production capacity to 45 million pounds a year. The gamble is the biggest in Du Pont's history. The firm will invest $250 million in Kevlar plant expansion, over 50 percent more than Du Pont has ever spent at one time on a single product. When that amount is added to what Du Pont has already spent on Kevlar, the total investment will reach about $500 million.[1]

It should be obvious that marketing a new fiber to industrial customers differs from marketing a new product to ultimate consumers. Industrial marketers nevertheless experience some problems similar to those of consumer product marketers and rely on basic marketing concepts and decisions. Those concepts and decisions are, however, applied in unique ways to take into account the nature of industrial markets and industrial products.

Industrial marketing is a set of activities directed toward facilitating and expediting exchanges involving industrial products and customers in industrial markets. As discussed in Chapter 2, an *industrial market* consists of individuals, groups, or organizations that purchase a specific kind of product for direct use in producing other products or for use in day-to-day operations. Industrial markets are made up of numerous types of customers including producers, governments, and institutions.

This chapter focuses on dimensions that are unique to the marketing of industrial products. Initially, we examine the nature of industrial marketing

1. Lee Smith, "A Miracle in Search of a Market," *Fortune*, Dec. 1, 1980, p. 92.

Figure 20.1   Advertisement for Kevlar
Source: Compliments of Du Pont, Kevlar R. Aramid Fiber.

by exploring the major characteristics of industrial transactions and industrial demand. Then we focus on the development of industrial marketing strategies, discussing the selection and analysis of industrial target markets and the distinctive features of industrial marketing mixes.

The nature of industrial marketing

As pointed out in Chapter 5, an *industrial product* differs from a consumer product in that it is purchased to be used directly or indirectly to produce other products or to be used in the operations of an organization. Industrial products fall into seven categories:

1. Raw materials actually become a part of a physical product. They are the basic materials provided from mines, farms, forests, oceans, and recycled solid wastes.
2. Major equipment includes large tools and machines used for production.
3. Though it does not become a part of the product, accessory equipment consists of standardized items used in production and office activities.
4. Component parts become part of the physical product and are either finished items ready for assembly or products that need little processing before assembly.

5. Process materials are used directly in production but, unlike component parts, are not readily identifiable.
6. Supplies facilitate a firm's production and operations but do not become an actual part of the finished product.
7. Services are the intangible products that organizations use in their operations.

Characteristics of industrial transactions

In some respects, industrial transactions are similar to consumer sales. Now, we will examine several characteristics of industrial transactions; then we will analyze selected dimensions of industrial demand. Industrial transactions differ from consumer sales in several ways. Industrial orders tend to be much larger than individual consumer sales. Industrial suppliers often must sell their products in large quantities to make profits; they therefore prefer not to sell to customers who place small, unprofitable orders.

Industrial sales are generally negotiated less frequently than are consumer sales. Some industrial sales involve large, expensive items, such as capital equipment, that are used for a number of years. Other industrial products, such as raw materials and component items, are used continuously in production and may have to be supplied frequently. However, the contract regarding the terms of sale and supply for these items may be negotiated only every third year.

In addition to infrequent sales negotiations, long negotiating periods may be needed to complete industrial sales. Industrial purchasing decisions are often made by a committee, orders are frequently large and expensive, and products may be custom-built. With an industrial transaction, there is a good chance that several people or departments in the purchasing organization will be involved. While one department might express a need for a product, a second department might develop its specifications, a third might stipulate the maximum amount to be spent, and a fourth might actually place the order.

One practice that is unique to industrial sales is *reciprocity,* an arrangement in which two organizations agree to buy from each other. Reciprocal agreements that threaten competition are illegal. The Federal Trade Commission and the Justice Department take action to stop reciprocal practices judged to be anticompetitive. However, a considerable amount of "innocent" reciprocal dealing occurs among small businesses, especially in the service industries. Some larger corporations engage in informal reciprocity to a lesser extent.[2] Because reciprocity forces or strongly influences purchasing agents to deal only with certain suppliers, its use can lower morale among agents and lead to less than optimal purchases.

Industrial demand

Several characteritics distinguish the demand for industrial products from the demand for consumer products. Industrial demand differs from consumer demand in that industrial demand is (1) derived, (2) inelastic, (3)

2. E. Robert Finney, "Reciprocity: Gone but Not Forgotten," *Journal of Marketing,* Jan. 1978, p. 55.

joint, and (4) more fluctuating. As we discuss each of these characteristics, remember that the demand for different types of industrial products varies. To put it another way, one should not expect the demand for component parts to be the same as the demand for major equipment.

Derived demand

The demand for industrial products is *derived demand* because industrial customers purchase products to be used directly or indirectly in the production of goods and services to satisfy consumers' needs. Therefore, the demand for industrial products derives from the demand for consumer products. In the long run, no industrial demand is totally unrelated to the demand for consumer goods.

The derived nature of industrial demand is usually multilevel. Industrial sellers at different levels are affected by a change in consumer demand for a particular product. For example, a few years ago, fiber makers were turning out large quantities of doubleknits; but consumers stopped buying doubleknits, and the demand for equipment used in manufacturing doubleknits also dropped. Therefore, factors influencing consumer buying of doubleknit fabrics affected fiber makers, equipment manufacturers, and other suppliers. Changes in derived demand are the result of a chain reaction. When consumer demand for a product changes, a wave is set in motion that affects the demand for all firms involved in the production of that consumer product.

Inelasticity of demand

The demand for many industrial products at the industry level is *inelastic demand;* that is, a price increase or decrease will not significantly affect demand for the item. Since a lot of industrial products contain a great many parts, price increases that affect only one or two parts of the product may yield only a slightly higher per unit production cost. Of course, when a sizable price increase for a component part represents a large proportion of the product's cost, then demand may become more elastic because the price increase of the component part causes the price at the consumer level to rise sharply.

The inelasticity characteristic applies only to market or industry demand for the industrial product, not to the demand for an individual industrial supplier. Suppose, for example, that a sparkplug producer increases the price of sparkplugs sold to small-engine manufacturers while its competitors continue to maintain their same lower prices. The sparkplug company probably would experience reduced sales because most small-engine producers would switch to lower-priced brands. A specific firm is quite vulnerable to elastic demand, even though industry demand for a particular product is inelastic.

Joint demand

The demand for a number of industrial products, especially raw materials and component parts, is affected by joint demand. *Joint demand* occurs when two or more items are used in combination to produce a product. For example, a firm that manufactures axes needs the same number of ax handles as it does ax blades; these two products are demanded jointly. If the supplier of ax handles cannot furnish the required number of handles and the ax producer cannot obtain them elsewhere, the producer will stop buying ax blades.

Understanding the effects of joint demand is particularly important for an industrial marketer that sells multiple, jointly demanded items. Such a marketer must realize that when a customer begins purchasing one of the jointly demanded items, a good opportunity exists to sell other related products. Likewise, when customers purchase a number of jointly demanded products, the producer must exercise extreme caution to avoid shortages of any item, because such shortages jeopardize the marketer's sales of all the jointly demanded products.

Demand fluctuations

The demand for industrial products may fluctuate enormously because it is derived demand. In general, when particular consumer products are in high demand, producers of those products buy large quantities of raw materials and component parts to ensure that long-run production requirements can be met. In addition, these producers may expand their production capacity, which entails the acquisition of capital goods.

A fall in the demand for certain consumer goods works in the same way to significantly reduce the demand for industrial products used to produce those goods. In fact, under such conditions, an industrial marketer's sales of certain products may come to a short-run standstill. When consumer demand is low, industrial customers not only cut their purchases of raw materials and component parts but also stop purchasing equipment and machinery, even for replacement purposes.

An industrial marketer may notice substantial changes in demand when its customers change their inventory policies—perhaps because of expectations about future demand. For example, if several dishwasher manufacturers who buy timers from one producer increase their inventory of timers from a two-week to a one-month supply, the timer producer will have a significant immediate increase in demand.

Sometimes, price changes can lead to surprising short-run changes in demand. A price increase for an industrial item may initially cause industrial customers to buy more of the item because they expect the price to rise further. Similarly, demand for an industrial product may be significantly lower following a price cut, because buyers are waiting for further price reductions. Fluctuations in demand can be significant in industries in which price changes occur frequently.

Selection and analysis of industrial target markets

Marketing research is becoming more important in industrial marketing. Most of the marketing research techniques that we discussed in Chapter 4 can be applied to industrial marketing. Here, we will focus on some important and unique approaches to selecting and analyzing industrial target markets.

Industrial marketers have considerable information about potential customers, much of which appears in government and industry publications; comparable data are not available regarding ultimate consumers. Even though industrial marketers may use different procedures to isolate

Table 20.1 Example of product classification through the Standard Industrial Classification system

Level	SIC Code	Description
Division	D	Manufacturing
Major group	22	Textile mill products
Industry subgroup	225	Knitting mills
Detailed industry	2251	Women's full-length and knee-length hosiery
Product category	22513	Women's finished seamless hosiery
Product item	2251311	Misses' finished knee-length socks

Sources: *1972 Standard Industrial Classification Manual,* Office of Management and Budget; and *Census of Manufacturers 1972,* Bureau of the Census.

and analyze target markets, most follow a similar pattern of (1) determining who potential customers are and how many there are, (2) locating where they are, and (3) estimating their purchase potential.[3]

Determining who potential customers are and how many there are

A lot of information about industrial customers is based on the **Standard Industrial Classification (SIC) system,** which was developed by the federal government to classify selected economic characteristics of industrial, commercial, financial, and service organizations. This system is administered by the Statistical Policy Division of the Office of Management and Budget. Table 20.1 shows how the SIC system can be used to categorize products. Various types of business activities are separated into lettered divisions, and each division is divided into numbered, two-digit, major groups. For example, major group 22 includes all firms that manufacture textile mill products. Each major group is divided into three-digit-coded subgroups, and each subgroup is separated into detailed industry categories that are coded with four-digit numbers. In the most recent SIC Manual, there are 84 major groups, 596 subgroups, and 976 detailed industry categories.[4] To categorize manufacturers in more detail, the *Census of Manufacturers* further subdivides manufacturers (Division D) into five- and seven-digit-coded groups. The fifth digit denotes the product class, and the sixth and seventh digits designate the specific product.

A large amount of data is available for each SIC category through various government publications, such as *Census of Business, Census of Manufacturers,* and *County Business Patterns.* Table 20.2 shows some types of information that can be obtained through government sources. Some data are available by state, county, and metropolitan area. Industrial market data also appear in such nongovernment sources as Dun & Bradstreet's

3. Robert W. Haas, *Industrial Marketing Management* (New York: Petrocelli Charter, 1976), pp. 37–48.
4. *1972 Standard Industrial Classification Manual,* Office of Management and Budget.

Table 20.2 Types of government information available about industrial markets (based on SIC categories)

Value of industry shipments
Number of establishments
Number of employees
Exports as a percentage of shipments
Imports as a percentage of apparent consumption
Compound annual average rate of growth
Major producing areas

Market Identifiers, Sales and Marketing Management's Survey of Industrial Purchasing Power, and other trade publications.

The SIC system is a ready-made tool that allows industrial marketers to divide industrial firms into market segments based mainly on the types of products produced or handled. Although the SIC system provides a vehicle for segmentation, it must be used in conjunction with other types of data to allow a specific industrial marketer to determine exactly which customers it is possible to reach and their number.

In conjunction with the SIC system, input-output analysis can be used effectively. It is based on the assumption that the output or sales of one industry is the input or purchases of other industries. *Input-output data* report which types of industries purchase the products of a particular industry. A major source of national input-output data is the *Survey of Current Business,* published by the Office of Business Economics, U.S. Department of Commerce. These data are presented in matrix form with eighty-three industries listed horizontally across the top of the table. To determine which industries purchase the output of a specified industry, one simply reads down the left column to the specified industry and then reads across the horizontal row, which shows how much each of the eighty-three industries spends on the output of the specified industry. For example, sixty-two of the eighty-three industries purchase paints and allied products (industry number 30). However, the purchases of three industries (new construction, maintenance and repair construction, and motor vehicles and equipment) account for 54 percent of the total purchases of paint and allied products. Each of the remaining fifty-nine industries buys less than 4.7 percent of the total.

After finding out which industries purchase the major portion of an industry's output, the next step is to determine the SIC numbers for those industries. Because firms are grouped differently in the input-output tables and the SIC system, ascertaining SIC numbers can be difficult. However, the Office of Business Economics does provide some limited conversion tables with the input-output data. These tables can assist industrial marketers in assigning SIC numbers to the industry categories used in the input-output analysis. For example, the motor vehicle and equipment industry—one industry that buys significant quantities of paint and allied products—can be converted into SIC categories 3711 and 3715.

After determining the SIC numbers of the industries that buy its output, an industrial marketer is in a position to ascertain the number of firms that are potential buyers nationally, by state, and by county. Government publications such as the *Census of Business,* the *Census of Manufacturers,* and *County Business Patterns* report the number of establishments within SIC classifications, along with other types of data such as those shown in Table 20.2. For manufacturing industries, *Sales and Marketing Management's Survey of Industrial Purchasing Power* contains state and county SIC information regarding the number and size of plants and shipment sizes. The *Survey of Industrial Purchasing Power,* unlike most government sources, is updated annually.

Locating industrial customers

At this point, an industrial marketer knows what types of industries purchase the kinds of products his or her firm produces, as well as the number of establishments in those industries and certain other information. However, that marketer has still to find out the names and addresses of potential customers.

One approach to identifying and locating potential customers is to use state or commercial industrial directories such as *Standard & Poor's Register* and Dun & Bradstreet's *Middle Market Directory* or *Million Dollar Directory.* These sources contain such information about a firm as its name, SIC number, address, phone number, annual sales, and other data. By referring to one or more of these sources, an industrial marketer can isolate industrial customers that have SIC numbers and determine their locations. Industrial marketers can use these sources to develop lists of potential customers by city, county, and state.

A second approach—which is more expedient but also more expensive—is to use a commercial data company. Dun & Bradstreet, for example, can provide a list of firms that fall into a particular four-digit SIC group. For each firm on the list, Dun & Bradstreet identifies the name, location, sales volume, number of employees, type of products handled, names of chief executives, and other information.

Either approach can effectively identify and locate a group of potential industrial customers. However, an industrial marketer probably cannot pursue all firms on the list. Since some firms have a greater purchase potential than others, the marketer must determine which segment or segments to pursue.

Estimating purchase potential

To estimate the purchase potential of industrial customers or groups of customers, an industrial marketer must find a relationship between the size of potential customers' purchases and a variable available in SIC data, such as number of employees. For example, a paint manufacturer might attempt to determine the average number of gallons purchased by a specific type of potential industrial customer relative to the number of persons employed. If the industrial marketer has no previous experience in this market segment, it will probably be necessary to survey a random sample of potential customers to establish a relationship between purchase sizes and numbers of persons employed. Once this relationship has been established, the relationship can be applied to potential customer segments to estimate their purchases. After deriving these estimates, the industrial marketer selects the customers to be included in the target market.

Although SIC data can be quite helpful in isolating and analyzing industrial target markets, several problems can arise. First, a few industries do not have specific SIC designations. Second, because a transfer of products from one establishment to another is counted as a part of total shipments, double counting may occur when products are shipped between two establishments within the same firm. Third, since the census bureau is prohibited from publishing data that would identify a specific business organization, some data—such as value of total shipments—may be understated. Finally, since SIC data are provided by government agencies, there is usually a significant lag between the time the data are collected and when that information becomes available.

Characteristics of industrial marketing mixes

After selecting and analyzing a target market, an industrial marketer must create a marketing mix that will satisfy the customers in that target market. In many respects, the general concepts and methods involved in developing an industrial marketing mix are similar to those used in consumer product marketing. Let us focus here on the features of industrial marketing mixes that differ from the marketing mixes for consumer products. We will examine each of the four components in an industrial marketing mix: product, distribution, promotion, and price.

Product

Compared with consumer marketing mixes, the product ingredients of industrial marketing mixes often include a greater emphasis on services, both before and after sales (see Figure 20.2). Services, including on-time delivery, quality control, custom design, and a nationwide parts distribution system, may be important components of the product. (See the Application on p. 623.)

Before making a sale, industrial marketers provide technical advice regarding product specifications, installation, and application. Many industrial marketers depend heavily on long-term relationships with customers that perpetuate sizable repeat purchases. Therefore, industrial marketers also make a considerable effort to provide services after the sale. Because industrial customers depend heavily on having products available when needed, on-time delivery is another service included in the product component of many industrial marketing mixes. An industrial marketer who is unable to provide on-time delivery can't expect the marketing mix to satisfy industrial customers. Availability of parts must also be included in the product mixes of many industrial marketers. The lack of parts can result in costly production delays. The industrial marketer who includes availability of parts within the product component has a competitive advantage over a marketer who fails to offer this service. Customers whose average purchases are large often desire credit; thus, some industrial marketers include credit services in their product mixes.

When planning and developing an industrial product mix, an industrial marketer of component parts and semifinished products must realize that a customer may decide to make the items instead of buying them. In some

You're a professional.
You need professional service
with your personal computers.

WELCOME TO
DIGITAL'S
COMPUTER-BASED
INSTRUCTION.

Digital gives you
the best support package
in the industry. Training
for your people. Hot lines
for your questions. A full
range of services for your
peace of mind.

Up to now, personal computers
have not been noted for their after-
sale support.
    Digital changes that.
    We've created three new personal
computers, intended for professionals.
That means they do more than most
personal computers. And they're
supported better than anybody else's.
    We offer a total service package,
giving you all the support you need,
right at your place of business.
From computer-based instruction to
instant-access hot lines to guaranteed
response times to software updates,
we provide everything.
    We have over 20,000 service people
worldwide and all the resources and
experience to deliver superior service
across the board: hardware, software,
education. Not even the world's
largest computer company can offer
you so much.
    So if you're looking into personal
computers, don't just compare the
goods, compare the services. You'll
find that when it comes to support
after the sale, nobody can do more
for your peace of mind than Digital.

d|i|g|i|t|a|l

Computers for professionals
from professionals.

© Digital Equipment Corporation 1983

Figure 20.2   Product with an emphasis on service
Source: Courtesy of Digital Equipment Corporation.

cases, then, industrial marketers compete not only with each other but also
with their own potential customers.

Industrial products frequently must conform to standard technical
specifications desired by industrial customers. For this reason, industrial
marketers tend to concentrate on product research that is directed at functional features rather than on market research.[5] This focus has led to some
less than successful marketing mixes. For example, Steel Company of
Canada (Stelco) sold trainloads of common nails to a market it did not
really know. Its marketers did not know who bought Stelco nails; nor did
they know for what applications the nails were used. Stelco introduced a
revolutionary nail, an inexpensive spiral-threaded nail that is stronger than
common nails, has more holding power, and is easier to drive. However,
the new nails have not sold as well as management expected.[6] The primary
reason is that Stelco's research focused on nails rather than on the people
in the nail market.

5. Jon G. Udell, *Successful Marketing Strategies in American Industries*
   (Madison, Wis.: Mimir Publishers, 1972), pp. 48–49.
6. Peter M. Banting, ''Unsuccessful Innovation in the Industrial Market,''
   Journal of Marketing, January 1978, p. 100.

United States automakers, losing market shares to foreign producers both at home and abroad, are fighting to gain back market shares and an ability to compete in a global market. Industrial marketers who provide parts to automakers face increased demands for quality, delivery, productivity, and pricing. To rebuild consumer confidence, U.S. automakers are specifying higher quality standards and are awarding and renewing contracts on the basis of a supplier's ability to meet these new requirements and deliver parts on time.

In the past, auto parts suppliers operated on a bid-on-it-and-run approach. The contracts were made on a yearly basis and an automaker typically had two to three thousand different suppliers. Today's new contracts are for a longer period, from three to eight years, drastically reducing the number of suppliers. The agreements are similar to partnerships. Automobile parts marketers attempt to gain a competitive edge by providing customer satisfaction through quality parts and services. The survival of the U.S. auto industry is dependent on the success of this relationship between suppliers and automakers.

Hoover Universal, a supplier of car and truck seats, has implemented changes in its sales force. Sales representatives spend less time in direct sales efforts with purchasing agents and more time in design and engineering discussions with customers. Hoover has been able to gain a competitive edge through capital investments in manufacturing facilities and effective industrial marketing. The supplier established a multi-year contract with Nissan's production plant in Tennessee and, to provide efficient service, built a manufacturing plant twenty miles from Nissan, which enables Hoover to provide just-on-time delivery of inventory. Hoover's sales force meets directly with engineers, designers, and production managers from the Nissan plant to better supply seats that meet the needs of Nissan's market.

Success for a supplier in the auto industry depends on its ability to produce high quality products and provide the right type of services. Success requires a technically knowledgeable sales force that can interact effectively regarding many aspects of production.

Source: Based on Bob Woods, "Selling Parts with Services," *Sales and Marketing Management,* July 4, 1983, pp. 29–30.

Since industrial products often are sold on the basis of specifications and are rarely sold through self-service, the major consideration in package design is protection. Less emphasis is placed on the package as a promotional device.

Distribution

The distribution ingredient in industrial marketing mixes differs from that of consumer products with respect to the types of channels used; the kinds of middlemen available; and the transportation, storage, and inventory policies in effect.

Distribution channels tend to be shorter for industrial products than for many consumer products. Four commonly used industrial channels are shown in Figure 20.3 (a similar diagram was presented earlier in Figure 7.3). Other, less popular channels also may be available. Although *direct distribution channels,* those in which products are sold directly from producers to users (see channel 1, Figure 20.3), are not employed frequently in the distribution of consumer products, they are the most widely used channels for industrial products. Over half of all industrial products are sold through direct channels. Industrial buyers like to communicate di-

Figure 20.3
Four major types of
industrial marketing
channels

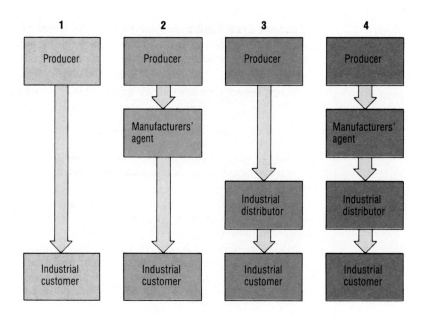

rectly with producers, especially when expensive or technically complex products are involved. In these circumstances, an industrial customer wants the technical assistance and personal assurances that only a producer can provide.

In channel 2 (Figure 20.3), a manufacturers' agent is employed. As described in Chapter 8, a *manufacturers' agent* or representative is an independent business person who sells complementary products of several producers in assigned territories and is compensated through commissions. A manufacturers' agent does not acquire title to the products and usually does not take possession. Acting as a salesperson on behalf of the producers, a manufacturers' agent has no latitude, or very little, in negotiating prices or sales terms.

Using manufacturers' agents can benefit an industrial marketer. These agents usually possess considerable technical and market information and have an established set of customers. For an industrial seller with highly seasonal demand, a manufacturers' agent can be an asset because the seller does not have to support a year-round sales force. That manufacturers' agents are paid on a commission basis also may present an economical alternative for a firm with highly limited resources that cannot afford a full-time sales force.

Certainly, the use of manufacturers' agents is not free of problems. Even though straight commissions may be cheaper for an industrial seller, the seller may have little control over manufacturers' agents. Because of the compensation method, manufacturers' agents usually want to provide service on their larger accounts. They are frequently reluctant to spend adequate time following up sales, to put forth special selling efforts, or to provide sellers with market information when such activities reduce the amount of productive selling time. As they rarely maintain inventories, manufacturers' agents have a limited ability to provide parts or repair services quickly to customers.

Channel 3 in Figure 20.7 shows an *industrial distributor* between the producer and the customer. Like manufacturers' agents, industrial distributors are independent business organizations. However, they do take title to products, and they do carry inventories. Industrial distributors usually sell standardized items such as maintenance supplies, production tools, and small operating equipment. Some industrial distributors carry a wide variety of product lines; others specialize in one or a small number of lines. Industrial distributors can be most effectively used when a product has broad appeal, is easily stocked and serviced, is sold in small quantities, and is needed rapidly to avoid high losses (such as a part for a machine in an assembly line).[7]

Industrial distributors offer several advantages. They can perform the needed selling activities in local markets at relatively low cost to a manufacturer. They can reduce a producer's financial burden by providing credit services to their customers. And because industrial distributors usually maintain close relationships with their customers, they are aware of local needs and can pass on market information to producers. By holding adequate inventories in their local markets, industrial distributors reduce the producers' capital requirements.

The Apeco Corporation—a small Des Plaines, Illinois, copier manufacturer—effectively used industrial distributors to compete with the heavyweights in the copier industry. Apeco had discovered that as a small copier succeeded in a given territory, the manufacturer, usually Japanese, would move in and sell direct. Therefore, Apeco offered industrial distributors (dealers) exclusive territories.[8] Apeco guarantees forty-eight-hour service and supports its distributors in many other ways. By treating industrial distributors fairly, Apeco has succeeded in a very tough market. It could easily have failed in the face of intense competition.

There are, though, several disadvantages to using industrial distributors. Like manufacturers' agents, industrial distributors may be difficult to control, since they are independent firms. They frequently stock competing brands, so an industrial seller cannot depend on them to sell a specific brand aggressively. Since industrial distributors maintain inventories—for which they sustain numerous expenses—they are less likely to handle items that are bulky, that are slow sellers relative to profit margin, that need specialized facilities, or that require extraordinary selling efforts. In some cases, industrial distributors lack the technical knowledge necessary to sell and service certain industrial items.

As shown in Figure 20.3, channel 4 has both a manufacturers' agent and an industrial distributor between the producer and the industrial customer. This channel may be appropriate when the industrial marketer wishes to cover a large geographic area but maintains no sales force because of highly seasonal demand or because the firm cannot afford a sales force. This type of channel also can be useful for an industrial marketer

7. James D. Hlavacek and Tommy J. McCuistion, "Industrial Distributors: When, Who, and How?" *Harvard Business Review,* March–April, 1983, p. 97.
8. Ellen M. Kleinberg, "Improving Distributor Relations," *Industrial Marketing,* Feb. 1981, p. 73.

that wants to enter a new geographic market without expanding the firm's existing sales force.

Selecting an industrial channel or channels requires careful analysis along several dimensions. So far, our discussion has perhaps implied that all channels are equally available and that an industrial producer can select the most desirable option. However, in a number of cases, only one or perhaps two channels are available for the distribution of certain types of products.

An important issue in channel selection is the manner in which particular products are normally purchased. If customers ordinarily buy certain types of products directly from producers, it is unlikely that channels with middlemen will be effective. Other dimensions one should consider are the cost and physical characteristics of the product, the costs of using various channels, the amount of technical assistance needed by customers, and the size of product and parts inventory needed in local markets.

Physical distribution decisions regarding transportation, storage, and inventory control are especially important for industrial marketers. The continuity of most industrial buyer-seller relationships depends on the seller's having the right products available when and where the customer needs them. This requirement is so important that industrial marketers must sometimes make a considerable investment in order-processing systems, materials handling equipment, warehousing facilities, and inventory control systems. Like marketers of consumer products, industrial marketers try to use the proper mix of these resources to minimize total physical distribution costs while maintaining a satisfactory level of service.

Promotion

The combination of promotional efforts used in industrial marketing mixes generally differs considerably from those used for consumer products, especially convenience goods. The differences are evident both in the emphasis placed on various promotion mix ingredients and in the activities performed in connection with each promotion mix ingredient.

For several reasons, most industrial marketers rely on personal selling to a much greater extent than do consumer product marketers (except, perhaps, marketers of consumer durables). Since an industrial seller often has fewer customers, personal contact with each customer is more feasible. Some industrial products have technical features that are too numerous or too complex to explain through nonpersonal forms of promotion. Because industrial purchases frequently are high in dollar value and must be suited to the job and available where and when needed, industrial buyers want reinforcement and personal assurances from industrial sales personnel. Since industrial marketers depend on repeat purchases, sales personnel must follow up sales to make certain that customers know how to use the purchased items effectively, as well as to ensure that the products work properly.

As Table 20.3 illustrates, the average cost of an industrial sales call varies from industry to industry. Selling costs were defined as salaries, commissions, bonuses, and travel and entertainment expenses. The average cost of closing an industrial call is $907.80, based on an average of 5.1

Table 20.3   The cost of closing a sale differs among industries

SIC	Industry	No. of Cases	Average Number of Calls to Close a Sale (by SIC)	Average Cost Per Sales Call (by SIC)	Average Cost to Close a Sale* (by SIC)
25	Furniture & Fixtures	9	3.3	$239.90	$ 791.67
26	Paper & Allied Products	13	4.8	106.20	509.76
27	Printing, Publishing & Allied Industries	7	5.1	66.10	337.11
28	Chemicals & Allied Products	45	4.9	133.00	651.70
29	Petroleum/Refining & Related Industries	7	5.0	142.00	710.00
30	Rubber & Misc. Plastic Products	12	5.6	98.80	553.28
32	Stone, Clay, Glass & Concrete Products	16	4.5	95.30	428.85
33	Primary Metal Industries	19	3.7	117.90	436.23
34	Fabricated Metal Products	58	5.0	126.10	630.50
35	Machinery (Except Electrical)	155	5.9	182.10	1,074.39
36	Electrical & Electronic Machinery Equipment	83	4.9	210.90	1,033.41
37	Transportation Equipment	30	6.7	367.20	2,460.24
38	Instruments; Photographic & Optical Goods	31	4.5	150.60	677.70
45	Transportation by Air	6	3.0	83.80	251.40
49	Utilities & Sanitary Services	6	3.5	170.20	595.70
63	Insurance	5	3.6	64.40	231.84
73	Business Services	8	4.6	195.00	897.00
75	Automotive Repair Services	5	4.8	93.80	450.24

*This is determined by multiplying the average number of calls to close a sale by the average cost per sales call for each SIC.

Source: Laboratory of Advertising Performance (LAP), Report #8052.1, McGraw-Hill Research, McGraw-Hill Publications Co., 1221 Avenue of the Americas, New York, NY, 10020.

calls at a cost of $178.00 per call.[9] Because of the escalating cost of personal selling, telemarketing—the creative use of the telephone to enhance the salesperson's function—is on the upswing.[10] Some of the activities in telemarketing include toll-free 800 phone lines and data-terminal-assisted personal sales work stations that take orders, check stock and order status, and provide shipping and billing information.[11]

Although not all industrial salespeople perform the same sales activities, they usually can be grouped into the following categories, as described in Chapter 13: technical, missionary, and trade or inside order

9. Laboratory of Advertising Performance (LAP) Report #8051.1, McGraw-Hill Research.
10. Rick Roscitt, "Telemarketing Helps Industrial Marketers Increase Sales, Productivity, Profitability," *Marketing News,* May 1, 1981, p. 1.
11. Ibid.

Application

Celanese produces fibers and yarns for a number of end-use applications. Its advertising program is designed to stimulate demand of both its products and its customers' products in the apparel market, and to build broader awareness of its Fortrel polyester and Arnel triacetate fibers and yarns. Celanese tries to accomplish this goal by communicating with each link in the apparel merchandising chain through the fashion and apparel trade press, consumer magazines, newspapers, and other media.

Since Celanese produces industrial products, much of its advertising is not aimed at consumers but is directed at industrial buyers instead. Celanese fibers, for example, are playing an increasingly important role in many industrial end-use applications. Thus, Celanese advertises in several business publications that are widely read by management in manufacturing, transportation, communications, and service industries.

Source: Based on "Ads, Ads, Ads," *Celanese World,* Vol. 6, No. 4, p. 10.

takers. Telemarketing could be used effectively by an inside order taker. Regardless of how sales personnel are classified, industrial selling activities differ from consumer sales efforts. Because industrial sellers frequently are asked for technical advice regarding product specifications and uses, they often need, and are more likely to have, technical backgrounds. Compared with typical buyer-seller relationships in consumer product sales, the interdependence that develops between industrial buyers and sellers is likely to be stronger, with sellers counting on buyers to purchase their particular products and buyers depending on sellers to provide information, products, and related services when and where needed. Although industrial salespeople do market their products aggressively, they almost never employ "hard-sell" tactics, because of both their role as technical consultants and the interdependency between buyers and sellers.

Advertising tends to be emphasized less in industrial sales than in consumer transactions. Some of the reasons given earlier for the importance of personal selling in industrial promotion mixes explain the relative lack of importance of advertising. Industrial advertising rarely sells the product per se. Rather, it paves the way for other selling efforts, especially personal selling.[12] (The Application above focuses on related dimensions.)

Advertising often supplements personal selling efforts. Since the cost of an industrial sales call is high and continues to rise, advertisements that allow sales personnel to perform more efficiently and effectively are quite worthwhile for an industrial marketer. Advertising can make industrial customers aware of new products and brands; inform buyers about general product features, representatives, and organizations; and isolate promising prospects by providing inquiry forms or the addresses and phone numbers of company representatives.

The advertising message can be sufficiently selective to elicit a response only from customers who are interested in the product. Chemetron Corporation, for example, processes over fifteen thousand inquiries monthly regarding products that range from welding electrodes to medical

12. Marianne Paskowski, "Industrial Advertising . . . ," *Industrial Marketing,* May 1981, p. 78.

Figure 20.4
Consumer advertise-
ment aimed at deriving
demand for an indus-
trial product
*Source: Du Pont
Company.*

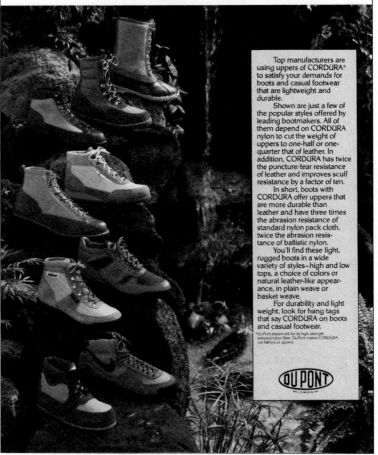

Leading bootmakers rely on Cordura® for durability and light weight.

Top manufacturers are using uppers of CORDURA® to satisfy your demands for boots and casual footwear that are lightweight and durable.

Shown are just a few of the popular styles offered by leading bootmakers. All of them depend on CORDURA nylon to cut the weight of uppers to one-half or one-quarter that of leather. In addition, CORDURA has twice the puncture/tear resistance of leather and improves scuff resistance by a factor of ten.

In short, boots with CORDURA offer uppers that are more durable than leather and have three times the abrasion resistance of standard nylon pack cloth, twice the abrasion resistance of ballistic nylon.

You'll find these light, rugged boots in a wide variety of styles—high and low tops, a choice of colors or natural leather-like appearance, in plain weave or basket weave.

For durability and light weight, look for hang tags that say CORDURA on boots and casual footwear.

Du Pont trademark for its high-strength textured nylon fiber. Du Pont makes CORDURA not fabrics or uppers.

(DU PONT)

equipment.[13] To ensure that appropriate information is sent to a respondent, it is crucial that the inquiry be specific as to the type of information
desired, the name of the company and respondent, the company's SIC
number, and the size of the organization.

Because the demand for most industrial products is derived demand,
marketers can sometimes stimulate demand for their products by stimulating consumer demand. Thus, an industrial marketer occasionally sponsors
an advertisement that promotes the products sold by that marketer's customers. In Figure 20.4, for example, Du Pont is promoting several bootmakers' products that are made with Cordura,® a high-strength, air-tex-
tured nylon fiber made by Du Pont. Du Pont does not make the boots

13. Don Gruening, "Chemetron Uses Inquiry Leads to Provide Multiple
Benefits," *Industrial Marketing,* Jan. 1978, p. 46.

shown in Figure 20.4, but it does produce Cordura. By stimulating demand for boots made with Cordura, Du Pont is also stimulating demand for Cordura.

When selecting advertising media, industrial marketers primarily choose such print media as trade publications and direct mail; they seldom use broadcast media. Trade publications and direct mail reach precise groups of industrial customers and avoid wasted circulation. In addition, they are best suited for advertising messages that present numerous details and complex product information (which are frequently the type of messages that industrial advertisers wish to get across).

Compared with consumer product advertisements, industrial advertisements are usually less persuasive in nature and are more likely to contain a large amount of copy and set forth numerous details. In contrast, marketers that advertise to reach ultimate consumers sometimes avoid extensive advertising copy, because consumers are reluctant to read it. Industrial advertisers use long copy, however, because they believe that industrial purchasers who have any interest in the product will search for information and read long messages.

Sales promotion activities can play a significant role in industrial promotion mixes and include such efforts as catalogs, trade shows, and trade-type sales promotion methods like merchandise allowances, buy-back allowances, displays, sales contests, and other methods discussed in Chapter 13. Industrial marketers go to considerable effort and expense to provide catalogs that describe their products to customers. Customers refer to these catalogs to determine specifications, terms of sale, delivery times, and other information about products offered by various sellers. Catalogs thus assist buyers in deciding which suppliers to contact.

Trade shows can be effective vehicles for making many customer contacts in a short time. Although trade shows can be expensive, industrial marketers can use them for various purposes: to show and demonstrate new products, to find new customers, to take orders, to develop mailing lists, to promote the company image, and to find out what competitors are doing.

The manner in which industrial marketers use publicity in their promotion mixes may not be much different from the way that marketers of consumer products use it.

Price

Compared with consumer product marketers, industrial marketers face many more constraints from legal and economic forces. As indicated in Chapter 16, the Robinson-Patman Act significantly influences the pricing practices of producers and wholesalers by regulating price differentials and the use of discounts. When the federal government invokes price controls, the effect ordinarily is to regulate industrial marketers' prices directly and to a greater extent than consumer product prices. With respect to economic forces, an individual industrial firm's demand is often highly elastic, requiring the firm's price to approximate competitors' prices. This condition often results in nonprice competition and in a considerable amount of price stability.

Figure 20.5
Advertisement illustrating a product sold on total value rather than low price
Source: Caterpillar Tractor Company.

Today's route to sustainable competitive advantage lies in offering the customer better value, even at a slightly higher price.[14] Customers are used to buying on the basis of price, which is visible and measurable, and producers are used to competing on the same basis; but a strategic advantage based on the total value delivered is far less easily duplicated by competitors.[15] Companies like Caterpillar and Hewlett-Packard have shown that a value-based strategy can effectively garner a commanding lead over competition. Both firms emphasize the highest quality products at slightly higher prices. Consider the advertisement in Figure 20.5 in which Caterpillar stresses the value of its products and their long-term cost-effectiveness.

Although there are a variety of ways for determining prices of industrial products, the three most common are administered pricing, bid

14. John L. Forbis and Nitin T. Mehta, "Value-Based Strategies for Industrial Products," *Business Horizons,* May–June 1981, p. 32.
15. Ibid.

pricing, and negotiated pricing. With *administered pricing,* the seller determines the price (or series of prices) for a product, and the customer pays that specified price. Marketers that use this approach may employ a one-price policy in which all buyers pay the same price, or they may set a series of prices that are determined by one or more discounts. In some cases, list prices are posted on a price sheet or in a catalog. The list price acts as a beginning point from which trade, quantity, and cash discounts are deducted. Thus, the actual (net) price paid by an industrial customer is the list price less the discount(s). When a list price is used, an industrial marketer sometimes specifies the price in terms of list price times a multiplier. For example, the price of an item might be quoted as "list price × .78," which means the seller is discounting the item so that the buyer can purchase the product at 78 percent of the list price. Simply changing the multiplier allows the seller to revise prices without having to issue new catalogs or price sheets.

With *bid pricing,* prices are determined through sealed bids or open bids. When a buyer uses sealed bids, sellers are notified that they are to submit their bids by a certain date. The bids are opened and made public at a designated time. Usually, the lowest bidder is awarded the contract, providing that the buyer believes the firm is capable of supplying the specified products when and where needed. Under an open bidding approach, several but not all sellers are asked to submit bids. This differs from sealed bidding in that the amounts of the bids are not made public. Finally, an industrial purchaser sometimes uses negotiated bids. Under this arrangement, the customer seeks bids from a number of sellers, screens the bids, and then negotiates the price and terms of sale with the most favorable bidders until a final transaction is consummated or until negotiations are terminated with all sellers.

Sometimes, a buyer will be seeking either component parts to be used in production for several years or custom-built equipment to be purchased currently and through future contracts. In such a circumstance, an industrial seller may submit an initial, less profitable bid to win "follow-on" (subsequent) contracts. The seller that wins the initial contract is often substantially favored in the competition for follow-on contracts. In such a bidding situation, an industrial marketer must determine how low the initial bid should be, the probability of winning a follow-on contract, and the combination of bid prices on both the initial and the follow-on contract that will yield an acceptable profit.[16]

For certain types of industrial markets, a seller's pricing component may have to allow for *negotiated pricing.* That is, even when there are stated list prices and discount structures, negotiations may determine the actual price paid by an industrial customer. Negotiated pricing can benefit seller and buyer because price negotiations frequently lead to discussions of product specifications, applications, and perhaps product substitutions. Such negotiations may give the seller an opportunity to provide technical assistance to the customer and perhaps sell a product that better fits the customer's requirements; the final product choice might also be more prof-

16. Douglas G. Brooks, "Bidding for the Sake of Follow-on Contracts," *Journal of Marketing,* Jan. 1978, p. 35.

itable for the seller. The buyer benefits by gaining more information about the array of products and terms of sale available and may acquire a more suitable product at a lower price.

Some industrial marketers sell in markets in which only one of these general pricing approaches prevails. Such marketers can simplify the price components of their marketing mixes. However, a number of industrial marketers sell to a wide variety of industrial customers and must maintain considerable flexibility in pricing practices.

Summary

Industrial marketing is a set of activities directed at facilitating and expediting exchanges involving industrial products and customers in industrial markets. Industrial markets consist of producers, governments, or institutions that purchase a specific kind of product for direct use in producing other products or for use in day-to-day operations.

Industrial transactions differ from consumer transactions in several ways. The orders tend to be considerably larger. Negotiations occur less frequently but are often lengthy when they do occur. Industrial transactions sometimes involve more than one person or one department in the purchasing organization.

Industrial demand differs from consumer demand along several dimensions. Industrial demand derives from the demand for consumer products. At the industry level, industrial demand is inelastic; if the price of an industrial item changes, demand for the product will not change as much proportionally. In some cases, an industrial product is demanded jointly with another product. Demand for industrial products can fluctuate widely.

Industrial marketers have a considerable amount of information available to them for use in planning their marketing strategies. Much available information about industrial customers is based on the Standard Industrial Classification (SIC) system developed by the federal government. This system categorizes businesses into major industry groups, industry subgroups, and detailed industry categories. The SIC system provides industrial marketers with information needed to identify market segments. It can best be used for this purpose in conjunction with other information, such as input-output data. After identifying target industries, the marketer can locate potential customers by using state or commercial industrial directories or by employing a commercial data company. The marketer then must estimate the potential purchases of industrial customers by finding a relationship between a potential customer's purchases and a variable available in published sources.

Like marketers of consumer products, an industrial marketer must develop a marketing mix that satisfies the needs of customers in the industrial target market. The product component frequently emphasizes services, since they may be of primary interest to industrial customers. The marketer also must consider that the customer may elect to make the product rather than buy it. Industrial products must meet certain standard specifications desired by industrial users.

The distribution component for industrial products differs from that for consumer products in the types of channels used; the kinds of middlemen available; and transportation, storage, and inventory policies. A direct distribution channel is common in industrial marketing. Industrial marketers also use channels containing manufacturers' agents, industrial distributors, or both. Channels are chosen on the basis of availability, the typical mode of purchase for a product, and several other variables. The primary objective of the physical distribution of industrial products is to ensure that the right products are available when and where needed.

Personal selling is a primary ingredient of the promotional component in industrial marketing mixes. Sales personnel often act as technical advisors both before and after a sale. Advertising sometimes is used to supplement personal selling efforts. Industrial marketers generally use print advertisements containing a larger amount of information but less persuasive content than consumer advertisements do. Other promotional activities include catalogs, trade shows, and trade-type sales promotion methods.

The price component for industrial marketing mixes is influenced by legal and economic forces to a greater extent than it is for consumer marketing mixes. Pricing may be affected by competitors' prices as well as by the type of customer who buys the product.

Important terms		
Industrial marketing	Input-output data
Industrial market	Direct distribution channels
Industrial product	Manufacturers' agent
Reciprocity	Industrial distributor
Derived demand	Administered pricing
Inelastic demand	Bid pricing
Joint demand	Negotiated pricing
Standard Industrial Classification (SIC) system	

Discussion and review questions

1. List some characteristics that differentiate industrial transactions from consumer sales.
2. How does industrial demand differ from consumer demand?
3. As our society becomes more aware of environmental and health hazards, it is possible that a change in demand will occur in the type of foods we buy. Explain how a change in demand for processed foods and canned vegetables could affect industrial demand.
4. Explain why the demand for many industrial products at the industry level is inelastic.
5. What function does the SIC system perform for industrial marketers?
6. List some sources that an industrial marketer can use to determine the names and addresses of potential customers.
7. How do industrial marketing mixes differ from those of consumer products?
8. What are the major advantages and disadvantages of using industrial distributors?
9. Why would an industrial marketer spend resources on advertising aimed at stimulating consumer demand?
10. Compare and contrast three methods for determining the price of industrial products.

Cases

Case 20.1

Georgia-Pacific Building Products[17]

Georgia-Pacific Corp. is the world's largest plywood producer. Despite a downturn in the building products market in the early 1980s, Georgia-Pacific has continued to develop new plants, products, and programs that should improve the company's competitive position in building markets. While new residential construction still accounts for a large portion of Georgia-Pacific's building products sales, the remodeling, repairs, and additions market has been the sales leader for Georgia-Pacific products for the past three years.

Georgia-Pacific has stayed at the leading edge of product development in the 1980s and is now actively involved in all three of the new structural panels, waferboard, composite plywood, and oriented-strand board, as well as plywood.

1. *Plywood.* This staple of the construction industry is made by peeling logs and laying up the veneers at right angles to each other for rigidity and strength.
2. *Composite plywood.* This structural panel closely resembles plywood, except that the middle "ply" is a core made of oriented wood fibers.
3. *Oriented-strand board.* OSB is made of toothpick-size strands of wood laid up in layers at right angles to each other.
4. *Waferboard.* This product is made from wood flakes or "wafers" that are bonded into a panel with resin.

Composite plywood products allow for better use of the company's wood supply and also allow the company to take advantage of new market opportunities. The company recently constructed a composite plywood plant in Dudley, North Carolina, where the major focus is on manufacturing waferboard and oriented strand board. It has recently doubled the capacity of its Dudley OSB plant and has plans to build or expand nine other structural panel plants, two of which are already under construction and nearing completion.

In addition to manufacturing wood building products, Georgia-Pacific is one of the ten largest producers of roofing materials nationwide. It now has ten roofing plants throughout the United States. These facilities are among the industry's most efficient and modern. That company's goal is to double roofing sales in the early 1980s as part of an ambitious and aggressive marketing program to increase sales of many key product lines.

Georgia-Pacific anticipates substantial growth in sales of lumber, metal products, and paneling over the next few years. One factor that will help it attain this growth is its strong distribution division. That division's strength benefits the company both in terms of its support for the manufacturing operations and its ability to move quickly in the marketplace.

In summary, Georgia-Pacific has come through the latest economic recession and building downturn in a position to benefit from any surge in the market for building products. Its modern plants make products vital to

17. Many of the facts in this case are from the Georgia-Pacific *1980 Annual Report,* pp. 10, 20–21. Updated by Georgia-Pacific in 1984.

the building trades, and it has the industry's most comprehensive distribution network.

The remodeling/repair market has been Georgia-Pacific's sales leader. If this market continues to grow and if the demand for residential and industrial construction continues to increase, as it already has thus far in the decade, Georgia-Pacific will be able to keep its sales balanced in response to fluctuations in demand. Georgia-Pacific must keep abreast of the changing environment, and its marketing strategies must deal effectively with the upturns and downturns in the demand for building products.

Questions for discussion
1. What are the characteristics of industrial demand for building products made and sold by Georgia-Pacific?
2. How should Georgia-Pacific locate their industrial customers and estimate purchase potential for their new structural panels?
3. Do the current marketing strategies and plans for expansion and growth fit the environment of the building industry today?
4. Suggest a marketing strategy for structural panels if there is a downturn in the economy.

Case 20.2

NutraSweet[18]

NutraSweet is an artificial sweetener produced by G.D. Searle. It tastes like sugar, looks like sugar, contains fewer calories than sugar, but does not have the bitter aftertaste of most artificial sweeteners. NutraSweet is Searle's brand name for the new sweetener, aspartame. G. D. Searle, which is a pharmaceutical firm, has patent rights on aspartame until 1987.

NutraSweet is made from a combination of two amino acids. It is a highly concentrated sweetener—200 times sweeter than sugar and six times sweeter than cyclamate. NutraSweet contains no sodium, and it is not a carbohydrate. It can easily be used by diabetics, and it can also be used safely by pregnant women. Although it is a sweetener, it does not promote tooth decay. Compared with sugar, NutraSweet's only shortcomings are that it does not hold together under high heat, and it cannot be used as a thickening agent the way that sugar can.

Approved by the FDA in 1981, NutraSweet is an industrial product found in a variety of food products normally containing sugar or sugar substitutes. Products sweetened with NutraSweet can be reduced in calories by about 95 percent. It can extend a product's shelf life and it enhances certain fruit flavors. NutraSweet currently is found in the following product categories:

Beverages: Diet Pepsi, Diet Coke, Hires Root Beer, Orange Crush, Diet 7Up, Diet Squirt, RC Cola, Dad's Root Beer, Sugar Free Dr Pepper

18. The information in this case is from Gene Bylinski, "The Battle for America's Sweet Tooth," *Fortune,* July 26, 1982, pp. 28–32; "NutraSweet Fact Sheet," *Advertising Age,* May 9, 1983, p. M-21; "NutraSweet: What It Is and What It Isn't," Searle Food Resources, Inc., 1983; and Jayne Pearly, "Technology," *Forbes,* Nov. 7, 1983, pp. 256–258.

Beverage Mixes: Lipton's Ice Tea Mix, Swiss Miss, Carnation cocoa mix, Ovaltine, Alba, Kool-Aid, Crystal Light, Wyler's Drink Mix
Candies: Wriggley's peppermint gum, Wriggley's spearmint gum
Cereal: Halfsies
Desserts: Whipped toppings, Shimmer, D-Zerta gelatin mix

All products that contain NutraSweet must display the "NutraSweet" name.

Thus far, Searle's marketing efforts have been effective. The firm promoted NutraSweet, an industrial product, to a consumer market. Searle spent $1 million on consumer advertising using the theme "Introducing NutraSweet—You can't buy it, but you're gonna love it." Searle advertised both on TV and in magazines. To demonstrate the excellent taste of NutraSweet, Searle used direct mail to provide free samples of gumdrops sweetened with NutraSweet to a large number of consumers. Trial of the gumdrops was encouraged through television commercials.

Searle sells NutraSweet for $90 a pound, which is more than twenty times the price of saccharine. The price is expected to decline, and it is predicted to be as low as $40 a pound in 1990. Despite NutraSweet's high price, it is faring quite well in the market. Searle's biggest challenge so far has been how to meet the rising demands for NutraSweet.

In 1982 NutraSweet sales were $158.3 million, and in 1983 they increased to $424.8 million. Profits went from $64.9 million in 1982 to $178.5 million in 1983. Searle plans to open a new aspartame plant costing $100 million next year.

Questions for discussion
1. Why is NutraSweet considered to be an industrial product? What type of industrial product is NutraSweet?
2. Why did Searle promote NutraSweet to consumers when the average consumer cannot buy even a pound of NutraSweet?
3. Why is Searle able to charge a price that appears to be so much higher than the prices for competing products?

21

Nonbusiness Marketing

Objectives

To explore the concept of marketing in nonbusiness situations.

To examine how organizational or individual goals determine whether an organization is a business or a nonbusiness.

To understand the development of marketing strategies in nonbusiness organizations.

To describe methods for controlling nonbusiness marketing activities.

To provide real-life examples of nonbusiness marketing strategies.

It should not surprise anyone studying marketing that the American Heart Association and other voluntary service, nonprofit health organizations use marketing concepts and activities to achieve their goals. Public support is needed to gain the financial and voluntary aid necessary to keep the organization running. Thus knowledge of public attitudes toward an organization can have an important impact on goal attainment.

One survey indicated that contributors to the American Heart Association are likely to be older, with either low or high income, and to have lived more than twenty years in an area. The same study discovered that only 25 percent of the respondents could identify the American Heart Association slogan, "We're Fighting for Your Life."[1] Obviously, these data can help the American Heart Association select its target market and focus its marketing efforts where they are most needed. As shown in Figure 21.1, the American Heart Association is now trying to emphasize its slogan and message by demonstrating the benefits the organization offers society.

Figure 21.1   An American Heart Association poster illustrating its commitment to public health   *Source: Reprinted with permission of The American Heart Association.*

1. F. Kelly Shuptrine and Ellen M. Moore, "The Public's Perceptions of the American Heart Association: Awareness, Image and Opinions," in *Evolving Marketing Thought for 1980, Proceedings of the Southern Marketing Association,* ed. John H. Summey and Ronald D. Taylor (Nov. 19–22, 1980), p. 281.

Consider the following events: A planned parenthood organization launches a program to inform mothers-to-be about the importance of medical care during early pregnancy. The Air Force encourages young people to contact an Air Force recruiter, as illustrated in Figure 21.2. The YMCA determines which market segments need and want its services. A major state university creates the position of vice president of marketing to plan strategies during a period of low enrollments.

These situations all involve nonbusiness marketing activities. *Nonbusiness marketing* includes marketing activities conducted by individuals and organizations to achieve some goal other than ordinary business goals such as profit, market share, or return on investment. Remember that we broadly defined marketing as a set of individual and organizational activities aimed at facilitating and expediting exchanges within a set of dynamic environmental forces. Although most examples used in this text involve business enterprises, this chapter examines the unique aspects of marketing in nonbusiness situations. Most of the previously discussed concepts and approaches to managing marketing activities apply to nonbusiness situations.

We will first examine the concept of nonbusiness marketing and see how organizational and individual goals determine whether an organization is a business or a nonbusiness. Next, we will explore the overall objectives of nonbusiness organizations, their marketing objectives, and the development of their marketing strategies. Then we will illustrate how an audit of marketing activities can promote marketing awareness in a nonbusiness organization. Finally, we will look at some real-life examples of how nonbusiness marketing strategies have been implemented.

Marketing applied to nonbusiness organizations

As discussed in Chapter 1, an exchange situation exists when individuals, groups, or organizations possess something that they are willing to give up in an exchange. In nonbusiness marketing, obligations or rewards often are not clearly specified in advance. Also, the objects of the exchange may not be specified in financial terms. Usually, exchange is facilitated through *negotiation* (mutual discussion or communication of terms and methods) and *persuasion* (convincing and prevailing upon by argument). Acceptance of nonbusiness products is attained through constant efforts to further an organization's goals. Often negotiation and persuasion are conducted without reference to or awareness of the role that marketing plays in transactions. We are concerned with nonbusiness performance of marketing activities, whether or not the exchange is consummated.

Why is nonbusiness marketing different?

We devote a separate chapter to nonbusiness marketing because people traditionally have not thought of nonbusiness exchange activities as marketing. Only organizations that attempt to make a profit—including those such as mutual insurance companies that try to gain or maintain market share—have been viewed as the type that must perform marketing activities.

Some nonprofit organizations have business-like goals but lose productivity and efficiency in attempts to serve their members. For example, Teachers Insurance and Annuity Association-College Retirement Equities Fund (TIAA-CREF), is a nonprofit organization and the second largest pension fund in the United States. This organization controls $25 billion in assets and nearly monopolizes pension management for private universities and other nonprofit educational institutions. Profit-oriented companies and some TIAA-CREF members participating in retirement plans feel that the organization has recently been too conservative or failed to be creative in investing in high-growth companies that outperform the market.[2]

Profit is a variable that only indirectly changes the nature of marketing activities. Many organizations strive for effective marketing activities. Charitable organizations and supporters of social causes are major non-

2. Christopher Conte, "More Schools Break Longtime Ties to Academe's Major Pension Fund," *Wall Street Journal,* September 14, 1983, p. 35.

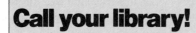

What was the price of stock in AT&T on April 1, 1944? ☎ **Do men waste more time on the job than women?** ☎ **Do eskimos really rub noses?** ☎ **How nutritional are TV dinners?** ☎ **How many bones do dogs have?** ☎

Have a question?

Call your library!

American Library Association

business marketers in this country. Political parties, unions, religious sects, and fraternal organizations also perform marketing activities; yet they are not considered businesses. Whereas the chief beneficiary of a business enterprise is its owner, in theory the only beneficiaries of a non-business organization are its clients, its members, or its public at large. For example, as illustrated in Figure 21.3, the American Library Association urges its beneficiary, the public, to use the library. It is assumed that this activity will contribute to the public's welfare.

In a business, the owner or board of directors delegates authority to executives and holds them accountable for achieving the company's goals—for example, profits. In nonbusiness organizations, such direct-line accountability is difficult to achieve because it is often unclear who the "owners" are or to whom one should be accountable.[3] Therein lies one of the major differences between a business and a nonbusiness. Nonbusinesses have a greater opportunity for creativity, but their weaknesses lie in

3. Cecily Cannan Selby, "Better Performance from Nonprofits," *Harvard Business Review,* Sept.–Oct. 1978, p. 93.

the loss of productivity and efficiency because of less direct accountability to an owner. For example, trustees or board members of nonbusinesses have trouble judging performance when services can be provided only by trained professionals. It is harder for administrators to evaluate the performance of doctors, professors, or social workers than it is for sales managers to evaluate the performance of salespersons.

The marketing concept in nonbusiness organizations

Nonbusiness organizations sometimes fail to implement the marketing concept. The marketing concept tells us that all of an organization's planning should be guided by the clients, members, or publics being served. The success of nonbusiness organizations that have adopted the marketing concept has reinforced the value of this concept. By adopting the marketing concept, Population Services International has been able to sell more birth control products in Bangladesh than government workers had been able to give away. Marketing research was conducted to select brand names, colors, point-of-purchase displays, and advertising messages. In contrast, governmental family planning relied on patriotic exhortations that did not appeal to individuals.[4]

Other organizations have been less successful. Some welfare agencies, police forces, and other government agencies have problems in dealing with the public. Almost everyone complains about the quality of government services received for the taxes paid. Nonbusinesses clearly have marketing problems; but the problems can be solved. Many universities, for example, are adopting the marketing concept to overcome enrollment problems created by declining birth rates and increased costs of education. In a formal research study, marketing and nonmarketing materials sent by American colleges and universities were categorized. To the extent that materials supported product, price, promotion, or distribution they were defined as marketing materials. Such materials included promotional brochures, events advertisements, career development brochures, and personal letters supporting the college or university.[5]

Today there are a number of marketing consulting firms that help universities to develop marketing strategies. Table 21.1 outlines the responsibilities and activities of the director of marketing for a major university.

Governments can modify or adapt marketing principles to meet the desires of society. In fact, marketing research was used to formulate policy proposals for planning and developing tourism in Canada.[6] Figure 21.4 illustrates an advertisement for travel to Ontario, Canada. Note that this advertisement appeals to the out-of-doors market segment. Marketing concepts and techniques can be used effectively in policy decisions regarding the nature and type of products that government provides for its citizens.[7]

4. Kevin Higgins, "Marketing Enables Population Control Group To Boost Results," *Marketing News,* Oct. 14, 1983, p. 12.
5. John A. Bradford, "Marketing and Non-Marketing Materials Sent by American Colleges and Universities," *Journal of the Academy of Marketing Science,* Spring 1983, p. 126.
6. J. R. Brent Ritchie and Roger J. LaBreque, "Marketing Research and Public Policy: A Functional Perspective," *Journal of Marketing,* July 1975, p. 17.
7. Ibid., p. 12.

Table 21.1   Job description: Director of marketing for a university

Position title: Director of Marketing

Reports to: A vice president designated by the president

Scope: University-wide

Position concept: The director of marketing is responsible for providing marketing guidance and services to university officers, school deans, department chairmen, and other agents of the university.

Functions: The director of marketing will:
1. Contribute a marketing perspective to the deliberations of the top administration in their planning of the university's future
2. Prepare data that might be needed by any officer of the university on a particular market's size, segments, trends, and behavioral dynamics
3. Conduct studies of the needs, perceptions, preferences, and satisfactions of particular markets
4. Assist in the planning, promotion, and launching of new programs
5. Assist in the development of communication and promotion campaigns and materials
6. Analyze and advise on pricing questions
7. Appraise the workability of new academic proposals from a marketing point of view
8. Advise on new student recruitment
9. Advise on current student satisfaction
10. Advise on university fundraising

Responsibilities: The director of marketing will:
1. Contact individual officers and small groups at the university to explain services and to solicit problems
2. Prioritize the various requests of services according to their long-run impact, cost-saving potential, time requirements, ease of accomplishment, cost, and urgency
3. Select projects of high priority and set accomplishment goals for the year
4. Prepare a budget request to support the anticipated work
5. Prepare an annual report on the main accomplishments of the office

Major liaisons: The director of marketing will:
1. Relate most closely with the president's office, admissions office, development office, planning office, and public relations department
2. Relate secondarily with the deans of various schools and chairmen of various departments

Source: Philip Kotler, "Strategies for Introducing Marketing into Nonprofit Organizations," *Journal of Marketing,* Jan. 1979, p. 42. Reprinted with permission of the publisher, the American Marketing Association.

Although most organizations should accept the marketing concept, the purposes or reasons for servicing customers, clients, members, or the public at large differ. Nonbusiness organizations serve clients, members, or the public to achieve some social or organizational goal. Nonbusiness organizations have no owners, stockholders, or members who are supposed to make a financial profit, although employees usually receive fair compensation for their work.

Figure 21.4
Ontario, Canada encourages tourism
Source: Ontario Ministry of Tourism and Recreation.

Northern Ontario/Canada

The Sounds of Silence

The dip and pull and ripple of the paddle, the whistle whirring of the reel, the echo of the loon. This is the place to refresh your senses far and away from the workaday world. Come North to 400,000 lakes, to wilderness excursions or fly-in fishing camps, or resorts of all sorts in our great out-of-doors. North to greet the dawn and the call of the wild. Phone TOLL FREE 1-800-828-8585 or from New York State 1-800-462-8404 or write: Ontario Travel, Queen's Park, Toronto M7A 2E5, Ontario/Canada.

ONTARIO yours to discover!

In nonbusiness organizations, goals—and sometimes clients—are difficult to define. Universities, philanthropic foundations, museums, police, and welfare agencies have many complex, interrelated reasons for existence. For such organizations, planning marketing activities and implementing the marketing concept may require more coordination and refinement of goals than is necessary for a business.

The publics or target markets it serves reflect an organization's unique philosophy and mission. Most universities have goals other than merely attracting students and granting degrees; research, service, and contributions to society are also goals. Religious sects often base their goals on faith and the divine guidance of leaders. Other nonbusiness organizations, such as the U.S. Postal Service, are supposed to serve the needs and desires of their clients.

Nonbusinesses may be controversial

Nonbusiness organizations may have goals that are not accepted by some members of society. Opposing organizations may spring up to combat the success of a movement or social cause with which they disagree. Nonprofit groups such as Common Cause, the American Postal Workers Union, the National Association of Independent Colleges and Universities, and Gun Owners of America spend lavishly on lobbying efforts to persuade Congress, the White House, and even the courts to support their interests.[8] Few persons, however, oppose the basic goals of the American Cancer Society (to prevent cancer and treat victims) or of the March of Dimes (to prevent birth defects).

The professional who manages marketing activities that promote the cause of a controversial group must make more value judgments about participation than do marketers in most business enterprises. Also, the use of marketing by controversial groups may be called into question by various members of society.

Marketing as a field of study does not attempt to state what an organization's goals should be, nor to debate the issue of nonbusiness versus business goals. Marketing only attempts to provide a body of knowledge and concepts to help further an organization's goals. Individuals must decide whether they approve or disapprove of a particular organization's goal orientation. Most marketers would agree that profit and consumer satisfaction are appropriate goals for business enterprises, but there probably would be considerable disagreement about the goals of a controversial nonbusiness organization.

Nonbusiness marketing objectives

The basic aim of nonbusiness organizations is to obtain a desired response from a target market (public). The response could be a change in values, a financial contribution, the donation of services, or some other type of exchange.

Even cities market themselves to achieve prosperity or improve overall living conditions. Birmingham, Alabama, has changed its image of racial disharmony; city government, civic groups, and businesses worked together to solve problems and create a new environment. Today, the city is encouraging high-technology businesses and promoting community services, educational institutions, and a new civic center that covers six square blocks.[9]

Nonbusiness marketing objectives are shaped by the nature of the exchange and the goals of the organization. Figure 21.5 illustrates how the exchange transactions and the purpose of the organization can influence marketing objectives. (These objectives are used as examples and may or may not apply to specific organizations.)

8. "Lobbyists: Washington's 'Hidden Persuaders,' " *U.S. News and World Report,* Sept. 19, 1983, p. 63.
9. "Birmingham: A City Forging New Hopes," *U.S. News and World Report,* Sept. 9, 1983, pp. 56–57.

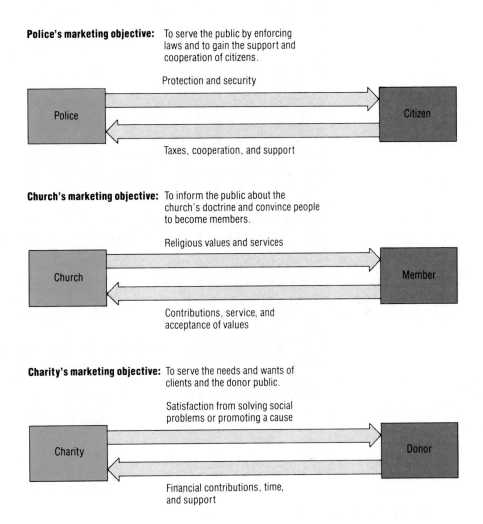

Police's marketing objective: To serve the public by enforcing laws and to gain the support and cooperation of citizens.

Protection and security

Police → Citizen

Taxes, cooperation, and support

Church's marketing objective: To inform the public about the church's doctrine and convince people to become members.

Religious values and services

Church → Member

Contributions, service, and acceptance of values

Charity's marketing objective: To serve the needs and wants of clients and the donor public.

Satisfaction from solving social problems or promoting a cause

Charity → Donor

Financial contributions, time, and support

Figure 21.5 Examples of marketing objectives for different types of exchanges
Source: Philip Kotler, Marketing for Nonprofit Organizations, *2nd ed., © 1982, p. 38. Adapted by permission of Prentice-Hall, Inc., Englewood Cliffs, N.J.*

Nonbusiness marketing objectives should state the rationale for an organization's existence. An organization that defines the marketing objective as providing a product can be left without a purpose if the product becomes obsolete. However, serving the perceived needs and wants of a target public, or market, enhances an organization's chance to survive and to achieve its goals.

Developing nonbusiness marketing strategies

A marketing strategy encompasses (1) defining and analyzing a target market and (2) creating and maintaining a marketing mix. A nonbusiness organization may find it difficult to think in terms of the needs, perceptions, or preferences of its market or public. It is very easy for an organization to assume that it knows what the public needs or wants. For example, an interest group may assume that it is only right to protect endangered animals such as seals, whales, or wolves. Figure 21.6 promotes an interest group

SOME FOLKS CAN'T AFFORD A GOOD LAWYER.

Folks who often need one. . .like deer and eagles and wolves, and the wilderness they need to live in.

Places like forests and swamps, rivers and plains and seacoasts. . .wild places and things that so benefit humankind in their natural state. But they need an assist from us.

The Sierra Club's Legal Defense Fund provides it. . .lawyers and scientists to defend nature's rights and advance her needs. But we must have your help if we are to give nature all the help it must have. Your generous contribution to the Sierra Club Legal Defense Fund will be tax-deductible. And effective.

To make a deductible contribution or for additional information, please write to:

The Sierra Club Legal Defense Fund
2044 Fillmore Street   San Francisco, CA 94115

that wants to conserve wildlife's natural habitat. Another interest group, the Center for Science in the Public Interest (CSPI), has petitioned the FTC to curb alcohol advertising directed at young people. The CSPI objective calls for the elimination of alcohol advertisements in broadcast media, printed health warnings similar to those found in cigarette advertisements, elimination of celebrities in advertisements, and restricted channels of distribution for beer, wine, and distilled spirits. This objective is designed to minimize the appeal and availability of alcohol for young people and to make them aware of the effects associated with drinking.[10] Obviously, CSPI's objective is intended to achieve what the group considers best for society.

Similarly, people who work for hospitals, welfare organizations, municipal transportation systems, and the like, often assume that they have

10. Kevin Higgins, "Debate Rages over Marketing and Alcohol Problems," *Marketing News,* Sept. 30, 1983, p. 1.

the technical competence to decide what services the public needs. How-ever, hospitals often offend or frighten patients by failing to explain pro-cedures; welfare organizations are sometimes patronizing; and city buses can be dirty and overcrowded. From such examples, it is clear that an or-ganization's strategy failures often can be traced to its neglect of the basic desires and concerns of target markets.

Target markets

We must revise the concept of target markets slightly when we examine nonbusiness organizations. Whereas a business is supposed to have target groups that are potential purchasers of its product, a nonbusiness organi-zation may attempt to serve many diverse groups. For our purposes, *target public* is broadly defined as a collective of individuals who have an interest in, or a concern about, an organization, a product, or a social cause. It follows that the terms "target market" and "target public" are difficult to distinguish for many nonbusiness organizations. Once an organization is concerned about exchanging values or obtaining a response from the pub-lic, it views the public as a market.[11]

In nonbusiness organizations, direct consumers of the product are called *client publics,* and indirect consumers are called *general publics.*[12] For example, the client public for a university is its student body, while its gen-eral public includes parents, alumni, trustees, and other groups. The client public usually receives most of the attention when an organization devel-ops a marketing strategy. Techniques and approaches to segmenting and defining target markets were discussed in Chapter 2. These techniques ap-ply to nonbusiness target markets.

Table 21.2 exemplifies behavioral segmentation of the performing-arts market in a large urban area. By delineating markets for classical, country/folk, theater, pop, and recital art forms, arts administrators can provide more and better performances for defined audiences and develop new pro-grams for unique market segments.[13] Notice that Table 21.2 indicates not only the types of performances attended but also the types of performances that particular market segments are more likely not to attend. Arts admin-istrators know, therefore, that the country/folk market segment is unlikely to attend musicals, plays, or symphonies.

Developing a marketing mix

A marketing mix strategy limits alternatives and directs marketing activi-ties toward achieving organizational goals. The strategy should outline or develop a blueprint for making decisions about product, distribution, pro-motion, and price. These decision variables should be blended to serve the target market.

A successful strategy requires careful delineation of a target market through marketing research and the development of a complete marketing mix. For example, many states have established agencies that use promotional

11. Philip Kotler, *Marketing for Nonprofit Organizations* (Englewood Cliffs, N.J.: Prentice-Hall, 1982), p. 37.
12. Ibid.
13. John R. Nevin and S. Tamer Cavusgil, "Audience Segments for the Performing Arts," *Marketing of Services,* ed. James H. Donnelly and William R. George (Chicago: American Marketing Association, 1981), p. 128.

Table 21.2   Art-form audience segments

Market Segment	Type of Performance Attended	Type of Performance Not Attended
Classical	Symphony Chamber music Opera Ballet	Experimental theater Rock Comedians
Country/folk	Country-western Folk/bluegrass Rock	Musicals Plays Symphony
Theater	Musicals Traditional plays Experimental theater	Rock Chamber music
Pop	Jazz Big bands Pop vocalist/group	Gospel
Recital	Instrumental recitals Solo vocal recitals	Musicals Pop

Source: John R. Nevin and S. Tamer Cavusgil, "Audience Segments for the Performing Arts," *Marketing of Services,* ed. James H. Donnelly and William R. George (Chicago: American Marketing Association, 1981), p. 127. Reprinted with permission of the publisher.

methods to attract foreign investment for continued economic growth of the state. Some concrete examples include the following methods:

1. Personal selling—U.S. or foreign-based individuals directly contact potential investors.
2. Sales promotion—direct investment is encouraged through seminars and investment missions.
3. Advertising—printed and audiovisual promotional materials are utilized in foreign countries, along with advertisements in newspapers and magazines.
4. Publicity—the press is utilized systematically.

Through the examination of various state departments in Southeastern states and their attempts to attract foreign investment, it was found that none of the states determined the wants and needs of potential investors. Instead, their selection of target markets was based on such factors as past investment levels and the feelings of agency representatives. Another major problem was the agencies' neglect to evaluate feedback from foreign investors regarding their states' promotional programs. Also, product was not emphasized as much as the promotion variable.[14]

14. Spero C. Peppas, "An Application of Marketing Theory to the Attraction of Foreign Investment," *A Spectrum of Contemporary Marketing Ideas,* ed. John H. Summey, Blaise J. Bergiel, and Carol H. Anderson (Carbondale, Ill.: Southern Marketing Association, 1982), pp. 204–208.

Table 21.3 Opportunity assessment for nonbusiness marketing mix[a]

Nonbusiness Industry	Level of Application			
	Product	Distribution	Price	Promotion
Health care organizations	High	Medium-High	Low-Medium	Low-Medium
Educational facilities	High	Medium	Low-Medium	High
Political organizations	High	Medium	Low-Medium	High
Cultural organizations	Medium	Low-Medium	High	Medium-High
Public service agencies	Medium-High	High	Low	Low-Medium
Professional organizations	High	Low	Medium	Low-Medium
Religious organizations	High	Medium	Low-Medium	Low
Human services organizations	High	Low-Medium	Low	Medium-High

[a]The contents of each line represent an assessment of one major mid-western city as an example only.

Source: Philip D. Cooper and George E. McIlvain, "Factors Influencing Marketing's Ability to Assist Non-Profit Organizations," *Evolving Marketing Thought for 1980, Proceedings of the Southern Marketing Association,* ed. John H. Summey and Ronald D. Taylor (Nov. 19–22, 1980), p. 317. Used by permission.

The level of application for any given marketing mix variable may range from low to high (see Table 21.3), depending on the needs of the non-business industry.[15] As Table 21.3 indicates, however, a marketing mix should always involve some decision about each of the four major elements—product, distribution, promotion, and price. For example, ethical and legal considerations tend to limit the use of promotional tools in the health-care industry. Keep in mind that Table 21.3 is based on a survey of nonbusiness organizations in one city—the marketing mix emphasis can vary from organization to organization.

Product

Nonbusiness organizations deal with ideas and services more often than with goods. Problems in developing a product configuration evolve when an organization fails to define what is being provided. In product-oriented businesses, the physical reality of the product provides a simple but powerful base on which to build a description of what is being provided.

15. Philip D. Cooper and George E. McIlvain, "Factors Influencing Marketing's Ability to Assist Non-Profit Organizations," *Evolving Marketing Thought for 1980, Proceedings of the Southern Marketing Association,* ed. John H. Summey and Ronald D. Taylor (November 19–22, 1980), p. 316.

Figure 21.7
Maryland's promotion
of pro-business
attitudes
*Source: Maryland Office
of Business and Indus-
trial Development.*

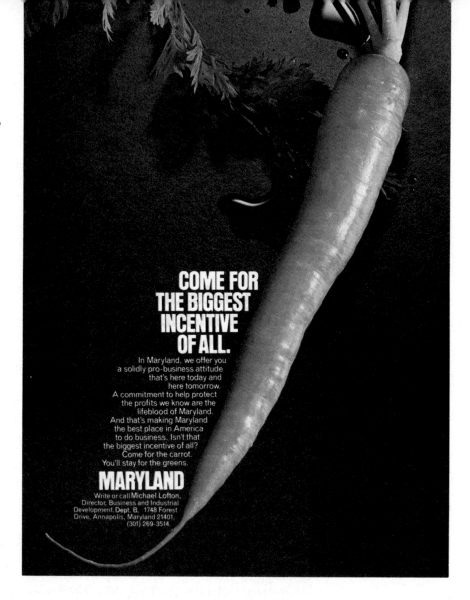

Because of the abstract nature of services, it is far more difficult for a service-oriented organization to describe what it is providing.[16] What product
does the Peace Corps provide? Its services include vocational training,
health services, nutritional assistance, and community development. Ideas
include international cooperation and the implementation of U.S. foreign
policy. The Peace Corps' product is more difficult to define than the average business product. The marketing of ideas and concepts is more abstract than the marketing of tangibles, and it requires much effort to present benefits. Consider the advertisement in Figure 21.7 that promotes
Maryland's probusiness attitude. This abstract concept is promoted to attract new industry.

16. Dan R. E. Thomas, "Strategy Is Different in Service Businesses," *Harvard
Business Review,* July–Aug. 1978, p. 159.

Distribution

Nonbusiness products must be available before an exchange can take place. Marketers usually analyze distribution as it relates to decisions about product and promotion. Since most nonbusiness products are ideas and services, distribution decisions relate to how these ideas and services will be made available to clients. If the product is an idea, selecting the right media (the promotional strategy) to communicate the idea will facilitate distribution. The availability of services is closely related to product decisions. By nature, services consist of assistance, convenience, and availability. Availability is part of the total service (product). For example, making a product such as health services available calls for knowledge of such retailing concepts as site location analysis.

Most nonbusiness organizations in capitalist nations do not get involved in the physical distribution of goods. If goods must be moved, a facilitating agency such as the postal service or United Parcel Service may carry out the task. One exception is the U.S. Geological Survey which arranges for sporting-goods stores and other commercial outlets to sell its maps. Also, the Geological Survey has joined with another government office to sell colorful satellite images of the globe.[17]

Developing a channel of distribution to coordinate and facilitate the flow of nonbusiness products to clients is a necessary task, but the traditional concept of the marketing channel may need to be reviewed. The independent wholesalers available to a business enterprise do not exist in most nonbusiness situations. Instead, a very short channel—nonbusiness organization to client—is prevalent because manufacturing and the movement of goods are rarely necessary to make ideas and services available; that is, production and consumption are often simultaneous.

Promotion

Making promotional decisions may be the first sign that nonbusiness organizations are performing marketing activities. Nonbusiness organizations use advertising and publicity to communicate with clients and the public. Although personal selling may be called something else, it is used by many nonbusiness organizations. Churches and charities rely on personal selling when they send volunteers to recruit new members or request donations. The U.S. Army uses personal selling when its recruiting officers attempt to convince potential enlistees to join. Special events to obtain funds, communicate ideas, or provide services are sales promotion activities. Contests, entertainment, and prizes offered to attract donations resemble the sales promotion activities of business enterprises.

Price

The broadest definition of price (valuation) must be used to develop the marketing strategy. Financial price, an exact dollar value, may or may not be charged for a nonbusiness product. Economists recognize the giving up of alternatives as a cost. *Opportunity cost* is the value of the benefit that is given up by selecting one alternative rather than another. This traditional

---

17. Paul Harris, *Sales and Marketing Management,* Feb. 14, 1983, p. 50.

economic view of price means that if a nonbusiness organization can convince someone to donate time to a cause or to change his or her behavior, then other alternatives are forgone, and this is a cost to (or a price paid by) the individual.

This concept of price can be used to determine what price is paid by a new recruit to join the all-volunteer army. The price is the giving up of both personal freedom (by submitting to army rules and regulations) and earning potential, if any, outside the armed service. In planning the marketing strategy of the all-volunteer army, price is not viewed as a major controllable aspect of the marketing mix, although a consideration of what the new recruit is giving up is programmed into product and promotion decisions.

For other nonbusiness organizations, financial price is an important part of the marketing mix. The U.S. Postal Service has a special advisory commission to help set prices; government-owned transportation systems and utility services are priced to recover most costs while providing benefits. Pricing strategies of nonbusiness organizations often stress public and client welfare over equalization of costs and revenue. If additional funds are needed to cover costs, then donations, contributions, or grants may be solicited.

Controlling nonbusiness marketing activities

To control marketing activities in nonbusiness organizations, managers use information obtained in the marketing audit to make sure that goals are achieved. Table 21.4 lists several helpful summary statistics. It should be obvious that the data in Table 21.4 are useful for both planning and control. Control is designed to identify what activities have occurred in conformity with the marketing strategy and to take corrective actions where any deviations are found. The purpose of control is not only to point out errors and mistakes but also to revise organizational goals and marketing objectives as necessary. For example, universities view alumni as one of their most important markets. In most cases, little is known about former students' motivation to provide assistance to their alma mater. In one study, it was learned that graduates with applied majors, such as agriculture, and those who participated in university activities are more likely to provide long-term continuing support to the university. These results indicate that universities might be able to gain more support from alumni in the long run by encouraging student participation in activities.[18]

To control nonbusiness marketing activities, managers must make a proper inventory of activities performed and prepare to adjust or correct deviations from standards. Knowing where and how to look for deviations and what types of deviations to expect are especially important in nonbusiness stiuations. Since nonbusiness marketing activities may not be perceived as marketing, managers must clearly define what activity is being examined and how it should function.

18. Steven W. Hartley and Eric N. Berkowitz, "Identifying Membership Strategies: An Investigation of University Alumni," *1983 Educators' Proceeding,* ed. Patrick E. Murphy, et al. (Chicago: American Marketing Association, 1983), p. 352.

Table 21.4   Examples of data useful in controlling nonbusiness marketing activities

1. **Product mix offerings**	B. Number of employees
A. Types of product (services)	1. By organization
B. Number of organizations offering the product (service)	2. Total industrywide
	C. Number of volunteers
2. **Financial resources**	1. By organization
A. Types of funding used	2. Total industrywide
1. Local grants	D. Number of customers serviced
2. State grants	1. By type of service
3. Federal grants	2. By organization
4. Foundations	3. Total industrywide
5. Public solicitation	
6. Fees charged	4. **Facilities**
B. Number using each type of funding	A. Number and type
C. Number using combinations of funding sources	1. By organization
	2. Total industrywide
3. **Size**	B. Location
A. Budget (cash flows)	1. By address
	2. Zip code
	3. Census tract

Source: Adapted from Philip D. Cooper and George E. McIlvain, "Factors Influencing Marketing's Ability to Assist Non-Profit Organizations," *Evolving Marketing Thought for 1980, Proceedings of the Southern Marketing Association,* ed. John H. Summey and Ronald D. Taylor (Nov. 19–22, 1980), p. 315. Used by permission.

It may be difficult to control nonbusiness marketing activities because it is often hard to determine whether goals are being achieved. A mental health center that wants to inform community members of its services may not be able to determine whether it is communicating with persons who need assistance. A growing case load does not guarantee that all needs have been met. Surveying to determine the percentage of the population that is aware of a mental health program can show whether or not the awareness objective has been achieved; but it fails to indicate what percentage of the persons with mental health problems has been assisted. The detection and correction of deviations from standards is certainly a major purpose of control, but standards must support the organization's overall goals. Managers can refine goals by examining the results that are being achieved and by analyzing the ramifications of those results.

Techniques for controlling overall marketing performance must be keyed to the nature of the operations. Obviously it is necessary to control the marketing budget in most nonbusiness organizations, but budgetary control is not tied to profit-and-loss standards. Responsible management of funds is the objective. Nonbusiness organizations have diverse missions; there is no hard-and-fast formula to determine what control techniques are appropriate or how to use them.

Central control responsibility can facilitate orderly, efficient administration and planning. For example, Illinois Wesleyan University evaluates graduating students' progress in order to control and improve the quality of the educational product. The audit phase relies on questionnaires sent to students and their employers after graduation. The employer completes a questionnaire to indicate the student's progress; the student completes a questionnaire to indicate which additional concepts or skills were needed to perform duties. In addition, a number of faculty members interview certain employers and students to obtain information for control purposes. Results of the audit are used to develop corrective action if university standards have not been met. Corrective action might include an evaluation of the deficiency and a revision of the curriculum.

Examples of nonbusiness marketing strategies

Let us take a closer look at the activities of strategy implementation to see just how marketing activities are used in nonbusiness situations. The examples here do not cover all the different areas in which marketing activities are used. Keep in mind, too, that many nonbusiness organizations will not admit that they perform marketing activities. They assume that their ideas and services would lose value if the public thought that they were "marketed."

The marketing of public health services

Although the core element of health services in the United States is provided by physicians and clinics in private enterprise for profit, the delivery of health services to the general public is provided in part by nonbusiness sectors of the economy.

Administrators in health organizations perform many tasks that can be related to marketing: they determine the health needs of clients, construct a distribution system to make services available, obtain financial support, and alter the values and behavior of the public. After determining clients' health needs, administrators must delineate target markets and develop a health services marketing mix. To implement the program, they must coordinate product, distribution, promotion, and price. As they develop a strategy, they must consider such environmental variables as legal, political, technological, and social forces. *Health services marketing* ranges from supporting causes—such as antismoking and antidrug programs—to providing physicians' services and hospital care. To gain a better understanding of health services marketing, we will examine the marketing of family planning. The nonbusiness organization Planned Parenthood is one health service that provides physicians' services, counseling, and birth control devices. See the Application on page 657.

The marketing of political candidates

Political candidate marketing focuses on the ideas, philosophies, personality, and appearance of an individual seeking an elective office. The candidate attempts to gain the support—and votes—of a target public. Candidates for the U.S. Senate commonly spend over one million dollars on advertising, personal appearances, and opinion research during a campaign. Political advertising has a strong direct effect on voting behavior in certain situations. Data show, for example, that voter turnout for low-in-

Application

Planned Parenthood's Marketing Strategy

Planned Parenthood's marketing strategy involves all marketing decision variables. The product centers on ideas (the concept of planning births); clinical services (physical examinations); and goods (birth control pills and devices). Planned Parenthood is organized around the philosophy that individuals should be free to determine the size of their families. Therefore, its marketing activities are not as concerned with goods as with the idea of getting people to take action in family planning.

Planned Parenthood's services are distributed through facilities in convenient locations. The distribution of information about family planning is coordinated through promotional activities. Promotion includes publicity (public service announcements by radio, television, and newspapers) as well as advertising and personal communication with groups and individuals. It also uses direct mail advertising in the form of simple brochures, both to obtain members (financial donations) and to encourage people to use the services.

Pricing is one of Planned Parenthood's most visible marketing activities, and its policy differs from that of most business enterprises. Although the agency must charge clients in order to provide services and to obtain government grants, its rates are figured on a sliding scale. A client's income determines the price paid for a service. If the client has no income, the service may be provided without charge. The client's own statement of income is accepted, and no attempts are made to run credit checks or to turn delinquent accounts over to collection agencies. Expenses that are not covered through clients' fees must be paid for through grants and donations.

Obviously, Planned Parenthood needs good public relations if it is to have the most effective impact on a community. Brochures and other forms of communication—when effective and inoffensive—serve a definite need. By informing the public about services relating to adoption, infertility, and early detection of cancer, the agency can promote the noncontroversial programs that most people support.

volvement contests such as state legislature races relates positively to the level of advertising in the campaign.[19]

The public is generally aware that political candidates are performing marketing activities by using persuasion to convince citizens to exchange votes for some desired political goal (better government, lower taxes, improved programs, and so on). A political candidate's marketing strategy concerns all elements of the marketing mix. As in other marketing situations, selecting a target market and developing the marketing mix are two main tasks in strategy development. See the Application on p. 658 for an example of how campaign planners used market research to "sell" their candidate. Implementation requires day-to-day tactics to channel the overall marketing strategy toward securing the desired marketing objective.

The product concept is very important in political candidate marketing. Often, an issue, personal feature, or campaign theme provides the product image. In a way, the candidate becomes the product—he or she is a concept, a person who promises to provide a service, and a physical being that can be seen. Individual voters "buy" the candidate who seems to offer the most benefits.

19. Michael L. Rothschild, "Political Advertising: A Neglected Policy Issue in Marketing," *Journal of Marketing Research,* Feb. 1978, pp. 63–67.

Application

Campaign Planners Use Market Research to Set Strategy

In a fairly recent presidential race, a campaign research report was prepared for a candidate in a three-person race. The candidate's marketing research consisted of eight hundred personal interviews with registered voters in North Carolina. Studies were conducted in other key states. The development of a marketing strategy followed easily after target markets were defined and components of the marketing mix were suggested. These were the conclusions of the campaigners.

1. At this point, the campaign should concentrate on his strengths. (He is not trying to develop consensus but only to win a plurality of the vote.) While there do not appear to be any outstanding target groups, we suggest concentrating on the following:

   Women. Extra television time (using the national spots locally) during morning, afternoon, and late-evening hours.
   Older voters. Communicate with these people about the prosperity issues— no recessions, new jobs and industry, and social security.
   Low-income voters. Our opponents do well here and, by all rights, should not. Again, communicate with voters about prosperity issues.

2. Given the present rate of change in voters' preferences, we do not feel that our candidate can overtake the other two candidates. In order to win, something new and dramatic must happen. Discounting any favorable, exogenous event, we recommend that he schedule a half-day appearance in the state—if North Carolina is considered one of the essential states. A rousing speech to Asheville residents and a side trip to Charlotte (and/or Hickory, if possible) are recommended. The speech and all press comments should be about job training and economic prosperity. Steer completely clear of foreign aid, Medicare, and federal aid to education.

3. We realize that demands on the candidate's time are enormous. We also realize that we have already suggested he visit two other states—Kentucky and Maryland. We feel, however, that he still does not stand a good chance of carrying North Carolina unless the target groups above are hit hard and visits are made to the state.

Campaign planners accepted the research findings that the candidate could not win in North Carolina, and so they directed the resources and personal visits to Kentucky and Maryland. This paid off in that victory was achieved in one of these states. Many potential political candidates use opinion surveys to avoid the costly efforts of conducting a campaign when they have only a limited chance of success. A political candidate gathers market information for the same reasons that a business uses research to try to avoid launching products that fail—neither wants to waste resources.

Promotion is used to convince voters to support, campaign for, and vote for the candidate. Advertising usually involves the following media: outdoor displays, television, radio, newspapers, and direct mail. Publicity is managed carefully through press conferences, press releases about key issues, and public appearances that create newsworthy stories. Special events, such as fund-raising dinners, raise revenue to cover campaign expenses. Distribution is coordinated closely with promotion. The candidate's availability and personal exposure permit voters to have direct contact with the product. Some voters want to touch, shake hands with, or talk with the candidate.

The price of supporting and voting for a candidate tends to be a value exchange rather than a financial cost. The price for support could be the cost of going to the polls and voting. It might involve campaign donations or volunteer work. Other exchanges include the voters' acceptance of the candidate's values or the candidate's modification of values to satisfy the target public.

Summary

Nonbusiness marketing includes marketing activities conducted by individuals and organizations to achieve some goal other than normal business goals. Nonbusiness marketing uses most concepts and approaches that are applied to business situations. An exchange situation exists when individuals, groups, or organizations possess something that they are willing to give up in an exchange.

While the chief beneficiary of a business enterprise is its owner, the beneficiary of a nonbusiness enterprise should be its clients, its members, or its public at large. The goals of a nonbusiness organization reflect its unique philosophy or mission. Some nonbusiness organizations have very controversial goals, but many organizations exist to further generally accepted social causes.

The marketing objective of nonbusiness organizations is to obtain a desired response from a target market. Developing a nonbusiness marketing strategy consists of defining and analyzing a target market and creating and maintaining a marketing mix. In nonbusiness marketing the product is usually an idea or service. Distribution is not involved as much with the movement of goods as with the communication of ideas and the delivery of services, which results in a very short marketing channel. Independent wholesalers usually are not available to control distribution activities. Promotion is very important in nonbusiness marketing; personal selling, sales promotion, advertising, and publicity are all used to communicate ideas and inform people about services. Price is more difficult to define in nonbusiness marketing because of opportunity costs and the difficulty of quantifying values exchanged.

It is important to control nonbusiness marketing strategies to reach desired goals. Control is designed to identify what activities have occurred in conformity with marketing strategy and to take corrective actions where any deviations are found.

Important terms

Nonbusiness marketing
Negotiation
Persuasion
Target public
Client publics

General publics
Opportunity cost
Health services marketing
Political candidate marketing

Discussion and review questions

1. Compare and contrast the controversial aspects of nonbusiness versus business marketing.
2. Relate the concepts of product, distribution, promotion, and price to a marketing strategy aimed at preventing drug abuse.

3. How should nonbusiness marketers address the problem of values? For example, do marketers have a responsibility to make value judgments about a social cause that is being marketed?
4. Discuss the impact of publics in developing nonbusiness marketing programs. What are some methods for isolating target publics?
5. Is there any guarantee that nonbusiness organizations are oriented more toward clients, publics, or consumers than business organizations are? Why or why not?
6. What are the differences among clients, publics, and consumers? What is the difference between a target public and a target market?
7. Much nonbusiness marketing seeks to increase the acceptability of a social idea or practice in a target group. In addition, nonbusiness marketers usually market ideas and services rather than physical products. What are the merits of the following social causes: (a) gun control, (b) prevention of venereal disease, (c) antismoking campaigns, and (d) efforts to increase usage of seat belts? Why might you hesitate to market them vigorously?
8. How do marketing concepts relate to society? How do exchanges structure our everyday lives?
9. What is the function of control in a nonbusiness marketing strategy?
10. What is the role of the environment in nonbusiness marketing? How does it relate to implementation of marketing strategy?
11. Discuss the development of a marketing strategy for a university. What marketing decisions should be made in developing strategy?
12. How do nonbusiness organizations set prices?
13. Apply the marketing channel concept to hospitals, universities, state parks, and forest fire prevention.

Cases

Case 21.1

River County Nursing Home

River County Nursing Home, located in a central Iowa city of 95,000 people, is a rural nursing home for the public. Although fees are charged, taxes pay for most of the services provided. The new administrator of the nursing home, Mr. Bill Setten, is concerned about the community's negative image of and attitudes toward the nursing home. One year ago the local newspaper had published a series of articles about how poorly residents were treated. A young reporter had infiltrated the staff as a dishwasher and exposed what he felt was unfair treatment of residents. Mr. Setten considered the newspaper reports biased because the young reporter had no previous experience in nursing homes and did not know how to judge specific work tasks as they relate to the operation of a nursing home.

Mr. Setten contacted a marketing professor at the local state university and asked if a marketing research class would conduct a survey to investigate local public opinion toward River County Nursing Home. Mr. Setten hoped to use the results of the survey to improve the image of and public support for River County Nursing Home.

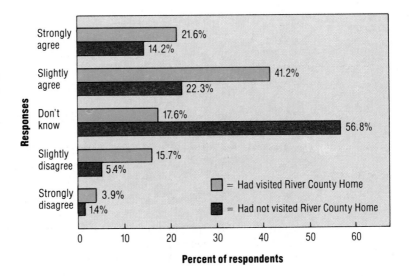

Figure 21.8
Results when people from the surrounding communities were asked "Does the River County Nursing Home meet the needs of the county?"

Responses

- Strongly agree: 21.6%, 14.2%
- Slightly agree: 41.2%, 22.3%
- Don't know: 17.6%, 56.8%
- Slightly disagree: 15.7%, 5.4%
- Strongly disagree: 3.9%, 1.4%

☐ = Had visited River County Home
■ = Had not visited River County Home

Percent of respondents

The professor agreed to conduct the research (a) to obtain an accurate picture of the attitudes of the River County residents toward the River County Nursing Home, and (b) to determine through what channels these residents have received the information on which their attitudes are based.

Any organization, especially a service organization such as a nursing home, must maintain good communications with the public. Attitudes of the county residents are vital for adopting new programs, phasing out obsolete ones, or merely in approving tax support for additional funding required to maintain services at the present level. Therefore, the research attempted to uncover unknown attitudes or possible negative attitudes by surveying a random sample of the River County residents.

Marketing research students constructed a questionnaire and conducted telephone interviews with 576 River County residents. They proportioned the sample to prefixes used by the telephone company. So, if 50 percent of River County was assigned an 829-prefix, this was the percentage used in this study. The suffixes were obtained from random number tables. The telephone interviews revealed:

1. Among the respondents, 30.5 percent had visited the River County Nursing Home. They were better informed about the facility's policies and procedures than respondents who had not visited the nursing home. When the statement was made that River County Nursing Home meets the needs of the county, those who had visited the facility more strongly agreed than those who had not, as shown in Figure 21.8.

2. The data indicated that although over 90 percent of the sample who had not visited the home were aware of the River County Nursing Home, most people were uncertain about the quality of care or how well it served the community. Figure 21.8 indicates that 56.8 percent of those respondents who had not visited River County Nursing Home answered "don't know" to an item rating "Nursing home meets the needs of the county."

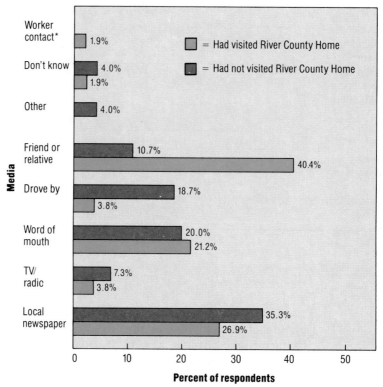

Figure 21.9
Media through which
rural respondents be-
came aware of the
River County Nursing
Home

Worker contact* 1.9%

= Had visited River County Home

Don't know 4.0%
1.9%

= Had not visited River County Home

Other 4.0%

Friend or relative 10.7%
40.4%

Drove by 18.7%
3.8%

Word of mouth 20.0%
21.2%

TV/ radic 7.3%
3.8%

Local newspaper 35.3%
26.9%

Media

0   10   20   30   40   50

Percent of respondents

*Worked there or a relative or friend worked there.

3. The four major sources of information about the facility were friend or relative (24.2 percent); newspaper (19.5 percent); driving by the location (19.3 percent); and word of mouth (16 percent). Figure 21.9 shows the media through which respondents became aware of the facility. Personal contact is the major opinion former, both positive and negative. Those who found out about the nursing home from a friend or relative held the widest spread of opinions as to quality and whether or not the facility met the county's needs. Apparently the newspaper's negative articles had little impact on people's opinions.

Figure 21.10 indicates what respondents think River County Nursing Home does for its residents. Note that persons of all ages are admitted to the nursing home. Most residents are ill and do need medical care; maintenance care is an important service.

Questions for discussion
1. How might River County Nursing Home inform the public about the service it provides and the quality of its care? Consider the major sources of information on which opinions about the nursing home are based.
2. Compare and contrast what respondents think the nursing home does and what it actually does. (Look at Figure 21.10.)
3. Suggest a marketing strategy for River County Nursing Home to improve its image and correct its identity in the county.

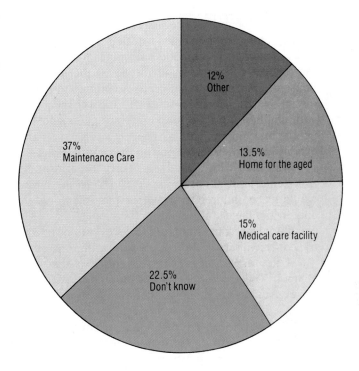

Figure 21.10
What respondents think the River County Nursing Home does for its residents

37%
Maintenance Care

12%
Other

13.5%
Home for the aged

15%
Medical care facility

22.5%
Don't know

Case 21.2

Developing a New Poison Prevention Program[20]

It is a sad fact that in the United States over 700,000 children each year are the victims of accidental poisoning. The most tragic aspect of this situation is that 95 percent of the children poisoned are under adult supervision at the time, and so most incidents could be averted if the parents of the victims took ordinary safety precautions.

These statistics have prompted the development of poison control centers based in hospitals throughout the country. Brokaw Hospitals's Poison Control enter in Normal, Illinois, is typical of many of these facilities; it is coordinated through the hospital's pharmacy department. Brokaw Hospital's pharmacy staff decided they had an obligation to do more than merely be efficient in treating poisonings as they occurred. They felt that active attempts had to be made to lower the number of accidental poisonings within the community. This resolution among the pharmacy staff initiated a movement to investigate the basic problem and implement an effective marketing strategy to prevent poisonings.

Through marketing research, it became apparent to the staff members that children will eat or drink just about anything. It found that most poisoning agents are located in and around the house. The most commonly

20. The material in this case was contributed by Terry Trudeau, Associate Professor, Department of Pharmacy Practice, Howard University College of Pharmacy and Pharmacal Sciences, Washington, D.C. Reprinted by permission of the author.

ingested substances were plants, household cleaning products, aspirin, vitamins, and cold medicines—in that order. Four basic factors were identified as leading to childhood poisonings: (1) accessibility of toxic agents, (2) the inquisitive nature of children, (3) the limited environment of a small house or apartment, which causes children to play near poisonous products (as in the kitchen or basement), and (4) the problems of communicating with children who are too young to understand the dangers of toxic products. The communications aspect was seen as the most crucial factor in establishing an effective poison prevention program.

Presented with these facts, Terry Trudeau, director of the Poison Control Center, set about the task of developing an educational program that would teach children to avoid poisons and would instruct teachers and parents in the basics of poison prevention. This year-round program drew on existing ideas concerning poison prevention, and innovation was provided by staff members and professionals within the community.

A key aspect of poison prevention is the use of an easily recognized symbol. The traditional symbol for poison has been the skull and cross-bones, but research shows that children often are attracted to this symbol because it suggests "playing pirate for fun" rather than danger and death. Symbols developed by other poison control centers in the United States also were ruled out, since none had sufficient impact to inspire a year-round poison prevention effort. It was decided to develop a new poison symbol that would be easily recognized yet repellent to all age groups.

Designed with the help of the Illinois State University art staff, the symbol shown in Figure 21.11 has proven effective in tests with preschool and kindergarten children, Named "SIOP," the symbol is a stylized green snake against a bright orange, circular background. The symbol is effective both because of its colors (green has proved to be repellent, and orange is among the hues that are first recognized) and because of its shape (the circle is the first shape children recognize and remember). The SIOP symbol comes with an adhesive band that is long enough to fit around most household products. The band is also orange, a color not frequently used in commercial packaging, thus increasing the visibility of the symbol from all angles.

SIOP was designed to be as frightening to children as possible. This improves the chances that children will stay away from the symbol, even though they might not know what it stands for. However, the key to making the SIOP symbol an effective deterrent to all children was the creation of an educational program that conditions children to stay away from SIOP. Whenever and wherever children see the fanged green snake, they are taught to say, "No! SIOP!" (which is *poison* spelled backward). In addition, "Happy," the Poison Prevention Dog (see Figure 21.12), was developed to serve as a foil to SIOP and teach children to avoid poisons. Happy barks whenever SIOP is near. This theme of good versus bad is carried throughout the program.

A wide range of materials was developed for the prevention program. For children, the program includes a story pamphlet, Happy's song, Happy's activity book, Happy and SIOP puppets, and Happy buttons, Frisbees, balloons, iron-on decals, and posters. For teachers and parents

Figure 21.11
Educational pamphlet with the SIOP symbol
Source: Terry Trudeau, R.Ph., M.B.A., Associate Professor, Department of Pharmacy Practice, Howard University College of Pharmacy and Pharmacal Sciences, Washington, D.C.

A PARENT AND TEACHER'S INTRODUCTION TO THE

SIOP

POISON PREVENTION PROGRAM

there are pamphlets about poison-proofing the home, poisonous plants, the use of Ipecac syrup, a SIOP poison first-aid chart, and SIOP poison prevention rules. Audio-visual shows, educational lesson plans, and SIOP stickers have also been developed.

The launching of the SIOP program coincided with the beginning of the National Poison Prevention Week. Much publicity was used in the area, including newspaper, television, and radio coverage of the new poison symbol. Distribution of the first SIOP symbols was accomplished by using the telephone company's mailing list to send SIOP stickers and a guide to poison prevention to each family in the county. Educational materials were delivered to all kindergartens, nursery schools, and day care centers. Teachers received a packet of materials containing instructions for using the program year-round. Each child received an activity book, a story pamphlet, a poison prevention guide, and a button. Additional materials were supplied on request.

Today, when new residents arrive in the community, they are sent SIOP stickers and pamphlets. The materials are also distributed in the school system. Natural childbirth classes, the public health department, and Brokaw's pediatrics ward help perpetuate the program by distributing SIOP materials. Grants from such organizations as the Jaycees and the

Figure 21.12
Educational pamphlet
with the "Happy"
symbol
*Source: Terry Trudeau,
R.Ph., M.B.A., Associate
Professor, Department
of Pharmacy Practice,
Howard University Col-
lege of Pharmacy and
Pharmacal Sciences,
Washington, D.C.*

THE
LEGEND OF

™

HAPPY
THE POISON
PREVENTION DOG

Brokaw Hospital Service have enabled free distribution of the materials. Many pharmacists serve on a speaker's bureau to present educational programs to schools and PTA groups.

Terry Trudeau and others involved in developing the SIOP program feel greatly rewarded since the program's inception. Among the many awards received is a federal grant from the Consumer Product Safety commission for continued service in poison prevention. Most important has been the decrease in the number of calls made to the center. And the severity of reported poisonings has diminished to an appreciable extent.

New ways are constantly sought to improve and spread the SIOP program and materials. The program is now becoming a national effort; Texas and Louisiana have adopted it, and other areas are in the process of doing so. Worldwide recognition is extending the program, with inquiries coming from as far as Australia and France. New ideas about distribution and target markets (such as industrial chemicals) are being explored in an effort to develop a single, comprehensive poison prevention program for the country. While accidental poisonings will always be a problem, the SIOP program is taking positive steps to prevent them.

Questions for discussion

1. Describe the basic elements of the marketing strategy used in the SIOP program.

2. Terry Trudeau took several university courses in marketing while obtaining his master's degree and developing the SIOP program. How do you think these marketing courses helped Trudeau in developing SIOP?

3. How could the SIOP symbol be promoted successfully as the national symbol for poison prevention?

22

International Marketing

Objectives

To define the nature of international marketing.

To describe the use of international marketing intelligence in understanding foreign markets and environments.

To examine the potential of marketing mix standardization among nations.

To describe adaptation of the international marketing mix when standardization is impossible.

To look at ways to become involved in international marketing activities.

Astute marketing, innovative design, and good timing have enabled Nike to become one of the top-selling athletic-shoe manufacturers in the United States. At one time, Nike was a small importer of a single Japanese running shoe line. Today, the company manufactures all types of athletic shoes, for competition or recreation. The company also markets sports apparel and accessories including running shorts and shirts, tennis clothes, warm-up suits, and athletic bags. Top athletes in arenas all around the world wear the Nike "swoosh" trademark.

In 1980, Nike's sales surpassed those of Adidas, even though Adidas is decades older, is more than twice Nike's size, and has very strong brand identity. Nike sales increased from $14.1 million in 1976 to over $880 million in 1983. The U.S. market experienced its first slow-growth year in 1981, after the jogging craze of the late 1970s leveled off.

To counter the domestic market slowdown, Nike is launching a worldwide marketing offensive to increase foreign sales, which could possibly equal its $400-million volume in the United States. The company anticipates that Europe and Japan will account for most of the growth abroad. Attempts are also being made to position Nike in markets throughout Asia, Latin America, and Africa. In 1983, foreign revenues were over $90 million, up $50 million from the year before.

Nike is planning to attack the European market by using professional and world class athletes as promotional tools. Though running is not presently as popular in Europe as it is in this country, Nike anticipates a running boom. Running shoes make up 43 percent of Nike's sales. Additionally, Nike is not ignoring the largest sport-shoe category in Europe, soccer. Nike management realizes that Adidas and Puma have a stronghold on the soccer market. Between them, they outfit 90 percent of professional soccer players, have many players under promotional contracts, and have a great deal of clout at the retail level. To strengthen its marketing efforts in Europe, Nike is buying out its distributors in Great Britain and Austria. To avoid stiff Common Market tariffs, Nike plans to supply the European market through its recently constructed factory in Ireland.

In Japan, Nike should benefit from its American name. The Japanese like American-made goods and view them as quality products. Nike has allied itself with Nissho-Iwai Corporation, Japan's sixth-largest trading company, giving Nike instant credibility and access to valuable contacts within the Japanese business community. The two companies formed Nike Japan Corporation. The company will concentrate on marketing top-of-the-line shoes, since Nike already has part of the low-priced sports-shoe market in Japan (see advertisement in Figure 22.1).[1]

1. "Fitting the World in Sport-Shoes," *Business Week*, Jan. 25, 1982, p. 73; Nike, Inc., *1983 Annual Report;* "Nike Looks to Europe," *Sales and Marketing Management*, March 15, 1982, p. 92; and Victor F. Zonana, "Jogging's Fade Fails to Push Nike Off Track," *Fortune*, Nov. 1, 1982, pp. 158–162.

Figure 22.1 Nike advertisement in Japanese
Source: Courtesy Nike Japan Corporation.

Management of international marketing activities such as those at Nike requires an understanding of marketing variables and a grasp of the environmental complexities of foreign countries. In many cases, serving a foreign target market requires more than minor adjustments of marketing strategies.

International marketing is marketing activities performed across national boundaries.[2] The planning and control of such marketing activities can differ significantly from marketing within national boundaries. This chapter looks closely at the unique features of international marketing and at the adjustment of marketing mixes when businesses cross national boundaries.

We begin by examining the levels of commitment and the degree of involvement of American firms in international marketing. Then we analyze several examples to see why international marketing intelligence is necessary when a firm is moving beyond its domestic market. Next, we analyze marketing mix standardization and adaptation. Finally, we describe a number of ways of getting involved in international marketing.

2. Vern Terpstra, *International Marketing*, 3rd ed. (Hinsdale, Ill.: Dryden Press, 1983), p. 4:

Table 22.1 Revenues and profits of the fifteen largest U.S. multinationals (in millions)

Company	Foreign Revenue	Total Revenue	Foreign as % of Total	Foreign Operating Profit[a]	Total Operating Profit[a]	Foreign as % of Total
Exxon	$69,386	$97,173	71.4%	$2,208	$4,343	50.8%
Mobil	37,778[b]	60,969[b]	62.0	880[c]	1,380[c]	63.8
Texaco	31,118	46,986	66.2	833[c]	1,281[c]	65.0
Standard Oil Calif	16,957	34,362	49.3	404[c]	1,377[c]	29.3
Phibro-Salomon	16,600	26,703	62.2	218[c]	337[c]	64.7
Ford Motor	16,526	37,067	44.6	460[c]	−658[c]	P/D
IBM	15,336	34,364	44.6	1,646[c]	4,409[c]	37.3
General Motors	14,376	60,026	23.9	−107[c]	963[c]	D/P
Gulf Oil	11,513	28,427	40.5	300[c]	900[c]	33.3
E I du Pont de Nemours	11,057	33,223	33.3	488[f]	1,491[f]	32.7
Citicorp	10,865	17,814	61.0	448[c]	723[c]	62.0
Intl Tel & Tel[d]	9,824	21,922	44.8	851	1,194	71.3
BankAmerica	8,051	14,955	53.8	253[e]	389[e]	65.0
Chase Manhattan	6,207	10,171	61.0	215	307[c]	70.0
Dow Chemical	5,544	10,618	52.2	143	356	40.2

[a]Unless otherwise indicated. [b]Includes other income. [c]Net income. [d]Includes proportionate interest in unconsolidated subsidiaries or investments. [e]Income before security gains or losses. [f]Profit before interest and after taxes.
Source: *Forbes,* July 4, 1983, p. 114. Reprinted by permission.

International marketing involvement

Among the technological developments needed to support international marketing, worldwide transportation and communication systems are critical. Equally important is the ability to analyze different environments and determine market potentials in foreign countries. Before international marketing could achieve its current level of importance, enterprises with resources had to develop an interest in expanding their businesses beyond national boundaries. Global marketing strategies then developed to increase profits and to increase the size and influence of firms.

The term *multinational enterprise* refers to the organizational aspects of firms that have operations or subsidiaries located in many countries to achieve a common goal. Often the parent firm is based in one country, and the multinational company is developed by cultivating production, management, and marketing activities in other countries. Such petroleum companies as Exxon, Shell, and Mobil are multinational companies that have worldwide operations. International Telephone and Telegraph (ITT) is a multinational giant with subsidiaries in many countries. ITT subsidiaries that operate on a multinational basis include Avis (car rentals), Telecommunication Equipment (a manufacuring division in Europe), Sheraton (an international motel and hotel chain), and World Communications (foreign telephone and telegraph operations).

Table 22.1 lists fifteen U.S.-based multinationals that depend on foreign revenue for a significant proportion of their total operating profit. Look at the contribution of foreign profit as a percentage of total profit to see how important international involvement can be. As Table 22.1 indicates, Exxon earned almost 51 percent of its 1982 profit on foreign opera-

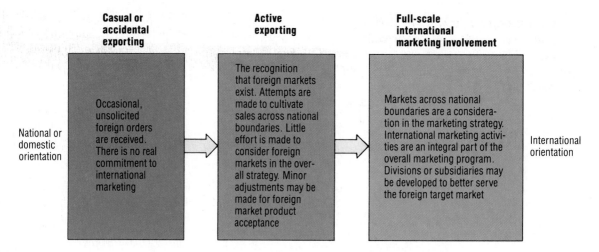

Casual or accidental exporting	Active exporting	Full-scale international marketing involvement

National or domestic orientation

Occasional, unsolicited foreign orders are received. There is no real commitment to international marketing

The recognition that foreign markets exist. Attempts are made to cultivate sales across national boundaries. Little effort is made to consider foreign markets in the overall strategy. Minor adjustments may be made for foreign market product acceptance

Markets across national boundaries are a consideration in the marketing strategy. International marketing activities are an integral part of the overall marketing program. Divisions or subsidiaries may be developed to better serve the foreign target market

International orientation

Figure 22.2 Levels of involvement in international marketing
Source: From International Marketing *by Vern Terpstra, pp. 10–12. Copyright © 1983 by Holt, Rinehart and Winston, Inc. Reprinted by permission of Holt, Rinehart and Winston, CBS College Publishing.*

tions. In recent years, many of these firms could not operate at an acceptable profit without their foreign operations.

Multinational firms have gained acceptance as they have become more sensitive to national customs, to labor-relations practices, and to governments' desires for capital, tax revenues, employment, technical skills, foreign exchange, and access to new products from abroad.[3] Multinational firms, often regarded as exploiters of impoverished countries, could prove to be the very tool by which those countries build prosperity. South Korean multinationals are paving roads in Nigeria; Filipino firms operate all over the globe.[4]

The level of involvement in international marketing covers a wide spectrum (see Figure 22.2). "Casual or accidental exporting" represents the lowest level of commitment to international marketing. "Active exporting" concentrates on selling activities to gain foreign market acceptance of existing products. "Full-scale international marketing involvement" means that top management recognizes the importance of developing international marketing strategies to achieve the firm's goals.

Foreign opportunities should be assessed as potential target markets. Once an international marketing commitment is made, management should design marketing strategies to serve foreign markets. This commitment should be based on the firm's goals and resources and on its ability to cross national boundaries to find the best market opportunities. As shown in Figure 22.3, Anaconda-Ericsson Information Systems has made a definite commitment to international marketing. Ericsson has found marketing opportunities in over one hundred countries.

3. Lawrence G. Franko, "Multinationals: The End of U.S. Dominance," *Harvard Business Review,* Nov.–Dec. 1978, pp. 94–95.
4. David A. Heenan and Warren J. Keegan, "The Rise of World Multinationals," *Harvard Business Review,* Jan.–Feb. 1979, pp. 101–102.

Where in the world are people getting the most advanced information systems today?

It takes an experienced company to meet the worldwide demand for advanced information systems.

And nobody can meet that demand better than Ericsson.

Today Ericsson offers one of the broadest, most advanced lines of information products and services in the world, all over the world. From Saudi Arabia and Australia to Mexico and the United States.

More than 100 countries in all.

And wherever you find Ericsson you find a total commitment to customer needs. We have made that commitment in the United States by establishing a sales and service network, backed by our own manufacturing plants, research laboratories, training centers, maintenance and diagnostic centers.

If you're wondering who in the world can meet your information

systems needs, the answer is simple. For your information, it's Ericsson.

Anaconda-Ericsson Information Systems, 7465 Lampson Avenue, P.O. Box 938, Garden Grove, CA 92642, (714) 895-3962.

In Canada, Anaconda-Ericsson Communications Inc., 1799 Argentia Road, Mississauga, Ontario L5N 3B1, (416) 821-9400.

For your information. It's **ERICSSON**

International marketing intelligence

Most American firms perceive international markets as differing in some ways from domestic markets. International markets can be analyzed in terms of culture, institutions, and behavior of buyers. Table 22.2 lists types of statistical data that may help marketers to ascertain whether buyers are able, willing, and authorized to purchase products. To determine the willingness to buy, marketers must investigate buying behavior and environmental influences.

Gathering secondary data (see Table 22.2) should be the first step in analyzing a foreign market. Sources of statistical data include U.S. government publications, international organizations such as the United Nations,

Table 22.2 Types of statistical data used to define international markets

A. Cultural
1. Distribution of the population by educational level
2. Distribution of the population by occupations
3. Distribution of the population by religions

B. Economic
1. Total personal income
2. Per capita income
3. Income distribution
4. Disposable income
5. Discretionary income
6. Distribution of wealth
7. Availability of consumer credit
8. Availability of capital
9. Rate of savings and capital formation

C. Demographic
1. Population size, persons and families
2. Age distribution
3. Regional distribution
4. Urban versus rural distribution
5. Marriage rate
6. Rate of family formation
7. Birth rate
8. Death rate
9. Distribution of families in various stages of the family life cycle

D. Geographic
1. Climate—temperate, jungle, arid
2. Elevation above sea level—lowlands, highlands
3. Access to transportation—seacoast, waterways, railroads, highways
4. Terrain—hilly, flat, rocky, grassland, forest

E. Technological
1. Advances in the physical sciences— applicable to agriculture, manufacturing, transportation, communication
2. Advances in the social sciences— applicable to governmental and political practices, business organization practices

F. Commercial (manufacturers, retailers, wholesalers, and service industries)
1. Number
2. Types
3. Location
4. Labor conditions
5. Employment record
6. Stage of technical advancement, especially mechanization, automation
7. Rate of growth
8. Management progressiveness

Source: Adapted from Gordon E. Miracle and Gerald S. Albaum, *International Marketing Management* (Homewood, Ill.: Richard D. Irwin, 1970), pp. 190–191. © 1970 by Richard D. Irwin, Inc. Reprinted by permission of Gordon E. Miracle.

governments of foreign countries, and international trade organizations. (The Application on p. 676 discusses certain types of information available through the Department of Commerce.) The shortcomings of secondary data include (1) unavailability of detailed data, (2) unreliability of some secondary data, and (3) lack of comparability and currency of available data.[5] Also, some statistics can be misleading. Although China has 23 percent of the world's population, it accounts for less than 1 percent of the trade.[6]

To overcome these shortcomings, marketers may need primary data if they are to understand consumers' buying behavior in the country under investigation. Figure 22.4 illustrates the services of an international marketing research firm. After analyzing secondary and primary data, marketers should plan a marketing strategy. Finally, after market entry, review and control will result in decisions to withdraw from the foreign market, to continue to expand operations, or to consider additional foreign markets.

5. David T. Kollat, Roger D. Blackwell, and James F. Robeson, *Strategic Marketing* (New York: Holt, 1972), pp. 175–176.
6. "China Trade's Harsh Realities," *China Trade Report*, February 1978, p. 2.

Marketers may need to adjust techniques of collecting primary data for foreign markets. Attitudes toward privacy, unwillingness to be interviewed, language differences, and low literacy rates can present serious research obstacles. In a bicultural country, such as Canada, a national questionnaire that uses identical questions is impossible because of cultural and language differences. In Bolivia and in most areas of Africa, where the literacy rate is low, self-administered questionnaires are out of the question.

In many developing countries, purchasing behavior is based on unique symbols. It may be necessary to investigate basic patterns of social behavior, values, and attitudes to plan a final marketing strategy. Pepsodent's promise of white teeth was unsuccessful in Southeast Asia, for example, where it is a habit to chew betel nuts, and black or yellow teeth are symbols of prestige.[7] Primary research should have uncovered this cultural characteristic before the product was launched, so that the marketing strategy could have been modified.

Environmental forces in international markets

A detailed analysis of the environment is an absolute necessity before a company enters foreign markets. If a marketing strategy is to be effective across national boundaries, the complexities of all environments must be understood. In this section, we will see how the cultural, social, economic, technological, political, and legal forces in other countries differ from those found in the United States.

By moving from the analysis of individual behavior to the more abstract level of institutions, we can better understand foreign markets. Institutions serve as structures for achieving some necessary societal goals. For example, *social institutions* include the family, education, religion, health, and recreational systems. *Economic institutions* are made up of producers, wholesalers, retailers, buyers, and other organizations that

7. David Ricks, Marilyn Y. C. Fu, and Jeffrey Arpan, *International Business Blunders* (Columbus, Ohio: Grid, 1974), p. 15.

Application

Standard Instrumentation Becomes Successful Through Exporting

One way to increase sales volume without adding additional product lines and personnel is through exporting. The Department of Commerce has an International Trade Administrative branch that offers services and information such as the following: locating foreign buyers for U.S. exporters; promoting products and services of U.S. industries in publications; providing valuable information on foreign importing companies, agents, end-users, and other potential customers; and assisting companies in determining if a foreign company will be interested in a specific export proposal. The Department of Commerce also puts out a text, *A Basic Guide to Exporting,* for additional information on foreign markets. It is recommended that a company investigate the full potential of a market before seeking help, or be prepared to pay for the market research involved.

Standard Instrumentation, in West Virginia, is a good example of a smaller company that achieved success through exporting abroad. The company exports specialized coal-testing instrumentation. After the oil crisis abated, the domestic coal-testing market was growing slowly. The company was able to foresee a potential world market ten times greater than the present domestic market. The decision was made to go international.

The advertisements aimed at end-users yielded limited response; so the company advertised to reach independent sales agents. The large number of qualified leads received was then verified through a Department of Commerce publication, *World Trader's Data Report.*

The strategy to sell overseas through sales agents was superior. Distributors were reluctant to carry the stock because of its low-volume, high-ticket quality. It is also very difficult to provide follow-up service to end-users. Standard Instrumentation management was selective in choosing agents, and has not had to travel abroad. Today, export sales represent over 50 percent of Standard Instrumentation's total sales volume.

Source: Based on Steven Mintz, "Standard Instrumentation Gives Exports Full Measure," *Sales and Marketing Management,* Sept. 12, 1983, pp. 52–56.

produce, distribute, and purchase products. ***Political and legal institutions*** include public agencies, laws, courts, legislatures, and government bureaus.

Cultural forces

Concepts, values, and tangible items, such as tools, buildings, and foods, make up *culture*. Culture is passed on from one generation to another; in a way, it is the blueprint for acceptable behavior in a given society.

When products are introduced into one nation from another, acceptance is far more likely if there are similarities between the two cultures. For example, almost 40 percent of Italians are overweight, and only recently have many of them started to do something about it. Today Weight Watchers International, a U.S. firm, is offering Italians a sensible approach to dieting. As Italians' cultural values toward weight approach American values, then Weight Watchers' products will become more successful.[8]

The connotations associated with body motions, greetings, colors, numbers, shapes, sizes, and symbols vary considerably across cultures. A few examples are shown in Table 22.3. For multinational marketers, these cultural differences have implications that pertain to product development, personal selling, advertising, packaging, and pricing.

8. Elizabeth Guider, "WW Is Getting Fat on Italy's Diet Craze," *Advertising Age,* Nov. 23, 1981, p. 66.

Table 22.3 Cultural variations on selected dimensions

Areas	Body Motions	Greetings	Colors	Numbers	Shapes, Sizes, Symbols
Japan	Pointing to one's own chest with a forefinger indicates one wants a bath. Pointing a forefinger to the nose indicates "me."	Bowing is the traditional form of greeting.	Positive colors are in muted shades. Combinations of black, dark gray, and white have negative overtones.	Positive numbers are 1, 3, 5, 8. Negative numbers are 4, 9.	Pine, bamboo, or plum patterns are positive. Cultural shapes, such as Buddha-shaped jars should be avoided.
India	Kissing is considered offensive and not seen on television, in movies, or in public places.	The palms of the hands are placed together and the head is nodded for greeting. It is considered rude to touch a woman or shake hands.	Positive colors are bold colors such as green, red, yellow, or orange. Negative colors are black and white if they appear in relation to weddings.	To create brand awareness, numbers are often used as a brand name.	Animals such as parrots, elephants, tigers, or cheetahs are often used as brand names or on packaging. Avoid sexually explicit symbols.
Europe	Raising only the index finger signifies a person wants two items. When counting on one's fingers, "one" is often indicated by thumb, "two" by thumb and forefinger.	It is acceptable to send flowers in thanks for a dinner invitation, but do not send roses (associated with sweethearts) or chrysanthemums (associated with funerals).	Generally, white and blue are considered positive. Black often has negative overtones.	Numbers of 3 or 7 are usually positive. 13 is a negative number.	Circles are symbols of perfection. Hearts are considered favorably at Christmas time.
Latin America	General arm gestures are used for emphasis.	The traditional form of greeting is a hearty embrace followed by a friendly slap on the back.	Popular colors are generally bright or bold yellow, red, blue, or green.	Generally, 7 is a positive number. Negative numbers are 13, 14.	Religious symbols should be respected. Avoid national symbols such as flag colors.
Middle East	The raised eyebrow facial expression indicates "yes."	The word "no" must be mentioned three times before it is accepted.	Positive colors are brown, black, dark blues, and reds. Pink, violets, and yellows are not favored.	Positive numbers are 3, 7, 5, 9, while 13, 15 are negative.	Prefer round or square shapes. Avoid symbols of 6-pointed star, raised thumb, or Koranic sayings.

Sources: James C. Simmons, "A Matter of Interpretation," *American Way,* April 1983, pp. 106–111; and "Adapting Export Packaging to Cultural Differences," *Business America,* Dec. 3, 1979, pp. 3–7.

Figure 22.5
Oil of Olay advertise-
ment used in Saudi
Arabia
Source: Olay Company.

A society's attitude toward the body also affects international marketers. The American custom of patting a child on the head would not be considered a sign of friendliness in the Orient, where the head has been held
sacred. In contrast, the illustration of feet is regarded as despicable in
Thailand.

An international marketer also must know a country's customs regarding male-female social interaction. Advertising that is based on the togeth-
erness of married life could backfire in Japan and Western Europe, where
husbands and wives often lead separate lives. In Italy it is unacceptable for
a salesman to call on someone's wife if the husband is not home. In Thailand, Listerine's television commercials, which portrayed boy-girl roman-
tic relationships, were unacceptable. The Oil of Olay advertisement in Figure 22.5 ran with a woman's photograph in all Persian Gulf countries
except Saudi Arabia. In that country, the use of women's photographs in
advertisements is prohibited. Thus, the line drawing in the figure was
substituted.

Social forces
Marketing activities are primarily social in purpose; therefore, they are structured by the institutions of family, religion, education, health, and recreation. In every nation, these social institutions can be identified. By finding major deviations in institutions among countries, one can gain insights into the adaptation of marketing strategy. For example, in a Bic Pen television commercial in Mexico, viewers see a mummy break out of his sarcophagus, using the pen—the pen keeps on writing. Research indicated that Mexican viewers would not believe a serious "torture" test, so the commercial pokes fun at a test while making a point about durability. Because of different socialization, U.S. viewers would probably believe a serious torture test.[9]

Economic forces
Economic differences dictate many of the adjustments that must be made in marketing across national boundaries. Most prominent are those adjustments caused by standards of living, availability of credit, discretionary buying power, income distribution, national resources, climate, and conditions that affect transportation.

In terms of the value of all products produced by a nation, the United States has the largest *gross national product (GNP)* in the world. GNP is an overall measure of the nation's economic standing, but it does not take into account the concept of GNP in relationship to population (GNP per capita). The aggregate GNP of a very small country such as Abu Dhabi (population 100,000) is low, but the GNP per capita (a measure of the *standard of living* is very high. The Soviet Union has the second highest GNP in the world, but it ranks twenty-third in GNP per capita.[10] This fact means that the average Soviet citizen has less discretionary income than do citizens in countries with higher GNPs per capita. Knowledge about per capita income, aggregate GNP, credit, and the distribution of income provides general insights into market potential.

Opportunities for international marketers are not limited to those countries with the highest incomes. For example, Litton's microwave cooking products are selling in Mexico and Brazil, international markets in which microwave ovens have had no impact.[11]

Some nations are progressing at a markedly faster rate than they were a few years ago, and these countries—especially in Latin America, Africa, and the Middle East—have tremendous market potential for specific products. However, marketers must understand the political and legal environment before they can convert buying power into actual demand for specific products. For example, Coca-Cola is boycotted in most of the Middle East for political reasons, but Coke has found a haven in Egypt, where sidewalk peddlers and space-strapped shop owners keep the soft drink in full view.[12]

9. Debra Beachy and Tad Gage, "Bic Is First Univas Stop in Mexico," *Advertising Age,* Nov. 16, 1981, p. 84.
10. *Statistical Yearbook 1978* (New York: United Nations, 1979), p. 742.
11. Dennis Chase, "Litton Expanding Microwave in Latin America," *Advertising Age,* Aug. 11, 1980, p. 12.
12. John R. Thompson, "Foreign Marketers Rush into Sadat's Open Arms," *Advertising Age,* Aug. 18, 1980, p. 52.

Technological forces   Much of the marketing technology used in North America and other industrialized areas may be ill suited for developing countries. Mass marketing techniques, for instance, are too complex and expensive to create the jobs needed to absorb the rapidly expanding labor forces of developing countries.[13] When supermarkets are introduced in developing countries, they are limited to high- and middle-income areas because there is too little buying power in low-income neighborhoods; therefore, they do not create many jobs. An institution that caters to the needs of the masses in North America becomes exclusive in developing countries, bringing benefits to those who least need them.[14]

In addition, the export of technology of strategic importance to the United States may require U.S. Department of Defense approval before foreign sales can occur. For example, the Soviet Union wanted to buy Boeing 747 jet engines, made by General Electric, for Russian airlines. When GE applied for the license to export these jet engines to the Soviet Union, its request was denied,[15] Yet General Electric was licensed to sell these same engines to Israel for use on jet fighters.

Political and legal forces   A country's political system, national laws, regulatory bodies, national pressure groups, and courts all have great impact on international marketing. A government's policies toward public versus private enterprise, consumers, and foreign firms influence marketing across national boundaries. As Figure 22.6 suggests, international marketers should consider insuring against the unexpected acts of a government. For example, France forced International Telephone and Telegraph to sell a profitable operation in telephone equipment and telecommunications to the government a few years ago. When France elected a socialist president, many firms feared nationalization.[16]

Figure 22.7 summarizes categories of political and legal risk in international markets. Political experts individually rated sixty-one countries according to (1) a nation's likelihood of restricting business and (2) its relative political instability. A "high" ranking on either scale means a greater than 30-percent chance of regime change or further business restriction. "Low" is defined as less than 20-percent risk. Thus China, whose regime is considered secure, nonetheless rates high on restrictions.

Differences in political and governmental ethical standards are illustrated by what the Mexicans call *la mordida*—"the bite." The use of payoffs and bribes is deeply entrenched in many governments. Since U.S. trade and corporate policy—as well as U.S. law—prevents direct involvement in payoffs and bribes, American firms may have a hard time competing with foreign firms that engage in this practice. Some U.S. firms that

13. Frank Meissner, "Rise of Third World 'Demands' Marketing Be Stood on Its Head," *Marketing News*, Oct. 6, 1978, p. 1.
14. Ibid.
15. "How Do You Get Approval from the U.S. Department of Defense to Export Sophisticated Products and Technology, For Example?" *Marketing News*, Oct. 6, 1978, p. 10.
16. Carolyn Pfaff and Peter Dewhirst, "U.S. Interests in France Threatened," *Advertising Age*, May 25, 1981, p. 64.

WHAT YOU NEED TODAY IS AN INTELLIGENT FOREIGN POLICY.

If you do business in foreign countries you have a lot more on your mind than mere profits and losses.

Political changes beyond your control can add a shocking degree of risk to normal business life. Governments can suddenly and arbitrarily confiscate your property, block currency or repudiate contracts, to mention only a few of the many challenges encountered by businesses operating around the world.

Furthermore, every overseas enterprise runs its own unique set of potential risks, which vary according to what it does and where it's located.

That's why our Political Risk Insurance for Overseas Investors, as well as our new Comprehensive Export Credit Insurance, can be invaluable. We know that when you do business abroad just about anything can go wrong. And since 1974 the AIG Insurance Companies have developed the kind of policies needed to help protect exporters, investors, contractors and virtually anyone else who has business interests just about anywhere in the world.

Today, no other insurance company comes close to matching the amount of political risk insurance we write. No one else offers such high limits of coverage. No one else has as many underwriters and claims specialists solely dedicated to this unique field. Nor does any other company have a staff as experienced in writing insurance to help protect you against the hidden dangers that may be inherent in your particular situation.

In short, no other underwriter, private or government, can offer greater flexibility in meeting all of your overseas insurance needs.

To learn more, just contact AIG Political Risk, Inc.

You'll see why it's smart to let an insurance company help take the intrigue out of foreign investment.

ONCE AGAIN THE ANSWER IS AIG.

THE AIG COMPANIES: American International Underwriters, American Home Assurance Co., Commerce and Industry Insurance Co., National Union Fire Insurance Company of Pittsburgh, Pa., American International Life Assurance Co., North American Managers, New Hampshire Insurance Co. and over 250 other companies operating around the world to meet your insurance needs.

Figure 22.6 Advertisement for political risk insurance
Source: Courtesy of the American International Group, Inc.

refuse to make payoffs are forced to hire local consultants, public relations firms, or advertising agencies—which results in indirect payoffs. The ultimate decision about whether to give small tips or gifts where they are customary must be based on a firm's code of conduct; it is illegal for U.S. firms to attempt to make large payments or bribes to influence policy decisions of foreign governments.

Strategic adaptation of marketing mixes

Strategic planning for marketing was discussed in detail in Chapter 18. You can plot competitive strengths and market attractiveness on a two-dimensional matrix. Such a device is most useful for analyzing products within the international context. As Figure 22.8 illustrates, each axis is a linear combination of factors that can be used to define a country's attractiveness from a market view and to assess the level of competition in that country.[17]

To develop a matrix, marketers must gather data for a specific product and country. Research style, methodology, and approach to data gathering vary by company.[18] Ford Tractor, for example, employs four basic

17. Gilbert D. Harrell and Richard O. Kiefer, "Multinational Strategic Market Portfolios," *MSU Business Topics,* Winter 1981, p. 6.
18. David C. Pring, "Filling Overseas Gaps," *Advertising Age,* Oct. 26, 1981, pp. 5–18.

	High	Medium	Low
High	El Salvador Iran Zaire	Philippines	Bolivia
Medium	Libya Kenya Nicaragua Nigeria Zambia	Argentina Dominican Republic Canada Ecuador, Egypt Indonesia Morocco, Pakistan Panama, Peru Portugal Tunisia, Turkey Yugoslavia	Brazil Colombia India, Italy Israel South Africa Spain Thailand Uruguay Zimbabwe
Low	China	Algeria Greece Mexico Saudi Arabia Venezuela	Australia Austria Chile, Denmark Finland, France Ireland Japan Kuwait Malaysia Netherlands New Zealand Norway Singapore South Korea Sweden, Taiwan United Kingdom United States West Germany

Political instability (vertical axis) — Restrictions on business (horizontal axis)

Figure 22.7 Sixty countries classified by instability and restrictions on business
Source: From Bob Donath, "Handicapping and Hedging the Foreign Investment," Industrial Marketing, February 1981, p. 58. Based on the Frost and Sullivan (F&S) World Political Risk Forecast.

variables—market size, market growth rate, government regulation, and economic and political stability—as measures of country attractiveness.[19] Ford Tractor executives estimate potential market share, product fit (how well a product fits a particular market need), contribution margin (profit per unit), and market support (quality and quantity of personnel in marketing, technical, and service areas) to assess competitive strength.[20]

Once a U.S. firm determines foreign market potentials and understands the foreign environment, it develops and adapts its marketing mix. Creating and maintaining the marketing mix is the final step in developing the international marketing strategy. Only if foreign marketing opportunities justify the risk will a company go to the expense of adapting the marketing mix. Of course, in some situations new products are developed for a specific country. In these cases, there is no existing marketing mix and no extra expense to consider in serving the foreign target market.

19. Harrell and Kiefer, "Multinational Strategic Market Portfolios," p. 8.
20. Ibid.

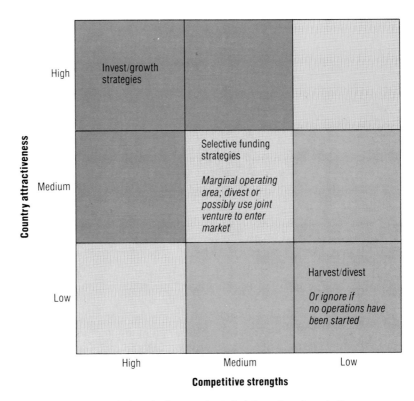

Figure 22.8 Matrix for plotting products in international marketing
Source: Adapted from Gilbert D. Harrell and Richard O. Kiefer, "Multinational Strategic Market Portfolios," MSU Business Topics, Winter 1981, p. 7. Reprinted by permission.

Product and promotion

As shown in Figure 22.9, there are five possible strategies for adapting product and promotion across national boundaries: (1) keep product and promotion the same worldwide; (2) adapt promotion only; (3) adapt product only; (4) adapt both product and promotion; and (5) invent new products.[21]

Keep product and promotion the same worldwide
This strategy attempts to use in the foreign country the product and promotion that have been developed for the U.S. market. This approach seems desirable wherever possible, since it eliminates the expenses of marketing research and product redevelopment. Despite certain inherent risks that stem from cultural differences in interpretation, exporting advertising copy does provide the efficiency of international standardization.

Germany and Austria are independent and distinct in national characteristics, but because of their proximity and language similarities, the same newspapers, television, and other media are targeted to both nations.[22]

21. Adapted from Warren G. Keegan, "Multinational Product Planning: Strategic Alternatives," *Journal of Marketing,* Jan. 1969, pp. 58–62; and Philip Kotler, *Marketing Management: Analysis, Planning and Control,* 5th ed. (Englewood Cliffs, N.J.: Prentice-Hall, 1984), pp. 455–456.
22. Keegan, "Multinational Product Planning," p. 11.

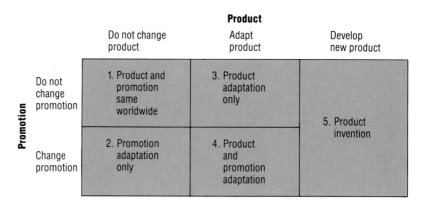

Product

	Do not change product	Adapt product	Develop new product
Do not change promotion	1. Product and promotion same worldwide	3. Product adaptation only	5. Product invention
Change promotion	2. Promotion adaptation only	4. Product and promotion adaptation	

(left axis label: **Promotion**)

Figure 22.9 International product and promotion strategies
Source: Adapted from Warren J. Keagan, "Multinational Product Planning Strategic Alternatives," Journal of Marketing, *January 1969, pp. 58–62. Published by the American Marketing Association.*

Unilever blundered when it sold one of its detergents under the Radion brand name in Germany and under a different brand name in Austria. Unilever failed to take advantage of the fact that Austrian consumers were exposed to its German advertising, because the product (Radion) could not be found in Austrian retail stores.

Adapt promotion only
This strategy leaves the product basically unchanged but modifies its promotion. This approach may be necessary because of translation problems with advertising copy. Although Pepsi-Cola has been able to introduce its product unchanged in foreign markets, the promotional messages have been altered. In Germany "Come alive with Pepsi" was translated clumsily as "Come out of the grave with Pepsi."[23] An American airline operating in Brazil advertised plush "rendezvous lounges" on its jets; only later did it learn that "rendezvous" in Portuguese quite specifically means a room that is rented for sexual purposes. Promotional adaptation is a low-cost modification compared with the cost of redeveloping engineering and production and the cost of physically changing products.

Adapt product only
Soap and detergent manufacturers have adapted their products to local water conditions and washing equipment without changing their promotion. Household appliances have been altered to use different types of electricity. The basic assumption in modifying a product without changing its promotion is that the product will serve the same function under different conditions of use.

A product may have to be adjusted for legal reasons. Japan has some of the most stringent automobile emission requirements in the world. These requirements mean that American automobiles that cannot meet the emission standards cannot be marketed in Japan.

23. Ricks et al., *International Business Blunders*, p. 12.

Sometimes, products must be adjusted to overcome social and cultural obstacles. Jello introduced a powdered gelatin mix that failed in England because the English were used to buying gelatin in a jelled form. Resistance to new technology is frequently based on attitudes and ignorance about the nature of a product. It is often easier to change the product than to overcome technological biases.

Adapt both product and promotion

When a product serves a new function in a foreign market, then both the product and its promotion need to be altered. In Europe, greeting cards provide a space for senders to write messages in their own words; and European greeting cards are cellophane wrapped, which also calls for a product alteration. Both the product and promotion must be changed because the product's function is different. Adaptation of both product and promotion is the most expensive strategy discussed thus far, but it should be considered if the foreign market appears large enough.

Create new products

This strategy is selected when existing products cannot meet the needs of a foreign market. General Motors has developed an all-purpose, jeeplike motor vehicle that can be assembled in underdeveloped nations by mechanics with no special training. The vehicle is designed to operate under varied conditions; it has standardized parts and is inexpensive. Colgate-Palmolive has developed an inexpensive, all-plastic, hand-powered washing machine that has the tumbling action of a modern automatic machine. The product was invented for households in underdeveloped countries that have no electricity. Strategies that involve the invention of products are often the most costly, but the payoff can be great.

Distribution and pricing

Decisions about the distribution system and pricing policies are important in developing an international marketing mix. Figure 22.10 illustrates different approaches to these decisions.

Distribution

A firm can sell its product to an intermediary that is willing to buy from existing marketing channels in the United States, or it can develop new international marketing channels. It must consider distribution both between countries and within the foreign country.

In determining distribution alternatives, the existence of retail institutions and wholesalers that can perform marketing functions between and within nations is one major factor. If a foreign country has a segmented retail structure consisting primarily of one-person shops or street vendors, it may be difficult to develop new marketing channels for such products as packaged goods and foods.

If the product being sold across national boundaries requires service and information, then control of the distribution process is desirable. Caterpillar sells over half its construction and earth-moving equipment in foreign countries. Because it must provide services and replacement parts, Caterpillar establishes its own dealers in foreign markets. Regional sales

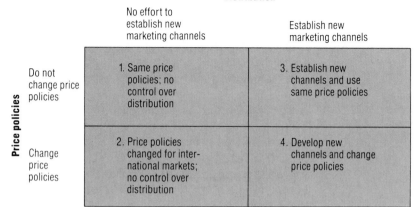

Distribution

	No effort to establish new marketing channels	Establish new marketing channels
Do not change price policies	1. Same price policies; no control over distribution	3. Establish new channels and use same price policies
Change price policies	2. Price policies changed for international markets; no control over distribution	4. Develop new channels and change price policies

Price policies (vertical axis label)

Figure 22.10   Strategies for international distribution and pricing

offices and technical experts are also available to support local dealers. A manufacturer of paintbrushes, on the other hand, would be more concerned about agents, wholesalers, or other manufacturers that would facilitate the product's exposure in a foreign market. Control over the distribution process would not be so important for that product.

Several international marketing channels are available to American businesses (see Figure 22.11). These marketing channels are not all-inclusive, nor do they exist for all product types. Marketers planning to sell products across national boundaries must work with available intermediaries or bridge the gaps.

Pricing

Prices are usually different for foreign markets than for home markets. The increased costs of transportation, supplies, taxes, tariffs, and other expenses necessary to adjust a firm's operations to international marketing can raise prices. A key decision is whether the basic pricing policy will change (as discussed in Chapter 15). If it is a firm's policy not to allocate fixed costs to foreign sales, then lower foreign prices could result.

American drug manufacturers have been accused of selling drugs in foreign markets at low prices (without allocating research and development costs) while charging American customers high prices that include all research and development expenses. The sale of U.S. products in foreign markets—or vice versa—at lower prices (when all costs have not been allocated or when surplus products are sold) is called *dumping*. Dumping is illegal in many countries if it damages domestic firms and workers.

A cost-plus approach to international pricing is probably the most common method used because of the compounding number of costs necessary to move products from the United States to a foreign country. Of course, our discussion of pricing policies in Chapter 15 pointed out that understanding consumer demand and the competitive environment is a necessary step in selecting a price.

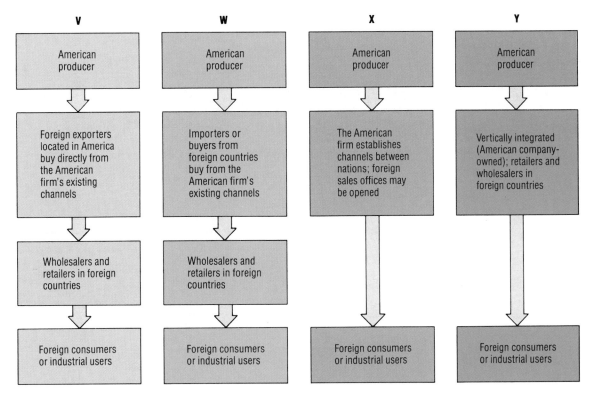

Figure 22.11   Examples of international channels of distribution for an American firm

The price charged in other countries is also a function of foreign currency exchange rates. Fluctuations of the international monetary market can change the prices charged across national boundaries on a daily basis. There has been a trend toward greater fluctuation (or float) in world money markets. A sudden variation in the exchange rate—which occurs when a nation devalues its currency, for example—can have wide-ranging effects on consumer prices. U.S. devaluation of the dollar in the 1970s resulted in lower prices for American products in foreign countries and higher prices for imports in the United States.

Standardization of international marketing mixes

Most of the environmental and marketing mix decisions discussed thus far have emphasized differences among nations in developing the marketing program. If it is possible to standardize the marketing mix for at least a major region of the world, the potential economic payoffs for a standardized product, distribution, promotion, or price are great. If a universally acceptable marketing strategy could be developed, it would decrease the expense and effort involved in designing a separate marketing mix for each foreign country. Figure 22.12 illustrates the standardization of the marketing mix for a Kellogg's cereal in French-speaking countries. Admittedly, gross differences in legal and political systems, economic development, and social institutions make standardization difficult.

Figure 22.12
Advertisement from a standardized international marketing approach
Source: © 1983 Kellogg Company. KELLOGG'S and KRISPI are registered trademarks of Kellogg Company.

Despite real differences among nations, a number of multinational companies are finding significant gains in an integrated approach to marketing strategy. Avis Rent-A-Car has used "We Try Harder," with minor variations, throughout Europe, as well as in the United States. Radio and television stations carry advertising messages across national boundaries. For example, Radio Luxembourg reaches buyers in France, Belgium, Switzerland, and the Netherlands.[24]

24. Saul Sands, "Can You Standardize International Marketing Strategy?" *Journal of the Academy of Marketing Science,* Spring 1979, pp. 130–131.

Table 22.4 Index of marketing mix standardization among European operations of selected multinational corporations (percent)[a]

Elements of Marketing Programs	Standardization		
	Low	Moderate	High
Total marketing program	27	11	63
Product characteristics	15	4	81
Brand name	7	0	93
Packaging	20	5	75
Retail price	30	14	56
Basic advertising message	20	6	71
Creative expression	34	4	62
Sales promotion	33	11	56
Media allocation	47	10	43
Role of sales force	15	10	74
Management of sales force	17	10	72
Role of middlemen	13	7	80
Type of retail outlet	34	7	59

[a]Percent = total number of paired countries showing comparisons (rounded off).

Source: Adapted by permission of the *Harvard Business Review*. An exhibit from "How Multinationals View Marketing Standardization," by Ralph Z. Sorenson and Ulrich E. Wiechmann (May/June 1975), p. 39. Copyright © 1975 by the President and Fellows of Harvard College; all rights reserved.

A survey of leading multinational corporations based mainly in the United States does indicate that, for consumer products at least, standardization can be performed on a wide, regional basis.[25] Leading multinationals, such as General Foods, Coca-Cola, and Procter & Gamble, which operate in Europe (England, Germany, France, Italy, Belgium, Holland, Sweden, and Switzerland) and the United States, have indicated that a high degree of standardization was possible for those two regions.[26]

Table 22.4 highlights that brand name and product characteristics are easy to standardize. Media allocation, retail outlet, or price may be more difficult. Multinational corporations indicate that if possible it is highly desirable to have uniformity in brands, packages, and labeling. Competitive advantages can be gained through standardization because of increased mobility on the part of consumers. In the end, however, the degree of similarity among environmental and market conditions determines the feasibility of standardization.

25. Ralph Z. Sorenson and Ulrich E. Wiechmann, "How Multinationals View Marketing Standardization," *Harvard Business Review*, May–June 1975, pp. 38–54.
26. Ibid.

Developing international marketing involvement

The level of commitment to international marketing is a major variable in deciding what kind of involvement is appropriate. A firm's options range from occasional exporting to expanding overall operations (production and marketing) into other countries. (The Application on p. 691 mentions a new device that should facilitate international marketing involvement for some organizations.) Here, we will examine exporting, licensing, joint ventures, and direct ownership as approaches to marketing across national boundaries.

Exporting

Exporting represents the lowest level of commitment to international marketing and the most flexible approach. The firm may find an exporting middleman that can perform most marketing functions associated with selling to other countries. This approach entails minimum effort and cost. Modifications in packaging, labeling, style, or color may be the major expenses in adapting a product. There is limited risk in using export agents and merchants, since there is no direct investment in the foreign country.

Export agents bring buyers and sellers from different countries together; they collect a commission for arranging sales. Export houses and export merchants purchase products from different companies, then sell them to foreign countries. They are specialists at understanding customers' needs in foreign countries.

Foreign buyers from companies and governments provide a direct method of exporting and eliminate the need for a middleman. Foreign buyers encourage international exchange by contacting domestic firms about their needs and about the opportunities available in exporting. Domestic firms that want to export with a minimum of effort and investment seek out foreign importers and buyers.

Licensing

When potential markets are found across national boundaries—and when production, technical assistance, or marketing know-how is required—*licensing* is an alternative to direct investment. The exchange of management techniques or technical assistance are primary reasons for licensing agreements. The licensee (the owner of the foreign operation) pays commissions or royalties on sales or supplies used in manufacturing. An initial down payment or fee may be charged when the licensing agreement is signed. Licensing is an attractive alternative to direct investments when the political stability of a foreign country is in doubt or when resources are unavailable for direct investments. Sometimes, unique political and economic conditions may make licensing the only alternative.

Joint ventures

In international marketing, a *joint venture* is a partnership between a domestic firm and foreign firms or governments. Joint ventures are often a political necessity because of nationalism and governmental restrictions on foreign ownership.

Joint ventures are especially popular in industries that call for large investments, such as the extraction of natural resources or automobile manufacturing. Control of the joint venture can be split equally, or one party

Application

Small U.S. Manufacturers May Become Multinationals Through Export Trading Companies

Following World War II, the United States' export sales of manufactured goods dominated the foreign marketplace. In the 1970s, the industrial systems of Western Europe and Japan entered the competition and eroded U.S. domination in the world and domestic markets.

The Export Trading Company Act (ETC) of 1982 allows U.S. companies to be more competitive in foreign markets. U.S. export activities are dominated by large multinational companies; four-fifths of all U.S. manufactured exports are produced by only two hundred U.S. firms. Department of Commerce estimates indicate that more than twenty thousand smaller companies could profitably sell manufactured products abroad. The ETC Act is designed to encourage these businesses to export their products.

The strongest of the foreign competitors is Japan, which achieved success through the organization and integration of technological and industrial strengths, the financial capability of banks, government assistance, and the expertise of international marketing companies. The ETC Act has two features that will create U.S. trading teams with expertise similar to that in Japan. First, the act permits banks to invest in ETCs. The information system of international banks will provide strategic planning, data processing, legal services, and political and foreign contacts. A second feature of the act is the protection it provides against antitrust actions; export activity that affects only foreign commerce will not be viewed as violating U.S. antitrust laws.

Investments for locating markets, distributors, consultants, customs agents, and export sales representatives are expensive and risky to the smaller company acting alone. With the ETC Act, services to meet these needs exist on a "one-stop basis" and at lower costs and reduced risks.

Source: Based on Tom Becker and James L. Porter, "Selling, ETC," *Sales and Marketing Management*, July 4, 1983, pp. 44, 46.

may control decision making. Once a joint venture succeeds, there is an increasing trend toward nationalism and toward expropriating or purchasing foreign shares of the enterprise. On the other hand, a joint venture may be the only available means to enter a foreign market. American construction firms bidding for business in Saudi Arabia, for example, have found that joint ventures with Arab construction companies gain local support among the handful of people who make the decisions.

Direct ownership

Once a company makes a long-term commitment to marketing in a foreign nation that has a promising political and economic environment, *direct ownership* of a foreign subsidiary or division is a possibility. Although most discussions of foreign investment concern only manfacturing equipment or personnel, the expenses of developing a separate foreign distribution system can be tremendous. The opening of retail stores in Europe, Canada, or Mexico can require a large investment in facilities, research expenditures, and management costs.

A wholly owned foreign subsidiary may be allowed to operate independently of the parent company so that management can have more freedom to adjust to the local environment. Cooperative arrangements are developed to assist in marketing efforts, production, and management. A wholly owned foreign subsidiary may export products to the home nation. Some American automobile manufacturers import into the United States cars built by their foreign subsidiaries. A foreign subsidiary offers important tax, tariff, and other operating advantages. One of the greatest advantages is the cross-cultural approach. A subsidiary usually operates under foreign management, so it can develop a local identity. The greatest danger in such an arrangement comes from political uncertainty—a firm may lose its foreign investment.

Summary

Marketing activities performed across national boundaries are usually significantly different from domestic marketing activities. International marketers must have an in-depth awareness of the foreign environment. The marketing strategy ordinarily is adjusted to meet the needs and desires of foreign markets.

Global marketing strategies are developed to expand a business beyond national boundaries and to achieve a corporate goal of long-term growth. Marketers must understand the complexities of the international marketing environment before they can formulate a marketing mix. Environmental aspects of special importance include cultural, social, economic, political, and legal forces. Cultural aspects of the environment that are most important to international marketers include customs, concepts, values, attitudes, morals, and knowledge. Social institutions influence human interaction. International marketers must understand such social institutions as family, religion, education, health, and recreation.

The most prominent economic forces that affect international marketing are those that can be measured by income and resources. Credit, buying power, and income distribution provide aggregate measures of market potential. The level of technology helps define economic development within a nation and indicates the existence of methods to facilitate marketing. The level of technology can dictate the structure of the marketing mix.

Political and legal institutions include the political system, national laws, regulatory bodies, national pressure groups, and courts. Foreign policies of all nations involved in trade determine how marketing can be conducted. Ethical standards and internal politics must be dealt with effectively; a firm must decide whether to use a domestic code of ethics or the foreign country's code of ethics.

After a country's environment has been analyzed, marketers must develop a marketing mix and decide whether to adapt product or promotion. Foreign distribution channels are nearly always different from domestic ones. The allocation of costs, transportation considerations, or the costs of doing business in foreign nations will affect pricing. Standardization of international marketing mixes is highly desirable, but most evidence indicates that standardization is regional at best.

There are several ways of getting involved in international marketing. Exporting is the easiest and most flexible international marketing method. Licensing is an alternative to direct investment. It may be necessitated by political and economic conditions. Joint ventures or partnerships are often appropriate when outside resources are needed or when there are governmental restrictions on foreign ownership. Direct ownership of foreign divisions or subsidiaries represents the strongest commitment to international marketing and involves the greatest risk.

Important terms

International marketing
Multinational enterprise
Social institutions
Economic institutions
Political and legal institutions
Culture

Gross national product (GNP)
Standard of living
Dumping
Licensing
Joint venture
Direct ownership

Discussion and review questions

1. How does international marketing differ from domestic marketing?
2. What must marketers consider before deciding whether or not to become involved in international marketing?
3. Why are the largest industrial corporations in the United States so committed to international marketing?
4. Why was so much of this chapter devoted to an analysis of the international marketing environment?
5. A manufacturer recently exported peanut butter with a green label to a nation in the Far East. The product failed because it was associated with jungle sickness. How could this mistake have been avoided?
6. Relate the concept of reference groups (Chapter 3) to international marketing.
7. How do religious systems influence marketing activities in foreign countries?
8. Which is more important to international marketers, a country's aggregate GNP or its GNP per capita? Why?
9. If you were asked to provide a small tip (or bribe) to have a document approved in a foreign nation where this practice was customary, what would you do?
10. In marketing dog food to Latin America, what aspects of the marketing mix would need to be altered?
11. What should marketers consider as they decide whether to license or to make a joint venture in a foreign nation?

Cases

Case 22.1

The Gillette Company[27]

Gillette is a major multinational corporation that develops and produces a wide variety of high quality products. The primary product lines include blades and razors, toiletries and grooming aids, writing instruments, Braun products (a German subsidiary), and small appliances. Gillette also sells other products—the single largest category of which is lighters. Originally

27. Many of the facts in this case are from Gillette Company, *1980 Annual Report,* p. 13; Bruce A. Mohl, "Sticking It to the Baron: Gillette Attacking Bic Where It Hurts—The Pen Market," *Boston Globe,* Jan. 19, 1982, pp. 43, 48; "Opportunism Pays," *Financial World,* Sept. 15, 1980, p. 39; Jamie Talon, "Yankee Goods—and Know-How—Go Abroad," *Advertising Age,* May 17, 1982, pp. M14–M16; and from *Forbes,* February 16, 1981, pp. 86–87.

Gillette's primary business was the manufacture and marketing of razors and blades. In 1926, King C. Gillette wrote of the safety razor, "There is no other article for individual use so universally known or widely distributed. In my travels, I have found it in the most northern town in Norway and in the heart of the Sahara Desert." Gillette's international marketing was initiated to fulfill the wants and needs of the blade-and-razor market.

Gillette began full-scale international marketing only four years after the company was founded. Expanding rapidly, Gillette successfully marketed high-quality shaving products at a reasonable price. Gillette has always tried to convince consumers to trade up for quality and sophistication, allowing the company to sell a more expensive product at a higher profit margin. Manufacturing operations are conducted at more than fifty facilities in twenty-six countries, and products are distributed in over two hundred countries. International operations contribute 60 percent of Gillette's sales and 52 percent of its operating profits.

Although some Gillette products are developed abroad, most are established in the United States and later adapted to meet the needs of the international market. The international market has been a fertile testing area for those few new products tried there, however. For instance, Gillette's original Cricket lighter had a flame adjuster with four moving parts. To accommodate the portion of the market that was more concerned with economy, Gillette redesigned Cricket, allowing the company to offer the lighter at a lower price. Gillette's new Cricket, with no flame adjuster, was introduced in Europe to monitor acceptance and has since been introduced to the domestic market.

Often Gillette products are marketed abroad under familiar brand names—Atra, Soft & Dri, and Eraser Mate are among them—but elsewhere Gillette creates new names for the same products: examples include Contour (Atra), Trinity (Soft & Dri) and Replay (Eraser Mate). The name Replay was developed because the concept of erasing is only understood in English-speaking countries. Products developed and launched in the United States can be successfully marketed in European countries. But cultural differences must not be overlooked. For example, many Europeans react negatively toward a product that inhibits perspiration, considering it unhealthy.

One product that Gillette successfully marketed in Europe was the TracII shaving system. Before entering this market, Gillette carefully developed a marketing plan to fit the European lifestyle. The TracII was renamed GII after research revealed that *trac*, in the romance languages, means fragile. Rodney Mills, executive vice president at Gillette International, said, "We wanted our target audience—men—to know that they could count on a good strong razor and not one that would easily break."

Gillette also had to develop a promotional campaign for the GII. In the United States, advertisements illustrated the concept of hysteresis—the first blade would raise the whisker and the second would cut before the whisker could retract. A sports analogy was utilized in Europe instead of the animated ads used in the United States. The sports ad conveyed the synchronization of movement and the end goal of scoring with a close shave. Mr. Mills observed that "this analogy gave us high impact advertising. For years our demand exceeded our supply." Gillette's market was young, active men. Techniques such as consumer receptivity and preference tests were utilized. "We used the successes of the U.S. advertising while adapting the message to individual cultures," said Mr. Mills. Gillette realized that the print media were more successful than the video because of the low number of television sets in many European countries.

Selective international diversification is part of Gillette's plan for achieving sustained profitable growth. Although generally successful, Gillette has experienced some failures. One example would be Gillette's seemingly logical acquisition of Sterilon hospital razors. Milton Glass, Gillette treasurer, remarked on their promotional error. "You don't advertise Sterilon razors to the patient. You know, "Ask for it by name when you enter the surgical ward' sort of thing." Gillette failed to recognize that industrial advertising cannot always be directed toward the end users.

One of Gillette's stronger operations is based in West Germany. Braun AG produces and sells a wide variety of consumer products including electric shavers, household appliances, photo products, hi-fi equipment, and clocks. In 1967 Braun was doing $67 million in business; after acquisition by Gillette, sales rose to $500 million. Despite the fact that sales rose in 1980, profits fell below the previous year's level. Major factors influencing profitability include the depressed state of the German economy and intense competition. Pressure on price decreased the opportunity for profitable growth.

Braun has been successful in the household appliance market. A significant upward trend was noted recently. Sales of the Multiquick food processing system. Braun juicer, and the Minipimer hand mixer rose markedly. Personal-care appliances have performed well, with sales of the hand-held hair dryer, the electric shaver, and Quick Style hair curler exceeding previous levels. Performance of photo products and hi-fi equipment has not achieved the expected levels.

In the past decade, Gillette established nine joint ventures with business partners in developing countries. Gillette's sales are increasing most rapidly in Asia, Africa, and Latin America. With a population of 3 billion, a growth rate of 3 percent annually, and a median age of 18, the emerging nations offer considerable opportunity. Due to the industrialization and urbanization of many Third World countries, the demand for personal grooming products and writing instruments is growing. Gillette is currently looking at expansion opportunities in Egypt and India, which have a combined population of approximately 750 million. Marketing management must decide on the best strategy for current international operations, such as Braun AG, as well as on expansion into new international markets.

Questions for discussion
1. Why has Gillette been successful in international marketing? Relate domestic success in the blade-and-razor market to international success in this market.
2. What does this chapter tell us about brand names? Why do you think Atra, Soft & Dri, and Eraser Mate use different brand names in some countries?
3. What benefits does Braun AG bring to Gillette? How could this German operation improve its profits?

4. Prior to the introduction of the TracII to the European market, what kind of research did Gillette perform? How could they have expanded research?

Case 22.2

Procter & Gamble's European Marketing[28]

During the 1950s and 1960s, Procter & Gamble expanded its operations to include a greater number of European countries. New operations were started in Switzerland, Holland, Italy, Germany, Greece, Austria, Spain, and Scandinavia. Today, consumers can purchase Procter & Gamble products in over 130 countries.

Despite worldwide economic problems and fluctuations of foreign currencies in relation to the U.S. dollar, Procter & Gamble's 1983–1984 net earnings from international operations amounted to $125 million last year, which is a 19 percent increase over the previous year. About a third of Procter & Gamble's total business is done outside the United States. One-third of its employees work in operations abroad, and a fifth of the company assets are outside the United States. Procter & Gamble's international operations continue to be important to the growth of the company.

Procter & Gamble's overall marketing plan is to offer superior products that meet consumer needs. Previously, Procter & Gamble products that were used in different European countries often were made of different formulas based on consumer preferences. Now, however, the company is changing its approach for its European markets. The product mix will now stress "multinational" or worldwide brands. For instance, Ariel laundry detergent has been reformulated to be accepted and used in all countries. Some of the products included in Procter & Gamble's international product mix include:

Pampers/Luvs diapers   Top Job laundry additive
Dash/Bold/Ariel laundry detergents   Head & Shoulders shampoo
Vizir liquid laundry detergent   Crest toothpaste

In addition to being more adventuresome, the new approach involves being much more aggressive. Procter & Gamble has been nicknamed the "sleeping giant" in Europe. This nickname may soon become obsolete. Advertising and promotional expenditures recently have skyrocketed. Five years ago, Procter & Gamble spent $19.2 million on promotion compared to an expenditure of $79.5 million last year. The company now plans to advertise heavily and establish more versatile advertisements. It wants some of its advertisements to be usable in several different European countries. Recently, one of its ad agencies used the same advertisement in France and Germany successfully. It also plans to use other promotional tech-

28. Portions of the information in this case are from Howard Sharman, "P&G on the Warpath Throughout Europe," *Advertising Age,* May 23, 1983, pp. 4, 54; Dagmar Mussey, "P&G Gambles on Shampoo Market in German Launch," *Advertising Age,* Oct. 3, 1983, p. 62; *Procter & Gamble's International Business,* 1980; and *The Procter & Gamble 1983 Annual Report.*

niques extensively. For example, trial size samples are being used to introduce Head & Shoulders shampoo in Germany. Finally, test marketing time has been cut drastically. Previously, Procter & Gamble test marketed products for many months. Vizir liquid detergent was launched nationally after being test marketed for a mere six months. Procter & Gamble is taking its foreign competitors by surprise and gaining market shares quite rapidly.

Questions for discussion

1. Evaluate Procter & Gamble's approach of marketing in several European countries in the same way.
2. Is the marketing environment fairly consistent across most European countries?
3. Through the use of back issues of the *Wall Street Journal,* find out the degree of variation in exchange rates in the currencies of countries mentioned in this case. Discuss how these fluctuations might affect Procter & Gamble's operations.

Careers
in Marketing

Some general issues

As noted in Chapter 1, between one-fourth and one-third of the civilian work force in the United States is employed in marketing-related jobs. Although there obviously are a multitude of diverse career opportunities in the field, the number of positions in its different areas varies. For example, millions of workers are employed in many facets of sales, but relatively few people work in advertising and marketing research jobs.

Many nonbusiness organizations now recognize that they do, in fact, perform marketing activities. For that reason, marketing positions are increasing in government agencies, hospitals, charitable and religious groups, educational institutions, and similar organizations. Traditionally, women have, for the most part, occupied marketing positions in retail organizations, but job opportunities for women are increasing rapidly in many other areas of marketing, especially in industrial sales.

Even though financial reward is not the sole criterion for selecting a career, it is only practical to consider how much you might earn in a marketing job. Table A.1 illustrates some top twelve salary positions for middle managers in marketing. Note that all of these careers relate directly to marketing. A national sales manager may earn from $50,000 to $75,000 or even higher salaries. Brand managers make $30,000 to $65,000 or a media manager could earn $30,000 to $55,000. Generally, entry-level marketing personnel earn more than their counterparts in economics, finance, and liberal arts, but not as much as people who enter accounting, chemistry, or

Table A.1 Top salary ranges for middle managers in marketing

Position	Salary Range
Corporate Strategic Market Planner	$55,000–$75,000
National Sales Manager	50,000– 75,000
International Sales	45,000– 60,000
Advertising Account Executive	40,000– 60,000
Sales Promotion	40,000– 55,000
Purchasing Manager	35,000– 55,000
Product/Brand Manager	30,000– 55,000
Media Manager	30,000– 50,000
Retail Sales	20,000– 40,000

engineering positions. Employees who advance to higher-level marketing positions often earn high salaries, and a significant proportion of corporate executives have held marketing jobs before attaining top-level positions.

Another important issue is whether or not you can enjoy the work associated with a particular career. Since you will spend almost 40 percent of your waking hours on the job, you should not allow such factors as economic conditions or status to override your personal goals as you select a lifelong career. Too often, people do not weigh these factors realistically. You should give considerable thought to your choice of a career, and you should adopt a well-planned, systematic approach to finding a position that meets your personal and career objectives.

After determining your objectives, you should identify the organizations that are likely to offer desirable opportunities. Learn as much as possible about these organizations before setting up employment interviews. Job recruiters are generally impressed with applicants who have done their homework.

A brief, clearly written letter of introduction is needed when making initial contact with potential employers by mail. After an initial interview you should send a brief letter of thanks to the interviewer. The job of getting the right job is important, and you owe it to yourself to take this process seriously.

The resume

The resume is one of the keys to achieving a good job. By stating your qualifications, experiences, education and career goals, the resume provides the opportunity for a potential employer to assess your compatibility with the job requirements. For the employer's benefit and the individual's the resume should be accurate and current.

To be effective, the resume can be targeted toward a specific position, as shown in Figure A.1. This document is only one example of an acceptable resume. The job target section is specific and leads directly to the applicant's qualifications for the job. Capabilities show what the applicant can do and that he or she has an understanding of the job's requirements. Skills and strengths should be highlighted in terms of how they relate to the specific job. The achievement section indicates success at accomplishing tasks or goals within the job market and at school. The work experience section includes educational background, which adds credibility to the resume but is not the major area of focus. The applicant's ability to function successfully in a specific job is the major emphasis.

Common suggestions for improving resumes include deleting useless information, improving organization, utilizing professional printing and typing, listing duties (not accomplishments), maintaining grammatical perfection, and avoiding an overly elaborate or fancy format.[1]

1. Tom Jackson, "Writing the Targeted Resume," *Business Week's Guide to Careers,* Spring 1983, pp. 26–27.

```
                              LORRAINE MILLER
                              2212 WEST WILLOW
                            BERKELEY, CA  10410
                               (416) 862-9169


      EDUCATION:  B.A. Arizona State University  1985  Marketing

      POSITION DESIRED:  PRODUCT MANAGER WITH AN INTERNATIONAL FIRM PROVIDING
                         FUTURE CAREER DEVELOPMENT AT THE EXECUTIVE LEVEL.

      QUALIFICATIONS:

        * communicates well with individuals to achieve a common goal

        * handles tasks efficiently and in a timely manner

        * knowledge of advertising, sales, management, marketing research, packaging,
          pricing, distribution, and warehousing

        * coordinates many activities at one time

        * receives and carries out assigned tasks or directives

        * writes complete status or research reports


      EXPERIENCES:

        * Assistant Editor of college paper

        * Treasurer of the American Marketing Association (student chapter)

        * Internship with 3-Cs Advertising, Berkeley, CA

        * Student Assistantship with Dr. Steve Green, Professor of Marketing,
          Arizona State University

        * Achieved 3.6 average on a 4.0 scale throughout college


      WORK RECORD:

      1984 - Present        Blythe and Co., Inc.
                               * Junior Advertising Account Executive

      1982 - Present        Assistantship with Dr. Steve Green
                               * Research Assistant

      1980 - 1982           The Men
                               * Retail sales and consumer relations

      1976 - 1980           Tannenbaum Trees, Inc.
                               * Laborer
```

Types of marketing careers

In considering marketing as a career, the first step is to evaluate broad categories of career opportunities in the areas of marketing research, sales, public relations, industrial buying, distribution management, product management, advertising, retail management, and direct marketing.[2] Keep in mind that the categories described here are not all-inclusive and that each of them encompasses hundreds of marketing jobs.

Marketing research

Clearly marketing research and information systems are vital aspects of marketing decision making. The information about buyers and environmental forces that is provided through research and information systems improves a marketer's ability to understand the dynamics of the marketplace and to make effective decisions.

2. Much of this information is adapted from *Occupational Outlook Handbook*, 1978–1979 edition, U.S. Department of Labor, Bureau of Labor Statistics, Bulletin 1955.

Marketing researchers gather and analyze data relating to specific problems. Marketing research firms are usually employed by a client organization, which could be a provider of goods or services, a nonbusiness organization, the government, a research consulting firm, or an advertising agency. The activities performed include concept testing, product testing, package testing, advertising testing, test-market research, and new product research.

A researcher may be involved in one or several stages of research, depending on the size of the project, the organization of the research unit, and the researcher's experience. Marketing research trainees in large organizations usually perform a considerable amount of clerical work, such as compiling secondary data from a firm's accounting and sales records and from periodicals, government publications, syndicated data services, and unpublished sources. A junior analyst may edit and code questionnaires or tabulate survey results. Trainees also may participate in primary data gathering by learning to conduct mail and telephone surveys, conducting personal interviews, and employing observational methods of primary data collection. As a marketing researcher gains experience, he or she may become involved in defining problems and developing hypotheses; designing research procedures; and analyzing, interpreting, and reporting findings. Exceptional personnel may assume responsibility for entire research projects.

Although most employers consider a bachelor's degree sufficient qualification for a marketing research trainee, many specialized positions require a graduate degree in business administration, statistics, or other related fields. Courses in statistics, data processing, psychology, sociology, communications, economics, and English composition are valuable preparations for a career in marketing research.

The U.S. Bureau of Labor Statistics indicates that marketing research provides abundant employment opportunity, especially for applicants with graduate training in marketing research, statistics, economics, and the social sciences. In general, the value of information gathered by marketing information and research systems will become more important as competition increases, thus expanding the opportunities for prospective marketing research personnel.

Salaries in marketing research depend on the type, size, and location of the firm as well as the nature of the positions. Generally, starting salaries are somewhat higher and promotions are somewhat slower than in other occupations requiring similar training. Experienced research personnel earn above-average salaries. In addition, the role of marketing in overall corporate planning is growing more important as companies seek marketing information for strategic planning purposes. Marketing research directors are reporting to higher levels of management than ever before, and the number of corporate vice presidents who receive marketing research as regular input in decision making has doubled in recent years.

Sales

Millions of people earn a living through personal selling. Chapter 13 defined personal selling as a process of informing customers and persuading them to purchase products through personal communication in an exchange situation. Although this definition describes the general nature of many sales positions, individual selling jobs vary enormously with respect to the type of businesses and products involved, the educational background and skills required, and the specific activities performed by sales personnel. Because the work is so varied, sales occupations offer a large number of career opportunities for people with a wide range of qualifications, interests, and goals. In terms of compensation, a sales career offers the greatest potential. The following sections describe what is involved in wholesale and manufacturer sales.

Wholesale sales

Wholesalers perform a variety of activities to expedite transactions in which purchases are intended for resale or are used to make other products. Wholesalers thus provide services to both retailers and producers. They can help match producers' products to the needs of retailers and can provide accumulation and allocation services that save producers time, money, and resources. Some activities associated with wholesaling include planning and negotiating transactions; assisting customers with sales, advertising, sales promotion, and publicity; handling transportation and storage activities; providing customers with inventory control and data processing assistance; establishing prices; and giving customers technical, management, and merchandising assistance.

The background needed by wholesale personnel depends on the nature of the product that is handled. A drug wholesaler, for example, needs extensive technical training and product knowledge and may hold a degree in chemistry, biology, or pharmacology. A wholesaler of standard office supplies, on the other hand, may find it more important to be familiar with various brands, suppliers, and prices than to have technical knowledge about the products. A new wholesale representative may begin a career as a sales trainee or may hold a nonselling job that provides experience with inventory, prices, discounts, and the firm's customers. A college graduate usually enters the sales force directly out of school. Competent salespersons also transfer from manufacturer and retail sales positions.

The number of wholesale sales positions is expected to grow about as fast as the average for all occupations through 1985. Earnings for wholesale personnel vary widely because commissions often make up a large proportion of their incomes.

Manufacturer sales

Manufacturer sales personnel sell a firm's products to wholesalers, retailers, and industrial buyers; they thus perform many of the same activities handled by wholesale salespersons. As is the case with wholesaling, the educational requirements for manufacturer sales depend largely on the type and complexity of the products and markets. Manufacturers of nontechnical products usually hire college graduates who have a liberal arts or business degree and provide them with training and information about the firm's products, prices, and customers. Manufacturers of highly technical products generally prefer applicants who have degrees in fields associated with the particular industry and market involved.

More and more sophisticated marketing skills are being utilized in industrial sales. Industrial marketing originally followed the commodity approach to complete a sale, whereby the right product is in the right place at the right time and for the right price. Now, there is a much stronger service attitude and emphasis on warranties and the entire support network such as parts and service availability.[3]

Employment opportunities in manufacturer sales are expected to experience average growth. Manufacturer sales personnel are well compensated and earn above-average salaries. Most of them are paid a combination of salaries and commissions, and the highest salaries are paid by manufacturers of electrical equipment, food products, and rubber goods. Commissions vary according to the salesperson's efforts, abilities, and sales territory and the type of products sold.

Public relations

Public relations encompasses a broad set of communication activities designed to create and maintain favorable relations between the organization and its publics—customers, employees, stockholders, government officials, and society in general. Communication is basic to all public relations programs. To communicate effectively, public relations practitioners first must gather data about the firm's client publics to assess their needs, identify problems, formulate recommendations, implement new plans, and evaluate current activities.

Public relations personnel disseminate large amounts of information to the organization's client publics. Written communication is the most versatile tool of public relations, and good writing ability is essential. Public relations practitioners must be adept at writing for a variety of media and audiences. It is not unusual for a person in public relations to prepare reports, news releases, speeches, broadcast scripts, technical manuals, employee publications, shareholder reports, and other communications aimed at both organizational personnel and external groups. In addition, a public relations practitioner needs a thorough knowledge of the production techniques used in preparing various communications.

Public relations personnel also establish distribution channels for the organization's publicity. They must have a thorough understanding of the various media, their areas of specialization, the characteristics of their target audiences, and their policies regarding publicity. Anyone who hopes to succeed in public relations must develop close working relationships with numerous media personnel to enlist their interest in disseminating an organization's communications.

A college education combined with writing or media-related experience probably is the best preparation for a career in public relations. Most beginners hold a college degree in journalism, communications, or public relations, but some employers prefer a business background. Courses in journalism, business administration, psychology, sociology, political science, advertising, English, and public speaking are recommended. Some employers require applicants to present a portfolio of published articles, television or radio programs, slide presentations, and other work samples.

3. Nicholas Basta, "Marketing Managers," *Business Week's Guide to Careers,* Spring 1983, p. 46.

Manufacturing firms, public utilities, transportation and insurance companies, and trade and professional associations are the largest employers of public relations personnel. In addition, sizable numbers work for health-related organizations, government agencies, educational institutions, museums, and religious and service groups.

Although some larger companies provide extensive formal training for new personnel, most new public relations employees learn on the job. Beginners usually perform routine tasks such as maintaining files about company activities and searching secondary data sources for information that can be used in publicity materials. More experienced employees write press releases, speeches, and articles and help plan public relations campaigns.

Employment opportunities in public relations are expected to increase faster than the average for all occupations through the mid-1980s. One caveat is in order, however. Competition for beginning jobs is keen. The prospects are best for applicants who have solid academic preparation and some media experience. Those who land jobs in public relations can expect to earn above-average salaries.

Industrial buying

Industrial buyers, or purchasing agents, are responsible for maintaining an adequate supply of the goods and services that an organization needs for operations. In general, industrial buyers purchase all items needed for direct use in producing other products and for use in the day-to-day operations. Industrial buyers in large firms often specialize in purchasing a single, specific class of products—for example, all petroleum-based lubricants. In smaller organizations, buyers may be responsible for purchasing many different categories of items, including such goods as raw materials, component parts, office supplies, and operating services.

An industrial buyer's main job consists of selecting suppliers who offer the best values in terms of quality, services, and price. When the products to be purchased are standardized, buyers may compare suppliers by examining catalogs and trade journals, making purchases by description. Buyers who purchase highly homogeneous products often meet with salespeople to examine samples and observe demonstrations. Sometimes, buyers must inspect the actual product before purchasing; in other cases, they invite suppliers to bid on large orders. Buyers who purchase specialized equipment often deal directly with manufacturers to obtain specially designed items made to specifications. After choosing a supplier and placing an order, an industrial buyer usually must trace the shipment to ensure on-time delivery. Finally, the buyer sometimes is responsible for receiving and inspecting an order and authorizing payment to the shipper.

Training requirements for a career in industrial buying relate to the needs of the firm and the types of products purchased. A manufacturer of heavy machinery may prefer an applicant who has a background in engineering; a service company, on the other hand, may recruit liberal arts majors. Although it is not generally required, a college degree is becoming increasingly important for buyers who wish to advance to management positions.

Employment prospects for industrial buyers are expected to increase faster than average through the 1980s. Opportunities will be excellent for individuals with a master's degree in business administration or a bachelor's degree in engineering, science, or business administration. In addition, companies that manufacture heavy equipment, computer equipment, and communications equipment will need buyers with technical backgrounds.

Distribution management

A distribution (or traffic) manager arranges for the transportation of goods within firms and through marketing channels. Transportation is an essential distribution activity that permits a firm to create time and place utility for its products. It is the job of the distribution manager to analyze various transportation modes and to select the combination that minimizes cost and transit time while providing acceptable levels of reliability, capability, accessibility, and security.

To accomplish this task, a distribution manager performs a wide range of activities. First, the individual must choose one or a combination of transportation modes from the five major modes available: railways, motor vehicles, inland waterways, pipelines, and airways. Then the distribution manager must select the specific routes the goods will travel and the particular carriers to be used, weighing such factors as freight classifications and regulations, freight charges, time schedules, shipment sizes, and loss and damage ratios. In addition, this person may be responsible for preparing shipping documents, tracing shipments, handling loss and damage claims, keeping records of freight rates, and monitoring changes in government regulations and transportation technology.

Distribution management employs relatively few people and is expected to grow about as fast as the average for all occupations in the near future. Manufacturing firms represent the largest employers of distribution managers, although some traffic managers work for wholesalers, retail stores, and consulting firms. Salaries of experienced distribution managers vary but, in general, are much higher than the average for all nonsupervisory personnel.

Most employers prefer graduates of technical programs or seek people who have completed courses in transportation, logistics, distribution management, economics, statistics, computer science, management, marketing, and commercial law. A successful distribution manager must be adept at handling technical data and must be able to interpret and communicate highly technical information.

Product management

In firms that use the product manager form of organization, the product manager occupies a staff position and is responsible for the success or failure of a product line. Product managers coordinate most of the marketing activities required to market a product; however, because they hold a staff position, they have relatively little actual authority over marketing personnel. Even so, because they take on a large amount of responsibility, product managers typically are paid quite well relative to other marketing employees. Being a product manager can be rewarding both financially and psychologically, but it also can be frustrating because of the disparity between responsibility and authority.

A product manager should have a general knowledge of advertising, transportation modes, inventory control, selling and sales management, sales promotion, marketing research, packaging, pricing, and warehousing. The individual must be knowledgeable enough to communicate effectively with personnel in these functional areas and to make suggestions and help assess alternatives when major decisions are being made.

Product managers usually need college training in an area of business administration. A master's degree is helpful, although a person usually does not become a product manager directly out of school. Frequently, several years of selling and sales management are prerequisites for a product management position, which often is a major step in the career path of top-level marketing executives.

Advertising

Advertising pervades our daily lives. As detailed in Chapter 12, business and nonbusiness organizations use advertising in many ways and for many reasons. Advertising clearly needs individuals with diverse skills to fill a variety of jobs. Creative imagination, artistic talent, and expertise in expression and persuasion are important to copywriters, artists, and account executives. Salesmanship and managerial ability are vital to the success of advertising managers, media buyers, and production managers. Research directors must have a solid understanding of research techniques and human behavior.

Advertising professionals disagree on the most beneficial educational background for a career in advertising. Most employers prefer college graduates. Some seek individuals with degrees in advertising, journalism, or business; others prefer graduates with broad liberal arts backgrounds. Still other employers rank relevant work experience above educational background.

"Advertisers look for generalists," says Kate Preston, a staff executive of the American Association of Advertising Agencies, "thus there are just as many economics or general liberal arts majors as MBAs. Many of the larger agencies want MBAs in their account management position, but there is a trend away from that at other agencies."[4]

A variety of organizations employ advertising personnel. Although advertising agencies are perhaps the most visible and glamorous of employers, many manufacturing firms, retail stores, banks, utility companies, and professional and trade associations maintain advertising departments. Advertising jobs also can be found with television and radio stations, newspapers, and magazines. Other businesses that employ advertising personnel include printers, art studios, letter shops, and package-design firms. Examples of specific advertising jobs are advertising manager, account executive, research director, copywriter, media specialist, and production manager.

Employment opportunities for advertising personnel are expected to increase faster than average through the mid-1980s. However, general eco-

4. Nicholas Basta, "Marketing Managers," *Business Week's Guide to Careers,* Spring 1983, p. 40.

nomic conditions strongly influence the size of advertising budgets and, hence, employment opportunities.

Retail management
Although a career in retailing may begin in sales, there is more to retailing than simply selling. Many retail personnel occupy management positions. Besides managing the sales force, they focus on selecting and ordering merchandise, promotional activities, inventory control, customer credit operations, accounting, personnel, and store security.

The manner in which retail stores are organized varies. In many large department stores, retail management personnel rarely get involved with actually selling to customers; these duties are performed by retail salespeople. However, other types of retail organizations may require management personnel to perform selling activities from time to time.

Large retail stores offer a variety of management positions besides those at the very top. A few examples include assistant buyers, buyers, department managers, section managers, store managers, division managers, regional managers, and vice president of merchandising. The following describes the general duties of a few of these positions. The precise nature of duties will vary from one retail organization to another, though.

A section manager coordinates inventory and promotions and interacts with buyers, salespeople, and ultimate consumers. The manager performs merchandising, labor relations and managerial activities and can rarely expect to get away with as little as a forty-hour work week.

The buyer's task is more focused. In this fast-paced occupation, there is much travel, pressure, and need to be open-minded with respect to new and potentially successful items.

The regional manager coordinates the activities of several stores within a given area. Sales, promotions, and procedures in general are monitored and supported.

The vice president of merchandising has a broad scope of managerial responsibility and reports to the president at the top of the organization.

Traditionally, retail managers began their careers as salesclerks. Today, many large retailers hire college-educated people, put them through management training programs, and then place them directly into management positions. They frequently hire people with backgrounds in liberal arts or business administration. Sales and retailing provide the greatest employment opportunity for marketing students. Usually, a successful background in a variety of retailing jobs is needed for store managers.[5]

Retail management positions can be exciting and challenging. Competent, ambitious individuals often assume a great deal of responsibility very quickly and advance rapidly. However, compensation programs for entry-level positions (management trainees) are usually below average. In addition, a retail manager's job is physically demanding and sometimes entails long working hours. Nonetheless, positions in retail management often provide numerous opportunities to excel and advance.

5. Kevin Higgins, "Economic Recovery Puts Marketers in Catbird Seat," *Marketing News,* Oct. 14, 1983, p. 8.

Direct marketing   One of the most dynamic areas in marketing is direct marketing. Direct marketing involves activities by which the seller uses one or more direct media (telephone, mail, print, or television) to solicit a response. For example, Shell Oil uses its credit card billings (direct mail) to sell a variety of consumer products. Telemarketing involves the use of direct selling to buyers using a variety of technological improvements in telephone services. The telephone is a major vehicle for selling many consumer products, such as magazines. The use of direct mail catalogs appeals to market segments such as working women or people that find going to retail stores difficult or inconvenient. Newspapers and magazines offer great opportunity especially in special market segments. *Golf Digest* for example is obviously a good medium for selling golfing equipment. Cable television provides many new opportunities for selling directly to consumers. Interactive cable will offer a new method to expand direct marketing by developing timely exchange opportunities for consumers.

The volume of goods distributed through direct marketing is a strong indicator of opportunity for careers in this growing area. H. B. Crandall, president of Crandall Associates, New York, has stated that job candidates with experience could "write their own ticket." He continued, "People with five years' experience are getting phenomenal salary offers. People with one year's experience are getting offers unheard of in any other marketing field."[6]

The most important asset in direct marketing is experience. Employers often look to other industries to locate experienced professionals. In a choice between an MBA or an individual with a direct marketing background, the experienced individual would be hired.[7] This preference means that if you can get an entry-level position in direct marketing, you will have a real advantage in developing a career.

The executive vice president of the advertising agency Young & Rubicam, Inc. in New York stated that direct marketing will have to be used "not as a tactic, but as a strategic tool."[8] Direct marketing's effectiveness is enhanced by periodic analysis of advertising and communications at all phases of contact with the consumer. Direct marketing involves all aspects of the marketing decision. It is becoming a more professional career area that provides great opportunity.

6. Higgins, "Economic Recovery Puts Marketers in Catbird Seat," pp. 1, 8.
7. Ibid.
8. "Wonderman Urges: Replace Marketing War Muskets with the Authentic Weapon—Direct Marketing," *Marketing News,* July 8, 1983, pp. 1, 12.

Financial Analysis in Marketing

Our discussion in this book has focused more on fundamental concepts and decisions in marketing than on financial details. However, marketers must understand the basic components of selected financial analyses if they are to explain and defend their decisions. In fact, they must be familiar with certain financial analyses if they are to reach good decisions in the first place. We will therefore examine three areas of financial analyses: cost-profit aspects of the income statement, selected performance ratios, and price calculations.[1] To control and evaluate marketing activities, marketers must understand the income statement and what it says about the operations of their organization. They also need to be acquainted with performance ratios, which compare current operating results with past results and with results in the industry at large. In the last part of the appendix, we discuss price calculations as the basis of price adjustments. Marketers are likely to use all these areas of financial analysis at various times to support their decisions and to make necessary adjustments in their operations.

The income statement

The income, or operating, statement presents the financial results of an organization's operations over a period of time. The statement summarizes revenues earned and expenses incurred by a profit center, whether it is a department, brand, product line, division, or entire firm. The income statement presents the firm's net profit or net loss for a month, quarter, or year.

Table B.1 shows a simplified income statement for a retail store. The owners of the store, Rose Costa and Nick Schultz, see that net sales of

Table B.1   Simplified income statement for a retailer

Stoneham Auto Supplies Income Statement for the Year Ended December 31, 1984	
Net Sales	$250,000
Cost of Goods Sold	45,000
Gross Margin	$205,000
Expenses	122,000
Net Income	$ 83,000

1. We gratefully acknowledge the assistance of Jim L. Grimm, Professor of Marketing, Illinois State University, in writing this appendix.

$250,000 are decreased by the cost of goods sold and by other business expenses to yield a net income of $83,000. Of course, these figures are only highlights of the complete income statement, which appears in Table B.2.

The income statement can be used in several ways to improve the management of a business. First, it enables an owner or manager to compare actual results with budgets for various parts of the statement. For example, Rose and Nick see that the total amount of merchandise sold (gross sales) is $260,000. Customers returned merchandise or received allowances (price reductions) totaling $10,000. Suppose the budgeted amount was only $9,000. By checking the tickets for sales returns and allowances, the owners can determine why these events occurred and whether the $10,000 figure could be lowered by adjusting the marketing mix.

After subtracting returns and allowances from gross sales, Rose and Nick can determine net sales from the statement. They are pleased with this figure because it is higher than their sales target of $240,000. Net sales is the amount the firm has available to pay its expenses.

A major expense for most companies that sell goods (as opposed to services) is the cost of goods sold. For Stoneham Auto Supplies, it amounts to 18 percent of net sales. Other expenses are treated in various ways by different companies. In our example, they are broken down into standard categories of selling expenses, administrative expenses, and general expenses.

The income statement shows that the cost of goods sold by Stoneham Auto Supplies during fiscal year 1984 was $45,000. This figure was reached in the following way. First, the statement shows that merchandise in the amount of $51,000 was purchased during the year. In paying the invoices associated with these inventory additions, purchase (cash) discounts of $4,000 were earned, resulting in net purchases of $47,000. Special requests for selected merchandise throughout the year resulted in $2,000 of freight charges, which increased the net cost of delivered purchases to $49,000. Adding this amount to the beginning inventory of $48,000, the cost of goods available for sale during 1984 was $97,000. However, the records indicate that the value of inventory at the end of the year was $52,000. Since this amount was not sold, the cost of goods that were sold during the year was $45,000.

Rose and Nick observe that the total value of their inventory increased by 8.3 percent during the year.

$$\frac{\$52,000 - \$48,000}{\$48,000} = \frac{\$\ 4,000}{\$48,000} = \frac{1}{12} = .0825 \text{ or } 8.3\%$$

Further analysis is needed to determine whether this increase is desirable or undesirable. (Note that the income statement provides no detail concerning the composition of the inventory held on December 31; other records provide this information.) If Nick and Rose determine that inventory on December 31 is excessive, they can implement appropriate marketing action.

Gross margin is the difference between net sales and cost of goods sold. Gross margin reflects the markup on products and is the amount available to pay all other expenses and provide a return to the owners.

Table B.2 Operating statement for a retailer

Stoneham Auto Supplies
income statement
for the year ended December 31, 1984

Gross Sales		$260,000
Less: Sales returns and allowances		10,000
Net Sales		$250,000

Cost of Goods Sold

Inventory, January 1, 1984 (at cost)		$48,000	
Purchases	$51,000		
Less: Purchase discounts	4,000		
Net purchases	$47,000		
Plus: Freight-in	2,000		
Net cost of delivered purchases		$49,000	
Cost of goods available for sale		$97,000	
Less: Inventory, December 31, 1984 (at cost)		52,000	
Cost of goods sold			$ 45,000
Gross Margin			$205,000

Expenses

Selling expenses			
Sales salaries and commissions	$32,000		
Advertising	16,000		
Sales promotions	3,000		
Delivery	2,000		
Total selling expenses		$53,000	
Administrative expenses			
Administrative salaries	$20,000		
Office salaries	20,000		
Office supplies	2,000		
Miscellaneous	1,000		
Total administrative expenses		$43,000	
General expenses			
Rent	$14,000		
Utilities	7,000		
Bad debts	1,000		
Miscellaneous (local taxes, insurance, interest, depreciation)	4,000		
Total general expenses		$26,000	
Total expenses			$122,000
Net Income			$ 83,000

Stoneham Auto Supplies had a gross margin of $205,000:

Net Sales	$250,000
Cost of Goods Sold	− 45,000
Gross Margin	$205,000

Stoneham's expenses (other than cost of goods sold) during 1984 totaled $122,000. Observe that $53,000, or slightly more than 43 percent of the total, is direct selling expenses.

$$\frac{\$53,000 \text{ selling expenses}}{\$122,000 \text{ total expenses}} = .434 \text{ or } 43\%$$

The business employs three salespersons (one full time) and pays competitive wages for the area. All selling expenses are similar to dollar amounts for fiscal year 1983, but Nick and Rose wonder whether more advertising is necessary, since inventory increased by more than 8 percent during the year.

The administrative and general expenses are also essential to operate the business. A comparison of these expenses with trade statistics for similar businesses indicates that the figures are in line with industry amounts.

Net income, or net profit, is the amount of gross margin remaining after deducting expenses. Stoneham Auto Supplies earned a net profit of $83,000 for the fiscal year ending December 31, 1984. Note that net income on this statement is figured before payment of state and federal income taxes.

Income statements for middlemen and for businesses that provide services follow the same general format as that shown for Stoneham Auto Supplies in Table B.2. The income statement for a manufacturer, however, is somewhat different, in that the purchases section is replaced by a section called cost of goods manufactured. Table B.3 shows the entire cost-of-goods-sold section for a manufacturer, including cost of goods manufactured. In other respects, income statements for retailers and manufacturers are similar.

Selected performance ratios

Rose and Nick's assessment of how well their business did during fiscal year 1984 can be improved through selective use of analytical ratios. These ratios enable a manager to compare the results for the current year with data from previous years and with industry statistics. Unfortunately, comparisons of the current income statement with income statements and industry statistics from other years are not very meaningful, since factors such as inflation are not accounted for when comparing dollar amounts. More meaningful comparisons can be made by converting these figures to a percentage of net sales, as this section shows.

The first analytical ratios we will discuss, the operating ratios, are based on the net sales figure from the income statement.

Operating ratios

Operating ratios express items on the income, or operating, statement as percentages of net sales. The first step is to convert the income statement into percentages of net sales, as illustrated in Table B.4.

After making this conversion, the manager looks at several key operating ratios. These ratios include two profitability ratios (the gross margin ratio and the net income ratio) and the operating expense ratio.

Table B.3   Cost of goods sold for a manufacturer

Cost of Goods Sold

Finished goods inventory, January 1, 1984			$ 50,000
Cost of goods manufactured			
Work-in-process inventory, January 1, 1984		$20,000	
Raw materials inventory, January 1, 1984	$ 40,000		
Net cost of delivered purchases	240,000		
Cost of goods available for use	$280,000		
Less: Raw materials inventory, December 31, 1984	42,000		
Cost of goods placed in production		$238,000	
Direct labor		$32,000	
Manufacturing overhead			
Indirect labor	$12,000		
Supervisory salaries	10,000		
Operating supplies	6,000		
Depreciation	12,000		
Utilities	10,000		
Total manufacturing overhead		$ 50,000	
Total manufacturing costs			$320,000
Total work-in-process			$340,000
Less: Work-in-process inventory, December 31, 1984			22,000
Cost of goods manufactured			$318,000
			$368,000
Cost of goods available for sale			
Less: Finished goods inventory, December 31, 1984			48,000
Cost of Goods Sold			$320,000

For Stoneham Auto Supplies these ratios are determined as follows (see Tables B.2 and B.4 for supporting data):

$$\text{Gross margin ratio} = \frac{\text{gross margin}}{\text{net sales}} = \frac{\$205,000}{\$250,000} = 82\%$$

$$\text{Net income ratio} = \frac{\text{net income}}{\text{net sales}} = \frac{\$83,000}{\$250,000} = 33.2\%$$

$$\text{Operating expense ratio} = \frac{\text{total expense}}{\text{net sales}} = \frac{\$122,000}{\$250,000} = 48.8\%$$

The gross margin ratio indicates the percentage of each sales dollar available to cover operating expenses and to achieve profit objectives. The

Table B.4 Income statement as a percentage of net sales

Stoneham Auto Supplies income statement as a percentage of net sales for the year ended December 31, 1984

			Percentage of net sales
Gross Sales			103.8%
Less: Sales returns and allowances			3.8
Net Sales			100.0%
Cost of Goods Sold			
Inventory, January 1, 1984 (at cost)		19.2%	
Purchases	20.4%		
Less: Purchase discounts	1.6		
Net purchases	18.8%		
Plus: Freight-in	.8		
Net cost of delivered purchases		19.6	
Cost of goods available for sale		38.8%	
Less: Inventory, December 31, 1984 (at cost)		20.8	
Cost of goods sold			18.0
Gross Margin			82.0%
Expenses			
Selling expenses			
Sales salaries and commissions	12.8%		
Advertising	6.4		
Sales promotions	1.2		
Delivery	0.8		
Total selling expenses		21.2%	
Administrative expenses			
Administrative salaries	8.0%		
Office salaries	8.0		
Office supplies	0.8		
Miscellaneous	0.4		
Total administrative expenses		17.2%	
General expenses			
Rent	5.6%		
Utilities	2.8		
Bad debts	0.4		
Miscellaneous	1.6		
Total general expenses		10.4%	
Total expenses			48.8
Net Income			33.2%

net income ratio indicates the percentage of each sales dollar that is classified as earnings (profit) before payment of income taxes. The operating expense ratio indicates the percentage of each dollar needed to cover operating expenses.

If Nick and Rose feel that the operating expense ratio is higher than historical data and industry standards, they can analyze each operating expense ratio in Table B.4 to determine which expenses are too high. They can then take corrective action.

After reviewing several key operating ratios, in fact, managers will probably want to analyze all the items on the income statement. For instance, by doing so, Nick and Rose can determine whether the 8-percent increase in inventory was necessary.

Inventory turnover

The inventory turnover rate, or stockturn rate, is an analytical ratio that can be used to answer the question, "Is the inventory level appropriate for this business?" The inventory turnover rate indicates the number of times that an inventory is sold (turns over) during one year. To be useful, this figure is then compared to historical turnover rates and industry rates.

The inventory turnover rate can be computed on cost as follows:

$$\text{Inventory turnover} = \frac{\text{cost of goods sold}}{\text{average inventory at cost}}$$

Rose and Nick would calculate the turnover rate from Table B.2 as follows:

$$\frac{\text{Cost of goods sold}}{\text{Average inventory at cost}} = \frac{\$45,000}{\$50,000} = 0.9 \text{ time}$$

They find that inventory turnover is less than once per year (0.9 time). Industry averages for competitive firms are 2.8 times. This figure convinces Rose and Nick that their investment in inventory is too large and that they need to reduce inventory.

Return on investment

Return on investment (ROI) is a ratio that indicates management's efficiency in generating sales and profits from the total amount invested in the firm. For example, Stoneham Auto Supplies' ROI is 41.5 percent, which compares well with competing businesses.

We use figures from two different financial statements to arrive at ROI. The income statement, already discussed, gives us net income. The balance sheet, which states the firm's assets and liabilities at a given point in time, provides the figure for total assets (or investment) in the firm.

The basic formula for ROI is

$$\text{ROI} = \frac{\text{net income}}{\text{total investment}}$$

For Stoneham Auto Supplies, net income for fiscal year 1984 is $83,000 (see Table B.2). If total investment (taken from the balance sheet for December 31, 1984) is $200,000, then

$$\text{ROI} = \frac{\$ 83,000}{\$200,000} = 0.415 \text{ or } 41.5\%$$

The ROI formula can be expanded to isolate the impact of capital turnover and the operating income ratio separately. Capital turnover is a measure of net sales per dollar of investment; the ratio is figured by dividing net sales by total investment. For Stoneham Auto Supplies,

$$\text{Capital turnover} = \frac{\text{net sales}}{\text{total investment}}$$

$$= \frac{\$250,000}{\$200,000} = 1.25$$

ROI is equal to capital turnover times the net income ratio. The expanded formula for Stoneham Auto Supplies is

$$\text{ROI} = (\text{capital turnover}) \times (\text{net income ratio})$$

or

$$\text{ROI} = \frac{\text{net sales}}{\text{total investment}} \times \frac{\text{net income}}{\text{net sales}}$$

$$= \frac{\$250,000}{\$200,000} \times \frac{\$\ 83,000}{\$250,000}$$

$$= (1.25)\ (33.2\%) = 41.5\%$$

Price calculations

An important step in setting prices is selecting a pricing method, as indicated in Chapter 15. The systematic use of markups, markdowns, and various conversion formulas helps in calculating the selling price and in evaluating the effects of various prices. The following sections provide more detailed information about price calculations than was offered in Chapter 15.

Markups

As indicated in the text, markup is the difference between the selling price and the cost of the item. That is, selling price equals cost plus markup. The markup must cover cost and contribute to profit; thus, markup is similar to gross margin on the income statement.

Markup can be calculated on either cost or selling price, as follows:

$$\text{Markup as a percentage of cost} = \frac{\text{amount added to cost}}{\text{cost}} = \frac{\text{dollar markup}}{\text{cost}}$$

$$\text{Markup as a percentage of selling price} = \frac{\text{amount added to cost}}{\text{selling price}} = \frac{\text{dollar markup}}{\text{selling price}}$$

Retailers tend to calculate the markup percentage on selling price.

Examples of markup

To review the use of these markup formulas, assume that an item costs $10 and the markup is $5.

$$\text{Selling price} = \text{cost} + \text{markup}$$

$$\$15 = \$10 + \$5$$

Thus

$$\text{Markup percentage on cost} = \frac{\$\,5}{\$10} = 50\%$$

$$\text{Markup percentage on selling price} = \frac{\$\,5}{\$15} = 33\frac{1}{3}\%$$

It is necessary to know the base (cost or selling price) to use markup pricing effectively. Markup percentage on cost will always exceed markup percentage on price, given the same dollar markup, so long as selling price exceeds cost.

On occasion, we may need to convert markup on cost to markup on selling price, or vice versa. The conversion formulas are

$$\text{Markup percentage on selling price} = \frac{\text{markup percentage on cost}}{100\% + \text{markup percentage on cost}}$$

$$\text{Markup percentage on cost} = \frac{\text{markup percentage on selling price}}{100\% - \text{markup percentage on selling price}}$$

For example, if the markup percentage on cost is $33\frac{1}{3}$ percent, then the markup percentage on selling price is

$$\frac{33\frac{1}{3}\%}{100\% + 33\frac{1}{3}\%} = \frac{33\frac{1}{3}\%}{133\frac{1}{3}\%} = 25\%$$

If the markup percentage on selling price is 40 percent, then the corresponding percentage on cost would be

$$\frac{40\%}{100\% - 40\%} = \frac{40\%}{60\%} = 66\frac{2}{3}\%$$

Finally, we can show how to determine selling price if we know the cost of the item and the markup percentage on selling price. Assume that an item costs $36 and the usual markup percentage on selling price is 40 percent. Remember that selling price equals markup plus cost. Thus, if

$$100\% = 40\% \text{ of selling price} + \text{cost}$$

then

$$60\% \text{ of selling price} = \text{Cost}$$

In our example, cost equals $36. Then

$$0.6X = \$36$$

$$X = \frac{\$36}{0.6}$$

$$\text{Selling price} = \$60$$

Alternatively, the markup percentage could be converted to a cost basis as follows:

$$\frac{40\%}{100\% - 40\%} = 66\frac{2}{3}\%$$

Then the computed selling price would be as follows:

$$\text{Selling price} = 66\frac{2}{3}\% \text{ (cost)} + \text{cost}$$

$$= 66\frac{2}{3}\% \text{ (\$36)} + \$36$$

$$= \$24 + \$36$$

$$= \$60$$

By remembering the basic formula—selling price equals cost plus markup—you will find these calculations straightforward.

Markdowns

Markdowns are price reductions on merchandise by a retailer. Markdowns may be useful on items that are damaged, or priced too high, or selected for a special sales event. The income statement does not express markdowns directly, for the change in price is made before the sale takes place. Therefore, separate records of markdowns are needed to evaluate the performance of various buyers and departments.

The markdown ratio (percentage) is calculated as follows:

$$\text{Markdown percentage} = \frac{\text{dollar markdowns}}{\text{net sales in dollars}}$$

In analyzing their inventory, Nick and Rose discover three special auto jacks that have gone unsold for several months. They decide to reduce the price of each item from \$25 to \$20. Subsequently, these items are sold. The markdown percentage for these three items is

$$\text{Markdown percentage} = \frac{3 \text{ (\$5)}}{3 \text{ (\$20)}} = \frac{\$15}{\$60} = 25\%$$

Net sales, however, include all units of this product sold during the period, not just those marked down. If ten of these items have already been sold at \$25 each, in addition to the three items sold at \$20, then the overall markdown percentage would be

$$\text{Markdown percentage} = \frac{3 \text{ (\$5)}}{10 \text{ (\$25)} + 3 \text{ (\$20)}}$$

$$= \frac{\$15}{\$250 + \$60} = \frac{\$15}{\$310} = 4.8\%$$

Sales allowances also are a reduction in price. Thus, the markdown percentages should also include any sales allowances. It would be computed as follows:

$$\text{Markdown percentage} = \frac{\text{dollar markdowns} + \text{dollar allowances}}{\text{net sales in dollars}}$$

1. In what way does a manufacturer's income statement differ from a retailer's income statement?
2. Use the following information to answer questions a through c:

Company TEA
fiscal year ended June 30, 1985

Net Sales	$500,000
Cost of Goods Sold	300,000
Net Income	50,000
Average Inventory at Cost	100,000
Total Assets (total investment)	200,000

    a. What is the inventory turnover rate for TEA Company? From what sources will the marketing manager determine the significance of the inventory turnover rate?

    b. What is the capital turnover ratio for fiscal year 1985? What is the net income ratio? What is the return on investment (ROI)?

    c. How many dollars of sales did each dollar of investment produce for TEA Company in fiscal year 1985?

3. Product A has a markup percentage on cost of 40 percent. What is the markup percentage on selling price?
4. Product B has a markup percentage on selling price of 30 percent. What is the markup percentage on cost?
5. Product C has a cost of $60 and a usual markup percentage of 25 percent on selling price. What price should be placed on this item?
6. Apex Appliance Company sells twenty units of product Q for $100 each and ten units for $80 each. What is the markdown percentage for product Q?

Name Index

Arnold and Company Marketing and
  Advertising, 276(illus.)
Arnold Palmer Sportswear, 259
Arnston-American Standard, 248
Arpan, Jeffrey, 675n
Arrid deodorants, 163
ASEA (Allmana Svenska Electriska), 558
Aspinwall, Leo, 222n
Assael, Henry, 86n
Associated Grocers (AG), 252
Association of American Railroads,
  298(illus.)
Atari, Inc., 16, 452, 453(illus.), 553
Atari home computer, 452, 453(illus.), 529,
  530(illus.)
Ativan, 187
Atra razors, 694
Athlete's Foot, The, 271
AT&T (American Telephone and Telegraph)
  Co., 13, 23, 326, 359(table), 468–470,
  607–608
Austin Nichols & Co., 455(illus.)
Avis Rent-A-Car, 276, 671, 688
Avon Products Incorporated, 271, 272,
  417–418
A&W Root Beer, 586

Bacardi Imports, Inc., 565(illus.), 566
Bailey, Earl L., 59n, 60n, 62n, 201n
Baker, R. C., 164n
Balanced Investment Planning Inc., 389
Ballou, Ronald H., 293n
BankAmerica, 671(table)
Banks, Howard, 499n
Banks, Sharon K., 129n
Banting, Peter M., 622n
Barban, Arnold M., 366n, 371n, 372n
Bardi, Edward, 298n
Barry, John, 583
Barton, Robert, 367n
Basic Guide to Exporting, A, 676
Baskin Robbins Company, 153
Basta, Nicholas, 703n, 706n
Bates, Albert D., 268n, 271n, 306n
Batus Inc., 359(table)
Baxter's Restaurant, 287(table), 289
Bayer, Tom, 383n
Bayer aspirin, 157
Bay State Machine Company, 68–69
B. Dalton Bookseller, 221
Beam, James B., Distilling Company, 163
Beatrice Foods Co., 358(table)
Beckenstein, Alan R., 458n
Becker, Tom, 691n
Beckman, Theodore N., 236n, 305n
Beecham Group Ltd., 359(table)
Beachy, Debra, 679n
Beech-Nut baby food, 25
Behavior Scan company, 124

Bell, Martin L., 183n, 428n, 604n
Bellizzi, Joseph A., 265n
Beman, Lewis, 296n
Ben Hogan Radial Irons (AMF), 544
Bennigan's Tavern and Restaurant, 30–31
Benson & Hedges cigarettes, 411
Bergen Brunswig Corporation, 237, 308
Bergiel, Blaise J., 650n
Berkman, Harold W., 89n
Berkowitz, Eric N., 654n
Bermans—The Leather Experts, 287(table),
  289
Bernstein, Sanford C., 469n
Berry, Dick, 94n
Berry, Leonard L., 91n, 271n
Besnier USA, Inc., 20(illus.)
Bessom, Richard M., 260n
Best, Roger, 263n
Bic Pen Corporation, 26, 470–471, 510, 679
Bigelow, R.C., Inc., 328, 329(illus.)
Bill Blass clothing, 51, 52(illus.), 432
Billig, Stephen M., 128n
Biphase Energy Systems, 581
Birds Eye frozen vegetables, 310
Bisquick biscuit mix, 156
Bivens, Jacquelyn, 270n
Black Flag insecticides, 187
Blackwell, Roger D., 72n, 89n, 221n, 674n
Blankenship, Albert B., 119n
Bloomingdale's, 266
Bloomingdale's by Mail, Ltd., 274,
  275(illus.)
Blue Stratos cologne, 409
Boeing Co., 570, 680
Bohmbach, Dwight, 91n
Bold detergent, 153, 162, 227, 696
Bonanza steakhouses, 544
Bonaventure Hotel, Los Angeles, 214
Bonoma, Thomas V., 250n
Bonus detergent, 153, 162
Boone, Louis E., 8n, 280n
Borden Inc., 177, 577, 583
Borkum Riff smoking tobacco, 249
Bose Corporation, 19
Boston Consulting Group (BCG), 561–562,
  571
Boswell, Dan A., 592n
Body, Harper W., Jr., 113n, 132n, 134n
Bradford, John A., 643n
Bradlees stores, 268(table)
Braniff Airlines, 14, 451
Braun AG, 695
Breen, George E., 119n
Breyers ice cream, 201–202
Brigade toilet bowl cleaner, 155
Bristol Bar & Grill, 287(table), 289
Bristol-Myers Co., 174, 359(table)
British Columbia Railways, 558
Britt, Steward Henderson, 119n
Brokaw Hospital (Normal, Illinois), 663–667

E.I. du Pont de Nemours & Co., 79, 359(table), 583, 613, 614(illus.), 629(illus.), 629–630, 671(table)

Ekco kitchen ware, 187

Ektaprint copier, Kodak, 537, 550

El-Ansary, Adel I., 225n, 227n, 237n, 248n, 281n, 283n

Electrolux Company, 271

Electronic Data Systems Corporation, 37

Elephant Memory Systems, 244

Eli Lilly & Company, 499–500

Elkins, John, 23n

Elrick & Lavidge, Inc., 115(illus.), 129(illus.)

El Torito dinnerhouses, 287(table)

Enfield Square Mall (Enfield, Connecticut), 389

Engel, James F., 72n, 89n

Engel, Peter H., 183n

English, Mary McCabe, 85n, 409n

Enis, Ben M., 572n

Enrick, Norbert L., 61n

Eraser Mate, 694

Ericcson Information Systems, 672, 673(illus.)

E.R.I.M. Consumer Research (A.C. Nielsen), 140

Esmark Inc., 358(table)

Etherea Fine Fragrances, 51

Ethernet (Xerox), 538

Etzel, Michael J., 271n

Ex-Cell-O Corporation, 60

Express Mail, 311(illus.), 311–312

Exxon Corp., 55, 158, 546, 671(table), 671–672

Exxon Office Systems Company, 546 and *illus.*

E-Z Go vehicles, 255

Fahey, Liam, 553n

Family World motels, 264

Fannie May Candy Shops, 261

Faris, Charles W., 96n

Farst, Debra, 544n

Felly's Flowers, 213

Fendel, Alyson, 279n

Ferrari North America, 41, 42(illus.)

Ferrell, O. C., 184n, 489n, 560n

Figuia, James S., 124n

Filene's department store, 265

Filiatrault, Pierre, 76n

Fine, Phyllis, 265n

Finney, E. Robert, 615n

Fisher, Anne B., 450n

Fisher, Gerald H., 77n

Fisher-Price Toys, 200

Fisk, George, 220n

Flying Tigers airline, 299, 300(illus.)

Foltz, Kim, 342n

Foot Locker store, 271

Forbis, John L., 631n

Ford, Glenn, 322

Ford Motor Co., 5, 358(table), 449–450, 555, 671(table), 681–682

Foremost-McKesson, Inc., 237

Foster, J. Robert, 294n, 295n

Foster, Thomas, 292n, 309n

Four-Phase Systems, Inc., 552

Fraker, Susan, 187n

Franges and Company, 430(illus.)

Franko, Lawrence G., 672n

Fran Murphy, Inc., 251(illus.)

Fred Meyer stores, 268(table)

Fred S. James and Company, Inc., 578, 579

Frey, Albert Wesley, 378n

Friedman, Walter F., 302n

Frisbee brand discs, 229, 230

Frito-Lay, 177, 178(illus.)

Froman, Arthur H., & Company, 249

Frontier Airlines, 451

Fu, Marilyn Y. C., 675n

Fuji American, 429, 430(illus.)

Fuller Brush Company, 271, 272

Gabel, H. Landis, 458n

Gable, Myron, 282n

Gablingers beer, 67

GAF company, 253

Gage, Tad, 679n

Gage, Theodore J., 71n

Gain detergent, 153, 162, 227

Gallo, E&J, Winery, 359(table), 449

Gallup & Robinson, Inc., 374

Gap, The (store), 271

Gardner, Samuel R., 201n

Garino, David P., 167n

Gates, Roger, 130n

Gemco Membership Department Stores, 268(table)

Gemveto Jewelry Co., Inc., 272(illus.)

General Battery Corporation, 256

General Electric Co., 92, 163, 180, 359(table), 577, 680

General Foods Corp., 82, 178, 184, 185, 186, 187, 188, 190, 310, 352, 358(table), 485, 689

General Grocer (wholesale), 158

General Mills, Inc., 104, 156, 358(table), 485

General Motors Corp., 5, 19, 108, 299, 358(table), 428, 446, 671(table), 685

Genuine Parts Company, 237

George, William R., 649n, 650n

Georges Marciano clothing, 51, 52(illus.)

Georgia-Pacific Corp., 635–636

Gerber's, 151–152

GETS (Guaranteed Emergency Transportation Service), 300

Getz, Malcolm, 466n

Gillette, King C., 694

Hutt, Michael D., 265
Hyatt Corporation, 451

IBM Corp., 207 and *illus.*, 208, 359(table),
    450, 538, 591, 671(table)
IBM personal computers, 207 and *illus.*,
    429, 450, 566, 591
IGA (Independent Grocers' Alliance), 158,
    227, 252
Illinois Wesleyan University, 655–656
Indata Corp., 294
Inderal, 187
Industrial Marketing magazine, 133
Ingrassia, Lawrence, 179n, 184n, 222n
Inman, Virginia, 13n
Instant camera, Kodak, 536
Intelmatique, 503
Intermountain Power Agency (Salt Lake
    City), 558
International Coffee Organization, 21
"International Entrees" (Swift), 71
International Harvester Co., 548
International Silver silverware, 278
ITT (International Telephone and Telegraph)
    Corp., 359(table), 469(table), 671 and
    table, 680
ITT Longer Distance, 607
Ivie, Robert, 302n
Ivory brand softsoap, 174
Izod Limited, 432

Jack-in-the-Box restaurants, 232
Jackson, Donald W., 260n
Jackson, George C., 310n
Jackson, Michael, 342–343, 553
Jackson, Tom, 699n
Jacobs, Sanford L., 443n
Jacobsen Turf products, 255–256
James, Don L., 271n
Jartran Inc., 209
J.C. Penney Co., 109, 158, 159 and *illus.*,
    200, 211, 227, 257, 266, 282, 359(table)
Jell-O products, 82, 310, 352, 685
Jennings, Waylon, 108
Jerrey, Gay, 76n, 183n, 535n
Jewel Companies, Inc., 270(table)
Johns Hopkins University, 185
Johnson, E.F., Company, 392(illus.)
Johnson, James C., 305n, 307n
Johnson, Robert, 57n
Johnson, S.C., & Son, 359(table)
Johnson & Johnson, 48, 174–175, 182,
    358(table)
jojo's (restaurants), 287(table)
Jolimar, Anwar, 289
Jonas Berger Associates, 308(illus.)
Jones, Ana Loud, 283n

Karger, Theodore, 196n, 197n
Kato, Hajima, 430n
K cars, 5, 14
Keane, John G., 548n
Keegan, Warren J., 672n, 683n, 684n
Kellogg Co., 221, 358(table), 485, 687,
    688(illus.)
Kelly, J. Patrick, 282n
Kendall Oil, 168
Kenmore brand, 158
Kentucky Fried Chicken, 196, 221, 275, 276
Kenworth trucks, 555
Kesselman-Turkel, Judi, 411n
Kevlar, 613, 614(illus.)
Kichen, Steve, 343n
Kiefer, Richard O., 681n, 682n, 683n
Kimberly-Clark Corp., 360(table), 407
King, Allen S., 109n
King, Michael, 196n
Kingman, Merle, 326n
Kinney Shoe Corporation, 271, 482
Kirin beer, 214
Kirkpatrick, C. A., 369n
Kitty Litter, 161
Klein, Heywood, 250n
Kleinberg, Ellen M., 625n
K mart Corp., 158, 211, 227, 263, 267,
    268(table), 359(table), 511, 552
Kodak, *see* Eastman Kodak Co.
Kollat, David T., 89n, 221n, 674n
Komatsu America Corporation, 544,
    545(illus.)
Kool-Aid, 637
Kool cigarettes, 564
Koten, John, 342n
Kotler, Philip, 11n, 57n, 209n, 265n, 266n,
    522n, 523n, 554n, 604n, 644n, 647n,
    649n, 683n
Kraft Inc., 71, 180, 201–203
Kroger Company, 270(table)
Kurtz, David L., 8n, 280n
KYST, AM (radio station), 45

La Barbara, Priscilla, 489n
LaBreque, Roger J., 643n
LaGarce, Raymond, 489n
LaMarca, Lou, 499n
Land, Edwin, 183
Landon, E. Laird, Jr., 129n
Lands' End (direct sales merchandiser), 273
    and *illus.*
Lane, W. Clayton, 89n
Langenscheidt Publishers, Inc., 239(illus.)
Langer, Judith, 130n
Langley, Monica, 607n
Larson, Erik, 208n
Laven, Betty, 416
Lawn and Garden Division of AMF, 543
Lay's Potato Chips, 177
Lazer, William, 489n

Leading Edge Products, Inc. (LEP), 244
"Lean Cuisine," 71 and *illus.*
L'eggs hosiery, 593
Lemon Concentrate, 696
Leonard, Frank S., 181n
Leslie Salt Company, 168
Lever Brothers, 48, 351
Levi Strauss & Co., 29–30, 159 and *illus.*,
　　161, 184, 185(illus.), 259, 278, 411, 510,
　　552
Levitt, Theodore, 147n, 169n
Levitz Furniture Corporation, 269
Levy, Sidney J., 523n
Light n' Lively cheese products, 180
Lilly, Eli & Company, 499–500
Limited, The (stores), 271, 278
Linden, Fabian, 513n, 514n, 518n
Lipton's Ice Tea Mix, 637
Lisa computer (Apple), 208, 429
Listerine, 678
Littlefield, James E., 369n
Litton Industries, Inc., 679
Loews Corp., 359(table)
Londro, Laura, 41n
Lopata, Richard S., 240n
Lorsch Group, 90(illus.)
Louis Joliet Mall (Illinois), 278
Löwenbrau beer, 67
Lowe's, Inc., 162(illus.)
Luck, David J., 156n, 560n
Lucky Stores, Inc., 270(table)
Lucky Whip, 195
Luick, John F., 334n, 406n, 408n
Lundstrom, William J., 138n
Lusch, Robert F., 225n
Luv diapers, 696
Lynch, Mitchell C., 181n
Lyons, George R., Company, 249
Lysol Disinfectant, 161

Maaco, 276
McCammon, Bert C., Jr., 220n
McCarthy, E. Jerome, 292n
McCartney, Paul, 343
McConnell, D. H., 417
McCormick Place Graphic Expo, 250
McCuffrey & McCull advertising, 159(illus.)
McCuiston, Tommy J., 311n, 625n
McDaniel, Carl, 164n
McDonald, James B., 282n
McDonald's Corporation, 26, 27, 221, 275,
　　276, 282, 358(table), 552
McGregor brand clothing, 259
McIlvain, George E., 651n, 655n
McKeon, James C., 252n
McLaughlin, Frank S., 295n
McMenamin, Michael, 496n
McNeal, James U., 157n, 160n, 167n, 332n
McNeilab, Inc., 174–175
Macy's department store, 266

Magee, John F., 305n
Magnavox (electronic products), 221
Magnet, Myron, 549n
Mahajan, Vijay, 180n
Maher, Philip, 535n
Maisel, Jay, 24n
Makro Self Service Wholesale Corporation,
　　243
Makrotest Limited, 675(illus.)
Mallen, Bruce, 253n
Mannington Mills, Inc., 389
March of Dimes, 646
Market Facts, Inc., 123, 127(table)
Market Identifiers, 619
Marketing Models Group, 123
Marketing News, 503n
Marketing and Research Counsellors, Inc.,
　　135(illus.)
Marketing Research Group (A.C. Nielsen),
　　140, 141
Market Research Corporation of
　　America,(MRCA), 134
Market Search, 134
Marlboro cigarettes, imitations of, 161
Mars, Forrest, 16
Mars, Inc., 359(table)
Marshall, Christy, 49n, 552n
Marshall Field department store, 266, 278
Mary Kay Cosmetics, 418
Maryland Office of Business and Industrial
　　Development, 652 and *illus.*
Mason, Joseph Barry, 277n, 280n, 309n
Mastercard, 274
Mather, Hal F., 296n
Mattel Inc., 200, 360(table)
Maverick Division of Blue Bell, Inc., 239,
　　240(illus.)
Maxim coffee, 178
Maxwell House coffee, 178
Mayer, Morris Lehman, 280n, 309n
Mazda Motors of America, 358(table)
MCA Inc., 358(table)
MCI Communications Corporation, 13, 468,
　　469 and *table,* 607
Media Research Group (A.C. Nielsen), 140
Medicaid, 463
Medicare, 463
Mehta, Nitin T., 631n
Meijer, Inc., 268(table)
Meisaner, Frank, 680n
Meister Brau Light beer, 67
Mellon Bank, 12(illus.)
Memorex disks, 244
MetroFone, 469
Metzger, Gale D., 128n
Miaoulis, George, 160n
Michael Jackson, Incorporated, 342–343
Michelob beer, 163
Mid-Continent Bottlers, Inc., 394
Middle Market Directory, 620

Miles Laboratories, 358(table)
Millanes, Robert, 139
Miller, Fredrick, 66
Miller Brewing Company, 66–68, 224, 411(illus.)
Million Dollar Directory, 620
Mills, Rodney, 694
Minipimer hand mixer, 695
Minnesota Mining and Manufacturing (3M), 150 and *illus.*, 184, 186(illus.), 329, 330(illus.), 583
Minnetonka, Inc., 173–174
Mintz, Steven, 104n, 676n
Miracle, Gordon E., 674n
Mitsubishi Aircraft International, Inc., 211–212
Mitsubishi Bank of California, 213–214
Mitsubishi Corporation, 213
Mitsubishi Heavy Industries, 212
Mitsubishi International Corporation, 238
Mitsubishi Motor Sales, 213
Moberg, Patricia E., 129n
Mobil Corp., 359(table), 370(illus.), 371(illus.), 671 and *table*
Mohl, Bruce A., 693n
Monsanto Company, 483
Montgomery Ward, 257, 266, 276(illus.), 282
Moon Drops cosmetics, 51
Moor, Paul, 256
Moore, Ellen M., 639n
Moore, Geoffrey H., 520n
Moore, Thomas, 174n, 535n, 550n
Moore Business Forms, 387
Morris, Desmond, 454
Morrison, Ann M., 259n, 432n
Morse, John, 259n
Morton's table salt, 38, 350(table)
Motel 6, 264
Motorola, Inc., 552
Mountain Red wines, 449
Multiquick food processing system, 695
Munsingwear, 278
Murphy, Patrick E., 48n, 654n
Muse Air Corporation, 21
Museum Tower, 333(illus.)
Mussey, Dagmar, 696n
Mustang automobile, 449–450

Nabisco Brands, Inc., 177, 358(table)
Nader, Ralph, 23, 505
Nagle, Thomas, 450n
Naked Ape, The (Morris), 454
Namath, Joe, 322
Naor, Jacob, 556n
Naraganan, Vodake K., 553n
Nashua Corp., 537, 538
National Association of Independent Colleges and Universities, 646
National Coffee Association, 21

Natural Wonder cosmetics, 51
NBC (National Broadcasting Company), 489
Neal, Bruce, 376n
Needham, Harper and Steers Advertising, Inc., 273(illus.)
Neiman Marcus department store, 444
Nelson, Willie, 108
Neodata Services Group (A.C. Nielsen), 140
Nestlé Company, Inc., 553
Nestlé Enterprises, Inc., 358(table)
Nevin, John R., 493n, 649n, 650n
Newsweek, 642
NFO Research Inc., 131n
Nickelodeon cable channel, 361
Nielsen, A.C., Company, 111(illus.), 134, 140–141
Nike (athletic shoes), 155–156, 669
Nike Japan Corporation, 669, 670(illus.)
Nikon cameras, 214
Nissan Motor Co., Ltd., 446, 500–501
Nissan Motors Corporation, U.S.A., 160, 358(table), 623
Nissho-Iwai Corporation, 669
Noble, John, 370n, 371n
Norris, Eileen, 410n
North American Phillips Co., 359(table)
Norton Simon Inc., 358(table)
Noxell Corp., 359(table)
Noxzema, 197
NPD Group, 123(illus.)
Nulty, Peter, 428n, 429n
Nutech (consultant firm), 23, 24(illus.)
NutraSweet, 435, 636–637
Nutrilite Products, Inc., 314

Occidental Life, 578, 579
Ocean Spray (juice producer), 166
Ohio State University, Marketing Staff of, 9n
Olay Company, 678 and *illus.*
Old Milwaukee beer, 431
Oldsmobile automobiles, 19
Omnidentix Systems Corporation, 276(illus.)
Ontario Ministry of Tourism and Recreation, 643, 645(illus.)
Opien (drug), 500
Oraflex, 499–500
Orange Crush, 636
Orchard home center, 287(table)
Oxydol, 153, 162
Ovaltine, 637
Oyer, M. Sm, 309n

Paccar (truck manufacturer), 555
Pace dentrifice gel, 155
Pac-Man cereal, 158
Paganetti, JoAn, 417n
Pampers, 183, 696
Pan American World Airways, 11, 358(table)
Parasuraman, A., 107n

Robeson, James F., 221n, 674n
Robicheaux, Robert, 226n
Robinson, J.B., Jewelers, 287(table), 288–289
Robinson, Joel R., 189n
Robinson, Patrick J., 96n
Rockwell International Corp., 63
Rockettes, 322
Roegiers' Tourage men's wear, 552
Rogers, Everett M., 192n, 328n, 331n
Rolls-Royce Motors, Ltd., 40
Ronson lighters, 26
Roscitt, Rick, 627n
Rosenbloom, Bert, 218n
Rose's Stores, Inc., 268(table)
Rosewood Hotel, Inc., 265, 265(illus.)
Rothschild, Michael L., 657n
Rothschild, Steven G., 409n
Rowan, Roy, 451n
Royal Crown Cos., 276, 359(table)
Rubin, Ronald S., 49n
Ruffles (snack food), 177
Ryder, James A., 209

Safeway Stores, Inc., 270(table)
Saks Fifth Avenue, 51, 52(illus.), 263 and *illus.*
Sales and Marketing Management, 133
Salmon, Julie, 425n
Salmon, Walter J., 270n
Sanders Cutlery Company, 416, 417(table)
Sands, Saul, 688n
Sanger-Harris department store, 363
Sapit, Donald, 576, 576n
Sara Lee foods, 163, 362(illus.)
Saran Wrap, 189
Sasser, W. Earl, 181n
Satellite Business Systems, 607
Savalas, Telly, 322
Savin Corp., 537, 538
SBS (telephone company), 469(table)
Scherer, James, 165n
Schering-Plough Corp., 358(table)
Schick razors, 189
Schiffres, Manuel, 468n
Schlitz beer, 20, 194, 430
Schlumberger, Jean, 433n
Schuchman, Abe, 601n
Schumacher, Fritz A., 186n
Sciglimpaglia, Donald, 138n
"Scotchtab" closure tape, 150 and *illus.*
Scott, J. D., 146n
Scott, William G., 594n
Scottish Inns, 264
Scrabble, 161
Sea Fresh Seafood Corporation, 608–609
Seagram, Joseph E. & Sons, Inc., 62, 506, 507(illus.)
Seagram Co., Ltd., 359(table)

Sealtest Ice Cream, 163, 201–203
Searle, G.D. (pharmaceutical firm), 636–637
Sears, Roebuck and Co., 158, 159, 200, 207, 221, 226, and *illus.*, 227, 257, 259, 263, 266–267, 278, 280, 282, 305, 359(table), 469, 580
Security Bank & Trust, 103–104
Seitz, Barry, 309n
Selby, Cecily Cannon, 642n
Sell Area Marketing, Inc. (SAMI), 134
Semlow, Walter J., 397n
Serax (drug), 187
Serta Mattress, 577
7-Eleven Stores, 286–287
Seven-Up Company, 194, 195(illus.), 276
Sewall, Gilbert, 449n
Shama, Avraham, 523n, 525n
Shapiro, Leo J., 91n
Sharman, Howard, 696n
Shell Oil Company, 55, 475, 671, 708
Sheplers western wear, 287(table), 289
Sherwin-Williams paints, 253
Sheth, Jagdish N., 72n
Shields, Brooke, 6
Shimmer dessert, 637
Southland Corporation, 270(table), 286–287, 430
Shower Mate liquid soap, 174
Shulman's drugstore (Eastgate Shopping Center, Cleveland), 269
Shuptrine, F. Kelly, 639n
Sierra Club Legal Defense Fund, 648(illus.)
Sigma Press, Inc., 576–578
Simmons, James C., 677n
Simon, Herbert, 527n
Sims, J. Taylor, 294n, 295n, 314n
Sisters International, Inc., 196
Six Flags Over Texas amusement park, 376(illus.), 379
Skolnik, Rayna, 166n, 388n
S*k*ool, The, 138–139
Sloan, Pat, 417n
Slurpee frozen carbonated drink, 286
Smart, John, 468–469
Smith, Lee, 182n, 613n
Smith, Wendell R., 39n
SmithKline Beckman, 358(table)
Smurf cartoon characters, 554
Smurfs cereal, 158
Snackin' Cake, 156
Soft and Dri, 694
Softsoap, 173–174
Solo liquid detergent/fabric softener, 155
Soloman, Paul J., 130n
Sony Corporation, 369(illus.)
Sorenson, Ralph Z., 689n
Southwest Airlines, 21
Spray-Rite (herbicide service), 483
Sprint Service (GTE), 13, 461(illus.), 468, 469 and *table*, 607

Standard Instrumentation, 676
Standard Oil of California, 671(table)
Standard Register Company, 387–388
Stanley, Richard E., 324n, 376n, 406n
Stanton, William J., 8n
Staples, William A., 48n
Star computer (Xerox), 538
Stasch, Stanley F., 113n, 132n, 134n
Steak and Ale restaurants, 30
Steel Company of Canada (Stelco), 622
Stein, Karen, 138
Steinbrink, John P., 402n
Sterilon razors, 695
Sterling Drug, 358(table)
Stern, Louis W., 225n, 237n, 248n, 281n, 283n
Stevens, Charles W., 5n
Stevens, Lawrence, 389n
Stevens, Ron, 249n
Stouffer Corporation, 71 and *illus.*, 167
Strategic Planning Institute, 571
Strawberry Shortcake cereal, 158
Stroh Brewery Company, 16, 359(table),430, 431(illus.)
Stuckey's stores, 78
Sturdivant, Frederick D., 220n
Sugar Free Dr Pepper, 636
Summey, John H., 639n, 650n, 651n, 655n
Sunkist, 350(table), 495–496
Survey of Current Business, 619
Survey of Industrial Purchasing Power, 620
Sweeney, Daniel J., 260n
Sweeney, Robert E., 592n
Swift, 71
Swiss Miss beverage, 637
Sylvania, 158

Tab Cola, 321
Talarzyk, W. Wayne, 236n, 305n
Talley, Walter J., 396n
Talon, Jamie, 693n
Tandem Computers, 533(illus.)
Tandy Corporation, 207
Target Stores, 221, 267, 268(table), 282
Taylor, Ronald D., 639n, 651n, 655n
Teachers Insurance and Annuity Association-College Retirement Equities Fund (TIAA-CREF), 641
Telecommunication Equipment (ITT subsidiary), 671
Telstar call-control system, 608
Tender Vittles, 231
Tenneco Corporation, 557
Tequila Willie's dinnerhouses, 287(table)
Terpstra, Vern, 670n, 672n
Texaco, 671(table)
Texas Instruments Incorporated, 16, 58, 155, 196, 253, 458
Textron, Inc. Outdoor Products Group, 255–256

T.G. & Y. Stores Co., 268(table)
Thomas, Dan R. E., 652n
Thompson, John R., 679n
3M (Minnesota Mining and Manufacturing), 150 and *illus.*, 184, 186(illus.), 329, 330(illus.), 583
Tic Tac candies, 161
Tide detergent, 153, 162, 227
Tiffany & Co., 433(illus.)
Time Inc., 358(table)
Time magazine, advertisement in, 332
Timex Corp., 16, 156, 509(table), 510, 511
Timken Company, 554, 555(illus.)
Top Job cleaner, 696
Topmost brand, 158
Toshiba Television, 170(illus.)
Tostitos, 177
Touber, Edward M., 265n
Toyota Industrial Trucks, U.S.A., Inc. 95(illus.)
Toyota Motor Corp., 5, 446, 500
Toyota Motor Sales, 358(table)
Toys "Я" Us, Inc., 200, 208
Trac II razors, 189, 694
Transamerica Airlines, Inc., 579, 580
Transamerica Corporation, 556, 557, 559, 578–581
Transamerica Delaval Inc., 579, 580–581
Transamerica Financial Corporation, 579–580
Transamerica Financial Services, 578
Transamerica Insurance Co. Inc., 578, 579
Transamerica Interway, Inc., 578, 580
Transamerica Title Insurance Co., 578, 580
Transway International Corporation, 302, 303(illus.)
Trans World Corp., 358(table)
Trimprint film (Kodak), 536
Trinity (Soft and Dri), 694
Trojan Yacht, 223, 224(illus.)
Trudeau, Terry, 663n, 664, 665n, 666n
Tuna Helper, 156
Turicchi, Thomas E., 108n
TV Guide, 417
20th Century-Fox Film Corp., 359(table)
Tyco Industries, Inc., 338(illus.)
Tylenol, 161, 174–175

UAL Inc., 358(table)
Udell, Jon G., 622n
U-Haul International, Inc., 209, 210
Ultima II cosmetics, 51
Ultra Brite toothpaste, 161, 193
Underwood Deviled Ham, 196
Unilever U.S., 359(table), 684
Union Carbide Corp., 359(table)
Union Pacific, 304(illus.)
United Air Lines, Inc., 451
United Parcel Service (UPS), 219, and *illus.*, 245, 250, 302, 653

United States Tobacco Company, 249
Urbanski, Al, 407n
USAIR, Inc., 451, 460
U.S. Air Force, 640 and *illus.*
U.S. Army, 326, 653
USA Today, 560, 561(table)
U.S. Geological Survey, 653
U.S. Government, 360(table)
U.S. Postal Service, 311(illus.), 654
U.S. Telephone, 468, 469(table)

Van Andel, Jay, 314
Van Halen, Eddie, 343
Van Heusen brand, 278
Varig Brazilian Airlines, 308(illus.)
Venture stores, 268(table)
Visa (credit card), 274
Vizir liquid detergent, 696, 697
Vogue, 363
Voit, W. J., 229
Volkswagen of America, 358(table)
Volkswagenwerk, A.G., 5, 41
Volvo, Inc., 555

Waldholz, Michael, 463n
Walker, Bruce J., 271n
Walker and Associates Advertising, 390(illus.)
Walkup, Tracy, 576n, 578
Wal-Mart Stores, Inc., 57, 267, 268(table), 298, 315–317
Walt Disney Productions, 17
Walters, C. Glenn, 237n, 262n
Wang, Chih Kang, 324n
Ward's, *see* Montgomery Ward
Warner Amex Communications, Inc., 453(illus.)
Warner Communications, 358(table)
Warner Lambert Company, 340(illus.), 358(table)
Warner records, 553
Warshaw, M. R., 146n
Washington Apple Commission, 351(illus.)
Wasson, Chester R., 154n, 194n
Waterman, Robert H. Jr., 17n
WATS (Wide Area Telecommunications Service), 25, 127(table), 128
Watson, Donald S., 466n
WD-40 Company, 583–584
Webster, Frederick E., Jr., 96n, 98n
Weigand, Robert E., 225n
Weight Watchers, 11
Weight Watchers foods, 166
Weight Watchers International, 676
Wendy's International Inc., 27, 195–196, 358(table)
Werner, Ray O., 485n
Western Electric Co., Inc., 607
Western Union, 468, 469
Westfall, Ralph, 113n, 132n, 134n

Westinghouse Electric Corp., 248, 567
Whalen, Bernie, 504n, 531n
Wham-O-Manufacturing Co., 229, 230
Wheaties cereal, 179
Wheel Goods Division of AMF, 543
Whipped Toppings, 637
Whirlpool Corporation, 14, 15(illus.)
White Consolidated Industries, 548, 549(illus.)
Wickes Furniture stores, 269
Wiechmann, Ulrich E., 689n
Wild Turkey bourbon, 455 and *illus.*
Williams, Andrew M., 45n
Wilson, Ann and Nancy, 21
Wilson apparel, 259
Wind, Yoram, 96n, 98n, 180n, 544n
Winn-Dixie Stores, Inc., 270(table)
Winter, Ralph E., 445n
Wittebarr, Suzanne, 287n
WJIM-TV (Lansing, Michigan), 486
Women's 501 jeans (Levi Strauss), 29–30
Wood, Donald F., 305n, 307n
Woods, Bob, 438n, 623n
Woodside, Arch G., 294n, 295n, 314n
Woolco discount division, 281
Woolite, 187
Woolworth, F.W., Co., 281
World Communications, 671
World Trader's Data Report, 676
Wrangler brand clothing, 259, 278, 552
W.R. Grace & Co., 287–289
Wrigley, Wm., Jr., Co., 359(table)
Wrigley's gum, 637
Wyler's Drink Mix, 637

Xerox Corporation, 113–114, 359(table), 537–538, 557
Xerox Learning Systems, 399, 400(illus.)

Yamaha motorcycle company, 438
Yapp, Donald, 483
YMCA, 640
Yovovich, B. G., 363n

Zale Corporation, 383–383
Zaltman, Gerald, 124n
Zayre stores, 268(table)
Zenith, 566
Zeren, Linda M., 157n, 160n
Ziegler, William L., 334n, 406n, 408n
Zikmund, William G., 138n
Zinszer, Paul H., 225n
Zonana, Victor F., 156n, 669n

Subject Index

Buying center, organizational, 96–97
Buying power, 511, 514–515
Buying power index, 515 and *table*

Cabbage Patch Kids, 200–201
Cable television
  child audience for, 361
  "Daytime" on, 40
  direct marketing through, 708
California wine industry, prices in, 449
Camcorder (Kodak), 536
Cameras
  disc, 107, 183, 452, 536
  Polaroid, 180–181, 183
  see also Eastman Kodak Co.
Candidates, political, marketing of, 656–659
Capabilities and resources of firm, 554–556
Captioned photographs, 377
Careers, in marketing, 698–708
Carling O'Keefe, Ltd., 224
Cash-and-carry wholesalers, 243
"Cash cows," products as, 562–563, 564
Cash discounts, 464
Cash flow, as pricing objective, 429
Castle and Cooke Food, 586
Catalog retailing, 274, 275(illus.), 418
  showrooms, 269
Caterpillar Tractor Company, 458, 511, 544,
  631 and *illus.*, 685–686
Celanese Corporation, 7, 8(illus.), 628
Channels of distribution, *see* Marketing
  channels
Causal studies, in marketing research, 118
Celler-Kefauver Act (1950), 477(table), 491
Census Bureau, U.S., 49, 124
Cents-off offers, 408, 410
Cereal industry
  new brands in, 158
  "shared monopoly" alleged in, 484–485
Certified Grocers of California Limited, 235
  and *illus.*, 306 and *illus.*
Channel capacity (communication), 327
Channel, marketing, *see* Marketing channels
Channel conflict, 225
Channel cooperation, 224
Channel leadership, 226(illus.), 226–227
Channel power, 226
Chicago Law School, on price fixing, 483
Child Protection Act (1966), 481(table)
Child Protection and Toy Safety Act (1969),
  481(table)
Children's TV, advertising in, 361
Chrysler Corporation, 5, 14, 213, 358(table)
Cigarette Labeling Act (1965), 481(table)
Civil Aeronautics Board (CAB), 423,
  487(table)
Class, social, *see* Social class
Clayton Act (1914), 477(table), 478, 491,
  492, 493
Client publics, 649

Closing, in personal selling, 393
Coca-Cola and Coca-Cola Co.
  and brand infringement, 161
  and international standardization, 689
  and pricing, 464
  and product positioning, 194
  sales volume/advertising expenditure for,
    359(table)
Coding process, 325
Cognitive dissonance, 76
Coleco Industries, Inc., 200–201, 208, 554
Colgate-Palmolive Co., 163, 359(table), 685
Combination compensation plan, 401
Commercialization phase of new-product
  development, 190–193
Commercials
  and channel capacity, 327
  jingles and slogans in, 326
  see also Television commercials
Commission, and price, 425
Commission merchants, 247(table), 248
Common Market, 669
Communication, 324–328
  kinesic, 334
  within marketing unit, 591–592
  proxemic, 334
  tactile, 334
  in warehousing, 308–310
Community shopping centers, 278
Compact cars, pricing of, 445–446
Company sales
  forecast, 59–63
  potential, 58–59
Comparative advertising, 351
Compensation, for salespersons, 401,
  402(table)
Competition, 509(table), 509–511, 532
Competition-matching approach, for
  advertising appropriation, 357
Competition-oriented pricing methods, 461
Competitive advertising, 349–350
Component parts, as industrial product, 150
Comprehensive spending patterns, 516–518
Computerland, 207 and *illus.*
Computers
  in analysis of attitudes , 82
  artificial intelligence through, 526
  and AT&T, 608
  government modernization of, 37
  by Kodak, 536–537
  for marketing-data bank, 110
  and personal selling, 389
  in physical distribution, 294, 306–307,
    308–310
  in telephone interviewing, 128, 129(illus.)
  and wholesaling by LEP, 244
  by Xerox, 538
  see also Personal computers
Concentration strategy, 40–41, 45
Conference Board, 182, 517, 518

Marketing objective, 557
Marketing-oriented organization, 584, 585(illus.)
Marketing plan, 546, 559–561
Marketing planning cycle, 559
Marketing productivity, audit of, 603(table)
Marketing program, 548
Marketing research, 107–108, 110, 115(illus.), 115–120
  and Bangladesh birth control, 643
  careers in, 700–701
  cases in, 138–141
  data gathering in, 116–118, 124–134
  and decision making, 111–114, 114(table)
  design of, 120–124
  ethical and educational standards in, 136
  executives' opinion of, 119
  and MIS, 109 (see also Marketing information system)
  for political candidate, 658
  practical application of, 134–136
  problem definition in, 116
Marketing strategy, 25–26, 544, 546–548, 647
  audit of, 602–603(table)
  differential, 510
  nonbusiness, 656–659
  see also Strategic market planning
Marketing systems, audit of, 603(table)
Market manager, 179
Market opportunity, 551–553
Market requirements, 552
Market sales potential, 58
Market Search, 134
Market segmentation approach, 39–40
  concentration strategy in, 40–41, 45
  conditions for effectiveness of, 43
  in jewelry market, 282
  multisegment strategy in, 41–42
  for performing arts, 649, 650(table)
  and product positioning, 194
  single-variable or multivariable segmentation in, 55–57
  variables in, 44–45
Market share, as pricing objective, 428–429
Market share analysis, 595–596
Market tests, 62–63
Markup pricing, 459–460
Markups, 717–719
Mars, Forrest, 16
Mass merchandisers, 267–271
Materials handling, 307–308
Maternity wear, by Levi's, 185
Mature products, marketing strategy for, 196–197
Maturity stage, of product life cycle, 155–156
MCI Communications Corp., 13, 468, 469 and illus., 607
Measurement of sales, 595–596
Mechanical observation devices, 132

Media plan, for advertising, 357, 360–363, 364–367(table)
Medications, see Drugs
Medium-range plans, 561
Medium of transmission, 325
Merchandise allowances, 412–413
Merchandising, 282, 283(illus.)
Merchant wholesalers, 240–245, 252
Merchants, 208
  commission, 247(table), 248
Microscience, 526
Mid-Continent Bottlers, Inc., 394
Middle East, 679
Middleman, 208, 245
Miller, Fredrick, 66
Miller Brewing Company, 66–68, 224, 411(illus.)
Miller-Tydings Act (1937), 480
Mini-vans, 5–6
Minnesota Mining and Manufacturing (3M), 150 and illus., 184, 186(illus.), 329, 330(illus.), 583
Minnetonka, Inc., 173–174
MIS, see Marketing information system
Missionary salespersons, 394–395
Mitsubishi Corporation, 213
Modified rebuy purchase, 96
Monetary policies, 521
Money refunds, 409–410
Monopolistic competition, 509(table), 510
Monopoly, 509 and table
  see also Antitrust legislation; Procompetitive legislation
  "shared," and cereal industry, 484–485
Monsanto Company, 483
Morris, Desmond, 454
Motels, image of, 264(illus.), 264–265
Motivating
  of marketing personnel, 590–591
  of salespersons, 402–404
Motivation research, 80–81, 82–83
Motives
  and consumer buying behavior, 79–80
  in market segmentation, 51
Motorcycle market
  glutting of, 438
  Harley-Davidson in, 343–344
  and Honda, 83
Motorola, Inc., 552
MRO (maintenance, repair, operating) items, 151
Multinational companies, 671(table), 671–672, 689, 691. See also International marketing
Multiple packaging, 165–166
Multisegment strategy, 41–42
Multivariable segmentation, 56(illus.), 56–57
Mustang automobile, 449–450

Percent of sales approach, for advertising appropriation, 357
Perception, and consumer buying, 77–79
Perfect competition, 509(table), 510
Performance
  evaluation of, 592–593, 595–601
  ratios, 713–717
  standard, 592
Periodicals, for market data, 133–134, 618–620
Personal computers
  by Apple, 207, 208, 355, 591
  by Atari, 452, 453(illus.), 529, 530(illus.)
  by IBM, 207 and *illus.*, 429, 450, 566, 591
  and marketing, 531
  marketing channels for, 207–208
Personal interview surveys, in marketing research, 125–126(table), 127(table), 130–131
Personality, and consumer buying, 83–84
Personal Pan Pizza, 145–146
Personal products, advertising of, 339, 340(illus.)
Personal relationships, in organizational buying, 93
Personal sales, 271–273
Personal selling, 333–334, 388–393
  and advertising, 352
  careers in, 701–702
  cases on, 416–418
  elements of, 390–393
  industrial, 628
  and regulatory forces, 494
  and sales force management, 395–405
  and sales promotion, 406
  and types of salesperson, 393–395
Person-specific influences on consumer buying, 76–77
Persuasion, in exchange, 641
Philip Morris, Inc., 16, 67, 359(table), 429, 509(table)
Physical distribution, 292–293
  cases in, 314–317
  communications and data processing in, 308–310
  industrial, 626
  by intermediaries, 209(table)
  inventory planning and control in, 293–297
  marketing strategy in, 310–312
  materials handling in, 307–308
  transportation in, 297(illus.), 297–303
  warehousing, 303–307
Piggyback services, 303
Pillsbury Co., 30, 185, 358(table)
Pillsbury restaurants, 30–31
PIMS (Profit Impact on Marketing Strategy), 561, 567–570, 571, 572
Pioneer advertising, 349
Pioneer pricing, 451–453

Pizza Hut, Inc., 49, 145–146
Place utility, 260, 292
Planned Parenthood, 656, 657
Planned shopping centers, 277–279
Planning
  for inventory, 293–297
  marketing, 559
  see also Marketing plan; Strategic market planning
Playboy Enterprises, Inc., 56–57, 161
Playboy magazine, 363, 367, 368(illus.)
Plymouth automobiles, 5 and *illus.*, 213
Point-of-purchase displays, 408–409
Point-of-sale terminal (POS), 309
Poison prevention program, 663–667
Polaroid Corp., 180–181, 183, 359(table)
Political candidate marketing, 656–659
Political and legal forces
  and international marketing, 676, 680–681, 682(illus.), 684
  as marketing variable, 22
  see also Regulation of business
Politics, and marketing environment, 476, 495–496
Population
  Hispanics in, 47 and *table*
  in sampling, 120
  U.S. projection for, 50(illus.)
Population density, and product needs, 49
Possession utility, 260
Postpurchase evaluation
  in consumer buying behavior, 75–76
  in organizational buying, 97–98
Posttest, for advertising, 373
Premiums, 410, 413, 425
Presentation, in personal selling, 391–392
Press conference, 377
Prestige pricing, 455–456
Pretests, for advertisements, 372
Price, 424–427
  calculations, 717–720
  controls, 492
  and demand, 617
  differentiation, 460, 479, 492
  discounting, 463–465
  discrimination, 465–466, 479
  elasticity of demand, 434–435
  leaders, 457
  lining, 456 and *illus.*
  and organizational buyer, 94
  penetration, 452–453
  product image and, 21
  skimming, 452
Pricing, 10(table), 21, 427(illus.), 427–429, 430, 449–450, 462
  in airline industry, 451
  audit of, 603–604(table)
  of bank services, 425
  breakeven analysis in, 439–440

Pricing *(cont.)*
  cases on, 443–447, 468–471
  and competition, 423–424, 450, 451, 461
  cost-oriented, 458–459
  cost-plus, 459
  customary, 454–455
  for declining products, 198
  and demand, 431–435, 460, 461(illus.)
  of Dream Whip, 188
  from experience curve, 458
  geographic, 465
  in growth stage, 196
  for industrial markets, 462–466, 630–633
  by intermediaries, 209(table)
  in international marketing, 686(illus.),
    686–687
  marginal analysis in, 436–439
  markup, 459–460
  for mature products, 197
  for medical practice, 463
  method for, 458
  and nonbusiness marketing, 651(table),
    653–654
  objectives in, 427–429
  odd-even, 453–454
  pioneer, 451–453
  by Planned Parenthood, 657
  prestige, 455–456
  professional, 456–457
  promotional, 457–458
  psychological, 453–456
  and regulatory forces, 492, 494
  and Robinson-Patman Act, 465,
    477(table), 479, 492, 630
  and shortages/inflation/recession,
    524(table)
  special-event, 457
  transfer, 462
  as wholesaling activity, 237(table)
Pricing policy, 450
Primary data, 116
  for foreign markets, 674–675
Private distributor brands, 158–160
Private warehouses, 305–306
"Problem children," products as, 562–563,
  564–565
Problem definition, in marketing research,
  116
Problem recognition
  in consumer buying, 73–74
  in organizational buying, 97
Process materials, as industrial product, 151
Procompetitive legislation, 477(table), 477–
  480
Procter & Gamble, 6–7
  as consumer-oriented, 16, 33 and *illus.*
  as multinational, 689, 696–697
Producer markets, 35
Producers, wholesalers' services for, 238
Product adoption process, 191–192, 328–331
Product advertising, 349

Product assortments, 261–262
Product awareness, advertising for, 329,
  330(illus.)
Product characteristics, and promotion mix,
  338–339
Product deletion, 181–182, 183(illus.)
Product development, as new-product
  development phase, 188 (*see also* New-
  product development)
Product differentiation, 38–39
Product image, and price, 21
Product introduction, 191, 192. *See also*
  New-product development
Production costs, and penetration pricing,
  453
Production orientation, 14–15
Production-oriented organization, 584
Product item, 151
Product life cycle, 153–154
  decline stage of, 156
  growth stage of, 155
  introduction stage of, 154–155
  maturity stage of, 155–156
  and strategic planning, 572
Product line, 151–152, 153
Product management, 178–180
  careers in, 705–706
  in deletion of products, 181–182,
    183(illus.)
  in new-product development, 182–193
  in post-commercialization stages, 194–198
  and product mix, 179–193
  in product modification, 180–181
  and product positioning, 193–194
Product manager, 178
Product mix, 152–153
  adjustments in, 177, 179–180
  deletion of products from, 181–182,
    183(illus.)
  development of new products for, 182–193
  modification of products in, 180–181
  and regulatory forces, 491–492
Product modification, 180–181
Product-portfolio analysis, 562
Product portfolio approach, 180
Product positioning, 177, 193–194, 201–203
Product quality, as pricing objective, 429
Product-related variables, in market
  segmentation, 52–53
Products, 10(table), 11, 19, 146–147
  audit of, 603(table)
  branding of, 156–163
  cases on, 173–175
  consumer, 147–149, 210(illus.), 211
  industrial, 147, 149–151, 614–615, 621–623
  in international marketing, 683–685
  labeling of, 168, 491–492
  from new technologies, 528
  and nonbusiness marketing, 651(table),
    651–652, 653
  organizing by, 586–587, 587(illus.)